SATAN
AND THE
PROBLEM OF
EVIL

CONSTRUCTING
A TRINITARIAN
WARFARE
THEODICY

GREGORY A. BOYD

IVP Academic

An imprint of InterVarsity Press
Downers Grove, Illinois

How was this received in the evangelical world?

[Handwritten notes at top of page:]

p.162 - Don't accept everything as p[art of] God's plan

p.164 - potential to love involves poten[tial] for harm

p.165 · love requires freedom ①, freedom requires ② risk, risk entails moral responsibility ③

p.170 ④ responsibility is proportionate to the potential to influence others

God's way of helping us to [?]

InterVarsity Press
P.O. Box 1400, Downers Grove, IL 60515-1426
World Wide Web: www.ivpress.com
E-mail: mail@ivpress.com

InterVarsity Press® is the book-publishing division of InterVarsity Christian Fellowship/USA®, a student movement active on campus at hundreds of universities, colleges and schools of nursing in the United States of America, and a member movement of the International Fellowship of Evangelical Students. For information about local and regional activities, write Public Relations Dept., InterVarsity Christian Fellowship/USA, 6400 Schroeder Rd., P.O. Box 7895, Madison, WI 53707-7895, or visit the IVCF website at <www.intervarsity.org>.

Scripture quotations, unless otherwise noted, are from the New Revised Standard Version of the Bible, copyright 1989 by the Division of Christian Education of the National Council of the Churches of Christ in the USA. Used by permission. All rights reserved.

Cover photograph: Erich Lessing/Art Resource, N.Y.

ISBN-10: 0-8308-1550-3
ISBN-13: 978-0-8308-1550-0

Printed in the United States of America ∞

Library of Congress Cataloging-in-Publication Data

Boyd, Gregory A., 1957-
    Satan and the problem of evil : constructing a trinitarian warfare theodicy / Gregory A. Boyd.
        p. cm.
    Includes bibliographical references and index.
    ISBN 0-8308-1550-3 (pbk. : alk. paper)
        1. Theodicy. 2. Spiritual warfare. 3. Trinity. 4. Devil. I. Title.
BT160.B665 2001
231'.8—dc21

                                                                                    2001024838

| P | 21 | 20 | 19 | 18 | 17 | 16 | 15 | 14 | 13 | 12 | 11 | 10 | 9 | 8 | 7 | 6 | 5 | 4 | 3 |
| Y | 21 | 20 | 19 | 18 | 17 | 16 | 15 | 14 | 13 | 12 | 11 | 10 | 09 | 08 | 07 | 06 | | | |

p.140 his use of scripture and science → very modern?

p.147 - divine sovereignty isn't exhaustive, God takes adventure, God controlling everything undermines God's sovereignty - we can say 'no'

p.151 - no coercion in God

p.158-156 - God's prediction of having a bride

161 hints of eschatology

's love of us

✗ use of scripture

p.55 Out of love, God created a world in which evil was possible

p.58 - Is his reading of Augustine accurate Is compatibilist similar to predestination

p.116 - love requires freedom to freedom requires risk. good summation of argument

p.127 - God doesn't have exhaustive def. foreknowledge

p.111 omniresourceful God → not anthropomorphic

p.130 - God isn't limited as humans - neo Molinist perspective - God has control yet we have freedom

p.124 - Molinist perspective

p.134 - EDF undermines moral responsibility

p.138 - God knows the future as a realm of possibility

p.174 – ① Moral responsibility is shared
p.176 – ② love is worth the risk
p.178 ③ wisdom of a risk can't assess
p.181 ⑤ the power to influence is irrevocable
p.186 ⑥ power to influence is finite
p.196 – we don't know – why it seems [?] a satisfactory answer mistrust p.216 – complexity

A Word of Appreciation

The ideas and arguments found in this book have been developed in dialogue with a number of people, to whom a sincere expression of appreciation is in order.

The perpetual debate I've had with my good friend Paul Eddy has greatly helped me to refine my thoughts. Moreover, his compulsion for research and willingness to share his findings with me have saved me years of library work. I am forever indebted.

The dialogues I've had with my colleagues at Bethel College and Woodland Hills Church (St. Paul, Minnesota), and more recently with the lively and challenging participants in the discussion at my Christus Victor website (<www.gregboyd.org>) have been extremely beneficial and fun. Thanks to them for the stimulating debates, which have sharpened my thinking on a number of points.

A number of others have helped to further my thinking as well. John Sanders's remarkable insight into the Bible and knowledge of history have been helpful. Tyler and Chelsea DeArmond have been invaluable in editing this work, helping me clarify concepts and assisting me in running a crazy, overbooked life. They are dear friends with servant spirits and keen minds whom I respect and appreciate profoundly. Randy Barnhart and Jim Beilby have also influenced my thinking, especially as it concerns middle knowledge.

Gary Deddo and the InterVarsity staff have done an outstanding job and have been a joy to work with. I must also extend a word of thanks to George Brushaber, president, and Jay Barnes, provost of Bethel College, and Leland Eliason, provost of Bethel Seminary. I appreciate the challenges you each have offered to my views but also your defense of academic freedom that has supported me over the last several years.

Two more people must be mentioned. First, I am profoundly indebted to my loving father, Edward K. Boyd, to whom this book is dedicated. He has always challenged me and been an example to me. One of the greatest joys in my life is seeing how his new relationship with Jesus Christ is constantly transforming him—at the age of eighty-four! And finally, I am blessed beyond words to have a committed, loving wife, Shelley Boyd, who supports my work, encourages my spirit, stimulates my thinking and just plain loves me like crazy. How can I express my gratitude to you?

a jump into an FCH meeting — use of male pronouns is striking.

p. 205 — new summary
p. 213 — God has restricted Ge's omniscience.
p. 218 — Does χ was theory really answer natural disasters?

229 God, prayer, process thought

Abbreviations

AB	Anchor Bible
ANF	The Ante-Nicene Fathers. Edited by A. Roberts and J. Donaldson. 10 vols. Grand Rapids, Mich.: Eerdmans, 1979.
ATJ	*Ashland Theological Journal*
BARev	*Biblical Archaeology Review*
BASOR	*Bulletin of the American Schools of Oriental Research*
BSac	*Bibliotheca sacra*
BTB	*Biblical Theology Bulletin*
BWANT	Beiträge zur Wissenschaft vom Neuen Testament
CBQ	*Catholic Biblical Quarterly*
CD	Karl Barth. *Church Dogmatics.* Edited and translated by Geoffrey W. Bromiley and Thomas F. Torrance. Edinburgh: T & T Clark, 1936-1977.
CTQ	*Concordia Theological Quarterly*
CurTM	*Currents in Theology and Mission*
EBC	*Expositor's Bible Commentary.* Edited by F. E. Gaebelein. 12 vols. Grand Rapids, Mich.: Zondervan, 1976-1992.
ETSMS	Evangelical Theological Society Monograph Series
FC	The Fathers of the Church: A New Translation. Washington, D.C.: Catholic University of America Press, 1947.
FRLANT	Forschungen zur Religion und Literatur des Alten und Neuen Testaments
HAR	*Hebrew Annual Review*
HDR	Harvard Dissertations in Religion
JBL	*Journal of Biblical Literature*
JECS	*Journal of Early Christian Studies*
JETS	*Journal of the Evangelical Theological Society*
JSOTSup	Journal for the Study of the Old Testament Supplement Series
LCC	Library of Christian Classics
LCL	Loeb Classical Library
LTQ	*Lutheran Theological Quarterly*
NIB	The New Interpreter's Bible. Nashville: Abingdon, 1994-.
NICOT	New International Commentary on the Old Testament
NovT	*Novum Testamentum*
NPNF	Nicene and Post-Nicene Fathers
POS	Pretoria Oriental Series
RelS	*Religious Studies*
RQ	*Römische Quartalschrift für christliche Altertumskunde und Kirchengeschichte*
ST	*Studia theologica*
Them	*Themelios*
ThTo	*Theology Today*
TJ	*Trinity Journal*
TS	*Theological Studies*
WBC	Word Biblical Commentary
WUNT	Wissenschaftliche Untersuchungen zum Neuen Testament

INTRODUCTION

I freely admit that real Christianity . . .
goes much nearer to Dualism than people think. . . .
The difference is that Christianity thinks this Dark Power was created by God,
and was good when he was created, and went wrong.
Christianity agrees with Dualism that this universe is at war.
But it does not think this is a war between independent powers.
It thinks it is a civil war, a rebellion,
and that we are living in a part of the universe occupied by the rebel.
C. S. LEWIS, *MERE CHRISTIANITY*

The Bible uniformly teaches that God is the Creator of all that is and the sovereign Lord of history (e.g., Gen 1:1; Deut 10:14; Ps 135:6-18; John 1:3; Acts 17:24-27; Eph 1:11; Col 1:16-17). At times he exercises unilateral control over what transpires in history, miraculously intervening to alter the course of nations or of individuals, even predestining some events long before they come to pass (e.g., Is 46:10-11; Acts 2:23; 4:28). Because God is omnipotent, his goal of acquiring a "bride" (the church) and establishing an eternal kingdom free from all evil certainly will be achieved someday (e.g., 1 Cor 15:25-28; Eph 1:16-23; Col 1:18-20; Rev 20:10). In sum, Scripture's majestic portrayal of God is that of a sovereign, omnipotent Creator who is confidently guiding the world toward his desired end.

Because of this clear biblical witness, many Christians have concluded that, in order for God to accomplish his goal for creation, *everything* that happens in world history must somehow fit into his sovereign plan. This assumption has permeated much of the church's theology and piety throughout most of its history. It is expressed, for example, in many traditional hymns that reassure us that God is in control and is working out his purposes no matter what happens to us.[1] The assumption is also expressed in clichés Christians are prone to recite in the face of suffering. When confronting tragedies such as cancer, crippling accidents or natural disasters, believers sometimes attempt to console themselves and others by uttering truisms such as "God has his reasons," "There's a purpose for everything," "Providence writes straight with crooked lines," and "His ways are not our ways." The same assumption to some extent permeates our broader culture as well, as evidenced, for example, by the fact that insurance policies customarily refer to natural disasters as "acts of God."

The assumption that there is a divine reason behind everything has also been frequently espoused by some of the church's chief theologians. For example, Augustine, arguably the most influential theologian in church history, expressed this assumption in strong terms when he wrote, "to God . . . all wills . . . are subject, since they have no power except what He has bestowed upon them. The cause of things, therefore, which makes but is not made, is God."[2] Again, "the will of the Omnipotent is always undefeated."[3] "Nothing happens unless the Omnipotent wills it to happen," according to Augustine.[4] Even evil deeds must be allowed by God for a specific good purpose.[5] Hence, Augustine encouraged Christians who had been victimized by others to find consolation in the knowledge that their oppressors could not have harmed them as they did unless God allowed it for a greater good.[6]

---

[1]Consider, for example, Lloyd's famous hymn, "My Times Are in Thy Hand": "My times are in thy hand / Whatever they may be/ Pleasing or painful, dark or bright / As best may seem to thee / My times are in thy hand / Why should I doubt or fear? / My Father's hand will never cause / His child a needless tear." To cite another example, with Sandell's famous hymn, "Day by Day and with Each Passing Moment," we sing: "The protection of his child and treasure / Is a charge that on himself he laid / As thy days, thy strength shall be in measure / This the pledge to me he made . . . / Help me, Lord, when toil and trouble meeting / E'er to take, as from a father's hand / One by one, the day, the moments fleeting / Till I reach the promised land."

[2]Augustine City of God 5.9 (NPNF 1 2:92).

[3]Enchiridion, Library of Christian Classics, ed. J. Baille, J. McNeill and H. P. Van Duren, trans. A. C. Outler (Philadelphia: Westminster Press, 1955), 7:400.

[4]Ibid., p. 395.

[5]"In their very act of [wicked people] going against [God's] . . . will," Augustine holds, "his will is thereby accomplished . . . for it would not be done without his allowing it—and surely his permission is not unwilling, but willing" (ibid., p. 389).

[6]According to Augustine, the victim "ought not to attribute [his suffering] to the will of men, or of angels, or of any created spirit, but rather to His will who gives power to wills" (City of God 5.10 [NPNF 1 2:93]). Even the premature death of little children fulfills a divine purpose, according to Augustine. When parents experience "the suffering and death of their little ones so dear to them," he suggests, God is disciplining the parents ("The Free Choice of the Will," FC 59).

Calvin made a similar point when he wrote:

> Suppose a man falls among thieves, or wild beasts. . . . Suppose another man
> wandering through the desert finds help in his straits. . . . Carnal reason
> ascribes all such happenings, whether prosperous or adverse, to fortune. But
> anyone who has been taught by Christ's lips . . . will look farther afield for a
> cause, and will consider that all events are governed by God's secret plan.[7]

Another classic expression of this traditional perspective came from the six-teenth-century monk Brother Lawrence, who wrote:

> God knows best what we need and everything He does is for our good. If we
> knew how much He loves us, we would always be ready to receive from Him,
> without equanimity, the sweet and the bitter, and even the most painful and
> most difficult things would be pleasing and agreeable . . . when we believe that
> it is the hand of God acting on us, that it is a Father filled with love who sub-
> jects us to this humiliation, grief and suffering then all bitterness . . . is forgot-
> ten and we rejoice in them. We must believe unquestioningly that . . . it is
> pleasing to God to sacrifice ourselves to Him, that it is by His divine Provi-
> dence that we are abandoned to all kinds of conditions, to suffer all kinds of
> sufferings, miseries and temptations.[8]

I call this understanding of God's relationship to the world the "blueprint
worldview,"*[9] for it assumes that everything somehow fits into "God's
secret plan"—a divine blueprint. The view takes many different forms, some
saying, for example, that God *ordains* all things, others that he simply *allows*
tragic events to occur. But each shares the assumption that, whether
ordained or allowed, there is a *specific divine reason* for every occurrence in
history. If God wanted to prevent the event from taking place, the reasoning
goes, he could have prevented it. Since he did not, he must have had a good
reason for not doing so.

Questioning the Blueprint Worldview

As traditional and popular as the blueprint worldview is, it is not without significant difficulties. For one thing, this view makes it exceedingly difficult to

---

[7]John Calvin, *Institutes of the Christian Religion,* ed. James T. McNeill, trans. Ford L. Battles
(Philadelphia: Westminster Press, 1960), pp. 198-99 [1.16.2].
[8]Brother Lawrence, *The Practice of the Presence of God,* trans. John J. Delaney (Garden City,
N.Y.: Image, 1977), pp. 95-96, 100.
[9]I place an asterisk after the first use of terms or concepts that may be unfamiliar to lay readers
or that are unique to the theodicy developed in this book. A short definition of the term or
concept and an explanation of how it fits into the trinitarian warfare theodicy is found in the
glossary.

reconcile the evil in our world with the omnipotence and perfect goodness of God. It is not easy to believe—and for some of us, not possible to believe—that there is a specific providential purpose being served by certain horrifying experiences.

For example, dozens of small children were recently buried alive by a mudslide in Mexico. Can we conceive of a specific reason why God might have deemed it better to allow this tragedy than to prevent it? To cite another example, several years ago a young girl was abducted from her own yard in a rural town in Minnesota. Her parents now live in a perpetual nightmare, wondering every day if their daughter is alive and, if she is, what is being done to her. Can we theorize a possible "good" providential reason why God might have thought it better to allow this nightmare rather than to prevent it? Is it possible to accept the advice of Augustine, Calvin and Brother Lawrence and encourage these parents to accept this nightmare as coming from their loving Father's hand?

To some of us, the suggestion that God has a "higher reason" for allowing children to suffocate in mud or be kidnapped is insulting to those who experience the horror as well as to the character of God.[10] Indeed, on the assumption that believing in God means accepting a "higher harmony" in which horrifying events somehow fit, some have abandoned belief in God altogether. Like Ivan in Dostoyevsky's novel *The Brothers Karamazov,* these people abandon belief in God on moral grounds. "I renounce the higher harmony altogether," Ivan announces. "It's not worth the tears of . . . one tortured child."[11] Any design that intentionally includes the suffering of innocent children for a "greater purpose" is intrinsically immoral, he argues, and we are obliged to renounce it.

The Warfare Worldview

From my perspective, Ivan's rage is justified, but his rejection of God unnecessary. For, despite the above mentioned motif stressing God's sovereignty, Scripture does not support the view that there must be a specific divine reason behind all events. This brings us to a second and even more fundamental problem with the blueprint worldview: it is, I contend, rooted in an imbalanced reading of the Bible.

---

[10]See, e.g., Kenneth Surin, *Theology and the Problem of Evil* (Oxford: Blackwell, 1986); Terrence W. Tilley, *The Evils of Theodicy* (Washington, D.C.: Georgetown University Press, 1990); and M. Scott, "The Morality of Theodicies," *RelS* 32 (1996): 1-13.

[11]See Walter Kaufmann, ed., *Religion from Tolstoy to Camus* (New York: Harper & Row, 1961), pp. 137-44.

While Scripture emphasizes God's ultimate authority over the world, it also emphasizes that agents, whom God has created, can and do resist his will. Scripture does not teach that God controls all the behavior of free agents, whether humans or angels. Humans and fallen angels are able to grieve God's Spirit and to some extent frustrate his purposes (e.g., Gen 6:6; Is 63:10; Lk 7:30; Acts 7:51; Eph 4:30; Heb 3:8, 15; 4:7). While his *general will* for world history cannot fail, his *particular will* for individuals often does. God does not will any individual to eternally perish, for example, yet multitudes of individuals thwart this will and choose this destiny for themselves (1 Tim 2:4; 2 Pet 3:9).

Indeed, as I shall show in chapter one, there is a dominant motif running throughout Scripture—I have elsewhere argued that it is the *central* motif of Scripture—that depicts God as warring against human and angelic opponents who are able in some measure to thwart his will.[12] While the previously mentioned biblical motif stresses that God is in control of the overall flow of world history, this other motif qualifies this truth by depicting God as *striving to establish* his will "on earth as it is in heaven" (Mt 6:10).

God genuinely strives against rebellious creatures. According to Scripture, the head of this rebellion is a powerful fallen angel named Satan. Under him are a myriad of other spiritual beings and humans who refuse to submit to God's rule. Scripture refers to this collective rebellion as a kingdom (Mt 12:26; Col 1:13; Rev 11:15). It is clear that God shall someday vanquish this rebel kingdom, but it is equally clear that in the meantime he genuinely wars against it.

This motif expresses what I call the "warfare worldview"* of the Bible. I argue that the narrative of the Bible and all events in world history are best understood against the backdrop of this worldview. The world is literally caught up in a spiritual war between God and Satan. The main difference between the warfare worldview and the blueprint worldview is that the former does not assume that there is a specific divine reason for what Satan and other evil agents do. To the contrary, God fights these opponents precisely because *their* purposes are working *against his* purposes. The reason why they do what they do is found in them, not God.

Suffering takes on a different meaning when it is viewed against the backdrop of a cosmic war, as opposed to a context that assumes everything is part of God's "secret plan." In the warfare worldview we would not wonder about the specific reason God might have had in allowing little

---

[12]For a thorough analysis of this motif, see Gregory A. Boyd, *God at War: The Bible and Spiritual Conflict* (Downers Grove, Ill.: InterVarsity Press, 1996).

children to be buried alive in mud or a young girl to be kidnapped. Instead, we would view these individuals as "victims of war" and assign the blame to human or demonic beings who are opposing God's will. Following Scripture, we would of course look to God for our comfort in the midst of our suffering, trust that he is working to bring good out of the evil, and find consolation in our confidence that the war will someday come to a glorious end. But we would not look to God's purposes for the *explanation* of why this specific evil occurred in the first place. In a warfare worldview, this is understood to be the result of the evil intentions and activity of human and angelic agents.

The Thesis of This Work

As is the case with the blueprint worldview, the warfare worldview is not without difficulties. Foremost among these is the question of how this view can be reconciled with the biblical teaching that God is the all-powerful Creator of the world. Since the warfare worldview denies that God always has a specific reason for allowing evil deeds to occur, must it not deny that God is *able* to prevent events he wishes would not take place? We may state the dilemma as follows: It seems we must either believe that God does not prevent certain events because he *chooses* not to or because he is *unable* to. The warfare worldview denies that God always chooses not to intervene, for this would require the belief that there is a specific divine purpose behind everything. Hence the warfare worldview must accept that at least sometimes God is *unable* to prevent them. But how then can we continue to affirm that God is all-powerful?

In essence, the goal of this book is to answer this question. How are we to conceive of an all-powerful God creating beings who to some degree possess the power to thwart his will, and thus against whom he must genuinely battle if he is to accomplish his will? The attempt to answer this question is the attempt to render philosophically coherent the warfare worldview of Scripture as well as the war-torn appearance of our world.

My conviction is that, unlike the questions that the blueprint worldview raises, this question has a plausible answer. The thesis of this book is that the answer lies in the nature of love. As Father, Son and Holy Spirit, God's essence is love (1 Jn 4:8, 16). God created the world for the purpose of displaying his triune love and inviting others to share in it (cf. esp. Jn 17:20-25). I shall argue that it was not logically possible for God to have this objective without risking the possibility of war breaking out in his creation. By definition, I will contend, the possibility of love among contingent creatures such as angels and humans entails the possibility of its antithesis, namely, war. If God wanted the former, he had to risk the latter.

More specifically, throughout this work I will submit and defend six theses that I believe are entailed by the conviction that God created the world to invite others to share in his triune love. If accepted, these six theses make sense of the warfare worldview of the Bible and of the war-torn nature of the world.

The Title of This Work

As should already be clear, this work is not focused exclusively on the identity and activity of Satan. I nevertheless decided to title this work *Satan and the Problem of Evil* for the following three reasons.

First, as we will see in the next chapter, the New Testament repeatedly identifies the originator and head of the rebellion against God as Satan. Indeed, although it does not locate the entire responsibility for all evil on Satan, it does trace all evil back to him. Hence, for example, the New Testament identifies illness, diseases, spiritual blindness and episodes of demonization as part of Satan's work (Lk 13:10-17; Acts 10:38; 2 Cor 4:4; 1 Jn 3:8).[13] The war that currently ravages the creation involves all angels and humans, but it is first and foremost a struggle between Satan and God. Thus, insofar as our goal is to render this cosmic struggle intelligible and understand evil in our lives in the light of it, it made sense to express it as centered on Satan and the problem of evil.

Second, and closely related to this, because Scripture depicts Satan as being far more powerful than any of the demonic or human agents that are under him, he represents the ultimate challenge for our theodicy. The challenge of explaining how God could create beings who can resist his will and genuinely war against him is epitomized in Satan. If we can account for his existence, we shall have thereby accounted for the existence of all lesser evil agents. So again, it made sense to express the subject matter of this work as being about the connection between Satan and the problem of evil.

Third, I will argue that there is a class of evils in the world that cannot be explained adequately except by appealing to Satan. When people inflict harm on other people, we can perhaps fully account for the evil act by appealing to their free will. But how are we to account for the fact that people as well as animals suffer from "natural" causes? While appealing to

---

[13]Cf. ibid.

Satan is not itself sufficient to explain "natural" evil,* I shall argue that no explanation that ignores his activity is adequate.[14]

Constructing a "Trinitarian Warfare Theodicy"

I label the position I develop in this work the trinitarian warfare theodicy.* It is a *warfare* theodicy because it attempts to make philosophical sense of the warfare worldview of Scripture and to understand our own experience of evil in this framework.

I call it a *trinitarian* warfare theodicy for two reasons. First, I want clearly to distinguish the warfare worldview I espouse and defend the warfare worldview that most other cultures in history have in some form espoused.[15] The biblical warfare worldview is unique in that it has at its foundation the belief in a triune Creator God who is all-powerful and all-good. This is why the trinitarian warfare worldview* is unique: it must reconcile the reality of spiritual war with the belief in an all-powerful and all-good God.

Yet the belief in the omnipotent, triune God that leads to the problem of evil also leads to its solution, which constitutes the second reason I call this theodicy a *trinitarian* warfare theodicy. We are not talking about any omnipotent deity; we are speaking specifically of the Father, Son and Holy Spirit who created the world as an expression of love and as an invitation to love. We are speaking of the Father who sent his Son to defeat the devil and rescue humans through the power of the Spirit (1 Jn 3:8; 4:7-16). I contend that if we think consistently about the loving purposes and sovereign power of *this* God, we will understand why the creation had to include the possibility of the kind of war and the type of suffering we and God are now in the midst of.

The Trinitarian Warfare Theodicy and Other Theodicies

This work is intended to be a constructive work in philosophical theology, not primarily a polemical work. While I shall at points need to establish my perspective over and against others (especially chapters two, eight and nine), space will not allow me to interact critically and in depth with the multitude of other theodicies that have been put forth. For the purpose of clarification,

---

[14]Philosophers and theologians customarily distinguish between "moral" and "natural" evil, the former being evil that results from free agents, the latter being evil that comes from "natural" causes. I ultimately deny the distinction. Hence, throughout this work I place quotation marks around the word *natural* when referring to "natural evil." My argument is that there is in fact nothing "natural" about it. Ultimately, it is as much the result of free agents exercising their will as is "moral evil."

[15]Cf. Boyd, *God at War*, pp. 11-17.

however, it may prove helpful to offer an overview of how my work generally contrasts with other approaches to the problem of evil. Three points may be made.

First, as suggested above, the trinitarian warfare theodicy contrasts with theodicies predicated on the blueprint worldview, that is, that assume there must always be a specific divine reason for each specific evil in the world. I do not deny that in the context of this war zone God *sometimes* may allow, or even ordain, suffering for a particular higher purpose. Scripture teaches this much. I can therefore affirm much in those traditional theodicies that explain suffering as, for example, God's way of punishing sin, of building our character, or of contributing to some other "greater good." However, I deny that Scripture, reason or experience requires the belief that suffering must *always* serve a divine purpose.

Second, almost all theodicies predicated on the blueprint worldview affirm the reality of human and angelic free will. The church has unanimously affirmed that the angels who fell and the humans who followed them chose to do so of their own volition and that they should not have done so. These agents are morally responsible for their misdeeds. To this extent these theodicies are compatible with the trinitarian warfare theodicy advocated in this work.

The trinitarian warfare theodicy constructed in this work differs from these theodicies, however, in its claim that agents are genuinely free only if the agents themselves are the *ultimate explanations* of their own free activity (see chapter two). If we understand the purpose an agent had in mind in freely carrying out a particular deed, we have understood the *ultimate reason* for the deed. We thus need not assume that there is also a divine reason explaining its occurrence, either as to why it was ordained or specifically allowed. Theologians who espouse some form of the blueprint worldview assign the *responsibility* for evil deeds to the agents doing them but the *ultimate reason* for why these particular evil deeds were ordained or allowed to God. I will rather argue that the ultimate reason for a deed is inextricably connected to the agent who is morally responsible for it.

Defenders of blueprint theodicies have made valiant attempts to argue that it is logically possible to affirm that agents are free and that there is a specific divine purpose behind their behavior, whether they believe this behavior is specifically ordained or specifically allowed by God. I do not believe any of these attempts have been successful, but aside from several criticisms that shall be made in chapter two, it lies outside the parameters of this work to demonstrate this. I will be content rather to offer a view that, if accepted, renders these attempts unnecessary. That is, if we reject the assumption that there is a specific divine reason behind all free actions, attempts to demonstrate its logical possibility become superfluous.

Third, a number of philosophers and theologians in recent times have attempted to avoid the blueprint worldview by affirming that events with no divine reason behind them can happen. On a number of different grounds these thinkers affirm that gratuitous suffering (i.e., suffering that has no specific divine reason behind it) is consistent with belief in an all-powerful God.[16] To this extent, these approaches are consistent with the one I develop in this book. Indeed, I make significant use of these approaches in developing my own perspective.

However, my approach differs from most of these approaches in at least two respects. First, the most fundamental reason why I believe suffering is often gratuitous—devoid of a divine reason—differs from these other approaches. Within my system the possibility of gratuitous suffering is necessarily built into the possibility of love for contingent creatures.

Second, my reading of Scripture and my approach to understanding evil in the world, especially "natural" evil, leads me to place far more emphasis on the importance of nonhuman free agents than these other approaches have typically done. To be sure, a few philosophers and theologians in recent times have suggested that we need to appeal to Satan and demonic agents to account for the full scope of evil in the world (see chapter ten). But none have yet developed this thesis fully. I shall attempt to do so in this work.

Method

The method I employ to arrive at the six theses that constitute the core of the trinitarian warfare worldview is based on Wesley's methodological quadrangle of Scripture, reason, experience and tradition as the criteria for theological truth.[17] A brief word should be said about each of these criteria.

---

[16]As shall be more clear, to say that there is no specific divine reason behind a particular evil act is not to say that God doesn't *respond* to a particular evil act in such a way that a good purpose is brought out of it (Rom 8:28). It is worth noting that even some theologians within the Reformed tradition have moved away from the blueprint worldview. See, for example, Vincent Brümmer, *Speaking of a Personal God: An Essay in Philosophical Theology* (Cambridge: Cambridge University Press, 1992); Adrio König, *Here Am I: A Christian Reflection on God* (Grand Rapids, Mich.: Eerdmans, 1982); and Nicholas Wolterstorff, "Does God Suffer?" *Modern Reformation* 8 (October 1999): 45-47.

[17]On Wesley's quadrangle see Donald Thorsen, *The Wesleyan Quadrilateral: Scripture, Tradition, Reason and Experience as a Model of Evangelical Theology* (Grand Rapids, Mich.: Zondervan, 1990); W. Stephen Gunter et al., *Wesley and the Quadrilateral: Renewing the Conversation* (Nashville: Abingdon, 1997).

First, I assume that Scripture is divinely inspired and therefore trustworthy on all matters that it intends to teach. I believe this assumption is defensible on rational and historical grounds, though it lies outside the scope of this work to demonstrate this.[18] Granted, because this is a work in philosophical theology, reason will play a more dominant role than it would if this were a work in biblical theology. Still, it is my conviction that whatever we arrive at by means of reason must square with the teaching of Scripture.

Second, as was just suggested, I assume that reason, if employed correctly, is also a trustworthy guide in seeking after truth. Scriptural revelation goes *beyond* reason, but I do not believe it ever goes *against* reason. Scripture may lead us to accept *paradoxes* (such as the incarnation and the Trinity), but it never requires that we accept *contradictions,* which are devoid of meaning.

Third, I assume that experience has a legitimate role to play in our quest for truth. This assumption is rooted in the scriptural teaching that God is truthful and that we are made in his image. We are "wired," as it were, to experience the world accurately. I thus believe that our theologizing and philosophizing should square with and illuminate the way we actually experience the world on a day-by-day basis. For example, I will argue in chapter two that the fact that we must assume we are self-determining with every decision we make is a very good reason to accept the conclusion that we are self-determining agents. Similarly, I shall argue in chapter four that, since we must assume that the future is partly open as well as partly settled with every decision we make, there is good reason for concluding that the future is in fact partly open and partly settled. Indeed, throughout this work I will suggest that the fact that the world *looks* like a war zone between good and evil is a very good reason for believing that the world *is* a war zone. Unless we have irrefutable reasons for thinking otherwise, we should accept that things are the way they appear.

We must be careful here, of course, especially in these postmodern times, when some are inclined to make experience the final arbiter of all truth claims. Although we are made in God's image and "wired" to experience the world accurately, we are also fallen. Consequently, experience can deceive us. It should therefore never be placed above or even considered apart from Scripture and reason. But when considered in the light of Scripture and reason, I believe that experience can contribute to our search for truth.

Finally, I assume that church tradition has a dialectical role to play in our

---

[18]In my view the inspirational authority of Scripture attaches to the canonical form of Scripture and does not itself resolve any historical-critical issues regarding the editorial histories of various texts. For the purposes of this work, such issues may therefore be left aside.

quest for truth. As a Protestant I am careful to place Scripture above tradition. I hold to the Reformation principle of *sola scriptura,* believing that Scripture is the final arbiter of theological truth. But I nevertheless hold that all theological and philosophical reflection must be conducted in critical dialogue with church tradition. Concerning the development of the trinitarian warfare theodicy, I find that the early postapostolic church has a great deal to contribute, insights that were obscured in the tradition after Augustine (see chapters one and ten).[19]

These four assumptions constitute the method I employ as I work out the implications of love and thereby attempt to render the warfare worldview of Scripture intelligible. In short, I shall be reflecting on the nature of love in the light of Scripture, reason, experience and church tradition. As I seek to identify the a priori conditions that make love among contingent creatures possible, all four of these criteria will be employed simultaneously.

I do so because these four criteria provide checks and balances on one another. If our thinking about the conditions of love contradict our reading of Scripture, for example, this is a sure indication that we are either reasoning improperly or interpreting the Bible incorrectly. Similarly, if our interpretation of Scripture contradicts our experience, this also is a sure indication that we are either misinterpreting Scripture or our experience. And when aspects of the church's theological tradition come into conflict with either Scripture, reason or experience, this too is an indication that we need to question either the church's tradition or our use of these other three criteria.

Employing the four criteria simultaneously also ensures that our use of any of the criteria will not be myopic. Attending to our experience may illuminate aspects of Scripture that we might otherwise miss, for example, and thinking through the metaphysical implications of love among contingent creatures may bring to our awareness aspects of our experience, of Scripture or of the church's theological tradition that we might otherwise overlook.

Outline of My Argument
This work is structured in two parts. Part one develops the six theses that

---

[19]In a forthcoming volume (*The Myth of the Blueprint* [Downers Grove, Ill.: InterVarsity Press, forthcoming]) I shall develop the thesis that the postapostolic fathers generally reflect a warfare worldview which contrasts at significant points with the blueprint worldview developed by St. Augustine. I shall trace the philosophical influences that contributed to this shift and argue that it led much of the classical-philosophical tradition in the church in an unbiblical and philosophically untenable direction.

structure the trinitarian warfare theodicy. Part two works through the implications of this theodicy in relationship to prayer, "natural" evil and the doctrine of eternal punishment.

I will develop my argument as follows: Since my entire project is an attempt to make philosophical sense of the warfare worldview of Scripture, it will be necessary first to survey the biblical material that expresses this worldview. Unless the significance of this material is adequately appreciated, my efforts to make sense of it will not be understood. This is the primary goal of chapter one ("The World at War"). I shall also take this opportunity to root my own reflections on the problem of evil in church history by briefly discussing the manner in which the trinitarian warfare theodicy was anticipated in the thinking of the early postapostolic fathers.

With this foundation in place, I will proceed to develop the six theses that form the core of my position. The first thesis of the trinitarian warfare theodicy (TWT1) is that love must be freely chosen. I shall argue that we can conceive of beings possessing the capacity to love only if we conceive of them as possessing self-determining freedom.* Correlatively, I argue that the warfare worldview of Scripture presupposes that angels and humans possess self-determining freedom. Many today argue that this concept of freedom is implausible, incoherent or theologically misguided. Chapter two ("The Free Fall") thus spells out TWT1 and defends it against these objections.

In chapters three ("A Risky Creation") and four ("A Question of Balance") I develop and defend the second thesis of the trinitarian warfare theodicy. I argue that love entails risk (TWT2). God could not have created a world in which creatures possess a measure of self-determining freedom without risking some loss. His free creatures might not choose as he wants them to choose. On both theological and philosophical grounds, however, many object to the concept of a risk-taking God. I therefore set forth the biblical and philosophical case for viewing risk as a legitimate and important attribute of God. In the course of making my case I will address the implications of attributing risk to God for our understanding of God's knowledge of, and relationship to, the future.

The next two chapters develop and defend the remaining four theses of the trinitarian warfare theodicy. In chapter five ("Love and War") I submit the thesis that love, and thus freedom, entails that we are to some extent morally responsible for one another (TWT3). We could not have the capacity to love unless we also possessed the power to influence one another, for better or for worse. I further argue that the power to influence for the worse must be roughly proportionate to our power to influence for the better (TWT4). I address a number of possible objections in the course of developing these two theses and conclude that accepting them renders intelligible aspects of Scripture and of our experience that are otherwise difficult to understand.

I develop the final two theses of the trinitarian warfare theodicy in chapter six ("No Turning Back"). I contend that not only does love entail freedom but that this freedom must be, within limits, irrevocable (TWT5). This thesis, if accepted, explains why God cannot always prevent evil deeds he would otherwise prevent. To some extent God places an irrevocable limitation on himself with his decision to create beings who have the capacity to love and who are therefore free. I further argue, however, that this limitation is not infinite, for our capacity to freely choose love is not endless (TWT6). Angels and humans are finite beings who thus possess only a finite capacity to embrace or thwart God's purposes for our lives. This final thesis of the trinitarian warfare theodicy renders intelligible why God must genuinely war against rebellious creatures at the present time, though he is certain to overcome them in the future.

Having established the framework of the trinitarian warfare theodicy in part one, I spend the next six chapters (part two) applying it to various issues important for any theodicy. Chapter seven ("Praying in the Whirlwind") addresses whether or not the trinitarian warfare theodicy makes sense of the Scripture's teaching regarding the urgency of petitionary prayer. I argue that it does so better than any alternative.

The next three chapters address the problem of "natural" evil. This is where the centrality of Satan and his rebellious army within the trinitarian warfare theodicy is most clearly seen. I argue that ultimately there is no such thing as "natural" evil (which is why I place quotation marks around the word). In my view, *all* evil ultimately derives from the wills of free agents. What cannot be attributed to the volition of human agents should be attributed, directly or indirectly, to the volition of fallen angels.

In chapters eight ("Red in Tooth and Claw") and nine ("When Nature Becomes a Weapon") I review and critique seven different ways philosophers and theologians have attempted to explain "natural" evil. I attempt to show that while there are important principles found in each of these views, they are all inadequate as a comprehensive explanation for "natural" evil because they fail to recognize and emphasize the wills of spiritual agents behind the forces of nature. I then attempt to provide this missing element in chapter ten ("This an Enemy Has Done").

Finally, arguably the most challenging aspect of the problem of evil is the reality of hell—at least as it has traditionally been conceived. If earthly suffering is hard to reconcile with an all-loving God, how much more difficult is it to reconcile the reality of hopeless eternal suffering with this understanding of God? The issue is of particular interest to us because it does not seem that the trinitarian warfare theodicy could be of any value in resolving this dilemma. Gratuitous suffering at the present time is inevitable and intelligible, I argue, because we are presently engaged in a cosmic war, and the possibility of the suffering we consequently experience was metaphysically required by the possibility of love. But what explains suffering—unending suffering—once the war has ceased? Unlike suffering in this present age, it seems that suffering in hell can only exist *because God wills it.*

The final two chapters of this book address this challenging issue. In chapter eleven ("A Clash of Doctrines") I examine why the church has traditionally believed that hell is characterized by eternal, conscious suffering and discuss the problems involved in this view. I then examine an increasingly popular understanding of hell called annihilationism,* which avoids these problems by maintaining that unsaved people and rebellious angels are eternally extinguished, not tormented, by God after being judged for their sins. While the view has much to be said for it, however, it also has some problems of its own.

In the final chapter of this book ("A Separate Reality") I propose an alternative model of hell that modifies both the traditional and the annihilationist models, retaining the value but avoiding the difficulties found in both. Utilizing Karl Barth's concept of "the nothingness" (das Nichtige*) as well as insights from C. S. Lewis, I attempt to construct an internally consistent and experientially plausible model of hell that allows us to say both that those who reject God's love suffer eternally, in one sense, and that they have been annihilated, in another sense.[20]

The Style of This Work
Finally, a word should be said about the style of this work. As in *God at War,* the first volume in this Satan and Evil series, I have attempted to make this

---

[20]I include five appendixes at the end of this work that consider issues relevant to the trinitarian warfare theodicy. Appendix one offers brief responses to objections that can be raised against this theodicy. Appendix two offers four philosophical arguments for the incompatibility of self-determining freedom and the view that the future is exhaustively definite in the mind of God. Appendix three deals with the issue of what becomes of people who never had the chance to resolve themselves for or against God's love. Appendix four briefly develops a "theology of chance," since chance is important to the trinitarian warfare theodicy but ruled out by most of the church tradition. Appendix five briefly addresses passages of Scripture often cited in support of compatibilism.

work as accessible to nonspecialists as possible without compromising its academic integrity. I believe that the subject matter is too important to be restricted to specialists in philosophical theology. Besides, most of what is said in highly specialized philosophical works can, with some effort, be translated into common language without much loss of meaning or precision.

I have thus attempted to balance concerns for popular communicability with concerns for academic rigor. Whenever possible, I have "tucked" technical discussions that are likely to be of interest only to specialists in the notes. Laypersons could bypass this material without losing much of the substance of this work, though it is possible that certain questions may arise for them that are only addressed in the notes.

Despite my efforts to use ordinary language as much as possible, however, lay readers should be forewarned that several sections in the body of this work required more technical jargon than the rest of the work. The middle subsection of chapter two ("A Philosophical Objection") is the most technical section of this work. It contains a rather philosophical defense of self-determining freedom. I deemed this defense indispensable inasmuch as this conception of freedom is foundational to the central thesis of this work. Nevertheless, lay readers who already agree that humans possess self-determining freedom (i.e., who agree that compatibilism* is misguided) may want to consider this section optional and skip forward to the next subsection ("A Theological Objection").

Beyond this, a few sections of chapters four and nine deal with philosophical issues that some may consider demanding. Sections of chapter twelve may be difficult for some as well, simply because of the heavily nuanced nature of the discussion. I encourage lay readers not to worry too much about this. This material is important, but I believe the articulation and defense of the trinitarian warfare worldview sustained throughout this work can be adequately understood even if this particular material is not.

Having said all this, and having laid out the map of how we shall proceed, we now embark on the project. Our first step is to survey the warfare worldview of the Bible and of the early postapostolic church.

PART I

1

THE WORLD AT WAR

The Warfare Worldview of the Bible & the Early Church

> And war broke out in heaven; Michael and his angels fought
> against the dragon. The dragon and his angels fought back,
> but they were defeated, and there was no longer any place for them in heaven.
> The great dragon was thrown down, that ancient serpent,
> who is called the Devil and Satan, the deceiver of the whole world—
> he was thrown down to the earth, and his angels were thrown down with him.
> REVELATION 12:7-9

> No one . . . who has not heard what is related of him who is called "devil,"
> and his "angels," and what he was before he became a devil,
> and how he became such, and what was the cause of the simultaneous apostasy
> of those who are termed his angels, will be able to ascertain the origin of evils.
> ORIGEN, FIRST PRINCIPLES

> No theodicy that does not take the Devil fully into consideration
> is likely to be persuasive.
> JEFFREY B. RUSSELL, MEPHISTOPHELES

> War is the father of all and the king of all.
> HERACLITUS

*A*s noted in the introduction, this work is an attempt at making philosophical sense of the warfare worldview of the Bible. How can the scriptural depiction of God striving to accomplish his will against agents who genuinely resist it be reconciled with Scripture's uniform testimony that God is all-powerful? The answer, I will argue, lies in the necessary conditions of creatures possessing the capacity to love. Before exploring these conditions, however, we must first have an adequate appreciation of the biblical material that gives rise to the question.

Toward this end, I first consider various ways the Old Testament expresses a warfare worldview. I then discuss the manner in which Jesus' ministry reflects a warfare worldview, followed by an examination of how it gets reflected throughout the remainder of the New Testament. I conclude with a brief examination of the warfare mindset reflected in the writings of the postapostolic fathers. This chapter's thesis is that, as much as Scripture emphasizes God's control of the world, this pervasive warfare motif suggests that he does not control everything. One important implication of this is that one cannot posit a *specific* divine reason for the behavior of beings who resist God's will.

The Warfare Worldview of the Old Testament

In sharp contrast to the New Testament, Satan plays a minor role in the Old Testament. Instead, the warfare worldview in the Old Testament is expressed in terms of God's conflict with hostile waters, with cosmic monsters, and with other gods. We will examine these three motifs in this order.

Rebuking hostile waters. Like their ancient Near Eastern neighbors, ancient Jews believed that the earth was founded on and encircled by water (e.g., Ps 104:2-3, 5). And, as was the case with these neighbors, ancient Israelites often depicted these waters as a chaotic or hostile force. This was one of the ways ancient authors expressed the conviction that there was something that opposes God and his creation in the cosmic environment of the earth. The Creator thus had to fight to preserve the order of creation.

Whereas other cultures credited one of their chief god(s) with preserving order against hostile forces of chaos, biblical authors always acknowledge Yahweh as the earth's defender. It is Yahweh's "rebuke" (i.e., not the rebuke of a pagan god) that causes the hostile waters to "flee." It is "at the sound of [his] thunder" that "they take to flight" (Ps 104:7). Indeed, these hostile waters take flight at the very sight of God (Ps 77:16).

Moreover, it was the Lord who assigns these rebel waters a "boundary that they may not pass" (Ps 104:9, cf. Job 38:6-11; Prov 8:27-29). It is the Lord and none other who defeats these enemies, who tramples on the sea with his warring horses (Hab 3:15), and who sits enthroned above "the mighty waters" (Ps 29:3-4, 10).

In sum, as Jon Levenson notes, the view here is that "the Sea [is] a somewhat sinister force that, left to its own, would submerge the world and fore-stall the ordered reality we call creation. What prevents this frightening possibility is the mastery of YHWH, whose blast and thunder . . . force the Sea into its proper place."[1]

Biblical authors are of course confident that the Lord is capable of con-taining, and ultimately defeating, these rebel waters. But there is no sugges-tion here that Yahweh's war against these forces is prescripted or inauthentic. To the contrary, as a number of exegetes have noted, biblical authors exalt God's sovereignty precisely *because* they are certain that these raging forces are real, formidable foes.[2]

Leviathan and Rahab. Another common ancient Israelite way of expressing the Creator's warfare against anticreational forces was to depict them as cosmic monsters. Here too the Jews share much in com-mon with the mythology of their Near Eastern neighbors. The two most frequently mentioned "monsters" in the Old Testament are Leviathan and Rahab.

As in Canaanite mythology, Leviathan was believed to be a ferocious, twisting serpent of the sea encircling the earth. He had (on some accounts) many heads (Ps 74:14) and could blow smoke out of his nose(s) and fire out of his mouth(s) (Job 41:18-21). Humans could not defeat or control this beast, for human weapons were useless against a creature of such power. Indeed, this monster could eat iron like straw and crush bronze as if it were decayed timber (Job 41:26-27).

Nevertheless, biblical authors were confident that Leviathan was no match for Yahweh. At the time of creation as well as in subsequent battles against Israel's enemies, Yahweh "broke the heads of the dragons in the waters [and] crushed the heads of Leviathan" (Ps 74:13-14). Looking for-ward to God's ultimate victory wherein all of creation would be freed from evil, Isaiah writes: "On that day the LORD with his cruel and great and strong sword will punish Leviathan the fleeing serpent, Leviathan the twist-

---

[1]Jon Levenson, *Creation and the Persistence of Evil: The Jewish Drama of Divine Omnipotence* (San Francisco: Harper & Row, 1988), p. 22.

[2]Levenson, *Persistence of Evil;* John Gray, *The Biblical Doctrine of the Reign of God* (Edinburgh: T & T Clark, 1979); Adrio König, *Here Am I! A Christian Reflection on God* (Grand Rapids, Mich.: Eerdmans, 1982); Adrio König, *New and Greater Things: Re-evaluating the Biblical Message on Creation* (Pretoria: University of South Africa, 1988); C. J. Labuschagne, *The Incomparability of Yahweh in the Old Testament,* POS 5 (Leiden: E. J. Brill, 1966); Tremper Longman III and Daniel G. Reid, *God Is a Warrior* (Grand Rapids, Mich.: Zondervan, 1995); T. N. D. Mettinger, "Fighting the Powers of Chaos and Hell—Towards the Biblical Portrait of God," *ST* 39 (1985): 21-38.

ing serpent, and he will kill the dragon that is in the sea" (Is 27:1).[3]

Given the mythical-poetic nature of this literature, we should not suppose any contradiction between the claim that Leviathan's heads *were* crushed in the primordial past and the claim that someday Yahweh *will* kill this dragon. The point of such passages is that the Creator *has had* and *will continue to have* strong opposition from cosmic forces and that he has been able and will continue to be able to contain, and ultimately defeat, these forces.

Rahab is portrayed in similar terms. This cosmic creature inhabiting the waters that encircle the earth threatened the whole earth but was no match for Yahweh. When Yahweh expressed his wrath against evil, "the helpers of Rahab bowed beneath him" (Job 9:13). In the primordial past Yahweh's power "churned up the sea," his wisdom "cut Rahab to pieces," and his hand "pierced the gliding serpent" (Job 26:12-13 NIV). The psalmist also celebrated Yahweh's sovereignty over "the raging of the sea" by announcing that he had "crushed Rahab like a carcass" and "scattered [his] enemies with [his] mighty arm" (Ps 89:9-10). In similar fashion Isaiah reassured himself that Yahweh would "awake" to deliver Israel by remembering that in the primal past he had "cut Rahab in pieces" and "pierced the dragon" (Is 51:9).

Contrary to the convictions of most contemporary Western people, but in keeping with the basic assumptions of ancient people and primordial people groups today, Old Testament authors did not draw a sharp distinction between "spiritual" and "physical" realities. The world "above" and the world "below" were seen as intertwined. Hence biblical authors frequently see battles between nations as participating in God's ongoing battle with cosmic forces. For example, the evil character and threatening power of Rahab on a cosmic level was understood to be revealed in and channeled through the evil character and threatening power of Egypt (Ps 87:4; Is 30:7; cf. Jer. 51:34; Ezek 29:3; 32:2).

For this reason, Israel's defeat of an opponent was sometimes construed as the Lord once again defeating cosmic forces of chaos (Is 17:12-14). When Yahweh freed the children of Israel from Egypt, for example, this was considered his defeat of the raging waters (Hab 3:12-13; cf. Nahum 1:4).[4] And when he further delivered Israel by parting the Red Sea, this was seen as a

---

[3]The same vision of Leviathan and his ultimate defeat is expressed in Revelation 12, which speaks of the "great red dragon, with seven heads," who is "the deceiver of the whole world." This "great dragon" is explicitly identified as "the Devil and Satan" (Rev 12:3, 9).

[4]A. Yarbro Collins, *The Combat Myth in the Book of Revelation,* HDR 9 (Missoula, Mont.: Scholars Press, 1976), p. 11.

new application of Yahweh's victory over Rahab (Ps 77:16; Is 51:9-10).[5]

Conversely, Israel's defeat by an enemy could be described as being devoured by the mighty sea serpent (Jer 51:34, cf. v. 55). Similarly, David identified the enemies who opposed him with the forces that have opposed God since the beginning of creation (Ps 93:3-4). Moreover, when David's life was threatened he asked the Lord to reenact his primordial victory over sinister cosmic forces on his behalf. He called on Yahweh to deliver him "from my enemies and from the deep waters. Do not let the flood sweep over me, or the deep swallow me up" (Ps 69:14-15). Again he asks, "Stretch out your hand . . . set me free and rescue me from the mighty waters, from the hand of aliens" (144:7).

As before, biblical authors were confident of the Lord's ultimate sovereignty over his cosmic foes and thus over their earthly foes. But biblical authors also assumed that the Lord nevertheless entered into genuine battle against his foes, just as they assumed that they must enter into genuine battle against their foes.

Battle among the "gods." Beyond cosmic waters and monsters, Old Testament authors also assumed the existence of multitudes of other powerful heavenly beings called "gods," the "sons of God" or, less frequently, "angels."[6] Together they formed a "heavenly council" in which decisions affecting humans were made (1 Kings 22:20; Job 1:6; 2:1; Ps 82:1; 89:7). They were supposed to carry out God's will and fight on God's behalf (2 Sam 5:23-24; 2 Kings 2:11; 6:16-17; Ps 34:7; 68:17; 82:1-8; 103:20; Dan 7:10). For our purposes, the most significant aspect of these gods, however, is that they were considered personal agents who exercised a significant influence on the flow of history and who did not necessarily carry out Yahweh's will. Because they were personal agents, they could choose to oppose God's will—and sometimes they did.

For example, in opposition to God's will, some of these "sons of God" copulated with human women and produced hybrid giants in the days prior to the flood (Gen 6:1-4).[7] The author(s) of Genesis provided this account in part to explain why the Lord started over with the human race at this point. Similarly, a "prince of Persia" opposed God's will by delaying his response to one of Daniel's prayers (Dan 10). The Lord had to dispatch another powerful angel to battle this "prince" in order to get the message through.

---

[5]Ibid., p. 117. See also Levenson, *Persistence of Evil*, pp. 20-21.
[6]Gregory A. Boyd, *God at War: The Bible and Spiritual Conflict* (Downers Grove, Ill.: InterVarsity Press, 1996), pp. 114-42.
[7]Ibid., pp. 176-77.

Along similar lines, a national god named Chemosh was apparently able to rout Israel on behalf of the Moabites when the king of Moab sacrificed his son to him (2 Kings 3:21-27).[8] Indeed, a case can be made that all the "gods of the nations" were originally servants of God assigned to care for particular nations. But instead of using their position to lead the nation to Yahweh, they made themselves the object of the nation's allegiance.[9]

Perhaps the most disclosive passage reflecting both the personal nature of these beings as well as their significant influence over what transpires on earth is Psalm 82. Here we find the psalmist proclaiming:

> God has taken his place in the divine council;
>   in the midst of the gods he holds judgment:
> "How long will you judge unjustly
>   and show partiality to the wicked?
> Give justice to the weak and the orphan;
>   maintain the right of the lowly and the destitute.
> Rescue the weak and the needy;
>   deliver them from the hand of the wicked." . . .
>
> I say, "You are gods,
>   children of the Most High, all of you;
> nevertheless, you shall die like mortals,
>   and fall like any prince." (Ps 82:1-4, 6-8)

This passage depicts a discussion that transpired in the heavenly council. These gods (perhaps national gods) had apparently been given various duties to perform among humans: to help administer justice, to defend the weak, and to help the poor. But at least some of these gods had rebelled and decided to serve the wicked instead. Consequently, Yahweh threatened them with the same fate that befalls mortals and earthly princes. Though they were truly gods, if they did not conform to God's will, they would die like the mortals they were supposed to protect.[10]

The point is that Old Testament authors did not assume that things always went as God planned in the heavenly realm any more than they always

---

[8]Cf. Judg 11:24, which seems to assume that Chemosh was able to acquire land for the Moabites through battle.

[9]On angelic beings as "gods of the nations," see Boyd, *God at War*, pp. 135-40. For further discussions, see Daniel I. Block, *The Gods of the Nations: Studies in Ancient Near Eastern National Theology*, ETSMS 2 (Jackson, Miss.: Evangelical Theological Society, 1988); Walter Wink, *Unmasking the Powers: The Invisible Forces That Determine Human Existence* (Philadelphia: Fortress, 1986), pp. 87-107.

[10]On Yahweh's interaction and conflict with other "gods," see Boyd, *God at War*, pp. 114-42.

went as he planned on earth. While the Lord always accomplishes his general will in the end, there is often significant opposition along the way. His sovereignty, in other words, is a sovereignty that has to be defended.

Warfare in the Ministry of Jesus

The theme of God striving to establish his sovereign will (his kingdom) on earth over and against forces that oppose him becomes far more pronounced in the New Testament. In keeping with the apocalyptic climate of the time, we read much more about angels at war with God and other angels, about demons that torment people and, most importantly, about the powerful being who leads this rebellion against the Creator. His name, of course, is Satan.

Jesus' view of the satanic kingdom. A theme that underlies Jesus' entire ministry is the apocalyptic assumption (already intimated in the Old Testament, as we have seen) that creation has been seized by a cosmic force and that God is now battling this force to rescue it. Jesus understood himself to be the one in whom this battle was to be played out in a decisive way. The assumption is evident in almost everything Jesus says and does.

Jesus refers to Satan as "the prince" *(archōn)* of this present age three times (Jn 12:31; 14:30; 16:11). The term *archōn* was used in secular contexts to denote the highest official in a city or region.[11] In short, Jesus acknowledges that Satan is the highest power of this present fallen world, at least in terms of his present influence. When Satan offers Jesus all "authority" over "all the kingdoms of the world," Jesus does not dispute his claim that it was his to offer (Lk 4:5-6). Other writings explicitly teach that the whole world is "under the power of the evil one" (1 Jn 5:19), for Satan is "the god of this world" (2 Cor 4:4) and "the ruler of the power of the air" (Eph 2:2). *Gub language*

Jesus addresses this evil "prince" as the leader of a relatively unified and pervasive army of spiritual powers and demons. Satan is thus called "the ruler of the demons" (Mt 9:34), and fallen angels are called "his angels" (Mt 25:41). On the basis of this assumed military unity, Jesus refutes the Pharisees' contention that he exorcises demons by the power of Satan rather than the power of God. If this were so, Jesus argues, Satan's kingdom would be working against itself (Mk 3:24) and could not exhibit the power it exhibits in this world.

Correlatively, Jesus taught that those who wish to make headway in tear-

---

[11]Clinton E. Arnold, *Powers of Darkness: Principalities and Powers in Paul's Letters* (Downers Grove, Ill.: InterVarsity Press, 1992), p. 81. See the discussion in Boyd, *God at War,* p. 181.

ing down this evil kingdom and in taking back the "property" of this kingdom must first tie up "the strong man" who oversees the whole operation (Mk 3:27). This could only be done when "one stronger than he attacks him and overpowers him" and thus "takes away his armor in which he trusted" (Lk 11:22). This, in a nutshell, is what Jesus understood himself to be doing by his teachings, healings, exorcisms and especially by his death and resurrection. His whole ministry was about overpowering the "fully armed" strong man who guarded "his property" (Lk 11:21)—the earth and its inhabitants who rightfully belong to God.

Demonstrating the kingdom of God. Jesus tied up the strong man so that he (and later, his church) could pillage the strong man's kingdom. In fact, this is what Jesus' teaching about the kingdom of God is all about. In the context of Jesus' ministry, it is a warfare concept. "If it is by the finger of God that I cast out the demons," Jesus teaches, "then the kingdom of God has come to you" (Lk 11:20). Where God reigns, Satan and his demons cannot. Put otherwise, if the earth is to become the domain in which God is king (the kingdom of God), then it must cease being the domain in which Satan is king. This is what Jesus came to accomplish. He came to "destroy the works of the devil" (1 Jn 3:8; cf. Heb 2:14) and to establish God's domain on earth.

Every exorcism and every healing—the two activities that most characterize Jesus' ministry—marked an advance toward establishing the kingdom of God over and against the kingdom of Satan.[12] Consequently, in contrast with any view that would suggest that disease and demonization somehow serve a divine purpose, Jesus *never* treated such phenomenon as anything other than the work of the enemy. He consistently treated diseased and demonized people as casualties of war. Furthermore, rather than accepting their circumstances as mysteriously fitting into God's sovereign plan, Jesus revolted against them as something that God did not will and something that ought to be vanquished by God's power.

---

[12]Susan Garrett writes, "Every healing, exorcism, or raising of the dead is a loss for Satan and a gain for God" (*The Demise of the Devil: Magic and the Demonic in Luke's Writings* [Minneapolis: Fortress, 1989], p. 55). James Kallas also captures the motif well when he notes that "the arrival of the kingdom is simultaneous with, dependent upon, and manifested in the routing of demons" (*The Significance of the Synoptic Miracles* [Greenwich, Conn.: Seabury, 1961], p. 78). See also O. Böcher, *Christus Exorcista: Dämonismus und Taufe im Neuen Testament,* BWANT 5.16 (Stuttgart: Kohlhammer, 1972); L. Sabourin, "The Miracles of Jesus (II): Jesus and the Evil Powers," *BTB* 4 (1974): 115-75; Graham H. Twelftree, *Jesus the Exorcist: A Contribution to the Study of the Historical Jesus,* WUNT 2.54 (Tübingen: Mohr [Siebeck], 1993), pp. 217-24; Rikki Watts, *Isaiah's New Exodus and Mark,* WUNT 2.88 (Tübingen: Mohr [Siebeck], 1997), pp. 137-82.

When confronted with a woman who had a deformed back, for example, Jesus did not wonder why God had allowed this to happen. Rather, he immediately diagnosed her as being bound by Satan and freed her from this bondage (Lk 13:11-16). Indeed, many times Jesus diagnosed illnesses as being directly caused by demons, as when he cast out demons of muteness or deafness (Mk 9:25; Lk 11:14). In other cases no exorcism was performed, but Jesus nevertheless opposed the illness as something that was not part of God's kingdom. He assumed that it was at least the indirect result of Satan's pervasive influence in the world. Hence Peter later summarized Jesus' healing ministry by noting that he "went about doing good and healing all who were oppressed by the devil" (Acts 10:38). All sickness and disease was considered a form of satanic oppression, and so in freeing people from it Jesus demonstrated the presence of the kingdom of God.

It is curious that the evil one to whom the Bible directly or indirectly attributes all evil has played a rather insignificant role in the theodicy of the church after Augustine. This, I contend, is directly connected to the fact that the church generally accepted the blueprint worldview that Augustine espoused. If we assume that there is a specific divine reason for every particular event that transpires, including the activity of Satan, then the *ultimate* explanation for evil cannot be found in Satan. It must rather be found in the reason that God had for ordaining or allowing him to carry out his specific activity.[13] The New Testament, I submit, does not share this assumption.

Warfare in the New Testament Church

Jesus' entire ministry, we have seen, reflects the belief that the world had been seized by a hostile, sinister lord. Jesus had come to take it back. Contrary to any view suggesting that everything has a divine purpose behind it, Jesus' ministry indicated that God's purposes for the world had to be fought for and won. Jesus taught his disciples to pray that God's will *would be* done "on earth as it is in heaven" (Mt 6:10). This presupposes that, to a signifi-

---

[13]David Griffin summarizes the point well when he notes, "It has been a widespread conviction of Christians generally and theologians in particular that, in spite of appearances to the contrary, God is actually in complete control of all events. The New Testament, however, knew better" ("Why Demonic Power Exists: Understanding the Church's Enemy," *LTQ* 28 [1993]: 224). Against classical theodicies, atheist Michael Martin insightfully comments, "That things appear to us to be a certain way is itself justification for thinking things are this way" (*Atheism: A Philosophical Justification* [Philadelphia: Temple University Press, 1990], 339). The trinitarian warfare theodicy in principle agrees with Martin against classical theodicies. The world looks like it is not meticulously controlled by God because its not meticulously controlled by God. Indeed, the world *looks* like a battlefield between good and evil because the world *is* a battlefield between good and evil.

cant extent at least, God's will is *not now* being done on earth.

According to the New Testament, Jesus in principle defeated Satan and established God's kingdom. Through his ministry of exorcism and healing, and especially through his death and resurrection, he destroyed the power of the devil (1 Jn 3:8; Heb 2:14), disarmed the principalities and powers (Col 2:14-15), and put all God's enemies under his feet (Eph 1:22; Heb 1:13). But the New Testament does not on this account conclude that Satan has ceased being in control of this world. This is the paradox of the already-not yet tension* within the New Testament.[14] While Satan has *in principle* been defeated by Christ, God's victory has not yet been fully *realized* on the earth. Applying this victory to the rest of the world is the primary business of the church, the body of Christ.

As was the case with Jesus' ministry, and as has always been the case with God's good purposes for the world, the church's efforts to apply God's victory to the world invariably encounters strong opposition from the enemy. Though they believed him to be mortally wounded, New Testament authors never underestimated the power and craftiness of this foe.

Consequently, New Testament authors refer to Satan, demons, fallen angels and various levels of evil principalities and powers as being quite active in the world (Eph 1:21; 3:10; Col 1:16). In addition, exorcism and healing continued to play an important role in the ministry of the early church (Acts 3:1-10; 8:6-7, 13; 14:3, 8-10; 19:11-12; 28:5). The world was conceived of as being in bondage to the evil one (Gal 1:4; Eph 5:16; 1 Jn 5:19). In the thinking of these New Testament writers, Satan's influence continued to be so pervasive that putting someone outside the church as a disciplinary measure was tantamount to turning that one over to Satan (1 Cor 5:1-5; 1 Tim 1:20; cf. 1 Tim 5:15).

The New Testament authors also portrayed the devil as "a roaring lion" who "prowls around, looking for someone to devour" (1 Pet 5:8). He was regarded as "the tempter" who influences people to sin (1 Thess 3:5; cf. Acts 5:3; 1 Cor 7:5; 2 Cor 11:3) and the deceiver who blinds the minds of unbelievers (2 Cor 4:4). Satan and his legions were understood to be behind all types of false teaching (Gal 4:8-10; Col 2:8; 1 Tim 4:1-5; 1 Jn 4:1-2; 2 Jn 7). He could appear as an "angel of light" (2 Cor 11:14) and even perform "lying wonders, and every kind of wicked deception for

---

[14]On the already–not yet tension in New Testament eschatology, see Werner G. Kümmel, *Promise and Fulfillment: The Eschatological Message of Jesus,* 3rd ed., SBT 1.23 (London: SCM Press, 1957); George E. Ladd, *Jesus and the Kingdom: The Eschatology of Biblical Realism,* 2nd ed. (Waco, Tex.: Word, 1964); B. Wiebe, "The Focus of Jesus' Eschatology," in *Self-Definition and Self-Discovery in Early Christianity: A Study in Changing Horizons,* ed. David J. Hawkins and Tom Robinson (Lewiston, N.Y.: Mellen, 1990), pp. 121-46.

those who are perishing" (2 Thess 2:9-10).

Paul understood that Satan, because of his ongoing power and in spite of his mortal wound, was able to hinder the work of the church, as when he prevented Paul from preaching at Thessalonica (1 Thess 2:18). Satan discourages Christians and entraps church leaders (1 Thess 3:5; 1 Tim 3:7). He establishes strongholds of deception in the minds of believers, which Christians must war against (2 Cor 10:3-5). For this reason Paul warns us that warriors of God must never be "ignorant of [Satan's] designs" (2 Cor 2:11). Indeed, Paul summarizes the Christian life as a battle "against the cosmic powers of this present darkness" (Eph 6:12; cf. vv. 10-18).

In sum, the world of the New Testament authors was a world at war. Granted, they expressed great confidence that Jesus had in principle defeated Satan and that Satan and all who followed him would eventually be defeated when Christ is enthroned as Lord of the cosmos. But they were just as certain that in this present fallen world order *God does not always get his way.* He desires all to be saved, for example, but many will perish (1 Tim 2:3-4; 2 Pet 3:9). Similarly, God wants believers to be conformed to the image of Christ, but our minds and behavior are usually to some degree conformed to the pattern of the world and under demonic strongholds (Rom 12:2; 2 Cor 10:3-5). God's Spirit can be, and frequently is, resisted by our wills (Eph 4:30; 1 Thess 5:19). Clearly, the Lord and his church continue to face strong opposition in carrying out God's will as we seek to establish his kingdom on the earth.

The Warfare Worldview of the Postapostolic Church

The warfare worldview of the Bible was adopted and even expanded by the first generation of believers who succeeded the apostles. Their reflections on evil differ significantly from the theology of the post-Augustinian church. They generally assume that the *final explanation* for evil is to be found in the free wills of Satan, fallen angels and human beings, as opposed to concluding that every particular evil has a divine purpose behind it.

A mediated providence. While the postapostolic fathers unequivocally affirmed that God is sovereign over the world, they also believed that his providential control was mediated by angels who possessed free will. Justin Martyr summarizes the prevailing view:

> God, when He had made the whole world, and subjected things early to man
> . . . committed the care of men and of all things under heaven to angels whom
> He appointed over them. But the angels transgressed this appointment.[15]

---

[15] Justin Martyr *2 Apology* 5 (ANF 1:190).

Along the same lines, Athenagoras notes that the "office of the angels is to exercise providence for God over the things created and ordered by Him." In his view, then, God exercises a "universal and general providence of the whole," but the control of "the particular parts are provided for by the angels appointed over them."[16] Likewise, Origen argues that every particular aspect of the earth, from the growing of fruit to the flow of streams and the purity of the air, are under "the agency and control of certain beings whom we may call invisible husbandmen and guardians."[17]

For these authors everything within the physical creation is under the mediated authority of some divinely appointed spiritual agent. While sovereignly ruling the creation in a "universal and general" sense, God does not ordinarily micromanage the affairs of creation.

Angels as free moral agents. Unfortunately, as Justin noted above, some of "the angels transgressed this appointment." These divinely appointed administrators were free moral agents who could, and to some extent did, rebel against the divine order. Pre-Augustinian writers stress the freedom and moral responsibility of both angels and humans as the ultimate explanation for their rebellious behavior.[18] Athenagoras expresses this consensus

---

[16]Athenagoras *A Plea for the Christians* 24 (ANF 2:142).

[17]Origen *Against Celsus* 8.31 (ANF 4:650-51). On angels in charge of foundational elements, see Origen *Homily on Jeremiah* 10.6; cf. *Homilies on Luke* 12, 13. According to Origen, every angel and human being was assigned a realm of authority in creation on the basis of the virtue and/or vice displayed in a preexistent state. He writes, "in the case [or, perhaps better translated, 'in the position'] of every creature it is a result of his own works and movements. . . . [T]hose [angelic] powers which appear either to hold sway over others or to exercise power or dominion, have been preferred to and placed over those whom they are said to govern or exercise power over . . . not in consequence of a peculiar privilege inherent in their constitutions, but on account of merit" (*First Principles* 1.5.3 [ANF 4:258]; cf. 2.9.2-4, 6).

[18]So, for example, Clement of Alexandria says, "This was the law from the first, that virtue should be the object of voluntary choice" (*Stromata* 7.2 [ANF 2:525]). The theme recurs among all the apologists, especially in Clement and Origen. See, for example, Clement *Stromata* 1.17; 2.3; 2.6; 2.15; 4.12; 4.22; 6.12; 7.2; Origen *On Prayer* 6.1-3; Origen *First Principles*, preface, 1.5.3; 1.8; 2.9.2; 3.1.3; 3.1.6; 3.1.18-22; Justin *1 Apology* 58; Theophilus *To Autolycus* 27; Irenaeus *Against Heresies* 4.37. Tatian goes so far as to say that it was "the demons . . . who laid down the doctrine of Fate" (*Address of Tatian* 9 [ANF 2:68]; see also chapters 8 and 11 of this work). Tatian has in mind here specifically the form of fatalism that was attached to the motions of planets, a view common in his day. On Tatian's and other early apologists' association of astrology with demonology, see Jean Daniélou, *Gospel Message and Hellenistic Culture*, ed. and trans. John A. Baker (Philadelphia: Westminster Press, 1973), pp. 431-33. Justin also suggested that the doctrine of fate is of demonic origin (*1 Apology* 14). On this see the discussion in Elaine Pagels, *The Origin of Satan* (New York: Random House, 1995), pp. 132-33. On the emphatic role that freedom played among all pre-Augustinian fathers, see D. Stoffer, "The Problem of Evil: An Historical Theological Approach," *ATJ* 24 (1992): 60-62; and especially Roger Forster and V. Paul Marston, *God's Strategy in Human History* (Wheaton, Ill.: Tyndale House, 1973), pp. 243-57.

well: "Just as with men, who have freedom of choice as to both virtue and vice, so is it among the angels." He continues:

> Some free agents, you will observe, such as they were created by God, continued in those things for which God had made and over which He had ordained them; but some outraged both the constitution of their nature and the government entrusted to them.[19]

Because they were free, they could rebel, and for Athenagoras and other early fathers, this is the ultimate explanation for why creation now exists in a war-torn condition.

Tatian argues along similar lines. He stresses the all-important role of freedom within God's creation:

> The Logos . . . before the creation of men, was the Framer of angels. And each of these two orders of creatures was made free to act as it pleased, not having the nature of good, which again is with God alone, but is brought to perfection in men through their freedom of choice, in order that the bad man may be justly punished . . . but the just man be deservedly praised. . . . Such is the constitution of things in reference to angels and men.[20]

Unlike God, who alone possesses goodness as an inherent quality, contingent beings such as angels and humans must bring it "to perfection . . . through their freedom of choice." Moral virtue, in other words, cannot be built into contingent beings as a matter of necessity. For Tatian, this freedom explains why things have gone wrong in creation.

> When men attached themselves to one who was more subtle than the rest [Satan, referring to Gen 3:1], having regard to his being the first-born, and declared him to be God, though he was resisting the law of God, then the power of the Logos excluded the beginner of the folly and his adherents from all fellowship with Himself. And so he who was made in the likeness of God [humans] . . . becomes mortal; but that first-begotten one through his transgression and ignorance becomes a demon; and they who imitated him . . . are become a host of demons, and through their freedom of choice have been given up to their own infatuation.[21]

---

[19]Athenagoras *A Plea for the Christians* 24 (ANF 2:142).

[20]Tatian *Address to the Greeks* 7 (ANF 2:67).

[21]Ibid., 2:68. On the freedom of Satan, Irenaeus writes that "he apostatized from God of his own free-will" (*Against Heresies* 5.26.2 [ANF 1:555]), and Clement says, "Now the devil, being possessed of free-will, was able both to repent and to steal." From this he concludes, "So in no respect is God the author of evil. But since free choice and inclination originate sins . . . punishments are rightly inflicted" (*Stromata* 1.17 [ANF 2:319]). Likewise Origen says that, "every Rational creature . . . is capable of earning praise and censure. . . . And this also is to be held as applying to the devil himself, and those who are with him, and are called his

Tatian's references to Satan being God's "first-born," to Satan being "more subtle" than humans, and to humans making Satan their "God" give us some idea of the remarkable authority and sinister nature he believed this fallen angel to have. When Satan rebelled of his own free will, multitudes of angels chose to follow him, thereby becoming demons. Consequently, according to Tatian, the earth is now under the power of Satan and is populated by multitudes of demons.[22] Indeed, Tatian elsewhere states that human life is life in slavery to ten thousand demonic tyrants.[23] Such was the common view of the early church.

For Tatian, the tragic nature of the world in its present condition is the result of angels and humans misusing their free will. The reason God gave them free will was because they, being contingent beings, could not possess "the nature of good" as a matter of necessity. If moral virtue was the goal, freedom had to be the means. Hence, evil as a possibility is built into the possibility of moral virtue.

Irenaeus provides yet another example of this postapostolic emphasis on the freedom and authority of angels. After reiterating the pre-Augustinian view of divine sovereignty by saying "there is no coercion with God, but a good will is present with Him continually," he continues:

> And in man, as well as in angels, [God] has placed the power of choice (for angels are rational beings), so that those who had yielded obedience might justly possess what is good, given indeed by God, but preserved by themselves. On the other hand, they who have not obeyed shall, with justice, be not found in possession of the good, and shall receive condign punishment: for God did kindly bestow on them what was good . . . but [they] poured contempt upon His super-eminent goodness.[24]

For Irenaeus, God's providential will is unequivocally and unambiguously good. There is no "mystery" as to how God's goodness might lie behind children being buried in mudslides or kidnapped. In his view, this goodness is reflected in the fact that God gave humans and angels the gift of freedom. But for Irenaeus this bestowal involves an element

---

angels" (*First Principles* 1.5.2 [ANF 4:256]; see also 1.8.3 [ANF 4:265-66]).

[22]See esp. *Address to the Greeks*, chs. 7-14, for Tatian's preoccupation with demons. See Pagels, *Origin of Satan*, pp. 131-35.

[23]Tatian *Address to the Greeks* 28.

[24]Irenaeus *Against Heresies* 5.37 (ANF 1:518). See also *Epistle to Diognetus* 7.4, which states that God sent his Son "as one who saves by persuasion, not compulsion, for compulsion is no attribute of God" (*The Apostolic Fathers: Greek Texts and English Translations of Their Writings*, ed. and trans. J. B. Lightfoot and J. R. Harmer, ed. and rev. by M. W. Holmes (Grand Rapids, Mich.: Baker, 1992), p. 545.

of risk. It means that "rational beings" have the capacity either to go along with God's providential design or not. For Irenaeus, this risk did not in any way compromise God's sovereignty, for neither Irenaeus nor any other pre-Augustinian theologian defined God's sovereignty merely in terms of control. Many of these early authors argue explicitly against this notion.[25] Thus with perfect consistency Irenaeus and other post-apostolic fathers affirm that the Creator is omnipotent even though he does not always get his way. Things go wrong, sometimes very wrong, and when they do these early fathers do not look for a divine reason to explain it.[26]

God's moral rule. This understanding of sovereignty and free will is articulated clearly in Origen. In response to the pagan claim that "whatever happens in the universe, whether it be the work of God, of angels, [or] of other demons . . . is regulated by the law of the Most High God," Origen argues:

> This is . . . incorrect; for we cannot say that transgressors follow the law of God when they transgress; and Scripture declares that it is not only wicked men who are transgressors, but also wicked demons and wicked angels. . . . When we say that "the providence of God regulates all things," we utter a great truth if we attribute to that providence nothing but what is just and right. But if we ascribe to the providence of God all things whatsoever, however unjust they

---

[25]For example, Tertullian maintains that "it is not the part of good and solid faith to refer all things to the will of God . . . as to make us fail to understand that there is a something in our power" (*Exhortation on Chastity* 2 [ANF 4:50-51]).

[26]These early theologians take it for granted that evil arises solely from creaturely free wills and thus cannot be understood as in any sense designed by God. If it were so designed, God would be responsible for it. Origen, for example, says that it "certainly is absurd [to say] that the cause of their [fallen angels'] wickedness should be removed from the purpose of their own will and ascribed of necessity to their Creator" (*First Principles* 1.5.3 [ANF 4:258]). Tatian argues in a similar fashion when he says that "our free-will has destroyed us. . . . Nothing evil has been created by God; we ourselves have manifested wickedness" (*Address to the Greeks* [ANF 2:70]). Cf. Theophilus, *To Autolycus* 17, for a similar statement. As noted before, Clement of Alexandria writes, "So in no respect is God the author of evil. But since free choice and inclination originate sins . . . punishments are rightly inflicted" (*Stromata* 1.17 [ANF 2:319]). Similarly, Irenaeus argues that "in man, as well as in angels, [God] has placed the power of choice. [For] if some had been made by nature bad, and others good, these latter would not be deserving of praise for being good, for such were they created; nor would the former be reprehensible, for thus they were made" (*Against Heresies* 4.37 [ANF 1:518-19]). All therefore agree that, as Clement puts it, God "is in no respect whatever the cause of evil" (*Stromata* 7.3 [ANF 2:526]) and that God's providential rule involves granting creatures freedom of choice. This thinking is far removed from Augustine's later doctrine of predestination and his understanding of evil as always mysteriously fulfilling a positive divine role.

may be, then it is no longer true that the providence of God regulates all things.[27]

The point is that the law of God's providence is a moral law, not a deterministic law. To say that "God regulates all things" is not to say that "God controls all things." Rather, God's governance is one that is consistent with "the preservation of freedom of will in all rational creatures."[28] Hence, God's sovereign will "regulates all things" not by controlling events but by imposing a moral law on them, such as the law that sin has consequences. If God's sovereignty in fact included sin, Origen argues, then it would no longer be a rule by moral law; that is, it would no longer be true that the "providence of God [morally defined] regulates all things." This line of thought is very close to Athenagoras's view, alluded to above, that God's providence is "general and universal," not meticulous. It is antithetical, however, to the blueprint model of providence that came to dominate the church's theologizing after Augustine.

Fallen angels and the problem of evil. We have seen that for the authors of this period the ultimate explanation for evil was located in the free will of creatures, not in any mysterious purposes of God. To be sure, all these fathers agree that God gave these creatures their freedom. But insofar as they address the topic, they also agree that God is not responsible for the fact that this freedom gives creatures the power to resist his will, if they so choose. As Tatian argued, the possibility of abusing freedom had to exist in order for the possibility of using it correctly to exist. When creatures abuse their God-given freedom to oppose God, the ultimate reason for their misdeed is found in them, not in God who gave them the gift they now abuse.

---

[27]Origen *Against Celsus* 7.68 (ANF 4:638). Cf. *Commentary on John* 2.7 (ANF 10:330-31), where Origen attempts to reconcile Jn 1:3, which affirms that the Word made all things, with the truth that God never creates evil. His answer, in a nutshell, is that God created the devil insofar as the devil has being but not insofar as the devil has made himself the devil. "It is," he says, "as if we should say that a murderer is not a work of God, while we may say that in respect he is a man, God made him." He combines this insight with a platonic understanding of evil as privation and thus concludes that "all . . . who have part in Him [God] who is . . . may properly be called Beings; those who have given up their being, by depriving themselves of Being, have become Not-beings. . . . Thus we have shown . . . what are the 'all things' which were made through the Logos, and what came into existence without Him, since at no time is it Being, and it is, therefore, called 'Nothing.' " This conclusion anticipates both Augustine and, even more markedly, Barth. In chapters nine and twelve of this work I will argue that this definition of evil is defective as an ontological analysis of evil but not as an eschatological analysis of evil.

[28]Origen *First Principles* 3.5.8 (ANF 4:344), in speaking about God's governance in restoring all creatures.

This perspective significantly influenced the way these early fathers addressed the problem of evil. Justin Martyr brings out this significance as clearly as anyone. After repeating the common theme that God appointed angels as morally responsible agents in charge of administering segments of his cosmos, he declares:

> But the angels transgressed this appointment. . . . They afterwards subdued the human race to themselves . . . and among men they sowed murders, wars, adulteries, intemperate deeds, and all wickedness. Whence also the poets and mythologists, not knowing that it was the angels and those demons who . . . did these things . . . ascribed them to God himself, and to those who were accounted to be his very offspring.[29]

This passage is significant for a number of reasons, not least of which is the fact that Justin is in this context expressly giving his explanation for the problem of evil raised by various opponents. The specific objection he addresses is the issue of how Christians can claim that God is "our helper" when, in fact, they are being viciously "oppressed and persecuted."[30] Reflecting the warfare worldview of the New Testament, Justin's answer is that this persecution is to be expected, for the world has been besieged by fallen angels and demons. The reason these angels fell and besieged the earth is to be found in their own free decisions. Pagan "poets and mythologists" do not understand this, however, and so mistakenly attribute "all wickedness" that fallen angels and demons perform to "God himself."

Origen argues along similar lines. Not only does Origen agree with Justin that persecutions are demonically inspired, he develops the general understanding of the relationship between the freedom of authoritative angels and evil in the world to the furthest extent found in the early church.[31] In discussing the problem of evil and, more specifically, while explaining why the

---

[29]Justin Martyr 2 *Apology* 5 (ANF 1:190). Justin is here tapping into a version of the "Watcher Tradition." See *The Book of Enoch,* trans. Matthew Black (Leiden: E. J. Brill, 1985), pp. 132, 161, who argues that Justin is here largely following *1 Enoch* 9:9 and 19:1, though he omits all talk about the Nephilim. In Justin's account, demons are the children, not the grandchildren, of the hybrid marriages of humans with fallen angels. See also Everett Ferguson, *Demonology of the Early Christian World* (New York: Mellen, 1984), pp. 105-11. For an overview of the Watcher Tradition, see Boyd, *God at War,* pp. 176-77. For helpful introductions to the demonology of the early church, see Ferguson, *Demonology;* Jeffrey B. Russell, *Satan: The Early Christian Tradition* (Ithaca, N.Y.: Cornell University Press, 1981); Leo Jung, *Fallen Angels in Jewish, Christian and Mohammedan Literature* (Philadelphia: Dropsie College, 1926; reprint, New York: Barnes & Noble, 1995), pp. 73-86.

[30]Justin Martyr 2 *Apology* 5 (ANF 1:190).

[31]On persecutions, see Origen *Against Celsus* 1.43. See also Pagels, *Origin of Satan,* pp. 143-46.

problem has been unsolvable to pagan philosophers, Origen writes:

> No one . . . who has not heard what is related of him who is called "devil,"
> and his "angels," and what he was before he became a devil, and how he
> became such, and what was the cause of the simultaneous apostasy of those
> who are termed his angels, will be able to ascertain the origin of evils. But
> he who would attain to this knowledge must learn more accurately the
> nature of demons, and know that they are not the work of God so far as
> respects their demoniacal nature, but only in so far as they are possessed of
> reason; and also what their origin was, so that they became beings of such a
> nature, that while converted into demons, the powers of their mind
> remain.[32]

If Satan and demons are evil, Origen suggests, it is not because God created them that way. They made themselves that way by the God-given power
of their own volition. Then, most significantly, against the Gnostic understanding that matter is evil Origen adds:

> Evils do not proceed from God. . . . But to maintain that matter . . . is the
> cause of evils, is in our opinion not true. For it is the mind of each individual
> which is the cause of the evil which arises in him, and this is evil . . . while the
> actions which proceed from it are wicked, and there is, to speak with accuracy,
> nothing else in our view that is evil.[33]

For Origen, the key to understanding evil in the world is found in a biblical understanding of the origin of Satan and demons. "No one . . . who has
not heard what is related of him who is called 'devil,' and his 'angels' . . . will
be able to ascertain the origin of evils." The crucial ingredient in understanding the devil is understanding that all evil—the only real evil there is!—
originates in the will of self-determining creatures. It cannot be traced back
to the Creator.

For these early fathers this was as true of "natural" evil as it was of
moral evil. Against all who attributed "natural" disasters to God, for
example, Origen insists, "famine, blasting of the vine and fruit trees, pestilence among men and beasts: all these are the proper occupations of
demons."[34] So too demons are "the cause of plagues . . . barrenness . . .
tempests . . . [and] similar calamities."[35] Similarly, Tertullian argues that

---

[32]Origen *Against Celsus* 4.65 (ANF 4:527). For Origen, to be "possessed of reason" and to
possess free will are synonymous.
[33]Ibid., 4.66 (ANF 4:527).
[34]Ibid., 8.31 (ANF 4:651).
[35]Ibid., 1.31 (ANF 4:409). Interestingly enough, Origen relates the power of demons in the
natural world to the "nourishment" they gain from "the savor of burnt sacrifices, blood, and

"diseases and other grievous calamities" are the result of demons whose "great business is the ruin of mankind."[36]

For these early authors, there really is no such thing as "natural" evil, if by that one means evil that arises from natural or impersonal causes. Rather, it was generally assumed that there was an evil will behind *all* evil.

The fall of the "prince of matter." Perhaps the most comprehensive integration of the view of angels as free mediators of God's providence with the problem of evil is found in the second-century apologist Athenagoras. According to this insightful early writer, Satan was originally "the spirit which is about matter who was created by God, just as the other angels were . . . and entrusted with the control of matter and the forms of matter."[37] This spirit, however, has chosen to exercise its freedom to abuse "the government entrusted to [him]" and thus, "the prince of matter, as may be seen merely from what transpires, exercises a control and management contrary to the good that is in God."

From this premise, and against Euripides and other ancient pagan authors, Athenagoras further argues that the presence of evil in the world

---

incense" offered to them in the context of pagan religions. See Origen *Prayer: Exhortation to Martyrdom* 4.45 (trans. J. J. O'Meara [New York: Paulist, 1954], p. 188). For Clement of Alexandria, the connection between evil spirits and natural calamities was less clear (see, e.g., *Stromata* 6.3). Nonetheless, Clement had a well-developed demonology that played an important role in his theological worldview. For a discussion of Clement's demonology, see W. E. G. Floyd, "Malleus Maleficarum," in his *Clement of Alexandria's Treatment of the Problem of Evil* (Oxford: Clarendon, 1971), pp. 61-73; F. Andres, "Die Engel- und Dämonenlehre des Klemens von Alexandrien," *RQ* 34 (1926): 13-37, 129-40, 307-29.

[36]Tertullian, *Apology* 22 (*ANF* 3:36).

[37]Athenagoras *A Plea for the Christians* 24 (ANF 2:142). Neil Forsyth maintains that Athenagoras's account "brings . . . the Christian view of demons very close to the Gnostic view" (*The Old Enemy: Satan and the Combat Myth* [Princeton, N.J.: Princeton University Press, 1987], p. 353). Athenagoras does not, however, claim that matter itself is evil. This is crucial. His point is not about matter as such but about the power of the spirit put in charge over it—a spirit who has, catastrophically, now turned hostile to the Creator he was supposed to serve. What is more, while this "prince of matter" rules demons and while they "hover about matter" (*A Plea for the Christians* 27 [ANF 2:143]) these demons are not (contra Forsyth) themselves intrinsically associated with matter by Athenagoras, though they are ambiguously identified with other aspects of creation (they are "placed about this first firmament" [matter], *A Plea for the Christians* 24 [ANF 2:142]). Hence, it does not seem to me that Athenagoras is "very close to the Gnostic view." I would rather argue that Athenagoras's idea of Satan as the "prince of matter" most likely is rooted in the New Testament title of Satan as "the ruler of the cosmos" *(archōn tou kosmou)*. As Francis X. Gokey notes, "every kingdom is concerned with space and time. The devil as *archōn tou kosmou* is regarded as presiding over the physical and material world as opposed to the spiritual kingdom of God; the devil as *archōn tou aionos* is regarded as presiding over the present time as opposed to God who will come in glory at the *parousia*" (*The Terminology for the Devil and Evil Spirits in the Apostolic Fathers*, Patristic Studies 93 (Washington, D.C.: Catholic University of America Press, 1961), p. 74 n. 2.

does not imply that there is no Supreme Being "to whom belongs the administration of earthly affairs." Athenagoras is clearly sympathetic to this atheistic perspective to the point of conceding that, given the vast amount of evil in the world, it does seem as though there is no Supreme Administrator. But he rather argues that this evil is not due to God's absence but to Satan's presence. The earth is afflicted by "a ruling prince" and "the demons his followers" who are, of their own free volition, incessantly working against the good administration of the Creator.[38] The world *looks like* a war zone because it *is* a war zone. The will of the Supreme Administrator is not the only will that affects things.

This second-century identification of Satan with "the spirit about matter" who is in control of "matter and the forms of matter" constitutes a profound development of the biblical warfare worldview. Evil is not simply something that happens *within* the (otherwise pristine) cosmos; it rather is a force that corrupts *the cosmos itself!* There is something hostile to God that has affected creation to the core, and God must fight it.

While not endorsing any of the particulars of Athenagoras's view, I believe it is essentially biblical. It is consistent with the biblical motif that God fights against cosmic threatening waters and powerful chaotic monsters such as Leviathan and Rahab. It constitutes another way of saying that Satan is "the ruler of the power of the air" (Eph 2:2), "the ruler *[archōn]* of this world" (Jn 12:31; 14:30; 16:11), and the "god of this world" (2 Cor 4:4). It is another way of explaining why Christians must fight against spiritual "rulers," "authorities," "powers of this present darkness" and "forces of evil in the heavenly places" (Eph 6:12).

As "may be seen merely from what transpires"—just look around, Athenagoras is saying—something other than God's will and design is at work in creation. From mudslides that bury children alive to diseases that kill multitudes of people, it is clear—at least it was clear to Athenagoras and the early church—that God's good will is not being uniformly carried out in history. Atheists argue on this basis that there is no Creator. Early church fathers rather argued on this basis, and from God's Word, that there is a Creator God but that he must battle a formidable opponent who has of his own volition made himself evil.

If this opponent was indeed the one originally entrusted with matter itself, and if the powers and demons who follow him were originally assigned other areas of creation to guard, then it is not surprising that creation is cor-

---

[38]Athenagoras *A Plea for the Christians* 25 (ANF 2:142-43).

? His view of Y in contrast w/ Yoder

rupt to the core. When morally responsible free agents choose to oppose God's will, all that they are responsible for suffers accordingly. In Athenagoras's view, matter itself has been polluted with an evil influence, and the whole physical realm suffers accordingly.

Conclusion

In this chapter we have seen that the Bible exhibits a strong warfare motif and that this motif was embraced in the early church. Neither the New Testament nor the early postapostolic fathers assume that there must be a divine purpose behind evil deeds. They treat agents as the final explanations of their own behavior. Insofar as the early fathers reflect further than this, they suggest that the possibility of evil is built into the nature of freedom and that creatures had to possess freedom if they were to be capable of moral virtue.

My conviction is that these early fathers were headed in the right direction. Unfortunately, in my view, this direction was significantly lost with the advent of Augustine's blueprint theology. The church, of course, continued to assign the blame for evil on free agents, including angels and demons. But to a large extent it ceased viewing agents as the ultimate explanation of their own behavior. The theodicy I construct in this work is an attempt to continue in the direction of the church fathers who preceded Augustine.

The place to begin reclaiming this perspective is with the concept of freedom assumed by the early church. Hence, in the next chapter I defend the notion that we possess self-determining freedom and therefore function as the ultimate explanations of our own behavior. I shall argue that our capacity for love requires this kind of freedom.

OT - God at war w/ cosmos
NT - Jesus at war through healing
AC - warfare motif adopted.
evil ≠ freedom of creature ≠ w/ evil   divine purpose
importance of other creatures/
divine, at w/ PhD

2

THE FREE FALL

Free Will & the Origin of Evil

The greatest gift that God . . . made in Creation,
and the most formidable to His Goodness,
and that which he prizes the most, was the freedom of the will.
DANTE, *THE DIVINE COMEDY*

The Devil's favorite axiom is the deterministic excuse for evil.
JEFFREY B. RUSSELL, *MEPHISTOPHELES*

Free will is what has made evil possible.
Why, then, did God give [creatures] free will?
Because free will, though it makes evil possible,
is also the only thing that makes possible any love or goodness or joy worth having.
C. S. LEWIS, *MERE CHRISTIANITY*

We have to believe in free will. We have no choice.
ISAAC SINGER

*M*y goal in this chapter is to begin to make philosophic sense of the warfare worldview of the Bible and the war-torn nature of the world by reflecting on the nature of love. How is it that God created a world in which he must genuinely fight to accomplish his will and in which his will is in fact sometimes thwarted? How is it that God created a world that is so radically out of sync with his character? Why should one assume that love holds the key to unlocking this mystery? Because love is the reason God created the world.

The Goal of Creation
God is love (1 Jn 4:8, 16). His essence is constituted by perfect love eternally

shared between the Father, Son and Holy Spirit (e.g., Jn 17:24). Throughout its narrative the Bible shows us that God created the world out of his triune love with the goal of acquiring for himself a people who would
participate in and reflect the splendor of his triune love. More specifically,
God's goal from the dawn of history has been to have a church, a bride, who
would say yes to his love, who would fully receive this love, embody this
love, and beautifully reflect this triune love back to himself. In the words of
H. D. McDonald, "The world is built for [God's] love. God is the Great
Cosmic Lover. . . . He is the ultimate Agape. . . . He loves and wants to be
loved by us."[1] Expressing and expanding the unfathomable triune love that
God eternally is was the chief end for which God created the world.[2]

This ultimate goal of creation is beautifully expressed in Jesus' prayer in
John 17:

> I ask not only on behalf of these, but also on behalf of those who will believe in
> me through their word, that they may all be one. As you, Father, are in me and I
> am in you, may they also be in us, so that the world may believe that you have
> sent me. The glory that you have given me I have given them, so that they may
> be one, as we are one. I in them and you in me, that they may become com-
> pletely one, so that the world may know that you have sent me and have loved
> them even as you have loved me. Father, I desire that those also, whom you have
> given me, may be with me where I am, to see my glory, which you have given
> me because you loved me before the foundation of the world. . . . I made your
> name known to them, and I will make it known, so that the love with which you
> have loved me may be in them, and I in them. (Jn 17:20-24, 26)

In essence, Jesus prays that his people—among whom he would wish to
include the whole world (Jn 3:16; 12:32; 1 Tim 2:4; 2 Pet 3:9)—would participate in the triune love of God, reflect this love back to God, and manifest
this love toward each other. He longs for people who are indwelt by the tri-

---

[1]H. D. McDonald, *The God Who Responds* (Minneapolis: Bethany House, 1986), p. 26.
[2]A classic work on this theme is Jonathan Edwards's *Concerning the End for Which God Created
the World*, in *Jonathan Edwards: Ethical Writings*, ed. Paul Ramsey (New Haven, Conn.: Yale
University Press, 1989), pp. 405-536. For an appreciative but critical assessment of Edwards's
philosophical theology, see my *Trinity and Process: A Critical Evaluation and Reappropriation
of Hartshorne's Di-polar Theism Towards a Trinitarian Metaphysics* (New York: Lang, 1992).
Others who strongly express the view that the purpose of creation is love are Eberhard Jüngel,
God as the Mystery of the World, trans. Darrell L. Guder (Grand Rapids, Mich.: Eerdmans,
1983); Clark Pinnock and Robert Brow, *Unbounded Love* (Downers Grove, Ill.: InterVarsity
Press, 1994); Adrio König, *Here Am I! A Christian Reflection on God* (Grand Rapids, Mich.:
Eerdmans, 1982), pp. 35-52; Mildred B. Wynkoop, *A Theology of Love: The Dynamic of Wesley-
anism* (Kansas City, Mo.: Beacon Hill, 1972); and George Newlands, *Theology of the Love of
God* (Atlanta: John Knox Press, 1980).

une love of God and who dwell within the triune love of God. This is the kingdom of God that the biblical narrative articulates and toward which world history is driving.

If love is the goal, what are its conditions? What must creatures be like if they are to be capable of participating in the love of the Trinity? My hope is that in answering this question we will arrive at an understanding of how and why the omnipotent Creator could have and would have created a world that could come under Satan's evil dominion and be as saturated with suffering and evil as our present world is.

In this chapter I will submit what I regard to be the first condition of love: it must be freely chosen. It cannot be coerced. Agents must possess the capacity and opportunity to reject love if they are to possess the genuine capacity and opportunity to engage in love. This, I shall argue, is confirmed by Scripture, reason and experience.

After putting forth my thesis, I next explore its implications. I first offer a critique of compatibilism*—the view that morally responsible freedom is compatible with determinism. Against this view, I argue that Scripture's warfare motif and the war-torn nature of the cosmos is explicable only on the assumption that angels and humans possess self-determining freedom, a view that is sometimes referred to as libertarian or incompatibilistic freedom.*[3] Following this, I examine a number of objections that have been raised against this understanding of freedom. These objections can be classified into three groups. I first consider a scientific objection, namely, that modern science suggests that we do not determine our own choices. Next I consider a philosophical objection that argues that the notion of self-determining freedom is incoherent. Finally I conclude by addressing a theological objection that contends that self-determining freedom conflicts with the biblical teaching that humans are fallen and can be saved only by grace through faith.

As mentioned in the introduction, my critique of compatibilism and

---

[3]Galen Strawson distinguishes between incompatibilism, the belief that morally responsible freedom is logically incompatible with determinism (without asserting whether or not such freedom actually exists), and libertarian freedom, which asserts that such freedom actually exists. Libertarianism thus "purports to show that we are free and so assumes (or argues) that determinism is false" ("Libertarianism, Action, and Self-Determination," in *Agents, Causes and Events: Essays on Indeterminism and Free Will*, ed. Timothy O'Connor [New York: Oxford University Press, 1995], p. 27). The distinction is irrelevant to our purposes, however, and so, following the usage of these terms in much of the literature, I will consider libertarian, incompatibilist and self-determining freedom to be equivalent concepts. I should note that this understanding of freedom is also often referred to as "indeterministic freedom." I choose to avoid this label because it suggests that free will is either uncaused or random.

defense of self-determining freedom in this chapter are unavoidably somewhat technical. Lay readers with little philosophical background may find this section demanding. While I encourage all readers to persevere, I want to acknowledge that this material may be considered optional to those who do not need to be convinced of the philosophical viability of the concept of self-determining freedom. After the opening section ("Love and Freedom"), these readers might consider skipping down to the last subsection ("A Theological Objection").

LOVE AND FREEDOM
Love in Contingent Agents
The first thesis of the trinitarian warfare theodicy is that *love must be chosen* (TWT1). If God's goal is to have agents participate in his triune love, these agents must possess the capacity to refuse his love. This is not to say that *God* must possess the capacity not to love. As church tradition has almost unanimously affirmed, God is a necessary being whose essence could not be other than it is. His character is therefore unalterable (Mal 3:6; Heb 1:12; Jas 1:17). God cannot fail to love for the same reason that he cannot lie (Heb 6:18). As we saw Tatian argue in the last chapter, however, it seems that this cannot hold true for contingent beings such as humans and angels. By definition, a contingent being could be other than it is. By definition, therefore, a contingent being could not be *necessarily* loving or virtuous.

Scripture and the Possibility of Saying No
I believe that Scripture confirms this insight. Volumes could, of course, be written on this topic, but presently it must suffice simply to summarize the biblical data pertaining to creaturely freedom. The very fact that throughout Scripture people and angels sometimes say no to God implies that God created agents with the capacity to say no to him. Moreover, I see nothing in Scripture that requires us to believe, as some would argue, that this no is itself part of God's design. For example, Scripture repeatedly affirms that God does not want any person to be lost (e.g. 1 Tim 2:4; 4:10; 2 Pet 3:9). But it also states in no uncertain terms that multitudes of people will in fact be lost. From this it seems reasonable to conclude that if God *could have* designed the world in such a way that all would say yes to him and no one would be lost, he *would have* done so. The fact that he did not do so suggests that he could not do so. The possibility of saying no to God must be metaphysically entailed by the possibility of saying yes to him.

As I read it, the biblical narrative repeatedly confirms this point. Granted, there are biblical texts that can be interpreted to support a compatibilist perspective, but doing so renders the biblical motif of God's frustration over human stubbornness in the face of his loving-kindness incoherent.[4] People can and do resist God (e.g., Is 63:10; Acts 7:51; Heb 3:8, 15; 4:7, cf. Eph 4:30). The Lord is frequently grieved, sometimes even amazed, at how "stiff-necked" people are in resisting him (e.g., Ex 33:3, 5; 34:9; Deut 9:6, 13; 10:16; 31:27; Judg 2:19; 2 Kings 17:14; 2 Chron 30:8; 36:13; Neh 9:16; Is 46:12; 48:4; Jer 7:26; Hos 4:16).[5] In my view, the entire biblical narrative describes God's sometimes frustrating but ultimately victorious pursuit of a people who will accept and be transformed by his loving lordship.

As far as I can see, there are only two possible stances we can take regarding this material. We may conclude that God intentionally designed the world to be grieving and frustrating to him. The implication of this conclusion is that God's design for the world included rebellion, sin and all its horrors, for these are the things that grieve and frustrate him. Or we may conclude that God prefers not to be grieved or frustrated and prefers the world to be free from sin. However, he created a world in which this grief over sin was possible simply because he could not rule this possibility out if he wanted a world that contained the possibility of love.

The first supposition is difficult on a number of accounts. For one thing, it is hard to understand why anyone, including God, would *choose* to be grieved and frustrated if one possessed the power and wisdom to avoid such an outcome. Even more to the point, Scripture unanimously informs us that God does *not* want sin and suffering in his creation. This is why throughout the biblical narrative God strives to get rid of it and is genuinely grieved when it persists. The second supposition carries with it no such difficulties. It simply suggests that love must be chosen. If the possibility of saying no to God's love is a necessary correlary to the possibility of saying yes to God's love, then there is no mystery in the fact that people often say no and that God is genuinely grieved and frustrated when they do so.

Our Experience of Love and Freedom

Experience confirms TWT1 as well, I believe. Is it possible to force people to

---

[4]For a compatibilistic analysis of such texts, see D. A. Carson, *Divine Sovereignty and Human Responsibility* (Atlanta: John Knox Press, 1981). For some critical discussion on the compatibilist interpretation of Rom 9, see the second and third objections in appendix one. For a discussion of other biblical texts often cited in support of compatibilism, see appendix five.
[5]On God's amazement at Israel's stubbornness and sin, see Is 5:1-7; Jer 3:6-7, 19-20; 7:31; 19:5; 32:35.

love? Powerful people may be able to force others to do just about anything. Through psychological or physical torture, they may succeed in forcing them to curse their own children or deny their faith. They may even succeed in forcing others to *act* and *say* loving things to them. But no one can force another person to *actually* love them.

But God created us, someone might respond, so he need not coerce us to love him. He could simply create us with an unquenchable desire to love him. In this case we would choose to love God simply by virtue of how we were created. I suggest that this supposition also conflicts with our experience.

Consider this analogy: Suppose I were able to invent a computer chip that could interact with a human brain in a deterministic fashion, causing the person who carries the chip to do exactly what the chip dictates without the person knowing this. Suppose further that I programmed this chip to produce "the perfect wife" and inserted it in my wife's brain while she was sleeping. The next morning she would wake up as my idea of the perfect wife. She would feel, behave and speak in a perfectly loving fashion. Owing to the sophistication of this chip, she would believe that she was voluntarily choosing to love me in this fashion, though in truth she could not do otherwise.

Would my wife genuinely love me? I think not. Proof of this is that I (and hopefully all husbands) would eventually find this "love" unfulfilling. I would know that my wife was not experiencing these loving feelings or engaging in this loving behavior on her own. In reality, I would simply be acting and speaking *to myself* through this sophisticated computer chip. My wife's behavior would not be chosen by *her*, so *she* would not really be loving me at all. She would become the equivalent of a puppet. If I want love from *her*, she must personally possess the capacity to choose *not* to love me.

If God desires a bride made up of people who genuinely love him— who do not just *act* lovingly toward him—he must create people who have the capacity to reject him. He must endow agents with self-determination. They, not he, must determine whether or not they will love him and each other. And this, I submit, explains why God created a world in which evil was possible. If love is the goal, it could not be otherwise. God chose to create a world in which evil was possible only in the sense that he chose to create a world in which love was possible. The possibility of evil is not a second decision God makes; it is implied in the single decision to have a world in which love is possible. It is, in effect, the metaphysical price God must pay if he wants to arrive at a bride who says yes to his triune love.

The Nature of Self-Determining Freedom

The nature of the freedom TWT1 postulates is self-determining freedom. It is distinct from compatibilistic freedom, which I will discuss below. This conception of freedom affirms that "given the same causal conditions, [free agents] could have chosen or done otherwise than we did."[6] "The agent might have done otherwise," Robert Kane argues, "*all past circumstances* (including the agent's motives and willings) *and all laws of nature remaining the same.*"[7]

In this view, we see, the total set of antecedent causes does not determine a truly free action. While factors outside the agent are *influential* in every decision an agent makes, such factors are never *coercive* when the decision is in fact free. Thus, appealing to factors external to the agent can never *exhaustively* explain the free choice of the agent. In light of all influences and circumstances, agents ultimately *determine themselves.*[8]

In this sense, free agents are the "ultimate creators and sustainers of their own ends or purposes."[9] Our basic intuitions regarding the nature of personhood, moral responsibility, human dignity and individuality depend on the con-

---

[6]B. Reichenbach, "Evil and the Reformed View of God," *International Journal for Philosophy of Religion* 24 (1988): 69.

[7]Robert Kane, *The Significance of Freedom* (New York: Oxford University Press, 1996), p. 57. Emphasis in original.

[8]In chapters six and seven we will discuss a number of factors that condition the self-determining freedom of a person. These same variables, I shall argue, explain the *apparent* arbitrary manner in which God sometimes overrides creaturely freedom while other times letting it play itself out.

[9]Kane, *Significance of Freedom*, p. 32. Defenders of incompatibilist or libertarian freedom (also sometimes labeled indeterministic or contracausal freedom, though I regard these terms to be somewhat misleading) vary greatly in their understanding of precisely *how* free agents are free. But they all fundamentally agree that incompatibilist freedom entails that nothing outside of the agent *exhaustively* determines the willing of the agent. Given the exact same circumstances, the agent could will differently and thus could behave differently. For various defenses of incompatibilist freedom that I have found helpful, see the essays by Ginet, Chisholm, Nozick, Kane, Rowe, O'Connor and Clarke in Timothy O'Connor, ed., *Agents, Causes and Events;* Peter Van Inwagen, *An Essay on Free Will* (Oxford: Oxford University Press, 1983); Peter Van Inwagen, "The Incompatibility of Free Will and Determinism," *Philosophical Studies* 27 (1975): 185-99; Timothy O'Connor, "Indeterminism and Free Agency: Three Recent Views," *Philosophy and Phenomenology Research* 53 (1993): 499-526; Charles A. Campbell, *In Defense of Free Will* (London: Allen & Unwin, 1967); Richard Taylor, *Action and Purpose* (Engelwood Cliffs, N.J.: Prentice-Hall, 1966); C. Ginet, "In Defense of Incompatibilism," *Philosophical Studies* 44 (1983): 391-400; C. Ginet, *On Action* (Cambridge: Cambridge University Press, 1990); D. Wiggins, "Towards a Reasonable Libertarianism," in *Essays on Freedom and Action,* ed. T. Honderich (London: Routledge & Kegan Paul, 1973); D. Lamb, "On a Proof of Incompatibilism," *The Philosophical Review* 86 (1977): 20-35; and the exceptionally clear and insightful essay on the concept of self-determining (indeterministic) free will by Robert Nozick in his *Philosophical Explanations* (Cambridge, Mass.: Harvard University Press, 1981), ch. 4.

viction that our deeds are *in our control*. It is *up to us*. Again, as Kane argues:

> The source or ground (*arche*) of action [is] . . . in the agent or self, and not outside the agent. . . . If we were to trace the causal or explanatory chains of action backward to their sources, they would terminate in actions that can only and finally be explained in terms of the agent's voluntarily or willingly performing them.[10]

This view of freedom, I submit, is the one presupposed in Scripture and the one required if love is to be possible for contingent creatures. We must possess the power to do otherwise. We must be able to *determine ourselves* in relation to God's invitation to participate in his triune love and in relation to all our morally responsible actions.[11] However, many argue that this view of freedom is both unnecessary and untenable. Thus I will now briefly discuss the nature of compatibilistic freedom and three sets of objections raised against the concept of self-determining freedom.

COMPATIBILISTIC FREEDOM
The Nature of Compatibilistic Freedom
According to compatibilism, an agent need not be self-determining to be

---

[10]Kane, *Significance of Freedom*, p. 79. Defenders of self-determining freedom usually postulate a self ("soul," "spirit") that transcends the "causal or explanatory chains" that constitute natural history. For Kant's famous argument for a noumenal self, see Immanuel Kant, *Critique of Practical Reason*, trans. L. W. Beck (Indianapolis: Bobbs-Merrill, 1956), p. 100. Kane attempts to render indeterministic freedom intelligible without postulating any "transempirical power centers, nonmaterial egos, noumenal selves, nonoccurrent causes, [or] . . . a litany of other special agencies whose operations were not clearly explained" (*Significance of Freedom*, p. 11). He regards all such appeals to be premodern (212-13). He rather attempts to appeal only to the "complex chaotic processes in the brain, involving neural networks that are globally sensitive to quantum indeterminacies at the neuronal level." In his view, "persons experience these complex processes phenomenologically as 'efforts of will' they are making to resist temptation in moral and prudential situations" (130). He labels theories like his "Teleological Intelligible Theories," as opposed to "Agent Cause Theories" in which a transcendental agent is postulated. See his "Two Kinds of Incompatibilism," in O'Connor, ed., *Agents, Causes and Events*, pp. 115-50.

In my estimation, Kane's depiction of freedom reduces it to an epiphenomenal reality—persons *experience* neuronal indeterminacy as morally responsible freedom—but he has not yet explained how such indeterminacy could make one genuinely morally responsible. As I have elsewhere argued in relation to process thought, chance occurrences can never add up to morally responsible freedom. See my *Trinity and Process*, pp. 151-68. Nevertheless, Kane's analysis of what needs to be true if morally responsible free will is to be rendered intelligible is most helpful.

[11]This position raises the question of what becomes of individuals who were unable to resolve themselves either for or against God's love in this lifetime, such as babies who die or severely retarded people. The issue is crucial for all who hold to the free-will defense. I address the topic in appendix three.

genuinely free. Agents are free if there is nothing that constrains them from doing what they want. But they need not be—and, most would argue, cannot be—free to determine *what they want*. As Bertrand Russell argued, "you can act as you please, [but] you can't please as you please."[12] Most compatibilists argue that this concept of freedom is sufficient to render agents morally responsible for their actions.

Throughout Christian tradition, compatibilists have frequently held that God ultimately orchestrates the disposition of each agent though each agent is morally responsible for how he or she acts on this disposition.[13] To return to an example cited in the introduction, Augustine taught that when a person unjustly suffers at the hands of another person, "he ought not to attribute [his suffering] to the will of men, or of angels, or of any created spirit, but rather to His will who gives power to wills," for in God "resides the power which acts on the wills of all created spirits, helping the good, judging the evil, controlling all, granting power to some, not granting it to others"[14] Though God ultimately controlled the event, however, Augustine believed that the perpetrator was nevertheless morally responsible for acting as he or she did. The free decision of the criminal functions as the *immediate* explanation and locus of responsibility for the misdeed, but God "who gives power to wills" and was thus ultimately in control of the crime functions as

---

[12]Quoted by Strawson in "Libertarianism," p. 24.

[13]A classic philosophical and theological defense of compatibilism is Jonathan Edwards's *Freedom of the Will,* ed. Paul Ramsey (New Haven, Conn.: Yale University Press, 1957). For several recent biblical defenses of compatibilism, see D. A. Carson, *Divine Sovereignty and Human Responsibility;* D. A. Carson, *How Long O Lord? Reflections on Suffering and Evil* (Grand Rapids, Mich.: Baker, 1990), pp. 201-28; R. C. Sproul, *Willing to Believe: The Controversy over Free Will* (Grand Rapids, Mich.: Baker, 1997); and Thomas Schreiner and Bruce Ware, *The Grace of God, The Bondage of the Will,* 2 vols. (Grand Rapids, Mich.: Baker, 1995). The philosophical literature defending some form of compatibilism is voluminous. Some of the works that I have found helpful are Alfred J. Ayer, "Freedom and Necessity," in *Philosophical Essays* (London: Macmillan, 1954); H. Frankfurt, "The Problem of Free Action," *American Philosophical Quarterly* 15 (1978): 157-62; R. B. Hobart, "Free Will as Involving Determination and Inconceivable Without It," *Mind* 43 (1934): 1-27; Galen Strawson, *Freedom and Belief* (Oxford: Oxford University Press, 1986); Strawson, "Libertarianism"; Daniel C. Dennett, *Elbow Room: The Varieties of Free Will Worth Wanting* (Cambridge, Mass.: MIT Press, 1984); Susan Wolf, *Freedom Within Reason* (Oxford: Oxford University Press, 1990); J. Narverson, "Compatibilism Defended," *Philosophical Studies* 32 (July 1977): 99-105; and Ted Honderich, *A Theory of Determinism* (Oxford: Oxford University Press, 1988).

[14]Augustine *City of God* 4.10 (NPNF 1 2:92-93). So too, about evil agents Augustine says, "In their very act of going against his will, his will is thereby accomplished." Hence, "However strong the wills either of angels or of men, whether they will what God willeth or will something else, the will of the Omnipotent is always undefeated. . . . Even when [the will of God] . . . inflicts evils, it is still just. . . . The omnipotent God never doth anything except what he doth will, and doth everything that he willeth" (*Enchiridion,* LCC 7:399-400).

the *final* explanation of the event. We must now consider whether or not this view of freedom is plausible.

Self-Determining Freedom and Moral Responsibility
This view of freedom has a number of difficulties, two of which are presently worth mentioning. First, this view does not adequately explain moral responsibility. As Robert Kane and others have argued, the intelligibility of our convictions about moral responsibility depends on the supposition that the *agent* is the *final* cause and explanation for his or her own behavior.[15] Unless agents have the power "*to be the ultimate creators (or originators) and sustainers of their own ends or purposes,*" he argues, our sense of morally responsible self-determination cannot be rendered intelligible.[16] In other words:

> when we trace the causal or explanatory chains of action back to their sources in the purposes of free agents, these causal chains must come to an end or terminate in the willings (choices, decisions, or efforts) of the agents, which cause or bring about their purpose.[17]

---

[15]Kane, *Significance of Freedom,* passim, but esp. pp. 79-101. See also his "Two Kinds of Incompatibilism," pp. 115-50. This is what he terms "the Ultimacy Condition" of freedom. Many others have argued along similar lines. Especially helpful is Timothy O'Connor's "Agent Causation," in O'Connor, ed., *Agents, Causes and Events,* pp. 173-200. See also Immanuel Kant, *Religion Within the Limits of Reason Alone,* trans. Theodore M. Greene and Hoyt H. Hudson (New York: Harper & Row, 1960), who says that "man *himself* must make or have made himself in whatever, in a moral sense, whether good or evil, he is to become. Either condition must be an effect of his free choice; for otherwise he could not be held responsible for it and could therefore be morally neither good nor evil" (p. 40). Even some compatibilists concede that moral responsibility requires that agents must originate their own free decisions, whether or not they think compatibilism is able to render intelligible this requirement. See, e.g., Daniel Dennett, "On Giving Libertarians What They Say They Want," in O'Connor, ed., *Agents, Causes and Events,* pp. 43-55.
[16]Kane, *Significance of Freedom,* p. 15 (emphasis in original). See also Randolfe Clarke, "Toward a Credible Agent-Causal Account of Free Will," in O'Connor, ed., *Agents, Causes and Events,* p. 203.
[17]Kane, Significance of Freedom, p. 4. To be ultimately responsible "the agent . . . [must] be responsible for anything that is an *arche,* or sufficient ground, reason or explanation for the agent's responsible action" (ibid., p. 73). Alvin Plantinga puts it this way: "if I am Free with respect to an action A, then causal laws and antecedent conditions determine neither that I take A nor that I refrain" (*The Nature of Necessity* [Oxford: Clarendon, 1982], p. 171). See also Mortimer Adler, *The Idea of Freedom,* 2 vols. (New York: Doubleday, 1961), vol. 2, esp. pp. 232, 292-93; Clarke, "Toward a Credible Account"; Peter Van Inwagen, "When Is the Will Free?" in O'Connor, ed., *Agents, Causes and Events,* pp. 210-11, 221-22; W. Sellars, "Thought and Action," in *Freedom and Determinism,* ed. Kevin Lehrer (New York: Random House, 1966), pp. 105-40; and W. P. Alston, "Divine Actions, Human Freedom, and the Laws of Nature," in *Quantum Cosmology and the Laws of Nature: Scientific Perspectives on Divine Action,* ed. Robert Russell, Nancey Murphy and C. J. Isham (Vatican City: Vatican Observatory Publications, 1993), pp. 185-96.

If agents are to be free and morally responsible, Kane is arguing, the buck must stop with them in terms of what ultimately produces and thus explains their behavior. They must be, to some extent, *self*-determining beings. The power to decide between alternatives, to turn possible courses of actions into actual courses of action, must ultimately lie within themselves.

In a very real sense a theist might say that self-determining, morally responsible agents must possess something of God's power to create new realties.[18] They create the reality of what they do and thus who they become. Their choices create new states of affairs that would not have otherwise existed. It seems that this must be true for agents to be truly responsible for what they do and who they become.

But if we follow the compatibilist conviction that causal chains can be traced beyond an agent's willing "to heredity or environment, to God, or to fate, then "the ultimacy would not lie with the agents but with something else."[19] Kane refers here to the "ultimacy" of the *explanation* for why a deed is what it is and thus the "ultimacy" of who is *responsible* for the deed being what it is. Separating responsibility and ultimate explanation, as the compatibilist view does, undermines the authenticity of both freedom and moral responsibility.[20]

The mere fact that there is nothing outside of agents that prevents them from doing what they want is not sufficient to render moral responsibility intelligible. Simply being able to do what you want does not render one free or morally responsible *if the want itself is outside of one's control.* My earlier analogy of the computer chip inserted into my wife's brain illustrates the point. The fact that there were no external restraints on the way my computerized wife loved me does not thereby make her free in loving me, for the ultimate source and explanation of her "perfect" love resided outside of herself. If I rather programmed this computer chip to cause her to murder someone, no jury would convict her of the crime. For her love to be genuine and for her moral responsibility to be intelligible, the ultimate source and explanation for her deeds must reside *within herself.*

---

[18]Philo construed this as the Creator giving humans some of his miraculous power to upset the laws of nature. See Harry A. Wolfson, *Philo: Foundations of Religious Philosophy in Judaism, Christianity, and Islam,* 2 vols. (Cambridge, Mass.: Harvard University Press, 1947), 1:431, 436. I affirm Philo's point that our creativity mirrors in a small way God's creativity, though contrasting our creativity with otherwise inexorable laws of nature is not helpful.

[19]Kane, *Significance of Freedom,* p. 4; see p. 74.

[20]William Rowe raises similar objections against "Lockean freedom" (compatibilistic freedom) in "Two Concepts of Freedom," in O'Connor, ed., *Agents, Causes and Events,* pp. 153-57.

Compatibilist Freedom and the Problem of Evil

The failure to consistently affirm agents as the ultimate producers and ultimate explanations of their own actions intensifies the problem of evil, which is the second difficulty with compatibilism. If the ultimate explanation for why anything and everything is the way it is lies in God, not free agents, then it is difficult to avoid the conclusion that God is ultimately responsible for everything.[21] For the same reason it is also difficult to render intelligible the warfare motif of Scripture within this view.[22] If Augustine is correct in holding that every will that opposes God actually fulfills God's will in its very act of opposition, is not God's battle against Satan and all who follow him ultimately disingenuous?[23]

From my perspective, compatibilism and the problem of evil are inextricably connected. God's character is rendered ambiguous to the extent that the warfare between God and Satan's kingdom is rendered disingenuous, and this warfare is rendered disingenuous to the extent that the self-determining freedom of those who oppose God is denied. If we agree that agents are self-determining, however, there is no difficulty understanding why God's character is not impugned by the evil in the world and, not coincidentally, why the war between God and Satan's kingdom is rendered authentic.

Compatibilist Objections to Self-Determining Freedom

Though the compatibilist understanding of freedom has its difficulties, it still is preferable, in the minds of many, to the concept of self-determining freedom, which they regard as at best implausible, at worst incoherent. In

---

[21]See J. Sennett, "The Free Will Defense and Determinism," *Faith and Philosophy* 9 (1991): 340-53. We might here note that theologians often use the compatibilistic understanding of free will to argue that God is ultimately responsible for all evil (including evil that "free" agents carry out). In my estimation, their argument is decisive. See J. Mackie, "Evil and Omnipotence," *Mind* 64 (1955): 100-115; Anthony Flew, "Divine Omnipotence and Human Freedom," in *New Essays in Philosophical Theology*, ed. Anthony Flew and Alasdair MacIntyre (London: SCM Press, 1955); A. Flew, "Compatibilism, Free Will and God," *Philosophy* 48 (1973): 231-44. For an attempted response by a theistic compatibilist, see J. Feinberg, "And the Atheist Shall Lie Down with the Calvinist: Atheism, Calvinism and the Free Will Defense," *TJ* 1 (1980): 142-52.

[22]David Griffin forcefully makes the point that "the realism of the New Testament image of the demonic is lost in the theology of Augustine and other classical theologians because of their monistic monotheism according to which there is only one center of power." He further notes that "the battle between the divine and the demonic is, accordingly, a mock, not a real, battle" ("Why Demonic Power Exists: Understanding the Church's Enemy," *LTQ* 28 [1993]: 227).

[23]"In their very act of going against his will, his will was thereby accomplished" (*Enchiridion* 399).

defense of TWT1 I must now address these charges.

A scientific objection: genes, environment and self-determination. Some have argued that the self-determining conception of freedom conflicts with certain aspects of modern science. More specifically, recent research regarding the role of genes and environment in influencing human personality and behavior suggests to many that everything about humans is exhaustively determined by factors outside of, and antecedent to, the agents. On this basis, many argue that our subjective experience of self-determination is illusory.[24] If we had exhaustive knowledge of the variables responsible for the formation of any particular agent, and if we possessed exhaustive knowledge of every experience that the agent would undergo during her lifetime, the behavior of the agent would be perfectly predictable.

Galen Strawson summarizes the essence of this argument:

> (1) It is undeniable that one is the way one is as a result of one's heredity and experience. (2) One cannot somehow accede to true responsibility for oneself by trying to change the way one is as a result of heredity and experience. For (3), both the particular way in which one is moved to try to change oneself, and the degree of one's success in the attempt at change, will be determined by how one already is as a result of heredity and experience.

If the premise of this argument (1) is accepted, the conclusion seems unavoidable. There is no place for self-determining freedom. And if this is so, it seems that the first thesis of the trinitarian warfare theodicy must be abandoned. I do not think the premise of the argument is valid, however. I offer six arguments against it.

Angelic freedom. First, as a preliminary word, one could argue that even if the premise were accepted it would not logically require abandoning the trinitarian warfare approach to evil altogether, for in Scripture and among the postapostolic fathers evil was not just a human phenomenon. It was first

---

[24]See, e.g., Robert E. Brooks, *Free Will: An Ultimate Illusion* (Lake Oswego, Ore.: CIRCA, 1986). Thomas Nagel contrasts the "internal" or "subjective" view of freedom (i.e., we are self-determining) with the "objective" view (i.e., we cannot be self-determining) in "The Problem of Autonomy," in O'Connor, ed., *Agents, Causes and Events,* pp. 33-42. See also Thomas Nagel, *The View from Nowhere* (New York: Oxford University Press, 1986), pp. 110-37. One of the most popular recent representations of the scientific objection to freedom is Richard Dawkins, *The Selfish Gene* (New York: Oxford University Press, 1976). For discussions that incorporate this objection, see John Searle, *Minds, Brains, and Science* (Cambridge, Mass.: Harvard University Press, 1984); Roy Weatherford, *The Implications of Determinism* (London: Routledge, 1991); Honderich, *Theory of Determinism,* and Richard Double, *The Non-reality of Free Will* (Oxford: Oxford University Press, 1991). Samuel Johnson captures something of the modern dilemma when he says, "All theory is against freedom of the will; all experience for it" (quoted in W. Rowe, "Two Concepts of Freedom," p. 151).

of all the result of the misuse of angelic free will. Whatever else may be true about angels, they are not tied to genes and environment the way humans are. Hence, though the position would be admittedly odd, one could in principle accept that humans are not free in a self-determining sense while affirming that angels are and that evil in the world is ultimately the result of their free activity.

Inconclusive evidence. We need not embrace such an odd position, however, for the evidence supporting genetic or environmental determinism is simply not conclusive, which is my second argument. While empirical evidence proves that genes and environment strongly *influence* human behavior, this evidence fails to prove that these factors *determine* our behavior.

Indeed, some research suggests evidence to the contrary. According to several recent studies on criminal behavior, for example, there is often no discernable criminal tendency in the family history of a convicted criminal and no childhood environmental factors that would explain the criminal's mindset. In many cases, a criminal is best described as a "victimizer, a molder of his environment, rather than a mere product of that mold."[25] Hence, while genetic and environmental influences may contribute to a person developing criminal characteristics, there is nothing that requires us to believe that this influence is determinative. In some cases, at least, it is at least as true to say that criminals *make themselves* as it is to say that they *are made* by forces outside of themselves.

Determinism and moral responsibility. The third argument against the scientific objection to self-determinism has already been made in our earlier critique of compatibilism, namely, that if genes and environment determine behavior, how could we hold others morally responsible for what they do? How can criminals be held any more responsible for their behavior than they are for, say, the color of their eyes or texture of their hair? We do not blame others for unalterable features of their appearance because we understand that the cause of this feature lies outside of themselves. But this means that if behavior is determined by factors outside of our control, we have no more moral responsibility for it than we do our eye color.

As noted above, our fundamental sense of moral responsibility is that

---

[25]Samuel Yochelson and Stanton Samenow, *The Criminal Personality,* 2 vols. (New York: Aronson, 1977), 1:104. For an expanded version of the case here, see S. Samenow, *Inside the Criminal Mind* (New York: Times Books, 1984). Peter Van Inwagen argues that methodologically, empirical studies never could conceivably prove determinism. See *Essay on Free Will,* pp. 198-202. See also J. Thorp, *Free Will: A Defense Against Neurophysiological Determinism* (London: Routledge & Kegan Paul, 1980).

agents can only be held responsible for their behavior if they *could have done otherwise*. Kane formalizes this assumption when he writes:

> An agent is *ultimately responsible* for some E's [event or state] occurring only if
> . . . something the agent voluntarily . . . did or omitted, and for which the
> agent could have voluntarily done otherwise, either was, or causally contrib-
> uted to, E's occurrence and made a difference to whether or not E occurred.[26]

Only if things *could* have been different, and only if it was ultimately up to the agent to make this difference, can we consistently say that things *should* have been different and that it is *the agent's fault* for their not being different.[27] If all our behavior is determined by our genes or our environment (or God, for that matter), however, we cannot with logical consistency affirm this. As Peter Van Inwagen argues, the fact that we all assume that we are morally responsible thus constitutes "an unsurpassably good reason for believing in free will."[28]

The self-refuting nature of physical determinism. Fourth, if everything about us is genetically and environmentally determined, then of course a person's belief that everything about us is genetically and environmentally determined must itself be genetically and environmentally determined. But as C. S. Lewis and others have argued, it is not clear that physically deter-mined effects of physically determined causes can possess any truth value.[29] Chemical reactions and environmental effects just occur; they are neither true nor false. We do not assess a belch or a clap of thunder in terms of its truth value.

---

[26]Kane, *Significance of Freedom,* p. 35. On this topic, see P. Bertocci, "Personality, Free Will and Moral Obligation," in *The Problem of Free Will,* ed. William Enteman (New York: Charles Scribner's Sons, 1967), pp. 19-31; Willard James, "The Dilemma of Determinism," in Ente-man, ed., *Problem of Free Will,* pp. 47-75. Using this same logic, but arguing in a different direction, is G. Strawson, "The Impossibility of Moral Responsibility," *Philosophical Studies* 75 (1994): 5-24.

[27]See Kane, *Significance of Freedom,* pp. 32, 79, 190. Clarence Darrow is celebrated for his legal ability to argue on the basis of environmental conditions that his clients could not have done otherwise and thus should not be convicted. In my view, he was simply being a consistent compatibilist. See Clarence Darrow, *Crime: Its Cause and Treatment* (New York: Colwell, 1922). See also P. Edwards, "Hard and Soft Determinism," in *Determinism and Freedom in an Age of Modern Science,* ed. Sidney Hook (New York: Collier, 1961), pp. 117-25.

[28]Van Inwagen, *Essay on Free Will,* p. 206.

[29]C. S. Lewis, *Miracles* (New York: Macmillan, 1978), pp. 12-24. Lewis revised his argument in the light of criticisms raised by Elizabeth Anscombe on February 2, 1948, at the Oxford Socratic Club. For a discussion of the Lewis-Anscombe debate, see V. Reppert, "The Lewis-Anscombe Controversy: A Discussion of the Issues," *Christian Scholars Review* 19 (1989): 32-48. This argument, it should be noted, only refutes *physical* determinism. It does not con-stitute a refutation of other forms of determinism.

If this is so, however, and if the physical determinist is correct, then the assertion that everything about humans is genetically and environmentally determined cannot be true or false. The assertion itself is simply a physically determined phenomenon. It too "just occurs." Though the thought process behind the assertion is far more complex than a belch, it can possess no more truth value than a belch. Both are reducible to chemical reactions. Hence, if the belief that everything is physically determined is true, the assertion that everything is physically determined cannot be. In other words, the position is self-refuting, and hence necessarily false.

Explaining the phenomenon of freedom. Fifth, if the goal of any philosophical or scientific theory is to render puzzling phenomenon intelligible, then compatibilism must be judged to be a poor theory. Not only does it fail to explain our basic sense of morality, it also fails to explain our phenomenological experience of ourselves as self-determining personal agents. Indeed, compatibilism dismisses this as illusory.[30]

Now, compatibilists often point out that we also experience ourselves as significantly affected by factors outside our control. We do not choose our parents, for example, nor do we choose our environment, our basic personality traits, our basic physical traits or even many of our life experiences. Much of life, past and present, happens *to* us. This is true, and defenders of self-determining freedom have sometimes damaged the plausibility of their own case by minimizing these facts.[31]

Nevertheless, it is equally clear though ultimately denied by compatibilists, that *within the parameters set by these externally determined factors* we uniformly experience ourselves as self-determining, morally responsible agents. Within the parameters of all the variables that are beyond my control but that contribute to who I am at this present moment, I experience myself

---

[30]Related to this is the observation of Van Inwagen: "Careful investigation, philosophical or scientific . . . may indeed yield information about what freedom of choice really consists in, but it cannot show us that there is no such thing as freedom of choice" (*Essay on Free Will,* p. 107). In this context, Van Inwagen's observation is actually a correction of an argument by Anthony Flew. For a meticulous (though, in my view, too frequently opaque) analysis of the self from a phenomenological perspective, see Paul Ricoeur, *Freedom and Nature* (Evanston, Ill.: Northwestern University Press, 1973). Kane correctly notes that what drives the libertarian view of freedom is the inescapability of our phenomenological experience of choices being really up to us (*Significance of Freedom,* p. 190, cf. pp. 58-59, 80-101).

[31]So argues Kane, *Significance of Freedom,* pp. 212-13. "What is needed for a mature libertarianism," Kane correctly argues, "is a recognition of the many ways in which circumstances of birth and upbringing can limit free will and responsibility . . . without yielding to the temptation that we are all always helpless victims of circumstances" (p. 214).

as having a degree of "say-so" in what will transpire in the next moment.[32] Within the parameters given to me I experience the future as a realm of possibilities whose actualization *depends on me.* I may not even theoretically believe that this is true; I may be a determinist. But this is nevertheless *how we experience the world,* and it is *this* experience that needs explaining.

This sense of self-determination amidst other-determination is not a peripheral matter. It is inextricably bound to our sense of value and worth. Robert Nozick refers to this when he writes:

> Without free will, we seem diminished, merely the playthings of external forces. . . . Determinism seems to undercut human dignity, it seems to undermine our value. . . . If our actions stem from causes before our birth, then we are not the originators of our acts and so are less valuable.[33]

This sense of being an "originator" lies at the core of the human experience and our sense of worth.[34] While a great deal of the world in which we live and even a good deal of our own lives is determined by forces outside of our control, the conviction that we possess self-determination remains. However much of life may be decided *for* us, some aspects of our life are decided *by* us. We have some degree of genuine say-so in what happens in our lives and in the world, and it is this that most fundamentally gives our lives dignity and worth. The failure of compatibilism to account for this fundamental feature of our experience seriously challenges its plausibility.

Determinism and the pragmatic criterion for truth. This leads to my final response to the scientific objection to self-determining freedom. Determinism cannot be illustrated or verified in our experience of decision making. This not only casts doubt on the truthfulness of the theory; it casts doubt on its very meaningfulness.[35]

---

[32]The scope of "say-so" within the variables that condition our freedom is what I will later identify as an agent's quality of freedom.* This quality must be irrevocable if the agent is truly to be morally responsible (see chapters six and seven).

[33]Nozick, *Philosophical Explanations,* p. 291. It should be noted, however, that Nozick nevertheless attempts (unsuccessfully, in my judgment) to integrate this insight with a compatibilist understanding of freedom. Kane gives a similar prognosis on the significance of indeterministic freedom in *Significance of Freedom,* pp. 80-101.

[34]Karl Popper argues along similar lines regarding our sense that we come up with genuinely new ideas and create new things. If determinism is true, nothing is ever truly novel ("Of Clouds and Clocks," in *Objective Knowledge* (Oxford: Oxford University Press, 1972), p. 222. This insight is expanded and integrated with recent scientific findings, especially in physics, in his *The Open Universe: An Argument for Indeterminism* (London: Hutchinson, 1982).

[35]On the pragmatic criterion of truth, see Charles Hartshorne, *Creative Synthesis and Philosophic Method* (reprint, Lanham, Md.: University Press of America, 1983), p. 81; Charles Hartshorne, *Creativity in American Philosophy* (Albany, N.Y.: SUNY Press, 1984), pp. 54-55, 284; Boyd, *Trinity*

It is unclear how one could make a decision in a manner that would illustrate the conviction that the decision is exhaustively determined by forces outside of oneself. Decision making requires that we deliberate between options, and, as Richard Taylor points out, it seems "one can deliberate only about what he believes to be within his own power."[36] The act presupposes the conviction that we are *not* determined, that it is *up to us* to determine which option shall be taken.[37] It is, it seems, virtually impossible to deliberate and illustrate any other belief.

For this reason, I argue, no one can genuinely deliberate about what is empirically, metaphysically or logically impossible—or at least about what one *believes* to be empirically or logically impossible.[38] For example, I am unable genuinely to deliberate about whether or not I should fly on my own power to work each morning, for I do not believe that I am able to fly on my own power. Nor do I (or can I) deliberate about possible courses of action I might take regarding a decision that is already past, for I cannot believe that it is now up to me to do anything about it. But I do genuinely deliberate some mornings about whether I should have eggs or cereal for breakfast, for I believe that both of these options are within my power to decide.

Now, if I genuinely believe that everything about me is determined by factors outside myself, whether this determination comes from genes, environment, fate or God, then I also believe that it is empirically or metaphysically impossible for me to do other than what I shall do. If I am a determinist, I must believe that it is never really *up to me* to determine things

---

and Process, pp. 65-67, 258. David Griffin captures the essence of the pragmatic criterion of truth well when he notes that "the ultimate criteria for testing philosophical doctrines are those notions that all people in fact presuppose in practice, even if they deny them verbally" ("Introduction: Time and the Fallacy of Misplaced Concreteness," in *Physics and the Ultimate Significance of Time,* ed. D. Ray Griffin [Albany, N.Y.: SUNY Press, 1986], p. 8). Griffin is applying this criterion as a way of arguing that time is ultimately real, not illusory.

[36] Richard Taylor, "Deliberation and Foreknowledge," in *Free Will and Determinism,* ed. Bernard Berofsky (New York: Harper & Row, 1966), p. 278.

[37] So argues Richard Taylor, *Metaphysics,* 2nd ed. (Englewood Cliffs, N.J.: Prentice-Hall, 1974), pp. 42-44; Van Inwagen *Essay on Free Will,* pp. 154-55; Boyd, *Trinity and Process,* p. 66; Hartshorne, *Creative Synthesis,* pp. 93, 204. Nozick provides an excellent analysis of self-determining deliberation in "Choice and Indeterminism," in O'Connor, ed., *Agents, Causes and Events,* pp. 101-14. Also insightful in this regard is Irving Janis and Leon Mann, *Decision Making* (New York: Free Press, 1977); Ricoeur, *Freedom and Nature;* and Taylor, *Action and Purpose.*

[38] Van Inwagen argues along these lines (*Essay on Free Will,* pp. 155-61). Likewise, Kane argues that "the ultimately responsible agent . . . cannot *believe* their free choices just happened to occur in a manner that is inexplicable by their reasons" ("Two Kinds of Incompatibilism," p. 132; emphasis added).

one way or another. Yet with every act of deliberation I engage in, *I presuppose that this belief is untrue.*

I thus conclude that it is impossible ever to illustrate one's belief that determinism is true by how one chooses between options. Strict Calvinists and deterministic behaviorists alike simply do not and cannot live in congruity with their beliefs about the nature of the world and of themselves. This strongly suggests that deterministic views are false, if not meaningless.

On the basis of these six arguments I conclude that the charge that modern genetic and sociological research has discounted self-determining freedom is mistaken.

A philosophical objection: to be caused or not to be caused, that is the question. We have not yet addressed the most fundamental objection to the concept of self-determining freedom. A number of philosophers argue that this notion is incoherent.[39] Obviously, if they are correct the first thesis of the trinitarian warfare theodicy is invalidated. Thus, in this section I will discuss this objection and contend that self-determining freedom can be rendered coherent.

The most forceful argument for the incoherence of self-determining freedom goes as follows: Either a person's decisions are caused or not. If they are caused, then they are determined and thus are not free in an incompatibilist sense. If they are uncaused, however, they still are not free, for, as Kant taught us, an uncaused event is inconceivable.[40] Even if uncaused decisions were conceivable, however, they still would not be free. They would rather be random and capricious. Uncaused decisions could be no more "free" and could possess no more moral quality to them than the involuntary twitching of an eyelash.[41]

Nozick nicely summarizes the argument when he writes:

> If an uncaused action is a random happening, then this no more comports with

---

[39]This objection is common among compatibilists. For several of the most compelling works incorporating this objection, see Strawson, *Freedom and Belief*; Strawson, "Libertarianism"; Dennett, *Elbow Room;* Wolf, *Freedom Within Reason;* Double, *Non-reality of Free Will;* Richard Double, "Libertarianism and Rationality," in O'Connor, ed., *Agents, Causes and Events,* pp. 57-65; Ayer, "Freedom and Necessity"; Charlie D. Broad, "Determinism, Indeterminism and Libertarianism," in *Ethics and the History of Philosophy* (London: RKP, 1952); and A. Goldman, *A Theory of Human Action* (Englewood Cliffs, N.J.: Prentice Hall, 1970). Also relevant is B. Waller, "Free Will Gone Out of Control," *Behaviorism* 16 (1988): 149-57, who argues that indeterministic freedom limits agents' control over their decisions.

[40]According to Kant, causation is one of the synthetic a prioris of the mind and as such functions as one of the preconditions for intelligibility (*Critique of Pure Reason,* trans. F. Max Müller [Garden City, N.Y.: Doubleday, 1966], pp. 366-80).

[41]See Richard Taylor's argument against "simple indeterminism" in his *Metaphysics,* pp. 51-52.

human value than does determinism. Random acts and caused acts alike seem to leave us not as the valuable originators of action but as an arena, a place where things happen, whether through earlier causes or spontaneously. . . . If our actions were random, like the time of radioactive decay of uranium 238 emitting an alpha particle, their being thus undetermined would be insufficient to ground human value or provide a basis for responsibility and punishment.[42]

As far as I can see, Nozick's argument is irrefutable. I must agree that if self-determining freedom is either incoherent or capricious, it cannot serve as a viable reckoning of our conviction that we are free and morally responsible agents. For reasons I shall now give, however, I do not believe that self-determining freedom needs to be construed as either incoherent or capricious, for I do not believe that it needs to be construed as being uncaused.

The freedom of God. My first observation is a preliminary one. I want to argue that the implications of denying self-determining freedom conflict with a central aspect of the historic Christian understanding of God, for the church has always ascribed to God self-determining freedom. The orthodox teaching of the church has been that God's decisions to create the world, to intervene in the world's affairs, and certainly to save the world were neither capricious nor caused by something outside of God. As Father Solokowski has insightfully argued, the most distinctive aspect of the traditional conception of God is that there is no necessity that attaches to his decisions to create or interact with the world. God is not forced to create and interact with the world, and he does not need to create and interact with the world.[43] If God decides to do so, it is a matter of sheer grace, and grace is as far removed from necessity as it is from capriciousness.[44] God's gracious decision to create and interact with the world can only be conceived of as a self-determining act.

---

[42]Nozick, *Philosophical Explanations,* p. 292. See also his "Choice and Indeterminism." Strawson expresses the dilemma succinctly: "we cannot be free agents . . . if determinism is true. . . . And surely we can no more be free if determinism is false and it is, ultimately, either wholly or partly a matter of chance or random outcome that we and our actions are as they are" ("Libertarianism," p. 13).

[43]Robert Sokolowski, *The God of Faith and Reason* (Notre Dame, Ind.: University of Notre Dame Press, 1982), p. 19. As I argue *in Trinity and Process,* this does not imply that the creation means nothing to God. It only means that its significance is nonutilitarian (pp. 274-76; 375-81).

[44]Richard Swinburne rightly argues that for the theist the ultimate explanation of things is "the choice of an agent," namely, God (*The Existence of God,* rev. ed. [Oxford: Clarendon, 1991], p. 103). My argument is that if free agency as an *ultimate explanation* is unintelligible, then this fundamental Christian teaching is unintelligible. Conversely, if we assume that the Christian teaching about creation is intelligible, we must assume that free agency as an ultimate explanation is intelligible.

Now, someone might argue that *God* might enjoy this sort of self-determining freedom but that humans and angels do not. Indeed, I would submit that this has been the position most commonly assumed by Christian compatibilists, for no one has wanted to affirm that God's decision to create and interact with the world was necessary or capricious. This reply does not support the contention that self-determining freedom is incoherent, however. It rather presupposes that it *is* coherent, for it is applied to God. Moreover, if it is coherent when applied to God, how does it become incoherent when applied to humans?

Indeed, if humans lack a logically consistent concept of self-determining freedom, what provides the analogical ground by which we can talk about *God's* gracious self-determining freedom? A concept devoid of all experiential content is vacuous. If we assume that it *is* meaningful to claim that nothing outside God's will caused him to create and interact with the world, that he could have done otherwise, and that his decisions are not capricious, then we *must* affirm that we experience something like this sort of freedom. In short, unless we were free in a self-determining sense, we could never meaningfully say that God is.

This argument stands even if we find it difficult to *explain* self-determining freedom. An inexplicable concept may be meaningful as long as it has an experiential basis and is not self-contradictory. We routinely experience and speak of self-consciousness, for example, even though it continues to prove difficult to explain. So too we experience self-determining freedom in every act of deliberation and in every moral judgment we make, and orthodox Christians at least assume it is intelligible to talk about self-determining freedom when they say that God created the world freely. But it is admittedly a difficult phenomenon and concept to explain.

The nature of causation. My second reply to the objection that self-determining freedom is incoherent concerns the concept of causation employed in this argument. The argument that self-determining freedom is equivalent to uncaused randomness works only on the assumption that causation is inherently deterministic. That is, the argument only works if saying that "x *causes* y" is equivalent to saying that "y is *determined* by x." But as a number of philosophers have argued, there is no logically necessary reason for concluding this.

Peter Van Inwagen illustrates the dubiousness of equating the concepts of causality and determination in the following scenario:

> Suppose someone throws a stone at a window and that the stone strikes the glass and the glass shatters in just the way we would expect glass to shatter

when struck by a cast stone. Suppose further that God reveals to us that the glass did not *have* to shatter under these conditions, that there are possible worlds having exactly the same laws of nature as the actual world and having histories identical with that of the actual world in every detail up to the instant at which the stone came into contact with the glass, but in which the stone rebounded from the intact glass. It follows from what we imagine God to have told us that determinism is false. But does it also follow that the stone did not break the glass, or that the glass did not break *because* it was struck by the stone? It is not easy to see why we should say this follows.[45]

As Van Inwagen goes on to argue, it is principally because of an assumption that "instances of causation simply *are* instances of universal, exceptionless laws" that we tend to suppose that "to cause" and "to determine" are equivalent concepts.[46] But this assumption is not necessary, as the hypothetical revelation of God in the above instance makes clear. In addition, the fact that we *can* understand causation in this instance without any deterministic connotations demonstrates the intelligibility of a nondeterministic concept of causation.

It is not logic alone, however, that demonstrates the intelligibility of nondeterministic causation; the concept is also supported by fundamental features of quantum mechanics.* The only concept of causation that has consistently proven useful at a quantum level is *statistical, probabilistic* and *nondeterminative* in nature.

We can, for example, specify ahead of time *the range* of possible behaviors of a quantum particle given a certain set of causal conditions, and we can thus specify a probability to the various possible behaviors of a quantum particle under these conditions. But we cannot *predict in detail* the behavior of any particular particle given those same causal conditions. The regularity of the world, at least at a quantum level, is *intelligible* in the light of causal conditions but not *exhaustively predictable* on the basis of these conditions.

---

[45]Van Inwagen, *Essay on Free Will,* p. 139.

[46]Ibid. "Universal causation," Van Inwagen argues, "does not entail determinism." See ibid., pp. 4-5. Elizabeth Anscombe has argued this point forcefully in "Causality and Determination," in *Metaphysics and the Philosophy of Mind: Collected Philosophical Papers,* vol. 2 (Minneapolis: University of Minnesota Press, 1981). Others who argue against this identification as it concerns free decisions are Nozick, *Philosophical Explanations,* pp. 295-97; Nozick, "Choice and Indeterminism"; Kane, "Two Kinds of Incompatibilism"; R. Chisholm, "Agents, Causes, and Events: The Problem of Free Will," in O'Connor, ed., *Agents, Causes and Events,* pp. 95-100; and O'Connor, "Agent Causation." For two more general explorations of the concept of indeterministic causation, see Ellery Eells, *Probabilistic Causality* (Cambridge: Cambridge University Press, 1991); and Michael Tooley, *Causation: A Reality Approach* (Oxford: Clarendon, 1987).

Unless one wishes to maintain that quantum physicists perpetually talk nonsense, this observation must be taken as demonstrating that an intelligible understanding of the relationship between cause and effect need not include a deterministic understanding of cause and effect. It also demonstrates that a behavior need not be futuristically predictable to be retroactively intelligible. At a quantum level it simply is not the case that an exhaustive knowledge of the causal conditions would produce the ability to predict the future perfectly. Causal conditions render their particular effects *intelligible* but not *necessary.*

Now, if this much is true of the fundamental physical properties of the world, why think that something like this cannot be true at an anthropological level—especially since our experience of ourselves as free agents lies at the very core of our self-identity, as was argued above.[47] Our actions have causal conditions—they are not capricious—and these causal conditions specify the parameters within which our behavior must operate and render our free actions retrospectively intelligible once they have been completed. Indeed, they do the latter because they do the former. But these causal conditions (including our reasons and desires) do not meticulously *determine* our particular actions. Given the exact same set of conditions, we could have done otherwise. It was *up to us* as free agents to decide.

Kane highlights this insight as the key to understanding self-determining freedom when he notes:

> What is required [for the intelligibility] of free choices . . . is not that they be completely explicable in terms of the past, but that they possess a "teleological

---

[47]Nozick ("Choice and Indeterminism," pp. 104-5) and Kane ("Two Kinds of Incompatibilism," p. 129; cf. *Significazznce of Freedom,* pp. 54-56) draw the analogy between a quantum particle in its superposition (i.e., prior to the wave collapse when measured) and an agent prior to her self-determination. See also Van Inwagen, *Essay on Free Will,* pp. 191-202. I apply the findings of quantum physics to the issue of how God can be sovereign over an indeterministic, risk-filled cosmos in chapters four and six.

It should perhaps be noted that some philosophers, especially within the Process movement, push the insight that our experience must provide the analogical key to understanding all of reality to the point of concluding that all of reality is something like experience. There is no such thing as "substance" that is utterly devoid of an experiential center. This position is known as panpsychism. I methodologically agree that our understanding of reality must be analogically rooted in the one slice of reality we know firsthand, namely, our own experience. I thus agree that our experience—including our experience of freedom—must be stretched to a universally generalized level if the nature of "substance" is to be understood (Hartshorne labels this "the Principle of Continuity"; see Boyd, *Trinity and Process,* pp. 40-42). But I am not yet convinced that this entails panpsychism. See my discussion in *Trinity and Process,* pp. 42-43, 121-29.

intelligibility" or "narrative continuity" which is to say the choices can be fit into meaningful sequences.[48]

Hence, free actions are not capricious, for they are retroactively intelligible. They possess a "narrative continuity" with what preceded them. But neither are they necessitated, for they are to some extent unpredictable. As Leibniz first recognized (but unfortunately did not himself carry out consistently), reasons can *incline* without *necessitating*.[49] Free actions can thus be judged reasonable and noncapricious without denying that other courses of action were possible, given the same antecedent conditions.[50] Hence, given identical conditions no one could have precisely predicted the free act. But given that the free act has occurred, it is perfectly intelligible in the light of the conditions that gave rise to it.

Let me again note that this is true whether or not we are able to give an adequate explanation for *how* self-determining freedom actually works. If the data we are trying to explain require the postulation of self-determining freedom, then that is grounds for accepting it. Here quantum physics provides another helpful analogy. Though the concept of indeterministic causation is conceptually difficult, it is necessary for explaining phenomena at a quantum level. But does not the phenomenon of the human self require it just as strongly? And if the concept of indeterministic causation is intelligible at a quantum level, how does it all of a sudden become unintelligible at an anthropological level?

We should, I think, rather conclude just the opposite. That is, the reason that indeterministic causality is intelligible at a quantum level is because it is intuitively intelligible at the anthropological level. Just as we can only talk about "higher" realities such as God by extending concepts rooted in our experience upward, so we can only talk about "lower" realities such as quan-

---

[48]Kane, *Significance of Freedom*, p. 146. A number of philosophers have argued that the intelligibility of self-determining acts is retroactive. Nozick, for example, argues along these lines with his concept of the "reflexivity" of free decisions (see "Choice and Indeterminism," p. 109). Why an agent "weighted" variables leading up to a decision is intelligible in the light of the decision, but the decision is not exhaustively predictable given this weighting. See also O'Connor, "Agent Causation."

[49]Gottfried Leibniz, *Selections*, ed. P. Wiener (New York: Scribner, 1951), p. 435. See the discussion in R. Chisholm, "Freedom and Action," in *Freedom and Determinism*, ed. K. Lehrer (New York: Random House, 1966), p. 25. This theme runs throughout Hartshorne's work. See, e.g., *Whitehead's View of Reality* (New York: Pilgrim, 1981), p. 4; *Creativity in American Philosophy*, p. 79; and *The Logic of Perfection and Other Essays on Neoclassical Metaphysics* (La Salle, Ill.: Open Court, 1962), pp. 162-64, 173.

[50]This is what Kane calls the "more-than-one-way-rationality" of free acts (*Significance of Freedom*, p. 108).

tum particles by extending concepts rooted in our experience downward. We can analogically describe quantum particles acting freely because all people experience themselves as being to some extent free—even when their own belief systems deny it.[51]

Indeterminism and the principle of sufficient reason. Perhaps a stronger argument can be made against self-determining freedom by maintaining, not that it violates the concept of causality, but that it violates the principle of sufficient reason. That is, one might argue that incompatibilist freedom cannot specify a sufficient reason why a given option A was chosen over and against another option B.[52] Or, conversely, if one *can* specify a sufficient reason why A was chosen over B, then, it seems, the choice of A was determined.

In short, it seems that the only way that the sufficient reason for A is "sufficient" to render A *intelligible* is by rendering it *determinate* in the light of the reason that makes it intelligible. What else could "sufficient" mean here? Items x, y, z are sufficient to render ß intelligible if and only if they render intelligible the fact that ß occurs *rather than* -ß. But this is what the concept of self-determining freedom seems to deny. It holds that given *all* antecedent conditions, ß or -ß could have occurred. The conditions sufficient to bring about ß are also sufficient to -ß. But is this not tantamount to admitting that there is no reason why ß was chosen over -ß? Hence, the choice of that ß is irrational.

This is a strong argument, but I do not believe it is decisive. It is based on a mistaken, necessitarian understanding of sufficient reasons. Proof that this necessitarian understanding is mistaken is that it results in a self-contradiction and the collapse of all modal distinctions.[53]

My argument, in a nutshell, is as follows: If *(a)* every contingent event has a sufficient reason, and *(b)* every sufficient reason necessitates what it explains, then *(c)* the totality of contingent events must have a sufficient reason (from *a*), and thus *(d)* the totality of contingent events is necessitated (from *b*). It seems that *d* constitutes a logical contradiction, however. For what is contingent is by definition *not* necessitated. Indeed, if all things are

---

[51]It should be clear that I am not at all *equating* indeterministic causality (or more specifically, quantum indeterminacy) with human freedom. Human freedom presupposes indeterministic causality, and there is an analogical relationship between the two. But human freedom goes far beyond indeterministic causality.

[52]The "reason" here need not be the subjective reason of the free agent doing the choosing. The sufficient reason is rather "that which renders x intelligible." This of course centrally includes the subjective state of the person doing the choosing, but it includes all other relevant conditions as well—everything that is "sufficient" for rendering the choice intelligible. The concept of incompatibilistic freedom, this argument is saying, denies this.

[53]A more thorough presentation of this argument is found in Van Inwagen, *Essay on Free Will,* pp. 202-4.

necessitated, then the very concept of contingency loses meaning. This would seem to entail further that its contrast—necessity—loses all meaning as well.[54] The modal distinction between necessity and contingency has collapsed. Either premise *a* or premise *b* must be mistaken. Either the principle of sufficient reason is not to be universally applied *(a)* or it does not necessitate what it explains *(b)*.

It does not seem that *a* is misconstrued. The notion of a contingent event occurring without a sufficient reason does indeed seem unintelligible (though some defenders of self-determining freedom deny this).[55] Contingent events are *by definition* what they are *because of something else*, and this something else is what constitutes the sufficient reason for their being what they are. The only thing that could conceivably lack a sufficient reason would be something that was noncontingent, something that was, so to speak, "its own reason," something that could not be other than it is and thus something that did not owe its being to something else. If anything like this is conceivable (and I am convinced that it is), it could only be God.[56] By definition, it could be nothing in this *contingent* world.

Sufficient reason and the parameters of intelligibility. The problem, therefore, seems to lie with premise *b*. We need to question the assumption that ß has a "sufficient reason" if and only if its occurrence *over and against -ß* has been rendered intelligible. Is there anything incoherent with the supposition that two differing events, ß and -ß, could have identical sufficient reasons? Is there something incoherent in the belief that sufficient reasons may govern more than one event? I do not see that there is. As Randolf Clarke has argued, actions do not necessarily require a "contrastive rational explanation" (why *this* rather than *that*) to be rational, that is, to have a sufficient reason.[57]

Consider an artist painting a landscape. Let us suppose that in the midst of her scenery she paints a wolf of a certain size, shape and color. Now, what is the sufficient reason for her incorporating that particular wolf into her painting? It is undoubtedly the fact that the wolf "fit" the aesthetic aim of

---

[54]On the necessity of concepts having a meaningful contrast, see Hartshorne, *Creative Synthesis,* pp. 32, 89-90, 166, 245. The point is discussed in my *Trinity and Process,* pp. 34-35, and is applied to the issue of determinism on pp. 63-65.

[55]See, e.g., Taylor, *Action and Purpose,* pp. 114-15.

[56]This is the insight that grounds the ontological argument. See my critical discussion of Hartshorne's version of the ontological argument in *Trinity and Process,* pp. 179-233.

[57]Clarke, "Toward a Credible Account," p. 207. See also his "A Principle of Rational Explanation?" *Southern Journal of Philosophy* 30 (1992): 1-12. Nozick also argues that "we can have an explanation and understanding of why something occurred even when we do not know of any reason why it, rather than something else, occurred that time, in that instance" ("Choice and Indeterminism," p. 107).

her work. Were we somehow able perfectly to analyze her aesthetic aim (and all other relevant influences, of course) we would thereby have identified the comprehensive sufficient reason that adequately renders this whole painting, with its particular wolf, intelligible.

But does this mean that we would have attained an understanding of why this artist painted *exactly* this particular wolf and not, for example, a wolf that was slightly darker, a hair taller, perhaps looking in a slightly different direction, and the like? The answer *may* be yes, if in fact the aim of her work centered on that particular wolf. Otherwise the answer would undoubtedly be no. A different wolf, and perhaps even a different animal altogether, may have satisfied her aesthetic aim just as well. In other words, the aesthetic aim that functions as the sufficient reason for the particular wolf that was actually painted could have functioned just as well as the sufficient reason for a number of other possible variations on that theme.

There are, however, obvious limits to this. Given the artist's aesthetic aim, it is possible that a *significantly* different looking wolf, or a *significantly* different kind of animal, or the absence of an animal altogether would not have fit. These variations lie outside the parameters within which possible aesthetic themes are intelligible in the light of the artist's particular aesthetic aim.

Hence, we may conclude that the sufficient reason for this particular painting with this particular wolf could have functioned as the adequate explanation for a range of similar paintings but not as the sufficient reason for any painting outside these parameters. This example suggests that sufficient reasons, no less than the previously discussed concept of causality, may specify *parameters of intelligibility* for a range of possibilities rather than one necessary actuality.

The sufficient reason for self-determining choices. To return to our original question, I would suggest that whether or not a sufficient reason renders ß as opposed to -ß intelligible depends on how broadly or narrowly ß is defined. As a formal principle, however, nothing requires us to hold that the sufficient reason for ß must exclude -ß.

In this light, it seems that defenders of self-determining freedom need not deny that free actions have a sufficient reason any more than they need deny that self-determining actions have a cause. An act of freedom (as with a quantum event) always has a sufficient reason that renders it *retroactively intelligible,* but it does so without rendering it *futuristically predictable.* Prior to the event, even an exhaustive knowledge of the surrounding circumstances could not have given us a determinate knowledge of what shall certainly occur—for the act is free. But *once the act occurs,* one can review all the factors and at least hypothetically discover the sufficient reason behind the act—for the act is free, not capricious. In short, the free act is intelligible, but not necessitated, by its sufficient reason.

The concept of free agency. Still, compatibilists might insist that if free actions are futuristically unpredictable but retroactively intelligible, then there must be *something* that transitions the unpredictable future into the retroactively intelligible past. In other words, if either ß or -ß could occur, and if either ß or -ß would be intelligible given the sufficient reason that governs both of them, then we must yet discover what it is that actually brings about ß rather than -ß. And the answer, one must note, cannot be the sufficient reason for ß or -ß all over again. We are looking for whatever it is that brings about the actuality of one *rather than* the other. If neither antecedent causal conditions nor present sufficient explanations determine the present, what does?

The answer most defenders of self-determining freedom give to these difficult questions is simply "the free agents." Free actions are not deterministically caused by the sum total of antecedent conditions, for they are free and not determined. Neither are they uncaused, for they are free and not capricious. Rather, insofar as they are free, they are caused by *the agent* who initiates them. The agent (together with all attending conditions) could be the sufficient reason for either ß or -ß, and, if the choice between ß or -ß is truly free, the agent alone ultimately decides the matter.

Hence, the agent is understood to be a volitional center of causation, an originating agent, an enduring, creative "I" who can deliberate between options and choose one of them, setting in motion a chain of causality *that it is not itself an effect of.* As Richard Taylor argues, "some . . . causal chains . . . have beginnings, and they begin with the agents themselves."[58] Only on

---

[58]Taylor, *Metaphysics,* p. 56. See also his *Action and Purpose.* Something like this is held by most libertarians, according to Alvin Plantinga. For such thinkers, "agent causation . . . is conceptually prior to event causation in that the latter can be understood only in terms of the former" ("Self-Profile," in *Alvin Plantinga,* ed. James E. Tomberlin and Peter Van Inwagen, Profiles: Contemporary Philosophers and Logicians 5 (Boston: D. Reidel, 1985), p. 47. For other defenders of some version of agency causation, see O'Connor, "Agent Causation"; O'Connor, "Indeterminism and Free Agency"; Clarke, "Toward a Credible Account"; Van Inwagen, *Essay on Free Will;* Campbell, *Defense of Free Will;* I. Thalberg, "How Does Agent Causation Work?" in *Action Theory,* ed. Myles Brand and Douglas Walton (Dordrecht, Holland: D. Reidel, 1976), pp. 213-38; J. Bishop, "Agent-Causation," *Mind* 92 (1983): 61-79; and J. Forster, *Ayer* (London: Routledge & Kegan Paul, 1985), pp. 283-98. It should be noted that not all defenders of incompatibilistic freedom are agent theorists. Some, such as Kane and Chisholm (in his most recent work), attempt to account for incompatibilistic freedom by seeing it as a variation of event causation (see Kane, "Two Kinds of Incompatibilism"; Chisholm, "Agents, Causes, and Events").

such a supposition can we view agents as the *ultimate* originators and *ultimate* explanation of their own actions, which, as we saw earlier, is the precondition for our being morally responsible.

Some attempt to argue that this concept of agent causation is incoherent, but their arguments are generally the same as those offered against incompatibilist freedom that we have already refuted.[59] Having said this, it must be admitted that this concept goes beyond what can be ascertained by empirical or reductionistic analysis. It is an irreducible transcendental postulate* that we must accept if we are to explain, not dismiss, the fact that we experience ourselves as free, morally responsible agents.[60]

On the basis of these arguments I conclude that the charge that self-determining freedom is incoherent is not compelling.

A theological objection. Thus far we have been concerned with scientific and philosophical objections to the concept of self-determining freedom. We must now consider a third objection. Some theologians argue that this concept is inconsistent with the biblical understanding of original sin and of salvation by grace alone. If humans can and must of their own will choose to accept or reject God's love revealed in Christ, then, they argue, we cannot affirm with Scripture that we are "dead" in sin (Eph 2:1) and "by nature children of wrath" (Eph 2:3). Nor can we affirm with Paul that we are saved by God's grace, through faith alone (Eph 2:8-9). If a self-determining deci-

---

[59]For reasons of space, I have not considered the objection that incompatibilistic freedom requires an infinite regress of choices. If we choose not only our actions but also the desires and reasons that lead to those actions, what renders our choice of desires and reasons intelligible? Further desires and reasons? See, e.g., Strawson, "Libertarianism," pp. 16, 24. For a classic statement of the infinite regress dilemma, see Edwards, *Freedom of the Will*, pp. 175-76. In my estimation, Nozick ("Choice and Indeterminism"), O'Connor ("Agent Causation") and Clarke ("Toward a Credible Account") adequately answer the charge with their concept of the agent as an originator of events. The supposition of an infinite regress only follows if one assumes that there can be no volitional center that *originates* a way of desiring, reasoning and choosing and that cannot be reduced to prior desiring, reasoning and choosing.

Several challenging critiques of agency causation are Broad, "Determinism, Indeterminism and Libertarianism"; Nagel, "The Problem of Autonomy"; Thalberg, "How Does Agency Causality Work?"; D. Davidson, "Agency," in *Essays on Action and Events* (Oxford: Oxford University Press, 1980), and L. Bonjour, "Determinism, Libertarianism and Agent Causation," *The Southern Journal of Philosophy* 14 (1976): 145-56.

[60]The type of reasoning I have used to argue for free agency as a "transcendental postulate" was referred to by Charles S. Peirce as "abduction" (in contrast to induction and deduction). See C. Peirce, *Collected Papers of Charles Sanders Peirce*, ed. Charles Hartshorne and P. Weiss (Cambridge: Harvard University Press, 1931-1935) B, 69a. In discussing Pascal's use of this type of reasoning, Douglas Groothuis summarizes it as "an appeal to a compelling explanation, a postulate that illuminates material not otherwise as intelligible or significant" ("Deposed Royalty: Pascal's Anthropological Argument," *JETS* 41 [1998]: 209).

sion is required for us to be saved, the argument goes, then faith is a "meritorious work" that we carry out.

This argument is articulated by, among others, R. C. Sproul, currently one of the most prolific exponents of this line of thinking.

> Why say that Arminianism "in effect" makes faith a meritorious work? Because the good response people make to the gospel becomes the ultimate determining factor in salvation.

He continues:

> I often ask my Arminian friends why they are Christians and other people are not. They say it is because they believe in Christ while others do not. Then I inquire why they believe and others do not? "Is it because you are more righteous than the person who abides in unbelief?" They are quick to say no. "Is it because you are more intelligent?" Again the reply is negative. They say that God is gracious enough to offer salvation to all who believe and that one cannot be saved without that grace. But this grace is cooperative grace. Man in his fallen state must reach out and grasp this grace by an act of the will, which is free to accept or reject this grace. Some exercise the will rightly (or righteously), while others do not. When pressed on this point, the Arminian finds it difficult to escape the conclusion that ultimately his salvation rests on some righteous act of the will he has performed. He has "in effect" merited the merit of Christ.[61]

In the end, Sproul and other such Calvinists argue that grace is only grace if God regenerates people without *any* cooperation on their part, which is what God must do if indeed we are truly "dead" in our sin prior to his saving work. Obviously, corpses cannot cooperate with God. While we cannot presently address all the complex issues that surround this debate, two brief responses should be made.

The problem of unconditional election. First, as many Calvinists freely admit, if there is nothing *in the human subject* that explains why a person is or is not saved, then the ultimate explanation for why any person is or is not saved must *lie in God.* Note further that this explanation must have nothing whatsoever to do with the person that would lead God to choose one way or the other. God chooses who will and will not be saved based on nothing other than his desire to save or not save someone. This is the classic Calvinistic doctrine of unconditional election.

As Arminians have argued, however, this view is problematic from a scriptural perspective. As we noted at the beginning of this chapter, Scripture uni-

---

[61]Sproul, *Willing to Believe,* p. 26.

formly teaches that God loves everyone and thus desires all to be saved. Though God's people have always had trouble accepting it, Scripture consistently portrays God's love as universal and impartial (Acts 10:34; cf. Deut 10:17-19; 2 Chron 19:7; Job 34:19; Is 55:4-5; Mk 12:14; Jn 3:16; Rom 2:10-11; Eph 6:9; 1 Pet 1:17).[62] The Lord explicitly tells us that he is not arbitrary or unfair (Ezek 18:25). He "does not willingly afflict or grieve anyone" (Lam 3:33). He takes no delight in the destruction of any wicked person but rather desires all to repent (Ezek 18:23, 32; 33:11). Peter tells us that God is patient, "not wanting *any* to perish, but all to come to repentance" (2 Pet 3:9). Paul tells us that God "desires *everyone* to be saved and to come to the knowledge of the truth" (1 Tim 2:4). God desires to be "the Savior of all people" (1 Tim 4:10), and thus, in the words of John, Christ died as "the atoning sacrifice for our sins, and not for ours only but also for the sins of the whole world" (1 Jn 2:2). It was because "God so loved *the world* that he gave his only Son," and he did this "so that *everyone* who believes in him may not perish but may have eternal life" (Jn 3:16, emphasis added).

This central motif of Scripture, a motif that reflects the very character of God, is undermined for the sake of a logical inference in the classical Calvinistic doctrine of unconditional election. Sproul and others *infer* that grace is incompatible with choosing for or against God and thus further *infer* that God unilaterally chooses who will or will not be saved. Nothing in Scripture explicitly teaches this, however. When a logical inference contradicts an explicit, unambiguous, pervasive teaching of Scripture, we must question the premise from which the inference is made or the logic of the inference itself.

Is a gift that is accepted less of a gift? The problem, I submit, lies in the premise. The conclusion that we cannot attribute our salvation to God's grace if we have to choose is mistaken. A gift is not less of a gift because it is accepted. For example, a woman recently donated several million dollars to help some Minnesotans who had been devastated by spring floods. Would

[62]Contrast this with W. E. Best, a Calvinist who understands "God's love" to mean that "God loves some and hates others. . . . God does not love everybody" (*God Is Love* [Houston: South Belt Grace Church, 1985], p. 39). Against this, see T. Talbott, "The Love of God and the Heresy of Exclusivism," *Christian Scholars Review* 27 (1997): 99-112. See also D. M. Lake, "He Died for All: The Universal Dimensions of the Atonement," in *Grace Unlimited*, ed. C. Pinnock (Minneapolis: Bethany House, 1975), pp. 31-50; Thomas C. Oden, *The Transforming Power of Grace* (Nashville: Abingdon, 1993), pp. 84-87. Though Calvin and Luther compromised the universality of God's salvific love, other strands of the Reformation emphasized it. See Alvin J. Beachy, *The Concept of Grace in the Radical Reformation* (Nieuwkoop: De Graaf, 1977); and Wynkoop, *Theology of Love*.

we not consider it absurd if someone claimed that her gift was not really a gift because the unfortunate victims of this flood chose to accept it?

So it is, I believe, with God's offer of salvation. The sacrificial gift is offered to all and is no less a gift because we must choose to accept it.

Is faith a work? Scripture seems to confirm this perspective. Throughout both the Old and New Testaments we find the Lord pleading with people to *make a choice* to accept his offer of salvation and to enter into a covenantal relationship with him. The motif is succinctly expressed in Deuteronomy, when the Lord, after laying out the terms of his covenant, challenges the people of Israel:

> See, I have set before you today life and prosperity, death and adversity. If you obey the commandments of the LORD your God that I am commanding you today, by loving the LORD your God, . . . then you shall live. . . . But if your heart turns away and you do not hear, . . . I declare to you today that you shall perish. . . . I have set before you life and death, blessings and curses. Choose life so that you and your descendants may live. (Deut 30:15-19)

We see that whether the children of Israel are blessed or cursed depends on what *they* choose to do. God graciously offers them life and pleads with all of them to accept it. But they are individually and collectively free to choose death. In my view, every passage that portrays the Lord or one of his spokespersons pleading with people to *believe* in the Lord, to *obey* his decrees, *not to resist* the Holy Spirit or to *repent* of their sins is suggesting the same thing. So is every passage that depicts people as morally responsible for their decisions. These texts are suggesting that it is ultimately up to people as morally responsible agents to choose to accept or reject God's offer of salvation.[63]

The fact that Scripture sees no conflict between this emphasis on human choice and the graciousness of God's offer suggests that there is no conflict. This implies that anyone who concludes that there *is* a conflict between

---

[63]A few of the verses that express the moral responsibility of people to choose to believe on the Lord are Num 14:11; Josh 24:15; Ps 78:22; 106:24; Mt 21:32; Mk 1:15; Jn 1:7, 12; 3:15-18; 5:46-47; 11:25-26; 16:9, 30-31; 19:35; 20:27, 31; Acts 10:43; 14:2; 16:31; 19:9; 28:24; Rom 10:10-14; 16:26; 1 Pet 2:7; 1 Jn 5:10. On the moral responsibility of people to choose to obey God, see, e.g., Ex 19:5; 34:11; Deut 11:27, 32; 27:10; 30:10; 1 Sam 12:14-15; 15:19-22; 1 Kings 3:14; Jer 7:23; 11:3-7; 22:3-5; 40:3; Dan 9:11; Mt 19:17; 28:20; Jn 14:15, 23-24; 15:10; Acts 7:39; 2 Thess 1:8; 3:14; Heb 5:9; 1 Pet 4:17; 1 Jn 2:3; 3:22-24; 5:3; Rev 3:3. In fact, the Lord frequently tested Israel to see whether or not they would choose to obey him (e.g., Judg 3:1-4). On the moral responsibility of people to choose not to resist God, harden their hearts, or grieve the Holy Spirit, see, e.g., 1 Sam 6:6; 2 Chron 36:12-13; Ps 95:8; Is 1:19-20; 63:10; Acts 7:51; Eph 4:30; Heb 3:8, 15; 4:7; Rev 3:20.

grace and free choice is drawing unwarranted inferences from the biblical teaching on grace or the need for human choice.

Along these same lines, Scripture never portrays a choice to receive a gift from God as a "work." When New Testament authors stress that salvation is not arrived at by "works," as first-century Jews they are referring to works *of the law*.[64] They are saying that God's righteousness does not come by external obedience to the law, as some Jews of their day supposed. God's righteousness cannot be earned. It can come only as a gift (Rom 4:4-16). But the New Testament nevertheless also teaches that the gift must be accepted. One must choose to place one's trust (faith) in God's gracious provision. This choice is not in any sense the *cause* of their salvation, but it is a *condition* that must be met for the gift of salvation to be applied to their life.

If people are *not* made righteous before God, the New Testament does not teach that this was because God decided to pass them over. They stand condemned before God solely on the grounds that they refused to meet the condition of placing their trust in Christ. If they are hardened against God, it is *because of their unbelief* (Rom 11:20, cf. Rom 10:3; 11:7, 25). This does not imply that they are less righteous or less intelligent than those who choose to accept the gift, as Sproul suggests. It only implies that out of the moral center of their being these people chose to resist the Holy Spirit and refused to submit to Christ as Savior and Lord (see, e.g., Lk 7:30).

Is the work of the Holy Spirit irresistible? Christians have usually believed that because we are slaves to sin and to Satan (Jn 8:34; Rom 6:16), we could never choose to accept God's offer of salvation unless God graciously enabled us to do so. Does this view not conflict with the idea that we are self-determining agents in the process of salvation? I do not believe that it does.

I agree that Scripture teaches that believers choose to place their trust in Christ only because the Father "draws them" and the Spirit enables them (Jn 6:44, 65; 1 Cor 12:3; Eph 2:8). But I, along with other Arminians, deny that the Father draws us and the Spirit enables us *in an irresistible manner.*

---

[64]For a helpful survey of various perspectives on Paul and the law see C. J. Roetzel, "Paul and the Law: Whence and Whither?" *Currents in Research: Biblical Studies* 3 (1995): 249-75. On understanding Paul's view of the law within the context of its Jewish background (which has not generally been the case within the Augustinian-Calvinist tradition) see M. G. Abegg, "Paul, Works of the Law and the MMT," *BARev* 20, no. 6 (1994): 52-55, 82; J. D. G. Dunn, *Jesus, Paul, and the Law: Studies in Mark and Galatians* (Louisville: Westminster John Knox, 1990); E. A. Martens, "Embracing the Law: A Biblical Theological Perspective," *Bulletin for Biblical Research* 2 (1992): 1-28; N. T. Wright, *The Climax of the Covenant: Christ and the Law in Pauline Theology* (Edinburgh: T & T Clark, 1991).

God graciously makes it *possible* for us to believe. But he does not make it *necessary* for us to believe. It is one thing to claim that without the Holy Spirit we *cannot* believe and quite another to say that with the work of the Holy Spirit we *must* believe. Scripture affirms the former but not the latter.

In the Arminian view, Scripture denies that the Holy Spirit works irresistibly by insisting that God's love is universal; by placing the responsibility for deciding for or against God on the person, not on God; and by explicitly informing us that people can and do resist the Holy Spirit (e.g., Is 63:10; Acts 7:51; Heb 3:8, 15; 4:7; cf. Eph 4:30). The fact that the Lord is frequently grieved, frustrated and even amazed at how stiff-necked people are toward him suggests the same (e.g., Ex 33:3, 5; 34:9; Deut 9:6, 13; 10:16; 31:27; Judg 2:19; 2 Kings 17:14; 2 Chron 30:8; 36:13; Neh 9:16; Is 46:12; 48:4; Jer 7:26; Hos 4:16).

Sproul thus seems mistaken in claiming that people who affirm self-determining free will cannot consistently affirm the Protestant doctrine of *sola gratia*.* There is no merit in accepting a gift, especially if even the ability to accept the gift is itself a gift. We can thus consistently affirm that God desires all to be saved and that everyone who is saved is saved solely by God's grace; on the other hand, everyone who is not saved has only himself or herself to blame.

CONCLUSION

We have in this chapter considered the first thesis of the trinitarian warfare theodicy: *love must be chosen* (TWT1). This choice, I have argued, implies that agents capable of love must possess self-determining freedom. I have argued that neither scientific, philosophical or theological objections to this concept are compelling. At the same time, I have contended that we have a number of reasons for accepting the notion of self-determining freedom.

Self-determining freedom is the only form of freedom consistent with our experience of ourselves as self-determining agents. Correlatively, it is also the only view consistent with our experience of moral responsibility and personal dignity. What is more, only by assuming that creatures possess self-determining freedom can we meaningfully affirm God's self-determining freedom in creating and interacting with the world. Finally, and most importantly, this view begins to render intelligible the warfare worldview of Scripture and thus the evil in a world created by an all-powerful and all-good God.

The ongoing warfare between God and agents who oppose him makes sense, I contend, only on the assumption that these agents were created with the capacity to *choose* to war against God. Within limits, the capacity of these agents to choose to war against God must genuinely rival God's own will. If we can understand why God has to create agents with this capacity, we can understand why he has to allow them to rebel and why he must, within limits, strategically fight against them when they do rebel. We can, in short, begin to understand how it is that God's creation has become a war zone and why it is not his fault that it is so. TWT1 asserts that the answer is love. It must be chosen, which introduces the possibility that it may not be chosen.

The remaining five theses of the trinitarian warfare theodicy follow from the first and will be considered throughout the next five chapters. The first of these is an elaboration on what it means to say that love may not be chosen. I contend that this implies genuine risk on God's part. This point of view is currently quite controversial, so the next two chapters will attempt to ground it in Scripture, reason and experience.

argues ag. compatibilism + determinism
(doesn't hold logically)

- love must be chosen, agents possess
self-det. freedom to otherwise

3

A RISKY CREATION

Divine Foreknowledge &
the Trinitarian Warfare Worldview

*In creating beings with free will, omnipotence from the outset
submitts to the possibility of . . . defeat. What you call defeat,
I call miracle: for to make things which are not Itself and thus to become . . .
capable of being resisted by its own handiwork, is the most astonishing and unimaginable
of all the feats we attribute to the Deity.*
C. S. LEWIS, THE PROBLEM OF PAIN

*The happiness God desires for His creatures is . . . ecstasy of love. . . .
And for that they must be free.*
C. S. LEWIS, MERE CHRISTIANITY

*Our freedom is our supreme dignity; that makes us children of the Most high;
we can enjoy it only by living in a partly chancy world.*
PETER GEACH, PROVIDENCE AND EVIL

*God knows all things. . . . The things he knows are partly divine and immortal,
partly perishable and temporal. . . . His knowledge of uncertain things . . .
cannot be different from their nature. . . . They are . . . possible in both directions
rather than subject to necessity. . . . So contingent things are not inflexibly arranged
and determined from the beginning with the sole exception of the very fact,
that they must be uncertain.*
CALCIDIUS, ON FATE

*I*n the last chapter I argued that the possibility of love requires self-determining freedom. Love must be freely chosen, which necessarily entails the
possibility that it may be rejected. In this and the next chapter I shall argue
that this possibility entails risk for God. In the same way that God could not

create two adjacent mountains without thereby creating a valley between them (for this is logically impossible), so God could not create a world in which love is possible without risking war. Leslie Weatherhead once said that this is not "the best of all possible worlds," but it is "the world of best possibilities."[1] I now want to submit that it can be the latter only because it cannot be assured of being the former. This constitutes the second thesis of the trinitarian warfare theodicy (TWT2): *Freedom implies risk.* TWT2 is crucial to the development of our theodicy, for unless we affirm that God takes genuine risks, we will not be able to acknowledge that the world is a war zone while also holding that this war is not God's will.

The claim that God takes risks is not uncontroversial, however. Most significantly, attributing risk to God seems to contradict the classical understanding of God's foreknowledge. In this view, God possesses exhaustively definite foreknowledge* (henceforth abbreviated EDF) of everything that shall ever come to pass. It is *exhaustively* definite because it consists exclusively of eternally definite facts: the future is, from all eternity, definitely this way and definitely not that way. There are no open possibilities for God. Even the future decisions of free agents are eternally settled in the mind of God. The EDF doctrine seems to rule out ascribing risk to God, for it is difficult to attribute risk to a being who engages only in activities for which the outcome is certain an eternity before he engages in them.

In this chapter I argue that this impression is essentially correct: the classical view of God's foreknowledge is indeed incompatible with ascribing risk to God. I shall first critically discuss one version of the EDF doctrine (simple foreknowledge) which may allow for divine risk but is untenable on other grounds. Following this, I shall propose and defend an alternative perspective, sometimes called the open view of God.* This view maintains that the future is to some degree open and is therefore perfectly known by God as such. In the next chapter I shall respond to scriptural and theological objections to the open view, and offer several philosophical and practical considerations in its support.

Before beginning, however, I wish to make two important comments. First, my point is not that believers cannot embrace the trinitarian warfare worldview without also embracing the open view of the future, that is, without denying that God possesses EDF. Many sisters and brothers in Christ embrace something like the trinitarian warfare worldview and are actively engaged in overt spiritual warfare who nevertheless hold to the EDF doc-

---

[1]Leslie Weatherhead, *Salute to a Sufferer* (Nashville: Abingdon, 1962), p. 37.

trine. I believe that they do so with a certain inconsistency, as I shall attempt to demonstrate. But I applaud their theology and practice. More than anything else, in light of the absolute preeminence Christ placed on the unity of his church (Jn 17:20-25), I pray that this issue would never be used by the enemy to bring disunity. My conviction is that the open view of the future has some distinct advantages for our understanding Scripture, making sense of the war zone we live in and living out the Christian life. But it is not an issue over which Christians should divide.

Second, it is not my intention to wager the entire credibility of the trinitarian warfare theodicy on my defense of the open view of the future. At its heart the trinitarian warfare theodicy is simply an expansion and fleshing out of the free will theodicy that Arminians have always appealed to. The question of the openness of the future, then, is an in-house Arminian discussion on how to render the freewill defense most coherent, biblical and credible. The open perspective on the future, however, is more biblical and logically more consistent with the warfare worldview of Scripture and the trinitarian warfare theodicy than the EDF doctrine.[2] This is what I attempt to establish in the next two chapters.

---

[2]Some Christian versions of the open view of God and the future are Keith Ward, *Rational Theology and the Creativity of God* (Oxford: Basil Blackwell, 1982); Richard Swinburne, *The Christian God* (Oxford: Clarendon, 1994); William Hasker, David Basinger, Richard Rice, Chris Pinnock and John Sanders, in *The Openness of God: A Biblical Challenge to the Traditional Understanding of God* (Downers Grove, Ill.: InterVarsity Press, 1994); John Sanders, *The God Who Risks: A Theology of Providence* (Downers Grove, Ill.: InterVarsity Press, 1998); Stephen Davis, *Logic and the Nature of God* (Grand Rapids, Mich.: Eerdmans, 1983); T. J. Gorringe, *God's Theatre: A Theology of Providence* (London: SCM Press, 1991); M. Garrigue, *Dieu sans idée du mal: La liberté de l'homme au coeur de Dieu* (Limoges, France: Critérion, 1982); Richard Foster, *Prayer: Finding the Heart's True Home* (San Francisco: HarperSanFrancisco, 1992); J. Randolph Lucas, *The Future: An Essay on God, Temporality, and Truth* (London: Basil Blackwell, 1989); Major Jones, *The Color of God: The Concept of God in Afro-American Thought* (Macon, Ga.: Mercer University Press, 1987); Peter Geach, *Providence and Evil* (Cambridge: Cambridge University Press, 1977); Vincent Brümmer, *What Are We Doing When We Pray? A Philosophical Inquiry* (London: SCM Press, 1984); W. O. Mundia, "The Existence of the Devil" (Ph.D. diss., Boston University School of Theology, 1994); Terence Fretheim, "The Repentance of God: A Key to Evaluating Old Testament God-Talk," *Horizons in Biblical Theology* 10, no. 1 (1988): 47-70; Adrio König, *Here Am I: A Believer's Reflection on God* (Grand Rapids, Mich.: Eerdmans, 1982); David Bartholomew, *God of Chance* (London: SCM Press, 1984); Richard Creel, *Divine Impassability* (Cambridge: Cambridge University Press, 1986); Peter Baelz, *Does God Answer Prayer?* (London: Darton, Longman & Todd, 1982). I have previously espoused this view in *The God of the Possible* (Grand Rapids, Mich.: Baker, 2000). See also Gregory Boyd and Edward Boyd, *Letters from a Skeptic* (Colorado Springs: Chariot Victor, 1994); Gregory Boyd, *Trinity and Process: A Critical Evaluation and Reconstruction of Hartshorne's Di-Polar Theism Towards a Trinitarian Metaphysics* (New York: Lang, 1992).

Risk and Exhaustively Definite Foreknowledge

Risk and eternal certainty. It seems that a decision cannot be risky if its outcome is certain an eternity before it is made. Consider this analogy: I have "inside information" on the future of a particular stock. I am absolutely certain about the future of this stock, and I buy or sell shares accordingly. Would I be risking anything in buying or selling my shares? Trading with such information is illegal precisely because it eliminates my element of risk in the trade.

If the EDF doctrine is true, however, this is precisely the kind of information God eternally has about the entire future. Consider the eternal destiny of the damned. If God eternally possesses "inside information" that certain individuals will end up in hell if they are created, can we also affirm that God *risked* their damnation when he created them? Doesn't the possibility that these people would be saved have to exist if we are to speak of God risking the possibility of their damnation for the sake of the possibility of their salvation? If their damnation was certain to God, the impossibility of their salvation was also certain, and there was no risk involved in God's decision to create them.[3]

This raises the difficult question of why God would create individuals he knows will end up in hell. Classical Calvinists are consistent in claiming that God does it for a higher purpose: his own glory. Those who cannot accept this conclusion are left in a quandary—unless they deny the EDF doctrine that raises the question in the first place. If the destiny of individuals is in fact open at the time they are created, then there is no puzzle as to why God creates individuals who choose hell. God doesn't will this destiny, but he is willing to risk it for the magnificent possibility that they will end up within his kingdom.

Simple foreknowledge. Some have proposed a model of divine foreknowledge which allows them to avoid the dilemma of affirming either that God creates people for the purpose of sending them to hell (Calvinism) or that he creates them without certain knowledge of their fate (open theism). In this alternative view God knows that certain individuals will be damned but cannot on this basis refrain from creating them. This is called "simple foreknowledge," for it holds that God simply knows what will take place but cannot alter it in the light of this knowledge. The fact that God foreknows what will occur does not increase his control over what occurs.

---

[3]On the problems which the traditional doctrines of EDF and predestination generate when combined with the traditional understanding of hell as eternal conscious suffering, see Jerry Walls, *Hell: The Logic of Damnation* (Notre Dame: University of Notre Dame, Ind. Press, 1992), pp. 33-55; John Hick, *Evil and the God of Love* (San Francisco: Harper & Row, 1966), pp. 113-20. Atheist Michael Martin raises similar objections against the traditional EDF doctrine in his *Atheism: A Philosophical Justification* (Philadelphia: Temple University Press, 1990), pp. 377-89.

This view is somewhat different from the classical Arminian position, in which divine foreknowledge was understood to increase God's control over what transpires without denying human freedom. Jack Cottrell articulates the classical Arminian position succinctly:

> What enables God to monitor people's plans and include such permission in his eternal decree? The answer is his foreknowledge. . . . God has a true foreknowledge of future free-will choices without himself being the agent that causes them or renders them certain. . . . This is how God maintains sovereign control over the whole of his creation, despite the freedom he has given his creatures.[4]

Indeed, the original disagreement between Arminius and his Calvinistic contemporaries concerned whether God predestines the elect on the basis of his foreknowledge of their faith, as Arminius held, or foreknows the elect on the basis of his having predestined them. The Arminian position presupposes that God acts responsively to his foreknowledge. Thus, he foreknows who will believe and then predestines them.

The simple foreknowledge position denies that God can respond to his foreknowledge in this way, thus avoiding the problem of God creating individuals he knows will go to hell. In this view, God's act of creating people is not affected by his knowledge of what will become of them. To return to our earlier analogy, it is as though God possesses "inside information" but must buy and sell stock *as though he did not*. For the same reason, this view does not require a divine reason behind every event that occurs. God eternally foreknows each particular evil that will ever take place, but he can do nothing about it.

This view can ascribe genuine risk to God and thus is fully compatible with the trinitarian warfare theodicy. But there are some problems with this view. First, as I shall attempt to demonstrate, this and every other version of the EDF doctrine cannot adequately account for the many passages of Scripture that depict God as facing a partly open future. Indeed, in one respect the simple foreknowledge perspective fares worse than classical Arminianism or Calvinism. As we shall see, whenever Scripture emphasizes God's foreknowledge of future events, it is to exalt his sovereign control over what is to come.[5]

---

[4]Jack W. Cottrell, "The Nature of Divine Sovereignty," in *The Grace of God, the Will of Man: A Case for Arminianism* (Grand Rapids, Mich.: Zondervan, 1989), p. 111.

[5]See John Sanders's excellent article "Why Simple Foreknowledge Offers No More Providential Control Than the Openness of God," *Faith and Philosophy* 14, no. 1 (1997): 26-40. In the next chapter I argue that the openness model of God and the future affords God *much greater* control than the simple foreknowledge perspective.

Second, while the simple foreknowledge position avoids some difficulties by denying that God can alter his behavior in response to his knowledge of the future, it invites other difficulties. How can God respond to anything? With all Christians, defenders of simple foreknowledge want to affirm that God sometimes intervenes to bring about events that are more in line with his will. But if God can't alter the future that he knows is coming, how can he respond to this same future when it becomes the present? Conversely, if God can respond to events when they occur, how can he not be able to respond to his knowledge that these events will occur if he doesn't intervene to alter them? In the simple foreknowledge view, God must first experience events in the present *as though* he had no foreknowledge and then foreknow what he experienced and how he responded. In other words, his foreknowledge functions as a sort of "hindsight."[6] In one respect this peculiar perspective places God on the same level as the tragic Cassandra in Hellenistic mythology.[7]

One might be inclined to pity God if this is his predicament. From all eternity he has seen what was coming—the cosmic war, the horror, the pain, the suffering, the unending plight of the damned. And he can even foresee how he will respond to these tragedies *once they occur*. But he cannot do anything ahead of time to avoid them. Like Cassandra, he's hopelessly locked into an unending vision he can do nothing about.

Third, this understanding of divine foreknowledge is irrelevant. In this view, God's exhaustive foreknowledge doesn't make any practical difference for God or for us concerning the flow of history. Everything proceeds *as though* God did *not* possess EDF. Indeed, if we hold to the pragmatic criterion of truth and insist that a belief must be able to make a conceivable difference in life to be meaningfully affirmed, then simple foreknowledge must be dismissed.

The open view of the future. The open view of God (or of the future,* as I prefer) avoids the difficulties associated with the EDF doctrine and allows us to consistently attribute risk to God.[8] With the whole of the Christian tradition, this view affirms that God is omniscient, knowing the past, present and future perfectly.[9] But it also affirms that the future decisions of self-deter-

---

[6]Ibid.

[7]See Homer's *Iliad* 6.13; *Aeneid* 2; and *Odyssey* 4.

[8]The label "open view of the future" is better than "open view of God" because, as we shall see, the distinctive aspect of this perspective has less to do with the nature of God than it does the nature of the future.

[9]I regard this belief to be not only sound biblical doctrine but, as I have elsewhere argued (*Trinity and Process,* pp. 244-53), a metaphysically necessary truth. God's knowledge and real-

mining agents are only possibilities until agents freely actualize them. In this view, therefore, the future is partly comprised of possibilities.[10] And since God knows all things perfectly—just as they are, and not otherwise—God knows the future as partly comprised of possibilities.[11]

The open view of the future thus affirms that in creating the world God faced the possibility, but not the certainty, that free creatures would choose to oppose him to the extent that they have. This view thereby allows us to

ity mutually define each other. Indeed, with Royce and Hartshorne I believe an argument can be made that our fallible knowledge of reality presupposes the reality of an infallible knower. See Josiah Royce, *The Conception of God* (New York: Macmillan, 1898), ch. 1; Charles Hartshorne, "Ideal Knowledge Defines Reality: What Was True in 'Idealism,' " *Journal of Philosophy* 43 (1946): 573-82; Charles Hartshorne, *Creative Synthesis and Philosophic Method* (1970; reprint, Lanham, Md.: University Press of America, 1983), pp. 286ff.

[10]The possibilities in question are ontological, not just epistemological. Those who affirm EDF may yet hold that the future consists of a realm of possibilities. But the indefiniteness of these possibilities, they must admit, is merely epistemological—due to our limited frame of reference. For God there are no genuine "maybes." Everything is *definitely* this way and *definitely* not another. It is not *for God* possibly this way and possibly another.

[11]The open view of the future is not a recent concept. While much research remains to be done on the extensiveness of this view in the ancient world and in the early church, we know that it was at times espoused. The most thorough treatment of the future as partly open in the early church that I am aware of is that of the fifth century theologian Calcidius. See J. den Boeft, *Calcidius on Fate: His Doctrine and Sources,* Philosophia Antiqua, ed. W. J. Verdenius and J. H. Waszink vol. 17 (Leiden: E. J. Brill, 1970), esp. pp. 52-53, 67-68 (162-63, 169-71 in Calcidius's original work). See also J. H. Waszink, *Commentarius: Corpus Platonicum Zmedi Aevi* (Leiden: E. J. Brill, 1962). Some argue that the African Christian tradition has usually assumed the open view of the future. For example, Major Jones writes, "We [in the African Christian tradition] believe human actions to be truly free, such that whereas God's knowledge of the past is total and absolute, God's knowledge of future events is not yet complete, particularly so far as acts of human freedom are concerned. The perfection of divine omniscience, then, must be construed to be God's always perfectly increasing knowledge taking in, with the passage of time, all knowable reality" (*The Color of God: The Concept of God in Afro-American Thought* [New York: Mercer, 1987], p. 95). Moreover, the view was given serious consideration in the late nineteenth century, being espoused in one form or another by such noteworthy theologians as G. T. Fechner, Otto Pfeiderer, and Jules Lequier. It was in various forms adopted by the great Bible commentator Adam Clarke (see *The Holy Bible . . . with a Commentary and Critical Notes* [London: J & T Clarke, 1810]), the popular circuit preacher Billy Hibbard (see *Memoirs of the Life and Travels of B. Hibbard,* 2nd ed. [New York: Piercy & Reed, 1843], pp. 372-414), the theologian Joel Hayes [see *The Foreknowledge of God: or, The Omniscience of God Consistent with His Own Holiness and Man's Free Agency* [Nashville: MECS, 1890]), the Disciples of Christ theologian T. W. Brents (*The Gospel Plan of Salvation* [Bowling Green, Ky.: Guardian of Truth Foundation, 1874]) and the esteemed Methodist professor and chancellor of Ohio Wesleyan University Lorenzo D. McCabe (see his *Divine Nescience of Future Contingencies a Necessity* [New York: Phillips & Hunt, 1882] and *The Foreknowledge of God, and Cognate Themes in Theology and Philosophy* [Cincinnati: Cranston & Stowe, 1887]). So far as I have been able to discover, from Calcidius through McCabe, no one was ever charged with heresy for denying that the content of God's foreknowledge was exhaustively definite. I am indebted to John Sanders of Huntington College for my information on Adam Clarke and Billy Hibbert.

consistently affirm that God entered into a somewhat risky endeavor in creating the world. For this and other reasons it is the perspective that best expresses and renders intelligible the trinitarian warfare worldview.

The sovereign Lord of history. For all biblical theists, the final court of appeal regarding any position is Scripture. As important as philosophical arguments may be, they do not take precedence over exegetical arguments. And so we must now consider whether Scripture supports the view that God faces a partly open future.

It is clear that *many* things about the future are portrayed as definite in the Bible, made so either by God's sovereign design or by inevitable consequences of present actions. The theme is strongest in Isaiah. As a way of distinguishing himself from the dead idols that the Israelites were inclined to chase after, Yahweh declares:

> I am the LORD, that is my name;
>   my glory I give to no other,
>   nor my praise to idols.
> See, the former things have come to pass,
>   and new things I now declare;
> before they spring forth,
>   I tell you of them. (Is 42:8-9)

The declaration is made as a challenge several chapters later when the Lord asks:

> Who is like me? Let them proclaim it,
>   let them declare and set it forth before me.
> Who has announced from of old the things to come?
>   Let them tell us what is yet to be.
> Do not fear, or be afraid;
>   have I not told you from of old and declared it? (Is 44:7-8)

Clearly the Lord is in command of the flow of history and therefore has a perspective on its future that mere human beings and worthless idols could never have. Several chapters later comes an even more dramatic declaration of this same truth.

> The former things I declared long ago,
>   they went out from my mouth and I made them known;
>   then suddenly I did them and they came to pass.
> Because I know that you are obstinate . . .
> I declared them to you from long ago,
>   before they came to pass I announced them to you,

so that you would not say, "My idol did them." (Is 48:3-5)

This motif is perhaps most emphatically expressed in Isaiah 46 when the Lord proclaims:

> Remember the former things of old;
> for I am God, and there is no other;
>   I am God, and there is no one like me,
> declaring the end from the beginning
>   and from ancient times things not yet done,
> saying "My purpose shall stand,
>   and I will fulfill my intention," . . .
> I have spoken, and I will bring it to pass;
>   I have planned, and I will do it. (Is 46:9-11)

The one true God is Lord of history, not some dead idol. Whatever Yahweh decides to do he can most certainly accomplish. And to prove it and distinguish himself from idols, Yahweh tells his people what he's going to do ahead of time.

The point of these passages is not, however, that God knows everything that is going to occur but that the Lord is the one *controlling* history. Similarly, when the Lord tells his people that it is he who "declares the end from the beginning," he immediately adds "*My* purpose shall stand, and *I* will fulfill my intention. . . . *I* have planned, and *I will do it*" (Is 46:10, emphasis added). Whatever the Lord is going to do he foreknows from the time he decides to do it. And so he declares this foreknowledge to prove that he, not some idol, is doing it.[12]

But do these passages teach that the future is *eternally and exhaustively settled* in the mind of God? Only if they also teach that the future is *exhaustively and unilaterally determined* by God. But nothing in these passages suggests this conclusion. The scope of each passage is quite specific: the Lord is speaking about his intention to bring the Jews back to their homeland. We outrun what the passages warrant if we universalize them.

Open-Ended Prophecies
The first piece of biblical material I will examine has sometimes been used to argue against the open view of the future. The Bible contains a number of

---

[12]On an openness view of this and other biblical predictions, see Sanders, *God Who Risks*, pp. 129-37. For a more extensive review of the biblical evidence supporting the classical view of foreknowledge, critiqued from an open view perspective, see Boyd, *The God of the Possible: Divine Foreknowledge and the Openness of the Future* (Grand Rapids, Mich.: Baker, 2000), ch. 1.

prophecies that were fulfilled long after they were given. Details about the Messiah, the destruction of particular cities and even predictions about end times are found throughout the Bible.[13] How can the Bible contain such accurate predictions, it is often argued, unless God possessed exhaustive knowledge of what was to come?

Some prophecies are simply declarations of what the Lord himself is going to do, as in the passages from Isaiah mentioned above. It's a matter not of God seeing into the future but of God knowing his own intentions in the present. Many prophecies involving free agents are not unconditional predictions of what will certainly happen but warnings of what *might* happen if things don't change. Such prophecies may *look like* unconditional predictions when the conditions for God's changing his mind aren't met. But their conditional nature is revealed when the conditions are met.

Jonah and the repentant Ninevites. The Lord instructed Jonah to proclaim, "Forty days more, and Nineveh shall be overthrown!" (Jon 3:4). This sounds like an unconditional declaration of a future event. The Ninevites fortunately did not accept it in those terms, however, for they repented of their evil: "Who knows? God may relent and change his mind; he may turn from his fierce anger, so that we do not perish" (Jon 3:9). According to the Bible, this is exactly what God did: "When God saw what they did, how they turned from their evil ways, God changed his mind about the calamity that he had said he would bring upon them; and he did not do it" (Jon 3:10).

If Nineveh had not repented, of course, the inspired decree that Nineveh would perish in forty days would have been fulfilled. This would have undoubtedly made it *look like* God had declared an unconditional prediction about the future; a number of prophecies *seem* unconditional for this reason: the conditions for God to alter his plans are not met. In this instance, however, the Ninevites repented, so God changed his mind, clearly demonstrating that God was declaring to Jonah his conditional *intention* to overthrow Nineveh (3:4), not disclosing his *foreknowledge* about Nineveh.

Passages such as this not only show that the open view of the future is compatible with biblical prophecy; they also challenge the classical view of foreknowledge. If God knew with certainty that Nineveh was going to repent, then his prophecy that the city would be destroyed in forty days seems disingenuous—it does not express a real intention. And if God didn't really change his mind regarding the future of Nineveh, then the explicit

---

[13]For an exhaustive survey of all possible biblical prophecies, see J. Barton Payne, *Encyclopedia of Biblical Prophecy* (New York: Harper & Row, 1973). I and many biblical scholars would hesitate in accepting many of the alleged prophecies Payne finds in Scripture, however.

biblical teaching that "God changed his mind about the calamity" is misleading. If we concede that the future can to some extent be open, however, the text can be understood straightforwardly.

Hezekiah's recovery. Another interesting illustration of the Lord's willingness to reverse his prophetic decrees in the light of human decisions is his healing of King Hezekiah. Hezekiah became fatally ill, and the Lord sent Isaiah to announce: "Thus says the LORD: Set your house in order, for you shall die; you shall not recover" (2 Kings 20:1; Is 38:1).

Hezekiah received this prophecy as coming from the Lord, but like the Ninevites, he did not regard the message as unalterable. On the contrary, as one who had a personal relationship with God, Hezekiah pleaded with God to change his mind (2 Kings 20:2-3; Is 38:2-3). As is often the case in Scripture, God granted his servant's request.[14] In response to Hezekiah's prayer the Lord told Isaiah:

> Turn back, and say to Hezekiah prince of my people, Thus says the LORD, the God of your ancestor David: I have heard your prayer, I have seen your tears; indeed, I will heal you; on the third day you shall go up to the house of the LORD. I will add fifteen years to your life. I will deliver you and this city out of the hand of the king of Assyria. (2 Kings 20:5-6; Is 38:5-6)

If the Lord didn't really change his mind, isn't Scripture misleading when it says the Lord *added* fifteen years to his life? Conversely, if God was truthful in declaring his intention to end Hezekiah's life, and if God's later statement was also truthful, then must we not accept that God truly changed his mind? And if God's mind can be truly changed, can his intentions be eternally settled, as the EDF doctrine stipulates?

The flexible potter. The motif of God's willingness to change even after decreeing his intention to take a particular course of action is explicitly taught and beautifully illustrated in Jeremiah 18. The Lord shows Jeremiah a potter refashioning a previously "spoiled" pot (vv. 1-4). He then says:

> Can I not do with you, O house of Israel, just as this potter has done? says the LORD. Just like the clay in the potter's hand, so are you in my hand, O house of Israel. (Jer 18:6)

Since Augustine, the analogy of a potter and his clay has frequently been employed in support of a deterministic model of divine providence. Focusing primarily on Paul's use of this analogy in Romans 9, many Christians

---

[14]On the Old Testament motif of people changing God's mind, see Walter Brueggemann, *Old Testament Theology: Essays on Structure, Theme, and Text* (Minneapolis: Fortress, 1992), pp. 35-37.

have concluded that God determines everything, including who will go to heaven and who will go to hell. Out of one lump of clay (humanity) God supposedly makes "objects of mercy" (elect humans) which he has "prepared beforehand for glory" (heaven) while making other "objects of wrath" (reprobate humans) which are "made for destruction," or hell (Rom 9:22–23).[15]

While many issues surround the exegesis of Romans 9, we should note that as the analogy is used in Jeremiah it actually has the *opposite* connotation. Rather than emphasizing the arbitrary power of a potter over his clay, this analogy demonstrates God's *willingness to be flexible and change* according to the situation. Hence, in Jeremiah 18 the Lord says:

> At one moment I may declare concerning a nation or a kingdom, that I will pluck up and break down and destroy it, but if that nation, concerning which I have spoken, turns from its evil, I will change my mind about the disaster that I intended to bring on it. And at another moment I may declare concerning a nation or a kingdom that I will build and plant it, but if it does evil in my sight, not listening to my voice, then I will change my mind about the good that I had intended to do to it. . . . Thus says the LORD: Look, I am a potter shaping evil against you and devising a plan against you. Turn now, all of you from your evil way, and amend your ways and your doings. (Jer 18:7–11)

Because the Lord is the potter and the potter has absolute authority over the clay, the Lord has the sovereign right *to change his mind whenever he chooses.* He is the master potter who is able and willing to alter his initial plans and refashion vessels according to a new plan. He has the authority and willingness to revoke a prophesied blessing or curse according to the situation. And so, Jeremiah decrees, even though the Lord has already prophesied against Israel, she should repent of her sin rather than despair and say "It is no use!" (Jer 18:12).

Jeremiah's use of this analogy is difficult to square with the EDF doctrine. It suggests that the future to some extent consists of possibilities, even after the sovereign "potter" has declared his intent to act in a certain way. If Israel would simply repent and turn to God, according to Jeremiah, God would change his mind regarding the disaster he has foretold and would bless Israel instead.

At a later date the Lord commanded Jeremiah to remind the Judeans of this truth: God is a God who is willing to change his mind.

---

[15]Sanders has a fine discussion of this and other "pancausal" texts in *God Who Risks,* pp. 81-87. See also Fredrik Lindström, *God and the Origin of Evil: A Contextual Analysis of Alleged Monistic Evidence in the Old Testament,* trans. F. H. Cryer (Lund, Sweden: Glerup, 1983). For a discussion of Romans 9 from a nondeterministic perspective, see appendix one, question 2.

> Stand in the court of the LORD's house, and speak to all the cities of Judah that come to worship in the house of the LORD; speak to them all the words that I command you. . . . It may be that they will listen . . . and will turn from their evil way, that *I may change my mind* about the disaster that I intend to bring on them because of their evil doings. (Jer 26:2–3, emphasis added)

Jeremiah obediently repeats this message almost verbatim to the elders of Judah.

> Now therefore amend your ways and your doings, and obey the voice of the LORD your God, and the LORD will *change his mind* about the disaster that he has pronounced against you. (v. 13)

The elders then repeated the message almost verbatim to the people, reminding them how the Lord changed his mind before when Hezekiah entreated his favor (Jer 26:19): in effect. if the Lord was willing to change his mind back then, he may be willing to change his mind again.[16] The Judeans should thus not demean God's character by assuming he would not alter his plans. While some evangelicals today dismiss the notion as "beneath" God or even as heretical, the central point of these passages is to drive home this very point: God is willing to change his mind.

Could these texts be anthropomorphic? Traditionally, defenders of the EDF doctrine consider passages that depict God as changing his mind to be anthropomorphisms.* The authors were portraying God in humanlike terms. These verses may *seem* to teach that God changes his mind, but in truth, the argument goes, God is above the sort of change these verses ascribe to him.[17] Four things may be said against this customary interpretation.

First, nothing in the texts themselves suggests that they were intended as anthropomorphisms. This conclusion rather seems to be driven by a philo-

---

[16]An example of the Lord changing his mind in the opposite direction—from blessing to curse—is in his treatment of Eli. The Lord had "promised" that Eli and his ancestors would minister before him "forever" (1 Sam 2:30). Yet because of Eli's sin and the sin of his sons, the Lord revoked his promise (vv. 27-36). It is difficult to affirm the genuineness of the original promise if God knew from all eternity that there was no possibility that Eli's family would minister before him forever.

[17]See, e.g., John Calvin, *Commentaries on the First Book of Moses*, trans. John King (Grand Rapids, Mich.: Eerdmans, 1948), 1:248-49. For contemporary restatements of this position, see Bruce Ware, *God's Lesser Glory: The Diminished God of Open Theism* (Wheaton, Ill.: Crossway, 2000); Bruce Ware, "An Evangelical Reformulation of the Doctrine of the Immutability of God," *JETS* 29 (1986): 442; Norman Geisler, *Creating God in the Image of Man? Neotheism's Dangerous Drift* (Minneapolis: Bethany House, 1997), pp. 90, 108.

sophical presupposition brought to the text. It is assumed that God cannot change his mind; hence verses that explicitly say that he does so can't be accepted at face value.

Second, this philosophical presupposition creates an arbitrary "canon within the canon." Texts that agree with the presupposition are granted the authority to depict God "as he truly is," while those which don't are not granted this authority. Isaiah, it seems, speaks more accurately about God than Moses, Jeremiah or Jonah. But Scripture does not suggest this distinction. To the contrary, in the very context where Moses is said to have changed God's mind, Scripture tells us Moses enjoyed an unprecedented intimate relationship with the Lord (Ex 33:11). This hermeneutic would have us believe we are in a better position to know what God is "really" like than Moses or Jeremiah.

The arbitrariness and presumptuousness of this hermeneutic is illustrated well in Calvin's treatment of the biblical passages which say that God changes his mind. Calvin argued that Scripture depicts God as changing his mind "because our weakness does not attain to his exalted state." Hence, "the description of him that is given to us must be accommodated to our capacity so that we may understand it." This "mode of accommodation is for him to represent himself to us not as he is in himself, but as he seems to us." Hence, while God seems to change his mind, in truth "neither God's plan nor his will is reversed, nor his volition altered."[18]

There is a flaw in Calvin's line of argumentation. If God must accommodate himself "because of our weakness" so "we may understand it," how is it that Calvin is able to argue that we are *not* to understand God according to his accommodation? Calvin apparently believes that *his* "weakness" does not preclude *him* from attaining to God's "exalted state." To the contrary, he seems confident that he has attained it and is capable of communicating it to others: "neither God's plan nor his will is reversed." But if Calvin is capable of attaining this "height," his argument is obviously undermined. Clearly, God does not have to accommodate himself "to our capacity so that we may understand." Indeed, just as clearly, God's accommodating himself to "our capacity" does not help us understand, according to Calvin. Otherwise

---

[18]John Calvin, *Institutes of the Christian Religion*, ed. John T. McNeill, trans. Ford L. Battles (Philadelphia: Westminster Press, 1960), 1.17.13, 227. This way of treating the "divine repentance" passages goes back at least to Philo and was adopted by several of the early church fathers, most notably Clement of Alexandria and Origen. See the discussion in Joseph C. McLelland, *God the Anonymous: A Study in Alexandrian Philosophical Theology*, Patristic Monograph Series 4 (Cambridge, Mass.: Philadelphia Patristic Foundation, 1976), pp. 37-40, 122-23.

Calvin wouldn't have to work so hard to make sure we do *not* understand that God changes his mind when God himself tells us that he does!

People who adhere to the Protestant principle of sola scriptura should judge this classical approach to these passages as presumptuous and unwarranted. If Calvin is indeed correct in asserting that God accommodates himself to our capacity so we may understand him, we have all the more reason not to try to outsmart God by supposing we can arrive at a "more exalted" understanding of him.

Third, the texts that speak of God changing his mind do not readily lend themselves to this interpretation. Like all metaphors, anthropomorphisms must connect with reality at some point if they are to communicate anything meaningful. Expressions like "the right hand of God" or "the eyes of the Lord," for example, communicate something of God's strength and knowledge. But if indeed it is an anthropomorphism, what does the concept of God changing his mind communicate? If God in fact never changes his mind, saying he does so doesn't communicate anything truthful; it is simply inaccurate.[19]

This observation is especially important in the light of Scripture's express encouragement to think about God as being capable of changing his mind. Through Jeremiah the Israelites were instructed *not* to assume that God can't or won't change his mind (Jer 26:2-3, 13; cf. 18:6-12). Indeed, Old Testament authors twice exalt God's willingness to adjust his plans as one of his praiseworthy attributes (Joel 2:13-14; Jon 4:2). This places the concept of God changing his mind in an entirely different category than anthropomorphic expressions like "the right hand of God." The teaching that God "may change [his] mind" *is the point of the admonition.* If God doesn't genuinely change his mind, the inspired admonition to think of him as doing so not only lacks content, it is positively deceiving.

I can perhaps make my point more forcefully by approaching it from another direction. Suppose that God *did* genuinely want to encourage us to see him as a God who can and will at times change his mind. How could he do so in terms that would be more explicit than the way he has already done in Scripture? If passages like Jeremiah 18 and 26 are not explicit enough, *what would an explicit admonition look like?* Nothing could be more explicit than the Lord's simply telling us, "I may change my mind." And this suggests that the classical interpretation of these passages has ruled out from the start the possibility of God telling us that he changes his mind. It is further

---

[19]See Sanders's similar argument in *God Who Risks*, pp. 69-70. His whole discussion on the matter of "divine repentance" is illuminating (pp. 66-75).

evidence that scriptural interpretation has been taken captive by philosophical presuppositions. What Scripture is and is not allowed to say is decided ahead of time.

Finally, we cannot take passages that depict God as changing his mind as anthropomorphisms without undermining the integrity of Scripture. For example, Scripture says that because of Moses' intercession, "the LORD changed his mind about the disaster that *he planned to* bring on his people" (Ex 32:14, emphasis added; cf. Deut 9:13-14, 18-20, 25; Ps 106:23). If the Lord didn't really change his mind, then neither did he really plan on bringing disaster on his people. Scripture thus misleads us when it explicitly tells us the Lord was planning just this before he changed his mind. Similarly, 1 Chronicles 21:15 tells us that the Lord in righteous anger dispatched "an angel to Jerusalem *to destroy it;* but when he was about to destroy it, the LORD . . . relented." If God never really changes his mind, however, the expressed purpose Scripture gives us as to why the Lord sent the angel cannot be correct, for God never really intended to destroy Jerusalem. How can one genuinely intend to do something one is certain one will not do?

Dozens of similar examples could be given, but the point is already clear. While other expressions such as "the right hand of God" are rightly taken as anthropomorphisms to preserve the integrity of Scripture, taking the portrayals of God changing his mind in this fashion has the opposite effect. Out of fidelity to Scripture we ought to abandon this classical interpretation.

The God Who Moves with Us in Time

The disappointed God. There are many other ways in which the Bible portrays God as facing a partly open future. Hear the frustration of the Lord, for example, as he expresses his amazement at Israel's stubbornness:

> The LORD said to me in the days of King Josiah: Have you seen what she did, that faithless one, Israel, how she went up on every high hill and under every green tree, and played the whore there? And *I thought*, "After she has done all this she will return to me"; but she did not return. (Jer 3:6-7, emphasis added)

And again:

> I *thought*
>   how I would set you among my children,
> and give you a pleasant land,
>   the most beautiful heritage of all the nations.
> And *I thought* you would call me, My Father,
>   and would not turn from following me.
> Instead, as a faithless wife leaves her husband,

so you have been faithless to me, O house of Israel. (vv. 19–20, emphasis added)

How could the Lord *genuinely think* that Israel would do one thing if in fact he eternally foreknew that Israel would not do this? The Lord's expression of disappointment can be authentic only if the future partly consists of possibilities and probabilities, not exclusively settled certainties. Only if it was possible—indeed, probable—that Israel would return to the Lord and call him "Father" can we make sense of the Lord telling us he thought Israel would do this and was disappointed when they did not.

The same is true of the Lord's expression of disappointment in Isaiah 5:1–4. Comparing himself to the frustrated owner of a vineyard, the Lord says he "expected [his vineyard] to yield grapes, / but it yielded wild [or "worthless"] grapes" (Is 5:2). The Lord than asks, "What more was there to do for my vineyard / that I have not done in it? / When I expected it to yield grapes, / why did it yield wild grapes?" (Is 5:4). The fact that the Lord did all he could do for his "vineyard" shows that his expectation and frustration were genuine. But how can this be if the Lord was eternally certain his vineyard would not "yield grapes"? Why strive for something you are already certain will never be?

Passages such as these need not imply that God was caught off guard, as though he didn't anticipate the *possibility* of the improbable. Nor do they imply that God was mistaken in thinking people would do one thing when it turns out they did another.[20] If God knows reality exhaustively, he eternally knows all future possibilities with their various probabilities, for these are objective realities. From all eternity, for example, it was logically possible that if God created a certain kind of world, and if the world proceeded in the direction it did, the situation described in these passages would come about. God would, then, eternally know this. And from all eternity it was logically possible (and, given the Lord's expectation, probable) that in this situation his people would respond positively to the Lord's leading. But it was from all eternity also logically possible (but improbable) that in this exact same situation his people would not respond positively. The omniscient Lord, having a perfectly accurate assessment of all probabilities, *thought* his people would do the former when this situation came about. But many of his people, being self-determining free creatures, opted for the more improbable course of action. Still, he was not caught off guard. Indeed, since God is infinitely

---

[20]Ware repeatedly charges that the God of open theism makes mistakes. See for example *God's Lesser Glory*, pp. 19-20.

intelligent—his intelligence doesn't get "spread out" by considering numerous possibilities—God had from eternity anticipated each situation as perfectly *as if* it were the only possibility that could take place. At the same time, since the remarkable stubbornness of the Israelites was improbable, the Lord was not mistaken in his expectation that his leading would *likely* cause his people to follow him.[21]

The God who asks questions. Sometimes the Lord expresses his frustration by asking questions about the future. This too suggests that the future is partly open. "How long will this people despise me?," the Lord asks. "And how long will they refuse to believe in me, in spite of all the signs that I have done among them?" (Num 14:11; cf. 1 Kings 22:20; Hos 8:5). The Lord had performed miracles expecting the Israelites to believe in him. His question suggests that he was genuinely taken aback when they persisted in their unbelief. The fact that the Lord continued trying to get the Israelites not to despise him—that is, that the Lord persistently tried to answer his own question—suggests that this question is not merely rhetorical.

The God who regrets. The openness of the future is also illustrated in the Bible's depictions of God as grieving the outcome of decisions *he himself has made.* Regarding the incredible wickedness of antediluvian humanity, for example, the Bible says "the LORD was sorry that he had made humankind on the earth, and it grieved him to his heart" (Gen 6:6). The fact that he destroyed them and started over with Noah's family demonstrates the genuineness of his regret. But how could the Lord possibly be sorry for making humankind if he was eternally certain they would turn out exactly this way when he created them?

Again, those who interpret this expression as anthropomorphic must ask, "What is this an anthropomorphic expression of?" If the Lord didn't *really* regret his decision to make humans, what does the expression that tells us he *did* regret making humans truthfully communicate to us? Suppose that God truly wanted to tell us that he sometimes truly regrets decisions. How could he do so in terms any clearer than in this passage? If telling us he was sorry he made humankind doesn't accomplish this, what would?

Another example when God experiences regret regards his decision to make Saul king of Israel. God had intended to bless Saul and his descendants

---

[21]On omniscience and future possibilities, see the discussions in Thomas Morris, "Properties, Modalities, and God," in *Anselmian Explorations* (Notre Dame, Ind.: University of Notre Dame Press, 1987), and Richard Creel, *Divine Impassability* (Cambridge: Cambridge University Press, 1986), pp. 98-99. In the next chapter I shall further develop the concept that God perfectly knows and anticipates all future possibilities, including counterfactuals of creaturely freedom.

(1 Sam 13:13) but Saul's behavior as king altered God's intentions. After his appointed king chose a rebellious course of action that brought him to a despicable state of wickedness, the Lord told Samuel, "I regret that I made Saul king, for he has turned back from following me" (1 Sam 15:11). The author reiterates this point at the end of his narrative: "And the LORD was sorry that he had made Saul king over Israel" (1 Sam 15:35). The only perspective that allows us to affirm the straightforward meaning of these texts is the acceptance that Saul's fate was not a foregone conclusion when God made him king. The Lord could only be sorry for making Saul king if he had hoped for a different outcome than what transpired (as his earlier statement regarding Saul indicates).

God took a risk in making Saul king. The risk depended on choices Saul made, and in this case God suffered a loss. God suffers this kind of loss whenever anyone thwarts his purpose for their lives (e.g., Lk 7:30). And it creates the kind of sorrow God now experiences over the war that is ravaging his cosmos. In the open view, God genuinely hopes each individual will turn to him and genuinely hoped the creation wouldn't fall into the war zone it has become. But if love is the aim, then freedom is the means and risk is the price. Things may not, and did not, turn out as God would have hoped.

However, God is never at a loss concerning his response to rebellious agents. God knows all future possibilities, all future certainties, and is in control of the overall flow of history. He is never unprepared, and in his infinite wisdom he is able to redeem good out of evil in ways we could never anticipate. Indeed, because the Lord possesses unlimited intelligence, he can attend to and anticipate numerous possibilities as thoroughly as if each one were the only future that could come about. Whichever possible course of action gets actualized, it is from God's perspective as though this were the only course he had to concern himself with. The open view sacrifices none of God's ability to respond to the future. It does not posit a "hand-wringing God" who worries about the future, as some who oppose this view suggest.[22] Finite creatures have their intelligence stretched thin the more possibilities they have to entertain, but not God. Hence, when a person like Saul fails, God already has a person like David waiting in the wings. Scripture reveals a God who is utterly confident of his ability to achieve his overall purposes despite (and sometimes by means of) the sinful rebellion of his creations. So confident is he, in fact, that he is willing to risk some loss with free agents in order to open the possibility of fellowship with them throughout

---

[22]Ware, *God's Lesser Glory,* p. 216, cf. pp. 20-21, 159.

eternity. He is willing to suffer frustration, disappointment and grief in order to share the joy of his triune being with others.

The Lord of the present. Another episode with Saul reveals the openness of the future God faces and touches once again on what looks like prophetic foreknowledge. In 1 Samuel 23 young David is fleeing for his life from King Saul to the town of Keilah. Hearing rumors that Saul might besiege the town in his attempt to capture him, David inquires of the Lord:

> "O LORD, the God of Israel, your servant has heard that Saul seeks to come to Keilah, to destroy the city on my account. And now, will Saul come down as your servant has heard?" . . . The LORD said, "He will come down." Then David said, "Will the men of Keilah surrender me and my men into the hand of Saul?" The LORD said, "They will surrender you." (1 Sam 23:10-12)

So far the narrative could be read as an example of how the Lord can see into the future. Interestingly enough, however, *none of this comes to pass.* Saul does not come down, and David is not handed over. On the basis of the information given him by the Lord, David and his men immediately leave Keilah. Hence, what the Lord said would happen now *can't* happen.

This passage offers another example of the sovereign Lord of history offering his servant insights into what will take place *if* things don't change. *Knowing the present perfectly,* the Lord knew Saul's heart and the dispositions of the people of Keilah and thus could accurately predict how they would behave *if David stayed.* But this prediction wasn't an example of exhaustively definite foreknowledge, for what the Lord predicted did not come to pass. It is rather an example of how the future is somewhat open to various possible courses of action and how the Lord perfectly anticipates these possible courses of action.

Acts 21:10-12 is another example. The prophet Agabus warns Paul that he will be bound by the Jews and handed over to the Gentiles if he goes to Jerusalem. On the basis of this prophecy Paul's comrades "urged him not to go up to Jerusalem"—they apparently did not take Agabus's prophecy in accordance with the EDF doctrine. Nonetheless, Paul's heart was resolved to go.

Things do not transpire quite as Agabus prophesied, however. The Jews do not bind Paul and hand him over to the Romans; rather, the Romans *rescue* Paul from the Jews who are about to kill him (21:27–33). Such a turn of events is puzzling if God possesses EDF and if Agabus's prophecy was truly inspired by the Holy Spirit. If God knows every detail about the future activity of free agents, there's no adequate explanation for the fact that things did not happen exactly as the Holy Spirit had prophesied through Agabus.

If we understand that the future is to some extent open, however, the narrative presents no problem. Through Agabus, God informs Paul and his comrades about what will happen *if* Paul chooses to go to Jerusalem (Paul has a choice in the matter) and *if* all the other individuals involved remain unchanged. Paul chooses to go to Jerusalem despite the warning, but apparently some Jews, by their own free choice, act more aggressively than God expects when they discover Paul in the temple. This may explain other prophecies in the Bible that are not fulfilled precisely as given.[23]

The God who finds out. Scripture consistently portrays God's knowledge as conforming to the way things really are (for his knowledge is perfectly accurate), and part of the way things really are is temporally conditioned. Plato and much of Greek philosophy after him held that time was somewhat illusory, and this conviction eventually became a staple of the classical-philosophical tradition after Augustine. But Scripture never expresses this sentiment. It rather portrays God's knowledge as conditioned by the past, present, and future. In other words, God "remembers" the past and anticipates the future. Insofar as he empowers humans to freely determine the future, this means that God waits "to see" what shall come to pass.

An intriguing example of this occurs when God authorizes Adam to name the animals he has created. Genesis 2:19 tells us that after God created the animals, he "brought them to the man *to see* what he would call them; and whatever the man called every living creature, that was its name" (emphasis added). As Del Ratzsch notes, "the original word for 'see' has the sense of 'discover.' That certainly makes it sound as though the plan had space to accommodate a wide range of names that Adam might have come up with."[24] The point Ratzsch is making is that God's sovereign control of the world doesn't rule out an element of uncertainty about the future. God empowers humans to be genuine partners in bringing about the future, and this means that the future is to some extent dependent on what we do.[25] But the passage also clearly shows that God's knowledge of the world is tempo-

---

[23]On the open nature of much biblical prophecy, see Terence Fretheim, "Divine Foreknowledge, Divine Constancy and the Rejection of Saul's Kingship," *CBQ* 47 (1985): 595-602; "The Repentance of God: A Study of Jeremiah 18:7-10," *HAR* 11 (1989): 31-56. Sanders, *God Who Risks*, pp. 129-37, is also helpful here.

[24]Del Ratzsch, *The Battle of Beginnings* (Downers Grove, Ill.: InterVarsity Press, 1996), p. 187; cf. p. 190. The responsive nature of God in the Genesis narrative is emphasized and nicely expounded on by Michael Welker in *Creation and Reality*, trans. John F. Hoffmeyer (Minneapolis: Fortress, 1999).

[25]Phyllis Trible notes that in this passage God is present "not as the authoritarian controller of events but as the generous delegator of power who even forfeits the right to reverse human decisions" (*God and the Rhetoric of Sexuality* [Philadelphia: Fortress, 1978], p. 93).

rally conditioned. God waits to see how humans will choose.

Another illustration of this is found in the theme of divine testing which runs throughout the Old Testament. The Lord frequently tests his covenant partners in order *to find out* whether or not they will remain faithful to him. For example, after Abraham passes God's "test" (Gen 22:1) by being willing to sacrifice his son, the Lord declares, "*now* I know that you fear God, *since* you have not withheld your son" (Gen 22:12, emphasis added). If God were certain that Abraham would "fear God" before the test, then his stated reason for giving the test, along with the time ("now") and source ("since") of God's knowledge of Abraham's character, cannot be correct.[26]

Similarly, the Lord forbids the Israelites from gathering more than a day's ration of bread from heaven when they were in the wilderness because he wants to "test them, whether they will follow my instruction or not" (Ex 16:4). By the Lord's own admission, there would have been no point for this testing if the Lord was already (from all eternity!) certain how the Israelites would behave.

Scripture abounds with similar statements. Moses tells the Israelites that the Lord has kept them in the desert forty years "in order to humble you, testing you *to know* what was in your heart, whether or not you would keep his commandments" (Deut 8:2, emphasis added). He also tells them that God allows false prophets to be correct sometimes because "the LORD your God is testing you, *to know* whether you indeed love the LORD your God with all your heart and soul" (Deut 13:3, emphasis added). The Lord temporarily withdraws support from Israel to "*find out* if they would obey the commandments of the LORD" (Judg 3:4 NASB, emphasis added; cf. 2:22). Similarly, God leaves Hezekiah "to himself" at one point "in order to test him and *to know* all that was in his heart" (2 Chron 32:31, emphasis added).

If we take these passages at face value they suggest that God was not certain how Abraham, the Israelites or Hezekiah would respond to his tests before he gave them. He tested them to find this out. If the Lord was certain ahead of time (let alone from all eternity) how these people would respond, the reason God gave the tests ("*to know* whether . . .") cannot be accurate. Again, suppose that God actually wanted to tell us that he tested people to truly find out how they would respond. How could he have done so in a manner that would be clearer than what he

---

[26]See Michael Carasik, "The Limits of Omniscience," *JBL* 119, no. 2 (2000): 221-32. Carasik unfortunately concludes that the testing motif rules out not only exhaustive divine foreknowledge but exhaustive present divine knowledge.

already gives us in these passages? If these passages do not teach this, in other words, what would a passage that *did* teach this say? If God telling us that he tests people "*to know* their heart" isn't enough to convince us that God in fact tests people to know their hearts, what would convince us?

Opponents of the open view often argue that God tests people not for his sake but for theirs. This interpretation would be possible except that each of the verses we just examined explicitly tells us that the testing was *for God,* not the people being tested. An interpretation that reverses what a text explicitly says is not a viable interpretation. Others argue that if we took these verses literally we would have to deny that God possesses exhaustive present knowledge, for the passages say God wanted to know "their heart." Since Scripture informs us that God knows all things while nevertheless teaching us that God tests people to know their heart, the understanding of "heart" which this objection presupposes cannot be correct.[27] The two teachings are easily rendered compatible by recognizing that the heart is the seat of a person's will. To discover a person's "heart" is to discover what their decision will be. Each of these passages, if read in context, makes this clear. The Lord tests people "*to know* what was in your heart, *whether or not you would keep his commandments*" (Deut 8:2, emphasis added). Since people are free agents, God wants to find out "whether they will follow my instruction or not" (Ex 16:4).

The search for an intercessor. Another example of God's knowledge being temporally conditioned is found in Ezekiel 22. Here the Lord declares his disappointment and righteous indignation with Israel. In a passage that emphasizes the urgency of prayer perhaps more emphatically than any other text in the Bible, the Lord says of his people:

> The people . . . have oppressed the poor and needy, and have extorted from the alien without redress. And I sought for anyone among them who would repair the wall and stand in the breach before me on behalf of the land, so that I would not destroy it; but I found no one. Therefore I have poured out my indignation upon them. (vv. 29-31).

If we take this passage at face value, the fate of Israel depends on whether or not the Lord finds anyone to "stand in the breach" before him as Moses had

---

[27]Because of this supposed contradiction, Ware concludes that "the straightforward meaning open theists commend simply cannot be the intended meaning of this text" (*God's Lesser Glory*, p. 73). If read in context, I argue, there is no contradiction between these two biblical motifs.

done centuries earlier (Ex 32:7-14).[28] Unfortunately, this time no Moses intercedes and alters God's declared intent.

The genuineness of the Lord's search for a person to stand in the breach is compromised if in fact God knew all along that no one would be found. Unless the Lord *genuinely hoped* he could raise up someone, *genuinely tried* to find that person and was *genuinely frustrated* at finding no one, it's not clear what this passage communicates. If God's hope, attempt and frustration were genuine, the question whether someone would stand in the breach had to be an open issue when God began his search. One can't hope and try to find something one is certain does not exist. As I shall argue subsequently (chapter seven), the open view renders the urgency which Scripture attaches to intercessory prayer intelligible precisely because it accepts at face value Scripture's teaching that things genuinely hang in the balance on whether or not people pray.

An open-ended eschatology. A final indication that God is genuinely affected by what takes place in time and that the future is partially open concerns the way Scripture sometimes speaks of eschatological matters. For example, several times the Lord threatens to "blot . . . out of the book of life" the names of all who abandon the faith (Rev 3:5; cf. Ex 32:33). We are elsewhere told that the names of the faithful have been in the process of being recorded since the foundation of the world (Rev 17:8). But despite God's desire to lose no one (2 Pet 3:9) and his strong commitments to preserve all his sheep (Jn 10:28-29; cf. Phil 1:6; 1 Thess 3:3; 1 Pet 1:4-5; Jude 24) this record is apparently probational throughout this present age. Believers can have their names blotted out of the book of life if they irrevocably recant their profession of faith (Heb 6:3-6; 2 Pet 2:20-22).

If the future is exhaustively settled and God possesses EDF, however, he would know from all eternity who would ultimately fall away. One thus wonders why their names were written in the book in the first place. Indeed, as argued earlier, if God wants no one to be damned but is eternally certain that some of those he creates will be damned, one must wonder why he creates them in the first place.

Another interesting passage suggesting that the Lord faces a partly open future is 2 Peter 3:9-12. Even though Jesus taught us that the Father alone

---

[28]The Bible contains many examples of the Lord's setting out on a course of judgment only to have that judgment called off or shortened in the light of intercessory prayer, e.g., Num 11:1-2; 14:12-20; 16:20-35, 41-48; Deut 9:13-26; 2 Sam 24:17-25; 1 Kings 21:27-29; 2 Chron 12:5-8; Amos 7:1-6. Such passages carry on the theme of God "changing his mind" in the light of human input and changing circumstances.

knows the day and hour of Christ's return (Mk 13:32), Peter suggests that God has delayed the second coming because he is "patient with you, not wanting any to perish" (2 Pet 3:9). Moreover, Peter encourages believers to be "waiting for and hastening *(speudō)* the coming of the day of God" (v. 12).[29] Similarly, Paul and the early Christians prayed for the Lord to come quickly (1 Cor 16:22; Rev 22:20). Two points may be made regarding these texts.

First, if it can be delayed by God and sped up by us, the time of the second coming cannot be eternally settled. When Jesus tells us the Father alone knows "the day and the hour" of the second coming, we can easily take this as an idiomatic way of affirming that the decision about this matter is the Father's. He alone will know when the time is right.[30] I may tell my daughter that I know the time when she'll be ready to drive a car, but I'm not thereby claiming that I have a preset date in mind. I am rather saying that I know the criteria I'm looking for in her life on which my decision is based. Judging from 2 Peter, it appears that the rate of the growth of the kingdom in the world is one important variable that the Father considers in deciding when to bring this age to a close.

Second, if the future is exhaustively definite and known by God as such, God would possess an unalterable knowledge of exactly when the second coming will take place. But this is difficult to square with what Peter explicitly says in this verse. How are we to understand God's delaying or our speeding up something that is eternally settled in God's mind?

The Omniresourceful God

The fact that the Lord often uses conditional and tentative terms about the future also suggests that he faces a future partially composed of possibilities. In Exodus 3, for example, the Lord commissions Moses to tell the elders of Israel that the Lord has heard their prayers and intends to deliver them out of Egypt (Ex 3:7-17).[31] He assures the insecure Moses, "They will listen to your voice" (Ex 3:18). Moses does not interpret God's statement as an infallible prediction of the future, however, for he quickly counters, "Suppose they do not believe me or listen to me" (Ex 4:1). The Lord does not respond by assuring Moses that he knows every detail of what is going to

---

[29]The NIV has "as you look forward to the day of God and speed its coming."

[30]This is likely the import of Paul's expression "at the right time" (Rom 5:6). Paul is saying that when the variables were in place, when the conditions were right, the Father sent the Son into the world (cf. Gal 4:4).

[31]I owe my insights concerning the open aspects of this passage to John Sanders.

take place before it comes about, as one might expect if he in fact possesses such knowledge. He rather shows Moses how he can turn a staff into a serpent and then back into a staff again (Ex 4:2-4). This miracle, the Lord tells him, is "so that they may believe that the LORD, the God of their ancestors, the God of Abraham, the God of Isaac, and the God of Jacob, has appeared to you" (Ex 4:5).

Moses is not convinced that the first miracle will suffice. So the Lord adds a second miracle: he shows Moses how he can make a hand leprous and then whole again (Ex 4:6-7). Then the Lord states, "*If* they will not believe you or heed the first sign, they *may* believe the second sign" (Ex 4:8, emphasis added). But the Lord quickly acknowledges the possibility that even this second miracle might not convince them. And so he continues:

> *If* they will not believe even these two signs or heed you, you shall take some water from the Nile and pour it on the dry ground; and the water that you shall take from the Nile will become blood on the dry ground. (Ex 4:9)

If we set aside the assumption that the future is exhaustively settled, the text clearly suggests that God is not certain how many miracles it will take to convince the elders of Israel that he has sent Moses. If we rather insist that the Lord knew all along that it would take exactly three miracles, then he seems disingenuous in telling Moses they *may* believe after the first *or* the second miracle (Ex 4:5, 8). How can the Lord tell Moses that something might happen if he knows for certain it will not happen?[32]

This lack of certainty regarding some aspects of the future is no defect on God's part, however. It's just that the only reality that exists for God to know is that the elders *may* believe after one, two or perhaps three miracles. *That* is what is real, and so *that* is what God perfectly knows as real. Until the elders resolve the issue by responding to Moses' miracles, there's nothing other than possibilities for God to know. God can hardly be faulted for not knowing something that does not exist.

However, this passage also makes it clear that God is absolutely confident he can convince the elders of Israel to follow Moses and escape Egypt. This much of the future *is* settled, for God has resolved it to be so. This episode is intended to teach Moses that God has more than enough resources to

---

[32]We should also note the episode that immediately follows the one we are discussing. The Lord becomes frustrated with Moses' persistent unbelief (Ex 4:10-17). He unsuccessfully tries to convince Moses that he can overcome his speech impairments. This episode is easier to reconcile with the view that Moses' remarkable obstinacy was not eternally certain than it is with the EDF perspective. If God eternally knew Moses would not be willing to speak, it's more difficult to understand the Lord's frustration and persistence in trying to get him to speak.

accomplish whatever he sets out to accomplish. He is an omniresourceful God. It's just that within the parameters of the future that God has already settled, there are unsettled features. The elders *will* become convinced. But it may take one, two or three miracles to bring this about.

The God who says maybe. Scripture contains many divine "maybes," though they often go unnoticed. Each one suggests that the future is partially open. For example, the Lord tells Jeremiah to stand in the court and preach to the Judeans, telling him, "It *may* be that they will listen . . . that I *may* change my mind about the disaster I intend to bring"(Jer 26:3, emphasis added). The subjunctive nature of the Lord's promise suggests that it isn't a foregone conclusion that the Judeans will listen to Jeremiah.

Similarly, the Lord instructs Ezekiel to enact a prophetic lesson for Israel, telling him, "*Perhaps* they will understand, though they are a rebellious house" (Ezek 12:3, emphasis added). As it turns out, they did not understand. If God was certain that the Israelites would not understand when he gave Ezekiel his instructions, it was misleading to say "perhaps they will understand." It was also a waste of Ezekiel's time when God motivated him to enact this prophetic lesson on the basis of this possibility.

Likewise, in Exodus 13:17 we read that the Lord decided not to take the children of Israel the shortest route to Canaan. This would be puzzling except that the Lord explains what led him to this decision. Scripture says the Lord thought (or said), "*if* they face war, they *might* change their minds and return to Egypt" (NIV, emphasis added). The conditional nature ("if . . . might") of this sentence suggests that it was not certain that Israel would do this. It was probable, however. Hence the Lord wisely refrained from putting Israel in this situation.

Finally, we must consider the numerous times the Lord presents options to humans and speaks in conditional terms. For example, the Lord says to the king of Judah:

> If you will indeed obey [my] word, then through the gates of this house shall enter kings who sit on the throne of David. . . . But if you will not heed these words, I swear by myself . . . that this house shall become a desolation. (Jer 22:4-5)

Similarly, after Solomon completes the temple the Lord says to him:

> If you will walk before me, as David your father walked, . . . doing according to all that I have commanded you, and keeping my statutes and my ordinances, then I will establish your royal throne over Israel forever. . . . If you turn aside from following me . . . and do not keep my commandments and my statutes that I have set before you, . . . then I will cut Israel off from the land that I

have given them; and the house that I have consecrated for my name I will cast out of my sight. (1 Kings 9:4-7)

God addresses his people in this "if . . . if not" manner throughout Scripture. It says something important about God's relationship to people. As Terrence Fretheim observes, it means that

> the way in which . . . human beings respond to God and God's ways makes a difference with respect to the shape the future takes for both God and Israel. Both of these futures must be considered genuine possibilities for God as well. For God to hold out the possibility of a positive human future, when it was not in fact a possibility, would be an act of deception.[33]

If God cannot deceive, the future must be partially open. Fretheim continues:

> If both futures are possible for God, then God has not established which future shall come to be, and God also does not finally know for certain which one shall occur. God knows these futures as genuine possibilities, though God may be said to know which future is more probable.[34]

God always works with humans to bring about the positive future. But where free agents are involved, some outcomes cannot be guaranteed. A certain amount of risk is involved.

The sovereign chess master. As noted above, the passages that suggest that God faces a partly open future do not conflict with those that depict God as the all-powerful, sovereign, majestic Lord of history. To the contrary, they further exalt this sovereignty. Together these two motifs show that God's providence is not merely a matter of controlling the ways things turn out. If he chose to, of course, God could operate this way. But it would not exalt his wisdom (how much wisdom does it take to control something within your power?) and would not allow for genuine love to exist (see TWT1). Because God has chosen to create a cosmos populated with free agents, God's sovereignty is established as much by his wisdom as it is by his power. He gives humans and angels the power to say no to him so that they might also have the power to say yes to him. But though these agents are able to thwart his will to some extent, God is nevertheless able to wisely accomplish his overall purposes in spite of, and sometimes by means of, their rebellion.

---

[33]Terence Fretheim, "Divine Dependence on the Human: An Old Testament Perspective," *Ex Auditu* 13 (1997): 9.
[34]Ibid.

We might compare this view of God to a master chess player.[35] We would ordinarily consider a chess player to be insecure to the extent that she would need to know ahead of time, or control if possible, all the moves of her opponent to ensure winning a match. Conversely, we would ordinarily consider a chess player wise and confident to the extent that she could ensure victory without relying on these aids. Her confidence is rooted in her ability to wisely anticipate all *possible* future moves her opponent might make together with all the possible responses she may make to each of these possible moves. She does not know exactly how many moves she will have to make, or what these moves will be, before the match begins, for she does not know exactly how her opponent will move his pieces. If her opponent is formidable, she may even have to place certain pieces "at risk" in order finally to checkmate him. But *by virtue of her superior wisdom* she is certain of victory. And precisely because her victory does not come from having a blueprint of her opponent's moves or otherwise controlling her opponent's moves, the wisdom she displays in achieving her victory is praiseworthy.

The fact that Scripture tells us the Lord sometimes speaks of the future in terms of what might take place instead of what will certainly take place suggests that the chess master analogy is appropriate. Like a wise chess master, the Lord knows that it *may* take more than one or two miracles to convince the elders of Israel that Moses is his messenger, but he is nevertheless certain that he will eventually convince them. He knows that the Israelites *may* heed the message he gives through Jeremiah, *might* understand the message Ezekiel enacts, *might* retreat if they face the Philistines, and *may* turn to him and call him Father—or they may not. While he hopes for the one, he anticipates the other. He "wins the game" not by meticulously controlling it or by possessing "inside information" but by being the infinitely wise God that he is.

This is, of course, an analogy. In reality, no humans can come close to foreknowing every possible combination of moves they and their opponents might make throughout the course of every conceivable match. These possibilities do exist ahead of time, however, so the omniscient God of course perfectly knows them. Indeed, to apply the analogy to the real world, we must conceive of God foreknowing and perfectly anticipating from all eter-

---

[35]The analogy of God as a chess master was first used by William James in *The Will to Believe and Other Essays in Popular Philosophy* (New York: Dover, 1956), pp. 181-82. Peter Geach uses it in *Providence and Evil* (Cambridge: Cambridge University Press, 1977), but in a questionable way. Though he denies meticulous providence and exhaustive definite foreknowledge, he seems to suggest that God's will can never be thwarted. For a critique of Geach, see Sanders, *God Who Risks*, pp. 230-31.

nity every possible event that might ever come to pass. For whatever in fact comes to pass was logically possible from all eternity. Consequently, God would eternally know it as such.

But this vast foreknowledge is of *possibilities*, not of future *certainties*. God may (and does) sovereignly delimit these possibilities as he sees fit by decreeing the parameters within which free agents can make decisions. There is no "risk" he enters into that he himself did not choose. But in the open view of the future he does not restrict these possibilities to one certain course of action. While that would be a risk-free course of action, it would rule out freedom, which in turn would rule out the possibility of love.

Though open theists are often accused of limiting God's knowledge or of undermining his sovereignty, this understanding of the future serves to *increase* our appreciation of God's knowledge and power.[36] To perfectly anticipate every possible combination of moves throughout all time—as easily as if one had only one certain combination of moves to attend to—requires infinite intelligence in a way that possessing a blueprint of what will certainly occur does not. In addition, achieving one's objectives while working with personal agents who possess free will requires a confidence and virtuous form of influential power which controlling everything lacks. When the "chess match" of this world history is concluded, it will look to us finite creatures as though God had only this one course of action to anticipate. The open view simply exalts God's wisdom by acknowledging that God possessed this perfect anticipation without this course of action being pre-fixed in his mind or his will from all eternity.

---

[36]The theme that the open view of the future assails God's knowledge and power (as well as most other attributes of God) is the central thesis of Ware's recent book *The Lesser Glory of God*. While this book is not without helpful criticisms, Ware's critique as a whole is predicated on the assumption that (1) God is sovereign only to the extent that God controls, and (2) the future exists as an exhaustively definite reality for God to know. If one accepts these starting points, some of Ware's criticisms of the open view stand—but are also unnecessary, since the outcome was presupposed in the starting point. To cite one of many possible examples, Ware argues that in the open view, God "of necessity lacks vital information that he has no access to because that information is located in an unknown future" (p. 180). Of course, if open theists believed that God lacked information about the future because he could not access it, Ware's criticism that open theists posit a "diminished God" would be correct. In point of fact, however, none of those Ware is critiquing has ever held anything remotely like this obviously untenable position. In the open view, there *is no* information "located in the future" about exactly how free agents will act. The future is partly composed of possibilities, so God perfectly knows it as such. Ware presupposes *his own view* of the future and then charges open theists with positing an ignorant God for not knowing it! Overall Ware's critique rarely engages open theists on their own terms, and this renders his work largely irrelevant to anyone who wants to seriously engage in critical dialogue with the open view at an academic level.

Conclusion: Risk and the Open Future

In this chapter I have tried to demonstrate that the God of the Bible is not a God who has or needs "inside information" on what is going to transpire. As Creator of the cosmos and sovereign Lord of world history, God sets the parameters within which all free activity must take place. He predestines whatever aspects of history need to be predestined to accomplish his objectives. He knows perfectly all possible future events as well as whatever is settled about the future as a consequence of the present. But within these parameters he allows free agents room to make their own decisions and to ultimately determine their own destinies. The open view of the future thus renders intelligible both the sovereign control and the partial openness that the Bible ascribes to God in the context of his relation to history.

If the case made in this chapter for a partially open future is accepted, it is possible to ascribe risk to God for the sake of love without concluding that God is not in control of the world. While Scripture assures us that the overall objectives of history are secure—the Lord shall certainly have a bride who will participate in his triune love—it also teaches us that the fate of any one of his free creatures is unsettled until they themselves choose to enter into the saving covenant with him. This is the ultimate risk the Lord takes in creating a world with the purpose of sharing his triune self with others.

If significant numbers of free agents (angels and humans) opt to rebel against him, or if crucially important, high ranking, morally responsible agents (such as Lucifer) decide to rebel against him, then the result will be a cosmos caught up in warfare. We may believe on the basis of Scripture that God genuinely hoped this would not occur. And we may believe on the basis of Scripture that God is genuinely grieved by the fact that it did occur. But we may also be confident, again on the basis of Scripture, that God knew of and anticipated these possibilities and yet deemed the risk worth it. The alternative is either no creation at all or what comes to almost the same thing: a creation that was incapable of love.[37]

But we have not yet completed our case in defending TWT2. There are a number of scriptural arguments that have been raised against this view which yet need to be addressed. And there are several other arguments in favor of this view which need to be considered. To this task we turn in the next chapter.

God risked in Creating

---

[37]This is the open theist's answer to the objection that God is more, not less, responsible for the evil that transpires in world history if he did not know exactly what would take place when he created the world but knew that it might involve great suffering. See the discussion in Walls, *Hell*, pp. 51-53.

4

A QUESTION OF BALANCE

Issues Surrounding
the Foreknowledge of God
& the Openness of the Future

*If even the omnipotent God cannot act to change the past,
it does not seem any more conceivable that the omniscient God can know
with certainty the unformed future.*
J. POLKINGHORNE, SCIENCE AND CREATION

*Why, if one act of knowledge could from one point take in the total perspective,
with all mere possibilities abolished, should there have been anything more than that act?
Why duplicate it by the tedious unrolling, inch by inch, of the foredone reality?
No answer seems possible.*
W. JAMES, "ON SOME HEGELISMS"

God saves by persuasion, not compulsion, for compulsion is no attribute of God.
EPISTLE TO DIOGNETUS

I have thus far argued that *love requires freedom* (TWT1) and *freedom requires risk* (TWT2). These are the first two theses that render the warfare worldview of Scripture intelligible and the trinitarian warfare theodicy plausible. Without these theses it is difficult to understand why the triune God would create a world where the sort of evil we presently experience could take place. As we all know intuitively if not from experience, love is risky business. If God's aim for creation was love, the metaphysical price he had to pay was the risk of having some creatures choose the opposite of love.

As I have shown, TWT2 contradicts the classical understanding that God possesses *exhaustively definite foreknowledge* (EDF).[1] I argued that the classical perspective stands in tension with Scripture at a number of points. This biblical material implies that while a good deal of the future is settled from God's perspective, some aspects of the future are not. The future consists of indefinite possibilities as well as definite realities.

The issue is not this simple, however. While many passages suggest that the future *is* partly open, defenders of the classical perspective argue that these passages must be interpreted in light of other passages that suggest the future is exhaustively settled. If my thesis is to be plausible, that the future must be partially open for God's risk to be genuine, these other passages must be considered.[2]

The first task of this chapter, therefore, is to consider the most convincing scriptural arguments against the open view. In the course of addressing these arguments I shall develop in greater depth certain aspects of this perspective, especially regarding its understanding of divine sovereignty. More specifically, I will flesh out and defend the understanding of divine sovereignty within the open view of the future by relating it to the view that God possesses "*middle knowledge.*"* Following this I shall consider three more arguments that support this view. The first is philosophical, the second based on contemporary physics and the third based on our phenomenological experience of ourselves. The goal in all of this is to ensure that TWT2 is biblically, rationally and experientially grounded.

A Foreknown Bride and a Foreknown Messiah

Foreknowledge of the church. One of the few biblical passages that explicitly mentions God's foreknowledge is Romans 8:29. Here Paul declares that "those whom [God] foreknew he also predestined to be conformed to the image of his Son, in order that he might be the firstborn within a large family." Does this verse imply that God foreknows all that shall come to pass, including who will and will not believe in Christ? Three brief considerations are relevant.

First, the scope of what is foreknown in this passage is limited. When Paul

---

[1]The issue is not whether God possesses exhaustive foreknowledge. It is rather whether the future God foreknows is exhaustively *definite*. In contrast to classical theists, open theists claim that the future is partly made up of possibilities and hence is perfectly known by God as partly made up of possibilities.

[2]In this chapter I am concerned only with passages that are frequently cited in support of the EDF doctrine. I briefly consider passages that are frequently cited in support of the view that God controls all things (and the compatibilistic understanding of freedom that accompanies this view) in appendix five.

refers to those who were "foreknown" as well as to those who were "predestined," "called," "justified" and "glorified" (Rom 8:29–30), he is clearly *distinguishing* this group of people (believers) from other people (nonbelievers). What is said about this group cannot be said about the others. "Those whom God foreknew" contrasts with those whom God did *not* foreknow. Hence, if Paul is using the verb *proginōskō* (lit. "to know before") in a cognitive sense—that is, to say that God possessed certain information ahead of time—then far from implying that God foreknows everything, this text would actually be *denying* that God foreknows everything.

My second point, however, is that there is no good reason to take *proginōskō* in a cognitive sense. It is more likely that Paul is using the term *know* in the customary Semitic sense of affection rather than in a merely cognitive sense. To "know" someone is to love that one. So to "foreknow" someone means to love that one ahead of time. Three chapters later Paul refers to Israel as "[God's] people whom he foreknew" (Rom 11:2). If this is in fact its meaning in 8:29, then Paul is simply claiming that God loved the church before he called them just as he loved Israel before he called them.

This leads directly to my third point. There is no more reason to think Paul is referring to particular individuals in this passage than there is to think he is discussing individual Jews in Romans 11:2. It is not that God foreloved select individuals (as opposed to other individuals whom God didn't forelove) and then called and predestined them. What God loved ahead of time (ultimately from the foundation of the world) was the bride of Christ, the body of Christ, the church *considered as a corporate whole.*

From the dawn of creation God's heart has been set on *the group* of all those who would say "yes" to the invitation of the King. God predestined *this group* to be saved (2 Tim 1:9), to be holy and blameless (Eph 1:4), to do good works (Eph 2:10), to be glorified (1 Cor 2:7) and to be conformed to the image of Jesus Christ (Rom 8:29). Once you or I freely align ourselves with this corporate whole, this new people of Israel (Gal 6:15-16; Phil 3:3), all that is predestined and foreknown about *the group* now applies to all of us who choose to believe.[3]

Suppose I decide at the last minute to attend a theology conference in which, to my surprise, a person delivers a paper on Milton's *Paradise Lost.* At the end of the presentation I ask, "When was it decided that we would listen to that paper?" to which the conference organizer responds, "It was decided

---

[3]On the corporate nature of election see William W. Klein, *The New Chosen People: A Corporate View of Election* (Grand Rapids, Mich.: Zondervan, 1970); and R. Shank, *Elect in the Son: A Study of the Doctrine of Election* (Springfield, Mo.: Westcott, 1970).

six months ago." It wasn't decided six months ago that I *individually* would hear this paper; rather, it was decided that whoever chooses to attend this conference would hear this paper. Now that I and others have decided to attend this conference, we can all say, "It was decided [predestined] six months ago that *we* would hear this paper." What was decided for the group as a whole gets individually applied as individuals choose to align themselves with the group.

So it is with the Bible's teaching on the predestined church. All who choose to become part of the bride of Christ can proclaim that *we* were loved by God and chosen in Christ "before the foundation of the world to be holy and blameless before him in love" (Eph 1:4; cf. Rom 8:29; 1 Pet 1:2). We were "destined " to be adopted "as his children through Jesus Christ" (Eph. 1:5). We were given grace from the foundation of the world (2 Tim 1:9) and destined to live eternally to the praise of God's glorious grace (Eph 1:11). But *individually* belonging to this group was ultimately our decision to make.[4]

The Messiah and the foreknowledge of God. Understanding the corporate nature of the foreknown and predestined church explains a significant group of texts in Scripture often cited in defense of EDF. But it doesn't explain all of them. A number of passages speak of particular events being foreknown by God, even events resulting from individuals' free will. Many of these surround the person and ministry of Jesus Christ.

For example, dozens of prophecies in the Old Testament accurately predict details about the coming Messiah (e.g., he would be born in Bethlehem; arise out of the lineage of Abraham, Isaac, Jacob, Jesse and David; be executed with criminals; have his side pierced; be buried with the rich; atone for the sins of many). Most of these predictions seem to involve future free decisions of individuals.[5]

---

[4]Jesus' parable of the king who "called" many to his wedding banquet but "chose" as guests only those who accepted his invitation and wore wedding robes illustrates the corporate nature of election (Mt 22:1-14). The king's guests could refer to themselves as "chosen" by the king, though *anyone* who had accepted his conditions could have claimed the same.
[5]See "Prophecy, as Proof of Bible," in Norman Geisler, *Baker Encyclopedia of Christian Apologetics* (Grand Rapids, Mich.: Baker, 1999), pp. 610-17. At the same time, it should be noted that sometimes a New Testament author claims that Jesus "fulfilled" an Old Testament verse to say that an aspect of Jesus' life illustrates or recapitulates the point of the passage. When Matthew claims that Jesus "fulfilled" Hosea 11:1 when he went to Egypt (Mt 2:15), for example, he was not thereby claiming that Hosea had the future Messiah in mind when he wrote that passage. Hosea was referring to Israel as the "son" called out of Egypt; Matthew was simply noting that the life of Jesus recapitulates the life of Israel, who also was called out of Egypt. On this see John Sawyer, *Prophecy and the Biblical Prophets*, rev. ed. (New York: Oxford University Press, 1993), pp. 142-46; John Sanders, *The God Who Risks: A Theology of Providence* (Downers Grove, Ill.:

Similarly, some of the central events that surround the life and death of Jesus Christ are identified as foreknown and preordained. One of the most explicit passages along these lines is Acts 2:23, where Peter refers to Jesus as being "handed over to you [Jews] according to the definite plan and foreknowledge of God" to be "crucified and killed." Similarly, in Acts 4:27-28 early Christians proclaimed that

> Herod and Pontius Pilate, with the Gentiles and the peoples of Israel, gathered together against your holy servant Jesus, whom you anointed, to do whatever your hand and your plan had predestined to take place.

The obvious question is, how are the messianic prophecies and statements about foreknown and predestined aspects of Jesus' life possible unless God possesses EDF? The problem is compounded by the fact that it seems impossible to appeal to "conditional prophecies" in these cases. If there was anything which was unconditionally promised throughout Scripture since the time of the Fall it was the coming of the Messiah (Gen 3:15; cf. Rev 13:8). Although conditional prophecies occur frequently in the Old Testament, their presence does not explain this category of prophecies.

In point of fact, however, these passages present no difficulty for the view of the future as partly open. While the open view holds that humans must be free to the extent that they are capable of love, this freedom obviously has limits. Indeed, the concept of freedom is only meaningful against the backdrop of limited determinism.[6] As I have already argued, our freedom is conditioned (but not extinguished) by our genes, our environment, our previous choices and acquired character, and most certainly God's will. (In chapters six and seven I argue that freedom is restricted by a host of other variables as well.) The open view of the future thus affirms that many aspects of the future are determined either by God or by inevitable consequences of present causes. It is therefore compatible with the biblical portrait of God as the sovereign Lord of history who knows all settled aspects of the future ahead of time, and who is able to determine whatever he wants to ahead of time to accomplish his objectives. There is therefore no logical problem in reconciling the biblical truth that the Lord predestined and foreknew various details about the Messiah as well as other matters

---

InterVarsity Press, 1998), pp. 133-34; John Goldingay, *Models for Interpretation of Scripture* (Grand Rapids, Mich.: Eerdmans, 1995), pp. 122-27, 146-48.
[6]This conclusion is based on the principle of contrast. See my *Trinity and Process: A Critical Evaluation and Reconstruction of Hartshorne's Di-Polar Theism Towards a Trinitarian Metaphysics* (New York: Lang, 1992), pp. 36-37. For Hartshorne's rejection of determinism on the basis of this principle, see pp. 61-65.

with the biblical data that suggests that the future is partly open.

Predestined wicked acts? In Acts 2:23 and 4:28, however, God seems to predestine a wicked deed (i.e., crucifying Jesus) while at the same time holding the perpetrators responsible for it. Does this undermine the claim that morally responsible free acts cannot be part of the future that is settled? Two points will suffice to show that it does not.

First, neither Acts 2:23 nor 4:28 suggest that *the individuals* who crucified Jesus were predestined and foreknown. These verses only affirm that it was preordained and foreknown that the Messiah would be crucified. *That* Jesus would be killed was predetermined. *Who* would do it was not. It might be objected that God can not predestine and foreknow a particular event without predestining and foreknowing the particular people who will carry out this event. But this conclusion follows only if a *mechanistic worldview** is presupposed. That is, if a one-to-one relationship between causes and effects is assumed, then a particular effect cannot be determined without its antecedent causes also being determined. But this assumption is not necessary. To the contrary, this assumption is at odds with the general direction most fields of science took throughout the twentieth century. In a multitude of differing ways we have discovered that reality is constituted as a balance between determinism and freedom, stable laws and chance, regularity and spontaneity, general predictability and an element of unpredictability about specifics.

In this context, there is no contradiction in claiming that an event is predestined while affirming that the individuals who carry it out are not.[7] I believe this nonmechanistic worldview is much closer to the Semitic worldview of the Bible, which is why they had no difficulty affirming that some, but not all, of the future is predestined and foreknown as settled. In the case of the crucifixion, as long as God knew that in certain circumstances there would be a certain percentage of people who would act as the wicked people

---

[7]There are a few exceptions to this in Scripture. It was prophesied that a particular man named Josiah would tear down the pagan altars and destroy the pagan priesthood which plagued Israel (1 Kings 13:2-3; cf. 2 Kings 22:1; 23:15-16). And it was prophesied that a pagan king named (or titled) Cyrus would help rebuild Jerusalem (Is 45:13). In these cases it seems that for providential reasons the Lord determined that he would exert whatever influence was necessary to accomplish these tasks through these individuals. The libertarian freedom of these individuals was thus restricted to this extent ahead of time. However, these passages do not suggest that everything about Josiah and Cyrus (let alone the whole scope of history) was settled ahead of time. Restricting a person's freedom in one respect no more undermines their general freedom than does any other restriction placed on individuals (e.g., their physical, emotional, intellectual makeup; their time, place and circumstances of birth). As I shall show in chapter six, freedom always takes place in a context of variables which condition and restrict it.

spoken of in these passages acted, he could predestine and thus foreknow that the Messiah would be crucified without undermining the freedom of any individuals.

Second, defenders of the open view of the future can further affirm that God at times predestines certain acts of wicked individuals. They would simply deny that this predestining occurred before these individuals had freely resolved their own characters. God would be morally culpable if he predestined people to carry out wicked acts prior to their birth. But he is not morally culpable if he chooses to direct the path of people who have already *made themselves* wicked.

We must remember that moral responsibility applies to the acquired character of self-determining agents even more fundamentally than it applies to the particular decisions agents make which reflect and reinforce their character. Traditionally theologians have distinguished the character a person receives from God *(habitus infusus)* from the character they freely acquire *(habitus acquirus)*. There is no contradiction in the claim that a person is morally responsible for an act even though they could not have done otherwise, so long as the character that now rendered their action certain flowed from a character they themselves acquired. It was not "infused" into them by God.

Hence, a person who has solidified his character *(habitus acquirus)* as a greedy person by making multitudes of free decisions is morally culpable not only for all the further greedy *acts* he performs but also and even more fundamentally for being *the kind of person he has freely become.* Moral culpability is not just about people *acting* certain ways when they could have and should have acted differently. It's more about people *becoming* certain kinds of people when they could have and should have become different kinds of people. Hence, if God decides that it fits his providential plan to use a person whose choices have solidified his character as wicked, God is not responsible for this person's wickedness.[8]

To illustrate, Scripture suggests that the Messiah's betrayal was predestined and Jesus foreknew that Judas would betray him (Jn 6:64, 70-71;

---

[8]With Calvinists, open theists can affirm that God can, if he chooses, sovereignly steer people who possess compatibilistic freedom. Open theists simply deny God's preordination that these individuals would have the solidified character that would render some of their behavior certain. Rather, these individuals are responsible for their own character, for they themselves acquired it by the use of their libertarian freedom. The view that libertarian freedom becomes compatibilistic freedom, that self-determining acts lead to a self-determined character, shall be more fully discussed in chapter six as I address the sixth thesis of the trinitarian warfare theodicy—namely, that libertarian freedom is finite.

13:18-19). These contentions do not contradict the view that morally responsible, self-determining actions cannot be predestined or foreknown as long as Judas was not *in particular* chosen to carry out this deed before Judas had *made himself* into the kind of person who *would* carry out this deed. After Judas unfortunately hardened himself into this kind of person, God wove his character into a providential plan. God thus used evil for a higher good (cf. Gen 50:20). Jesus could therefore foreknow that Judas would be the one to betray him. But nothing suggests that it was God's plan *from eternity* that Judas would play this role.[9]

In conclusion, there is no difficulty in understanding how God could predestine and thus foreknow that Jesus would be betrayed and crucified by wicked people without predestining or foreknowing who specifically would betray and crucify him. God orchestrated events to the extent that certain wicked people (and certain wicked spirits, Jn 13:27; 1 Cor 2:8) acted out their self-acquired characters and did what they wanted to do in conformity with his plan to have his Son betrayed and crucified. But they are still responsible for what they did, for they are responsible for the kind of agents they had freely become. God was simply employing their sinful intentions to his own end.

The Open View of the Future and Middle Knowledge

A number of critics insist that open theists cannot consistently acknowledge that God can have a significant role in steering human choices, such as Judas' betrayal. Nor can they consistently affirm that certain acts are predestined, such as the crucifixion of Jesus, while denying that the people who carried out these acts were predestined. Indeed, some critics insist that the God of open theism is limited to guesswork about the future. In his recent book *God's Lesser Glory*, Bruce Ware repeatedly makes this point. According to him, the open view of God posits a "limited, passive, hand-wringing God" who can do little more than hope for the best.[10] Again, he writes:

> What is lost in open theism is the Christian's confidence in God. . . . When we are told that God . . . can only guess what much of the future will bring . . . [and] constantly sees his beliefs about the future proved wrong by what in fact

---

[9]Mark 3:14-15 says that the Lord commissions the *Twelve* to preach, heal and exorcise demons, a point which may indicate that Judas was not yet a "son of perdition" (Jn 17:12 KJV). See G. Olson, *The Foreknowledge of God* (Arlington Heights, Ill.: Bible Research Corporation, 1941), pp. 23-25.

[10]Bruce Ware, *God's Lesser Glory: The Diminished God of Open Theism* (Wheaton, Ill.: Crossway, 2000), p. 216.

transpires . . . can a believer know that God will triumph in the future just as he has promised he will?[11]

This depiction is not at all accurate. To expand my defense of the consistency of the open view with the biblical depiction of God as sovereign over the world, it will prove helpful to briefly set the discussion of open theism in the context of the debate over God's "middle knowledge,"* a debate that began with Luis de Molina in the sixteenth century.[12] This necessary excursus will proceed in four steps. First I will briefly lay out the middle knowledge position and state its theological advantages. Second, I will discuss three problems which this position has difficulty overcoming. Third, I will demonstrate that by supplementing the classical Molinist position, the open view is able to solve these problems while retaining most of the advantages of the classical position. And fourth, I will show how open theists can consistently ascribe to God the control Scripture ascribes to God while also maintaining that the future is partially open. I will conclude this section by applying these insights to a paradigmatic test case: Peter's threefold denial of Jesus.

God's "middle knowledge." Defenders of middle knowledge hold that between (i.e., "in the middle of") God's knowledge of all logical possibilities and God's knowledge of what will come to pass is God's knowledge of counterfactuals of creaturely freedom, that is, what free agents would do if they were created in other possible worlds. There are two basic reasons for concluding that God has knowledge of counterfactuals. First, Scripture gives a number of examples of God's claiming to know what various people would do in different situations (e.g. 1 Sam 23:10-12; Jer 38:17-18). Second, since God is omniscient, he must know the truth value of all propositions. Hence he must know the truth value of all counterfactual propositions, including counterfactuals of creaturely freedom.

The theological advantage of this position is that it grants God much greater control over the world than simple foreknowledge while yet maintaining libertarian freedom. In this view, prior to creation God first knew how every free agent would respond to every conceivable situation they might be placed in—how they would act in any possible world.* On the basis of this knowledge, God actualized the one possible world that best suited his sovereign purposes. This view thus allows one to consistently hold that creatures are incompatibilistically free while also maintaining that there is a specific

---

[11]Ibid., pp. 20-21.
[12]Hence, advocates of middle knowledge are often referred to as Molinists. William Lane Craig provides an excellent introduction and defense of Molinism in *Divine Foreknowledge: Four Views*, ed. Paul Eddy and James Beilby (Downers Grove, Ill.: InterVarsity Press, 2001).

divine reason for all that takes place in creation.

Difficulties in the "middle knowledge" position. Despite its advantages, there are a number of problems with the classical Molinist position, four of which may be mentioned presently. First, the Molinist position must struggle with the classical problem of evil. Since God always does the best thing, the classical Molinist must accept that the world God actualizes must be the best possible, given that agents possess libertarian freedom. But it seems implausible that *this* actual world constitutes the one possible world in which free agents choose the least amount of evil.

Second, while there is some scriptural warrant for holding that God knows counterfactuals of creaturely freedom, Molinism is no better at explaining the "openness motif" in Scripture than any other version of classical theism. It has to take as anthropomorphic all passages in which God changes his mind, expresses regret, experiences surprise or disappointment, speaks and thinks of the future in terms of what may or may not happen, and so on. As I argued in the previous chapter, while Scripture certainly contains anthropomorphisms, there are no good grounds for concluding that all passages constituting the motif of future openness are in this category.

Third, it is difficult to render the Molinist account of middle knowledge philosophically cogent. In this view, every possible decision any possible free agent might ever make in any possible world is an eternal fact. From all eternity, the *facticity** not only of the future world but of all possible worlds, exists. How do we account for this eternal facticity? It cannot exist because God wills it to exist, for that would constitute determinism, something Molinists want to avoid. Indeed, the central advantage of middle knowledge is supposedly that it allows one to affirm total sovereignty while maintaining libertarian freedom. But neither can this eternal facticity exist because agents other than God will it to exist, for created agents are not eternal, and Molinists (and most others) generally deny retroactive causation. Moreover, agents never will the counterfactuals that are supposedly true about them. They are what the agents *would have* willed *had they* been created in a different possible world.

We are left then with the unappealing alternative of denying that *anything* grounds the eternal facticity of counterfactuals of creaturely freedom. From all eternity the fact of what free agents would do in every possible situation was simply there, without any sufficient reason to account for it. It is simply a metaphysical surd. This position is at best strongly counterintuitive. It could also be charged with dualism, for the facticity of the world, and of every possible world, is depicted as an uncreated reality that eternally coexists alongside of God.

It is thus not at all clear that the middle knowledge position is consistent with libertarian freedom, and this is the fourth problem with this position. As was argued in chapter two, agents can be said to possess libertarian freedom if it lies within their power to do otherwise given the exact same set of antecedent conditions. But how then can we meaningfully say that agents could have done otherwise if all they shall ever do, and all they would have ever done in any possible world, is an unalterable fact an eternity before they even exist? Stated otherwise, how can agents be said to be self-determining when *they* don't ground the facticity of what they do and ever would have done in different circumstances? The facticity eternally precedes them, created by nothing. If agents possess self-determining or libertarian freedom, *they* must be the ones who resolve possibilities into facts.

Would-counterfactuals and might-counterfactuals. Molinists are correct in their claim that propositions expressing counterfactuals of creaturely freedom have an eternal truth value, and thus that the omniscient God knows this truth value. Where classical Molinism erred, however, was in assuming that counterfactuals are exclusively about what agents would or would not do. These do not exhaust the logical possibilities of counterfactual propositions. The logical antithesis of the statement "agent *x* would do *y* in situation *z*" is not the statement "agent *x* would not do *y* in situation *z*." This is a contrary proposition, not a contradictory proposition. The logical antithesis of "agent *x* would do *y* in situation *z*" is rather the statement, "agent *x* *might not* do *y* in situation *z*." This latter statement also has an eternal truth value and hence must be known by God. The point is that would-counterfactuals do not exhaust the category of counterfactuals: there are also might-counterfactuals. Propositions about both categories of counterfactuals have an eternal truth value which must be known by an omniscient being.

If we include might-counterfactuals among God's middle knowledge, we arrive at the following neo-Molinist* position. Between God's precreational knowledge of all logical possibilities and God's precreational knowledge of what will come to pass is God's "middle knowledge" of what free agents *might or might not do* in certain situations as well as of what free agents *would do* in other situations. If it is true that agent *x* might or might not do *y* in situation *z*, it is false that agent *x* would do *y* in situation *z*, and vice versa. On the basis of this knowledge, God chose to actualize the possible world that best suited his sovereign purpose. If the world God created is a world in which some might-counterfactuals are true (as I argue is the case) then this world must by definition contain open possibilities. It is a world in which there are some things free agents might and might not do. To speak more precisely, this world would actually be a delimited set of possible worlds, any one of which *might be* actualized depending on the choices free agents make. In such a world, God's knowledge of what will be and what would be would not exhaust what God knows: God would also know what might or might not be.

To the best of my knowledge, classical Molinism never seriously entertained this possibility. They assumed that would-counterfactuals exhaust the category of God's counterfactual knowledge. They thereby assumed that all propositions expressing might-counterfactuals are false. They assumed, along with classical tradition as a whole, that omniscience *logically entailed* God's exhaustively definite knowledge of what *shall* come to pass. They simply added to this classical assumption the claim that God has exhaustively definite knowledge of what *would* come to pass in all other possible worlds. The discussion above reveals the arbitrariness of this assumption, however. There is no reason to conclude that God could not, if he wanted to, create a world in which some might-counterfactuals are true. Indeed, the very fact that might-counterfactuals are not self-contradictory (necessarily false) proves that God does not *by definition* have exhaustively definite foreknowledge.

The open view as neo-Molinism. If we grant that God created a world in which some might-counterfactuals are true, the four problems of classical Molinism mentioned above are avoided.

First, if the world God created is a world in which free agents might choose good or evil, there is no need to defend this world as the best possible world in which free agents act. This significantly lightens the burden of the problem of evil for the Christian theist.

Second, if we accept that some might-counterfactuals are true, we can easily account for the open motif of Scripture. We can accept Scripture's teaching that God sometimes thinks and speaks of the future in terms of what might or might not come to pass (e.g., Ex 4:7-9; 13:17; Ezek 12:3). We can accept its teaching that God sometimes regrets decisions he has made, for it might have (and should have) turned out differently (e.g., Gen 6:6; 1 Sam 15:11, 35). We can accept that God sometimes experiences surprise or disappointment, for we can understand how improbabilities that might not have occurred, and were thus expected not to occur by a God who knows all probabilities, can nevertheless come to pass (e.g., Is 5:1-4; Jer 3:6-7, 19-20). We can understand why God tests people to see what they will do, for they might or might not remain faithful to him (e.g., Gen 22:1, 12; Ex 16:4). We can understand how an omniscient God can experience frustration trying to get people to conform to his will (e.g., Ezek 22:29-30), for free agents might or might not choose to go along with his plans. And we can understand how an omniscicent God can change his mind, for his previous intentions were conditioned on what agents might or might not do (e.g., Jer 18:7-11; 26:2-3, 13, 19; Jon 3:10).

Third, if we accept that some might-counterfactuals are eternally true, we no longer have the problem of an ungrounded eternal facticity to possible worlds that include libertarian freedom, and there is no longer any problem accounting for libertarian freedom itself. On the one hand, the determinate aspects of any possible world, including worlds that include true might-counterfactuals, are grounded in God's will. For any possible world God might create, there are things that he decides would come to pass if he were to create them, and thus things that will come to pass in the world God decides to create.

On the other hand, if we accept that the world God created is a world in which some might-counterfactuals are true (in other words, it is not *exhaustively* determinate), there is no problem accounting for the eternal facticity of what free agents will do or would do in other circumstances. Insofar as might-counterfactuals are true—agents possess libertarian freedom—there is no eternal facticity. There are only eternal possibilities of what they might or might not do. To the extent that would-counterfactuals apply to future free agents, they do so because the actions of these agents flow either from the character God has given them *(habitus infusus)*, in which case they are not morally responsible for them, or from the character they will freely acquire *(habitus acquirus)* if they pursue a certain possible course of action, in which case they are responsible for them. In either case the would-counterfactuals are not ungrounded, as in classical Molinism. From all eternity God knows that if he chooses to create free agent *x*, she will have the basic characteristics of *a*, *b* and *c* *(habitus infusus)*. And from all eternity God knows that *if* agent *x* freely follows a certain possible life-trajectory, he will *become* the kind of person who would do *y* in situation *z* *(habitus acquirus)*. The would-counterfactuals for which agent *x* is morally responsible are contingent on the might-counterfactuals for which she is morally responsible.

The infinite intelligence of God. In the light of all this, it should be clear that Ware's criticism that the open view posits a God who can only wring his hands and guess at what will come to pass is altogether unfounded. According to this neo-Molinist perspective, God perfectly knows from all time what will be, what would be, and what may be. And he sovereignly sets the parameters for all three categories. Moreover, because God possesses infinite intelligence, his knowledge of might-counterfactuals leaves him no less prepared for the future than his knowledge of determinate aspects of creation. As we noted in the previous chapter, because he is infinitely intelligent, he does not need to "thin out" his attention over numerous possibilities as we do. He is able to attend to each one of a trillion billion possibilities, whether they be logical possibilities, would-counterfactuals or might-counterfactuals, *as though* it was the *only* possibility he had to consider. He is infinitely attentive to each and every one. Hence, whatever possibility ends up coming to pass, we may say that from all eternity God was preparing for *just this* possibility, as though it were the only possibility that could ever possibly occur. Even when possibilities occur that are objectively improbable—and to this extent surprise or disappoint God—it is not at all the case that he is caught off guard. He is as perfectly prepared for the improbable as he is for the probable.

The anthropomorphic God of Calvinism. In point of fact, Ware's criticism that the open view of the future reduces God to a "hand-wringing God" who can't assure us that he will win in the end says a great deal more about his view of God than it does about the view of God he purports to be criticizing. Ironically enough, Ware's criticism of the open view exposes his view of God to be *thoroughly anthropomorphic.*

We humans with our limited intelligence could not as confidently attend to a trillion billion possibilities as easily, and as perfectly, as we could attend to one certainty. Indeed, our focus is divided in half the second we have to attend to two possibilities instead of one certainty. And we humans with our limited wisdom and power could not assure anyone of a certain outcome unless we exhaustively controlled all the variables. Hence it is tempting to anthropomorphically assume that God must face similar difficulties. In his criticism Ware reveals that he has succumbed to this temptation, for his criticism assumes that God (like a finite human) can be more prepared for the future if he only has one certain future to attend to. Hence he criticizes a God who faces a multiplicity of futures as a "hand-wringing" deity. And his criticism assumes that God (like a finite human) can be assured of ultimate victory only if he controls all the variables. Hence he criticizes a concept of God who is not all-controlling as being out of control.

What is more, because Ware assumes that his anthropomorphic view of God is the epitome of divine perfection, he assumes that all the biblical passages not in agreement with this depiction are anthropomorphic. For Ware, it is "beneath" God to *really* (for example) think and speak of the future in a subjunctive mode, change his intentions in response to changing circumstances, experience regret, disappointment or surprise, and so on. This entire biblical motif, we are assured, consists of anthropomorphisms.

But the Bible tells us what God is truly like, in all of his unfathomable greatness—including his glorious flexibility in relation to his creation. Some, like Ware, can't fathom this infinite intelligence and thus anthropomorphically reduce God's future to one possible future and insist that even that one must be meticulously controlled. Only in this way can they conceive of God as sovereign over creation and assured of achieving his objectives in the end. And assuming their restricted view to be the standard of divine perfection, they criticize as "diminished" a view that God is intelligent and powerful enough to confidently move into the future and accomplish all his objectives without having to act like a human would, that is, without controlling, or at least knowing in advance, every detail. What is lacking in this critique is a faith-filled confidence that God is not limited like humans are. He can as confidently move into a multitude of possible futures as easily and as perfectly as he could move into one certain future.

In sum, the open view of the future does not undermine God's wisdom or sovereign control, as Ware and others argue: it rather infinitely exalts it. In this view God does not know *less* than the classical view: he knows *more*. He does not *under*-know the future, as it were: he *over*-knows it. And as with classical Molinism, the neo-Molinist perspective thereby grants God significant providential control while also affirming libertarian freedom. The neo-Molinist view does this while avoiding the problems that attend to classical Molinism, for it expands the scope of God's middle knowledge to include might-subjunctives.

A test case: Peter's denial. To substantiate the claim that neo-Molinism can affirm basically the same degree of providential control as classical Molinism, it may prove helpful to apply our reflections to an episode in Scripture that is frequently cited as a refutation of the open view of the future, namely, the episode of Peter's threefold denial of the Lord. The fact that Jesus predicted Peter would deny him three times (Mt 26:34) is often cited as proof that God possesses exhaustively definite knowledge of all that shall come to pass.[13]

Even before considering the specifics of the passage, we have reason to be cautious of this conclusion. Not only does the entire openness motif of Scripture count against it, but the conclusion far outruns what this episode warrants. The jump from Jesus' knowledge of what Peter will do in the next

---

[13]See, e.g., Ware, *Lesser Glory*, pp. 127-30.

twelve hours to the conclusion that God is from all eternity certain of every-thing every person will ever do is quite a leap. The conclusion seems espe-cially unwarranted when we consider that it is the incarnate Son giving this prediction, the same incarnate Son who confesses that he does not know the "day or hour" of his own return (Mk 13:32). What Jesus' foreknowledge of Peter's denial entails is a christological question before it is a theological question. The conclusion that Jesus knew everything about the future is rejected not only by open theists but by all who hold to a kenotic Christol-ogy.

This aside, it should be clear that this episode poses no significant prob-lem for the open view of the future. God knew and perfectly anticipated (as though it was the only possible outcome) that if the world proceeded exactly as it did up to the point of the Last Supper, Peter's character would be solid-ified to the extent that he would be the kind of person who would deny Christ in a certain situation. God eternally knows all might-counterfactuals, as we have said, and all would-counterfactuals that follow from might-coun-terfactuals. On the basis of this knowledge and his sovereign control as Cre-ator, God decides at some point to providentially ensure that just this situation would come about. For pedagogical reasons (see below), he informs Jesus of this future certainty and inspires him to share it with Peter.

This way of understanding this episode is in principle no different from the way a classical Molinist would understand it. Neo-Molinism modifies this view only in adding that at an earlier point in his life Peter could have (and should have) developed a different character, and if this had occurred, the Passion narrative would not have included Peter's denial.

Some might argue that the scriptural evidence indicates that Peter's char-acter was not solidified in this fashion, for he at other times seemed to be a fearless person. Indeed, it is not without significance that it was Peter's emphatic denial that he would *not* deny Christ that gave rise to Jesus' predic-tion (Mt 26:33). We have every reason to suspect that this bravado was false. Does not the fact that Peter denied Christ when under pressure demonstrate that he was in fact at heart a coward? But why did Peter *appear* so brave dur-ing Christ's ministry? Raising this question provides the clue as to why Jesus gives Peter this prediction in the first place.[14] Peter's displays of "courage" were rooted in his erroneous (but very common) expectation that the Mes-

---

[14]It is curious that so many treatments of this episode fail to ask *why* Jesus gave this prediction. They act as though the whole point was for Jesus to prove that he happened to possess knowl-edge of part of the immediate future. Yet asking this question is crucial to understanding both the purpose and the nature of the prediction.

siah would be a victorious military leader. This is why Peter emphatically refuses to accept Jesus' message that he came to serve and to suffer (cf. Mt 16:21-23). It is also why Peter seems so brave when his miracle-working master is around but is utterly crushed when Jesus is arrested.

God wanted to humble this future pillar of the church and correct his false understanding of the Messiah and of what leadership in the kingdom looks like (Mt 20:25-28). Given God's middle knowledge, God knew exactly what Peter would be like, and what Peter would do, if he freely acquired the kind of character he did. God thus knew precisely what it would take to bring Peter to his knees and make him receptive to the teaching he wanted him to receive. Three life-threatening blows to the ego, followed by three piercing questions to the heart, would cure Peter of his pride and false conceptions.

To this end the Father has Jesus inform Peter of what he is going to do in the next twelve hours. If any special divine influence would be necessary to ensure that three times people inquire about Peter's associations, that would be a minor accomplishment for the sovereign Creator. He knew all eternity all the would-counterfactuals of every person in the world at this time and could orchestrate their actualization however he saw fit, if this was necessary. Again, neo-Molinists do not assert anything different than what Molinists have always asserted except that it once could have gone differently, had Peter cultivated a different kind of character. It wasn't destined from the foundation of the world that Peter would have to undergo this painful chastisement.

From John we learn how this heavenly orchestrated lesson is consummated. After Peter's threefold denial, the crucifixion and the resurrection, Jesus asks Peter three times, "Do you love me?" This threefold inquiry is hardly coincidental. It corresponds to Peter's three denials. After each of Peter's responses Jesus instructs him, "Tend my lambs," teaching Peter that loving *Jesus* means serving *others*. Then, most importantly and most poignantly, Jesus completes his instruction by giving Peter yet another prediction—remarkably different from the earlier one. Now, instead of predicting Peter's denial, he predicts Peter's faithfulness. Peter shall in time be called on to undergo the same fate as his Master. He shall give his life for his sheep (Jn 21:15-19).

Because of what the Father brought Peter through, Peter's character was permanently changed. He had been humbled, and now that he had learned the true meaning of what Jesus came to do as well as the true meaning of servant leadership, he was in a position to understand and accept this invaluable lesson. Jesus' prediction of Peter's threefold denial was the loving but necessarily harsh means by which the Lord shattered the old Peter, with his false conceptions and false bravado, in order to build up a new Peter, a man willing to lay down his life for the lambs the Master entrusted to him.

Clearly the open view of the future has no more difficulty accounting for this episode than does classical Molinism. Indeed, these two schools of thought explain this and similar passages in nearly identical ways, the only difference being that the open view insists that the would-counterfactual truths were conditioned by previous might-counterfactual truths. Only because Peter at an earlier date *might have* become cowardly was it true that at this time and in this situation Peter *would act* cowardly. In any event, it should be evident that there is no internal contradiction between the view that the future is partly open and the understanding that God has ultimate control of the world.

A Philosophical Argument

Thus far I have addressed the biblical arguments for and against the open view of the future and have rendered the open view of sovereignty plausible by depicting it as a form of neo-Molinism. Now, are there any philosophical arguments that explicitly support the notion that libertarian acts are in principle unforeknowable as definite? As a matter of fact, there are several. Here I will consider only one. (See appendix two for a summary of four other arguments). This argument centers on the logical incompatibility of affirming the EDF doctrine while also affirming that agents possess libertarian or self-determining freedom.

The impossibility of changing the past. Let four things be granted: (1) God possesses EDF; (2) God's knowledge is infallible, hence unalterable; (3) the past by logical necessity cannot be changed;[15] and (4) we are not free or morally responsible in relation to what we cannot change.[16] These four pre-

---

[15]See, for example, R. Gale, *The Language of Time* (New York: Humanities Press, 1968), p. 107. Few philosophers dispute this. Some who deny this confuse *the past* with *our experience of the past.* God could of course change the latter. He could, for example, erase from our memories past event P1 and produce in our minds the memory of a past event P2. But even God can't then make it such that he *didn't* change P1 into P2. The past now *includes* the transition from P1 to P2, though *we* only remember P2. What happened is what happened, and God can no more make what happened a matter of what didn't happen than he can make A into -A. This is simply the law of self-identity: A thing is what it is. Stated otherwise, *the past is by definition not changeable.*

[16]Calvinists deny this premise. Hence this argument would not work for them. *Their* difficulty is rendering the denial of premise 4 intelligible. How can a person be free or morally responsible in relation to what they cannot change (in relation to what has been predestined about them).

mises seem to entail that agents are no more free and morally responsible with regard to future events (including their own future chosen actions) than they are with regard to past events. Among the totality of facts in any given moment in the past which we cannot change is the fact of what we shall do in the future—a facticity found in God's EDF and included in the totality of factual truths at any given moment in the past.

Suppose that God commissioned an angel to catalog all facts constituting the totality of reality on August 15, 1492. If God possesses EDF, this catalog includes not only all past and present facts but the facticity of all future realities as well, including *my* future decisions. For if my future decisions are facts in God's mind from all eternity, they certainly are facts in God's mind on August 15, 1492, and would thus be contained in his exhaustive catalogue of all facts recorded on this date.

The problem, of course, is that I am not free or morally responsible for *any* of the facts that constitute the totality of reality on August 15, 1492 (premise 4). It is past, unalterable and therefore outside the purview of my self-determining freedom. Yet, assuming God possesses EDF, the entirety of my future is part of this past totality. My future is as much a past fact as is Columbus's sailing on this date. I can no more change my future than I can affect Columbus' sailing itinerary. Hence, I can be no more free and morally responsible regarding *my* future than I am regarding Columbus's activity. In short, the EDF doctrine logically undermines morally responsible, self-determining freedom.

Seeing my future. Consider what would happen if God *gave you* his 1492 catalog of facts. Now you can read what was written five centuries ago about what you will do in the future. And you cannot alter what you read or avoid doing what the catalog says you will do; this is the catalog of an *infallible* omniscient mind.

Suppose you read in this book that on a certain date you will make a catastrophic immoral decision. What can you do about it? Absolutely nothing. Try as you might to alter this reality, you will certainly do exactly what the book infallibly predicts. Even your attempts to alter what is predicted about you are written in the book. Indeed, every thought, emotion and action you entertain while reading this exhaustive catalog constitute part of the content, for these are from all eternity past (hence, on August 15, 1492) part of the factual content of God's infallible, omniscient mind.

How does this view differ from determinism? How would a person who denied libertarian freedom construe this scenario differently? The facts are identical in both views. The only difference might be that the determinist could perhaps say God ordained this eternal facticity, while the defender of self-determining freedom would insist that the future acts which the reader shall unavoidably engage in are nevertheless acts she freely carries out. But this is arguably a distinction that makes no difference; it is merely semantic. One insists the future is determined, while the other insists that it is not. But the eternal facticity of the future is the same on both accounts.

Some may argue that this scenario simply demonstrates why God cannot reveal the content of his omniscient mind to us. As long as we don't know what we shall do, we do it freely. This argument fails, however, for the issue of self-determination is an ontological, not an epistemological issue. The question is whether we really *are* or *are not* free, not whether we *think* we are free or not. If all my future actions are in fact unavoidable—for they are as unalterable as my past—then I am not free even if God is the only being in the universe who knows it.

On the other hand, if we assume that we *do* determine aspects of our own future and *are* morally responsible for these aspects, it follows that what we will freely do in the future *cannot* be cataloged as a fact on August 15, 1492. To be sure, my future actions could be cataloged as might-counterfactuals (I might do *x* or *y*) or even as a would-counterfactual conditioned by antecedent might-counterfactuals (e.g., if Greg chooses a certain course of character development, he would at T1 become the kind of person who would do *x* in situation *z*). But the facticity of my future free decisions cannot eternally precede my making them.[17] This is what the term *self-determining* means if it has any self-consistent meaning at all.[18]

Can we affect the past? How might defenders of EDF respond to this argument? Taking their cue from William of Ockham, some have attempted to qualify the third premise, that we cannot change the past. To this end they make a distinction between "hard facts" about the past that are indeed unalterable and "soft facts" about the past that can in a sense be affected or at least "brought about."[19] "Soft facts" are past facts the truth of which is contingent

---

[17]So argues Richard Creel in his excellent work *Divine Impassability* (Cambridge: Cambridge University Press, 1986), pp. 98-99.

[18]See appendix two for an elaboration on the argument for an open future from the meaning of self-determination.

[19]E.g., B. Reichenbach, "Hasker on Omniscience," *Faith and Philosophy* 4 (1987): 86-92; Linda Zagzebski, *The Dilemma of Freedom and Foreknowledge* (Oxford: Oxford University Press, 1991), pp. 66-97; M. McCord Adams, "Is the Existence of God a 'Hard' Fact?" in *God, Foreknowledge, and Freedom*, ed. John M. Fisher (Stanford, Calif.: Stanford University Press, 1989), pp. 74-85; John M. Fisher, "Freedom and Foreknowledge," in *God, Foreknowledge, and Freedom*, ed. John M. Fisher (Stanford, Calif.: Stanford University Press, 1989), pp. 86-96; E. Zemach and D. Widerker, "Facts, Freedom, and Foreknowledge," in *God, Foreknowledge, and Freedom*, ed.

upon a future event, such as, "Mike correctly believed in 1991 that Bill Clinton would be elected president in 1992." The election of Bill Clinton made Mike's prior belief true and thus brought about the truth of a past fact. According to Ockham and his defenders, God's beliefs about the future are "soft facts." We bring about the truth of God's beliefs by what we do.

This response is problematic, however, for it is not clear that we can meaningfully be said to "bring about" the truth of God's beliefs the way the American populace "brought about" the truth of Mike's belief by voting Clinton into office. Since God is omniscient, his past beliefs about future activity are in no sense "soft" (assuming he possesses EDF). We can no more affect the content of God's past beliefs than we can affect any "hard" fact in the past. To return to the earlier illustration, if God were to reveal his beliefs in a catalog in 1492, the content of that catalog would constitute just as "hard" a fact as Columbus's sailing on this date.[20] Hence it does not seem that the distinction between "hard" and "soft" past facts is helpful in rendering libertarian freedom compatible with EDF.

Physics and the Open Future

If a position is true, *every* avenue of reflection ought to point in its direction, assuming that we are thinking cogently. I will conclude this exploration of the nature of divine risk, therefore, by briefly presenting two such pointers—the first from physics and the second from our experience of ourselves as free moral agents.

The quantum leap. A number of experts argue that quantum physics suggests a partly open future. The most relevant feature of quantum physics for our purposes is the indeterminate behavior of quantum particles. In quantum mechanics we can predict on a bell curve an individual particle's probable behavior under given experimental conditions, but we cannot in

---

John M. Fisher (Stanford, Calif.: Stanford University Press, 1989), pp. 111-22; J. Hoffman and G. Rosenkrantz, "Hard and Soft Facts," in *God, Foreknowledge, and Freedom*, ed. John M. Fisher (Stanford, Calif.: Stanford University Press, 1989), pp. 123-35; Anthony Kenny, "Divine Foreknowledge and Human Freedom," in *Aquinas: A Collection of Critical Essays*, ed. Anthony Kenny (Notre Dame, Ind.: University of Notre Dame, 1976), pp. 255-70; G. Mavrodes, "Is the Past Preventable?" *Faith and Philosophy* 1 (1984): 131-46. A seminal essay which serves as the springboard for contemporary discussions on ability or inability to in any sense affect the past is M. Dummett's "Can an Effect Precede Its Cause?" reprinted in his *Truth and Other Enigmas* (Cambridge, Mass.: Harvard University Press, 1978), pp. 319-32.

[20]Fisher argues that God's past beliefs are soft only if we have power to render them false. But this would be tantamount to having the power to render God nonexistent (John M. Fisher, "Ockhamism," *Philosophical Review* 94 [1985]: 81-100). But cf. also Adams, "Is the Existence of God a 'Hard' Fact?" pp. 74-85.

principle predict it precisely. The leap from the probability wave pocket (the state of being "possibly this or possibly that," what is sometimes called the particle's "superposition") to the actual state at the end of the experiment (the state of being "definitely this and definitely not that") cannot be exhaustively accounted for.[21]

Yet under the influence of the decaying mechanistic and deterministic worldview, Einstein insists that this unpredictability must only appear to be spontaneous due to our ignorance of all the variables. To cite his often quoted remark, there is no place for a God who "plays dice with the world."[22] Some continue to follow him in this conviction. The majority of quantum physicists, however, assume that indeterminacy is real, not just a function of our ignorance.[23] But this implies that the irreversibility of time is ultimately real as well. It is not, as Einstein thought, an illu-

---

[21]This is sometimes termed "the collapse of the wave pocket." On the relationship between this collapse and the view that time must be ontologically irreversible, see Peter Coveney and Roger Highfield, *The Arrow of Time* (New York: BasicBooks, 1990), pp. 181, 288. For a popular treatment of the concept of superposition, see David Lindley, *Where Does the Weirdness Go?* (New York: BasicBooks, 1996), pp. 168-72, 190-203, 213. I am not suggesting that there is no sufficient reason for the particle's behavior, only that the sufficient reason could have explained other particular behaviors as well.

[22]Quoted in Ronald W. Clark, *Einstein: The Life and Times* (New York: Hodder & Stoughton, 1973), p. 327. See N. Abrams and J. Primack, "Einstein's View of God," in *God for the 21st Century*, ed. Russell Stannard (Philadelphia: Templeton Foundation Press, 2000), pp. 153-56. Against Einstein, Abrams and Primack argue that modern science suggests that "dice is God's favorite game. . . . It now seems that God plays dice, but the universe is nevertheless rational because the game has rules" (p. 155). In the next chapter I show that the general thrust of recent science suggests that everything exemplifies the balance between chance, spontaneity and chaos, on the one hand, and order, stability and regularity on the other.

[23]"Indeterminism seems to have won the day in the field of quantum mechanics," concludes Mark W. Worthing, *God, Creation and Contemporary Physics* (Minneapolis: Fortress, 1996), p. 50. Mary Hesse argues, "It is important to notice that according to quantum theory this [indeterminism] is not merely a question of ignorance of laws which may after all be fundamentally deterministic, but of irreducible indeterminism in the events themselves" ("Miracles and the Laws of Nature," in *Miracles: Cambridge Study in Their Philosophy and History*, ed. C. F. D. Moule [London: A. R. Mowbray, 1965], p. 37). See also her defense of "ontological indeterminism" in her excellent essay "Physics, Philosophy and Myth," in *Physics, Philosophy and Theology: A Common Quest for Understanding*, ed. Robert J. Russell, William R. Stoeger and George V. Coyne (Notre Dame, Ind.: Notre Dame University Press, 1988), pp. 185-202. For a classic defense of a realistic interpretation of indeterminacy, see Karl Popper, *The Open Universe: An Argument for Indeterminism* (London: Hutchinson, 1982). Also relevant is his *Quantum Theory and the Schism in Physics* (London: Hutchinson, 1982). Other pertinent works are Alastair Rae, *Quantum Physics: Illusion or Reality?* (Cambridge: Cambridge University Press, 1986); Roland Omnés, *Physics World* (United Kingdom: Institute of Physics, 1995); Lindley, *Where Does the Weirdness Go*; Henry Stapp, *Mind, Matter, and Quantum Mechanics* (New York: Springer Verlag, 1993); J. Hobb, "Chaos and Indeterminism," *Canadian Journal of Philosophy* 21 (1991): 141-64; and Roger Penrose, *Shadow of the Mind* (Oxford: Oxford University Press, 1994).

sion.[24] Events *really do* transition from indefinite possibilities to actual realities, and the ultimate explanation as to what this actual reality shall be cannot be located outside the particle. Something genuinely new has taken place, something that could not have been exhaustively predicted, and something that cannot now be reversed.

This entails that the future partly consists of possibilities. As the past is by definition closed to possibilities, so the future, in this view, is by definition open to possibilities.[25] And since God knows reality perfectly, it entails that God knows the future partly as a realm of possibilities. John Polkinghorne summarizes the matter well when he notes that considerations of the role of indeterminacy in quantum physics

> emphasize how different time is from space [and] how seriously we must take its unfolding as a process of genuine becoming. The future is not already formed ahead of us, waiting to reveal itself to our exploration, as the fixed contours of a valley reveal themselves to the traveler who makes his ways through

---

[24]"For us believing physicists," Einstein said, "the distinction between past, present and future is only an illusion, even if a stubborn one." Cited in Banesh Hoffman (with Helen Dukas), *Albert Einstein: Creator and Rebel* (New York: Viking, 1972), p. 258. An excellent sympathetic treatment of Einstein's concept of time is given by Paul Davies in *About Time: Einstein's Unfinished Revolution* (New York: Simon & Shuster, 1995). For a comprehensive overview of discussions about the implications of contemporary physics for our understanding of time that tends toward the conclusion that Einstein was mistaken, see David R. Griffin, ed., *Physics and the Ultimate Significance of Time* (Albany, N.Y.: SUNY Press, 1986). On the irreversibility of time as an integral element in quantum mechanics, chaos theory and thermodynamics, see Coveney and Highfield, *Arrow of Time,* Peter Coveney, "The Second Law of Thermodynamics: Entropy, Irreversibility and Dynamics," *Nature* 333 (1988): 409-15; Peter Coveney, "Chaos, Entropy and the Arrow of Time," *New Scientist* 127 (1990): 49-52; Ilya Prigogine, *From Being to Becoming* (San Francisco: W. H. Freeman, 1980); Ilya Prigogine and Isabelle Stengers, *Order out of Chaos: Man's New Dialogue with Nature* (New York: Bantam, 1984); "Time, Dynamics and Chaos: Integrating Poincaré's 'Non-Integratable Systems,' " in *Chaos, The New Science: Nobel Conference 26,* ed. John Holte (Landham, Md.: University Press of America, 1993), pp. 55-88; "Irreversibility and Space-Time Structure," *Physics and the Ultimate Significance of Time*, pp. 232-49; Henry Hollinger and Michael Zenzen, *The Nature of Irreversibility* (Dordrecht, Holland: Reidel, 1985); Paul Horwich, *Asymmetries in Time* (Cambridge, Mass.: MIT Press, 1989). Coveney and Highfield argue forcefully that the paradoxes of quantum theory (such as the paradoxes of "Shrödinger's cat" and "Wigner's friend" are due to "the fact that the existing quantum formalism is based on time-reversible foundations, while measurement processes are intrinsically irreversible. . . . The problems posed by measurements can only be properly resolved with the help of a framework incorporating the arrow of time" (*Arrow of Time*, p. 138, cf. p. 288). The implications of quantum indeterminacy for our estimation of the fundamental nature of time was suggested early on by Hans Reichenbach, *The Direction of Time* (Berkeley: University of California Press, 1956).

[25]I develop an argument for the openness of the future on the basis of the past-future distinction in appendix two.

them. The future is in part our creation: its shape is responsive to our molding, as the clay is formed by the sculptor to create his irreducibly new thing, which is his work of art. If even the omnipotent God cannot act to change the past, it does not seem any more conceivable that the omniscient God can know with certainty the unformed future.[26]

It could of course be argued that science is forever changing and thus that what seems like a certain conclusion today might be revamped by new discoveries tomorrow. True enough. Too much should not be wagered on the vicissitudes of scientific discovery. At the same time, we cannot ignore the findings of contemporary science on this account. And on this matter it confirms what I have thus far been arguing from Scripture: the future is partly open.

Relativity theory and the open universe. Before moving to the second pointer to an open future, one aspect of contemporary science must be considered which some argue requires that the future *not* be indefinite: namely, Einstein's theory of relativity. Put most simply, Einstein proved that the flow of time is relative to the speed of light. The "when" of an occurrence is conditioned on the location and velocity of an observer. My "now" is your future. The question of precisely when my "now" will become your "present" depends on how fast you and I are traveling and how far we are from one another. According to relativity theory, therefore, it is impossible for us to coordinate events within a single all-encompassing "now."

The theological implications of this theory are controversial. According to some, it proves that God must exist outside of time. Since his knowledge of the cosmos is not dependent on the speed of light, since he does not travel at any speed, and since he is omnipresent and thus does not exist at a distance from what he creates, his "now" must simultaneously encompass all time. The future, therefore, is not in any sense open to God, it is argued, though it is to us. It has the same definiteness as the past, for God experiences it simultaneously with the past.[27]

---

[26]John Polkinghorne, *Science and Creation* (Boston: Shambala, 1989), p. 79. See also his *Quarks, Chaos & Christianity* (New York: Crossroad, 1996), p. 73.

[27]One of the first to argue along these lines was John Wilcox, "A Question from Physics for Certain Theists," *The Journal of Religion* 41 (1961): 293-300. Others who make some form of this argument are J. Baker, "Omniscience and Divine Synchronization," *Process Studies* 2 (1972): 201-8; F. Fost, "Relativity Theory and Hartshorne's Di-Polar Theism," in *Two Process Philosophers: Ford's Encounter with Whitehead,* ed. L. Ford (Tallahassee, Fla.: American Academy of Religion, 1973), pp. 89-99; Royce Gruenler, *The Inexhaustible God: Biblical Faith and the Challenge of Process Theism* (Grand Rapids, Mich.: Baker, 1983), pp. 75-100; Colin Gunton, *Becoming and Being: The Doctrine of God in C. Hartshorne and K. Barth* (Oxford: Oxford

There are four responses to be made to this objection. First, Scripture does not suggest that God exists in "an eternal now."[28] Every verse in the Bible that depicts God as personal and interacting with us on a moment-by-moment basis suggests the opposite. Even more to the point, all passages that depict God as changing his mind, regretting how decisions he made turned out, experiencing surprise and disappointment, and speaking about the future in subjunctive terms preclude such a notion, at least if we take these passages at face value (see chapter three). While the findings of science cannot be ignored, if a particular interpretation of a theory fundamentally conflicts with Scripture, Christians are obliged to stick with Scripture and judge that the interpretation of the theory is misguided.

Second, as a number of people have recently argued, Einstein's theory simply *doesn't* require or even suggest that time is unreal. There are a number of differing arguments offered, but the most compelling consideration is that Einstein's theory concerns how finite observers experience each other's "now," not each other's *future*. Indeed, the theory does not address the ontological status of the future.

More specifically, relativity theory stipulates that your "now" and my "now" cannot be experienced simultaneously by either of us. But it does not deny that we both have a future that neither of us (nor anyone else) have yet experienced. Relativity theory tells us that my observation of when your future becomes your "now" will be different from when you actually experience your "now," depending on how fast I am traveling and how distant I am from you, but it does not suggest that our individual futures are not actually future—to you or to anyone else.

Milic Capek, as esteemed an authority in this field as anyone, argues along

University Press, 1978), pp. 62-64; W. P. Alston, "Divine Action, Human Freedom, and the Laws of Nature," in *Quantum Cosmology and the Laws of Nature: Scientific Perspectives on Divine Actions,* ed. Robert J. Russell, Nancey Murphy and C. J. Isham (Berkeley, Calif.: Center for Theology and the Nature Sciences, 1993), pp. 185-206.

[28]Some have attempted to read this concept into Exodus 3:14 (quoted in its Septuagint version by Jesus in Jn 8:58). However one understands this passage, it must be conceded that it is a weak scriptural foundation for such a fundamental theological premise, especially in light of the fact that the rest of the biblical narrative presupposes that God exists in a sequence related to our time. In any event, the Hebrew of Exodus 3:14 simply cannot sustain this overly philosophical interpretation. For what follows see J. Randolph Lucas's fine essay, "The Temporality of God," in *Quantum Cosmology and the Laws of Nature: Scientific Perspectives on Divine Action,* ed. Robert J. Russell, Nancey Murphy and C. J. Isham (Berkeley, Calif.: Center for Theology and the Nature Sciences, 1993), pp. 235-46. On the relationship between being personal and temporality, see P. Brockelman, *Time and Self: Phenomenological Explorations* (New York: Scholars Press, 1985), who argues that "temporality is the very *form* of doing, the structure of action" (p. 24). If this is true, the notion of an atemporal personal agent is internally inconsistent.

these lines. His clear and forceful argument is worth quoting at length.

It is true that there are no objective "Now" lines [in relativity theory]; yet it is
not the whole truth, and this is precisely what makes the conclusion [that relativity theory requires a determinate future] wrong. Even a superficial inspec-
tion of relativistic time-space clearly shows that the past is separated from the
future *even more effectively* than in classical physics: the whole four-dimensional
region called "Elsewhere" (which could equally well be called "Elsewhen") is
interposed between the causal past and causal future. It is this region which is
differently divided by different observers and in which the "Now" lines do not
coincide. But no "Now" line of mine can ever cut my own causal past nor my
own causal future. . . . The apparently mysterious character of Einstein's universe disappears when we realize that this denial of absolute "Now" is [only] a
denial of *instantaneous* actions and of *instantaneous* space.

From this Capeck concludes:

Although there is no absolute "Now," there is such a thing as an *absolute
future*. This is quite obvious for my own "Here-Now," which I actually experience; I can never perceive my own future event, since there are no backward
causal actions, no effects preceding their causes. But more than that: my own
causal future cannot be *perceived by any other conceivable observer.* . . . By the
very definition of "Elsewhere," no causal actions from my own "Now"—*a for-
tiori* from my own future—can reach the observer unless they move with a
velocity greater than that of light, which is excluded by relativity. Conversely,
for the same reason, no event from the causal future of any observer located in
the "Elsewhere" region can reach my own "Here-Now." Consequently, future
events are *intrinsically unobservable.*[29]

A more theological way of arriving at this same conclusion—my third
response to this objection—is to note that Einstein's theory was concerned
only with the way time functions among *finite observers* within the finite universe. His theory does not address how an infinite, omnipresent being would
or would not experience time. This point is crucial, for if one believes that
there is a God who is present in every "now," then one can believe that there
is an encompassing "now" which is perfectly coordinated with the "now" of

---

[29]Milic Capek, "The Unreality and Indeterminacy of the Future in the Light of Contemporary
Physics," in *Physics and the Ultimate Significance of Time*," pp. 306-7. See also his *Concepts of
Space and Time*, Boston Studies in the Philosophy of Science, vol. 2 (Dordrecht, Holland:
Reidel, 1976). See also Coveney and Highfield, *Arrow of Time*, chap. 3, "How Time
Defeated Einstein," pp. 70-107, who argue that there is a flaw in Einstein's formulation pre-
cisely because he did not factor in the unidirectional flow of time. Others who argue against
the "block universe" implications of Einstein's theory are R. Gale, *The Language of Time*
(New York: Humanities Press, 1968); Lucas, "Temporality of God."

every finite observer. And this means that it is theologically meaningful, and even necessary, to speak about an absolute future which is future to every observer—including God. God's "now" encompasses all "nows," and God's future encompasses all futures.

Hence, while Einstein's theory precludes speaking about a cosmic "now" and "future" *as measured by any finite point,* it does not preclude our speaking about a cosmic "now" and "future" from God's all encompassing perspective.

Some have argued that this perspective limits God to time. Time was created when the cosmos was created, it is argued, and so if God is above the creation he must be "above time." This brings me to my fourth response. The only concept of time we have is the measurement of change. This perspective on change obviously could not exist without the creation, and hence if one believes that God is the Creator of all things, it is erroneous to say that God is bound by time. He does not have to measure change against any physical constant (such as the speed of light). This is not the issue, however. The issue rather is, Is God's experience *sequential?* Does God experience a "past," "present" and "future"? How he *measures* it (if it is even meaningful to speak this way) is inconsequential.[30]

Most scholars within the classical-philosophical tradition denied that there was sequence in God, primarily because they accepted the prevalent Hellenistic assumption that all change is either for better or for worse. Consequently, a perfect being cannot experience change, and thus can experience no before or after. But there are no biblical or logical grounds for accepting this assumption.

As I have noted, the entire narrative of Scripture presupposes that God experiences a before and after. Logically, change can express one's perfect character as easily as it can constitute an improvement or deteriorization of one's character. People who possess an unchanging sensitive character, for example, will change their demeanor appropriately as they interact with people. This change expresses the fact that they have a virtuously unchanging character; it does not improve or deteriorate their character.

So too Scripture depicts God as having a perfect, immutable character but as expressing this character through his wonderfully flexible interactions with his creations. His "now" encompasses the "now" of every point in space, but he is not bound to measure the successive "nows" the way any finite creature would.

---

[30]For an excellent nuanced discussion of issues surrounding the relationship between time and divine eternality, see Alan Padgett, *God, Eternity and the Nature of Time* (New York: St. Martin's Press, 1992).

Our Experience of Ourselves

The second pointer to the partial openness of the future has already been discussed in chapter two, so I will only briefly review it here. We assume that the future is partly open and partly settled every time we deliberate between options. It is impossible to illustrate the belief that *nothing* about the future is open by the way one deliberates about a choice. We cannot deliberate about matters that we do not believe are *within our power* to resolve. Conversely, it is impossible to illustrate the belief that *everything* about the future is open by the way one deliberates about a choice, for without a presupposed regularity to the world there is no stability from which decisions can be made. One can deliberate about buying a new car tomorrow, for example, only because one assumes (among many other things) that the laws of nature and the laws of economics will operate tomorrow pretty much the way they operated today. One can decide *some* things about the future only because one has neither the need or ability to decide *all* things about the future.

The same holds true for our sense of moral responsibility. We assume that an agent is morally responsible for an act to the extent that the ultimate source and explanation of the act was the agent herself. Our sense of moral responsibility presupposes that the future is to some extent open for us to decide. Yet our sense of moral responsibility also presupposes that some of the future is not up for us to decide. For example, a year from now I will still be responsible for acts I choose to carry out today because (we assume) I will be roughly the same person a year from now as I am today. This much is decided for me. Only because of this can those matters that are not decided for me be morally significant.

Therefore, our experience as free, moral agents who deliberate about decisions indicates that on a fundamental level we assume that reality is partly determined, partly undetermined. Reason and experience confirm what Scripture teaches.

Conclusion

In this chapter scriptural evidence used to support the view that the future is exhaustively settled, and thus that God possesses EDF, was found to be inadequate. Scripture clearly teaches that aspects of the future are settled either by God's will or by present circumstances, and so God knows them as settled. But some of the future is not, as is most clearly seen in the scriptural material examined in chapter three.

The objection that one can't affirm the biblical view of God as sovereign in history while also affirming that the future is partly open was found to be unwarranted, rooted in an anthropomorphic conception of God.

Finally, the view that the future is partly open and partly settled is confirmed by arguments from philosophy, physics and experience. When taken as a whole, the case for the open view of the future is quite strong.

With this perspective in place we are in a position to render intelligible the notion that a creation in which love is possible has to contain an element of risk for God. We are, therefore, also in a position to begin to understand how a world created by an all-good and all-powerful God could become the nightmarish battlefield that Scripture and our own experience say it is. This is not God's design, but it is his risk. He deemed the risk worthwhile for the sake of what it can achieve. Only by risking war can you have the possibility of love.

Many questions remain, however. For example, how can God be certain of achieving his goal (having a loving bride composed of multitudes of believers) if the destiny of every individual free agent in history is uncertain? If every part of a whole is risky, is not the whole risky? Moreover, while the possibility of love might entail the risky possibility that agents will rebel, why does God tolerate—for ages—these evil agents once they have rebelled? Why does he allow evil spirits and evil people to go on thwarting his plans and harming others? Indeed, why has God risked so much on the one whom Scripture traces all evil back to, namely, Satan? Does the fact that Satan has been ruling and harming this world for eons mean that God made a poor decision in risking this much authority on him?

If the trinitarian warfare theodicy, together with the central role it assigns to risk, is to be regarded as plausible, it is important to address these questions. To this task I turn in the next two chapters. In the course of addressing these questions I present and defend the third and fourth theses of the trinitarian warfare theodicy.

5

LOVE & WAR

Risk & the Sovereignty of God

For man, when perfected, is the best of animals,
but when separated from law and justice, he is the worst of all.
ARISTOTLE, POLITICS

Lilies that fester smell far worse than weeds.
SHAKESPEARE, NINETY-FOURTH SONNET

But what will not Ambition and Revenge Descend to?
Who aspires must down as low As high he sor'd,
obnoxious first or last To basest things.
MILTON, PARADISE LOST

The better stuff a creature is made of—the cleverer and stronger and freer it is—
then the better it will be if it goes right, but also the worse it will be if it goes wrong.
C. S. LEWIS, MERE CHRISTIANITY

*T*hus far I have argued that the metaphysical price God must pay for a creation in which love is possible is a creation in which evil is possible as well. This raises a host of questions that call for further probing into the meaning of love as the answer to the problem of evil. The remainder of this book is directed toward these questions.

In the next two chapters I will develop the heart of the trinitarian warfare theodicy by fleshing out several more important implications of the concept of contingent love and by addressing crucial issues pertaining to the understanding of divine providence within the trinitarian warfare worldview. In this chapter I first address the issue of how God can be guaranteed to win the war if he is not ensured of winning each of the particular battles, as the trinitarian warfare worldview holds. Following this, I discuss the issue of trusting a God who is not in meticulous control of the world. This leads to the important question of why God does not prevent humans or angels from harming other beings. In the course of addressing these questions, I develop the third and fourth theses of the trinitarian warfare theodicy.

General Control and Individual Freedom

A common objection to the concept of a risk-taking God is that it seems to undermine God's sovereignty. If God must risk the fate of individuals, it seems that he must also risk his overall goal of acquiring a bride. If any particular individual can opt out of God's plan, then every individual could conceivably opt out of God's plan. In other words, it seems that God's entire plan for world history could ultimately fail. Satan could conceivably win the war he has waged against God, at least insofar as it concerns the fate of the human race. Such a possibility undermines God's sovereignty and is obviously contrary to Scripture.

Along the same lines, it is sometimes argued that if anything is left up to the choices of free agents, then just about everything must be left up to the choices of free agents, for the choices of individuals sometimes affect the entire course of history. Henri Blocher states this argument well when he writes:

> God has to withdraw from an exceedingly vast area if he really wishes to allow free will to operate without him! The whole history of the world is constantly being switched from one direction to another by the choices made by freedom. As Pascal put it, had Cleopatra's nose been shorter, the whole face of the world would have changed. . . . Her pretty little face had such a hold over the mighty general, Mark Antony, that the fate of the Roman Empire hung in the balance. . . . At certain moments individual choices of apparent insignificance can decide the fate of the universe. . . . Either God does not interfere and no longer has control over anything very much; or else God contrives to limit the consequences of human choice, and so is not really playing the game and is reducing the drama of freedom to a superficial effect of no importance.[1]

Some have even argued that if God is not in control of everything, then something *must be in control of him* which is, they argue, tantamount to say-

---

[1]Henri Blocher, *Evil and the Cross*, trans. David G. Preston (Downers Grove, Ill.: InterVarsity Press, 1994), p. 59. See also Norman Geisler, *Creating God in the Image of Man? Neotheism's Dangerous Drift* (Minneapolis: Bethany House, 1997), pp. 132-45; T. Gray, "God Does Not Play Dice," *Them* 24 (May 1999): 21-34.

ing that God does not exist. In the words of R. C. Sproul, "If there is any part of creation outside of God's sovereignty, then God is simply not sovereign. If God is not sovereign, then God is not God."[2] Sproul consistently applies this line of reasoning to God's providence. If anything is not controlled by God, everything is in jeopardy. Thus he writes:

> If there is one single molecule in this universe running around loose, then we have no guarantee that a single promise of God will ever be fulfilled. Perhaps that one maverick molecule will lay waste all the grand and glorious plans that God has made and promised to us. . . . Maybe that one molecule will be the thing that prevents Christ from returning.[3]

Clearly, if there is any truth to this line of reasoning, the trinitarian warfare worldview is impossible. Four points may be made against it, however.

An adventurous sovereignty. First, the objection that God is not sovereign unless he controls everything assumes that sovereignty is synonymous with unilateral control. But why should we accept this understanding of divine sovereignty? As I have already argued, there are no rational or biblical reasons to suppose that divine sovereignty must or should entail exhaustive, meticulous, divine control.

To put it in Sproul's more extreme terms, why should we think that God would cease to be God because he decided to create something he did not meticulously control? On the contrary, this view seems severely to restrict God's omnipotence! It reduces the Creator to one possible mode of behavior: unilateral control. God *must* control everything in order to exist! Why should we suppose that this is the most exalted, let alone the only conceivable, form of sovereignty?

Can we not conceive of a God who is so great that he dares to create agents who can, to some extent, make autonomous decisions? Can we not conceive of a God who might *choose* to experience risk and adventure? Why should we assume that this is not the case—especially since Scripture itself indicates that God does at times experience surprise and disappointment (cf. chapter three)? Indeed, can we not imagine God growing tired of controlling, or even simply foreknowing, everything in meticulous detail from all

---

[2]R. C. Sproul, *Chosen by God* (Wheaton, Ill.: Tyndale House, 1986), p. 26. So too Sproul argues that if chance existed in any measure, "it would destroy God's sovereignty. If God is not sovereign, he is not God. If he is not God, he simply is not. If chance is, God is not. If God is, chance is not. The two cannot coexist by reason of the impossibility of the contrary" (*Not a Chance: The Myth of Chance in Modern Science and Cosmology* (Grand Rapids, Mich.: Baker, 1994), p. 3. Blocher argues along similar lines (*Evil and the Cross,* p. 59).
[3]Sproul, *Not a Chance,* p. 3.

eternity? If we who are made in God's image naturally desire a healthy element of novelty, risk and adventure, why should we assume that the opposite is true of God? Conversely, if the total absence of novelty, adventure and spontaneity would be torture for us, why should we assume it is heaven for God?[4] I know of no good answers to these questions.

The undermining of divine sovereignty. The definition of sovereignty as control is not only unwarranted; it is, for many of us, not sovereign at all. To speak frankly, it is hard to conceive of a *weaker* God than one who would be threatened by events occurring outside of his meticulous control. It is difficult to imagine a less majestic view of God than one who is necessarily limited to a unilateral, deterministic mode of relating to his creation. According to Sproul, God could not create a world that involved novelty and adventure for him even if he wanted to. He would cease to be God. If power is about having choices, does not any view that denies God the choice of creating an open creation completely undermine God's power?

But Sproul's is not the only view that undermines God's sovereignty in this way. The traditional view that God possesses exhaustively definite foreknowledge *as a necessary attribute* restricts God in the same fashion. In both views God *cannot* create a world that has a partly open future and in which he might experience risk, adventure and novelty. Unless the very idea of a partly open future is a logical contradiction, unless all might-counterfactuals are necessarily false (which is to say, unless an open world is a logically impossible world), we must conclude that both Sproul's and the traditional views restrict God's choices and thus undermine his omnipotence.

In any event, the view that God must control everything certainly undermines God's sovereignty. Even if we soften Sproul's claim that God *must* control everything, however, and hold rather that God simply *chooses* to control everything, it still does not seem to be a supremely praiseworthy form of sovereignty. What is praiseworthy about controlling something simply because you possess the innate power to do so? I have the power to exercise total and exhaustive control over my little finger as I twitch it, for example, but no one would think me praiseworthy on this basis. Yet, is this

---

[4]See W. Barrett's effective critique of determinism on the grounds that it does not allow for "novelty," "freshness" and creativity—though each of these things is extremely important to being authentically human ("Determinism and Novelty," in *Determinism and Freedom in the Age of Modern Science*, ed. S. Hook (New York: Collier-Macmillan, 1958), esp. p. 46. Karl Popper makes similar observations in "Of Clouds and Clocks," in *Objective Knowledge* (Oxford: Oxford University Press, 1972), p. 222.

not precisely what we do when we claim that God's sovereignty is praise-worthy because he controls everything? Of course, God *could* control everything if he wanted to, since it is *his* creation, just as my little finger is *my* finger.

As I see it, the central problem with this conception of sovereignty is that there is nothing intrinsically praiseworthy about sheer power. Praise has to do with character. What is praiseworthy about God's sovereignty is not that he exercises a power he obviously has but that out of his charac-ter he *does not* exercise all the power he *could*.[5] C. S. Lewis argued the point forcefully when he contended that the greatest "miracle" of divine omnipotence, and thus the greatest testimony to God's sovereignty, was the fact that God created beings who possessed the power to say no to him.[6]

Since our understanding of God is analogically rooted in our experience, consider what kind of sovereignty we ordinarily admire. Do we not ordi-narily view leaders who want to (or need to) meticulously control other peo-ple in order to ensure that things go exactly the way they want as insecure,

---

[5]It has been argued that worshiping a God who gets his way by sheer force inevitably inspires a people who attempt to get their way by force. Feminist theologians have been particularly insightful in noting this. See, for example, Susan Thistlethwaite's insightful essay, "I Am Become Death: God in the Nuclear Age," in *Lift Every Voice: Constructing Christian Theologies from the Underside,* ed. Susan B. Thistlethwaite and Mary P. Engel (San Francisco: Harper & Row, 1990). So too Tyron Inbody argues that classical theology was "deeply shaped by . . . a unilateral concept of power" that frequently "is driven to sacralize a concept of abusing power as somehow good" (*The Transforming God: An Interpretation of Suffering* (Louisville: Westminster Press, 1997), p. 117. C. R. Mesle argues along these lines in "Aesthetic Value and Relational Power: An Essay on Personhood," *Process Studies* 13 (1983): 59-70; as does Jürgen Moltmann in his classic work, *The Trinity and the Kingdom: The Doctrine of God,* trans. Margaret Kohl (San Fran-cisco: Harper & Row, 1981), esp. ch. 6. See also I. Thompson, "Liberal Values and Power Poli-tics," in *Ethics and Defense: Power and Responsibility in the Nuclear Age,* ed. Howard H. Davis (New York: Blackwell, 1987), pp. 82-102; Dorothee Soelle, *Christ the Representative: An Essay in Theology After the "Death of God,"* trans. David Lewis (Philadelphia: Fortress, 1967); *The Strength of the Weak: Toward a Christian Feminist Identity,* trans. Robert and Rita Kimber (Phil-adelphia: Westminster Press, 1984); and the fascinating (and largely unnoticed) work by Arthur C. McGill, *Suffering: A Test of Theological Method* (Philadelphia: Geneva, 1968).
[6]C. S. Lewis, *The Problem of Pain* (New York: Macmillan, 1962), p. 127. See also Leslie Weath-erhead's excellent discussion of the nature of omnipotence in *Salute to a Sufferer* (New York: Abingdon, 1962), esp. p. 87. Note as well William P. Alston's and Keith Ward's observation that the denial that God can limit himself if he chooses to constitutes a denial of divine sover-eignty ("Divine Action, Human Freedom, and the Laws of Nature," in *Quantum Cosmology and the Laws of Nature: Scientific Perspectives on Divine Actions,* ed. Robert J. Russell, Nancey Murphy and C. J. Isham [Vatican City: Vatican Observatory Publications, 1993], pp. 191-92; Keith Ward, "God As a Principle of Cosmological Explanation," in *Physics, Philosophy, and The-ology: A Common Quest for Understanding,* ed. Robert J. Russell, William R. Stoeger and George V. Coyne [Notre Dame, Ind.: Notre Dame University Press, 1988], pp. 249-54).

weak and manipulative people?[7] Conversely, do we not admire leaders who influence others by the respect that their character earns more than those who control others through coercion? Do we not admire leaders who not only influence others but empower others to influence them? Does not Bernard Loomer express an intuitive truth when he notes that "the capacity to receive from another or to be influenced by another is truly indicative of power"?[8]

I submit that a truly great leader who is sovereign over his kingdom in the most exalted fashion is a leader secure enough in the influence of his leadership and the character he possesses that he does not need to resort to coercion. Moreover, in this light, I contend, the omni-controlling understanding of divine sovereignty must be judged as actually constituting a *denial* of divine sovereignty.

---

[7]Inbody notes how the God of the classical philosophical tradition is equivalent to "a cosmic Caesar" (*Transforming God,* p. 183). It is curious that many Christians worship as supreme a leadership style that they otherwise find morally repugnant and that Jesus explicitly repudiated (Lk 22:24-30).

[8]Bernard Loomer, "Two Kinds of Power," *Criterion* (Winter 1976): 20. Loomer distinguishes between unilateral power and relational power. Unilateral power, the concept of power characteristic of the classical philosophical tradition, is a zero-sum game. The more one person has the less another must have. It is power *over* people and nature. Conceived in this light, God's omnipotence must entail omni-control. By contrast, relational power is not power *over* so much as it is power *with* another. It is not just power to produce an effect but also the capacity to undergo an effect (see pp. 14-20). When speaking of personal agents, Loomer argues that relational power is superior. Inbody agrees when he notes, "Strength is not the ability to control and hold things external to oneself or to get one's way, the ability to master through individual heroic might. Power, as a primary psychological, social, and ontological concept, is the ability to get along with others and to get things done, the ability to shape each other through the mutual empowerment of a relationship. . . . Authentic power is neither fusion nor control, but interconnectedness" (*Transforming God,* p. 136). Likewise Donald Wacome argues that it would be immoral even for an infinitely wise creator to "have complete control over another person's behavior, even if that person would behave in a better way and be happier than if he were permitted to act on his own." Such control would destroy personhood, he argues ("Evolution, Foreknowledge and Creation," *Christian Scholars Review* 26 [1997]: 316-17. See also Peter Baelz's insightful comments on divine power in *Does God Answer Prayer?* (London: Darton, Longman & Todd, 1982). Process theologians such as Inbody and Loomer have unfortunately concluded that they must postulate a necessary God-world relationship in order to ascribe the highest form of power (relational power) to God as an intrinsic divine attribute. For trinitarian theologians, however, relationality is the essence of the Godhead. What is necessary is not a God-*world* relationship but a God-*God* relationship, as I argue in *Trinity and Process: A Critical Evaluation and Reappropriation of Hartshorne's Di-Polar Theism Towards a Trinitarian Metaphysics* (New York: Lang, 1992). On the issue of maximally virtuous power, see N. Pike, "Over-Power and God's Responsibility for Sin," in *The Existence and Nature of God,* ed. Alfred J. Freddoso (Notre Dame, Ind.: University of Notre Dame Press, 1983); and T. P. Flint and Alfred J. Freddoso, "Maximal Power," in Freddoso, ed., *Existence and Nature of God,* pp. 81-114.

As we saw in chapter one, it seems that church theologians prior to Augustine generally shared this insight. Though they were remarkably diverse in many respects, they all agreed that "there is no coercion in God."[9] Several of them argue explicitly against the view that God's sovereignty should be equated with control on the grounds that this conception is fatalistic and pagan. In the words of Athenagoras, God rather exercises a "universal and general providence of the whole," but the control of "the particular parts are provided for by the angels appointed over them."[10] Or, as Origen more broadly puts it, God's governance is one that is consistent with "the preservation of freedom of will in all rational creatures."[11] For this reason he held that any view that ascribes to "the providence of God all things whatsoever" is a view that actually denies that "God regulates all things."[12] In other words, the omni-controlling model of providence undermines God's sovereignty.

Determinism and indeterminism. My third response to the charge that attributing risk to God undermines his sovereignty has already been alluded to in the previous chapter. The conclusion that everything is at risk if anything is at risk is simply misguided on a number of accounts. It is misguided from a scriptural perspective, for here God often declares *that* he is going to bring something about without knowing exactly *how* he is going to do so, for this latter point depends on what other personal agents do (e.g., Ex 3:18—4:10). It is misguided from a contemporary scientific point of view as well. In a wide variety of contemporary scientific disciplines we are finding that "chaos and order are complementary; the presence of one seems to imply the other."[13]

[9]Irenaeus *Against Heresies* 5.37 (ANF 1:518). See also *Epistle to Diognetus* 7.4, which states that God sent his son "as one who saves by persuasion, not compulsion, for compulsion is no attribute of God" (*The Apostolic Fathers: Greek Texts and English Translations of Their Writings,* ed. and trans. J. B. Lightfoot and J. R. Harmer, ed. and rev. by M. W. Holmes (Grand Rapids, Mich.: Baker, 1992), p. 545.
[10]Athenagoras *A Plea for the Christians* 24 (ANF 2:142).
[11]Origen *First Principles* 3.5.8 (ANF 4:344), in speaking about God's governance in restoring all creatures.
[12]Ibid. Cf. *Commentary on John* 2.7 (ANF 10:330-31).
[13]David J. Bartholomew, *God of Chance* (London: SCM Press, 1984), p. 95. See John Polkinghorne, *Quarks, Chaos and Christianity: A Common Quest for Understanding* (New York: Crossroad, 1996). It is this element of chance within order that makes temporality in order irreversible, according to an increasing number of scientists in different fields. For an overview, see Peter Coveney and Roger Highfield, *The Arrow of Time* (New York: BasicBooks, 1990). As with many other evangelical theorists, Sproul still works with a nineteenth-century understanding of cause and chance, typified by Laplace. For the transition from determinism to indeterminism in modern physics, see Arthur R. Peacocke, *Creation and the World of Science*

In complex systems theory, for example, it has been demonstrated that all "emergent properties," including life, consciousness and intelligence, are the result of order arising out of and dancing on "the edge of chaos," thereby producing creative complexity.[14] From a quantum mechanical perspective, all regularity in the phenomenological world is *statistical,* as I noted in the previous chapter. This does not undermine the real stability of nature's regularity, for within a range of possibilities the behavior of quantum particles *is* very predictable, and thus the behavior of large groups of such particles is highly predictable.

The crucial concept to understand is that this predictability is within *a range* of possibilities. The nature of the particles is such that we can say how they are *in general* disposed to act under such and such conditions (here the "laws" of nature apply), but we cannot say exactly how any *particular* particle *will* in fact act. The laws of nature "do not specify what must happen. . . . They specify what cannot happen. They are permissive laws."[15] Consequently, from quantum mechanics as well as from chaos theory, complexity theory and thermodynamics, "we are presented with a picture of the world that is neither mechanical nor chaotic, but at once both open and orderly in its character."[16]

(Oxford: Clarendon, 1979), pp. 52-59. In contemporary science, the order of the world is an order predicated on chaos. See John Polkinghorne, *Science and Creation* (Boston: Shambala, 1988), ch. 3. The world emerging from quantum physics is "a world of orderliness but not of clockwork regularity, of potentiality without predictability, endowed with an assurance of development but with a certain openness as to its actual form. It is inevitably a world with ragged edges, where order and disorder interlace each other and where the exploration of possibility by chance will lead not only to the evolution of systems of increasing complexity, endowed with new possibilities, but also to the evolution of systems imperfectly formed and malfunctioning" (ibid., p. 49; see also his *Quarks,* chaps. 3-4). Most recently, complexity theorists in a remarkable diversity of fields have been analyzing how dynamic systems (systems that incorporate chaos) of sufficient complexity can bring forth "emergent properties" when balanced with the right kind of order.

[14]See, e.g., Mitchell Waldrop, *Complexity: The Emerging Science at the Edge of Order and Chaos* (New York: Simon & Schuster, 1992); and Grégoire. Nicolis and Ilya Prigogine, *Exploring Complexity: An Introduction* (New York: W. H. Freeman, 1989).

[15]Gary Zukav, *The Dancing Wu Li Masters: An Overview of the New Physics* (New York: William Morrow, 1979), p. 213. On the statistically descriptive nature of laws in contemporary science, see William R. Stoeger, "Contemporary Physics and the Ontological Status of the Laws of Nature," in Russell, Murphy and Isham, eds., *Quantum Cosmology,* pp. 206-31, 235-46.

[16]John Polkinghorne, "The Quantum World," in *Physics, Philosophy and Theology: A Common Quest for Understanding,* ed. Robert J. Russell, William R. Stoeger and George V. Coyne (Notre Dame, Ind.: Notre Dame University Press, 1988), p. 341. In his *Quarks,* Polkinghorne relates this to God's love, which grants the world independence (hence a role for chance), as well as to God's faithfulness, which gives the world its regularity (pp. 41-42). See also David Bartholomew,

All of this exposes the false dichotomy involved in Blocher's argument that "either God does not interfere and no longer has control . . . or else God contrives to limit the consequences of human choice, and so is not really playing the game." What Blocher fails to appreciate is that both Scripture and the world suggest that the "game" is all about balancing control and freedom. God is in control precisely because he can and does limit creaturely freedom, and agents have freedom precisely because God does not exercise exhaustive unilateral control.

If we grasp the general trajectory of the areas of science we have been discussing, we should in principle be no more confounded by the fact that God can guarantee certain outcomes without meticulously determining their means than we are at how we can rely on the stability of the desk in front of us even though it is composed of quantum particles that are to some extent unpredictable. The laws that keep the world relatively predictable do not need to be meticulously coercive on a quantum level to be binding on a phenomenological level.[17] In the same way, God's providence does not need to be meticulously controlling on the level of free agents to ensure that his sovereign plan for the world will be accomplished.

The universality of deterministic-indeterministic complementarity. This leads directly to my final response to this objection. The notion that God's providential control must be meticulous for God to be in control of world history is misguided from the perspective of a common-sense phenomenological assessment of life. The complementarity of determinism and indeterminism is evidenced wherever we look.[18]

"God or Chance?" in *God for the 21st Century,* ed. Russell Stannand (Philadelphia: Templeton Foundation Press, 2000).

[17]For an excellent and accessible discussion of the paradox of how quantum indeterminacy produces phenomenological stability, see David Lindley, *Where Does the Weirdness Go?* (New York: BasicBooks, 1996). One of the central arguments sustained in this book is that Bohm and Einstein were incorrect in supposing that one needs to postulate "hidden variables" that make the indeterminacy of quantum mechanics determinate in order to account for the stability and predictability of the phenomenological world. "Quantum mechanics can give you as much determinism as anyone actually needs" he argues, "so the insistence of Bohm, and for that matter Einstein, that there must be something 'underneath' quantum mechanics has become empty" (p. 215). This issue directly parallels the thinking of those who suppose that God cannot control the world at a macro level unless he controls it at a micro level.

[18]The following discussion has been informed by a number of works that have examined the nonlinear, chance, chaotic dimension in everything from particles (Brownian motion) to economic systems. See, e.g., Ilya Prigogine and Michele Sanglier, *The Laws of Nature and Human Conduct* (Brussels: Task Force of Research Information and the Study of Science, 1985); Ilya Prigogine, *From Being to Becoming* (San Francisco: W. H. Freeman, 1980); Nicolis and Prigogine, *Exploring Complexity;* Waldrop, *Complexity;* Z. Nitecki and C. Robinson, eds., *Global*

The field of sociology, for example, is predicated on the fact that human behavior is statistically predictable. Yet individual behavior, to a significant extent, is not predictable. For example, we can within a range predict the percentage of people who will attempt suicide in a given year and the percentage of those who will succeed. We can within a range predict the percentage of people who will take up smoking, the percentage who will try to quit and the percentage who will actually succeed in their attempts. Likewise we can with significant accuracy predict the percentage of people who will commit violent crimes, cheat on their spouses, go to church, get in car accidents, develop a given disease, respond positively to particular advertisements, and so on.

But which *individuals* will and will not make various decisions or engage in any of these various behaviors is, with few exceptions, impossible to predict with certainty. The relationship between individuals and corporate wholes on a human level, we see, is similar to what we find at a quantum level. The behavior of groups is far more predictable than the behavior of individuals.

This is true of the animal and insect kingdoms as well. For example, we can accurately predict the working behavior of a colony of ants but cannot accurately forecast the exact behavior of any particular ant. We can accurately anticipate the formation of a flock of birds but cannot predict precisely which birds will form which part of that formation or which birds will join that formation. Along slightly different lines, we can predict what kind of song pattern a certain species of bird will sing, but any particular song always exhibits an element of unpredictable creativity and spontaneity.[19] We can accurately predict the

---

Theory of Dynamical Systems: Proceedings of an International Conference Held at Northwestern University, Evanston, Illinois, June 18-22, 1979 (Berlin: Springer Verlag, 1980); Bruce Weber, David Depew and James Smith, eds., *Entropy, Information and Evolution* (Cambridge, Mass.: MIT Press, 1988); Ian Stewart, *Does God Play Dice? The Mathematics of Chaos* (Oxford: Blackwell, 1989); Leon Glass and Michael Mackey, *From Clocks to Chaos: The Rhythms of Life* (Princeton, N.J.: Princeton University Press, 1988). I might incidentally note that the assumption that God must control each part to control the whole is misguided from a strictly logical perspective as well. If we accept that a concept has meaning only if its negation has meaning, the ontological affirmation of determinism presupposes the ontological affirmation of indeterminism. Hence the complementarity of determinism and indeterminism is a metaphysical, and therefore a universally instantiated, truth. See my discussion in *Trinity and Process*, pp. 34, 62-65.

[19]Hartshorne, who was an ornithologist as well as philosopher, integrates this metaphysical principle into his analysis of bird song in *Born to Sing: An Interpretation and World Survey of Bird Song* (Bloomington: Indiana University Press, 1973). See also his "Freedom, Individual, and Beauty in Nature," *Snowy Egret* 24 (Fall 1960): 5-14; and "Metaphysics Contributes to Ornithology," *Theoria to Theory* 13 (1979): 127-40. See also A. F. Skutch, "Bird Song and Philosophy," in *The Philosophy of Charles Hartshorne*, ed. Lewis E. Hahn, Library of Living Philosophers 20 (La Salle, Ill.: Open Court, 1991), pp. 65-76.

destinations and even the courses of flight of various kinds of bees on search expeditions as well as the migration pattern of various birds, fish, whales, and the like, but within these general patterns there are always elements of unpredictable spontaneity, especially on an individual level.

This principle is illustrated virtually everywhere we look. The old mechanistic assumption that exhaustive knowledge would lead to exhaustive predictability has always been just that: an assumption. The mechanistic, deterministic worldview of Newton was not a world anyone actually experienced; it was, rather, a world that could exist only in theory. In truth, this view has always been out of sync with what we know to be true about ourselves individually (we are self-determining) as well as a dimension of the world we observe around us (there is an element of spontaneity in everything). In this sense quantum physics is not discovering anything new; it is simply recognizing spontaneity at a new level of smallness.

We have every reason to believe that an element of unpredictability would remain even if we (like God) possessed exhaustive knowledge about everything. Granted, increased knowledge leads to increased predictability, especially at a phenomenological level. The Newtonian mechanistic model of the world reflects this truth. But it is not the whole truth. The more closely we observe the phenomenological world and the more we learn about the quantum world, the more reason we have for concluding that an element of unpredictability lies in the nature of things. Hence, the predictability of the world could never be exhaustive even if, like God, our knowledge of reality was.

I therefore conclude that there is in principle no contradiction between saying that God will certainly achieve his objectives for history, on the one hand, and that self-determining individuals are to some extent unpredictable, on the other. To the contrary, this claim squares perfectly with the way we experience ourselves and the world.

Can the Lord guarantee he will have a bride? Even though there is no contradiction between these two claims *in principle,* it still might be argued that the particular way Scripture portrays God's providential plan is incompatible with the belief that agents determine their futures to some extent. Scripture unequivocally depicts God as certain that he will have a people for himself, a bride. Indeed, he predestined that there would be a church before the world began (Eph 1:3-11; 2 Tim 1:9). But if God did not predestine or at least foreknow that anyone in particular would accept his invitation, then, it might be argued, he simply could not be certain of this. It seems that God's goal for world history could fail and that Satan could win this conflict after all.

While there is a certain common-sense appeal to this line of reasoning, I do not believe it is accurate. Two considerations will suffice to argue my point. First, in giving humans a nature that includes a self-determining will, God set the parameters of human freedom. As Creator, he knows humans exhaustively, infinitely better than any human could ever know them. Now, if sociologists, advertisers and insurance companies can accurately predict the behavior of large groups of people under certain conditions, though they are unable to predict the behavior of any particular individual within these groups, how much more should we assume that God is able to predict the behavior of large groups of people over long periods of time, that is, the whole human race throughout the whole of world history?

In my view, the Lord knew from the beginning that human rebellion was a possibility, if not an inevitability. As I argued in chapters three and four, this possibility was inherent in the gift of self-determination that God gave to humanity. The Lord also knew that *if* a fall were to occur, a certain percentage of people might reject his offer of salvation in spite of his incarnation and the constant, loving intervention of the Holy Spirit.[20] But the Lord also foreknew that a certain percentage range of people would, through faith and by means of his grace, accept his saving love. As Creator of humanity and the omniscient Lord of all creation, God knew that he would be able graciously to redeem a bride for himself. In addition, he was able to do this without determining, and thus foreknowing, which individuals would and would not belong to this bride. This is not a definite reality to be known until the agents themselves accept, or permanently reject, God's love.

Second, and even more fundamentally, the Lord could know from the start that he would certainly have a bride on the basis of his perfect knowledge of *his own character and ability*. As the biblical narrative testifies, he is

---

[20]Two subsidiary points may be made. First, there is no reason to suppose that the probability of Adam and Eve passing or failing their probationary period was 50 percent. Freedom requires a choice, but neither logic nor experience teaches us that it requires an evenly balanced choice. John Sanders may in fact be correct when he depicts the entrance of sin into the world through our first parents as being inherently "implausible" (*The God Who Risks: A Theology of Providence* [Downers Grove, Ill.: InterVarsity Press, 1998], pp. 46-47), but there is no contradiction in supposing that a fall was extremely likely, if not inevitable. Secondly, we need not suppose that God had an exact or fixed knowledge of the percentage of people who would and would not respond to his offer of grace in the event that humans fell. That is, his knowledge of this group behavior may be a wave probability, and this wave probability might fluctuate due to various contingencies over time. The objection we are considering, however, is avoided so long as this fluctuating wave probability could never include zero. Moreover, the wisdom of God is preserved so long as the wave probability could never be so low that the risk of creating this situation was not worth it.

the Lord of love who refuses to give up! Even if it were possible for entire generations completely to rebel against him, the Lord knew before he entered into this plan that he was willing to do whatever it took and to work for however long it might take to see his creation bear the fruit he was seeking. If he must delay consummating his plan to allow more people to enter into his eternal kingdom, he is willing to do this (see 2 Pet 3:9-10).

This aspect of God's character is continually revealed in Scripture. For example, prior to the flood humans and fallen angels steered the flow of history so far off course that it became almost hopeless. This level of depravity just prior to the flood had always been a possibility, so the omniscient Lord of course knew it as such from the foundation of the world. But the possibility seems to have been remote, judging from the fact that the Lord was so grieved that he regretted having made humans (Gen 6:6). The worst-case scenario had tragically come to pass: "The LORD saw that the wickedness of humankind was great in the earth, and that every inclination of the thoughts of their hearts was only evil continually" (Gen 6:5).

Even here, however, the Lord did not give up. Instead, he decided to start over. He destroyed all who opposed him and set out to rebuild the world with the remnant that could be salvaged.[21] He was not going to abandon his plan of having a people who share in his triune love and administrate his loving lordship on the earth (Gen 1:26-28). Though the Lord must sometimes use extreme measures, the all-powerful and all-wise God always finds a way to move toward his goals.

We find a similar state of affairs with Israel later in the biblical record. Since the time of Abraham, the Lord patiently had been building a people who would love him and function as a nation of priests to reach the whole world. But the people who belonged to this nation rebelled to the point where the Lord was ready to destroy all of them and start over with Moses (Ex 32:9-10). This degree of rebellion, which reoccurred later in Israel's history, surprised God presumably because the possibility of this level of obstinacy was so remote (see Jer 3:7, 19; cf. 7:31; 19:5; 32:35). But in a world of free agents, sometimes the improbable comes to pass. In this instance, Moses persuaded God to "change his mind" about the destruction he had planned

---

[21]On my reading of Scripture, it is possible that this was the second time the Lord destroyed the world and rebuilt it with the remains. The first may have occurred between Genesis 1:1 and 1:2. See my *God at War: The Bible and Spiritual Conflict* (Downers Grove, Ill.: InterVarsity Press, 1996), pp. 100-112. Scripture declares that God will do this one final time, prior to establishing his eternal kingdom (2 Pet 3:7). I discuss my reading of Genesis 1:1-2 in chapter ten.

for Israel. The episode demonstrates how the Lord is willing and able to move forward with his plans even when people choose to thwart his will for their lives.

On this basis we can understand how the Lord can have complete assurance that his overall goals will be accomplished, even while being uncertain as to who will and will not submit to these goals. God is determined—he has predestined—that there would be a bride, and he will not give up until this goal is achieved.

On Trusting God

Another common objection against views affirming creaturely self-determination and against the open view of the future in particular is that God cannot be trusted as our source of strength and comfort unless he meticulously controls the world, or at least foreknows in exhaustive detail what is going to happen. William Placher, for example, argues, "We could not trust in God and find peace in the midst of the world's chaos if there were any part of the world out of God's control."[22]

What can we trust God for? The first response to this objection is that it is not self-evident what it means to "trust God." When facing difficult situations, Christians frequently admonish one another, "Put your trust in God." But we need to define more precisely what it is we are to trust God for. If left undefined, the admonition can be misguiding if not wounding.

Allow me to offer an illustration of the ambiguity and harm that can be associated with this concept.[23] Several years ago a nineteen-year-old student I will call Laura confessed her feelings of guilt over the fact that she "just couldn't seem to truly trust God." In the course of our discussion I discovered that as a nine-year-old daughter of an American missionary to Brazil, Laura had been raped by a missionary "friend of the family." She reported the man, and he was duly "punished" by being put on leave for several months and then relocated to another mission field! Young Laura was told that even "men of God" sometimes do bad things and need God's grace, just like everyone else. She was instructed immediately to love and forgive this man and not to talk about the incident to anyone. If God forgives and forgets, she was instructed, so must we.

To make matters worse, as a typical (and unfortunate) means of comfort-

---

[22]William C. Placher, *The Domestication of Transcendence: How Modern Thinking About God Went Wrong* (Louisville: Westminster John Knox, 1996), pp. 123-24.

[23]As always, the name and details of this story have been altered to protect the anonymity of the person in question.

ing this victim, Laura's parents told her that God "always has his reasons" for allowing things like this to happen, though we of course may not understand these reasons until we get to heaven. Laura must simply believe that God was still "on his throne" and still "in control." She needed to trust God and believe that what the missionary intended for evil God intended for good. In time, she was told, she would actually be thankful for the experience.

When I asked Laura what she as a nineteen-year-old believed she was supposed to trust God for, her predictable Christian student answer was, "for God's perfect will for my life." When (to her increasing exasperation) I inquired further what *that* meant, she quoted one of the most quoted verses of the Bible by young Christians, Jeremiah 29:11: "For surely I know the plans I have for you, says the LORD, plans for your welfare and not for harm, to give you a future with hope." Finally, when I asked what she believed was included in the Lord's plan for her "welfare and not for harm," she exclaimed in an impatient matter-of-fact voice: "Well, to have a good marriage, of course, to have the right ministry or job and to do well in it, and to be healthy and safe. You know, just to prosper!"

"Safe?" I asked. "Do you mean, to be safe from rapists?" After a long pause she nodded a sheepish yes as her eyes began to tear up.

"No wonder you can't trust God, Laura," I said. "You already know that God *can't* be trusted to deliver on that one." Laura initially responded as though I had uttered a hideous blasphemy, yet she saw the obvious and painful truth of the point I was making. For ten years she had been encouraged by a Christian community to trust God for bodily protection when all the while she knew from personal experience that it was not only up to God to decide this matter. Intuitively, she knew that free agents like the missionary who had abused her also have a mind and will of their own. She intuitively knew that if there is no divine guarantee against little girls getting raped, there is no guarantee that nineteen-year-old women will not be raped. The result of this instruction was that Laura now blamed herself for not being able to "trust God" to protect her from being raped.

What is more, though she was too pious or simply too scared to admit it out loud to herself, Laura was privately enraged toward God. She understood her rape as a child ultimately to be God's fault. We are supposed to accept such tragedies as somehow fitting into God's plan—and yet we are supposed to trust God for protection from such tragedies! Could anyone have pieced together a more contradictory—and for victims like Laura, a more tormenting—theological puzzle? No wonder Laura was enraged. My experience has been that many who hold to the classical view of God's providence and who have had traumatic experiences hold similar sentiments toward God.

As this story illustrates, evangelical Christians often use the admonition to "just trust God" to encourage people to trust God for things that are not necessarily under his direct control and for things that he never unconditionally promises in his Word. We talk about trusting God to save and protect our families, to prosper us in our jobs or our ministries, to insulate us from spiritual attacks, and the like. And, as was initially the case with Laura toward me, people who dare to suggest that these things are not only up to God to decide are sometimes viewed as heretical. Yet, where in the New Testament does God leverage his character on any guarantee that evil will not befall us in this world? Where in the Bible are we promised that our children, families, jobs, ministries or even our very lives are guaranteed to be divinely protected?

As I pointed out to Laura, this question cannot be answered by appealing to Jeremiah 29:11. This chapter is addressed specifically to the exiled nation of Israel regarding what God's specific plan is for them in the near future. Besides, God's "plan" for them is just that: a plan. It expressed God's intention, not a foregone conclusion (as the subsequent history of Israel demonstrated). Nor is an answer found in the book of Job, for this entire book is a refutation of this notion (see chapter seven). Nor is the answer to be found in the Gospels where Jesus tells us to *expect* physical and emotional suffering, to be separated from families and even to be put to death for following him (Mt 5:11, 44; 16:24-25; Lk 12:53; 21:12; Jn 15:20; 21:18-19). Nor is the answer found anywhere in the Epistles, in which we are instructed to follow the example of Jesus in suffering for the sake of righteousness (Heb 12:3; Jas 5:10; 1 Pet 2:20-21).

Indeed, the New Testament promises that "in the world you face persecution" (Jn 16:33). This world is a spiritual war zone under the control of Satan (1 Jn 5:19), the "god of this world" (2 Cor 4:4). Soldiers who seek to overthrow his evil kingdom and establish the kingdom of God can expect to suffer in this war zone.

To say the least, then, the New Testament never makes our unconditional well-being in this probationary epoch part of the good news. The good news of the gospel is not that we will never suffer, get raped, be maimed or die an early death. The good news is rather that the Lord has given us something so marvelous that even if we suffer or die, our loss is ultimately insignificant. In the light of God's love, the grace of Jesus Christ and the life we have in the

Holy Spirit, the quality and duration of physical life itself dwindles in importance. While moth and rust—to say nothing of missionary rapists—might
ruin everything in this age, our treasure is laid up in a realm that is incor-
ruptible (Mt 6:19-20). Since we have this treasure, we do not need to fear
any earthly or spiritual authority who might be able to kill the body (Mt
10:28). These agents are indeed capable at times of wounding us or even of
killing us, but the only One believers need concern themselves with is the
One (God) who is able to "destroy both soul and body in hell."

Along similar lines, Paul tells us that no matter what happens, we cannot
be separated from the love of God toward us in Christ, either in this age of
warfare or in the age of God's coming kingdom. *This* is the good news.

> Who will separate us from the love of Christ? Will hardship, or distress, or per-
> secution, or famine, or nakedness, or peril, or sword? . . . No, in all these
> things we are more than conquerors through him who loved us. For I am con-
> vinced that neither death, nor life, nor angels, nor rulers, nor things present,
> nor things to come, nor powers, nor height, nor depth, nor anything else in all
> creation, will be able to separate us from the love of God in Christ Jesus our
> Lord. (Rom 8:35, 37-39)

Paul assumes that all these hardships can and do happen to Christians. In
this hellish war zone we may in fact be persecuted, suffer famine or be
assailed by demonic forces. Caught in the crossfire of this raging cosmic war,
children are forcibly abducted, women are violently raped, the poor are ruth-
lessly oppressed, minorities are systematically marginalized and godly people
are sometimes torturously murdered. On both a spiritual and a natural level,
bullets are flying, bombs are exploding, battles are raging—and little children, like this woman when she was nine, are not spared. General Sherman
was right: "War is hell."

We have no guarantee that tragedies will not happen to us in this war
zone. What we are guaranteed, what we can "trust God" for, and what
makes us "more than conquerors" amidst life's tragedies is that nothing can
"separate us from the love of God in Christ Jesus." Our trust in God and our
peace are not to be rooted in the up-and-down affairs of this war-torn world.
They are rather to be rooted in God's unchanging character and unconditional promise that his love for us in Christ is unwavering amidst life's
storms.[24]

---

[24]This raises the question of what role prayer plays in deciding what transpires in history. In
chapter seven I argue that the warfare worldview actually intensifies our appreciation of the
power and urgency that Scripture ascribes to prayer.

Revolt rather than resignation. Critics may grant that we cannot trust God to guarantee protection from life's nightmares but nevertheless argue that believers should find consolation in the belief that even the nightmares of life are allowed by God for a good divine reason. This is often part of what Christians mean when they encourage someone to "trust God" in the midst of a difficult situation.

Scripture certainly encourages the believer to find consolation in the fact that Christ suffers with us when we suffer (Rom 8:17; Phil 3:10; Heb 2:18; 4:15-16; 1 Pet 4:13; cf. Mt 28:20). It admonishes us to trust that God is always working to bring good out of whatever circumstance we find ourselves in, however tragic (Rom 5:3-5; 8:28). It encourages us to be steadfast when we are persecuted for our faith and when the Lord uses trials to build our character (Heb 12:3-13). Finally, as was just argued, the Bible certainly teaches that we can derive a peace that passes understanding from the fact that our eternal fellowship with God in his kingdom will more than make up for our sufferings in this present age (Rom 8:18; Phil 4:7). But I do not believe that Scripture teaches us to find consolation in trusting that everything that ever occurs has a divine reason behind it.

This belief not only goes beyond the teaching of Scripture; it fosters a mentality that is at odds with Scripture. If one holds that there is a divine reason behind all suffering, one is more likely to resign oneself to things that Scripture encourages us to revolt against. Jesus and the New Testament authors instruct us to revolt against evil as coming from the enemies of God rather than trying to find security and consolation in the hope that God is somehow secretly behind it.[25] Jesus never encouraged people to accept their sickness, disease or demonization as somehow fitting into his Father's plan.[26] Rather, he revealed that God's plan was to *overthrow* these things, and he

---

[25]David Griffin makes an insightful point in this regard. After pointing out that the Augustinian view of divine sovereignty reduces the "battle between the divine and the demonic" to "a mock, not a real, battle," he observes that "one of the motives of this monistic monotheism, with its doctrine of divine coercive omnipotence, was to convince us that we really had nothing to fear from the demonic power. That complacent belief, as history has revealed, is just what we do not need." ("Why Demonic Power Exists: Understanding the Church's Enemy," *LTQ* 28 [1993]: 227). Inbody also argues that the need for security often lies behind the omni-controlling view of sovereignty (*Transforming God*, p. 159). The atheist Michael Martin forcefully points out that "if evil is only an illusion from our limited perspective," as it is in the Augustinian system, "then acting to change something that appears evil to something that appears good will make no moral difference in the ultimate scheme of things" (*Atheism: A Philosophical Justification* [Philadelphia: Temple University Press, 1990], p. 443).

[26]Some have cited John 9:1-5 as a counterinstance to this claim. On both exegetical and theological grounds, their case is weak. See my *God at War: The Bible and Spiritual Conflict*, pp. 231-37.

taught his disciples (and us) to adopt the same attitude.[27] We are not to trust that God meticulously controls these things. We are rather to trust that God is against them, that he has empowered us to work with him in battling such evils and that God will ultimately overthrow all his foes and rid his creation of all forms of evil.

If we adopt a warfare worldview rather than a blueprint worldview, we are encouraged to trust God for everything God himself tells us to trust him for and to fight against everything God himself fights against. God's character is not tarnished by being entwined with the evil in the world, and the church's mission is not compromised by accepting things it ought to revolt against.[28]

The Dark Side of the Potential to Love

I have demonstrated that affirming God's providential control over the world is compatible with affirming a significant degree of self-determining freedom on the part of humans, but another fundamental question remains to be addressed. Even if we grant that God can control the world in general while allowing for freedom within the parameters of this control, we must ask why God does not narrow the parameters in certain cases. More specifi-

---

[27]If God, not Satan, is behind all the nightmares of the world, then far from trusting God we should rather follow the advice of W. Robert McClelland and consider it our moral obligation to "rage" against God as our "enemy" (*God Our Loving Enemy* [Nashville: Abingdon, 1982], p. 49). McClelland's work is an excellent assault on the unbiblical theology and lifestyle of resignation. He agrees that we should not accept all things as coming from God's hand. In his view, we should *revolt* against God *because* all things come from his hand. From the blueprint model of providence McClelland draws the logical conclusion that God can only be understood in the midst of suffering as "the enemy." In my estimation, all of McClelland's instincts are right except for the fact that he confuses God and Satan. If one grants McClelland's omni-controlling view of God, however, everything that he says about God follows.

[28]Brother Andrew—commonly known as "God's smuggler" because of his ministry of smuggling Bibles into closed countries—speaks forcefully against the apathy that results from viewing God as mysteriously behind everything. For example, he recounts hearing a conversation between two pious women regarding the fate of two people taken hostage by terrorists. One said, "I feel sorry for those poor men and their families, but really, this is God's problem not ours. We have to remember that he has already decided how their stories are going to turn out." Andrews regards this form of piety as "a paralyzing disease that has invaded the Body of Christ with dire consequences. It infects its victims with complacency and apathy that immobilize their will to resist evil while eroding their determination to accomplish the great work of Christ" (Brother Andrew and Susan DeVore Williams, *And God Changed His Mind Because His People Prayed* [reprint, London: Marshall Pickering, 1991], pp. 14, 22). According to Brother Andrew, the responsibility that God places on the church to accomplish his will makes sense and is carried out with passion only when Christians accept that the future is not exhaustively settled and God's will is not fixed. To a significant extent, whether God's will is accomplished or not genuinely depends on how Christians pray and what Christians do. (I discuss the issue of prayer within a warfare worldview in chapter seven.)

cally, we must wonder why God allows certain free agents the power to harm and even kill other free agents. Allowing for agents to choose against God and destroy themselves in the process is one thing; accepting that they may kill many others in the process is quite another. Why would God structure creation this way?

Michael Martin raises this question as part of his case against believing in God:

> God could have constructed natural laws in such a way that any attempt by a moral agent to do some morally objectionable act would end in failure; that is, the consequences of the act would not be morally objectionable. In this world a Hitler would choose to kill millions, but he would be unsuccessful.[29]

In short, even if we accept that love must be freely chosen and thus that creation must include risk, it is not clear why this risk should involve others.

The capacity to bless and the capacity to curse. The answer, I believe, lies in a further analysis of the nature of contingent love. Can contingent agents have the capacity to love other agents without also having the capacity to harm them? It seems to me that they cannot. For if the potential to choose love requires the potential to choose its opposite, as I have argued, then our capacity to freely love one another must imply that to some extent we have the capacity to freely harm one another. The opposite of helping others is not simply refraining from helping them; it is harming them.

This is the risk, and thus the moral responsibility, inherent in the potential to love.[30] This observation should not seem too controversial to us, for we experience it firsthand. We all know, for example, that our parents, friends, spouses and children have tremendous power to bless or hurt us, and we them, precisely because we have the capacity to love one another. The implicit (or in the case of marriage, explicit) covenant we enter into with those we love is that we will not abuse the power the beloved has given to us. The inherent risk involved in such covenants is that, because they are

---

[29]Martin, *Atheism,* p. 391.
[30]William Frankena argues forcefully that actions acquire a moral dimension to them only insofar as they knowingly bring about benefit or harm to sentient beings. See his *Ethics,* 2nd ed. (Englewood Cliffs, N.J.: Prentice-Hall, 1973), p. 113. The principle is exploited well for theodicy purposes by William Hasker in his essay "The Necessity of Gratuitous Evil," *Faith and Philosophy* 9 (1992): 23-44. Harold Kushner comes close to espousing the principle of moral responsibility that God must work with to attain his goal of love when he notes, "God has set Himself the limit that He will not intervene to take away our freedom, including our freedom to hurt ourselves and those around us" (*When Bad Things Happen to Good People* [New York: Schocken, 1981], p. 81). He also correctly notes that this insight is hinted at in Job (pp. 43-45).

made between free agents, the possibility of being hurt by our partners choosing against love is always present.

If I am correct, this is more than a mere observation. It could, in truth, be no other way. I submit that we cannot conceive of the potential to love without this concomitant potential to harm, which is why the freedom to love requires the risk of moral responsibility. For God to give us a capacity to love one another *is* for God to put us at risk with each other and thereby make us morally responsible for each other.

This claim forms the third structural thesis of the trinitarian warfare worldview. Just as *love requires freedom* (TWT1) and *freedom requires risk* (TWT2), *risk entails moral responsibility* (TWT3). For better or for worse, the potential to love or not is intrinsically relational. Others are affected by the choices we make.

If I am correct that this thesis forms part of the meaning of love, then it must be present wherever love is present. A parent's potential to love her child and thereby bless him, for example, is also her capacity to harm her child—which is to say, the parent is morally responsible for her child. A husband's potential to love and bless his wife is also his capacity to harm her—which is to say, the husband is to some extent morally responsible for the well-being of his wife. Indeed, every person's power to bless others is balanced by his or her power to harm them. To the extent that we can love, we can harm, and how we use this potential defines our moral character.

The scope of responsibility. Our moral responsibility extends beyond those with whom we have explicit relationships. We are commanded and equipped by our Creator to love everyone as well as to lovingly care for the whole animal and plant kingdom (Gen 1:26-28). This forms an implicit covenant between us and everyone and everything around us for which we are to some extent morally responsible.

This potentially beautiful tapestry of interlocking, morally responsible, free agents with every other free agent and with their whole environment can give humanity and creation a shared sense of oneness. But because it is a tapestry of *free* agents, it can potentially destroy itself to a significant extent and result in the destructive fragmentation of creation. For this reason Jesus taught us that we all share some responsibility for one another; we are neighbors (Lk 10:29-37). It is for this reason as well that every stranger we meet has some potential to harm us if he or she chooses to do so, and vice versa.

God cannot ordinarily guarantee that a child will not be abducted or raped because the price of such a guarantee would be that humans could not be morally responsible for one another, which would mean that we would not have the potential genuinely to love one another. Though it would be risk free and pain free, such a world, we have already noted, would hardly be worth creating. The consequence for creating a world that can produce good parents and neighbors who love and protect each other's children is that it must also be a world in which people may choose to despise, steal and abuse little children.

Why does God allow angels to influence humans? We should understand the interaction between humans and spiritual beings along similar lines. That is, it seems that the tapestry of morally responsible interaction includes spiritual free agents as well as human free agents. This ought not surprise us, for the Bible (and almost all primordial cultures) depicts the world "above" as very much like the world "below" and as inextricably interconnected with it.

Nor is this view difficult to process philosophically. In the words of Richard Swinburne, "If there is reason . . . for allowing humanly free agents to hurt other agents, then there is reason for allowing free agents other than men to inflict such hurt."[31] This reason, I have argued, lies in the nature of love and moral responsibility.

Hence, following the lead of the early church (see chapter one), we should conclude that angels have been entrusted with the capacity to bless or harm us for the same reason that parents have been given power over their children and leaders power over their followers. An angel's capacity and divine commission to lovingly protect a certain nation can damage that nation if that angel rebels (Dan 10:12-13). Other angels' capacity and divine commission to care for the poor works against the poor if those angels become evil or irresponsible in the administration of their duties (Ps 82). Spirits who once had the capacity to help preserve our health can contribute to our sickness when they fall (Mk 9:25; Lk 11:24). According to ancient tradition, certain angels who were charged with protecting and instructing humans prior to the flood turned evil and used their power to corrupt even the gene pool of the human race (Gen 6:1-4). In addition, perhaps, certain angels who could have helped protect our children (Mt 18:10) seek to destroy them when those angels set themselves against their Creator.

Taking their cue from Scripture, early church theologians concluded that much of the evil in the world is the result of "powers," "authorities" and "rulers" abusing their God-given potential to love. Most significantly, at the

---

[31]Richard Swinburne, *The Existence of God*, rev. ed. (Oxford: Clarendon, 1991), p. 202.

head of this rebellion is Satan, the angel who had the greatest potential for good and thus who now exercises the greatest power for destruction. While this agent could have administered God's loving plans for the whole cosmos, he now functions as the supreme architect for everything contrary to God. His evil intentions pollute everything.

In summary, Scripture and the postapostolic church generally depict angels as well as humans as participants in a society of free agents who share some degree of moral responsibility for one another. Angels are part of the moral tapestry that weaves all of creation together. They too have the power to love or destroy, bless or curse. Hence, when they freely rebel, all who could have been blessed by them suffer as a result. This conclusion helps render the warfare worldview of Scripture and the war-torn nature of our world intelligible.

The devil did not make you do it. Does this conclusion justify people who shun responsibility for their actions and claim that the devil or a demon made them sin? Martin Marty, among many others, argues that it does:

> The Devil, when invoked, stifles further inquiry because such a personal force can be blamed for everything. No examination of conscience is needed after the devil's name appears. I have isolated and defined the source of the problem. All I need do then is ignore it or exorcise the devil.[32]

Don Cupitt expresses a similar concern:

> Explanations of moral phenomena which have recourse to the Devil or devils must be repudiated because they are a device for shuffling off responsibility. Thus, when I commit a wicked act, I may be tempted to say "A devil made me do it." . . . Explanation by devils is a moral evasion. Instead of talking about devils, I should be reading Sigmund Freud, and admitting that there is that in me which the Gospel has not yet tamed and reordered. My "unconscious" is still me, it is not some other possessing me.[33]

It cannot be denied that appeals to Satan and demons are often illegitimately made in order to deny personal responsibility for sinful behavior. Indeed, this lame excuse is literally the oldest one in the book (Gen 3:13)! However, as Clement and Origen effectively argued against those who thought like

---

[32]Martin E. Marty, " 'The Devil, You Say. . .' 'The Demonic, Say I. . .'," in *Heterodoxy/Mystical Experience, Religious Dissent and the Occult*, ed. Richard Woods (River Forest, Ill.: Listening Press, 1975), p. 101.

[33]Don Cupitt, "Four Arguments Against the Devil," *Theology* 64 (1961): 413. Along similar lines (but within a theology that does not deny Satan's existence), see Paul M. Miller, *The Devil Did Not Make Me Do It* (Scottsdale, Penn.: Herald, 1977).

this in their day, there is no justification for this reasoning.[34] Admitting that
Satan and demons can sometimes *influence* our thinking and behavior does
not mean that they can *determine* our thinking and behavior.

There is no reason to think matters are different with spiritual agents than
they are with physical agents. When other people influence our behavior
they *share* the responsibility for our behavior to some extent. But it does not
entail that they *take away* our responsibility for our behavior. This is why
Adam and Eve were still held responsible for their rebellion, despite the fact
that the serpent was also held partly responsible for their fall (Gen 3:14-15).

Many circumstances and people influence our behavior every day, but
only in extraordinary cases do we consider these factors to undermine our
own responsibility for our behavior. For example, a twelve-year-old boy who
meticulously repeats a crime he viewed on television is not thereby excused
from his crime even though we would probably concede that what he saw on
television influenced his behavior. Perhaps the producers of the show bear
some responsibility for the crime. Perhaps the boy's parents as well as all who
support the program also share the responsibility. Indeed, everyone who
negatively influenced this young man as well as all who could have positively
influenced him but did not must bear some of the responsibility for the
crime. The same holds true for spirits who may have influenced this young
man. However, all things being equal, the onus of responsibility is on the
shoulders of the boy himself.[35] He could have and should have done otherwise, despite the influences on him.

So too people we love, respect, need or fear usually exercise a significant
influence on us, but only in the most extreme circumstances (e.g., brain-
washing, insanity) can we legitimately claim that our thinking and willing is
no longer our own. Again, others certainly share the moral responsibility of
the behavior they influence, but they do not own all of it.

Moral responsibility is always shared broadly, but generally not equally.
All things being equal, the self-determining agent most directly involved in

---

[34]Though Origen acknowledged that there may be particular demons involved in particular
vices (e.g., demons of lust, greed and so on.), he was careful to place the ultimate responsibility for how demons affect a person on the person who freely allowed demons to affect him or
her in a particular way (*Commentary on the Gospel of Matthew* 14.21; *Commentary on Romans*
10.31). For Clement's view of moral responsibility, see esp. *Stromata* 2.20 (ANF 2:371-72).
Both Origen and Clement understood that one being could *influence* another without
thereby undermining the moral responsibility of the person being influenced. On the centrality of free will for the early fathers, see chapter one.
[35]"All things being equal" here means barring extenuating circumstances such as exceptional
mental or emotional deficiencies, temporary insanity, and the like. The boy's maturity level is
of course also another variable that would affect our estimation of his responsibility.

the behavior is more responsible than others. It seems, then, that we have no grounds on which to cry "the devil made me do it" any more than we can legitimately cry "the television made me do it," "my upbringing made me do it," or "society made me do it." Though appeal to demonic influence can (and sometimes, I believe, must) at times help *explain* diabolic behavior, it rarely if ever excuses it.

Corruptio Optimi Pessima

Did God overplay his hand? Let it be granted that love entails freedom, that freedom entails risk and that this risk entails moral and social responsibility. Let it also be granted that both humans and angels participate in the cosmic tapestry of risky moral and social responsibility and that this does not undermine human responsibility. We must yet question why God would wager *so much* on both human and angelic freedom: If the wisdom of a poker player is reflected in the fact that he or she never overplays a hand, does it not seem that in the "poker game" of world history, as it were, God has played unwisely? Indeed, in light of the war that rages and the unthinkable tragedies that it produces, it sometimes seems that God has risked, and lost, far too much.

If God grants one agent enough freedom to destroy another agent's freedom—for example, by incapacitating or murdering that one—it seems God has wagered too much on the first agent's freedom. It looks like a bad "bet." After all, the point of giving freedom to an agent is supposedly so he or she would have the potential to love. But what is the point of giving one agent this potential if that agent can use it to override or destroy that same potential in another agent?

If this issue is puzzling regarding the potential destruction of one free agent by another, consider free agents such as Hitler, who have misused their morally responsible freedom to rob millions of people of their lives and thus of their potential to love. This agent was purportedly given freedom so he would have the potential to love, but he was allowed to use this freedom to undermine the same potential for millions of others. On the surface this appears to be outrageously bad providential planning.[36]

The principle of proportionality. The most plausible solution to this problem lies in a further analysis of the necessary implications of the possibility of love in contingent beings. I have argued that love entails freedom (TWT1), risk (TWT2) and moral responsibility (TWT3). I would now add

---

[36]So wonders Susan Anderson, "Plantinga and the Free Will Defense," *Pacific Philosophical Quarterly* 62 (1981): 279-80.

that the scope of this responsibility, this potential to bless or to curse, must be proportionate to the potential to love. As the fourth structural thesis of the trinitarian warfare theodicy, therefore, I submit that *moral responsibility is proportionate to the potential to influence others* (TWT4).

This thesis stipulates that the greater the potential a contingent agent has for love, the greater the potential this agent must have for the opposite of love. If TWT2 says, "Nothing ventured, nothing gained," TWT4 goes further and says, "The more that is ventured, the more that can be gained—or lost."

This insight is hardly new. Aristotle expressed it when he noted that because we are capable of "law and justice," humans have the potential to become better or worse than any other animal.[37] The thesis was essentially expressed in medieval theology by the phrase *corruptio optimi pessima:** "the corruption of the best is the worst." It is intimated in the words of Shakespeare's ninety-fourth sonnet: "Lilies that fester smell far worse than weeds."[38] It is also evidenced in Jesus' teaching that much is required from those to whom much is given (Lk 12:48) as well as in Paul's instruction that leaders must have higher qualifications and be held to a higher level of accountability than others (1 Tim 3; Tit 1:6-8). When people who have the capacity and moral responsibility to bless many fail to do so, their extraordinary potential to bless becomes an extraordinary capacity to harm. Hence these people require greater accountability and deserve more severe judgment if they fall.

The principle of proportionality in one form or another is evident everywhere we look. Careful observation shows that *"every increase in the capacity for good means a similar increase in the capacity for evil,"* as David Griffin has argued.[39] The benefits of television, for example, are balanced by the ill effects it can have on children, especially when unethical producers continually broadcast as much sexual immorality and violence as they can possibly get away with. So too the Internet has greatly increased the dissemination of

---

[37] Aristotle, *Politics,* in *The Basic Works of Aristotle,* ed. Richard McKeon (New York: Random House, 1941), p. 1130.

[38] Cited in Blocher, *Evil and the Cross,* p. 81.

[39] Griffin, "Why Demonic Power Exists," p. 229 (emphasis original). Richard Swenson recognizes the truth and extreme importance of this principle is in his book *Hurtling Toward Oblivion* (Colorado Springs: NavPress, 1999). Everything beneficial also has a potential to be harmful, he argues, including all areas of human progress. If one concentrates on the benefits of something without taking seriously its potential harm, the negative eventually destroys the good. Our culture, he attempts to demonstrate, has systematically ignored the negative potentiality inherent in our achievements, and there is evidence that our achievements are about to blow up in our faces because of it.

useful information but has also proportionately increased the availability of evil influences and information that can be destructive. Likewise, all the benefits of nuclear energy must be weighed against its capacity to destroy lives with demonic efficiency.

This principle is exemplified throughout creation, as C. S. Lewis observed: "The higher a thing is, the lower it can descend."[40] And again:

> The better stuff a creature is made of—the cleverer and stronger and freer it is—then the better it will be if it goes right, but also the worse it will be if it goes wrong. A cow cannot be very good or very bad; a dog can be both better and worse; a child better and worse still; an ordinary man, still more so; a man of genius, still more so; a superhuman spirit best—or worst—of all.[41]

The fact that certain humans and fallen angels behave in grotesquely evil ways testifies to the enormous potential for love and moral goodness they have, or at least had, in their original created natures.[42] A mother's potential to benefit her children is proportionate to her potential to harm them. The same charisma a leader can use to help thousands can also be used to hurt them. The same creativity and genius that can be used to cure diseases can also be used to invent biological weapons of mass destruction. The potential for diabolical evil in an Adolf Hitler is the inverse of the potential for Christlike love revealed in a Mother Teresa.

The catastrophe of the angel rebellion. The same principle is true of angels, I believe, for they too are (or at least were) free agents. The greater an angel's potential to soar, the greater its potential to fall: *corruptio optimi pessima.* The "stronger [the] angel," Lewis writes, "the "fiercer [the] devil" if the angel falls.[43] Daniel 10 may suggest that a fallen angel's ability to thwart God's will for a nation is directly proportionate to that angel's previous ability to administrate God's will for a nation. Indeed, as Wink observes, this rebel "prince of Persia" was simply continuing to use its God-given

---

[40]C. S. Lewis, *The Great Divorce* (New York: Macmillan, 1946), p. 124.

[41]C. S. Lewis, *Mere Christianity* (New York: Macmillan, 1979), p. 53. Lewis is specifically addressing the issue of why God would risk so much on the free will of Satan.

[42]The potential for love or destructiveness, I will later argue, needs a probationary period to be decided, but this probationary period is not eternal. Contingent creatures spend their potential one way or the other, and once spent we become what we choose. Libertarian freedom gives way to compatibilist freedom conditioned by the character an agent acquired by the use of their libertarian freedom. So far as we can discern, Satan and his fallen angels have finished their probationary period and are now destined to destruction. Psalm 82 may suggest that some of the unfallen angels are yet unsolidified in their character and thus in their destiny. They yet possess libertarian freedom, in other words.

[43]Lewis, *Great Divorce*, p. 97.

authority, but now toward a different end.[44] Along similar lines, according to the earliest interpretations of Genesis 6:1-4 certain angels inverted their God-given potential to bless humanity and thereby contributed to the decay and destruction of the antediluvian race.[45]

Similarly, according to the traditional interpretation of Scripture, Satan was once "the bright morning star" ("Lucifer," Is 14:12-15).[46] He was the pinnacle of God's creation, the one who possessed the greatest potential for good. For this same reason, however, Satan possessed the greatest potential for evil, for though he was the greatest of God's creation, he was nevertheless a contingent creature, which means that he possessed the capacity to choose one way or the other.

Thus, as with all contingent moral creatures, Lucifer's potentially magnificent relationship with God had to be chosen, as Tatian realized (see chapter one). In the traditional view, Lucifer tragically chose to exalt himself rather than offering himself as a gift of love to his Maker, and now Satan has fallen "down as low As high he sor'd, obnoxious first or last To basest things."[47] He has become the ultimate example of the *corruptio optimi pessima* principle!

Why does it seem that God risks so much—sometimes, seemingly, too much—on freedom? According to TWT4, *it is because he is aiming so high*. The depth to which an individual or group can sink is a function of the height to which such a one can soar. If God wants a world where a Mother Teresa is possible, he must be willing to contend with a world in which an Adolf Hitler is possible. Similarly, if God wants a world where a high-ranking angelic officer could wonderfully mediate his providential plan for the cosmos, he must be willing to accept a world that includes the possibility of having a high-ranking angelic officer use this same God-given authority to corrupt the cosmos.

This, I submit, is consistent with the understanding the early postapostolic fathers were working toward prior to the triumph of Augustine's blueprint theology. "The prince of matter" who was "entrusted with the control of matter and the forms of matter," says Athenagoras, now abuses "the gov-

---

[44]Walter Wink, *Unmasking the Powers: The Invisible Forces That Determine Human Existence* (Philadelphia: Fortress, 1986), pp. 89-90. On the nature of the powers involved, see G. L. Archer, "Daniel," in *EBC*, 7:124-25; J. J. Collins, *Daniel*, Hermeneia (Minneapolis: Fortress, 1993), pp. 374-76; J. E. Goldingay, *Daniel*, WBC 30 (Dallas: Word, 1989), pp. 291-92, 312-14; Louis F. Hartman and Alexandra A. DiLella, *The Book of Daniel*, AB 23 (Garden City, N.Y.: Doubleday, 1978), pp. 282-84; Ronald Wallace, *The Lord Is King: The Message of Daniel* (Downers Grove, Ill.: InterVarsity Press, 1979), p. 179.
[45]See Boyd, *God at War*, p. 138 and notes.
[46]I argue that the traditional understanding is justified from a historical-critical reading of Scripture in ibid., pp. 157-60.
[47]Milton, *Paradise Lost*, 9:163-71.

ernment entrusted to" him and "exercises a control and management contrary to the good that is in God."[48] No wonder Origen insists that any one "who has not heard what is related of him who is called 'devil' . . . will be able to ascertain the origin of evils."[49]

We have no idea of how glorious Satan might have appeared had he chosen to actualize his potential for loving service to God rather than his potential for rebellion. Neither can we acquire any clear idea of what Mother Teresa or Adolf Hitler might have looked like had they chosen each other's paths rather than the ones they in fact chose. But the extremity of Satan's evil is itself an indication of how much potential for love was thrown away by his fateful decision.

Creating Lucifer was certainly a high-stakes risk. In a microcosmic way, so is entrusting any child to a parent. In the end, such divine risk taking shall prove worth it, at least to God and to all who say yes to him. In the meantime, however, there is war, and, to quote General Sherman once again, "war is hell." For those in the midst of this war who know God, it must suffice to know that he does not will the war, that he is with us in the war, that he can use even our battle wounds to his advantage and that he shall someday end this war and reign victorious over his foes.

Has God wagered too much on freedom? Even if it is granted that the potential for love and goodness must correspond to a proportionate potential for war and evil (TWT4), some may still argue that putting millions of lives at risk for the sake of one person's freedom is an unwise risk, regardless of the potentiality of this person for good. Would any of the six million Jews who suffered under the Nazi regime agree that the possibility that Hitler could have greatly helped the world was worth the risk that he might choose rather to greatly harm the world? Wagering the potential destruction of six million people on how one person will use his freedom seems to be a very poor wager. Wagering the welfare of the entire creation throughout history on the will of one agent (Lucifer) seems even worse.[50]

---

[48]Athenagoras *A Plea for the Christians* 24 (ANF 2:142).
[49]Origen *Against Celsus* 55 (ANF 4:527).
[50]Michael Tooley expresses this objection when he argues that not even "the most ardent admirers of free will would wish to dissent from the claim that when it comes to gratuitously evil actions, it is a good thing to prevent people from successfully performing such actions, and thus to 'limit' the scope of their freedom. A world in which an omnipotent and omniscient being prevented people from performing gratuitously evil actions would still be a world in which people could do evil things—albeit not gratuitously evil things" ("Alvin Plantinga and the Argument from Evil," *Australasian Journal of Philosophy* 58 [1980]: 374-75). I believe my comments in the following sections adequately address this objection.

The objection is weighty and must be addressed.

The shared nature of moral responsibility. Three points may help soften the force of this objection. First, we grossly misrepresent the situation if we portray God as wagering millions of lives on what one free agent packed with potential for good or evil will or will not do. It is obviously as gross an oversimplification to blame, for example, the Holocaust completely on Hitler as it is to blame all the evil of the world on Satan. Evil on a grand scale, like goodness on a grand scale, always involves cooperation on a grand scale. As noted earlier, moral responsibility is always to some degree a shared social reality.

The Holocaust is an excellent case in point. While Hitler certainly bears more responsibility than any other individual for this atrocity, in truth the responsibility for it is widespread. Among other things, the Holocaust could never have occurred were it not for a longstanding tradition of anti-Semitism, mixed with a tradition of Prussian pride that goes back at least to the Middle Ages. Martin Luther in particular bears a good deal of responsibility for his influential, bitter and tragically anti-Semitic publications. Many adults in Nazi Germany and its occupied territories share some responsibility for allowing this nightmare to unfold as well. Even if we grant that many did not know the full scope of the evil they were a part of, and even if we acknowledge that most did not overtly contribute to the evil of the "final solution," relatively few did all they could have done to prevent the evil they saw taking place around them.[51] They were at the very least guilty of the "sin of omission."

Europe and America share some of the responsibility as well, for these nations did not respond as quickly and decisively as they could have to Hitler's advances and to the early reports of the atrocities taking place. Latent anti-Semitism, apathy and a self-absorbed nationalism contributed to this immoral indecisiveness. To a significant extent, the Christian church must also share some responsibility for this atrocity, for the church has entertained anti-Semitism throughout much of its history, and many churches at the time either endorsed Hitler's Nazism or failed to oppose it.

Hence, as influential as Hitler was, he did not possess the potential to slaughter millions of people on his own. It took millions of willing agents over centuries to set the stage for this debacle—and we have not even considered the multitude of fallen angelic agents who were also undoubtedly involved in this event.

---

[51]For a sobering analysis of the crucial role "ordinary Germans" played in the Nazi's "final solution," see Daniel J. Goldhagen, *Hitler's Willing Executioners and the Holocaust* (New York: Alfred A. Knopf, 1996).

The risk God takes in aiming at love, we see, is not unduly leveraged on individuals. The potential for love and the potential for destruction that God gives to his creation are shared potentials. Neither Hitler nor Mother Teresa could have accomplished what they accomplished without a great deal of help from others.

Moreover, we have no reason to assume that the spiritual realm is radically different from the physical realm. Satan's rebellion against God would not have had such an impact if it were not for a myriad of other high ranking dominions and powers who aligned themselves with him in his rebellion. The New Testament does not portray Satan as working alone. His destructive power is not only his own; it is the power of an entire kingdom spread throughout the world. This is why it stands or falls together, as Jesus taught (Mt 12:26).[52]

In sum, the capacity of an individual human or angel to singlehandedly love or destroy many others is somewhat illusory. While there are individuals who, by virtue of their innate potential and place in history, have a greater potential to benefit or harm others, the flow of history is more determined by a myriad of decision makers than by one or two decision makers.

How much is too much? Still, on the basis of the principle of proportionality, the amount of evil influence that individuals such as Hitler exercise seems to suggest that God sometimes wagers too much, even after due consideration has been given to the inherent sociological dimension of each individual's evil achievements. This brings me to my second point.

We must ask how much is too much freedom to give away, and how the "proper" amount is determined. It seems to me that wherever God could have placed the limit on our capacity to love or harm others, our capacity to harm would invariably seem too extreme when fully actualized. The most extreme examples of goodness impress us, and the corresponding extreme examples of evil horrify us, precisely because they are extraordinary. Hence, when we experience extreme examples of evil we naturally have difficulty understanding how any being created by God could be capable of such a thing and wonder why God would wager so much in giving us freedom. We experience it as being too much, precisely because it is far outside normal parameters.

The bottom line is that life is to some extent a gamble, even for God. And when a big gamble is lost it always feels, and should always feel, like too much was wagered. When we lose a person we love profoundly, either by

---

[52]On the Gospels' view of the unity and scope of the satanic kingdom, see Boyd, *God at War*, pp. 180-84.

death or by rejection, it can at the time seem that love was not worth the risk. When parents have children who rebel against them and hurt them profoundly, at the time it seems as though the risk involved in pouring their lives into their children was not worth it. Indeed, God himself seems to experience something like this sentiment when the beings he created and loves so dearly completely reject him. Hence, at one point he was genuinely "sorry that he had made humankind on the earth, and it grieved him to his heart" (Gen 6:6). Yet, while there are genuine loses, God knew that the *overall* risk of love is worth it. Consequently, he did not altogether give up on the human race but recreated them from Noah's family.

We who are created in God's image intuitively know that love is worth the risk. Despite the potential for enormous pain, all of us who are emotionally and psychologically healthy enter into loving relationships. Even after suffering painful rejections—some of which perhaps inspired promises that we will never risk in love again—most of us in time nevertheless choose to love again. Further, those who are healthy instinctively view those who choose not to risk in love as making a profoundly unhealthy decision.[53] Similarly, people continue to bring children into the world knowing full well the potential for pain these children bring with them. Every child is a testimony to our unquenchable faith that love is worth the risk.

If *we* have this faith, how can we question *God's* confidence that love is worth the risk despite the potential for pain? Like us, the Lord knew perfectly well that he repeatedly risked the pain of rejection by those he loved (e.g., Ezek 6:9; Hos 11; Mt 23:37), and he knew even from the start that this love affair would possibly require him to become a human and die a hellish physical and spiritual death on the cross (1 Pet 3:19-21; Rev 13:8). Yet, as with us who are made in his image, God deemed love worth this risk.

The risk and certainty of the prize. This leads to my third point. The wisdom of a risk cannot be accurately assessed by how much one can lose *in any particular instance.* As I have previously noted, when worst-case scenarios become reality, the risk is *not* worth it as it concerns *that particular loss.* However, the wisdom of the risk must be judged by the *quality* of the potential prize, on the one hand, and the *probability* of acquiring that prize, on the other.

We continue to love despite painful losses because we intuitively know that the potential reward of love is what makes life worth living. God does

---

[53]Indeed, if they persist in their self-protective, loveless wall of isolation we view them as sinking into a pathetic form of subhuman existence. I will argue in chapter twelve that hell can be best thought of as the end point of this sinking.

not need any love outside his own eternal, triune identity to make life worth living, but the Lord nevertheless regards the reward of created beings joining him in everlasting, triune celebration as worth whatever losses he and his creation might experience along the way. In other words, God deems the risk involved in creation as being *on the whole* worth it. In creating the world God judged that the quality of the prize was worth the possible, and perhaps even inevitable, pain the venture might cause him and others.

In addition, the probability of acquiring the prize makes the gamble worth it, for, as I have already argued, God was certain from the start that he would be able to acquire the loving bride he seeks. The risk he takes is that any one of his free creations may reject him and thereby destroy themselves and harm others. But as the Creator of their natures and as one who knows perfectly well his own uncompromising character, God could also be certain that this rejection would never be universal. He therefore judged that the probability of winning the prize (in this case, 100 percent) was worth the risk of possible losses along the way.

Conclusion
In this chapter we have examined *how* it is that God can be assured of attaining his overall objectives in creation though every individual agent who makes up this creation is something of a risk. We have also discussed *why* God would consider this objective worth it even though the risk for everyone involved, including himself, is great. He aims high, which means he must risk much, but the risk is wise, for the goal of love is worth it.

The convictions that risk implies moral and social responsibility for free agents (TWT3) and that moral and social responsibility is proportionate to the power to influence others (TWT4) in principle explain why God must allow individual agents, human and angelic, to harm other agents if they so choose. But there are several more particular but very important questions that still need to be addressed if the trinitarian warfare theodicy is to be rendered plausible. Why, for example, does a God who has the power to destroy his opponents at any time allow them to actualize their evil potential for such long periods of time? More specifically, why has God allowed Satan to reign over the cosmos throughout history? Why does he not simply destroy him? We must also question why God at times miraculously intervenes to alter the decisions of creatures while other times he does not. The answers to these questions lie in a further analysis of the metaphysical implications of love among contingent beings.

6

NO TURNING BACK

The Irrevocability &
the Finitude of Freedom

*T*hus far I have argued that love must be freely chosen (TWT1), that love therefore entails risk (TWT2), that this risk constitutes our moral responsibility (TWT3), and that our potential for morally responsible goodness must be proportionate to our potential for morally responsible evil (TWT4).

These four theses take us a long way in rendering intelligible the biblical warfare worldview and thus in understanding how a world created by an all-good and all-powerful God could have become such a nightmare. A number of difficult questions remain, however. This chapter will address three of them: (1) Why does God tolerate the ongoing activity of evil agents? That is, if God has the power to destroy the devil now, why does he wait until the end of the world to do it? (2) Why does God appear so arbitrary in his interactions with free agents, sometimes allowing them to go against his will, other times not? (3) If the potential for love entails a risky potential for evil, is heaven going to be eternally risky? In the course of addressing these questions I will submit the final two structural theses of the trinitarian warfare theodicy.

Why God Must War Against Rebel Agents

We can understand why agents must have the potential to resist God and others if they are to have the potential to love him and others. But why does God tolerate the ongoing evil influence of rebel creatures once they have chosen to rebel against him? Why does God not simply destroy them? Being omnipotent, God must have the power to do so, and it does not seem that doing so would undermine the genuineness of any agent's choice. The purpose of freedom could still be fulfilled, but no innocent people would have to suffer because of another agent's evil choice. So we must question why God chooses to engage in a prolonged and extremely painful warfare with his opponents, as though his resources were finite. I will first examine and critique two ways in which this question has been answered and then propose a third way that I believe is more plausible and more consistent with the trinitarian warfare theodicy.

The greater good. The dominant classical philosophical answer to this question is that God allows his enemies to persist in their evil activity because he can bring more good out of their evil than he could without it. Indeed, this is why he created beings he foreknew would become evil in the first place. In the words of Augustine, God deemed it "more befitting His power and goodness to bring good out of evil than to prevent the evil from coming into existence." Hence God creates and wars against evil agents.[1]

This perspective is traditional, but problematic. While Scripture certainly teaches that God works to bring good out of evil, it nowhere teaches that all evil is ordained or allowed for a specific greater good. This view is also difficult to justify on an experiential level. It forces us to accept that somehow

---

[1] Augustine *City of God* 22.1 (NPNF 1 2:479-80).

the balance of good over evil is increased because kidnappings, rapes and murders are not prevented. But, as Michael Tooley argues, this seems unreasonable. It is asking us to believe that

> if certain free actions of Stalin and Hitler [to say nothing of Satan] . . . had been interfered with, so that their lives had been shorter, or at least less productive, the result would have been a world that either contained more evil, or else a worse balance of good over evil, than that found in the actual world. I think that this claim may reasonably be described as highly improbable.[2]

Tooley's argument is persuasive. If there is another way of making sense of why God tolerates the ongoing activity of human and angelic evil agents, it should be given serious consideration.

A hoped-for universalism. An alternative way of answering this dilemma is to suppose that God tolerates the ongoing destructive influence of wicked humans and angels because he hopes (or knows with certainty) that these rebellious creatures will eventually be won over by his persistent love. This answer certainly resolves the dilemma and is not entirely without historical precedent in church tradition (e.g., Origen, Gregory of Nyssa). Unfortunately, the view is difficult to support from Scripture.[3]

True, there seems to be a certain class of angels whose destiny is not yet resolved for or against God. God thus corrects them, warns them and encourages them to follow his ways, lest they perish (e.g., Ps 82). But the Bible explicitly teaches that Satan and his angels are eternally doomed. These agents will be cast into hell where "they will be tormented day and night forever and ever" (Rev 20:10). As we will see in chapter twelve, the most horrifying dimension of this portrayal of hell is *its finality.* If there is any possibility of repentance and salvation in hell, the Bible does not tell us about it.

It seems that humans can also reject God to the bitter end and be cast into "the lake of fire" (Rev 20:15). Thus Jesus described those who will be rejected on judgment day and go into "the eternal fire prepared for the devil and his angels" (Mt 25:41). So too Jesus taught about a sin that will never be forgiven, "either in this age or in the age to come" (Mt 12:32). Teachings such as these are difficult to reconcile with the universalists' hope.

---

[2]Michael Tooley, "Alvin Plantinga and the Argument from Evil," *Australasian Journal of Philosophy* 58 (1980): 374.
[3]One of the best defenses of universalism in recent times is Jan Bonda, *The One Purpose of God,* trans. R. Bruinsma (Grand Rapids, Mich.: Eerdmans, 1993). See also Thomas Talbott, "The Doctrine of Everlasting Punishment," *Faith and Philosophy* 7 (1990): 19-42; J. R. Sachs, "Current Eschatology: Universalism, Salvation and the Problem of Hell," *TS* 52 (1991): 227-54.

This view also stands in tension with reason and experience as well. If love must be chosen, as I have argued, how could there be a guarantee that all creatures will eventually choose love? As Jesus himself suggests, is not the ability to reject God *now* evidence that the creature will reject God *later* (Lk 16:19-31)? Finally, does not experience confirm that the longer a person persists in a chosen disposition the less (not more) likely he or she is ever to change?

A third perspective. It thus does not seem that the explanation for why God tolerates the ongoing destructive activity of rebellious agents is that they mysteriously contribute to a greater good or that they will eventually turn to God. The remaining possibility, I suggest, is that God *cannot* immediately terminate their existence.

This may initially sound like a denial of God's omnipotence, but it is not. To be sure, if we were to hold that God's inability to immediately terminate evil beings was due to something *extrinsic to God* we would be denying God's omnipotence. But if God's inability is a necessary corollary of decisions he himself has made, then it is the *result* of God's omnipotence, not the denial of it. My contention is that one metaphysical implication of God's decision to create beings who have the potential to choose love or war is that they *must* have the power to exercise their influence over time, for better or for worse.

Agents cannot possess the power to love or harm others without some temporal duration to their power to influence. An influence devoid of temporal duration is a noninfluence. Temporal duration is thus built into the meaning of love, freedom and moral responsibility. Hence, in my view, once God gives the gift of self-determination, he *has to,* within limits, endure its misuse. This constitutes the fifth structural thesis of the warfare theodicy: *the power to influence is irrevocable* (TWT5).

According to TWT5, God engages in a prolonged struggle with creatures when they rebel, not because a greater good comes of it or because he hopes for their salvation (though this is true of human rebels who are not yet irrevocably hardened in their rebellion), but rather because the alternative of immediately revoking their power to influence would undo the morally responsible freedom that is necessary for love.

The irrevocability of self-determination. A simple analogy may help illustrate this thesis. Suppose I give my teenage daughter two hundred dollars for her birthday. If I genuinely give her this money I cannot dictate how she spends it. If I truly give it to her, *she owns it,* which means that she has the power to spend it as she sees fit. If I threaten to retract the money every time she wants to spend it in ways other than how I would spent it, I actually still own the money. I am just choosing to spend it through her.

In the same way, if God truly gives us the gift of self-determination, *we own it,* which means that we have the capacity to determine ourselves one way or another as we see fit. Unless we endure through time as an autonomous self in this decision, we cannot be said to have really been *given* the gift of self-determination. If God were to retract our freedom every time we were about to chose something against his will, then it cannot be said that he really gave us freedom or that we are in fact genuinely *self*-determining.

In short, the *genuineness* of the gift of self-determination hinges on its *irrevocability.* Moreover, since morally responsible self-determination implies a power to influence others, as we have seen, we must conclude that our power to influence others must be to some extent irrevocable. When free agents choose to harm others, to some extent God must tolerate this misfortune.

The extent to which God must tolerate this, it seems, depends on the potential he originally gave to the agent, just as the extent to which I must tolerate my daughter's spending habits depends on the amount of money I initially gave her. The more that is risked, I have argued, the more that can be gained and lost (TWT4). What I am now arguing is that this dual potentiality must have a temporal element to it. If Satan has the capacity to corrupt the cosmos for billions of years, it is only because he originally had the capacity to bless the cosmos for this same length of time. He could not have the former without having had the latter. When he chooses the former, it must be allowed, otherwise he never genuinely possessed the former. To a lesser extent, the same holds true for all free agents. Thus I will refer to each agent's domain of irrevocable freedom as that agent's quality of freedom.*[4]

The necessary ambiguity of moral options. The irrevocability of an agent's quality of freedom seems to be implied in the nature of moral decision making. For a choice to have a moral quality, it seems that the agent who makes the choice must be able to conceive of herself enduring through time as a

---

[4]Brian Hebblethwaite charges that there is a "grave incoherence in the idea that God might be thought to be sustaining a created universe containing fallen irredeemable, nonhuman spirits and allowing them to interfere with the human world" (letter to *Church Times* [June 6, 1975]: 12, quoted in G. Dow, "The Case for the Existence of Demons," *Churchman: Journal of Anglican Theology* 94 [1980]: 205). My thesis answers this charge. It should be noted that in saying that God gave people freedom I do not mean to suggest that God's will was the only variable in determining the quality of a person's freedom, any more than I would want to suggest that God's will was the only variable in determining other facets of their constitution. God works through the creation process, and the process incorporates many influences.

free agent in the decision she makes. That is, a moral deliberation is only possible when the options considered are *viable* options for the agent to live in. Conversely, morally responsible self-determination between options is not possible if one of the options entails immediate self-destruction.

If God's providential program for our world involved the immediate destruction of creatures when they freely turned against God, the decision not to turn against God would basically be coerced. The choice to follow God would be a matter of *survival*, not of *morality*. The choice to love God or not (as well as every other choice between godly and ungodly alternatives) would have the same moral character as the "choice" to breathe or not.[5]

God's design to have creatures who are capable of *moral* decision making requires a sort of covenant of noncoercion* with each of them.[6] Within the parameters of the gift that God has given his creatures—their "quality of freedom"—God allows them to endure as decision-making agents in the course they choose for themselves. This means that his response to their evil choices must, under ordinary circumstances, stop short of coercion. As the early postapostolic church recognized, God's providence must not be dictatorial if it is to be over agents who are free and morally responsible.

God's self-limitation. If we accept the claim that the freedom required by love is necessarily irrevocable, we may understand how it is that God must (given his previous choice to have free agents) tolerate the destructive power of Satan and his fallen angels as well as the evil influence of humans who align themselves with him. It is not that these evil agents mysteriously contribute to the greater good of the cosmos; they do not (though God certainly works to bring good out of evil). Neither is it the case that God holds out hope for their redemption; in the case of fallen angels, he does not. The ongoing destructive activity of rebel agents is simply the dark side of a beau-

---

[5]The choice to commit suicide is a moral decision (when it is done with a minimal level of sanity), but it is the exception that proves the rule. The decision to end one's life, when sane, is the result of either coming to the conclusion that a better state of existence awaits one beyond death or that ceasing to exist is a better alternative than continuing to exist.

[6]Jeremiah 33:20-25 depicts creation in terms of divine covenants. In this passage, the regularity of days and nights is portrayed as being the result of God's covenant with the day and night. The stability and integrity of the natural order, in other words, is the result of God promising to interact with creation in a certain way. For a given period of time God will not alter the regularity of day and night in creation (cf. Gen 9:8-17). I am suggesting that something like this occurs when God through the creation process (involving many variables) creates free creatures. For a given period of time God grants us self-determining authority and binds himself to interact with us in ways that honor that self-determination. He grants us a certain "quality of freedom" and thereby enters into a "covenant of noncoercion" with us. Within limits and for a period of time, he cannot *by his own choice* coerce our decisions.

tiful potential. It is against this potential for ongoing evil, actualized by free agents, that God must genuinely struggle. God could have ensured that this situation would not arise only by creating a risk-free robotic creation in which authentic love and moral goodness would also be impossible.

TWT5 answers the most compelling criticism raised against the notion of a self-limiting, omnipotent God. Tyron Inbody expresses the criticism well when he notes that *"omnipotent power that is self-limiting can also be in principle self-unlimiting any time and any place."*[7] This criticism further argues that there must always be a particular divine reason why God chooses to limit himself, but this leads us right back to the classical philosophical dilemma of wondering what particular good reason God might have had for allowing each particular evil to occur in the world.

The principle of irrevocability answers this charge. In short, there are metaphysical constraints that God cannot avoid when he decides to limit himself by giving nondivine creatures free will, just as there are metaphysical constraints that God cannot avoid when he decides to create anything. If God decides to create two adjacent mountains, he thereby decides to create a valley between them. If God decides to create a triangle, he thereby decides not to create a circle occupying that exact same space. Likewise, if God decides to create morally responsible free agents, he thereby decides to create beings who have the power to influence things for better or for worse *over time,* which entails that God is not free to "unlimit himself" any time he chooses.

Questions about TWT5. TWT5 in principle explains why God cannot always unilaterally intervene to prevent situations that are against his will, but it also raises a number of difficult questions. For example, if God enters into something like a "covenant of noncoercion" when he grants creatures self-determination, and if freedom is to some extent irrevocable, how can we explain biblical examples of God interfering with and even revoking the free decisions of some people? For example, I noted in chapter four that it is difficult to account for fulfilled prophecy unless we assume that the Lord can at times intervene to ensure that particular acts would occur. Similarly, it is difficult to make sense of the biblical certainty that in the *eschaton** God will defeat all those who oppose him unless we assume that God possesses the power to unilaterally revoke the freedom of his opponents. Moreover, the Bible also contains examples of God terminating the life (and thus obviously revoking the freedom) of free agents who had chosen evil. For example, the

---

[7]Tyron Inbody, *The Transforming God: An Interpretation of Suffering* (Louisville: Westminster John Knox, 1997), p. 143; cf. p. 149.

Lord struck Ananias and Sapphira dead for lying to the Holy Spirit (Acts 5:1-11), and Herod was struck dead for his arrogance (Acts 12:20-23). Indeed, on a much larger scale, God ordered the termination of the wicked Canaanite population and carried out destructive judgment on most of the human race when he sent the flood.

Where was God's "covenant of noncoercion" in these instances, one might ask? This brings us to the second question we are concerned with in this chapter: Why does God appear so arbitrary in his interaction with free agents, sometimes allowing them to go against his will, other times not? The answer to this question, I believe, is to be found in the innumerable contingent variables that surround an agent's quality of freedom. In order to expound these we must turn to the sixth and final thesis of the trinitarian warfare theodicy.

The Finitude of Freedom

TWT5 stipulates that *to the extent* that humans or angels are self-determining, to *that* extent their moral responsibility must be irrevocable. It does not stipulate how broad or narrow, how long or short, the extent of an agent's self-determination has to be. Nor does it stipulate the conditions on which an agent's self-determination is or is not irrevocable. TWT5 thus does not entail that God can *never* exercise coercive power in his interactions with free creatures. Nor does it entail that creatures have the power *eternally* to exercise an evil influence on the creation.[8] TWT5 simply says that self-determination and irrevocability are two sides of the same coin. A creature's potential for love must be balanced by an irrevocable potential for evil. The greater the one, the greater the other. The quality of freedom, in short, must cut both ways. *Corruptio optimi pessima.*

TWT5 thus does not contradict the biblical portrayal of God occasionally intervening unilaterally in the world or the clear biblical teaching that God will ultimately be victorious over his foes. God could only be prevented from intervening and winning in this way if the gift of freedom that he gave creatures was unconditional in nature and *unlimited* in scope or duration.

---

[8]This refutes Michael Martin's objection to the free-will defense that "since the evil that could result from the misuse of freedom is potentially unlimited, freedom would have to be considered virtually of infinite value." Freedom is not of infinite value, however, hence Martin concludes that God is not justified in permitting evil for this reason. The fact of the matter is that freedom among contingent agents is never unlimited, for contingent agents are, by definition, finite (*Atheism: A Philosophical Justification* [Philadelphia: Temple University Press, 1990], pp. 365-66). This will constitute the final thesis of the trinitarian warfare theodicy: freedom is finite.

This constitutes the sixth and final structural thesis of the trinitarian warfare theodicy: *the power to influence is finite* (TWT6). This thesis in principle explains why God can intervene in the world *sometimes*, but not *always*, and why God can be assured of *eventually* winning the cosmic battle, but not *immediately*. We will see that TWT6 in principle also explains why we can never know the extent of an agent's freedom and thus why God's interactions with free agents must usually *appear* arbitrary to us. Three considerations help confirm this thesis.

Arguments in favor of finite freedom

The argument from the nature of contingent creatures. TWT5 refers to the potential for love among contingent beings. Contingent beings are, by definition, beings who could be, or at least could have been, other than they are. Contingent beings are by definition finite, for they are delimited in every respect by what they are not.

If we consistently develop the nature of this contingency, I believe we will see the cogency of TWT6. It is impossible to conceive of contingent beings possessing a quality of freedom that is unlimited in time or scope. We would have to conceive of agents who are restricted in every respect except in their capacity to choose. The very notion of unlimited freedom for a contingent agent seems to contain a contradiction. A contingent being is by definition one who is *this* being rather than *that* being, which means that a contingent being is one who *does not choose* to be this being rather than that being. Their range of options is predicted on their contingent identity, which means it is inherently restricted. Stated differently, contingent beings are those who by definition could have been otherwise, and this entails that the range of options available to them (what I have been calling their "quality of freedom") could have been otherwise. Like every other process we observe in the world, our freedom is contingent and finite.[9]

The argument from the wisdom of God. Even if it were logically possible for God to give contingent beings a capacity to resist him that was unlimited in time and scope—that is, an unrestricted quality of freedom—it would be extremely unwise for him to do so. The owner of a company may give away or sell many shares of the company so that others might have say-so in the future of that company. But a wise owner who cares about the future of the company would not give away so many shares, so much say-so, that he or she becomes a minority stockholder.

---

[9]This is not to say that the *consequences* of free creatures' decisions cannot be eternal. The biblical teaching on heaven and hell would not be intelligible if this were the case.

Likewise, if we believe that God's aim in creation was to have nondivine creatures participate in his triune love, we may conceive of him, the original owner of all power, distributing "shares" of say-so among the participants in the vast human/angelic society of contingent creatures. These creatures must be capable of choosing *against* him if they are to be capable of choosing *for* him. But if God is in fact perfectly wise, we cannot conceive of him giving away more "shares" of his power than he could possibly control on a general scale. God is willing to take appropriate risks, as we have seen, but his risks are always wise. It seems that the all-wise Creator would at the very least keep enough "shares" so that the overall flow of history and the attainment of his ultimate aim in creation would remain within his power. He wants "shareholders" in his cosmic company, if you will, but he also wants to guard against a hostile takeover.

If God is perfectly wise, then, all free agents have *some* degree of irrevocable say-so, but none of them individually, nor all of them taken together, possess say-so greater than or equal to God's.[10] Their freedom is wisely limited in time and scope. The quality of their freedom can never rival the quality of God's freedom. Again, given what he could achieve by it, it was wise for God to take a genuine risk in giving creatures self-determining freedom, but given what he could lose in creation, God wisely restricted the extent of the risk he was willing to take. Consequently, although there is an irrevocable dimension to the quality of freedom of every morally responsible agent and God must genuinely struggle against it when agents use this freedom against him, the dimension itself is finite.

The argument from experience. The conviction that self-determining freedom is finite in scope and duration is confirmed by our own experience. We all know that the scope of our freedom is restricted by factors such as our genetic makeup, the environment we were raised in and the free will of other agents. We also know that the range of options available to us tends to decrease with time, which suggests that the duration of our self-determining freedom is finite as well. Augustine was simply reflecting familiar ancient wis-

---

[10]Some argue that if any entity is distinct from God, whether we are considering archangels or quantum particles, it must have *some* degree of autonomous say-so. A truly zero instance of power is equivalent to nothing distinct from what has power over it. Hartshorne argues, for example: "The idea of X making Y's concrete decisions or fully determining Y's action or change is merely verbal, says [sic] nothing consistent" (*Creative Synthesis and Philosophic Method* [reprint, Lanham, Md.: University Press of America, 1983], p. 271). On this basis I argue that strict Calvinism logically entails pantheism. See my *Trinity and Process: A Critical Evaluation and Reappropriation of Hartshorne's Di-Polar Theism Towards a Trinitarian Metaphysics* (New York: Lang, 1992), pp. 257-58.

dom when he noted that our choices become our habits, and our habits eventually become our character.[11] According to C. S. Lewis, this is the primary function of free will. It gradually determines the kind of person one will finally be.

> Every time you make a choice you are turning the central part of you, the part of you that chooses, into something a little different from what it was before. And taking your life as a whole, with all your innumerable choices, all your life long you are slowing turning this central thing either into a heavenly creature or into a hellish creature.[12]

We all experience this process of character solidification, according to Lewis. Speaking as George MacDonald trying to enlighten condemned people, he says:

> It begins with a grumbling mood, and yourself still distinct from it: perhaps criticizing it. And yourself, in a dark hour, may will that mood, embrace it. You can repent and come out of it again. But there may come a day when you can do that no longer. Then there will be no you left to criticize the mood, nor even to enjoy it, but just the grumble itself going on forever like a machine.[13]

According to Lewis, all people are ultimately in the process of becoming solidified either as "a creature that is in harmony with God . . . other creatures . . . and with itself," or as a creature "that is in a state of war and hatred with God, and with its fellow creatures, and with itself."[14] This is why I refer to life in this epoch as a "probationary period." We are now deciding the kind of eternal beings we will become. In this period we make

---

[11]Augustine, *Confessions*, trans. Henry Chadwick (Oxford: Oxford University Press, 1991), 8.5.141. Kant argued along these lines in *Religion Within the Bounds of Reason Alone*, trans. Theodore M. Greene and Hoyt H. Hudson (New York: Harper & Brothers, 1960), pp. 54-72; cf. Robert Kane, *The Significance of Freedom* (New York: Oxford University Press, 1996), pp. 34, 39, 42, 181. One of the most insightful analyses of the way in which human character can be irreversibly formed in its choices for sin is Søren Kierkegaard's *The Sickness unto Death*, trans. W. Lowrie (Princeton, N.J.: Princeton University Press, 1941), esp. pp. 236-62. On becoming irrevocably evil, see Richard Swinburne, "A Theodicy of Heaven and Hell," in *The Existence and Nature of God*, ed. Alfred J. Freddoso (Notre Dame, Ind.: University of Notre Dame Press, 1983). He notes that "the less we impose our order on our desires, the more they impose their order on us. . . . We may describe a man in this situation of having lost his capacity to overrule his desires as having 'lost his soul' " (pp. 48-49). See also E. Stump, "Sanctification, Hardening of the Heart, and Frankfurt's Concept of Free Will," *Journal of Philosophy* 85 (1988): 395-420; and Jerry Walls, *Hell: The Logic of Damnation* (Notre Dame, Ind.: University of Notre Dame Press, 1992), pp. 117-33.
[12]C. S. Lewis, *Mere Christianity* (New York: Macmillan, 1979), p. 86.
[13]C. S. Lewis, *The Great Divorce* (New York: Macmillan, 1946), p. 75.
[14]Lewis, *Mere Christianity*, p. 86.

choices, though in time our choices make us.

People who are now unalterably bitter, for example, were not born that way, nor did they become that way overnight. They lost their capacity to forgive by repeatedly choosing against it. In time their choice chooses them. "First they will not," C. S. Lewis explains, "in the end they cannot" open their hearts to God's love and forgive.[15] Happily, the same is true for people whose character has by the grace of God become loving. They begin by yielding to God's gracious influence to choose love. They end by *love* choosing *them*. For better or worse, *we irreversibly become the decisions we make*. And this, I submit, is why Scripture describes both heaven and hell as eternal, irreversible states.

In any event, it seems evident that time does not usually increase the availability of options for contingent beings such as us. It rather tends to resolve options one way or another, for better or for worse. Self-determining freedom is always finite and probational. As Lewis again observes, "Finality must come sometime."[16] Self-determining freedom is about what morally responsible contingent beings choose to *do* on their way to deciding what they are going to permanently *be*.[17] Our libertarian freedom is the probationary means by which we acquire compatibilistic freedom either for or against God. So long as we possess self-determining freedom we possess the power to do otherwise. But this power is provisional. It diminishes over time until our *doing* has determined our *being*. It is at this point no longer true that we *could be* other than we are. The only thing that can be said about us at this point is that we *could have been* otherwise.

Character development and grace. The goal of self-determining freedom, I have argued, is to become a person who eternally receives and reflects God's love. The risk is that people may choose to become the antithesis of this. It may prove helpful to place this understanding of probationary freedom in the context of the New Testament's teaching regarding the Fall and God's grace.

---

[15]Lewis, *Great Divorce,* p. 123.

[16]C. S. Lewis, *The Problem of Pain* (New York: Macmillan, 1962), p. 124. The whole of chapter 8 is instructive on this point.

[17]We will consider and illustrate this point further in chapter twelve, though a word of clarification is in order here. To say that our *doing* determines our *being* is only partially true for the believer. At a more fundamental level, what Christians *do* is determined by who they *already are* by virtue of what Christ has *already done for them*. For the Christian, then, *being* most fundamentally determines *doing*, not vice versa. Still, the choice to accept the work of the cross and the transforming power of grace was something the believer had to do (though even this God had to enable; see chapter two). The progress the believer makes in sanctification is also to a certain extent a matter of choice.

As I noted in chapter two, fallen humans are incapable of choosing God on their own. "In Adam," we are a race at war with God and in bondage to Satan (Rom 5:12-14). We are dead in sin and stand under God's judgment (Eph 2:1, 5). It is only because Jesus died for all and the Holy Spirit continually works in our hearts that we are able (but never forced) to say yes to God's love. When we do so we are freed from Satan's power, reconciled to the Father, given a new identity in Christ and empowered to live in right relationship with the Father and the Son. If we persevere in the faith, we are destined to become conformed to the image of Jesus Christ (Rom 8:29).

This clearly refutes any Pelagian notion that salvation or sanctification is something humans are able or required to achieve on their own. To the contrary, both are possible only because we have been graciously given a new identity in Christ that is increasingly manifested as we yield to God. Having been empowered by God, we must choose to accept and yield to God's grace in our life. In this life we do not do this perfectly, which is why we are continually in need of God's forgiveness. Yet as we persevere in this choice, we are increasingly changed "from one degree of glory to another" (2 Cor 3:18). If we do not abandon our faith and forfeit our birthright, we become children who are incapable of losing it, and this, I believe, is the goal of the whole process. God's grace, working through our choices, produces a bride who irrevocably loves Christ and reflects his character.

Conclusion regarding TWT6. I have argued that metaphysical considerations (the nature of contingency), theological considerations (God's wisdom) as well as our own experience affirms the truth of TWT6: *the power to influence is finite.* This implies that self-determining freedom is not an end in itself. Its role is always probational. It exists in this probationary period to irreversibly determine our eternal participation in or exclusion from the kingdom of God. Self-determining freedom ultimately gives way either to a higher form of freedom—the freedom to be creatures whose love defines them—or the lowest form of bondage—the inability to participate in love. We either become beings who are irrevocably open or irrevocably closed to God's love. The former is eternal life; the latter is eternal death.

TWT6 is crucial for the trinitarian warfare theodicy because it alone allows us to render coherent the clear scriptural teaching that the war that God fights in this present age is *not an eternal war.* While we cannot make sense of the genuineness of the war without affirming the irrevocability of morally responsible freedom (TWT5), we cannot make sense of the certainty of God's ultimate victory in this war without supposing that this irrevocability is finite (TWT6). In this way TWT6 allows us to avoid the classical philosophical problem of finding a higher reason for particular evils while also avoiding the Process perspective or the metaphysical dualistic perspective that evil can never be finally vanquished.

TWT6 also provides a plausible explanation of how it is that the possibility of love entails risk without holding that heaven will be eternally risky.[18] So far as it is revealed in Scripture, the final state of agents is irreversible, for better (heaven) or for worse (hell). But precisely because the goal is eternal love, this finality must be preceded by a time of decision making, a probationary period, in which every free agent fixes his or her heart either toward this goal or against it. Those who by God's grace used their irrevocable probational freedom as God intended ultimately become irrevocably aligned with him in love, while those who use their irrevocable probational freedom against God become irrevocably set against him in self-absorbed rebellion. "In the end," Jerry Walls notes, "one either perfects his moral freedom or he perverts it."[19] The possibility of going one way or the other does not last forever, though the irreversible consequences of how we actualize this possibility do (see chapter twelve).

Finally, appealing to the essential finitude of every agent's quality of freedom in principle explains why God sometimes overrules an agent's decisions, despite his general covenant not to do so. Beyond the parameters of the gift of freedom God has given, God may intervene as he sees fit. If I give my daughter two hundred dollars to spend as she chooses, I cannot exhaustively control how she chooses to spend it. But neither am I obliged to allow her to spend *three hundred* dollars as she chooses. I must with integrity honor my gift to her, but having honored it, I am under no further obligation. Likewise, after God's irrevocable gift of self-determination to an agent is "spent," as it were, God is under no obligation to refrain from intervening on the agent's freedom.

Variables conditioning the quality of freedom. Appealing to the finitude of creaturely freedom does not answer all the questions we might have about why God appears so arbitrary in his interactions with free agents, however. On the one hand, some might argue that the principle of irrevocability (TWT5) proves too much, even after being balanced with the principle of

---

[18]See the objection to the free-will defense made in D. A. Carson, *How Long O Lord? Reflections on Suffering and Evil* (Grand Rapids, Mich.: Baker, 1990), pp. 34-35; R. K. McGregor Wright, *No Place For Sovereignty* (Downers Grove, Ill.: InterVarsity Press, 1996), p. 192; cf. also Susan Anderson, "Plantinga and the Free Will Defense," *Pacific Philosophical Quarterly* 62 (1981): 279-80. A profound essay in defense of the view I am defending is J. F. Sennett, "Is There Freedom in Heaven?" *Faith and Philosophy* 16, no. 1 (1999): 69-82.

[19]Walls, *Hell*, p. 131.

finitude (TWT6), for it cannot adequately account for the extent to which Scripture depicts God as intimately involved in the free decisions of people. The suggestion that there is an area where God cannot go, even if only because of previous decisions he himself has made, seems deistic* to some.

Others might argue that the principle of finitude (TWT6) proves too little, even after being balanced with the principle of irrevocability (TWT5), for it does not explain why God's interaction with free agents seems so arbitrary. Let us grant that the scope and duration (the "quality") of our freedom is finite. And let us grant that this in principle explains how God can at times intervene, despite his covenant of noncoercion, on the free wills of agents. We still have made little progress in explaining why God killed Ananias and Sapphira for lying, for example, but does nothing to prevent a child from being abducted. There seems to be no rhyme or reason to God's involvement or lack of involvement in the decisions of free agents.

In what follows I will respond to both of these objections. I will argue that, far from implying deism, the supposition that God enters into a "covenant of noncoercion" when he gives the gift of freedom is what *allows* God to be intimately involved in the lives of creatures. I will also argue that there are discernable reasons why God's interaction with free agents must *appear* quite arbitrary to us.

The answer to both these questions is found by considering the innumerable contingent variables that condition God's interaction with the world. Some of these variables will be better addressed in the next chapter when we discuss the power of prayer, so we will presently consider only those contingent variables that surround every agent's quality of freedom.

What we shall now see is that freedom does not exist in a vacuum. It always exists in a context that significantly constrains and conditions it. By recognizing how these contingent variables do not *determine* the will, we avoid deism (and determinism). By recognizing how these contingent variables nevertheless significantly *condition* the will, we may appreciate why the quality of freedom, and thus the scope and duration of God's covenant of noncoercion toward a given agent, is in principle unknowable. Hence we may understand why God's interaction with creatures *appears* (but in reality is not) arbitrary.

For our present purposes we may organize these contingent variables affecting the exercise of an agent's quality of freedom into five categories.

The quality of freedom is conditioned by the ongoing influence of God. The parameters of an agent's quality of freedom are conditioned by God's ongoing providential influence in his or her life. To claim that an element of our self-determination must be free from God's coercive control does not imply that our self-determination must ever be free *from his influence*. To the contrary, if we are to have a personal relationship with our Creator we *must* be open to being influenced by him, and he by us. At the same time, the personal nature of this relationship also requires that there be a center to us that is not innately *controlled* by him. The genuineness of any personal relationship is found precisely in this balance between one's openness to being influenced by the other while preserving one's distinctness from the other. This principle applies as much to our relationship with God as it does with our spouses, friends and children.

This balance is illustrated both in Scripture and in the experience of believers in their relationship with God. As a passionate groom pursuing and loving his bride or a tender mother caring for her children (Is 49:15-16), God is personally involved in our lives at every moment. Our Lord leads us in ways that are best for us and best for his kingdom. But this leadership is person to person, not puppeteer to puppet. God leads personal beings with a persuasive call, not a controlling force. He wants to be Lord and Lover of persons, not of robots. As Irenaeus said in the second century, "there is no coercion with God."[20] So he graciously grants us the ability to accept or reject his loving lordship. It is, in the end, up to us.

This view of God is as far from deism as any view could be. Precisely *because* God ordinarily opts for a noncoercive relationship with his free subjects, he can be passionately involved in their lives in a personal, influential way. However much he may control aspects of our environment and perhaps even certain aspects of our lives, if his goal is to relate to persons and not robots, he must preserve within us a minimum defining parameter of self-determination that defines our basic autonomy, our nonnegotiable personhood.

By his own decision, the Lord cannot exhaustively control this center of the self. God must honor it with a covenant of noncoercion if we are to remain personal agents in our relationship with him. This freedom is, I believe, the core of what it means to be made in the image of God. Furthermore, far from threatening God, this freedom constitutes God's greatest achievement. As C. S. Lewis argued, God's omnipotence is most magnificently displayed in his ability and willingness to create beings who are actu-

---

[20]Irenaeus *Against Heresies* 5.37 (ANF 1:518). See also *Epistle to Diognetus* 7.4, in *The Apostolic Fathers: Greek Texts and English Translations of Their Writings*, ed. and trans. J. B. Lightfoot and J. R. Harmer, ed. and rev. M. W. Holmes (Grand Rapids, Mich.: Baker, 1992), p. 545.

ally capable of resisting him,[21] for it is this capacity alone that makes acceptance of him meaningful and rejection of him possible.

The quality of freedom is conditioned by our original constitution. Agents' quality of freedom is significantly conditioned by the nature they were created with and the parameters of possible roles that the Creator designed for them when they were created.

The Declaration of Independence states that it is a self-evident truth that all people are created equal. From a scriptural perspective this is undoubtedly true in terms of God's love for all people and thus in terms of their inherent worth. But in every other respect nothing could be further from the truth. People are radically *unequal* in terms of the possibilities and potential inherent in every area of their life. Some have outstanding physical or mental capacities others lack. Some even have inherent spiritual aptitudes that others lack. People are not equal in terms of their natural endowments.

The same must be said of people's innate quality of freedom. A person's potential to make a positive or negative impact in the flow of things—the parameters of one's morally responsible freedom—is directly connected to factors that one possesses by "nature." A person's natural intelligence, basic personality and physical abilities are all crucial variables in defining the parameters of one's say-so in the world. All other things being equal, a person of extraordinary intelligence, for example, will probably have broader parameters of possibilities, and thus a greater degree of say-so, than a person with exceptionally low intelligence. Things are never quite equal, of course, for we must also consider all the other variables that condition the moral potential of a person.

In any event, it is clear that people naturally possess unequal degrees of freedom and moral potentiality, just as (and precisely because) they possess unequal degrees of every other characteristic. Insofar as these differences flow from the reproductive process working in congruity with the design of the Creator, they are natural and beautiful. Insofar as they flow from other variables in this war zone that are incongruous with the Creator's design, they are unnatural and hideous (e.g., diseases and deformities).[22] In either

---

[21]"To become . . . capable of being resisted by its own handiwork, is the most astonishing and unimaginable of all the feats we attribute to the Deity" (Lewis, *Problem of Pain*, p. 127).

[22]In this war zone it is difficult, if not impossible, to determine with any confidence the line between what is and is not a part of the Creator's design as well as what is and is not the result of Satan's corrupting influence (on Satan and "natural" evil, see chapters eight through ten). For example, while we might agree that severe retardation is not part of the Creator's original design, since in these instances the brain does not work the way it was designed to work, we do not know what God's original design for a "normal" IQ range was. It may very well be

case, the point holds that though all people are equally loved and valued by God (as we should be toward one another), in all other respects we are profoundly different.

This is one of the many reasons we are unable to understand why God can intervene more decisively in some circumstances than in others. Allow me to illustrate by returning to the analogy of giving two hundred dollars to my sixteen-year-old daughter. If I genuinely give her this money, I noted, I empower her to spend it as she chooses. I give her economic say-so, as it were. If I subsequently intervene to dictate how she spends this money, I thereby reveal that I was disingenuous when I spoke and acted as though I gave her the money. In truth, I am spending my money through her. My gift to her, in other words, is only genuine to the extent that it is noncoercible and irrevocable.

But now consider the following scenario. Suppose I give my daughter this money and then seem to be inconsistent in my interactions with her as she spends it. Sometimes I allow my daughter to spend money however she chooses, even in ways I disapprove of, while other times I stop her from spending her money in the exact same way on the grounds that I do not approve of it! Sometimes I restrict *the kind* of thing my daughter may buy; other times I tell her *exactly* what she must buy. If you as an outside observer were watching me, I would seem totally inconsistent and arbitrary.

My apparent arbitrariness cries out for explanation. The more confidence you have in my character as a fair and consistent father, the louder the cry. This confusion reflects the problem (or at least one aspect of the problem) that we all face in trying to understand God's providential interaction with particular free agents. In both cases we are confined to judging *by external appearances.* Like a person who can only hear one end of a phone conversation, we do not know what went on behind the scenes to explain the behavior.

What actually happened may have been something like this: On my daughter's sixteenth birthday I gave her fifty dollars to spend however she

---

that higher functioning children with Down syndrome, for example, are simply part of God's diverse creational design. My own conviction on this matter is that a person's uniqueness is part of his or her creational design, part of being made in God's image, as long as this uniqueness incorporates some capacity to be self-determining. When an individual's mental capacity falls below this threshold, I believe we must judge this as being incongruous with God's ordinary design for human beings and thus the result of wills other than God's. We must again remember that Jesus always diagnosed birth defects (e.g., blindness, deafness, scoliosis) as Satan's design, not God's. See chapter one and my *God at War: The Bible and Spiritual Conflict* (Downers Grove, Ill.: InterVarsity Press, 1996), chaps. 6-8.

chose. I also gave her one hundred dollars to spend specifically on clothing for the upcoming school year, though I did not care at all what particular articles of clothing she purchased. Finally, I gave her another fifty dollars to buy a particular watch she had picked out ahead of time.

Now, suppose she spent the entire fifty dollars I had given her unconditionally by taking her friends to an arcade. I disapproved of this foolish waste of money, of course, and tried to *persuade* her to spend it differently. But I *gave* her this money with no strings attached. This commitment now formed part of the nonnegotiable givens* of the situation.[23] It was now *her* money, so I could not coercively intervene in the matter without going back on my word and undermining my integrity.

A line was crossed, however, when I caught her spending her clothing and watch money on more arcade games! Intervening in this case constituted no violation of my integrity, for I had stipulated ahead of time the kind of things the hundred dollars was to be spent on and the precise thing the last fifty dollars was to be spend on. This too was part of the "givens" of the situation. My intervention to stop the arcade spending was now justified, whereas it was not before—even though my disapproval for this wasteful expenditure was just as strong earlier as it was now.[24]

I believe our perception of God's interaction with free creatures is similar to this illustration. His mode of operation certainly appears arbitrary. Many times in Scripture and perhaps in our experience, God allows wicked agents to carry out their evil without any resistance. Other times in Scripture, and perhaps in our experience, God's intervening influence is strong, to the point of preventing particular evils from taking place. But this appearance, I submit, should not surprise us given what we know *about what we do not know.* We simply are ignorant of the "givens" of any particular situation. We do not know any agent's quality of freedom. We do not know what went on, and yet goes on, behind the scenes.

What I think we can know is this: If the goal of creation is love, free agents must possess a domain of self-determination that God has covenanted

---

[23]I discuss the concept of the "givens" of a particular situation more thoroughly in the next chapter.

[24]Something analogous to this may be implied when Scripture refers either to the sins of people or God's wrath becoming "full" or "complete." For example, the Lord tells Abraham that his descendants will eventually come back to the land of Canaan, "for the iniquity of the Amorites is not yet complete" (Gen 15:16). Paul likewise refers to the Jews of his day as "constantly . . . filling up the measure of their sins; but God's wrath has overtaken them at last" (1 Thess 2:16; see also Dan 8:23; Hos 13:12; Zech 5:5-11; Mt 23:32). Something like this may also implied by the concept of "the fullness of time" (e.g., Gal 4:4).

not to coerce. This domain is finite, because we are finite creatures. What we cannot know, however, is the quality of freedom any particular agent possesses at any given time. We do not know the scope of any agent's original potential or the extent to which this agent has solidified his or her character through the expenditure of this potential (see below). Nor can we know the extent to which an agent's present state is the result of variables outside of his or her control (e.g., decisions of other free agents) or how a particular agent's freedom is delimited by God's overall providential plan at the present time. In other words, to return to our analogy, we cannot know how much money the father gave the daughter, how much of it was given unconditionally, how much of it was given conditionally, what these particular conditions were, and the like. So of course the interaction of the father with the daughter—God with the free agent—is going to look arbitrary at times.

Now consider how much more arbitrary matters would appear if we were to play out this analogy with two or three other children at the same time. Lacking all the relevant information about who was given how much money under what conditions, and judging only from appearances, no sense could be made of the father's interaction with his children. This, I contend, is why we cannot understand the particulars of God's interaction with people. Indeed, even God's personal interaction with us individually must at times look arbitrary, for unlike my children in this analogy, we do not even know the "amount of money" we ourselves have been given or the terms under which we are allowed to "spend" it. Our own hearts are largely hidden from us (Jer 17:9). Hence, to a certain extent we must remain uniformed "outside observers" even of God's interaction with us (Deut 29:29).

In the end, it must be enough for us outside observers to know that when the father does not stop one of his children's spending, though he disapproves of it, he does so out of his own integrity. Conversely, when he does stop one of his children's spending because he disapproves of it, this too he does out of his integrity. Lacking all relevant information, and thus being incapable of making sense out of the father's interactions, we are forced simply to trust. But note, this trust presupposes that we are already confident that the father's will and character is not arbitrary. It presupposes that we understand that the mystery of the situation lies in our ignorance of the rules of the father's interaction with his children, not in the character of the father himself. So too, as I will subsequently argue, our trust in God's character largely depends on our understanding that the inscrutable mystery of the problem of evil is the mystery of a largely *unknowable creation*, not the mystery of an *unknowable God*.

The quality of freedom is conditioned by previous decisions. The particular decisions that a free agent makes condition the direction as well as the parameters of his or her future freedom. For example, when I was nineteen I believe that the Lord began distinctly to call me away from a career as a professional musician to pursue a career as a full-time teacher and preacher. I resisted the call for several months but finally buckled under the weight of conviction. Like Paul, I know I could have chosen to continue resisting God's call (Acts 26:19). Moreover, I sometimes wonder where I might be today had I chosen to do so. I yielded, however, and now live and minister in the peace of knowing that I am doing what God wants me to do.

That decision to yield to the Spirit's call changed the direction of my life in a monumental, and eventually irrevocable, way. My plans, aspirations, thought patterns and personality began to fundamentally change with this decision; so too the range of options available to me. The longer I journeyed down this new path, the more difficult it became ever to go back and the more unlikely it became that I would ever want to go back. The current of life gains momentum the further it flows.

There have been a handful of major direction-setting decisions like this in my life and (I would guess) seventy or eighty thousand smaller decisions that have played a significant role in bringing me to the place I am today. In this respect, I suspect that I am a rather typical forty-two-year-old. Every free decision I make now is conditioned by and largely constrained by this multitude of past decisions.

Decisions we make in the course of our lives shape the context of our future decisions. Possibilities are open to us now that would have otherwise been irrevocably closed had we previously chosen differently, while other possibilities are irrevocably closed to us now that would have otherwise been open had we previously chosen differently. Like every other process we observe in nature, the ever-quickening current of life flows in only one direction.[25]

---

[25]The observation that freedom is unidirectional and finite is consistent with a number of fields of contemporary science insofar as they are increasingly finding it necessary to incorporate irreversible, temporary processes in their explanations of things. As mentioned in the previous chapter, quantum mechanics is a case in point. The wave of possibilities that characterizes the quantum particle in its superposition "collapses" when measured, and the process cannot be reversed. Many argue that fundamental aspects of chaos theory, complex systems theory, thermodynamics and even recent cosmological theory require a similar postulation of irreversibility and temporality for their intelligibility. For an excellent overview of this tendency in a number of different fields, see Peter Coveney and Roger Highfield, *The Arrow of Time* (New York: BasicBooks, 1990). A seminal work arguing for the irreversibility of time is Ilya Prigogine's *From Being to Becoming* (San Francisco: W. H. Freeman, 1980).

These past decisions not only condition our future choices about what we will *do* in life; they also condition the kind of person we will *be* and even the amount of self-determination we have left to decide this matter. Decisions, however small, are not morally neutral activities. Certain decisions tend to create future possibilities, while other decisions tend to squelch them.

A single decision to love and forgive rather than to continue in hate, for example, begins to open up a world of possibilities in a person's life, whereas a single decision to hate rather than to forgive begins a process that, if continued, eliminates certain possibilities. A person's capacity to lovingly influence others and to be open to their love is significantly conditioned by the cognitive and emotional patterns that person has freely chosen in the past. So is a person's capacity to harm others or to be closed to their love.[26]

It should be evident, then, that a person's quality of freedom is not static. The amount of self-determination and say-so we have in deciding our own destiny and in influencing the destiny of others is partly a function of what we have done with our self-determination in the past. While some of the quality of freedom we enjoy is decided by factors outside of our control (see the first and second variables above), much of it is, or at least was, within our control. Thus our previous decisions form yet another "given" of every situation in which we are involved.

Our difficulty in utilizing this information to understand God's interaction with free agents is that we usually know as little about how other peoples' past decisions have affected their quality of freedom as we know about the quality of freedom originally given to them. To revisit my analogy, suppose that I not only give my daughter two hundred dollars under the conditions stipulated above but that I also stipulate that she must invest a certain percentage of her gift in the stock market. I offer her a number of incentives in this venture: the first hundred dollars she makes in the stock market she may spend on clothes; everything over and above this she may spend however she chooses. Suppose further that I, following Jesus' example (Mt 25:14-30), include a negative incentive: if she fails to make a certain amount of money by a certain date I will retract the money given to her for that purpose. Finally, imagine that I offer a similar, though scaled-down, arrangement to her two younger siblings.

Imagine how bewildering it would seem if you observed my interactions

---

[26]If heaven and hell are the zenith of both of these tendencies, we may construe heaven as maximum openness toward others (love) and hell as maximum closedness toward others (isolation, alienation and apathy). This, I argue in chapter twelve, is one of the most fundamental ways heaven and hell can and should be contrasted.

with my three children without possessing any of this information. The three children all have different amounts of money, but you do not know how much of it was originally given to them, how much of it (if any) they made for themselves or how much of it (if any) they have already spent. Sometimes I allow them to use their money however they please, even though I disapprove. Other times I stop them from using it however they please, precisely because I disapprove. You, however, have no idea why it is one way sometimes and a different way at other times. Sometimes I direct my children regarding how they can spend their money, other times not. Sometimes I direct one, but not the others—with no apparent equity between the three children. Finally, sometimes, apparently without notice, I simply retract portions of the money from one or more of them.

Though none of this would make any sense to an outside observer, *it is not arbitrary.* It actually makes perfect sense, *but only if one knows all the variables and the "givens" of the situation.* One of these variables is that the amount of money any particular child has, and the way I interact with his or her spending of this money, is conditioned on what that child has already done with his or her money. Knowing this principle will help you trust that I am a good and fair father, though I appear capricious to an outside observer. But you will not understand why I am acting one way toward one child and an apparently contradictory way toward another child. To understand this you would have to know not only the principles but also all the relevant variables (e.g., how much each was originally given, under what conditions, and so on).

This, I believe, is precisely the situation we are in as we observe God's interactions with free subjects from the outside. We can know some of the principles on which God operates and thus can trust God despite appearances, but we are simply not in a position to know most of the relevant facts that would explain the specifics of his interaction in any given instance. The principle that all free agents have a domain of self-determination that God cannot simply revoke is evident, in my opinion, but beyond this basic principle it is hard to say anything with certainty.

In the end we must trust that when the Father tolerates wickedness, he does so out of his integrity. When he puts an end to it, he does this out of his integrity as well. Whatever good he can do, he does. Whatever evil he can prevent, he prevents. Whatever he must out of integrity allow, he allows.

The quality of freedom is conditioned by other agents. As I have already observed, an agent's quality of freedom is conditioned by the freedom of other agents, human and angelic. I have argued that the potential to love that free agents are endowed with constitutes their moral responsibility (TWT3). Because we can love others (which means, at the very least, that we can influence their lives for the better), we also have the power to harm them (which means, at the very least, that we can influence their lives for the worse). We should now add that this further entails that an agent's quality of freedom is conditioned by the freedom of other agents. The free society of humans and angels is necessarily a morally responsible society.

This means that any particular free agent's actions affects the freedom of other agents, for better or for worse. This is illustrated in the relationship between a parent and a child. A father who consistently does loving things to his daughter, for example, will generally enhance her quality of freedom. The self-esteem and trust he has cultivated in her will assist her in becoming open to others and in pursuing loving possibilities. A father who consistently does unloving things to his daughter, however, will generally diminish her quality of freedom. Her low view of herself and mistrust toward others will make it less likely that she will be open to loving, healthy relationships with others or pursue loving possibilities. The nature of moral responsibility entails that we (and angels) can truly influence each other, for better or for worse.

This means that God's design, our original constitution and even our previous choices are not the only variables contributing to God's interaction with free agents. We must also consider what else is going on in the human and angelic society that might be affecting both the freedom of a particular agent and God's interaction with that subject. The quality of freedom, in other words, is not a static thing given at birth and remaining constant through life. Freedom is a dynamic reality largely defined by its relationship to everything else.

The amount of freedom a particular agent has at a particular moment, therefore, is a function of decisions other free agents have made as well as the result of God's planning and the agent's own previous decisions. All the people who have ever loved or hated that agent, and all those who could and should have loved that one but did not or even did not do so as consistently or as deeply as they should have, contributed to this person's present quality of freedom. They thus share some level of responsibility for who that agent is and who he or she is becoming.

As I have already argued, this principle of social responsibility applies to the angelic realm as well. After all, angels are given charge over us (Ps 91:11-12; Mt 4:6; 18:10; Heb 1:14) and can, according to Scripture, carry out this duty well or poorly (Ps 82). How they decide to carry out their duties affects our lives individually and corporately—including our quality of freedom.

Indeed, even their interaction with each other (e.g., warfare in heavenly places) can affect our lives (Dan 10).

The point to be taken from all of this is that TWT5 (the irrevocability of freedom) must be understood in light of TWT3 (the moral responsibility of freedom). More specifically, we cannot understand God's covenant of non-coercion with any individual agent without understanding God's covenant of noncoercion with every *other* agent. The choices any particular agent makes have consequences for the quality of irrevocable freedom for all the others. What is more, according to TWT4 (the principle of proportionality), the greater the quality of morally responsible freedom an agent has in relation to another (e.g., parent to child, Lucifer to humans), the greater the consequences the exercise of this freedom will be for the other agent.

To understand the specifics of God's interaction with a free agent, therefore, we would have to understand everything about that agent's relationship to *all other* human and angelic agents, especially those who are most closely associated with that particular agent. We may begin to realize how incomprehensibly complex the situation is by returning to our previous analogy regarding my monetary gifts to my children.

Suppose that in order to teach my children about the risky interconnectedness of morally responsible beings, I set things up so that all my financial interactions with them were not only dependent on the conditions and stipulations I gave them individually but also on, for example, what happened to various stock traded on the stock market. For example, suppose that I stipulated as part of my gift to my oldest daughter that whenever a certain stock rose more than 5 percent I would increase whatever money she had already earned by 10 percent. Whenever the stock dropped 5 or more percent, however, I would withdraw 10 percent. Imagine that I made similar arrangements with her in the event that the stock rose 10 or 20 or 30 percent and so on. Imagine, now, that I made similar arrangements with her in relation to every stock traded on the stock market. Finally, imagine that I did this under uniquely arranged terms with my other children as well.

If my financial interactions with my children seemed arbitrary to an uninformed observer before, they must now seem impossibly confusing. Unless observers were told about the connection between my behavior and the stock market, they could never surmise it from their own observations. Even after being informed of such a connection, they could not begin to understand any particular behavior of mine unless they knew how every *particular* stock affected every *particular* interaction and unless they knew on a moment-by-moment basis how each particular stock was performing.

In short, we can know the *principle* that there is a connection between our Father's interaction with us and the "stock market" of the cosmic society of free agents, as it were. We can even know *why* there *must* be this connection (i.e., moral responsibility). But in this probational epoch we cannot know much about the details of this broader "stock market" and how it impacts us. To be sure, Scripture offers some valuable information about how the cosmic network of relationships functions, and simple observation can teach us other things. For better or for worse, for example, parents affect children, spouses affect each other, friends affect friends, pastors affect congregations, government officials affect common citizens, angels affect humans and the war between God and Satan, which encompasses the war between all the angels, affects everything. However, we can know nothing beyond such general points.[27]

Once again we are led to the conclusion that we must trust in God's character, despite appearances, not because his character is mysterious, but because the world is so complex. For now we must be content knowing that the all-good God does all he can to further good and hinder evil. If we could see the big picture we could understand why this heart of love is sometimes manifested and sometimes not. We would also see the difference that our decisions make in how God's love is manifested in any particular situation. This leads to a fifth variable.

The quality of freedom is conditioned by prayer. That is, the quality of an agent's freedom can be strongly conditioned by God in response to prayer. Because this topic is so important, I devote most of the next chapter to it. At the present time I will simply mention it.

Scripture teaches and the experience of believers repeatedly confirms that one of the most important variables God has structured into the nature of creation is the power of prayer. God has significantly bound himself to the power of prayer, so much so that there are things he would like to do that will not be done unless people of faith pray. This means that in any given instance one of the factors determining the extent to which agents can carry out their own decisions is prayer: their own prayer, prayer for them and prayer by and for all parties who would be most affected by their decisions. Thus, prayer is one of the "givens" that factor into the if, when and how of God's intervention into any particular situation.

To return to my analogy one last time, imagine that my children were receiving anonymous financial gifts from friends and relatives all the time, gifts that had stipulations and conditions associated with them, just as my

---

[27]An exception to this is when God imparts a "word of knowledge" to a believer (1 Cor 12:8).

original gift of two hundred dollars had. Let us suppose that outside observers knew nothing about this. They could only see that sometimes one or more of the children had somehow acquired more money than they previously had, that sometimes they could spend this extra money as they wished, though sometimes not. An observer might assume that I was once again arbitrarily giving one or more of the children extra money and arbitrarily determining how they at times spent it. In truth, however, the seemingly capricious flow of extra cash was due to the financial condition and personal decisions of other people, not to my fickle character.

Something like this, I believe, is true of prayer. Part of the moral say-so with which God has endowed every human (and perhaps angelic) agent is the ability to influence things through prayer. According to Scripture, our petitionary prayer for people and for situations powerfully affects things. But, like the gifts my daughters received, it is a "behind the scenes" affect. It is therefore easily overlooked or underestimated. Yet the amount of freedom any agent has over another is partly conditioned by it. For example, who would have suspected that the flow of the Israelites' battle with the Amalekites was most decisively due to whether or not Moses had his hands raised in prayer (Ex 17:11-13)?

The quiet, unobserved and usually anonymous power of prayer provides yet another reason why we should not be surprised that we cannot understand the rhyme or reason of why God interacts with free agents as he does. Together with the unknown variables of God's providential guidance, our original constitution, our previous decisions and the freedom of other agents, prayer contributes to the total context in which any given free decision is made, for freedom never occurs in a vacuum. God seems arbitrary, not because he is arbitrary, but because the world he interacts with is unfathomably complex.

The blueprint worldview takes of all of these "givens" and all the mystery that surrounds them and packs them into God's plan for the world and his character. The world looks arbitrary because God's blueprint is so mysterious. By contrast, the trinitarian warfare worldview locates the mystery of the apparent arbitrariness of God and of life in the vast complexity of the world. If we saw what God sees, we would understand why God did what he did and we would see that he is always concerned with maximizing goodness and minimizing evil.

Conclusion

With this chapter I have completed my attempt to render intelligible the trinitarian warfare worldview and thus the trinitarian warfare theodicy. To the previously discussed theses that *love entails freedom* (TWT1), *freedom entails risk* (TWT2), *risk entails moral responsibility* (TWT3) and *moral responsibility is proportionate to the power to influence* (TWT4), I have added the theses that *the power to influence is irrevocable* (TWT5) and that *the power to influence is finite* (TWT6).

If these theses are accepted, I contend, we can make sense out of the fact that a world created by an all-good and all-powerful God could become a nightmarish war zone. In contrast to all blueprint theodicies, within the trinitarian warfare theodicy we need not assume that there is a specific, good divine reason why God ordains or allows each specific evil event to take place. The only reason God allows free agents to engage in evil deeds is that this possibility is *what it means* to create agents free. The specific reasons why these agents actualize this possibility in particular ways is found in them, not God. If God is justified in risking freedom in general, we need not ask why God allowed any particular event. To be sure, God can use evil agents to fulfill his purposes, and he always works to bring good out of evil. But God's specific way of *responding to* a particular evil must not be confused with God specifically ordaining or allowing a particular evil.

If the six trinitarian warfare theses are accepted, we can also begin to make sense of the fact that God is assured of winning the war, though many particular battles have yet to be decided. We can further understand why God must tolerate for a time the evil activity of rebellious agents, how it is that love must be risky now but not in heaven, and why it is that God's interaction with his creatures appears so arbitrary.

In short, these theses take us a long way in explaining Satan and the problem of evil, for Satan represents the paradigmatic case of a free agent turned bad. God created Lucifer free, for he created him with the potential to love (TWT1). This meant that there was a risk involved in creating Lucifer (TWT2), as there is with every free agent, for Satan's potential to become evil and to harm others had to be proportionate to his potential to become loving and to bless others (TWT3-4). Unfortunately, Lucifer chose an evil course that God must tolerate (TWT5) until the power of Satan's influence is spent (TWT6). The incredible amount of destruction Satan has brought about in God's creation is a testimony to the vast amount of love and benefit he could have brought had he chosen a different path. God could not have hoped for the former, however, unless he was willing to risk the latter.

The war-torn nature of our cosmos reflects this tragic fall and ongoing war. Satan's fall was catastrophic, which is ultimately why we experience catastrophic horrors in this world. Yet this fall was not altogether cataclysmic, for even in this worst-case scenario God is still victorious. Though he must now operate in a terrible war zone, God's goal of acquiring a bride cannot be thwarted. Satan and all who align themselves with him will ultimately be overthrown, and God and all who align themselves with him will ultimately reign victorious.

This completes part one of this work. What remains in part two is to apply these theses to four perennial issues related to the problem of evil: miracles, prayer, "natural" evil and hell. In the next chapter we will consider the first two of these issues. The question we will address is this: If humans and angels have as much irrevocable say-so as the trinitarian warfare theodicy ascribes to them, can we affirm the biblical truths that God can perform miracles and answer prayer? Given the centrality of miracles and prayer in the biblical witness and in the history of the church, this is no minor question.

In the following chapter I argue that, not only does the trinitarian warfare worldview allow for miracles and the effectiveness of prayer, but that it is the view that makes the most sense out of the apparent arbitrariness of God performing miracles and answering prayer. I believe it is also the view that makes the most sense out of the urgency that Scripture attaches to prayer. The very same reasoning that renders evil intelligible also renders miracles and prayer intelligible. I turn now to defend this claim.

PART II

7

PRAYING IN
THE WHIRLWIND

Miracles, Prayer &
the Arbitrariness of Life

My Father, if it is possible, let this cup pass from me;
yet not what I want but what you want.
JESUS, MATTHEW 26:39

If we are to take the biblical understanding seriously at all, intercession . . .
changes the world and it changes what is possible to God.
W. WINK, ENGAGING THE POWERS

Enemy-occupied territory—that is what this world is.
Christianity is the story of how the rightful king has landed,
you might say landed in disguise,
and is calling us all to take part in a great campaign of sabotage.
C. S. LEWIS, MERE CHRISTIANITY

While the past is fixed, the future remains open and we rediscover the arrow of time.
Chaos theory takes us from a deterministic description of the world
based on predictable behavior to one that is couched in terms of probabilities.
P. COVENEY AND R. HIGHFIELD, THE ARROW OF TIME

*I*n contrast to any view of God as detached from creation (e.g., deism), biblical theism emphasizes God's ongoing involvement in the world. In contrast to any view of God as inherently limited (e.g., Process thought), biblical theism teaches that God is the originator of all power and that he accomplishes seemingly impossible feats in the world (Mt 19:26; Mk 14:36; Lk 1:37). Finally, in contrast to any view of God as an impersonal principle (e.g., pantheism), biblical theism emphasizes God's love and personal involvement in our lives.

For these reasons, biblical theists hold that God miraculously intervenes in world history and responds to the prayers of his people. No understanding of divine providence can call itself "Christian" in any historic-orthodox sense of the word if it cannot allow for such personal divine activity. Everything from the doctrine of the supernatural inspiration of Scripture to the call to diligent prayer that has served as the foundation of the Christian worldview and lifestyle depends on affirming this understanding of divine activity. But, I submit, it does not depend on affirming the blueprint model of divine providence. To the contrary, I argue in this chapter that the trinitarian warfare model of providence is able to make better sense out of the biblical understanding of miracles and prayer than the blueprint model. I consider miracles first and then turn to prayer.

GOD ALWAYS DOES THE MOST GOD CAN DO
A Divine Reason for What Does Not Occur
Generally speaking, the classical understanding of omnipotence holds that God can intervene in the world anytime, anywhere and in any way he wants. This is partly why it assumes that God has a specific good divine reason for each event he allows to take place in history. If God wants, it is reasoned, he can prevent any particular event from taking place. Hence, there must always be a divine reason as to why God intervenes when he does and does not intervene when he does not. If one person is healed, for example, and another is not, the final reason for this difference must be located in God's will. If one child is miraculously protected while another is allowed to be abducted, it must ultimately be because it fit God's plan to protect the first but not the second.

This logic lies at the heart of the blueprint worldview and, not coincidentally, at the heart of the problem of evil. If God is all-good and all-powerful, why is his interaction in the world so selective and arbitrary? We touched on the problem in the last chapter and must now probe it more deeply.

The problem of divine arbitrariness is summarized well by Tupper:

> If God really has the power to intervene in nature and history whenever, wherever, and however God chooses, why does God not do so? The monarchical model of a do Anything, Anytime, Anywhere kind of God cannot account for the failure of God to act to prevent a colossal catastrophe or to deliver a segment of vulnerable humanity from some monstrous evil.[1]

---

[1]Francis Tupper, *Scandalous Providence: The Jesus Story of the Compassion of God* (Macon, Ga.: Mercer University Press, 1995), p. 60.

More specifically, the classical philosophical "monarchical model," as Tupper labels it, makes it difficult consistently to view God as the all-good God who is decisively revealed in Jesus Christ, for this monarchical model does not allow us consistently to say that God does all he can to bring the best for his children and to protect them from harm. To be sure, classical theologians have usually wanted to maintain the view that God always does the best thing. But the claim becomes problematic and the ascription of perfect goodness to God becomes ambiguous when God's "best" results in a young girl getting abducted and tortured. If Jesus is our central definition of God, as he must be, this perspective must be judged as untenable, for this is not the kind of "good" Jesus promoted. It is rather the kind of thing he spent his ministry revolting against.

The "Givens" of a Situation

The principle driving Tupper's "scandalous" understanding of providence is that "the God of love always does the most God can do" to prevent evil from taking place.[2] Anything less, he argues, would be less than perfect love and perfect goodness. But if God is omnipotent, why then does he not do more? Indeed, why does he not rid the world of everything that is inconsistent with his love? The answer, for Tupper, has to do with the "givens" of each particular historical situation. He writes, "*God always does the most God can do.* Whatever God does, it will be coherent with the givens in the situation, because these givens inevitably condition the action of human agents as well as the response of God."[3] Again, "In every critical situation with its multiple contextual variables God always does the most God can do."[4]

Perhaps because of his strongly narrative-oriented theological methodology, however, Tupper never thoroughly develops the nature and necessity of

---

[2]Ibid., p. 279. A similar assessment is made by Jerry Walls: "God's goodness entails that he loves all creatures, impartially desires that all of them be happy, and is willing to do whatever he can, short of overriding freedom, to give happiness to all" (*Hell: The Logic of Damnation* [Notre Dame, Ind.: University of Notre Dame Press, 1992], p. 111). The second-century theologian Athenagoras argued that, in contrast to all appearance of evil in the world (caused by free agents, human, angelic, and demonic), "God, being perfectly good, is eternally doing good" (*A Plea for the Christians* 26 [ANF 2:143]). In Athenagoras's view (and it is at some level shared by most pre-Augustinian church fathers), if something in creation is not good, that is reason enough to suppose that it arises from a will other than God's.

[3]Tupper, *Scandalous Providence*, p. 64.

[4]Ibid., p. 325. Peter Baelz also argues that in every situation "God is already doing all that Love can do" (*Does God Answer Prayer?* [London: Darton, Longman & Todd, 1982], p. 28). Were this not the case, God's love would not be perfect love.

these "multiple contextual variables." He does not probe behind the narrative of what God does to explore the possible metaphysical conditions that render this behavior intelligible. In my estimation, the depiction of a God who is purportedly all-powerful and perfectly loving but whose best effort is yet not ideal is plausible only to the extent that these metaphysical variables that condition his intervening behavior can be identified, developed and rendered plausible. When one believes that God is the Creator of all that is, as Tupper does, it is simply not enough to say *that* God does all he can do. One needs to explain *why* God cannot do more.

Tupper occasionally addresses this, as when he speaks of the self-limitation God imposes on himself in order to give space to the free creatures he has created.[5] This explanation is true enough, but it requires further investigation. For example, how does this principle alone explain why the prayers for one child's protection are answered while the prayers for another are not? We are left with Inbody's criticism of the self-limitation perspective, that "*omnipotent power that is self-limiting can also be in principle self-unlimiting any time and any place.*"[6] So why does God "unlimit" himself some times but not others? This is the same problem we face in the blueprint model of providence.

Understanding the "Givens" of a Situation
The model of providence I have constructed throughout the last few chapters is in most respects consistent with Tupper's (though he unfortunately does not make the connection with Scripture's warfare motif). However, I believe that the analysis of the nature of love developed throughout part one, and especially our previous discussion of the contingent variables of irrevocable freedom in chapter six, help render Tupper's view more coherent and plausible.

Why cannot God, the omnipotent Creator, do whatever he wants, wherever he wants, however he wants? In the terms we have established over the last several chapters, the answer would be that love involves freedom (TWT1) and that freedom involves genuinely open alternatives and thus genuine risks (TWT2). The risk involves other agents, which makes us morally and socially responsible for one another (TWT3). The power to use this responsibility for evil must be proportionate with an agent's potential to use it for good (TWT4), and this power must be, within limits, irrevocable

---

[5]Tupper, *Scandalous Providence*, pp. 324-31.
[6]Tyron Inbody, *The Transforming God: An Interpretation of Suffering and Evil* (Louisville: Westminster Press, 1997), p. 143 (emphasis original).

(TWT5), though finite (TWT6). In every situation, then, God must contend with the quality of irrevocable freedom he has given to each agent, together with all the contingent variables that condition each agent's quality of freedom.

In my view, therefore, God genuinely faces in every particular situation a reality distinct from himself that has some say-so over and against himself. By giving every free agent an irrevocable domain of genuine say-so in the flow of history, God has to that extent limited his own unilateral say-so in the flow of history. God is everywhere and at all times present in his creation maximizing good and minimizing evil. But to the extent that he has given creatures say-so, God has restricted the exercise of his own omnipotence.

The Sociological Nature of the Cosmos

For this reason, God cannot always get his way and cannot always do what he would like to do or what we would like him to do during this probational epoch. There are in fact as many variables to consider regarding any critical situation as there are personal agents involved. Each agent is a center of irrevocable self-determining freedom with which God must contend, and the decisions of each agent are to some extent relevant to all subsequent agents. The cosmos is woven together as a mutually dependent society within which moral and social responsibility is always somewhat shared.

In this sense we must conclude that *every single event* in the cosmos is to some extent a universally influenced, sociologically determined event. Every event within the whole is to some extent influenced by the whole and in turn influences the whole. That is, every act a free agent performs is in part influenced by how every other agent in the cosmos has ever acted, as well as by how the agent herself has acted in the past. Yet, as I argued in chapter two, this universal influence is not determinative insofar as the agent is free, and hence the onus of responsibility for any given act remains with the agent who carries it out.[7]

In this scheme of things, God is always the *most* influential agent

---

[7] My own reflections on the universal, inexhaustibly complex interrelatedness of being has been significantly influenced by systems theorists such as E. Lazlo, *The Systems View of the World: The Natural Philosophy of the New Developments in the Sciences* (New York: George Braziller, 1972); Justus Buchler, *Metaphysics of Natural Complexes* (Albany, N.Y.: SUNY Press, 1990); S. David Ross, *Transition to an Ordinal Metaphysics* (Albany, N.Y.: SUNY Press, 1980); and on a slightly different track, Harold Oliver, *A Relational Metaphysics* (Boston: Martinus Nijhoff, 1981).

directing the flow of history, but he is not and cannot be the *only* agent if, in fact, he wishes to have a cosmos that produces a loving bride and if, in fact, he wishes to preserve his own integrity. He of course predestines and thus foreknows general features of world history, as I argued in chapter four, and, for wise reasons he sometimes decides unilaterally to predestine and thus foreknow even particular events. As the sovereign author of the Choose Your Own Adventure novel of history, God certainly has the ability to do this. But predestining and foreknowing this much about world history still leaves a good deal of room for creatures to have a significant morally responsible "say" in how things transpire.

The Variable of Irrevocable Freedom: Why Doesn't the Lord Prevent Abductions?

With all this in mind, let us consider an actual nightmare in this war zone. Despite regular prayers for her protection by her parents, a seven-year-old girl named Greta was snatched from her neighborhood. Some months later her sexually assaulted, decapitated body was found in a plastic bag by a riverbed. In one moment, life for this young girl and for all who loved her became an unthinkable nightmare, a nightmare that her parents yet endure. How are we to understand this from the perspective of the trinitarian warfare theodicy?

From the perspective of this theodicy, we can be assured that the Lord who created Greta and gave his life on Calvary for Greta and her parents wishes this horror could have been prevented. We need not suppose that God had a particular "good" reason for ordaining or allowing this. Rather, God absolutely and unequivocally detests the terror and pain this little child suffered and the nightmare the parents continue to endure. Indeed, in this view we can assume that at every moment throughout this grisly ordeal God was doing all he could do to stop it. His Spirit was perpetually at work trying to influence the abductor to halt his wicked plan. God's angels also were undoubtedly battling whatever demonic agents were involved in influencing this person to carry out this hideous deed. But in the end, the will of this man was too hardened to the Spirit and too receptive to demonic influences to be altered. As a result, God's will to protect Greta was thwarted.

Why could not the Lord simply decide to override the wills of the human and angelic agents involved in this abduction? It was not because he lacked the power to do so, for sheer power is never the issue with

God. It was rather because of his ultimate goal for creation, because of his uncompromisable integrity and because of the historically contingent particularities (the "givens," as Tupper says) that constitute the situation. God's ultimate goal is to have creatures eternally participate in his triune love. The integrity with which he gives the risky gift of freedom is what makes this love possible (TWT1-3) and renders this freedom irrevocable (TWT4). But this freedom is also what makes nightmares possible. God cannot avoid the possibility of these nightmares without also canceling out the possibility of love. He must therefore tolerate the consequences of how agents use their freedom. Because of his own noble decision to have this kind of cosmos, God cannot guarantee that he will always get his way.

More specifically, we must consider the conditioning variables discussed in the previous chapter. The domain of irrevocable freedom that the abductor, demons and Satan possess factor into the givens of this situation. Indeed, because of the morally responsible interconnectedness of the cosmic society, the quality of freedom of *every other agent* in the cosmos, human and angelic, formed part of the "givens" of this situation as well. The manner in which these morally responsible influences converge to bring about this tragic episode could not simply be terminated by God without rendering the morally responsible nature of all these agents disingenuous. If the situation was to be prevented by God, it had to be by persuasion, not coercion, as the early church fathers understood (see chapter one).

In this light we must conclude that it is at least as true to say that God *could not* prevent Greta's abduction as it is to say that God *chose* not to prevent it. God chose not to prevent this abduction in the sense that he alone chose to create the kind of risky world where this kind of evil could happen. Moreover, because God made this choice, he now could not guarantee that this evil would be prevented. Where free agents are involved, God's omnipotent will can at times be thwarted (Lk 7:30).

The Mystery of Evil
Chaos theory and the mystery of everything. If we ask for specific reasons why God could not prevent Greta's abduction when at other times he intervenes and prevents tragedies, we must simply confess ignorance. To the finite mind it is an impenetrable mystery, pure and simple. But it is crucial to note that in the trinitarian warfare theodicy this impenetrable mystery is *not about God's character or plan,* as in the blueprint worldview.

It is rather a mystery about *the complexity of creation*. Relocating the mystery of evil is, I believe, one of the most distinct features of the trinitarian warfare theodicy.

Since every decision ever made by free agents eventually exercises some degree of morally responsible influence on all subsequent events, the specific givens that rendered Greta's abduction unpreventable are unknowable. They are as complex and unfathomable as all the particular relationships that have formed the morally responsible society of free agents since the beginning of time. While the majority of responsibility for Greta's abduction must be placed on her abductor, an exhaustive explanation of the "givens" that made this particular event unpreventable would necessarily require our having an exhaustive knowledge of the history of every free agent in the cosmos since the beginning of time.

Consequently, the mystery of why Greta was abducted when other children are spared is impenetrable. So is the mystery of any particular evil suffered in this war zone. Why did these particular children get buried in a mudslide and not others? Why did the mudslide occur exactly when it did and not earlier or later? Why did this particular person get cancer, and not another? Why was she healed when another was not? These questions are simply unanswerable from our limited, human perspective.

We can, I believe, attain a *general* understanding of the *kind of things* that render these events possible in God's creation. This is what the six trinitarian warfare theses and the statement of the variables that condition freedom attempt to do. We can therefore know that when evil occurs it is not necessarily the result of a particular good reason God has for allowing or ordaining it. All evil proceeds from wills other than God. But having said this much, we must also recognize that we can never exhaustively know the "givens" of any particular situation and thus can never fully understand why any particular episode unfolds one way while another episode unfolds a different way.

In this respect, evil events are on a par with all other events. That is, an element of impenetrable mystery surrounds every particular contingent feature of our world. Everything ultimately influences everything else, and, as we have seen, there is an element of spontaneity at every level of being. Thus an exhaustive explanation of anything would ultimately require an exhaustive explanation of everything, and even then we would have to acknowledge that things could have happened differently. Only the omniscient God can be certain of why particular events happen precisely as they do.

Chaos theory has something to teach us in this regard.[8] According to this theory, the slightest alterations in the "initial conditions" of any physical process may result in significant differences in the long-term consequences of that process. For example, the flap of a butterfly wing in China may be the crucial variable that produced a storm in New York the next month (this is sometimes referred to as "the butterfly effect"). This principle suggests that in the actual world initial conditions are never exhaustively knowable. Exhaustive knowledge of the initial conditions of any particular physical process would ultimately require an exhaustive knowledge of the history of the universe leading up to that point. One could not understand how the butterfly's flap of a wing produced a storm in New York unless one understood the innumerable variables that factored into this particular butterfly being exactly where it was at this particular time, together with the innumerable variables that factored into this wing flap having the powerful effect it had a month later in New York.

Such information is obviously beyond our finite cognitive capacities. Indeed, we can only experience such an infinite sea of variables as chaos (thus the label, "chaos theory"). This means that we cannot exhaustively

---

[8]For some helpful introductions, summaries and discussions of chaos theory, see James Gleick, *Chaos: Making a New Science* (New York: Penguin, 1987); John Holte, ed., *Chaos: The New Science: Nobel Conference XXVI* (Lanham, Md.: University Press of America, 1993); Grégoire Nicolis and Ilya Prigogine, *Exploring Complexity: An Introduction* (New York: W. H. Freeman, 1989); Ilya Prigogine and Isabelle Stengers, *Order out of Chaos: Man's New Dialogue with Nature* (New York: Bantam Books, 1984); and David Ruelle, *Chance and Chaos* (Princeton, N.J.: Princeton University Press, 1991). Closely related to chaos theory is the newly emerging complexity theory. For introductions, see Roger Lewin, *Complexity: Life at the Edge of Chaos* (New York: Macmillan, 1992); and Mitchell Waldrop, *Complexity: The Emerging Science at the Edge of Order and Chaos* (New York: Simon & Schuster, 1992). As with chaos theory, this field of study is very relevant for our theological understanding of the intricate balance between determinism and indeterminism in God's providence. Some of my own reflections on the implications of chaos and complexity theory for an understanding of providence have been influenced by theorists who have applied chaos and complexity theory to organizational management. Especially applicable to the trinitarian warfare model of providence are J. Colwel, "Chaos and Providence," *International Journal for Philosophy of Religion* 48 (2000): 131-38; Ralph D. Stacey, *Managing the Unknowable: Strategic Boundaries Between Order and Chaos in Organizations* (San Francisco: Jossey-Bass, 1992); and Margaret Wheatley, *Leadership and the New Science: Learning About Organization from an Orderly Universe* (San Francisco: Berrett-Koehler, 1992). See also L. Douglas Kiel, *Managing Chaos and Complexity in Government: A New Paradigm for Managing Change, Innovation, and Organizational Renewal* (San Francisco: Jossey-Bass, 1994); Jeffrey Goldstein, *The Unshackled Organization: Facing the Challenge of Unpredictability Through Spontaneous Reorganization* (Portland: Productivity, 1994); and H. Richard Priesmeyer, *Organizations and Chaos: Defining the Methods of Nonlinear Management* (Westport, Conn.: Quorum, 1992). For an interesting attempt to understand providence and miracles in the light of chaos theory, see Colwell, "Chaos and Providence."

explain *anything* and that all of our predictions about the future can only be approximations.[9] Our understanding of order must be conditioned by an appreciation of the vast chaos enveloping it, and all our beliefs about what we think we know must be conditioned by a humble appreciation for the endless domain of what we do not and cannot know.

The mystery of evil and an eight-second interval. One trivial illustration will emphasize the significance of chaos theory for our understanding of the mystery of evil. Let us try to explain why there is an eight-second interval between two particular cars on a particular freeway at a given moment. To assess this we would need to acquire an exhaustive knowledge of all the factors that led these two drivers to be on that freeway at just that moment, driving at just that speed. Had anything been different that day for either driver, the interval might have been longer or shorter—or perhaps nonexistent. The interval between these two cars was also affected by the speed of all the other drivers on the freeway at that time and before. Thus we would also have to acquire an exhaustive knowledge of all the factors that influenced all the drivers on the freeway that day, driving the exact speed they were driving.

We have not yet arrived at the initial conditions explaining the eight-second interval, however, for one cannot exhaustively understand the behavior of *any* driver on the freeway on this particular day without understanding all the factors that influenced this behavior on the previous day, week, months and years. Had anything been different—a career choice, a marriage choice, an unplanned pregnancy, an ice storm that altered the lives of a certain driver's parents in 1942—the eight-second interval may have been different. To understand such matters, we would have to consider all the variables that influenced everyone who ever influenced the drivers on the road that day, as well as the variables that influenced people who might have been on the road had things turned out differently. Every person, every decision, every physical and spiritual factor throughout history that exercised any influence on

---

[9]So far as chaos and complexity theory are concerned, our inability meticulously to predict the future is rooted solely in the number of unknowable variables that factor into every state of affairs (more specifically, in the initial conditions of every state of affairs). Chaos theory itself has thus far been worked out exclusively on a deterministic basis (so it is sometimes labeled "deterministic chaos"). If we add to this the understanding that there is an element of unpredictable spontaneity attending all things, from quantum particles to the animal kingdom to human behavior (as argued in chapter four), the unpredictability of the future grows greater still. For an excellent, succinct discussion of how chaos theory and quantum theory might interface, see H. Peitgen, "The Causality Principle, Deterministic Laws and Chaos," in Holte, ed., *Chaos*, pp. 35-43.

creating this eight-second interval would have to be fully understood if the interval was to be exhaustively explained.

Attaining anything like this understanding is obviously impossible for finite human beings. Thus we must conclude that we simply cannot know in any exhaustive sense why there was an eight-second interval between two given cars instead of a nine- or seven-second interval or no interval at all. For all we know, the interval would have been significantly different were it not for the flap of a butterfly wing in China in the thirteenth century. Whatever explanation we provide for the eight-second interval will of necessity be incomplete, conditioned by the impenetrable chaos of innumerable variables we are unable to examine. Our understanding of why there is an eight-second interval is thus enveloped by an infinite domain of mystery.

The same might be said for every contingent feature of our world. Why is a particular insect flying in a particular pattern in this particular place at this particular time? Why does a particular tornado destroy a particular house and not a different house? Why does a particular stock go up to a certain level at a particular time and down to a certain level at a different time? We can specify the kind of things that explain these facts, but we will never exhaustively explain the particular facts themselves.[10]

The mystery of why a particular child is abducted by a particular person at a particular time is no more or less mysterious than this. Here too we can specify the kind of things that explain these kinds of events, but we cannot explain any of their particularities. It is the direct result of a person's free will and the indirect result of innumerable other human and spiritual free wills. Beyond this, however, we can say little. From the perspective of the trinitarian warfare theodicy, it is enough for us to know that this mystery is not about God but about creation. Among the few things we can know with cer-

---

[10]This demonstrates that there is an irrational "surd" quality to all particularity. Particularity can never be exhaustively explained. The ultimate nonrational metaphysical fact is that every this is a this and thus not that, and there is no ultimate reason for it. Moreover, the number of contingent variables contributing to every this being a this (and thus not that) are beyond reckoning, with an element of freedom and/or spontaneity at each point. Colin Gunton has insightfully argued that the Western philosophical tradition (going back to the pre-Socratics), with its tendency to strive for one ultimate principle of explanation for everything, never adequately accounted for contingent particularity. In the "one-and-the-many" dilemma, it definitely favored the "one." Gunton argues for a more explicitly trinitarian understanding of ultimate reality as the means of providing an ontological grounding for the "many" (particularity) while nevertheless affirming the ontological necessity of the "one." See his *The One, The Three and the Many: God, Creation and the Culture of Modernity* (Cambridge: Cambridge University Press, 1993). Gunton's thesis is largely consistent with, and supplemental to, the thesis I advocate in this work.

tainty in this war zone is that God's character is unequivocally loving, holy and good, for he is clearly revealed in the person of Jesus Christ. Thus we can know that he revolts against this and all other forms of evil—as the ministry of Christ reveals—and that he calls on us to revolt against them as well. God is at war, and he calls on us to join him.

The lesson out of the whirlwind
The infinity of our ignorance. The book of Job confirms the point I am making. It teaches that evil must remain a mystery precisely because we are so small while the creation is so vast and complex. When the Lord finally speaks to Job out of the whirlwind (Job 38:1—41:34) it is not to proclaim that he has the right to do whatever he wants to do, as some believe. To be sure, God certainly wants to put Job in his place for accusing him of wrong doing (Job 40:2, 8), just as he even more sternly wants to put Job's friends in their place for thinking that they could neatly explain evil in their reward-and-punishment theology (Job 42:7-9). Further, God clearly wants to remind Job of who is control of the cosmos and who is not (Job 38:1—41:34).[11] But the main point of Yahweh's monologue from out of the whirlwind is to humble Job and all humans facing evil circumstances by pointing out *how little we know about the vast cosmos he has created.*

---

[11]One might take Job's statement that "no purpose of yours can be thwarted" (Job 42:1) to endorse an omni-causal view of God, but the verse does not specify what God's unthwartable will is. As I have admitted, if it were God's will to control each and every detail in history, God could certainly do that. But then one would wonder why he was angry with Job and his friends for the mistaken way they responded to Job's suffering. If everything is meticulously controlled by the will of God, their responses themselves would have been part of God's will. The verse could more easily be interpreted as either (a) God's unthwartable will is to have precisely the magnificent, complex, challenging kind of cosmos he describes in Job 38—41; or (b) whenever God unconditionally wills that something occurs in world history, this cannot be thwarted—leaving open the issue of how frequently or rarely this occurs.

A comment should also be made regarding Job 42:11, which says that Job's relatives consoled Job "for all the evil that the LORD had brought on him." In the light of the prologue, which informs us that Satan was the one who directly brought evil on Job, the verse should probably be taken to mean only that the Lord allowed Job to undergo his ordeal (see Job 1:12; 2:6). Nothing in the text suggests that the confrontation was part of a great divine plan. Indeed, the text suggests the opposite by poetically depicting Satan as an intruder to the heavenly court (1:6-7) and by noting that Satan challenges the Lord's *protection* of Job (1:10). At this early stage of special revelation in which God's uniqueness and unrivaled sovereignty had to be emphasized against all forms of polytheism, authors sometimes loosely characterized everything as coming from God in the sense that all events occur within a creation that comes from him and that he oversees. But they do not mean by this that God directly causes everything. See my discussion in *God at War: The Bible and Spiritual Conflict* (Downers Grove, Ill.: InterVarsity Press, 1996), pp. 143-52. For a discussion of other passages used to support a pancausal view of God, see appendix five.

Thus the Lord sarcastically chides Job when he asks:

Where were you when I laid the foundation of the earth? . . .
Who determined its measurements—surely you know! . . .
Have you comprehended the expanse of the earth?
    Declare, if you know all this. . . .
What is the way to the place where the light is distributed,
    or where the east wind is scattered upon the earth? (Job 38:4-5, 18, 24)

Our perspective of the cosmos is so limited, the Lord is saying, that we are simply not in a position to understand why things turn out the way they do. We should, then, be more hesitant than either Job or his friends were (and, we might add, more hesitant than many evangelical Christians are) in finding a divine reason for suffering or attributing evil to God.

The Lord also touches on our very limited understanding of cosmological and metaphysical principles when he asks:

On what were [the world's] bases sunk,
    or who laid its cornerstone?. . .
Do you know the ordinances of the heavens?
    Can you establish their rule on the earth? (Job 38:6, 33)

We know so little about anything regarding the physical ("bases") or metaphysical ("ordinances") structure of the cosmos that we are not in a position to think we could or should understand why particular events unfold as they do. But again, this mystery is a mystery about *the incomprehensibility of the world*, not about *the character of God*.

The unseen dimension of cosmic conflict. An important dimension of this incomprehensibility concerns the fact that God himself contends with forces of chaos. Hence the Lord continues his speech to Job by reminding him of his own battle against mighty cosmic forces of evil that Job and all ancient Near Eastern people believed in (see chapter one). All ancient Near Eastern people knew myths about a god of order fighting a god(s) of chaos, often symbolized by the sea. Hence the Lord reminds Job of his precreational battle with the chaotic cosmic sea that perpetually threatens the order of the world.[12]

Who shut in the sea *[yām]* with doors
    when it burst out from the womb . . .

---

[12]On the sea as hostile to God, see Boyd, *God at War,* pp. 83-89. Edwin Good notes a number of "disorderly" elements in Yahweh's speech, against which he must strive. See his *In Turns of Tempest: A Reading of Job* (Stanford, Calif.: Stanford University Press, 1990), p. 347. Harold Kushner has an interpretation of Job that is mostly consistent with mine. See his *When Bad Things Happen to Good People* (New York: Schocken, 1981), pp. 43-45. He unfortunately concludes from his reading of Job that God is not omnipotent.

and prescribed bounds for it,
    and set bars and doors,
and said, "Thus far shall you come, and no farther,
    and here shall your proud waves be stopped"? (Job 38:8, 10-11)

As Edwin Good points out, throughout this speech Yahweh "portrays an ambiguous world, whose order contains disorder, whose disorder undermines the order."[13] The point is that before Job critiques God's justice or effectiveness in running the cosmos, he should fully appreciate how difficult this chaotic sea can be and how impossible it would be for a human to attempt to control it.

The Lord then reminds Job of the menacing Behemoth and Leviathan with whom he must contend—threatening chaotic monsters of cosmic proportions familiar to ancient Near Eastern people.[14] The Lord asks Job, "Can you draw out Leviathan with a fishhook, or press down its tongue with a cord?" (Job 41:1). Only the Lord can contend with this malevolent creature (though even he needs a sword! Job 40:19), for this cosmic beast is indeed ferocious.[15]

Its sneezes flash forth light,
    and its eyes are like the eyelids of the dawn.
From its mouth go flaming torches;
    sparks of fire leap out.
Out of its nostrils comes smoke,
    as from a boiling pot and burning rushes.
Its breath kindles coals,
    and a flame comes out of its mouth. . . .
It counts iron as straw,
    and bronze as rotten wood. (Job 41:18-21, 27)

This cosmic beast fears nothing (Job 41:33). It cannot be captured or domesticated (Job 41:1-8). Even "the gods" are "overwhelmed at the sight

---

[13]Good, *Turns of Tempest*, p. 348. Terence E. Fretheim argues along similar lines. Through God's monologue, he notes, "images of wildness and strangeness are present, including the wild seas . . . the uncertainties of the night, and Behemoth and Leviathan. . . . For all the world's order and coherence, it doesn't run like a machine; a certain randomness, ambiguity, unpredictability, and play characterize its complex life" ("God in the Book of Job," *CurTM* 26 (1999): 89. As I will shortly show, images of conflict are present in the monologue as well.

[14]In my opinion, in the Old Testament these are demonic "principalities and powers" expressed in mythological terms that ancient Near Eastern people could understand. See my discussion in *God at War*, pp. 93-100.

[15]On Job 40:19, see J. C. L. Gibson, "On Evil in the Book of Job," in *Ascribe to the Lord: Biblical and Other Studies in Memory of Peter C. Craigie*, ed. Lyle Eslinger and Glen Taylor, JSOT-Sup 67 (Sheffield: Sheffield Academic Press, 1988), pp. 416-17.

of it" (Job 41:9, 25), and no one "under the whole heaven" can "confront it and be safe" (Job 41:11).

Why does the Lord remind Job of these ferocious cosmic beasts? Edmond Jacob identifies the reason:

> God wants to show Job how difficult the conduct of the world is with creatures so extraordinary and so mysterious which fear nothing . . . and against which he has to wage incessant war. By transposing that [battle] to his own plane, Job will be able to draw the conclusion . . . that God is not unjust by his lack of concern for him since he himself on a much higher plane struggles against evil.[16]

According to Fredrik Lindström, Yahweh's allusion to Leviathan and Behemoth as well as to the hostile waters and other chaotic forces of nature throughout his speech exposes the error in the theologies of Job and his "friends."

> YHWH in fact partially admits to Job that there are parts of Creation which are indeed chaotic; here we catch sight of an understanding of the world in which evil has independent existence. It neither comes directly from God, as Job maintains, nor can it be accommodated to a world order in which it is ultimately related to human behavior, as Job's friends claim.[17]

And again:

> Job explicitly held YHWH responsible for all the evil of existence, so YHWH rebuts this charge by pointing to his own continuous combat with evil as manifested in these chaos creatures.[18]

The cosmos is far more complex and combative than either Job or his friends assumed in their simplistic theologies.

J. C. L. Gibson expresses the point even more forcefully. He notes that "chapters 40 and 41 do not mention an open victory of God over Behemoth and Leviathan, but simply describe them as they are in their full horror and savagery." From this he concludes that the central point of these chapters is to draw attention

> to the Herculean task God faces in controlling these fierce creatures of his in the here and now. They are in fact set forth as worthy opponents of their Cre-

---

[16]Edmond Jacob, *Theology of the Old Testament,* trans. A. W. Heathcote and P. J. Allcock (New York: Harper & Row, 1958), p. 171.

[17]Fredrik Lindström, *God and the Origin of Evil: A Contextual Analysis of Alleged Monistic Evidence in the Old Testament,* trans. F. H. Cryer, ConBOT 21 (Lund: Gleerup, 1983), p. 154.

[18]Ibid., p. 156.

ator. They are quite beyond the ability of men to take on and bring to book. On the contrary, they treat men with scorn and derision, delighting to tease and humiliate and terrorize them. . . . Even God has to watch for them and handle them with kid gloves. It takes all his "craft and power" to keep them in subjection and prevent them from bringing to naught all that he has achieved. . . . It is of this divine risk as well as of the divine grace and power that Job is, in my view, being given an intimation in Yahweh's second speech: of the terrible reality of evil and (as Job himself was now only too well aware) of the dangers it presents to men.

From this Gibson draws his conclusion about the central point of this epic poem:

It is when Job realizes not only that God is on his side, and on the side of suffering and protesting humanity, but that God has a battle on his hands and a fierce and relentless foe to subdue before he can fully redress his, and their, grievances and heal his, and their, wounds—it is then and only then that in the midst of life's ongoing turmoil the erstwhile Prometheus finds himself strangely at peace.[19]

If this reading of Job is correct, then the popular line of interpretation of this book, which contends that humans must simply keep silent and accept the mysterious sovereignty of God, is mistaken. Early on Job expresses this form of piety (Job 1:21; 2:10), but the book does not condone this sentiment any more than it condones the theology of Job and his "friends" throughout the narrative.[20] In contrast to this theology, the book teaches that the mystery of evil stems from the complexity of creation and the warfare that engulfs it, not from the arbitrary sovereignty of God.[21]

---

[19]Gibson, "On Evil," pp. 416-17. For a similar perspective that highlights implications for liberation theology, see Gustavo Gutiérrez, On Job: God-Talk and the Suffering of the Innocent, trans. Matthew J. O'Connell (Maryknoll, N.Y.: Orbis, 1992), pp. 75-81.

[20]Fretheim notes that Job's two "confessions of faith . . . reflect Job's point of view, uttered in deep suffering. Do they also express the narrator's point of view? Probably not. Job's 'confessions' claim that God is responsible for both good and evil (a monistic view, also held by Job's friends). But, they reflect Job's falling back on a conventional piety. . . . Later (42:5) Job will stand in judgement over his prior piety, declaring it hearsay. The God speeches will finally present a more nuanced understanding of divine responsibility for a world in which one may be deeply hurt" ("God in the Book of Job," pp. 87-88).

[21]Gibson chides the traditional interpretation as "too 'Christian' " ("On Evil," p. 409). Lindström summarizes the speeches well when he writes: "We find in the dialogues a confrontation between the view that all evil comes from God as a reaction to human sin (the friends) and the view that a capricious and immoral God is the author of and bears the responsibility for all the evil in the world (Job). . . . Both of these views are put to shame in YHWH's two

Finally, we should note that the Lord never informs Job or his friends about Satan—the agent who was responsible for Job's misfortune. After the prologue he is not mentioned again. Some scholars argue that this silence is because the prologue was added after the main body of the text, but I find the arguments for this view unconvincing.[22] With Gibson, I rather argue that the prologue is vital to understanding the central point of the book.[23]

By giving the reader a glimpse of heaven that Job never becomes privy to, the work suggests in poetic fashion that things go on in heavenly realms that we are totally ignorant of but that nevertheless greatly affect our lives. If we knew more about the inscrutable society of the "sons of God" that exists between us and God, a world in which agents possess a degree of say-so, just as we do (but, it seems, usually on a grander scale), the world would appear far less arbitrary than it does now. (It would not, however, appear any more *fair*, since knowing that a free agent is acting does not imply that the agent will act fairly).[24]

In the end, the Lord does not give Job an explanation of his suffering. Job is simply humbled by having his vast ignorance, and thus his former arrogance, exposed. This is the point of this epic poem. But again, every-

---

speeches. In his first address YHWH points out that he has created a well-ordered cosmos which he continually renews. However, a region of existence does exist which is hostile to man and chaotic, although YHWH keeps it at bay. In his second address we encounter a somewhat dualistic picture of the world in which evil is hostile to God and self-sufficient; it is not directly related to the actions of God or man. Evil is characterized in such a way that only God is strong enough to resist it, which he in fact does" (*Origin of Evil*, p. 157). Another person who sees God's conflict with cosmic creatures in these chapters as the key to understanding the point of the book of Job is O. Keel, *Jahwes Entgegnung an Ijob*, FRLANT 121 (Göttingen: Vandenhoeck & Ruprecht, 1978). See also John Day, *God's Conflict with the Dragon and the Sea* (Cambridge: Cambridge University Press, 1985), pp. 62-87; and T. Mettinger, "The God of Job: Avenger, Tyrant, or Victor?" in *The Voice from the Whirlwind: Interpreting the Book of Job*, ed. Leo G. Perdue and W. Clark Gilpin (Nashville: Abingdon, 1992), pp. 39-49.

[22]See the discussions in D. J. A. Clines, *Job 1-20*, WBC 17 (Dallas, Tex.: Word, 1989), pp. lvii-lviii; and J. H. Hartley, *The Book of Job*, NICOT (Grand Rapids, Mich.: Eerdmans, 1988), pp. 21-24.

[23]Gibson, "On Evil," p. 412. In defense of the unity of the final work, see Nahum Sarna, "Epic Substratum in the Prose of Job," *JBL* 67 (1974): 17-34. My argument regarding the point of the silence about Satan in the body of the text could theoretically be accepted even on the assumption of multiple authorship. In this case the question regarding the silence would be attributed to the final redactor.

[24]There is almost unanimous agreement among biblical scholars that the genre of Job involves literary fictional techniques. This should caution us against inferring too much from the details of the prologue (e.g., must Satan literally get specific permission from God before afflicting someone?). On various views related to the literary role of the prologue in this work, see Fretheim, "God in the Book of Job," p. 87.

thing depends on our understanding of what this ignorance and arrogance is about. Job's ignorance is an ignorance of the complexity and warfare of creation, and his arrogance as well as the arrogance of his friends was in mistakenly thinking that they could trace everything directly back to God or human sin. Such logic inevitably results in people either concluding that people suffer because God is punishing them (Job's friends) or that God runs the cosmos arbitrarily (Job himself).

Peace comes to Job only when he learns that, though his suffering is a mystery, he can and must nevertheless humbly trust God. His suffering is not God's fault, and God is not against him. God's character is trustworthy.

THE POWER AND URGENCY OF PRAYER
The Problem of Prayer
The final issue we will address in this chapter concerns the role of petitionary prayer within a trinitarian warfare worldview. If we accept that God always does the most that he can to promote love and to prevent evil, and if we accept that God's power unilaterally to steer events according to his desires is restricted by the quality of each agent's freedom, what role can petitionary prayer play? One could argue that it is pointless, for if what a person prays for is something that is best for God to do, it seems God would already be trying to do it whether or not that person prayed. On the other hand, if one naively prays for something that is not best for God to do, then it seems that a God who always does the most good he can would not do it, regardless of the prayer. In other words, if what one is praying for is best, praying for it seems either unnecessary if God *can* carry it out or pointless if he *cannot*. Moreover, if what one is praying for is not best, God would not carry it out even if he could. So what is the point of petitionary prayer?

Scripture and Prayer
This is a very serious problem, to say the least, for the belief that prayer makes a difference with God and significantly influences the outcome of events is central to the biblical narrative. From Cain's plea for leniency (Gen 4:13-14) to the Israelites' cry for liberation (Ex 2:23-24; 3:7-10; Acts 7:34); from Moses' cry for help at the Red Sea and against the Amalekites (Ex 14:15-16; 17:8-14) to Hezekiah's prayer for an extension of life (2 Kings 20:1-7); and from Abraham's prayer for a son (Gen 15:2-3) to the leper's prayer to Jesus for healing (Mt 8:2-3), the biblical narrative is strung

together by examples of God's faithfulness in responding to the prayers of his people. Indeed, one of the most fundamental assumptions that runs throughout Scripture is that "the prayer of the righteous is *powerful* and *effective*" (Jas 5:16). Prayer moves God and makes an incredible difference in the world.

Jesus frequently taught on the importance of prayer. He repeatedly instructed us to ask God for things, promising that they will be given to us (Mt 7:7, 11; 18:19-20; Jn 14:13-16; 15:7, 16; 16:23). He encouraged us to pray with tireless persistence, *as though* God did not want to hear and answer our prayer (Lk 11:5-13; 18:1-8). This teaching only makes sense if prayer actually accomplishes things: the more we pray, the more good is accomplished. Indeed, there are more conditional promises attached to prayer in Scripture than to any other human activity.[25] John Wesley only slightly exaggerated the truth when he concluded that "God will do nothing but in answer to prayer."[26]

The bottom line is that conviction about the urgency of prayer and confidence in the power of petitionary prayer lies at the heart of biblical faith. Consequently, any theology that cannot render coherent the effectiveness and urgency of petitionary prayer in Scripture must, for this if for no other reason, be judged as being misguided at some level. Yet, as we saw above, one could argue that the trinitarian warfare worldview is unable to do just this. Three things may be said in response.

Prayer and the classical philosophical tradition. First, if petitionary prayer is problematic in the trinitarian warfare worldview, I believe it is more so in the classical philosophical tradition. This tradition does not answer the question posed earlier concerning how prayer can affect an all-good and all-powerful God. But beyond this it has the difficulty of explaining how prayer can affect a God who is altogether unchanging. How are we to render intelligible the biblical teaching that petitionary prayer is urgent and effective if nothing temporal and contingent affects God's eter-

---

[25]For an excellent discussion of the biblical material depicting God allowing us to influence him and thereby determine the future, see John Sanders, *The God Who Risks: A Theology of Providence* (Downers Grove, Ill.: InterVarsity Press, 1998), pp. 53-66, 100, as well as Terence E. Fretheim, "Divine Dependence upon the Human: An Old Testament Perspective," *Ex Auditu* 13 (1997): 1-13.

[26]Quoted approvingly in Paul E. Billheimer, *Destined for the Throne* (Minneapolis: Bethany House, 1975), p. 51. In my estimation, this little work remains one of the all-time classics on prayer. Others who express this conviction about prayer are Brother Andrew and Susan DeVore Williams, *And God Changed His Mind Because His People Prayed* (reprint, London: Marshall Pickering, 1991); and Watchman Nee, *What Shall This Man Do?* (London: Victory, 1961).

nal plans, as the classical philosophical tradition generally maintains?[27]

Many simply admit that this is mystery that must be accepted since, they believe, Scripture teaches both that prayer is efficacious and that God is absolutely unchanging. Whatever else may be said about this view, it certainly does not render petitionary prayer less problematic than views that hold that God's experience can change. Some within the classical philosophical tradition argue that prayer is primarily for *our* benefit, not God's. Prayer does not change God, but it is the means by which God changes us.[28] Others follow Aquinas and maintain that petitionary prayer is a valuable reminder of our dependence on God.[29] Still others hold that prayer is the ordained means by which God brings about ordained ends.[30] While there certainly is truth in all these perspectives, such explanations are not adequate in capturing the Bible's view of petitionary prayer as having a real contingent effect on God and thus on what transpires in history.

I submit that the effectiveness and urgency of petitionary prayer as it is commanded and illustrated throughout Scripture only makes sense if we are asking God to do something *he would not otherwise do* and if God at least sometimes *does this*. In the words of Peter Geach:

> Unless it is sometimes true that God brings about the course of events in a way that he would not had he not been asked, petitionary prayer is idle: just as it would be idle for a boy to ask his father for a specific birthday present if the

---

[27]Walter Wink argues the point effectively: "Before that unchangeable God, whose whole will was fixed from all eternity, intercession is ridiculous. There is no place for intercession with a God whose will is incapable of change. What Christians have too long worshiped is the God of Stoicism, to whose immutable will we can only surrender ourselves, conforming our wills to the unchangeable will of deity" (*Engaging the Powers: Discernment and Resistance in a World of Domination* [Minneapolis: Fortress, 1992], p. 301. The point is made by a number of theologians. See, e.g., Baelz, *Does God Answer Prayer?*; Vincent Brümmer, *What Are We Doing When We Pray? A Philosophical Inquiry* (London: SCM Press, 1984); Keith Ward, *Rational Theology and the Creativity of God* (Oxford: Basil Blackwell, 1982); Keith Ward, *Divine Action* (London: Collins, 1990); Sanders, *God Who Risks*; and David Basinger, *The Case for Freewill Theism: A Philosophical Assessment* (Downers Grove, Ill.: InterVarsity Press, 1996).

[28]See John Calvin, *Institutes of the Christian Religion,* ed. John T. McNeill, trans. Fred L. Battles (Philadelphia: Westminster Press, 1960), pp. 851-53 (3.20.3). So argues R. C. Sproul, *The Invisible Hand: Do All Things Really Work for Good?* (Dallas: Word, 1996), pp. 201-6. For an overview of various models of prayer in the Christian tradition, see Terrance Tiessen, *Providence and Prayer: How Does God Work in the World?* (Downers Grove, Ill.: InterVarsity Press, 2000).

[29]Brümmer, *What Are We Doing?* p. 45.

[30]Calvin, *Institutes,* p. 215 (1.17.3). So argues Paul Helm in *The Providence of God* (Downers Grove, Ill.: InterVarsity Press, 1994), p. 159. On this, see Sanders's critical discussion in *God Who Risks,* pp. 269-74.

father has made up his mind what to give irrespective of what the boy asks.[31]

If petitionary prayer is not idle, it must truly affect what God does. The classical philosophical model of providence has difficulty affirming this.

Prayer and Process theism. Second, I agree that prayer could make no difference if God is *exhaustively* constrained by creaturely free will. In Process thought, for example, God can *only* act in response to decisions of free agents and he must respond in accordance with metaphysical principles governing both him and creation.[32] God can never act *exceptionally* or *unilaterally* to bring about a state of affairs that otherwise would not have occurred. As a result, according to Process thought God cannot uniquely respond to petitionary prayers. Such a conclusion is entirely inadequate from a historic-orthodox Christian perspective and is due to the fact that Process thought places metaphysical constraints on God, that is, restrictions that God himself did not choose.

Prayer as morally responsible behavior. In contrast to Process thought, the trinitarian warfare model of providence does not place any metaphysical constraint on God, and this is my third point. Three things may be said in this regard.

First, while in the trinitarian warfare worldview God is indeed constrained by the integrity of his covenant not to exhaustively control free agents, this decision does not constrain him to exert the same influence at all times in all places, as in Process thought. If it helped achieve God's overall objectives for creation, therefore, God could arrange things so that communication with him (prayer) unleashes more divine influence in a certain direction than

---

[31]Peter Geach, *Providence and Evil* (Cambridge: Cambridge University Press, 1977), pp. 118-19. See also Brümmer, *What Are We Doing?* pp. 33-34. Wink has an even more critical assessment of the futility of intercessory prayer in the classical philosophical concept of God. See *Engaging the Powers*, 300-304. Bruce Epperly argues that "in order to pray wholeheartedly for persons in need, one must believe that prayer makes a difference, that is, one must have a vision of reality which affirms the positive role of prayer in physical and spiritual well being." The traditional view of God prevents this, he argues. The classical tradition has a "dysfunctional" view of prayer, he maintains, because it holds that "an omnipotent God is ultimately responsible for illness," that all illness is ordained or permitted by God "for the sake of correction, reproof, or punishment," and that "healing is a product of . . . God's omnipotent and arbitrary will" ("To Pray or Not to Pray: Reflections on the Intersection of Prayer and Medicine," *Journal of Religion and Health* 34 (1995): 142-43. I agree with Epperly's central thesis, though he unfortunately thinks he must deny God's omnipotence to sustain his thesis.

[32]See Gregory A Boyd, *Trinity and Process: A Critical Evaluation and Reconstruction of Hartshorne's Di-Polar Theism Towards a Trinitarian Metaphysics* (New York: Lang, 1992), pp. 288-89, 334; David Basinger, *Divine Power in Process Theism: A Philosophical Critique* (Albany, N.Y.: SUNY Press, 1988), pp. 85-98; *Case for Freewill Theism*, pp. 107-8. I will discuss Process thought more thoroughly in the next chapter.

would otherwise be unleashed. As I will argue shortly, I am convinced that this is precisely what God has done.

Second, in the last two chapters I suggested that God must consider all the relevant variables in deciding whether or not he can with integrity intervene in a particular situation. This view does not in any way undermine the efficacy and importance of prayer. On the contrary, I will argue that this view alone makes petitionary prayer intelligible, for *it allows prayer to be one of the central variables God takes into consideration.* Petitionary prayer can be understood to influence things for the same reason that all other morally responsible behavior influences things. Prayer is part of our moral say-so in influencing the flow of history and thus is a crucial variable that God considers in determining his response to situations.

Third, while much of the trinitarian warfare worldview can be embraced without accepting that the future is to some degree open, accepting the partial openness of the future is particularly advantageous when it comes to making sense of the power and urgency of prayer. If everything is eternally settled ahead of time either in the will or the mind of God, as the blueprint model of providence holds, then it is difficult to explain the urgency and efficacy that Scripture attributes to prayer.

For example, there are many instances where the Bible says that God intended to bring judgment on people or a city but reversed his course of action in the light of prayer (e.g., Ex 32:14; Num 11:1-2; 14:12-20; 16:20-35; Deut 9:13-14, 18-20, 25; 2 Sam 24:17-25; 1 Kings 21:27-29; 2 Chron 12:5-8; Jer 26:19). The motif is illustrated well in Psalm 106:23:

> Therefore [the Lord] said he would destroy them—
> had not Moses, his chosen one,
> stood in the breach before him,
> to turn away his wrath from destroying them.

Verses like this explain that the fate of many people depended on whether or not a person or group of people would intercede and pray. The Lord also tells us of a time when he "sought for" someone to "stand in the breech" for Israel but could not find anyone (Ezek 22:29-31). Consequently, Israel was judged.

These verses do not make sense if the future is eternally and exhaustively settled in God's mind or will. How can God genuinely reverse his declared intentions if he eternally foreknew or foreordained the outcome? Further, how could God genuinely seek someone to engage in intercessory prayer to save a nation if he eternally foreknew or foreordained that there would be no such person?

If we grant that the future is to some extent open, however, then whether or not people pray becomes part of the risk that God takes in creating a cosmos populated with free agents. The urgency and the efficacy of prayer is real—as real and at least as important as any other area of our life for which we are morally responsible.

Prayer as Creaturely Empowerment

However, we still have not answered the question of how prayer can genuinely affect God if we believe that God always does all he can do to bring about the best state of affairs. Before answering this question, however, I would like to point out that this question is hardly unique to the trinitarian warfare worldview. Unless one is willing to admit that God *does not* always do the best thing, one must answer this question. Yet if one embraces this conclusion, how can one consistently affirm that God is *perfectly* good? Is not God at least guilty of the sin of omission in this view? If this conclusion is not acceptable, then it seems one must concede that God always does the most he can do to promote good and prevent evil, which leads back to the problem of petitionary prayer we have been wrestling with.

I submit that the problem is resolved if we understand prayer to be part of the morally responsible potential, the spiritual say-so that God gives free agents in his desire to have a creation in which love is possible. I have argued that God is restricted in terms of what he can unilaterally carry out by the domain of irrevocable freedom he has given to agents. I have further argued that this entails that the short- and long-term implications of agents' behavior for all other agents must be allowed to unfold, for better or for worse. We may understand prayer as a central aspect of this moral responsibility. By God's own design, it functions as a crucial constituent in the "givens" of any particular situation that makes it possible for God more intensely to steer a situation toward his desired end. In the words of Peter Baelz, prayer is one of the central variables that "make it possible for God to do something that he could not have done without our asking."[33]

In other words, just as the Creator set things up so that we have genuine say-so on a physical level, so we can envisage him setting things up so that we have genuine say-so on a spiritual level—and this say-so is the power of prayer. As morally responsible agents, we are empowered to affect other people's lives and the flow of history by what we physically do and by what we do in prayer.

---

[33]Peter Baelz, *Prayer and Providence: A Background Study* (New York: Seabury, 1968), p. 118.

God's Need for Prayer

Furthermore, just as our freedom to effect things physically is irrevocable, so we may conclude that the power to effect things in prayer is also irrevocable. Prayer is part of the general covenant of freedom that the Lord grants us, and he genuinely binds himself to it. Scripture does not shy away from speaking of God sometimes needing humans to accomplish certain feats (Judg 5:23). Hence, we may understand that, by his own choice, God genuinely needs us to pray for certain things if they are to be accomplished, just as we may understand that God needs us to cooperate with him on a physical level for certain things to be accomplished.

Wink captures the genuine urgency of prayer well as he comments on the fascinating narrative of prayer and spiritual conflict found in Daniel 10:

> The point here seems to be that Daniel's intercessions have made possible the intervention of God. Prayer changes us, but it also changes what is possible for God. Daniel's cry was heard on the first day; it opened an aperture for God to act in concert with human freedom. It inaugurated war in heaven.[34]

Wink also writes, "If we are to take the biblical understanding seriously at all, intercession . . . changes the world and it changes what is possible to God."[35]

In my estimation, this empowering understanding of prayer makes the best sense out of the urgency with which Scripture commands us to pray. God could have created the world differently, of course. He could have created a world in which he did not need prayer, or any creaturely free decisions, to carry out his will. If God *needs* anything, it is because he chooses to. In my view, this is what God has done. He chose to create a somewhat risky world in which some things genuinely hinge on what free agents do, both physically and through the power of prayer.

The Rationale for Prayer

Though we cannot of course be certain, I do not think it is too difficult to suppose why God might have empowered us to have say-so both on a physical and a spiritual level. I shall offer three suggestions.

Personal relationships and empowerment. First, if we have correctly identified empowerment (possessing say-so) as the key to morally responsible

---

[34]Walter Wink, *Unmasking the Powers: The Invisible Forces That Determine Human Existence* (Philadelphia: Fortress, 1986), p. 91.

[35]Wink, *Engaging the Powers,* p. 302. Terence Fretheim asks, "Do not prayers make available to God some new ingredients (human will, energy, insight) with which to work the divine will in a situation, and without which the shape of the future wold be different?" ("Divine Dependence on the Human," p. 2).

personhood, then we can understand why God would empower us to influence things through prayer. Every true interpersonal relationship requires that the parties involved be genuinely empowered over and against one another. Where one party is wholly divested of power in relationship to the other, the dominated person becomes depersonalized. By definition, the relationship becomes *im*personal rather than *inter*personal.

This is as true of our personal relationship with God as it is with any other human. Though we are to be unequivocally under God's lordship, this lordship is a lordship of love that seeks to strengthen, not destroy, the personhood of the other.[36] God thus seeks not only to influence us but also to empower us to the extent that *we can influence him*. Prayer is a central aspect of this realm of influence. It preserves our personhood over and against our omnipotent Creator.

Communication and personal relationships. This arrangement also encourages us to maintain consistently and even pursue more passionately our personal relationship with our Creator, and this constitutes a second possible reason why God ordained that he be significantly influenced by prayer. The essence of any interpersonal relationship is mutually influential communication, and thus we can understand why God would set things up so that we need to communicate with him and that he needs us to communicate with him. By genuinely making things depend on whether or not we pray, God builds the necessity of a God-human communicating relationship into the very structure of creation.

Prayer as the power of God's viceregents. Thirdly, and closely connected to these first two points, the rationale for prayer becomes even clearer when we understand the purpose for which we exist on this earth. God wants us to participate in his unending, unsurpassable triune love and to mediate this love to the segment of the cosmos under our jurisdiction. He wants to establish his loving lordship over the whole cosmos, but he wants to do it *through mediaries:* in the case of the earth, through humans. In a word, he wants his bride to reign *with him* on the earth (2 Tim 2:12; Rev 5:10; 20:6). This was his goal from the start (Gen 1:26-27), and it will finally be accomplished in the eschaton.

In this light we may say that prayer is an essential aspect of our coreigning with God. God wants his will carried out on earth, but he wants it carried out in cooperation with us. Consequently, he orchestrates things such that

---

[36]Strict Calvinism fails in this regard, as Ben M. Carter argues in *The Depersonalization of God: A Consideration of Soteriological Difficulties in High Calvinism* (Lanham, Md.: University Press of America, 1989).

his will is not carried out unless we are in communication with him on it. To use an illustration from Paul Billheimer, God's will is like a business check that must be cosigned in order to be validated. We the church are the cosigning party, and prayer is our signing.[37] Hence the essence of prayer is, as Jesus taught, to align our will with the Father's will—to cosign his will, as it were—so that his rule is established "on earth as it is in heaven" (Mt 6:10). In prayer we begin our eternal job of mediating the Father's will and reigning with Christ on the earth.

Prayer, Risk and Divine Assurance

The problem of unanswered prayer. The trinitarian warfare worldview establishes a context in which the urgency and effectiveness of petitionary prayer makes sense. This context also makes sense out of why prayer is often *not* answered.

In the blueprint worldview, the ultimate reason why God does not answer a given prayer can only be that God does not will it to be answered. If God has a specific reason for all he ordains or permits, then we must suppose that he has a specific good reason for every prayer he answers and does not answer. Current popular evangelical theology has sometimes added another variable: perhaps God actually willed it but the person praying did not have enough faith to make the prayer effective.[38] In this case we are right back where Job and his friends were in their misguided speculations about why we suffer: either it is *God's* fault or *our* fault. Either God wanted Greta abducted or she or her parents lacked sufficient faith to prevent her abduction.

The trinitarian warfare worldview considers both of these approaches to be simplistic and misguided. The first is simplistic because it identifies God's

---

[37]Billheimer, *Destined for the Throne*, pp. 51-52. Watchman Nee has a similar understanding of prayer. "The water of divine deliverance," he writes, "depends upon the provision of human ditches" (*What Shall This Man Do?* p. 147).

[38]This is an especially strong tendency among Word of Faith churches, sometimes called "the positive confession movement." Believing that God never wills things such as sickness or poverty, they attribute these things to lack of faith. It constitutes the ultimate example of "blaming the victim" and obviously can be, and has been, extremely wounding. Its greatest error, I believe, is not that it claims that God opposes all forms of suffering (though this must be qualified) but that it reduces all the variables that might oppose God's will down to one, namely, the faith of the individual in need. Adherents of this movement thus become the most unambiguous representatives of the theology of Job's friends (which the book of Job refutes!). For a critical (though overly enthusiastic) assessment of this movement, see Hank Hanegraff, *Christianity in Crisis* (Eugene, Ore.: Harvest House, 1997). See also David R. McConnell, *A Different Gospel: A Historical and Biblical Analysis of the Modern Faith Movement* (Peabody, Mass.: Hendrickson, 1988); and C. I. Crenshaw, *Man as God: The Word of Faith Movement* (Memphis: Footstool Publications, 1994).

will as the only variable, when in fact there are a myriad of free agents who also contributed to every given situation. The second view is misguided because, though it recognizes variables other than God, it nevertheless reduces the multitude of cosmic variables down to the faith of the person praying.

It is, of course, consistent with Scripture to see conformity with the will of God and the quality of a person's faith as two variables that influence the answer to a prayer (Mt 17:20; 21:21; Mk 6:5-6; 1 Jn 5:14). But there are numerous other variables as well. Scripture also indicates, for example, that the persistence and fervency of prayer, as well as the number and agreement of people praying, can affect the efficacy of prayer (Mt 18:19-20; Lk 11:5-13; 18:1-8). Why should we think otherwise, since persistence, passion and large-group cooperation significantly affect what morally responsible creatures can and cannot accomplish on a physical level?[39]

Prayer and hostile angelic interference. We must also consider the possibility that things "behind the scenes" affect the when, where and how of a prayer getting answered. As neglected as it is in conservative evangelical circles—owing, I believe, to the ongoing influence of the blueprint worldview—the importance of the above noted variables of persistence and numbers in prayer only begins to make sense when we understand that prayer is fundamentally *a warfare activity.* To pray that the Father's will would be done on earth as it is in heaven (Mt 6:10) is to pray against all wills that want *their* own will done *against* the Father's will—and these opposing wills are significant. As Wink notes, again in relation to Daniel 10, "The angel of Persia actively attempts to frustrate God's will, and for twenty-one days succeeds. The Principalities and Powers are able to hold Yahweh at bay!"[40]

The reason why some prayers are not answered may have nothing to do with what God wills or with how profound or weak a person's faith is, for in this passage Daniel prays with effective faith and God wills to answer him. Why then is Daniel's prayer, or any prayer, not answered? "What we have left

---

[39]The relationship between the intensity and persistence of faithful prayer as well the number of people praying, on the one hand, and the effectiveness of prayer in bringing about healing, on the other, has recently been receiving scientific confirmation. See Larry Dossey, *Healing Words: The Power of Prayer and the Practice of Medicine* (San Francisco: HarperSanFrancisco, 1993); D. Matthews, *The Faith Factor: Proof of the Healing Power of Prayer* (New York: Viking, 1998); and T. Hudson, "Measuring the Results of Faith," *Hospitals and Health Networks* 70 (September 1996). Of related interest, see Epperly, "To Pray or Not to Pray," pp. 141-48.

[40]Wink, *Engaging the Powers,* p. 310.

out of the equation," Wink argues, "is the Principalities and Powers. Prayer is not just a two-way transaction. It also involves the great sociospiritual forces that preside over so much of reality."[41] He adds:

> Prayer involves not just God and people, but God and people and the Powers. What God is able to do in the world is hindered, to a considerable extent, by the rebelliousness, resistance, and self-interest of the Powers exercising their freedom under God.[42]

If Wink is correct, what goes on in the spiritual realm where good and evil "powers" reside may significantly affect how, when and even whether or not God can answer any given prayer. They are part of the givens of any particular situation that affect what can and cannot be done. Owing to the pervasive influence of an omni-controlling definition of sovereignty, much of the Christian theological tradition and a good deal of evangelical theology and praxis today lacks this insight. The result, as Wink sees, is that we tend to attribute to God what really belongs to the kingdom of Satan, on the one hand, and we tend to undermine the urgency of prayer in shaping the future, on the other. "Prayer that ignores the Powers," Wink writes, "ends up blaming God for evils committed by the Powers. But prayer that acknowledges the Powers becomes a form of social action."[43]

Prayer and chance. By affirming that the wills of humans and spirits influence what transpires in history, including answers to prayer, the trinitarian warfare theodicy is able to affirm the real power of prayer without depicting God as arbitrary. An episode out of Peter DeVries's novel *The Blood of the Lamb* may serve to illustrate this point. In this novel, a woman who has tuberculosis asks Wanderhope, the main character who also has tuberculosis, whether nor not he prays for her healing. Wanderhope adamantly replies that he does not.

> That would mean [that] the one I was addressing had done this to you to begin with, which I find hard to believe. . . . Asking Him to cure you—or me, or anybody—implies a personal being who arbitrarily does us this dirt. The prayer then is a plea to have a heart, to knock it off. I find the thought repulsive. I prefer to think we're victims of chance to dignifying any such force with the name of providence.[44]

---

[41]Ibid., p. 309.
[42]Ibid., p. 311.
[43]Ibid., p. 317.
[44]Peter DeVries, *The Blood of the Lamb* (Boston: Little, Brown, 1962), p. 104.

Wanderhope expresses a profound insight here, though unfortunately he draws a wrong conclusion from it. He assumes that either God controls all things and is therefore arbitrary—in which case praying for healing can only amount to twisting God's arm—or that history unfolds and evils must befall people strictly by chance—in which case praying for healing must be useless. The truth, I contend, lies between these two extremes.

Wanderhope correctly does not attribute to the will of God the arbitrary way in which some contract tuberculosis and others do not. He is therefore correct in rejecting prayer as a form of divine arm-twisting, asking God to "have a heart." I believe he also correctly concludes that people afflicted with tuberculosis and other diseases are largely victims of chance. As we argued above, no final explanation can be given as to why Wanderhope and this woman, as opposed to other individuals, contracted tuberculosis. A myriad of variables, all of which could have happened differently, converged to constitute the "givens" of the unfortunate plight of Wanderhope and his friend.

However, Wanderhope incorrectly concludes that prayer must be useless for two reasons. First, between the extremes of believing that God controls everything and that chance controls everything is the view that God *influences* all things. Though a myriad of contingent variables affect every particular situation, as Wanderhope understands, God sovereignly influences the whole process, working to bring about as much good and to prevent as much evil as possible.

Second, we can agree with Wanderhope that a myriad of contingent variables influence every particular situation but also affirm that we have genuine say-so in how we respond to these variables and thus influence what transpires in the future. Wanderhope assumes this element of say-so on a physical level, for he is willing to be treated by doctors. But he fails to see that we also have it on a spiritual level. The same Creator who set things up so that free agents can influence one another, for better or for worse, also set things up so that one of the ways we influence one another is by influencing God or created reality through the power of prayer. In the trinitarian warfare worldview, and in contrast to Wanderhope's conclusion, providence, prayer and chance may be seen as complementary concepts.

Thus, without altogether abandoning his concept of chance, Wanderhope should nevertheless have prayed for his friend's tuberculosis. Would he thereby be twisting God's arm to do what God would rather not do? By no means. He would rather be exercising his moral responsibility and thereby contributing to the possibility of God doing what God most likely already wanted to do. Would God be arbitrary in responding to this prayer either by healing or by not healing this woman? Or would it be the woman's fault if she was not healed? We have no reason to assume this. There are simply too many variables for us with our myopic, creaturely perspectives to discern why in any given instance one person was healed while another was not.

If this woman were healed, would this imply that God was the one who had given her tuberculosis in the first place? Jesus certainly did not think along these lines, for he healed many people by God's power whose diseases he explicitly attributed to Satan or to one of his demons (Mk 9:25; Lk 11:14; 13:11, 16; cf. Acts 10:38). Indeed, we can understand all of God's healing action in this war-torn creation to be acts of war, for the New Testament depicts sickness and disease as originating from the devil. Moreover, in praying against such matters we are siding with God against his enemy and exercising our God-given authority as joint heirs with Christ.

Praying in the Whirlwind

The power and humility of prayer. The trinitarian warfare understanding of prayer explains why prayer is necessary and urgent, why it works when it does and why at times it does not work. It thereby both empowers and humbles our prayer life.

It empowers our prayer life in that it explains how and why things genuinely depend on faith-filled, persistent prayer. Because of God's irrevocable gift of morally responsible communication with him, God genuinely needs prayer in order for his will to be done "on earth or in heaven." As Wink again puts it, "Prayer in the face of the Powers is a spiritual war of attrition. God's hands are effectively tied when we fail to pray. That is the dignity and urgency of our praying."[45]

In saying this, however, the trinitarian warfare view also humbles our prayer life, for we realize that as powerful as prayer is, it does not necessarily *guarantee* a certain result. In this war zone, there are few guarantees. Among other things, unseen developments in the spiritual realm may result in a ferocious whirlwind destroying our home and family (Job 1:19-20). We can and must believe on the basis of God's Word that prayer is crucial, vital and effective in furthering the kingdom of God. But prayer is, in most

---

[45]Wink, *Engaging the Powers,* p. 317.

circumstances, not a security blanket guaranteeing any particular outcome.[46]

The only eternally secure treasure. In a relational cosmos such as the one God has created, filled as it is with innumerable visible and invisible agents who each have a bit of irrevocable, self-determining say-so, we can sometimes pray intensely for a particular outcome and God may even will the same outcome, yet this outcome may fail to come to pass. Because of the innumerable variables that influence the cosmos and because of the present war-torn nature of the cosmos, the only activity of ours about which there is an unconditional divine guarantee is entrusting our soul to the Lord Jesus Christ.

> [No] hardship, or distress, or persecution, or famine, or nakedness, or peril, or sword . . . neither death, nor life, nor angels, nor rulers, nor things present, nor things to come, nor powers [are] able to separate us from the love of God in Christ Jesus. (Rom 8:35, 38-39)

While prayer and other factors can lower the probability and intensity of all these terrible things occurring in our life, Paul clearly assumes that such things *can* and *do* happen to believers. The good news is not that such things cannot happen to believers but that even when they do happen they cannot

---

[46]When prayer does constitute the decisive variable ensuring that a certain end will be achieved, God certainly knows this. Further, as Scripture (and for some of us, personal experience) illustrates, God is in these cases able to give believers a "word of knowledge" that guarantees a certain result for them (cf. 1 Cor 12:8). But in most circumstances there are no guaranteed outcomes. On the basis of God's promises (e.g., Jn 5:16), however, we may always be confident that our prayer is not wasted. It accomplishes something positive for the kingdom of God even if it doesn't bring about the specific outcome we prayed for. Though he does not integrate his reflections into a warfare perspective, Bruce Epperly substantially agrees with the point I am making about the power and limitations of prayer. On the one hand, he insists that we "must believe that prayer makes a difference" and "must have a vision of reality which affirms the positive role of prayer." It cannot simply be a pro forma activity, in other words. Things really do depend on prayer. On the other hand, we must concede that God's personal influence "is but one of many factors which influence our health and well-being in each moment of our lives. Along with the divine will toward wholeness, we are also being shaped by other factors, such as our physical condition, our conscious attitudes and thoughts, and the power of the providers, the food we eat, the culture we live in, its images of health and illness, our family-and-community matrix of relationships, and our prayers." Hence, Epperly appropriately concludes, "when prayer is not answered or healing does not occur in a strictly linear fashion, it is not due to God's arbitrary decision or lack of concern. . . . It is due to the interplay of a constellation of events, in which one or more of the many factors may be the source of the failure" ("To Pray or Not to Pray," pp. 144-45). What Epperly calls "the constellation of events" I (following Tupper) have called "the givens" of a particular situation. Epperly's reflections on this issue are expanded in his *At the Edges of Life: Toward a Holistic Vision of the Human Adventure* (St. Louis: Chalice, 1992).

separate us from the love of Christ. Hence Jesus tells us not to lay up for ourselves treasures on earth, for such treasures are vulnerable and will ultimately pass away. We are rather to lay up for ourselves treasures in heaven, where nothing is vulnerable and nothing perishes (Mt 6:19-21).

Finding peace in the whirlwind. This view admittedly does not offer the consolation many people seek in the face of this scary world. Indeed, the warfare worldview affirms that on a physical and emotional level the world is as scary and risky as it appears. Indeed, the unpleasantness of this affirmation is undoubtedly why many believers insist on clinging to the blueprint worldview despite its tension with the biblical view and the rather obvious ways in which it contradicts human experience.[47] Accepting this view means that one must accept more responsibility for what transpires in the world and must accept that there is no guaranteed security in this world, and this, quite frankly, is not an easy or popular thing to do. To cite Wink one more time, "It takes considerable spiritual maturity to live in the tension between these two facts: God has heard our prayer, and the Powers are blocking God's response."[48]

It is admittedly daunting to face the harsh reality of the war zone we live in, but this is what mature faith must do. Sometimes life in the midst of war can be a nightmare and, as much as each of us wish for it, there simply is no cosmic guarantee that the nightmare will not happen to us. Christian parents who pray for their children may still have their children abducted. Holding onto the myth of a divine blueprint is at least one way of closing our eyes to this reality and giving ourselves a false sense of security.

But as with all pseudosecurities this one can (and often does) backfire on the sincere people who hold it. When *I* am the mother who is haunted by the imagined screams of my abducted daughter for the rest of my life, when *I* am the wife whose ideal husband I prayed for all my life abandons me and my daughter, when *I* am the missionary girl who gets raped—then the same teaching that once gave me security now indicts me or enrages me or both. For now I must either blame myself for lacking faith or blame God for allowing the nightmare that I have suffered for a supposed "good" reason.

But if we are honest with ourselves, like Laura, the nine-year-old missionary child who as an adult intuitively knew she had no guarantee that she would not be raped again (chapter five), we all intuitively know that safety and security are not guaranteed in this life. We pray for protection and believe that

---

[47]The objection that the trinitarian warfare theodicy is inadequate as a practical theology because it offers no consolation and hope is more fully addressed in appendix one.
[48]Wink, *Engaging the Powers*, p. 311.

prayer is "powerful and effective" (Jas 5:16), but we still lock our doors at night. We pray for health but still take our vitamins. In the real world, things depend on many contingencies, and this applies to our communication with God as much as anything else, for prayer is part of the real world. What other people and spirits do, combined with many other variables, influences when, how and even whether or not any given prayer is answered.

One could argue, as Wink himself suggests, that this implies that God is not omnipotent.[49] But this conclusion is unnecessary. Whatever restrictions God faces he has placed on himself by choosing to create this kind of world. The risk of prayer no more implies that God is not omnipotent than does any other aspect of the morally responsible freedom of agents.

Conclusion

In this chapter we have explored the implications of the trinitarian warfare worldview with respect to why God's intervention in the world seems arbitrary and why God would make himself dependent on prayer. If our reasoning has been correct, we have shown that far from posing any insurmountable problems for the trinitarian warfare worldview, these issues are most effectively understood in the context of this view. Only when we understand the cosmos to be populated by visible and invisible agents who possess an element of irrevocable morally responsible say-so can the biblical portrayal of God's power and love be squared with both the biblical teaching on and our experience of God's providential activity.

In this way the trinitarian warfare worldview reconciles God's unequivocal desire to prevent evil and promote good with the reality that he often does not do this. It reconciles God's providential control over the world and the biblical assurance of his eschatological victory with the reality of self-determining free will. Finally, it reconciles God's universal desire to bring about good and his power to do so with the urgency that Scripture attaches to prayer.

Two further questions remain, however. The first is the question of how the trinitarian warfare worldview makes sense out of "natural" evil—evil not *obviously* associated with the willing of any free agent. The second is how we are to square the biblical teaching on God's total victory over Satan and evil with the traditional Christian understanding that hell involves eternal suffering. This latter question will be addressed in the final two chapters of this work (chapters eleven and twelve), but first we must address the thorny question of "natural" evil, to which we turn in the next three chapters.

---

[49]Ibid., p. 310.

8

"RED IN TOOTH & CLAW"

Perspectives on the Origin
of Natural Evil, Part 1

Man . . . trusted God was love indeed
And love Creation's final law—
Tho' Nature, red in tooth and claw
With ravine, shrek'd against his creed
TENNYSON, IN MEMORIAM

The Lucifer principle is a complex of natural rules,
each working together to weave a fabric that sometimes frightens and appalls us. . . .
Lucifer is the dark side of cosmic fecundity, the cutting blade of the sculptor's knife.
Nature does not abhor evil; she embraces it. . . .
Death, destruction, and fury do not disturb the Mother of our world;
they are merely parts of her plan.
HOWARD BLOOM, THE LUCIFER PRINCIPLE

He would be blind . . . who should suppose that the problem of evil,
including as it does the problem of sin, is wholly explicable in terms of human freedom. . . .
This is anything but the whole story. We have still to face the fact that there is evil
which is structural . . . in the very nature of created existence.
EDWIN LEWIS, THE CREATOR AND THE ADVERSARY

*T*he six theses discussed in part one attempt to render intelligible the warfare perspective of the Bible and early postapostolic church. By identifying the metaphysical conditions of the possibility of love, I have offered an answer to the question of how a cosmos created and governed by an all-powerful and all-good God could nevertheless be ravaged by a cosmic war and consequently filled with gratuitous suffering. These theses all revolve around the risky nature of freely chosen, morally responsible love, for love is God's central purpose for creation. God cannot hope to have agents who participate in his triune love without risking the possibility of the war.

However, the relevance of this answer regarding what is usually called "natural evil" remains to be seen. In contrast to moral evil, "natural evil," says John Hick, "is the evil that originates independently of human actions: in disease bacilli, earthquakes, storms, droughts, tornadoes, etc."[1] It is, in short, evil that lacks (or at least *seems* to lack) a moral agent behind it. Its apparent cause lies within the "natural" order of things.

Since nature itself is not personal, is not capable of love or freedom and thus is not morally responsible, how do our reflections on the nature of morally responsible love help explain this kind of evil within a trinitarian warfare worldview? In short, while we can perhaps understand why God would have to risk something on the morally responsible behavior of free agents, why should the natural world he presumably has direct control over be risky?

The Magnitude of "Natural" Evil

Evil inherent in the structure of creation. This issue is hardly peripheral, for pain and destruction in nature are not exceptions in an otherwise harmonious system. Rather, as with moral creatures, it seems that nature's potential for blessing is balanced by an equal capacity to curse. In the words of W. E. Stuermann:

> The web [of nature] unravels as often as it is woven in order. Frequently and brutally its threads are ripped in sudden and disconcerting manners, and the orderly tapestry of life unravels, leaving men broken by disaster and despair. Chaos looms before them and stretches to the horizons of their lives.

He continues:

> The biosphere is not a scene of unqualified friendliness and creativity. In it we discover uncountable injuries, disorders, and deaths. . . . The energies that incline toward order and creativity, are accompanied by . . . aggressive and

---

[1]John Hick, *Evil and the God of Love*, rev. ed. (New York: Harper & Row, 1978), p. 12; cf. Alvin Plantinga, *God, Freedom, and Evil* (Grand Rapids, Mich.: Eerdmans, 1977), p. 30. Wallace A. Murphree offers this minimalist distinction between moral and "natural" evil: "Moral evil is . . . any absolute, contingent evil which obtains by reason of human perversity; and natural evil is any absolute, contingent evil which obtains while all human beings are morally innocent with respect to it" ("Can Theism Survive Without the Devil?" *RelS* 21 ([1985]: 236). As I mentioned in chapter one, I argue that there is nothing "natural" about "natural evil" and hence put warning quotation marks around *natural* when used in this context. Cf. Edward Madden and Peter Hare, *Evil and the Concept of God* (Springfield, Ill.: Charles C. Thomas, 1968), p. 6.

destructive vectors and impulses. . . . Nature . . . does not in general display one grand purposiveness, untouched by decay and disaster. It is destructive and Dionysiac as well as creative and Apollonistic.[2]

In similar fashion, Edwin Lewis expresses the tension that lies at the heart of nature when he writes:

> Contradiction inheres in the structural framework of existence; it inheres in all organic life; it inheres in the nature of man. *Creation is creativity in strife with discreativity.* This is as nearly a correct account of what we everywhere observe and experience as can be condensed into seven words![3]

Whatever other form "discreativity" may take, as entropy it cuts to the core of every physical system. "The press of entropy," writes Robert J. Russell, is "the relentless disintegration of form, environment, organism," and it lies behind all "disorder," "dysfunction" and suffering in creation.[4] This pervasive influence of discreativity and the way it wars against order and creativity was expressed well by William Robinson in a little-known but valuable book entitled *The Devil and God.* Robinson writes:

> Nature always has a double aspect. It presents itself as benign, ready to do more than cooperate with man's endeavor to reach happiness. And it presents itself as hostile, destroying in a single night all that man has built up through long years of research and toil, sometimes appearing to take on even

---

[2]Walter E. Stuermann, *The Divine Destroyer: A Theology of Good and Evil* (Philadelphia: Westminster Press, 1967), p. 18. Noteworthy for our purposes, Stuermann later writes: "There is a wild antagonism at the heart of things. There is a madness there. Rationality, order, and creativity have as immortal adversaries chaos, disorder, and destruction. The countenance of Satan is indelibly inscribed in nature" (p. 24). I am largely in agreement with this, though I will subsequently argue that "the countenance of Satan" is neither "immortal" nor "indelible" in nature. Nature will be redeemed from its enslavement to the Adversary.

[3]Edwin Lewis, *The Creator and the Adversary* (New York: Abingdon-Cokesbury, 1948), p. 132 (emphasis original). Lewis goes on to argue from this that all attempts to explain this pervasive evil as lying within the will of God "either take out of evil its essential quality as evil, or they so root and ground evil in God as to require us to believe that evil is not evil or that God is not good" (ibid.). Lewis's argument is sound, though he unfortunately concludes that the only remaining alternative is eternal dualism. My contention is that a limited dualism can have the same explanatory force as eternal dualism, without the concomitant scriptural and philosophical problems. So long as we can specify why God cannot exercise exhaustive unilateral control over segments of the cosmos by virtue of the kind of creation he himself chose to bring into being, there is no need to hold that evil is an eternal principle God must contend with. The six theses of the trinitarian warfare theodicy are meant to provide this "why."

[4]Robert J. Russell, "Entropy and Evil," *Zygon* 19 (1984): 457. Russell later notes that "if evil is real in nature, entropy is what one would expect to find at the level of physical processes" (p. 465). This is true, but it leaves unexplained *why* evil is real in nature. This, I submit, requires the supposition of an evil will(s) influencing nature, even at the level of its fundamental laws.

a malignant aspect, as if she mocked and derided the high endeavor of man's spirit.[5]

He continues:

> We have quakes, volcanic eruptions, and tornadoes. We have learned to build better and stronger houses, but we still suffer from the effects of tempest. Here is something which presents itself as evil on a gigantic scale, which seems to say that within nature herself there is something like a cosmic warp, or that the devils had charge of creation and took a devilish delight in frustrating man's best efforts.[6]

This inextricable element of evil inherent in creation is what Howard Bloom has appropriately entitled "The Lucifer Principle." Though he does not himself believe in a personal devil, few have better captured the diabolical side of nature than he has:

> The Lucifer principle is a complex of natural rules, each working together to weave a fabric that sometimes frightens and appalls us. . . . Nature does not abhor evil: she embraces it. . . . Death, destruction, and fury do not disturb the Mother of our world; they are merely parts of her plan. Only we are outraged by the Lucifer Principle's consequences. And we have every right to be. For we are casualties of Nature's callous indifference to life, pawns who suffer and die to live out her schemes.[7]

For Bloom, the Lucifer Principle is simply part of the way things are. But no one who accepts that the cosmos was created by an all-good and all-powerful God can accept this. If the Creator is all-holy and all-powerful, one would at least expect that those aspects of creation with no autonomous will of their own would "display one grand purposiveness" and be "untouched by decay and disaster." To be sure, creation *does* display remarkable purposiveness and design, enough to proclaim the wisdom of a grand designer (Rom 1:20). But it also displays the antithesis of unified purposiveness and design.

Annie Dillard expresses the Lucifer Principle poignantly in *Pilgrim at Tinker Creek:* "The world is a monster." She continues:

> Any three-year-old can see how unsatisfactory and clumsy is this whole business of reproducing and dying by the billions. We have not yet encountered any god who is merciful as a man who flicks a beetle over on its feet. There is not a people in the world who behaves as badly as praying mantises. . . . We are

---

[5]William Robinson, *The Devil and God* (Nashville: Abingdon-Cokesbury, 1945), p. 16.
[6]Ibid., pp. 17-18.
[7]Howard Bloom, *The Lucifer Principle: A Scientific Expedition into the Forces of History* (New York: Atlantic Monthly, 1995), pp. 2-3.

moral creatures . . . in an amoral world. The universe that suckled us is a monster . . . a robot programmed to kill.[8]

I am writing this three days after a tidal wave drowned thousands of people who lived on the coast of Papua New Guinea. Such a catastrophe hardly reflects the perfect design of a perfect Designer. It reflects more the "design" of Lucifer (Bloom), a scheme of "discreativity" (Lewis) that is "destructive and Dionysiac" (Stuermann). It is "evil on a gigantic scale" (Robinson), the work of "a monster" (Dillard) that is all the more appalling to the theist because it seems to be the result of a perfectly "natural" process.

Animal suffering. Yet it is not humans alone who suffer at the hands of nature, a point that intensifies the problem even further. Innocent animals suffer as well. Indeed, in a sense the entire animal kingdom is a kingdom of pain. In Tennyson's memorable phrase, nature is "red in tooth and claw." Moreover, all the evidence indicates that it has been so from early in earth's history. Long before humans ever arrived on the planet, nature was characterized by

> teeth and talons whetted for slaughter, hooks and suckers molded for torment—everywhere a reign of terror, hunger, sickness, with oozing blood and quivering limbs, with gasping breath and eyes of innocence that dimly close in depths of cruel torture.[9]

One could even extend this observation down to the insect kingdom, as Robert Frost does in his poem "Design."

> I found a dimpled spider, fat and white,
> On a white heal-all, holding up a moth
> Like a white piece of rigid satin cloth—
> Assorted characters of death and blight
> Mixed ready to begin the morning right,
> Like the ingredients of a witch's broth—
> A snow-drop spider, a flower like a froth,

---

[8]A. Dillard, *Pilgrim at Tinker Creek* (New York: Harper Collins, 1974), p. 179.

[9]G. J. Romanes, quoted in Robert E. D. Clark, *The Universe: Plan or Accident?* (Philadelphia: Muhlenberg, 1961), p. 217. John Stuart Mill similarly notes, "If there are any marks at all of special design in creation, one of the things most evidently designed is that a large proportion of animals should pass their existence in tormenting and devouring other animals" ("Nature," in *Three Essays on Religion*, 3rd ed. [London: Longmans, Green & Co., 1923], p. 58). Interestingly enough, Ralph Winter, head of the Institute for the Study of the Origins of Disease, has recently called my attention to evidence suggesting that this violence was not present in the earliest stages of life. See Richard Fortey, *Life: A Natural History of the First Four Billion Years* (New York: Alfred A. Knopf, 1997), who argues that violence does not erupt on the scene until the end of the Precambrian period.

And dead wings carried like a paper kite.
What had that flower to do with being white,
The wayside blue and innocent heal-all?
What brought the kindred spider to that height,
Then steered the white moth thither in the night?
What but design of darkness to appall?—
If design govern in a thing so small.[10]

The obvious question such reflections pose to the Christian theist is why an all-good and all-powerful God would create such an inherently violent, frightening and painful "natural" system? Why is the design of nature largely a "design of darkness"? At the very least, why does nature not reflect the power and goodness of the Creator more perfectly, if not unambiguously? For as I have noted, in the case of "natural" evil, unlike the case of moral evil, there are no human agents whose free will can explain suffering.[11]

My argument over the next three chapters will be that this assumption is mistaken. Nature considered alone is indeed impersonal, but in reality it does not exist "alone." As the early church and almost every culture prior to modern Western culture has understood, it is subject to invisible agents who influence it for better or for worse. I thus argue that there is no such thing as "natural" evil. Nature in its present state, I believe, is not as the Creator created it to be, any more than humanity in its present state is as the Creator created it to be. When nature exhibits diabolical features that are not the result of human wills, it is the direct or indirect result of the influence of diabolic forces. Arguably, nowhere is the distinctiveness of the trinitarian warfare theodicy more apparent than on this point.

To make this case I will first critically evaluate seven traditional and contemporary approaches to "natural" evil, four in this chapter and three in the next. I will argue that these approaches contain valuable insights that must be appropriated if "natural" evil is to be adequately explained. But they are all inadequate in certain respects, primarily because they do not consider the possibility of evil agents influencing the natural system. Following this I will flesh out in chapter ten the implications of a trinitarian warfare approach to "natural" evil and attempt to demonstrate how it completes what is lacking in each of these theodicies.

The four views I examine in this chapter are the traditional Augustinian

---

[10]Robert Frost, "Design," in *Robert Frost Poetry and Prose,* ed. E. C. Lathan and L. Thompson (New York: Holt, Rinehart & Winston, 1972), p. 122. My thanks to my student and friend Dan Kent for reminding me of the theological significance of this poem.
[11]So argues, for example, H. J. McCloskey in "The Problem of Evil," *JBR* 30 (1962): 187-97.

view that "natural" evil fulfills a "higher" divine purpose; the traditional view that nature suffers because of human sin; John Hick's view that "natural" evil is the inevitable by-product of God's aim of developing souls with moral character; and Murphy and Ellis's view that "natural" evil is nature's way of participating in the self-sacrificial life of God.

"Natural" Evil and the "Higher Harmony" of Creation

Given the dominance of the blueprint worldview within the Christian tradition, we should not be surprised to find that "natural" evil has frequently been explained as fulfilling a higher divine purpose. This perspective can be traced back to Platonic and Stoic philosophy, but it found its way into the Christian tradition through Augustine.[12] The essence of Augustine's argument is that since all things occur in accordance with "Divine Providence," everything that happens by "natural" causes, including "monstrous births" and all things "injurious," must ultimately play a useful role within God's plan.[13] "The whole [of creation]," Augustine insists, "together is admirable."[14] Everything in creation, from "the entrails of the smallest and most contemptible animal" to the bloody carcass of a rooster killed in a cock fight, "has its own harmonious place in the cosmos," is "somehow consonant with the laws of nature" and is therefore "beautiful."[15]

Likewise all the apparently hostile aspects of nature, "fire, frost, wild beasts, and so forth," are all "beautifully adjusted to the rest of creation."[16] "That [God] is to be praised," writes Augustine, "is shown by dragons on earth . . . fire, hail, snow, ice, the hurricane and tempest, which perform your word."[17] It may be that such phenomena are being used by God to teach

---

[12]See Plotinus *Enneads* 3.2.11.17. This approach, in seminal form, goes back to Plato, who noted that a beautiful statue may not have beautiful eyes (*Republic* 420c). On the Stoic background to Augustine's concept, see John M. Rist, *Augustine: Ancient Thought Baptized* (Cambridge: Cambridge University Press, 1994), p. 261. In the third volume of this Satan and Evil series (entitled *The Myth of the Blueprint*), I will argue that Augustine's blueprint theology owes more to Stoic, Platonic and Manichean sources than it does the Bible.

[13]Augustine *City of God* 10.16 (NPNF 1 2:190-91). See his *Enchiridion* in *Augustine: Confessions and Enchiridion*, trans. A. C. Outler, LCC (Philadelphia: Westminster Press, 1955), pp. 394-96.

[14]Christopher Kirwan, *Augustine* (London: Routledge, 1991), p. 66. So too Augustine writes in his *Confessions*: "For you [God] evil does not exist at all, and not only for you but for your created universe, because there is nothing outside it which could break in and destroy the order which you have imposed upon it" (*Confessions*, trans. Henry Chadwick [Oxford: Oxford University Press, 1991], p. 125).

[15]Augustine *City of God* 5.10 (NPNF 1 2:93); cf. *Enchiridion* 11; *De ordine* 1.8.25.

[16]Augustine *City of God* 23.22 (NPNF 1 2:217). See also *Enchiridion* 342-44.

[17]Augustine *Confessions*, p. 125.

various people a lesson or to punish sin, or it may be that such "natural" phenomena simply serve as contrasts to the other beautiful aspects of the cosmos in order to embellish the whole as one uses antithesis to create "an exquisite poem."[18] Whatever the particulars, Augustine was certain that, although aspects of nature may appear ugly when considered alone, when viewed from God's all-encompassing perspective they in fact contribute to the beauty of the whole.

This is not to suggest that Augustine did not also attribute some aspects of "natural" evil to evil spirits, just as the early postapostolic fathers had done.[19] But unlike the earlier explanations, in Augustine's system the appeal to human and angelic free wills did not function as the *ultimate* explanation of whatever these wills brought forth. Because of Augustine's blueprint worldview, the ultimate explanation was rather traced further back to the purpose that God had in allowing or (the later Augustine emphasized) ordaining the free will to exercise itself as it did.

Several criticisms can be made against this perspective. First, the notion that horrendous aspects of nature contribute to a greater good is difficult to justify. With characteristic sarcasm, Mark Twain exposes the difficulty well as he tells his own version of the biblical story of Noah's ark.

> The microbes were by far the most important part of the Ark's cargo, and the part the Creator was most anxious about and most infatuated with. They had to have good nourishment and pleasant accommodations. There were typhoid germs, and cholera germs, and hydrophobia germs, and lockjaw germs, and consumption germs, and black-plague germs, and some hundreds of other aristocrats, especially precious creations, golden bearers of God's love to man, blessed gifts of the infatuated Father to his children.[20]

The point is well taken. Suggesting that "natural" evils like typhoid and cholera fit into a divine plan compromises both the goodness of God and the supposed evil of "natural" evil.[21] It is not even clear what the word *good* means if it is used to describe the "design" that orchestrates such things as killer diseases, mudslides that bury children alive or typhoons that drown thousands. If such things are in any sense good, what does evil look like? If

---

[18]Augustine *City of God* 10.18 (NPNF 1 2:215).

[19]Augustine *City of God* 2.23 (NPNF 1 2:38). See G. R. Evans's interesting discussion on Augustine's understanding of the relationship between evil wills and "natural" evil in *Augustine on Evil* (Cambridge: Cambridge University Press, 1982), pp. 97-98.

[20]Mark Twain, "Letter VII," *Letters from the Earth* (New York: Fawcett World Library, 1963), p. 34.

[21]See Terence Nichols's critique in "Miracles as a Sign of the Good Creation" (Ph.D. diss., Marquette University Graduate School, 1988), pp. 280ff.

such things are the work of a loving and all-good God, what would the work of a hateful devil look like?

Second, this perspective contradicts the Bible's portrayal of God as unequivocally and unambiguously *against* all forms of evil. To be sure, the Old Testament and the eschatological literature of the Bible portray God as sometimes using natural disasters to punish hardened sinners, as we will see when we examine the next approach. But this hardly supports the conclusion that *all* natural disasters or *every* monstrous aspect of nature is meant as discipline, punishment or any other higher divine purpose. Jesus' ministry uniformly reveals that the Father's will is to rid the world of all deformities, disease and illnesses. The work of God is not to design these into creation but to revolt against them. For these reasons I suggest that this way of making sense out of "natural" evil is simply not adequate.

Cursed Because of Sin

A second traditional approach to understanding "natural" evil, one that has often been considered alongside the first approach, is that it is the result of the human Fall. Citing Genesis 3, this view claims that God cursed nature as punishment for human rebellion. Diseases, earthquakes, hurricanes and the like are features of this punishment.

Nature and morally responsible willing. Three things may be said on behalf of this perspective. First, it is more consistent with Scripture than the previous approach, for Scripture often associates "natural" evil with human sin.[22]

Second, this view is not excessively mysterious, as is the higher harmony theory. Although this view is often embraced alongside the blueprint worldview, it does not logically require that we see destructive acts of nature fitting into a beautiful divine plan. Indeed, it is quite compatible with the perspective developed thus far in this work. If we accept that moral responsibility lies in the nature of free will, we could argue that nature is corrupted for no higher reason than because those free agents responsible for it have become corrupted. Jon Tal Murphree argues along these lines:

> The Fall of nature is roughly the natural consequence of the human Fall. Humankind held their natural world as a trust from God, so when their relationship with God was disrupted their relationship with the environment was distorted. The discord between human beings and nature reflects the tension

---

[22]See D. A. Carson, *How Long, O Lord? Reflections on Suffering and Evil* (Grand Rapids, Mich.: Baker, 1990), esp. pp. 41-132.

that has developed between them and God. When the foundation cracked the entire frame slumped.

Though he acknowledges that many modern people will not accept it, Murphree goes on to argue that the most crucial aspect of the failure of the earth's guardians is that they have allowed God's spiritual enemy to exercise his destructive influence. "If we were less sophisticated," he sarcastically notes, "we might even think that some sinister force just out of sight was consistently programming the world with evil."[23] I will subsequently argue that Murphee is on the mark with this observation.

The restoration of earth's rulers. A third positive aspect of this theodicy warrants a more extensive comment, for it has implications for our anthropology and Christology. A number of theologians have suggested that one major consequence of the human rebellion is that we lost much of the control over nature that we were originally intended to have. They maintain that the authority that Jesus manifested over nature was simply the natural authority humans were originally meant to have as nature's divinely appointed stewards. In this view, Jesus' miracles are to be considered temporary signs of what the human-earth relationship will be when the Fall is finally reversed and the kingdom of God has come.[24]

Humans were, after all, originally given a charge to rule over the animal kingdom, to subjugate and protect the earth (Gen 1:26, 28; 2:15), and thereby to manifest that we are created in the image and likeness of the supreme ruler and subjugator, God. We will someday reclaim this position, with the incarnate Christ as our coruler, when God's kingdom is fully established on earth (Rev 5:10). It thus seems reasonable to suppose that our present inability to master nature—indeed, our present bondage to hostile

---

[23]Jon Tal Murphree, *A Loving God and a Suffering World* (Downers Grove, Ill.: InterVarsity Press, 1981), p. 94. Two others who insightfully draw a connection between human sin and "natural" evil are Jacqueline Marina ("The Theological and Philosophical Significance of the Markan Account of Miracles," *Faith and Philosophy* 15 [1998]: 298-323) and R. J. Berry ("This Cursed Earth: Is 'The Fall' Credible?" *Journal of Science and Christian Belief* 11 [1999]: 29-49). Berry in particular draws a plausible connection between human moral responsibility and the well-being of nature. As with most free-will theists, however, Berry restricts his reflections to *human* moral responsibility and thus cannot adequately account for "natural" evils that clearly lie outside the human sphere of influence. By emphasizing that *spirits* have power to resist God's purpose and corrupt God's natural design, the trinitarian warfare theodicy is able to explain these other forms of "natural" evil.

[24]See Nichols, "Miracles as a Sign," esp. ch. 3. Even now, Nichols insists (correctly, I believe), "the prayers, faith, and holiness of humanity, by mediating God's grace, can influence not only war and peace . . . but even such physical realities as weather, earthquakes, disease, etc" (p. 291).

"natural" forces—is a result of our having lost an authority that once belonged to us. Had we remained in unbroken fellowship with the Father, as Jesus did, perhaps we too could have commanded storms to be stilled and food to be multiplied in his name (Mk 4:39; 8:1-8).[25]

Humans as fallen ecological stewards. This understanding of "natural" evil can to some degree be confirmed by simple observation. Even apart from losing in the Fall our supernatural capacity to control nature, much of the suffering at the hands of nature that befalls us and the animal kingdom is directly or indirectly our fault.[26] If we cared for the earth the way we were originally intended to, and if we cared about each other and the animal kingdom the way God intended, much of the suffering that occurs from nature could be avoided.

Starvation, for example, is more a result of the apathy and greed of those who have more than enough but refuse to share than a result of nature not producing enough. Further, how much of nature's inability to produce enough is at least indirectly due to the self-centered and shortsighted ways we have used it? What is more, how many fatal diseases are the direct or indirect result of our carelessly polluting our environment? And how many deaths by natural disasters could be prevented if human welfare on a global scale, rather than the individual accumulation of wealth, was made a top priority?

There is, then, a good deal to be said in favor of the traditional view that nature is hostile toward us as a result of human sin. This is not to say that the view is without problems, however. Several criticisms follow.

"Natural" evil and the blueprint worldview. To begin, because it was usually combined with a blueprint understanding of divine providence, the view that suffering at the hands of nature is divine punishment has traditionally

---

[25]Against this, one could argue that this understanding of Jesus' miracles as arising out of his perfect humanity rather than his divinity compromises his uniqueness. If we could at least hypothetically do what Jesus did, how is he qualitatively distinct from us? The answer, I submit, is that he was and is qualitatively distinct from us not so much by virtue of what he *did* but by virtue of *who he is.* Jesus is not only a perfect human; he is the divine Son of God. Hence, he is to be worshiped, though this can never be legitimately done in relation to any mere human being or even any angelic being (Mt 28:9, 17; Heb 1:6). Jesus' humanity is identical to our humanity, though his is unfallen. But what makes his human identity qualitatively unique is that as the eternal and fully divine Son of God, *he chooses it.* As God, and as a demonstration of God's self-defining love, he genuinely took on the nature of a human servant, and this is precisely how he exemplifies his glorious divinity (Phil 2:6-11).

[26]As Murphee notes, *A Loving God,* p. 94. Arthur Peacock has a good discussion of humans as God's viceregents on the earth in *Creation and the World of Science* (Oxford: Clarendon, 1979), pp. 294-318.

been interpreted in a meticulous way. It has usually been assumed that there is a *specific* divine reason behind each and every *specific* instance of suffering brought about by "natural" causes. If a particular nation or village experienced a catastrophic "natural" disaster, for example, it was often assumed that there must be a particular sin that this nation or village was being punished for.[27]

Although the Bible teaches that God sometimes chooses to discipline people this way, this does not warrant the conclusion that all "natural" evil is a form of divine punishment. Jesus affirms the message of the book of Job in several instances when he explicitly denies that certain "natural" evils were the result of divine punishment (Lk 13:4-5; Jn 9:1-4).[28] Even more significantly, Jesus denies this view by opposing all forms of "natural" infirmities and even a "natural" storm as being the direct or indirect result of demonic activity (e.g., Mk 4:35-41; 9:25; Lk 13:11, 16).[29]

Experience contradicts this theodicy as well. There is no discernible correlation between the amount of suffering a person or group of people experience at the hands of nature and the amount or intensity of their sinfulness. The insight of the psalmist that the wicked often prosper and the righteous suffer is at least as true today as it was when first written (e.g., Ps 10:2-11; 73:2-14). Hence, while we must yet leave open the possibility that God sometimes uses "nature" as a weapon against adversaries or to discipline people, we have no reason to conclude that this is always, or even usually, the explanation for why nature behaves as it does.

Prehumanoid animal suffering. Another difficulty with the punishment explanation of "natural" evil is that it fails to explain why, on the reckoning of most paleontologists, suffering and violence permeated the world millions of years before humans existed. Since the late Precambrian period the paleontological evidence reveals a nature "red in tooth and claw." Creatures

---

[27]For the classical satire on this prevalent assumption, see Voltaire, "Candide," in *Voltaire's Candide, Zadig and Selected Stories*, trans. D. M. Frame (Bloomington: Indiana University Press, 1961), pp. 3-101.

[28]Some read John 9:1-5 as an endorsement of the view that God ordains "natural" infirmities. But see my discussion in *God at War: The Bible and Spiritual Conflict* (Downers Grove, Ill.: InterVarsity Press, 1996), pp. 231-37.

[29]James Kallas contrasts the New Testament view with the common evangelical view when he writes, "We see polio or crippling and we piously shake our heads and cluck all the trite absurdities of a nonthinking people by saying, 'it is the will of God . . . hard to understand . . . providence writes a long sentence, we have to wait to get to heaven to read the answer.' Jesus looked at this and in crystal clear terms called it the work of the devil, and not the will of God" (*The Significance of the Synoptic Miracles* [Greenwich, Conn.: Seabury, 1961], p. 63). See the discussion in *God at War,* pp. 171-91; cf. pp. 205-14.

lived by devouring other creatures. The record also reveals that animals sometimes died slow and painful deaths by "natural" phenomena: suffocated in tar pits, burned by volcanic lava, buried by mud slides or earthquakes, frozen by drastic climate changes.[30]

If nature only started behaving in a hostile manner after the human Fall, how is this evidence to be explained? Is this violent prehumanoid state the way nature was originally created? Could such a painful system reflect the ideal, untainted plan of a benevolent, omnipotent Creator? Since the Lord cares for animals (e.g., Gen 1:26-28; Ps 36:6; Jon 4:11) and commands us to do the same (Deut 25:4; Prov 12:10; 27:23), why would he have pronounced such a painful state of affairs "good" (Gen 1:25)? Moreover, why does the Genesis 1 account suggest that all animals ate only vegetation prior to the Fall (Gen 1:29-30)?

Many have answered these questions by simply denying that animal suffering is evil. "We confuse it [animal suffering] with evil," says Blocher, "only in terms of an anthropomorphic projection on to the victim and of an imaginary identification." Without a "reflecting consciousness" such as humans possess, he argues, suffering cannot be called "evil." Thus he concludes, "There is no evil, properly speaking, except for persons."[31] Similarly, Peter Geach argues against sympathy for animal suffering and considering it an evil when he contends that "their [animal] life is too alien to ours for sympathy to be anything but folly or affectation."[32]

This conclusion raises several issues. First, it does not account for the bib-

---

[30]Some within the Creation Science movement attempt to argue that animals did not, in fact, suffer or die prior to the human Fall. See, e.g., John C. Whitcomb Jr. and Henry Morris, *The Genesis Flood: The Biblical Record and Its Scientific Implications* (Philadelphia: Presbyterian & Reformed, 1961); John C. Whitcomb Jr., *The Early Earth* (Grand Rapids, Mich.: Baker, 1986); Henry Morris, *The Beginning of the World* (El Cajon, Calif.: Master Books, 1977); Henry Morris, *The Genesis Record* (Grand Rapids, Mich.: Baker, 1976); and Ray Montgomery, *It's a Wonderful World—Naturally* (Washington, D.C.: Review and Herald, 1982). Such a view is beset with difficulties, not least of which is the fact that it requires the supposition of a very young earth (6,000-10,000 years old) and indeed the almost wholesale rejection of the findings of contemporary paleontology and geology.

[31]Henri Blocher, *Evil and the Cross*, trans. David G. Preston (Downers Grove, Ill.: InterVarsity Press, 1994), p. 33. Blocher also says, "As for the manifestations of violence in the animal kingdom . . . it is debatable whether they can be considered as *evil*" (p. 58).

[32]Peter Geach, *Providence and Evil* (Cambridge: Cambridge University Press, 1977), p. 80. So too Arthur C. Custance thinks there is no evil involved in suffering within the animal kingdom. See his "God Within Nature" in *Man in Adam and in Christ*, Doorway Papers 3 (Grand Rapids, Mich.: Zondervan, 1975), pp. 52-77. For a survey on views of animal pain, see Andrew Linzey and Tom Regan, eds., *Animals and Christianity: A Book of Readings* (New York: Crossroads, 1988), pp. 42-84.

lical data suggesting that animal suffering *is* evil. Second, it is not clear why a "reflecting consciousness" constitutes the all-important criteria as to whether or not suffering is evil. Blocher offers no explanation, though one is needed, for this criterion is not self-evident.

Third, if we grant this criterion and if we also grant that animals have no "reflecting consciousness," must we not also grant that human cruelty to animals is not evil? Conversely, if it seems intuitively right (to say nothing of biblically mandated, Gen 1:26-28; Prov 27:23) that it is indeed evil for humans to be cruel toward animals, how can we maintain that it is not evil if nature, under the Creator's direction, treats animals in this fashion? In my view, animal suffering at the hands of nature is as morally problematic as animal suffering at the hands of a sadistic human.

Fourth, if we grant Blocher's criterion, are we willing to concede further that the suffering of infants and severely mentally impaired people is not evil, for they often have less "reflecting consciousness" than many higher primates. This leads to a fifth objection: On what basis can one argue that only ordinary humans possess "reflecting consciousness"? Higher primates seem to possess a capacity to "reflect" and "feel"—a fact that contradicts Geach's claim that animals are "too alien" to us for us to have sympathy for their suffering. It is true that primates lack *the degree* of reflecting consciousness that ordinary humans possess. But even if we grant Blocher's criterion, this should lead to the conclusion that animal suffering, though somewhat less evil than human suffering, is evil nonetheless.

For these reasons I am compelled to regard animal suffering as evil, and since animals suffered before the Fall, this suggests that the punishment explanation is to some degree incomplete.[33]

Structural cosmic evil. Another problem with the punishment explanation is that the problematic aspects of creation seem to far outrun what would be called for in punishing humans for their crimes. It is, I have argued, not too difficult to understand why creation directly under human guardianship suffers when we fall, for such is the nature of morally responsible freedom. The explanation for why the earth is adversely affected by humans is in principle no different from the explanation for why children can be adversely affected by their parents. Given the principle of proportionality (TWT4), we may

---

[33]Some have suggested that the punishment for Adam and Eve's rebellion was applied retroactively to the creation and that this accounts for prehumanoid suffering. The view has at least two major difficulties: (a) it presupposes a view of foreknowledge that is debatable (see chapters three and four); (b) it reflects a bizarre form of justice, namely, that animals are punished millions of years ahead of time on the basis of the behavior of their future guardians.

agree that the potential of a morally responsible person or group to bless is also their potential to curse. When humans fall, our potential to bless nature and be blessed by nature was to some extent exchanged for a potential to curse nature and be cursed by nature.

This explanation can only be stretched so far, however. Violence and destruction were present in nature before humans existed, and they are present in places in the cosmos not under human authority. "The *whole creation*," the apostle Paul writes, "has been groaning in labor pains until now" (Rom 8:22). As Stuermann noted above, violence and destruction seem to be an integral part of the "natural" cosmic system. Everywhere order is balanced by chaos. Stars explode into supernovas and burn out other solar systems. Galaxies collide with other galaxies. The second law of thermodynamics, which describes everything as in the process of decaying, permeates creation. The cosmos as a whole is heading toward an energyless state of unending darkness.

We of course cannot be certain whether any form of life outside of the earth suffers as a result of this violence. Nevertheless, the theodicy problem remains either way. The point is that the structural nature of violence and destruction throughout the cosmos argues against the notion that the violence and destruction on *our* planet, *which obviously affects life adversely,* is only the result of human sin. Something bigger than ourselves seems to be involved.

There are, then, some weaknesses as well as strengths in the traditional punishment explanation for "natural" evil. While it cannot alone constitute a satisfactory explanation, it must play a central role in any explanation that will.

Nature as the Arena for Human Soul-Making

The hidden Creator of a hostile world. A third explanation of "natural" evil suggests that nature is designed by God to challenge creatures because the goal of creation is to produce souls of a certain kind of character. According to this view, this goal would be unattainable in a world without suffering. This perspective is generally attributed to the second-century theologian Irenaeus and has a number of defenders today. But the person most closely associated with this view and most responsible for its contemporary revival is John Hick.[34] Thus my discussion will center on his soul-making explanation for "natural" evil.

---

[34]Hick, *Evil and the God of Love.*

There are two closely related reasons why nature must have a dangerous and painful side to it, according to Hick. First, if the relationship that the Creator desires between himself and humans is to have a moral quality to it, there must be an epistemic distance* between us and the Creator. If the choice to love or reject God is to be morally responsible and free, Hick contends, "God must set man at a distance from Himself, from which he can then voluntarily come to God." This further implies that

> God must be a hidden deity, veiled by His creation. He must be knowable, but only by a mode of knowledge that involves a free personal response on man's part, this response consisting in an uncompelled interpretative activity whereby we experience the world as mediating the divine presence.[35]

The world, in short, must be "religiously ambiguous, both veiling God and revealing Him—veiling Him to ensure man's freedom and revealing Him to men as they rightly exercise that freedom."[36] It is necessary, then, for the natural environment of humans to have an "atheistic" character to it. This, for Hick, is partly why nature only ambiguously reveals the character of a loving Creator.

God also desires us to develop moral responsibility in relation to other people, which is another reason Hick believes nature must be ambivalent. According to Hick, "The development of human personality . . . moral, spiritual, and intellectual . . . is a product of challenge and response."[37]

So, for example, the challenge of cooperating with an unbending, impersonal, objective world enables us to become intelligent and morally responsible. If the objective natural world always conformed to our desires, Hick and others argue, we could never cultivate these qualities. Moreover, if humans never suffered at the hands of their environment, we would never develop virtues such as courage, patience and compassion. Hence, according to Hick, the possibility and even inevitability of "natural" evil is the price God must pay if he desires a world capable of producing creatures who could develop moral character in their relationship with him and in their relationships with each other.[38]

The necessity of epistemic distance and objective reality. There is much to commend this line of thinking. First, although it is somewhat problematic,

---

[35]Ibid., p. 281.
[36]John Hick, "An Irenaean Theodicy," in *Encountering Evil*, ed. S. David (Atlanta: John Knox Press, 1981), p. 46.
[37]Ibid.
[38]Michael Peterson argues along similar lines (*Evil and the Christian God* [Grand Rapids, Mich.: Baker, 1982], p. 113).

Hick's notion of a necessary epistemic distance between us and the Creator is consistent with my contention that love must be freely chosen and must be, within limits, irrevocable (TWT1, TWT4). Freedom of choice, I previously argued, requires that the alternatives under consideration be viable alternatives. If the choice is to be a matter of morality, not survival, it must be possible genuinely to project a future for oneself living out one's choices. If God in all his glory, power and splendor were perfectly obvious to us from the start, it is doubtful our choice to love him could have a distinctly moral quality to it.

In biblical terms, there may have been a metaphysical reason why God included a forbidden tree in the garden (Gen 2:15-17; 3:2-3). If Adam and Eve's choice to follow God was to have a moral dimension, the possibility of not following God had to exist. One might say that the serpent's lie that God's character was not impeccable—that God was actually threatened by Adam and Eve (Gen 3:4-5)—had to be believable. This plausibility would have been impossible, however, if there had been no epistemic distance whatsoever between God and his original creations.

Secondly, as we shall subsequently discuss more fully, Hick seems correct in suggesting that objective reality has to be impersonal and somewhat unbending if creatures are to live morally responsible lives within it. For us to be morally responsible in relation to the world, we must be able to influence the world, but the world must also be able to influence us. That is, it must be somewhat pliable but not immediately accommodating to our every whim.

To illustrate this in biblical terms again, before the Fall Adam was given the responsibility of tending a garden that existed independently of himself (Gen 2:5-17). He was responsible for the garden, which implies that the garden was pliable but not immediately subject to his every wish. For this reason, his caring had a moral quality to it. It was a responsibility he had to freely accept and work at.

So it must be, I argue, with all morally responsible agents. If the objective world was immediately subject to our wills, it could not function as the context in which agents could interact with it and with one another in morally responsible ways. Indeed, if objective reality was immediately subject to our every whim, it is doubtful whether we could call it "objective" reality at all. Would it not in fact simply be an extension of our subjective states? If this were the case, we would not exist over and against anything outside ourselves.

Nor could we genuinely exist over and against each other within such a world, for we are part of each other's objective environment. How could you exist independently of me, for example, if everything outside of myself immediately accommodated my wishes? You, like the rest of the "world," could in this case only be an extension of my own subjectivity.[39]

It thus seems that Hick and others are correct in arguing that the very possibility of moral agents interacting with each other requires the existence of an objective environment that is relatively neutral regarding the desires of any one of these agents. We need to be able to influence this environment, otherwise interaction would not be possible. But the world must also be able to exist over and against us.

C. S. Lewis illustrates this point well when he writes:

> As soon as we attempt to introduce the mutual knowledge of fellow-creatures we run up against the necessity of "Nature." People often talk as if nothing were easier than for two naked minds to "meet" or become aware of each other. But I see no possibility of their doing so except in a common medium which forms their "external world" or environment. . . . What we need for human society is exactly what we have—a neutral something, neither you nor I, which we can both manipulate so as to make signs to each other. . . . Society, then, implies a common field or "world" in which its members meet.[40]

In sum, it seems that Hick, Lewis and others are on the right track in maintaining that the Creator's aim in creation required some epistemic distance between himself and the world, on the one hand, and an objective reality that does not immediately conform to our wishes, on the other. Further, these two concepts, Hick believes, explain why the earth is not the "Edenic" paradise we might sometimes wish it to be.

Nightmares do not build character. Despite these important insights, I consider the soul-making explanation of "natural" evil inadequate. Chief among its shortcomings is the fact that the amount and intensity of suffering that humans and animals endure as a result of "natural" evil seems excessive

---

[39]Using this same line of reasoning, I would argue that strict Calvinism logically entails pantheism. If God exhaustively controls every aspect of creation, then the whole of the creation is simply an extension of himself. See Gregory A. Boyd, *Trinity and Process: A Critical Evaluation and Reappropriation of Hartshorne's Di-Polar Theism Towards a Trinitarian Metaphysics* (New York: Lang, 1992), pp. 67-70, 257-58.

[40]C. S. Lewis, *The Problem of Pain* (New York: Macmillan, 1962), pp. 30-31. Frederick R. Tennant makes the same point with a view toward explaining the preconditions for intelligence: "Without . . . regularity in physical phenomena there could be no probability to guide us: no prediction, no prudence, no accumulation of ordered experience, no pursuit of premeditated ends, no formation of habit, no possibility of character of culture. Our intellectual faculties could not have developed. . . . And without rationality, morality is impossible" (*Philosophical Theology*, 2 vols. [Cambridge: Cambridge University Press, 1928-1930], 2:199-200).

in the context of a divinely orchestrated soul-making agenda. Indeed, nature often seems orchestrated more for the crushing of souls than for their healthy development.

For example, several years ago a vicious tornado struck a small Kansas town without warning. While it did little other damage, it destroyed a small church, killing numerous parishioners. Among its victims were a dozen or so young children who were presenting an Easter pageant at the moment the tornado struck. The credibility of the soul-making theodicy depends on our ability to accept that this nightmare, and nightmares like it, are allowed in order to develop certain characteristics in people's lives.

Even if we grant that certain characteristics could be developed in response to this tragedy (e.g., compassion, empathy), can we argue that the price paid for this development was worth the lives that were lost? Would any of the victims or their parents concede this? Finally, what about God's concern to develop the characters of the children who were killed?

"Natural" disasters of this magnitude take the lives of innocent victims and leave their survivors emotionally and spiritually crushed as often as they develop character in them. Christians frequently hear testimonies of people who suffered enormous losses such as the one this church family endured but who proclaim that the loss, though incredibly painful, somehow increased their faith and built their character. We understandably celebrate such faith. What we often fail to hear, however, are the numerous testimonies of those who bitterly lost their faith, hope or character through such tragedies. We rarely give due consideration to voices like that of W. Somerset Maugham, who testify that their "suffering did not ennoble; it degraded" and who therefore conclude that as often as not suffering "made men selfish, mean, petty and suspicious."[41] If our theologies are to be rooted in reality and not wishful thinking, we need to hear these testimonies as well.

A story of spiritual degeneration. Allow me to provide one such story. A number of years ago I learned of a couple who discovered that their seven-year-old daughter had a rare and untreatable genetic disorder that was beginning to deteriorate her brain. Over the course of several years, the doctors informed them, these parents would have to helplessly watch their previously bright and creative child gradually lose all her mental capacities. It would ultimately leave her in an almost vegetative state. The news was understandably life-shattering.

What made the scenario even more nightmarish, however, was that this

---

[41]Quoted in Stuart Brown, ed., *Reason and Religion: A Royal Institute of Philosophy Symposium* (New York: Cornell University Press, 1977), p. 14.

particular genetic disorder was hereditary. Any subsequent children of this couple would most likely grow without any abnormality for the first five to seven years of their lives but would then begin to deteriorate as their older sister had. It so happens that in the previous year this couple had given birth to a beautiful set of twins.

As predicted, the first child began to deteriorate mentally over the course of the next several years. All the while her sister and brother were growing normally, sometimes asking about their older sister, who now spent her days in a special home, rocking back and forth and staring into space. The emotional strain on this couple as they lovingly raised these two beautiful children, all the while knowing their probable fate, was unbearable.

They and their friends persistently prayed and struggled to hope for a miracle. But a miracle never happened. Around the age of six both siblings began the same slow, torturous process of deterioration that their older sister had gone through. Some time in the second year of this macabre process the mother suffered a nervous breakdown. When she recovered she found that she had completely lost her faith. The husband's faith followed suit several years later. With their faith went all hope and eventually most of their character. The last I heard of the two, they had gone through a bitter divorce, both had become heavy drinkers, and the father had been fired from his previously successful career.

In my opinion, the suggestion that "natural" evils such as this degenerative disorder are allowed to build character is untenable. God will certainly seek to *use* tragedies like this to a higher end (Rom 8:28), but this does not mean that he allows them for this specific purpose. On the contrary, if there is any intentionality behind ordeals such as this one, it can only be that of a diabolic mind intent on destroying the people involved.

Two further objections. This example raises two related objections against the soul-making explanation of "natural" evil. First, God's failure to intervene in this tragedy, even after the persistent prayers of concerned people, cannot adequately be explained in this theodicy. As the atheist Michael Martin has cogently argued, the necessity of a neutral, objective, natural order is not vitiated by an occasional corrective miracle from the Almighty.[42] In chapter ten I will argue that only an understanding of the relative irrevocability of freedom, applied to spirits as well as humans, can explain why God does not prevent "natural" evils such as this.

Second, we may concede Hick's argument that there must be epistemic

---

[42]Michael Martin, *Atheism: A Philosophical Justification* (Philadelphia: Temple University Press, 1990), pp. 404-6.

distance between God and his free creatures if their relationship to him is to be chosen in a morally responsible manner. But epistemic distance alone does not adequately explain gratuitous "natural" evils such as the one the parents in our story endured. Nightmares such as this cannot be accounted for as merely the result of a necessary epistemic distance between us and God. It is one thing for circumstances to render God's presence obtuse, quite another for them to render God's absence obvious.

Nature as a Kenotic Process

Several scholars have recently developed a fourth intriguing approach to understanding "natural" evil, viewing nature as a *kenotic process*.* It suggests that nature is "red in tooth and claw" because it reflects and participates in the self-sacrificing nature of the Creator. The most recent, and in my estimation most noteworthy, exponents of this view are Nancey Murphy and George F. R. Ellis in their appropriately acclaimed work, *On the Moral Nature of the Universe*.[43] My exposition and critique of this view shall thus center on their reflections in this work.

A kenotic understanding of God is central to the view of Murphy and Ellis. Against the classical philosophical tradition's tendency to define omnipotence as control, the kenotic view understands God to limit himself by empowering other personal beings to exist over and against himself. What is more, against the classical philosophical view that God is immutable and impassable, the kenotic view sees God as being passionately involved in and profoundly affected by creation. Indeed, based on an understanding of Jesus Christ as the definitive revelation of God, the kenotic perspective emphasizes that God creates in order to give himself away in love and that God suffers in this loving self-giving.[44]

Murphy and Ellis aim to present in their work a unified worldview centered on this kenotic view of God. More specifically, they seek to demonstrate that a kenotic ethic, rooted in a kenotic understanding of ultimate reality (God), is presupposed in every branch of human understanding, including all the sciences. The reason for this presupposition is that creation exemplifies a kenotic structure.

The "cruciform" character of nature. Murphy and Ellis consider the problem of "natural" evil from this perspective. Following the lead of Holmes Rolston, Murphy and Ellis argue that suffering resulting from "natural" pro-

---

[43]Nancey Murphy and George F. R. Ellis, *On the Moral Nature of the Universe: Theology, Cosmology, and Ethics* (Minneapolis: Fortress, 1996).
[44]Ibid., pp. 118-22, 174-78.

cesses reflects the kenotic nature of the Creator. Quoting Rolston, they maintain that "the secret of life is that it is a passion play. Things perish in tragedy."
They continue:

> Things perish with a passing over in which the sacrificed individual also flows
> in the river of life. Each of the suffering creatures is delivered over as an inno-
> cent sacrificed to preserve a line, a blood sacrifice perishing that others may
> live. We have a kind of "slaughter of the innocents," a nonmoral, naturalistic
> harbinger of the slaughter of the innocents at the birth of the Christ, all per-
> haps vignettes hinting of the innocent lamb slain from the foundation of the
> world. They share the labor of divinity. In their lives, beautiful, tragic, and per-
> petually incomplete, they speak for God; they prophesy as they participate in
> the divine pathos.[45]

Suffering is a necessary part of the kenotic process of creation, according to
Rolston, Murphy and Ellis. "All things participate not only in the taking of
life in order to live," Murphy and Ellis write, "but in the painful *giving* of
their lives that others might live."[46] Nature thus has a universal "cruciform"
character to it. In a manner similar to the way that God offers himself up in
self-sacrificial love so others may have more abundant life, everything in
nature gives itself up so others might live and the whole of creation might
progress to more abundant life. The "red in tooth and claw" dimension of
nature that moves the evolutionary process toward the development of
higher life forms parallels the suffering quality of God's self-giving love that
moves the whole creation toward the end for which God created it.

I fully embrace Murphy and Ellis's understanding of God as kenotic love
over and against the classical philosophical understanding. Further, while not
agreeing with all the specifics, I endorse their ingenious attempt to arrive at a
unified worldview that encompasses all the sciences under the vision of ultimate reality as kenotic love. But I question the plausibility of their perspective on "natural" evil. I here offer three general criticisms of their view.

Why is nature so violent? First, while we must concede that some animals
and organisms survive by taking the life of other creatures, it is not clear why
this pain-filled "natural" order *has* to be the way it is. Murphy and Ellis assert
that they cannot see it operating otherwise. But, so far as I can tell, their
reflections are predicated on the assumption that the laws of nature we presently observe are inexorable. It seems to me that their argument is circular.
Certainly if the laws of nature presently governing the world are the laws

---

[45]Ibid., p. 212, quoting H. Rolston, "Does Nature Need to Be Redeemed?"
[46]Ibid., p. 213.

that *must* govern any world God could create, then the violent state of nature, or something like it, must be inevitable. But why assume this? For example, is there a metaphysical explanation for why the whole of nature exhibits the second law of thermodynamics? Must things decay? Is it not conceivable that creation could "naturally" move toward increased order rather than disorder?[47] Paul's statement that the *whole creation* will be set free from "its bondage to decay" (Rom 8:21) suggests that it is conceivable.

Moreover, are there *metaphysical* (not just empirical) reasons why certain animals must be carnivorous? Is there a necessary reason God could not accomplish his plan for creation without the millions of years of death and destruction that have gone into achieving these ends? More specifically, was all of this suffering really necessary to arrive at beings with the capacities humans now possess? Murphy and Ellis have not demonstrated the necessity of these things, and until they do their theodicy remains incomplete.

Is this perspective scriptural? Second, Murphy and Ellis's kenotic explanation of "natural" evil" is inconsistent with Scripture. Even if we grant their assumption that the early Genesis narrative is mythological, we must, if we consider it inspired, make *some* sense out of its depiction of the animal kingdom as being noncarnivorous before the Fall and some sense of the fact that in this narrative the Creator declared this original creation to be unequivocally "good" (Gen 1:29-31). However, Murphy and Ellis do not address this biblical motif.[48]

---

[47]See Q. Smith, "An Atheological Argument from Evil Natural Laws," *International Journal for Philosophy of Religion* 29 (1991): 159-74. Smith suggests that "evil natural laws" constitute evidence of God's nonexistence. I rather take such evil laws to be evidence for the devil's existence. We both agree that the laws of nature could and should be somewhat different than they presently are if they were established by an all-good Creator. On the gap between what is and what should be in nature, see S. Clark, "Is Nature God's Will?" in *Animals on the Agenda: Questions About Animals for Theology and Ethics,* ed. Andrew Linzey and Dorothy Yamamoto (Urbana: University of Illinois Press, 1998), pp. 123-36. Clark writes, "What should happen and what does happen are no closer in the world of nonhuman nature than in human history, despite the readiness of pantheists [and, we might add, many classical philosophical theologians!] to see 'beauty' in the subtle ways of death devised by parasite and predator" (p. 134). On the nonnecessity of death, see Osborn Segerberg Jr., *The Immortality Factor* (New York: E. P. Dutton, 1974).

[48]Interestingly enough, Plato also believed that the animal kingdom was once nonviolent, for "God was their shepherd" (*The Statesman,* trans. H. N. Fowler [Cambridge, Mass: Harvard University Press, 1962], p. 59). For various cosmological reasons, the world fell, according to Plato: "All the gods who share, each in his own sphere, the rule of the Supreme Spirit . . . let go the parts of the world which were under their care." Now, though the world still receives "only good things . . . from its Composer," it receives "all the elements of harshness and injustice" from this fall (pp. 62-63). This mythological view reflects some profound insight into the nature of spiritual reality.

What makes this omission surprising is that this motif fits well with other features of their theological system. Throughout their work Murphy and Ellis emphasize that the vision of God as self-giving entails a pacifistic ethic. Because God does not achieve his ends by resorting to coercion or violence but rather influences creation by self-sacrificial love, we should do the same, they argue. But if they are correct, should we not expect God's creation to reflect this, which is precisely what Genesis suggests about the prefallen world? Just as violence among humans suggests that we are out of sync with our Creator, would it not be logical to conclude that violence within the "natural" realm suggests that nature is out of sync with the Creator? Murphy and Ellis do not follow this logic, however. They rather attempt to justify the violence in nature and do not consider the pacifistic vision of the Genesis narrative.[49]

There are other tensions with the biblical revelation as well. For example, Paul declares that all of nature is fallen, that it groans and that it needs redemption (Rom 8:20-22). This fallen state contrasts strongly with God's pronouncement prior to the fall that the creation is "good" (Gen 1:31). The assumption in Romans 8 is that nature is no longer the way the Creator originally intended it to be.

Similarly, Jesus' ministry demonstrates that "natural" phenomena such as disease, illness, deformity and even life-threatening storms are the direct or indirect results of Satan's activity (see chapter one). Far from revealing God's character, such "natural" phenomena reveal the character of his archenemy, Satan, according to Jesus and the Gospel authors. As a result, instead of concluding that such "natural" evil participates in "the divine pathos," they assert that God's character and power—his kingdom—is revealed by *ridding* creation of such things.

Finally, if the violent state of the animal kingdom reveals the Creator's design and is "natural," why does Scripture portray such violence as disappearing when the Lord's kingdom is finally established? For example, in Isaiah we read:

The wolf shall live with the lamb,
    the leopard shall lie down with the kid,

---

[49]One possible explanation for this omission is that Murphy and Ellis take seriously the scientific evidence for an old earth filled with violence long before humans ever arrived on the scene. If we start here, then it seems that the Genesis account of a nonviolent world prior to the human fall need not be factored into our understanding of the natural world. In chapter ten, however, I will offer a means by which we can affirm both the Genesis view of a pacifistic supralapsarian creation but still accept the majority scientific view that the earth is billions of years old and was filled with violence long before humans came on the scene.

the calf and the lion and the fatling together,
    and a little child shall lead them.
The cow and the bear shall graze,
    their young shall lie down together;
    and the lion shall eat straw like the ox.
The nursing child shall play over the hole of the asp,
    and the weaned child shall put its hand on the adder's den.
They will not hurt or destroy
    on all my holy mountain;
for the earth will be full of the knowledge of the LORD
    as the waters cover the sea. (Is 11:6-9; cf. 65:25; Ezek 34:25-31)

This passage suggests that when nature is brought into perfect alignment with God's will—that is, when it is "full of the knowledge of the LORD"—there will be no violence in it. Animals will not survive by devouring other animals. This suggests that the violent state of the animal kingdom that we find today is not as it was originally created to be. It is "fallen."[50]

For all the insight embodied in their work, therefore, I conclude that in this respect Murphy and Ellis's view is inconsistent with Scripture and the rest of their system. The fundamental problem is that they do not consider the scriptural motif that something has gone seriously wrong with creation: it is fallen and under the bondage of violent spiritual agents who oppose the Creator's design.

Does nature reflect the self-giving Creator? Third, I am not convinced that the "red in tooth and claw" dimension of nature can justifiably be described as "cruciform." For no reason other than love God became a human and suffered a God-forsaken death on the cross. For no reason other than love God gives himself away so others may live. *That* is the cruciform quality of divine love. But where is this quality reflected in nature?

I suggest that nature exemplifies quite an opposite quality. Murphy and Ellis claim that the whole animal kingdom participates in "the labor of divinity" by engaging in "the painful *giving* of their lives that others might live."[51] On the contrary, I see only *taking*. Is it not the case that the suffering that takes place in nature is always a matter of one animal ripping life

---

[50]Stanley Hauerwas and John Berkman have argued somewhat along these lines in "A Trinitarian Theology of the 'Chief End' of 'All Flesh,' " in *Good News for Animals? Christian Approaches to Animal Well-Being*, ed. Charles Pinches and J. B. McDaniel (Maryknoll, N.Y.: Orbis, 1993), pp. 62-73. See also Charles Birch and Lukas Vischer, *Living with the Animals: The Community of God's Creatures* (Geneva: WCC Publications, 1977), esp. ch. 2, "Violence in Creation," and ch. 3, "The Fall and Its Consequences."

[51]Murphy and Ellis, *Moral Nature*, p. 213.

from another to ensure its own survival?

For example, I recently watched a nature video in which a pack of hyenas devoured an antelope. The antelope did not offer itself up to be eaten. Rather, despite the antelope's most vigorous attempts to survive, the vicious pack of hyenas violently robbed the pitiful beast of its life. And, as is often the case in nature, this killing was not merciful. Much of the antelope's skin was ripped off before it finally died.

What is "cruciform" about this? In my view, this gory aggression does not reflect the kenotic love of the Creator. If it reflects any transcendent design at all (I will subsequently argue that it does), it is that of a being that preserves itself by feeding on weaker prey regardless of the suffering such feeding produces (cf. 1 Pet 5:8). To put it in Rolston's terms, if this "slaughter of the innocents" is in fact a "naturalistic harbinger of the slaughter of the innocents at the birth of the Christ," it can only be because there is something equivalent to evil king Herod masterminding this "natural" slaughter. But in this case we must wonder what is "natural" about it?[52]

If we deny the influence of a "cosmic Herod" behind the scenes of nature, however, then we are left wondering why the innocents are slaughtered at all. In other words, the analogy Rolston draws between the slaughtered children of Bethlehem and the endless slaughter that characterizes the "natural" world does not work because he fails to acknowledge an evil free agent responsible for the slaughter in the latter case.

This criticism is significant to Murphy and Ellis's thesis because, as I have already suggested, their goal is an ethical vision that conforms to the nature of reality. The pacifistic ethical vision they prescribe for humans on the basis of their kenotic understanding of God is inconsistent with the "natural" order of the animal kingdom. Live by killing; eat or be eaten; survival of the fittest—*this* is the law of nature, and there is nothing pacifistic or self-sacrificial about it.

Again, I agree with Murphy and Ellis's ethical vision and the kenotic view of God on which it is based, but this should lead them to the conclusion that nature as it is now is not ruled solely by God and thus does not unambiguously manifest his loving character.

Spirits and a unified worldview. Murphy and Ellis's vision would be more consistent if they agreed that nature is not as the self-giving Creator intended it to be. In fact, the foundation for this conclusion is already

---

[52]For precisely this reason Murphree argues that theism must be as "committed to the existence of a devil" and to "the explanation of natural evil" as it is to the existence of human freedom as the explanation of moral evil ("Can Theism Survive?" pp. 231-44). I could not agree more.

present in their system, for they hold that humans possess self-determining freedom empowering us to work either with the Creator or against him in achieving his ends.[53] When we choose to act coercively or violently against the Creator's design (but in keeping with nature's pattern), we harm each other and nature. In this case things are not as they should be.

But why should we limit self-determining freedom to human agents? Along with Scripture, the early postapostolic church and most non-Western cultures, why not suppose that spiritual agents also possess a similar "power to influence"? Moreover, if *we* possess the ability to corrupt nature, why should we not suppose that these agents possess a similar, but more extensive, power? Such a postulation would posit the "cosmic Herod" necessary to explain the "slaughter of the innocents" within the Bethlehem of God's created "natural" order.

Conclusion

If spirits exist as free agents with power to influence people and nature, then any attempt to arrive at a comprehensive view of reality without taking them into consideration will inevitably be inadequate. The inherent difficulties in Murphy and Ellis's view of "natural" evil illustrate this fact, as do the inherent difficulties in the three views before it. In chapter ten I will develop the implications of an approach to "natural" evil that incorporates the activity of such spirits.

Before embarking on this, however, three other contemporary approaches to "natural" evil need to be considered. Each view, we shall see, offers important insights that help form a comprehensive approach to understanding "natural" evil. But each is inadequate for the same reasons the four views we have examined in this chapter are inadequate. Their theodicy omits the one to whom Scripture ultimately traces all evil: Satan. Demonstrating this claim is the goal of the following chapter.

---

[53]Murphy and Ellis, *Moral Nature*, pp. 34-37, 207-8, 213-18.

9

WHEN NATURE
BECOMES A WEAPON

Perspectives on the Origin
of Natural Evil, Part 2

Author of evil, unknown till thy revolt . . .
How hast thou disturbed
Heaven's blessed peace, and unto Nature brought
Misery, uncreated till the crime
Of thy rebellion.
MILTON, *PARADISE LOST*

Tiger! Tiger! burning bright
In the forest of the night,
What immortal hand or eye
Could frame thy fearful symmetry?
When the stars threw down their spears,
And watered heaven with their tears,
Did he smile his work to see?
Did he who made the Lamb make thee?
WILLIAM BLAKE, "THE TIGER"

A fertile world must be neither too rigid, nor too loose.
It needs both chance and necessity.
JOHN POLKINGHORNE,
QUARKS, CHAOS AND CHRISTIANITY

The theodicies examined in the previous chapter attempt to explain
"natural" evil by identifying a purpose that the Creator has for it. That is, it
contributes to the beauty of the whole, it punishes sinners, it builds our

character, or it participates in God's suffering, self-sacrificial love. For all their valuable insights, I believe, each of these perspectives is finally inadequate.

These and other difficulties have led some philosophers and theologians to seek alternative explanations of "natural" evil. If we cannot explain apparently diabolical aspects of nature by identifying a purpose the Creator supposedly has for them, perhaps an explanation is to be found in an inherent limitation of God or in creation. The three approaches to "natural" evil we will consider in this chapter argue along these lines.

We will first consider the view that "natural" evil exists because God is inherently limited. Following this we will examine two variations of the view that "natural" evil exists because there is a necessary limitation in creation. As with the four views examined in the previous chapter, I will argue that each of these views offers some positive contributions to resolving the problem of "natural" evil, though each has difficulties as well. These difficulties, I will argue, are primarily due to their failure seriously to consider the possibility of evil wills negatively influencing the natural order.

The Process View of God as Inherently Limited

The fifth approach to "natural" evil holds that nature is not perfect simply because the God who creates and sustains it is limited in his power. This approach has many variations, but its most compelling and influential expression is found in Process theology.[1]

I must confess that Process theology is not easy to summarize, especially if our desire is to stay as free from technical jargon as possible. What follows is an attempt to summarize a very complex system of thought as clearly and concisely as possible. As I mentioned in the introduction, lay readers who are unfamiliar with philosophical concepts may find this section demanding, but I believe their perseverance will be worth the effort.

---

[1]While many sources contributed to the formation of Process thought, the person usually credited with founding this movement is Alfred North Whitehead in his classic work, *Process and Reality: An Essay in Cosmology*, corrected ed. (New York: Free Press, 1978). Another variation of this type of theism (sometimes called "finite theism") that was influential early in the twentieth century is Personalism. See, e.g., Edgar S. Brightman, *A Philosophy of Religion* (New York: Prentice-Hall, 1940), pp. 286-301; and Peter Bertocci, "The Explanation of Excess Evil," in *An Introduction to the Philosophy of Religion* (New York: Prentice-Hall, 1951), pp. 420-40. Brightman's "finite God solution" is critiqued in Edward Madden and Peter Hare, *Evil and the Concept of God* (Springfield, Ill.: Charles C. Thomas, 1968), pp. 107-14. Undoubtedly the most well-known popularizer of this theological perspective today has been Rabbi Harold Kushner. His book, *When Bad Things Happen to Good People* (New York: Schocken, 1981), has been a bestseller for over a decade.

Perception and memory as analogical keys to reality. In order accurately to evaluate the Process explanation of "natural" evil, we must first acquire a basic understanding of its view of reality and of God, for these are inextricably connected within this metaphysical system. The key to understanding reality, according to Process thought, is to examine the slice of reality we know firsthand, namely, our own experience. We understand things only to the extent that we understand them in relation to our own experience.[2]

Process thought holds that perception and memory are the two components of our experience most crucial to understanding reality. Both perception and memory involve experiencing a past multiplicity of data in a newly unified way. When I observe a landscape, for example, my experience at any given moment is a single, unified experience. But what I am experiencing is actually a vast multiplicity of disparate individual data (colors, shapes, smells, etc.). My experience unifies this multiplicity of data into a single whole.

What is more, though my unified experience defines my conscious experience in this instant, the multiplicity of data unified in my present experience is actually in the past. The principle that what we experience in the present is actually in the past by the time we experience it is clearly illustrated when we are looking at stars, but Process thought holds that it is a universal metaphysical principle. Experience is always a novel unification in the present of a multiplicity of data from the past.

Finally, *the way* I am now unifying the past multiplicity in my present experience always includes an element of creativity. The multiplicity of data I perceive in a landscape did not determine exactly how I would experience it. Among other things, part of my unique experience of the landscape is constituted by the way I synthesize the data of my experience with every other experience that has ever contributed toward making me who I am. My unified experience of the landscape thus represents a creative advance over the multiplicity of data that form the landscape itself.

Memory exemplifies these principles. *What* we remember is the past. The memory is unified in the present, though the past data we remember are not. Moreover, *how* we remember the past is not strictly determined by what we

---

[2]Whitehead labeled this "the reformed subjectivist principle" (*Process and Reality*, pp. 157-67), while Hartshorne referred to it as "the principle of continuity" (e.g., *Beyond Humanism: Essays in the New Philosophy of Nature* [Chicago: Willet, Clark, 1968], p. 50, and *Creativity in American Philosophy* [Albany, N.Y.: SUNY, 1984], p. 206). Hartshorne argues that psychological concepts must provide the analogical key to understanding all of reality (*Beyond Humanism*, p. 116). See my discussion in *Trinity and Process: A Critical Evaluation and Reappropriation of Hartshorne's Di-Polar Theism Towards a Trinitarian Metaphysics* (New York: Lang, 1992), pp. 40, 121-31.

remember. Each memory of the past involves a creative advance over the past, for the past is always synthesized with a new present.

Becoming over being. The most fundamental conviction of Process thought is that *all of reality is structured this way.* Whereas classical metaphysics held that reality is composed of indivisible solid units (atoms), Process thought argues that reality is composed of indivisible dynamic *experiences.* The ultimate building blocks of reality are momentary, novel, unified "perceptions" or "memories" (called actual occasions*) of a past multiplicity of data.[3] Each actual occasion experiences (or, in Process terms, prehends*) a past multiplicity and in turn immediately becomes available to be experienced by subsequent actual occasions (as "objectified data").

For Process thought, then, reality is a perpetual process of experiences coming into being, only to quickly become the object of subsequent experiences. There are not things that *have* experiences, as in classical substantival metaphysics. Rather, things *are* experiences. Or again, beings do not become. Rather, becoming produces beings.

Everything that appears to have a stable, independent existence on a phenomenological level is actually perpetually becoming. Like a swarm of gnats dancing in the sunlight, thereby giving the appearance of being a solid ball floating in the air, every individual "thing" in our sense experience is in fact a "swarm" of actual occasions, a sea of momentary experiences.[4] It only appears stable because our senses are too dull to participate in the moment-by-moment units of becoming that constitute that thing at a most concrete level.

God as the unifying experience of the world. What is true of every actual occasion is also true of God, according to Process thought. "God is not to

---

[3]Whitehead expresses the heart of his cosmological vision when he writes, "The ultimate metaphysical principle is the advance from disjunction to conjunction, creating a novel entity other than the entities given in the disjunction. The novel entity [i.e., new actual occasion] is at once the togetherness of the [past] 'many' which it finds, and also it is one among the disjunctive 'many' which it leaves; it is a novel entity, disjunctively among the many entities which it synthesizes. The many become one, and are increased by one. In their natures, entities are disjunctively 'many' in process of passage into conjunctive unity" (*Process and Reality*, p. 21).

[4]The analogy of a swarm of gnats applies best to relatively uncoordinated entities such as inanimate objects, for they lack a strong organizing principle. The stronger the dominant organizing principle, however, the higher functioning is the togetherness of actual occasions. Such things are high-functioning "societies" or "nexus" of actual occasions. Donald Sherburne has a helpful discussion in *A Key to Whitehead's Process and Reality,* ed. Donald Sherburne (Chicago: University of Chicago Press, 1966), pp. 72-97. Joseph Bracken applies Whitehead's concept of "society" in interesting ways in *Society and Spirit: A Trinitarian Cosmology* (Selinsgrove, Penn.: Susquehanna University Press, 1991). He relates it to field theory in physics and the concept of "spirit" in theology.

be treated as an exception to all metaphysical principles," writes Whitehead; rather, "He is their chief exemplification."[5] Both are encompassed by the same metaphysical categories. At a most concrete level, then, God is to be understood as a moment-by-moment unit of experience.[6] Unlike any other actual occasion, however, God is the one actual occasion (or single *series* of actual occasions, some would argue) who creatively synthesizes in his present experience the entire multiplicity constituting the just-past cosmos. He is, in a word, the all-embracing experience that unifies the world.

Not only this, but God is the one actual occasion who is a part of the experience of every other actual occasion. God perceives or remembers ("prehends") the entire world, and to some degree the entire world perceives or remembers God. The innumerable actual occasions constituting the cosmos in one moment are thus unified in God's experience, and then God is experienced by the innumerable actual occasions constituting the cosmos the next moment.

As said above, each experience constitutes a creative advance over the data that it unifies. Hence the interplay of God experiencing the just-past world, and the world then experiencing God, constitutes a perpetually creative advancement. The cosmos, and God, are thus in the process of becoming. God enriches the world, and the world enriches God. God influences the world, and the world influences God. According to Process thought, this process has gone on and must continue to go on forever. This is not the result of a choice God makes. It is the metaphysically necessary structure of existence itself.

Moral and "natural" evil in Process thought. Because God can only influence the world, not control it, things do not always go as he would wish. To be sure, God directs each actual occasion (and each "society" of

---

[5]Whitehead, *Process and Reality*, p. 343. This is one of the most fundamental mistakes Process thought makes, according to Colin Gunton. See *Becoming and Being: The Doctrine of God in Charles Hartshorne and Karl Barth* (Oxford: Oxford University Press, 1978). See also J. Mannoia, "Is God an Exception to Whitehead's Metaphysics?" in *Process Theology*, ed. Ronald Nash (Grand Rapids, Mich.: Baker, 1987), pp. 253-80.

[6]It must be noted, however, that this does not exhaust who God is, according to Process thought. God is also constituted by an "abstract pole." God's consequent nature changes moment by moment, but his abstract or primordial pole is eternally fixed. This view, I have elsewhere argued, is extremely problematic (see *Trinity and Process*, pp. 211-17). See also John O'Donnell, *Trinity and Temporality: The Christian Doctrine of God in the Light of Process Theology and the Theology of Hope* (Oxford: Oxford University Press, 1983), pp. 73-86; Royce Gruenler, *The Inexhaustible God: Biblical Faith and the Challenge of Process Theism* (Grand Rapids, Mich.: Baker, 1983); Robert Neville, *Creativity and God: A Challenge to Process Theology* (New York: Seabury, 1980), pp. 57-66. I suggest an alternative, trinitarian understanding of God's "di-polarity" in *Trinity and Process*, pp. 218-33, 374-92.

occasions) as it is in the process of becoming.[7] This is what allows actual occasions to form the ordered societies that constitute individual, enduring things at a phenomenological level. But because each occasion is a *creative* advance over the past multiplicity it experiences, there must be an inherent element of spontaneity. Order can never be exhaustive. Conflict is thus inherent in the nature of things.

This is how evil originates, according to Process thought. Actual occasions are to some degree free either to align themselves with or to resist God's influence toward order (his "subjective aim"). When they opt to actualize themselves in ways that resist God's aim, conflict inevitably results. While we only attribute morally responsible behavior to human decision making, according to Process thought something analogous to this takes place at every level of being. *Everything* is to be understood by analogy with human experience. Hence moral evil at a human level is analogous to "natural" evil at all subhuman levels, extending all the way down to the unpredictable behavior of subatomic particles.

There are a number of positive features to Process thought, as I have argued elsewhere.[8] Among other things, its critique of classical substantival metaphysics is persuasive. It has arguably done a better job integrating metaphysical reflection with contemporary physics than any other metaphysical system. Its understanding that contingency and change can be part of God's perfection, and thus its view that God responds to the world, is both philosophically compelling and biblically sound. Finally, its insight that evil in all forms is always connected to creaturely freedom, and thus that the distinction between "moral" and "natural" evil is somewhat arbitrary, is sound, as I will subsequently argue.

But Process philosophy also has a number of theological and philosophical difficulties. The difficulties that warrant our attention in our present discussion are as follows.

Shortcomings of Process Philosophy

Problems in the Process ontology. First, the way Process thought understands the becoming of actual occasions is problematic. As we have seen, every actual occasion supposedly constitutes itself as a synthesis of the objectified data and a response to God's influence. Moreover, every actual occasion is to some degree "creative" or "free" in how it constitutes itself. Yet the actual

---

[7]God's influence on each actual occasion is usually termed the "subjective aim" that God offers each actual occasion.
[8]Boyd, *Trinity and Process,* passim.

occasion only exists as a *result* of this creative synthesis and response to God. So, we must wonder, what is it that decides how to become? What is it that God tries to influence? There is no subject available to influence until *after* the becoming is complete.[9]

Second, and closely related to this, there is a problem in the Process understanding of how each actual occasion comes into being and constitutes a creative advance over the previous multiplicity it experiences. What gives rise to the creativity that constitutes each new and novel actual occasion? It is not God, for in this case the new subject could not be autonomous from God and thus free over and against God. But neither can it be the previous multiplicity, for in this case the new subject could not be free over and against the previous multiplicity. What then is left?

Standard Process thought explains this by appealing to the metaphysical category of "creativity." The trouble with this category, however, is that it has no intelligible ontological grounding within the Process schema. It is rooted neither in God nor in the actual world, leaving it nowhere. It *describes* what occurs, but because it has no ontological grounding it cannot *explain* what occurs. Hence, Process thought requires us to believe that each actual occasion constitutes itself as a virtual creation *ex nihilo*.[10] I submit that this concept is incoherent.

Philosophical problems in the Process view of God. There are significant philosophical difficulties in the Process conception of God as well. Process thought cannot render intelligible the enduring nature of God. It is not clear what keeps God being God in Process thought. What accounts for God always experiencing the world fully and influencing the world perfectly? Since every actual occasion is to some degree free, what keeps God from veering off course, as it were, from his perfect status? If every actual occasion, including God, is new every moment, what is it that ensures that God-now will have the same God-defining characteristics as God-just-past? In short, what grounds the necessary nature of God?

Process theologians generally postulate a "primordial" or "abstract" pole in God to carry out this function. But this postulation is insufficient because

---

[9]See L. Kirkpatrick, "Subjective Becoming: An Unwarranted Abstraction?" *Process Studies* 3 (1973): 15-26; Wolfhart Pannenberg, "Atom, Duration and Form: Difficulties with Process Philosophy," *Process Studies* 14 (1984): 21-30; Boyd, *Trinity and Process*, pp. 148-51.

[10]The general category of "creativity" attempts to render this intelligible in Process thought, but it is unsuccessful, as Neville has convincingly argued (*Creativity and God*). I argue that the problems raised here can be avoided without returning to a substantival ontology by understanding the essence of every subject, including every actual occasion, as a unit of creativity, identical with God's "subjective aim" (see *Trinity and Process*, pp. 105-20 and passim).

the categories of the system dictate that only actual occasions are real.[11] Everything else that can be said about reality describes these occasions. So we can understand how the concept of a primordial or abstract pole of God *describes* how God concretely acts. But we are looking for a *prescription*, not a description. We do not need to know *that* God is an actual occasion (or series of actual occasions) with certain qualities. We want to know *how* God is an actual occasion who *necessarily* has certain qualities.

Unless God's essential nature is necessary and actual *apart from* his interaction with the world, neither the enduring nature of God nor the contingent nature of the world can be rendered intelligible. God must be self-sufficient within himself, creating and relating to the world out of love instead of metaphysical necessity.[12] Instead, Process thought assumes that God is part of a broader God-world reality, the whole of which can be encompassed by a single set of metaphysical principles. Both reason and revelation argue against this, I maintain.

This is also why Process thought concludes that the God-world relationship must be eternal. This conclusion is built into its methodology. If God must be understood in the same terms as the world and all of reality must be understood as analogous to human experience, then it could not be otherwise. God as a center of experience *must* have a world to experience, and the world as a society of experiences *must* have a God to direct it. Moreover, if reality *must* be structured like this, then the God-world relationship *must* be eternal. But I argue that it is not necessary to begin with these assumptions.

Reality only becomes intelligible when we understand God *to be* the explanation of all reality, not *part of* the explanation of all reality. This requires that we, in keeping with Scripture, understand God to be antecedently actual, necessary, self-sufficient and relational within himself.

Biblical problems with the Process view of God. As troublesome as the philosophical problems with the Process view of God are, however, from my perspective its most problematic features lie in its incompatibility with the inspired portrait of God in the Bible.[13] These features are all interconnected.

Because Process theology denies that God can exist apart from the world,

---

[11] " 'Actual entities'—also termed 'actual occasions'—are the final real things of which the world is made up. . . . God is an actual entity, and so is the most trivial puff of existence in far-off empty space. . . . The final facts are, all alike, actual entities" (Whitehead, *Process and Reality*, p. 18).

[12] I have elsewhere argued that this logically entails that God contain necessary internal relationships (i.e., God is triune), for a self-sufficient reality without relationality is inconceivable (*Trinity and Process*, pp. 208-31, 328-42, 374-86).

[13] See Gruenler, *The Inexhaustible God;* Nash, ed., *Process Theism.*

it also denies the biblical teaching that God freely created the world. Because it denies that the world unilaterally originates from God, it must deny the biblical view that all creaturely power comes from God and thus that God possesses the inherent ability to override creaturely power and supernaturally intervene in the world. For the same reason it also denies that God possesses the ability ultimately to vanquish evil, as Scripture teaches.

What is more, because Process theology denies that God can supernaturally intervene in the world, it must reject all the miracles in Scripture, including the miracle of the incarnation and the resurrection. It must for this same reason deny that God responds to petitionary prayer. God is bound by a metaphysical rule stipulating that he always be influenced by the world and in return influence the world in a uniform way. To the extent that we affirm the biblical portrait of God, therefore, we have reasons for denying key aspects of the Process portrait of God.

A critique of Process thought on "natural" evil. We may now consider the Process approach to understanding "natural" evil. First, if our critique of the Process view of actual occasions, creativity and God is sound, then the Process understanding of "natural" evil must be considered unsound insofar as it is rooted in these concepts. More specifically, if the concept of actual occasions as self-creative units of experience arising out of "creativity" is incoherent, then the view that evil arises from the free activity of these occasions must be considered incoherent as well. Likewise, if the view that God and the world are two coeternal realities necessarily sharing power is implausible, then the view that evil exists because God must share power with the world and thus must deal with chaotic features of the world must be considered implausible as well. From the perspective of biblical Christianity, aspects of God's creation that are outside God's meticulous control can only be because God created them with the capacity to be outside of his meticulous control.

But even if we were to accept the Process view of things, its explanation of "natural" evil may still be considered implausible. The Process view of actual occasions as exercising freedom, or at least spontaneity, can perhaps account for some relatively minor natural mishaps. God cannot in this view meticulously control everything. There must be an element of unpredictability permeating all of reality. As I have noted in previous chapters, I agree with this perspective.

But how does this insight account for "natural" catastrophes?[14] How does

---

[14]See the related critique of theodicies that limit God's power by Michael Martin, *Atheism: A Philosophical Justification* (Philadelphia: Temple University Press, 1990), pp. 436-40.

the spontaneity of actual occasions, atoms, molecules, and the like account for earthquakes, mudslides, famines, plagues and other natural disasters? If God exercises enough influence on individual actual occasions to keep them in relatively ordered "societies," as Process thought holds, why can God not have enough influence to keep these "societies" from interacting with each other in disastrous ways? If God is powerful enough to keep solid entities relatively intact at a phenomenological level, how is it that he is not powerful enough to prevent these phenomenologically solid entities from interacting in ways that cause creatures to suffer?

The pain nature inflicts on creatures has nothing to do with the sometimes erratic nature of subatomic particles, for as we saw in chapter five, an element of unpredictability at this level does not significantly affect stability at a phenomenological level. The intellectual problem nature poses is not that it is somewhat unpredictable. Nature is *hostile* to sentient creatures even when it is relatively predictable, precisely when it is "obeying" its laws.

Hence, while I concede with Process thought that the origin of "natural" evil is identical with the origin of moral evil—it lies in the free will of agents—I see little value in locating this evil-creating "freedom" in microscopic actual occasions. As I will argue in the next chapter, only wills that possess significant authority over nature can significantly disrupt God's design for nature.

Nature as Inherently Limited

We have seen that explaining "natural" evil either as serving a divine purpose or as due to an inherent limitation in God is problematic. Many contemporary philosophers and theologians have thus attempted to explain it by appealing to inherent limitations in creation. As with previous views, this perspective has many forms. For the purposes of our present discussion, however, I will group their various arguments under two general motifs.

The dual potentiality of created things. Some theologians and philosophers argue that an "objective world" that could function as a neutral medium in which free agents could relate in morally responsible ways metaphysically requires potentially hazardous qualities. We cannot conceive of any aspect of an objective world that could potentially benefit agents that could not also potentially harm agents. What makes something a blessing in one situation makes that same thing a curse in another situation. Furthermore, according to this view this is a metaphysically necessary truth. It could not be otherwise.

Michael Peterson illustrates this point well with several examples when he writes:

The same water which sustains and refreshes can also drown; the same drug which relieves suffering can cause crippling psychological addiction; the same sun which gives light and life can parch fields and bring famine; the same neural arrangements which transmit intense pleasure and ecstasy can also bring extreme pain and agony.[15]

Antithetical potentials in all natural objects and in all natural laws are necessary features of created things, argues Peterson. We cannot consistently conceive of it being otherwise. Hence we of course cannot conceive of an omnipotent God creating it otherwise. The elimination of undesirable potentialities in any object, Peterson argues, immediately necessitates the modification of all natural laws and thus the correlative immediate modification of all nature objects.[16] "The whole matter becomes so complex," he continues, "that no finite mind can conceive of precisely what modifications the envisioned natural world would have to incorporate in order both to preserve the good natural effects and to avoid the fortuitous evil ones." Hence Peterson concludes:

It is simply the character of any set of natural laws to occasion both good and evil. Therefore, it is not clear that even God can modify the natural system we have in order to remove its evil and destructive effects but retain its good and desirable effects.[17]

An omnipotent God must certainly work within the realm of logical possibilities, and these logical possibilities put empirical constraints on the possible combination of qualities exhibited by natural objects and natural laws. Among other things, this view universalizes the previously discussed principle that an agent's potential to bless is also that agent's potential to curse (TWT4). Thus we may affirm this view insofar as it holds that the potential benefit of any created entity is also a potential harm.

However, I do not believe that this insight alone adequately explains "natural" evil. It does not explain why God would tolerate the massacre of little children by a tornado. Granted, the general point that the power of the wind to benefit humankind must also entail that under certain conditions it will be able to destroy churches. Let us further grant that the solidity of the bricks that shelter the congregation from rain and keeps them warm must

---

[15]Michael Peterson, *Evil and the Christian God* (Grand Rapids, Mich.: Baker, 1982), p. 111. See also Frederick R. Tennant, *Philosophical Theology*, 2 vols. (Cambridge: Cambridge University Press, 1928-1930), 2:201-2; David Basinger, "Divine Omnipotence: Plantinga and Griffin," *Process Studies* 11 (1981): 21.

[16]Peterson, *Evil and the Christian God*, p. 115.

[17]Ibid., p. 116.

also possess the correlative potential to kill people if they strike them on the head with sufficient speed. Even so, why could God not have intervened just enough to prevent the actualization of these hazardous potentials?

Even if one maintains that, for whatever reason, the tornado *must* be allowed to occur, why could God not have shifted the tornado several yards in one direction or the other to spare the children? Would God's intervention have undone natural laws and natural objects equivalent to supposing that water lost its capacity to drown creatures or the sun lost its ability to scorch the ground? I cannot see that it would.

If on the basis of the necessary correlating qualities of created things we conclude that it was impossible for God to alter a tornado's path slightly, we cannot explain how God *ever* intervenes in the natural order. Nor can we ever credit God with blessings that come from the natural order.[18] We have, it seems, just argued ourselves into a deistic view in which God cannot supernaturally calm storms, resurrect the dead or part the Red Sea.

What is more, if "natural" evil is to be explained by the element of randomness inherent in creation, and if this randomness is a necessary feature of the world, it becomes impossible to conceive of a world devoid of "natural" evil. Yet the Bible suggests that the creation before the Fall as well as after the eschaton will not be plagued with "natural" evil. The "bondage to decay" (Rom 8:21) the creation now experiences is unnatural and temporary, according to Scripture. We thus have biblical grounds for concluding that the attempt to explain "natural" evil by appealing to nature's random processes is inadequate.

In sum, this view does a good job of explaining why natural objects and laws must have qualities that are threatening to humans and animals under certain conditions. But it does not adequately explain why God does not prevent those conditions from taking place, at least when these circumstances are due to natural processes. And it fails to explain how the Bible can offer us the hope that some day the creation shall be free of "natural" evil.

As I will argue in the next chapter, what is lacking in this perspective on "natural" evil is precisely what was lacking in the previous perspectives, namely, a warfare worldview. Nothing in the will of God or the power of

---

[18]Peter Baelz seems to be vulnerable to this criticism. If God cannot be blamed for harmful aspects of nature, neither can he be credited with beneficial aspects of nature: "If a prolonged drought is to be understood as a natural occurrence and not a divine visitation, so too is the coming of the rain which ends the drought" (*Prayer and Providence: A Background Study* [New York: Seabury, 1968], p. 68). I rather argue that we should credit God with blessings that come from nature but also, to some extent, blame Satan for evils that come from nature.

God or the nature of creation adequately explains why the necessarily hazardous potential of the natural order is allowed to be actualized in destructive ways. The *actualization* of the harmful potentials within nature only makes sense within a Christian theistic framework, I will argue, when we postulate a metaphysically necessary connection between nature's potential to bless or curse with the metaphysically necessary potential of free agents to bless and curse. Further, it only makes sense if we acknowledge that human agents are not the only beings who possess this morally responsible power. If morally responsible self-determining spirits who have a power to affect the "neutral medium" of the objective world for better or for worse exist, then we can understand why God cannot always prevent the conditions that manifest the hazardous potential of nature. In the hands of loving free agents, nature becomes a blessing. In the hands of evil free agents, however, it becomes a weapon.

The value and risk of randomness in nature. A second variation on the view that "natural" evil is due to inherent limitations in the natural order attempts to identify nature's random processes as the source of "natural" evil. This view is similar to Process theology, though its conclusions are not based on a Process analysis of reality. One of the most published exponents of this type of theodicy in recent times is the scientist-theologian John Polkinghorne. In keeping with quantum physics, Polkinghorne argues that nature illustrates a significant element of chance. "[God] is not the puppet master of men or of matter," he writes.[19] This element of chance is crucial if the creation is to contain certain desirous qualities.

For one thing, the inherent and pervasive randomness of the world is necessary for the world to have an ontological status autonomous from God.[20] It also allows for novelty and generates forms of life that otherwise could not be generated.[21] Most importantly, however, it allows for the

---

[19]John Polkinghorne, *Science and Creation* (Boston: Shambala, 1988), p. 67.

[20]Ibid., p. 66. See also his *Quarks, Chaos and Christianity: Questions to Science and Religion* (New York: Crossroad, 1996), p. 39. Process thought also argues this point. If true, it means that it is logically impossible for God to create a world that is ontologically distinct from himself but that is exhaustively determined by him (see chapter six, note 8).

[21]Polkinghorne writes, "Chance is the engine of novelty. Necessity is the preserver of fruitfulness" (*Quarks,* p. 40). So argues David J. Bartholomew, for example, in *God of Chance* (London: SCM Press, 1984), pp. 18-21, 34-36. See also Arthur R. Peacocke, *Creation and the World of Science* (Oxford: Clarendon, 1979), 94-103; and Arthur R. Peacocke, "Chance and Law in Irreversible Thermodynamics, Theoretical Biology, and Theology," in *Chaos and Complexity: Scientific Perspectives on Divine Action,* ed. Robert J. Russell et al. (Vatican City: Vatican Observatory Publications, 1995), pp. 123-43.

eventual evolution of conscious beings who possess the capacity to be self-determining, hence loving, hence morally responsible.[22]

But spontaneity within creation is costly, Polkinghorne and others note. For, as Process thought argues, wherever there is an element of chance, there is also an element of unpredictability and thus an inevitable element of chaos. One cannot have both guaranteed absolute order and genuine chance within creation. As in the previous view, randomness must possess correlative potentials. The potential of randomness to benefit the cosmos and enhance humankind necessarily entails the correlative potential to harm humankind and bring about disorder within the cosmos. Hence, if the Creator wants the benefits of randomness, he must be willing to sacrifice a corresponding degree of guaranteed order. This, argues Polkinghorne, is why nature is often disorderly.

> The presence in [nature] of physical evils (earthquakes, genetically induced malformations, disease) reflects the untidiness of disorder, just as the presence in it of physical goods . . . reflects the organizing power of order. Each is the inescapable complement of the other in the process of the world.[23]

Applying this insight more broadly, he writes:

> The open flexibility of the world's process affords the means by which the universe explores its own potentiality, humankind exercises its will, and God interacts with his creation. The first, through its limitation and frustration, gives rise to physical evil. The second, through its sinfulness, gives rise to moral evil.[24]

The value of open processes. As with Process thought, one of the most significant strengths of this position is that, in contrast to much conservative Christian theological reflection today, it takes the newly emerging paradigm of contemporary science seriously by affirming the reality of spontaneity, chance and freedom in the creational process. It insightfully argues that a

---

[22]So argues Robert J. Russell: "Since quantum chance is involved in the production of order and life, this suggests that even the random character of elementary processes contribute something essential to the greater panorama out of which emerges the conditions for genuine alternatives, and eventually the reality of free will and authentic relationship characterized by love" ("Quantum Physics in Philosophical and Theological Perspective," in *Physics, Philosophy and Theology: A Common Quest for Understanding*, ed. Robert J. Russell, William R. Stoeger and George V. Coyne [Notre Dame, Ind.: Notre Dame University Press, 1988], p. 362).

[23]Polkinghorne, *Science and Creation*, p. 49. Polkinghorne says that the only way natural evil can be explained is by "a variation of the free-will defense, applied to the whole created world. One might call it 'the free-process defense' " (p. 66).

[24]Ibid., p. 67.

good deal (if not everything) of value in the world, including the value of free will and human personhood, would have to be sacrificed if randomness and (at higher levels) freedom were judged by God to be too risky.[25] It captures the vision of contemporary science expressed most powerfully in chaos and complex systems theory that life proceeds as a dance between order and chaos, determinism and indeterminism.

Incorporating openness in the creation process not only reconciles our view with contemporary science; it also provides a way out of the otherwise unsolvable problem of evil, as I have already argued. The alternative belief that God exercises meticulous, exhaustive control over the world necessarily entails that either disorder and evil are merely apparent or that the Creator is not perfectly good. If neither of these alternatives is acceptable, then logic forces us to accept that there is in creation an openness to disorder. Beings other than God must have say-so in what transpires. The origin of everything the Creator opposes must lie here.

Are natural catastrophes random occurrences? Despite the significant contributions of Polkinghorne and others, however, I do not believe that this view is adequate. As I argued against Process thought, most of the significant "natural" catastrophes we seek to explain with our theodicies do not seem to be adequately addressed in this view. Macro-level disasters cannot be explained by appealing to micro-level processes alone, for the phenomenological stability of the world demonstrates that God is in any given instance perfectly able to preserve general order in the midst of quantum chaos.

So once again we question how appealing to random processes of nature explains a tornado that kills a number of children. Why could God not have intervened to shift the tornado several yards one way or another to prevent the disaster? There is no cogent answer to this question so long as we insist on locating the origin of "natural" evil either in God (as in the first five approaches) or in nature itself (as in this approach).

The alternative missed by both sets of views is one that locates "natural" evil in the irrevocable free wills of spiritual agents who have been given some authority over nature. Nature has no will of its own with which to oppose God. But if we accept that there are spiritual agents who can influence the objective world just as humans can, then we can begin to understand how nature could become hostile to God's purposes, even though it has no will of its own. In the hands of free agents, human or angelic, our neutral

---

[25]See appendix four, "A Theology of Chance," where I develop further the concept of chance as it relates to the trinitarian warfare theodicy.

medium of relationality* can become either a gift of love or a weapon of war.[26]

Humans use their environment (including our physical bodies) to bless and curse all the time. What prevents us from applying this principle to spirits? After all, theists often credit a nonhuman spirit (God) with being responsible for the way our neutral, objective environment sometimes blesses us. We thank God for good health and sunny days. So why should we not credit a nonhuman evil agent(s) for the way our otherwise neutral environment sometimes curses us?

I will not argue that appealing to evil spirits alone accounts for all "natural" evil. We have seen that insights in other approaches must be incorporated if our approach to "natural" evil is to be complete. But I will claim that no explanation of "natural" evil can be satisfactory unless it includes some such appeal. In this view, tornadoes that kill little children and genetic diseases that incapacitate children and morally destroy parents do not come from God or from intrinsic limitations in his creation. Ultimately, I will argue, they originate in the kingdom of Satan. They are acts of terrorism and war.

I will develop this thesis further in the next chapter, but first we must consider the seventh and final approach to understanding "natural" evil: the teachings of Karl Barth regarding the menacing nature of *das Nichtige*.

Barth and the Menace of *das Nichtige*

In many respects Barth's thinking on "natural" evil is similar to those who explain it as arising from inherent limitations in creation. His approach is distinctive and important enough, however, to warrant a separate discussion.

Being and nothingness. At the center of Barth's reflections on evil is his curious concept of "the nothingness" *(das Nichtige)*. According to Barth, when God said yes to creation (that is, when God created this particular world) he necessarily said no to everything he did not create. This *no* is "the nothingness" that stands over and against creation. All the possibilities that God bypassed in creating *this* particular world, as opposed to any *other* possi-

---

[26]Peter Geach argues against C. S. Lewis's "neo-Manichean" view that the devil and demons are partly responsible for "natural" evil by contending that there is no evidence "that pain as such is elaborately contrived, as by Lewis' Devil." He rather contends that "the Creator's mind, as manifested in the living world, seems to be characterized by mere indifference to the pain that the interlocking relationships of life involve" (*Providence and Evil*, p. 77; cf. pp. 69-70). It is odd for anyone within the parameters of the orthodox Christian tradition to appeal to the *indifference* of the Creator as the *answer* to the problem of "natural" evil. The *problem* is precisely the apparent indifference of God in the face of suffering.

ble world, acquire a kind of reality by their very negation. "Not only what God wills," Barth insists, "but what He does not will, is potent, and must have a real correspondence."[27] That is, in the very act of saying what he was *for* God declared what he was *against,* and this gave what God was against a "peculiar" kind of existence.[28]

Das Nichtige is thus not literally nothing, argues Barth, but neither is it a creation of God. Rather, it exists "in a third way of its own."[29] In a sense, it exists by virtue of not actually existing. Barth portrays this realm of "the nothingness" as the "potent" nonbeing that God must always resist in order to preserve creation. It is the ominous "formless and void" chaos of Genesis 1:2 that God opposes by fashioning the orderly world over and against it.[30] It is a perpetually "menacing" pervasive reality that is menacing precisely because it has no reality of its own. It is a realm of nonbeing perpetually trying to be, as it were, over and against the creation that God has chosen. Hence Barth can appropriately characterize *das Nichtige* as a realm of falsehood that becomes evil when it encroaches on the realm of creation. Indeed, in Barth's view, all the personifications of evil in Scripture (that is, the devil, demons, Leviathan) are mythological expressions of this cosmic menacing force.[31]

---

[27]Karl Barth, *Church Dogmatics* (henceforth *CD*) 3.3:352. The most extensive treatment of this concept is in section 50 of this work (3.3:289-368).

[28]Barth writes, for example, "That which is not is that which God as Creator did not elect or will, that which as Creator He passed over, that which according to the account in Genesis 1:2 He set behind him as chaos, not giving it existence or being. That which is not is that which is actual only in the negativity allotted to it by the divine decision, only in its exclusion from creation, only, if we may put it thus, at the left hand of God. But in this way it is truly actual and relevant and even active after its own particular fashion. . . . To this sphere there belongs the devil, the father of lies. To this sphere, too, there belongs the world of demons and sin and evil and death"(*CD,* 3.3:73-74). G. K. Chesterton, of all people, captures the logic behind Barth's concept when he writes concerning the human will: "Every act of will is an act of self-limitation. To desire actions is to desire limitation. . . . When you choose anything, you reject everything else" (*Orthodoxy* [Garden City, N.Y.: Doubleday, 1959], pp. 39-40). The element that Barth adds—and it is exceedingly curious—is that what is rejected *resists* what was not rejected. What is rejected is not "actual" even as "the negativity allotted to it." It is not clear to me that Barth's concept is meaningful. I will argue in chapter twelve, however, that the concept becomes very meaningful when *free agents choose* that which God has rejected.

[29]Barth, *CD,* 3.3:349. This is what Barth calls the "ontic peculiarity" of *das Nichtige* (3.3:353).

[30]Ibid., 3.3:74.

[31]Barth argues that the existence of Satan and demons is "null and void" (ibid., 3.3:523). H. Schwarz argues that Barth does not give the devil his due by linking him to Nothingness. He notes, for example, how Barth has to pass over John 14:30, which says that Satan is ruler of the world (*Evil: A Historical and Theological Perspective,* trans. M. W. Worthing (Minneapolis: Fortress, 1995), pp. 167-68.

The "shadow side" of creation and "natural" evil. The concept of *das Nichtige* forms the basis of Barth's view of "natural" evil in the following two ways. First, simply by virtue of being "this" and not "that," every aspect of the contingent creation is surrounded by "the nothingness." Every aspect of creation is limited by virtue of what it is not. According to Barth, this gives the whole of contingent creation "a shadow side."[32]

This aspect of Barth's theology is similar to the previously discussed views of created nature being necessarily limited in certain respects. The experience of emotional and physical pain, as well as the experience of death, are all part of the "shadow side" of the natural order.[33] For Barth, this shadow side of creation is not evil in and of itself, for it is an inevitable corollary to what God created and has a legitimate, though temporary, role to play in God's providential design. But it is nevertheless experienced by humans as "dark."[34] Barth explains much of what we call "natural" evil in this way.

Sometimes in the human experience, however, "the nothingness" encroaches on creation and chaos overcomes order. This constitutes the second aspect of Barth's view of *das Nichtige*. The legitimate shadow elements of creation can become genuinely evil. That to which God said no not only limits but to some extent actually perverts that to which God said yes. Chaos at the periphery of creation now becomes part of creation.

Francis Tupper summarizes this Barthian concept more clearly than Barth himself when he writes:

> God creates order out of chaos, which locates chaos always ever present on the boundaries of creation. The randomness of chaos within creation would include all the destructive forces that we call natural evil. . . . The dysteleological elements in creation precede human existence, but the destructive forces in creation become natural evil in the context of human life in the world. So we name these random elements that destroy human life and habitation "natural disasters": earthquakes, tornadoes, hurricanes, blizzards, drought, floods, forest fires, volcanic eruptions, mountain slides.[35]

---

[32]Barth, *CD*, 3.3:350.

[33]Ibid., 3.3:295-302.

[34]So argues Nigel Wright: "Properly described, this Shadow should not be called evil. It is dark, but it is not evil because it is created by God and provides the kind of environment in which mankind may learn to depend upon God" (*The Satan Syndrome* [Grand Rapids, Mich.: Zondervan, 1990], p. 94). The creation will eventually lose its shadow side and its evil (p. 95).

[35]Francis Tupper, *Scandalous Providence: The Jesus Story of the Compassion of God* (Macon, Ga.: Mercer University Press, 1995), p. 138. It should be noted, however, that Tupper more carefully distinguishes between chaos and Nothingness than does Barth.

Barth himself is not clear on exactly how and why the menacing force of "the nothingness" sometimes encroaches on creation. Barth seems content to leave the matter something of a mystery. Tupper, however, suggests that this encroachment is at least partly caused by human willing. "Whenever we violate the creaturely boundaries of human existence," he writes, "whatever the measure of intentionality, we unleash the destructive violence of chaos into human life."[36] The forces of chaos would be kept at bay, he suggests, if humans did not sinfully overstep the legitimate boundaries God has ordained for them.

The value of Barth's das Nichtige. Many aspects of Barth's reflections are insightful and useful. The insight that every *this* affirmed by God implies a *that* denied by God helps us understand some aspects of "natural" evil. It articulates the truth that even God must confront certain metaphysical constraints in creating any possible world. As mentioned earlier, water cannot have both the positive quality of quenching thirst and the quality of being breathable, for example. Hence we may understand why vulnerability is a necessary feature of creatures' contingency. This truth accounts for some of what we experience as dark in creation.

There is value in Barth's concept of *das Nichtige* as well. The insights that evil is a sort of "unreal reality" constituted by what God opposes, that this peculiar reality is utter falsehood and that its only power is the power of a lie are of paramount importance for any trinitarian system of thought. As Augustine recognized in his debate with the Manicheans, only by embracing these insights it is logically possible to avoid concluding either that evil is an eternal thing or that the eternal Creator is completely without evil.[37]

In short, if evil can be neither created by God nor coeternal alongside of God, it must indeed constitute some peculiar "third" ontological status between these two alternatives. We will later find this notion particularly helpful in resolving certain problems associated with the biblical understanding of hell (chapter twelve).

Problems with Barth's explanation
Why does God not keep chaos at bay? There are, however, problems in Barth's attempt to explain "natural" evil. First, while Barth's reflection on the finitude of created things helps us understand why creation *could* have a shadow side, it does not adequately explain why creation *does* have a shadow side.

---

[36]Ibid., p. 141.
[37]See Augustine's *The Catholic and Manichean Ways of Life,* trans. D. and I. Gallagher (Washington, D.C.: Catholic University of America Press, 1966).

Still less does it explain why *das Nichtige* sometimes encroaches on creation and produces diabolical evil. As with the view that "natural" evil is due to a limitation in creation, Barth's reflections do not adequately explain why nature's necessary *potential* to harm is sometimes *actualized*, often resulting in extreme gratuitous suffering. Barth does not explain why the omnipotent Creator fails to prevent the potential shadow side of creation from being actualized or, more seriously, the potential of chaos to overcome order from occurring.

If my earlier analysis of love was correct, however, there are discernible reasons why God is constrained from always intervening on the free wills of morally responsible agents. Hence, as I suggested, an explanation of God's noninterference with "natural" evil is available *if* we link "natural" evil with the activity of free agents.[38]

Tupper touches on this solution, as we saw above, but he only links "natural" evil with the activities of human free agents. A more adequate explanation is available if we follow Scripture, the postapostolic fathers and the insights of most primordial peoples and broaden our understanding of free agency to include spiritual agents. To adequately explain catastrophic events that transcend human influence, we need to appeal to wills that transcend human wills.

Empowering das Nichtige. Second, while we will later make use of Barth's concept of *das Nichtige*, the concept of evil as negation in Barth's theology is not coherent. I suspect this is why Barth has great difficulty describing it. For example, Barth contends that one cannot say that Nothingness "is," but neither can one say that it "is not."[39] But what meaning can we ascribe to such an assertion? So far as I can discern, none. Something (or better, "nothingness") either *is* or *is not*. Similarly, Barth insists that nothingness "has no basis" in creation or in God. "It has . . . no possibility," Barth insists, "except that of the absolutely impossible." He justifies this conclusion by asking, "How else can we describe that which is intrinsically absurd but by a formula which is logically absurd?"[40] I cannot fault either Barth's logic or his honesty: his concept, as it stands in his system, is definitely absurd. But how, then, can we accept it? He has, in truth, given us nothing meaningful to assent to.

---

[38]Wright criticizes Barth for displacing the biblical story of the angelic fall with his own incoherent reflections about "nothingness." The origin of evil, Wright correctly insists, resides in the free will of rebel superhuman forces (*Satan Syndrome*, pp. 61-65).

[39]Barth, *CD*, 3.3:353. On the difficulty of rendering the concept of *das Nichtige* coherent, see Wilfried Härle, *Sein und Gnade: Die Ontologie in Karl Barths Kirchlicher Dogmatik* (Berlin: Walter de Gruyter, 1974), pp. 227-69.

[40]Barth, *CD*, 4.1:410.

What nothingness *is* in Barth's system is simply a realm of bypassed possibilities. It is the realm of what could have been but is not. There is nothing particularly incoherent about *this* notion. Every *this* does indeed imply a *not that*. The trouble for Barth is that there is nothing "false" or "menacing," let alone potentially "evil," about bypassed possibilities. Indeed, bypassed possibilities can in and of themselves do nothing, good or evil. They are only possibilities, and negated ones at that.

Possibilities can *become* false, menacing and evil, however, if and when they are *chosen* over and against actual reality *by a free, morally responsible agent,* and here we discover the most fundamental missing element in Barth's understanding of evil. It is the same element lacking in the previously examined explanations of "natural" evil. Negated possibilities only become evil when rebellious free agents choose them over reality. Only when "the nothingness" is chosen and incarnated in an agent *as real* does it become real evil. Now it is no longer a mere "absence." It becomes a concrete embodied presence.[41]

Only in this way can we render intelligible Barth's claim that *das Nichtige* is a menacing force. That to which God says no becomes an evil yes *when a creature who has power to influence says yes to it.* When an agent chooses a reality of its own making over the Creator's chosen reality instead of actualizing its freedom in obedience to God and in conformity with the Creator's chosen reality—that is, when a creature says yes to God's no and no to God's yes—*das Nichtige* becomes something more than negated possibilities.

By virtue of being chosen, the *no* has become a *yes. Das Nichtige* borrows "power to influence," as it were, from the morally responsible agent who uses *its own* God-given power to influence to choose it. Further, owing to the necessary irrevocability of this morally responsible authority (TWT4), this evil choice must now be allowed to adversely affect everything and everyone under the sphere of this agent's moral responsibility. If the agents who choose this negated realm have a *cosmic* power to influence, then we can understand how *das Nichtige* could become the cosmic menacing force Barth describes it as being.

All of this makes sense if, but only if, God's say-so is not the only say-so

---

[41]I would submit that this is also the missing element in the traditional Augustinian definition of evil as "the absence of good." This definition describes the *potentiality* of evil but not the *actuality* of evil. Evil becomes actualized when it is chosen by an actual agent. This is also why I argue that evil can never be properly discussed in the abstract. We must always have concrete instances of evil before us if our discussion is truly to be about evil and not just the potential for evil. See my *God at War: The Bible and Spiritual Conflict* (Downers Grove, Ill.: InterVarsity Press, 1997), pp. 33-35.

operative in the cosmos. Barth's theology does not consistently allow for this creaturely say-so, however, which is why the concept of *das Nichtige* as a cosmic menacing force is not intelligible within his system. To be sure, his insight into the cosmic dimension of evil is profound and biblical. But this cosmic dimension is only intelligible if it is linked with cosmic free agents who can use their moral authority to create an alternative, false reality of their own choosing over against the reality that God has chosen.[42]

Conclusion

The seven approaches to "natural" evil we have examined in the last two chapters contain insights that must be incorporated into any comprehensive understanding of evil. From Augustine and Scripture we acknowledged that God allows "natural" evil for a greater good, though in contrast to Augustine I have argued that this greater good is not a "higher harmony" found in each particular evil but the general good of creaturely freedom for the sake of love. Also with Augustine and much of the church tradition, I agree that human sin has played a major role in corrupting nature and that God sometimes uses "natural" evil to punish sin.

What is more, with Hick and other soul-making theodicists, I agreed that the development of intelligent, morally responsible agents requires the existence of a neutral, objective medium of relationality that is relatively impervious to our individual wishes and thus that sometimes may work against us. I also conceded Hick's argument that God can't be unequivocally obvious to us in this probationary period if our choice for him is to be of a moral nature. There must be an "epistemic distance" between him and us. To some extent, the "atheistic" quality of the natural order can be accounted for in this way.

With Ellis and Murphy I argued that God is characterized by kenotic self-giving love and thus ordinarily interacts noncoercively with the world. He respects the integrity of the free creatures he has created. Furthermore, with Process thought I agreed that "natural" and "moral" evil do not have different origins. All evil arises from agents having say-so in how things transpire over and against God. I also agreed with those thinkers who have argued

---

[42]Barth unfortunately identified Satan and demons with nothingness rather than seeing them as free agents who *choose* nothingness. As strongly as he opposed demythologization, he is himself guilty of it at this point. When doing exegetical work, Barth seems to affirm the reality and significance of Satan and demons. See, for example, *CD*, 3.2:599-600, where Barth presents a thoroughly warfare understanding of Jesus' ministry. In his own reflections, however, he sees them as personifications of *das Nichtige*. See, for example, *CD*, 3.3:519-31; 4.2:229.

that randomness is (whether by metaphysical necessity or by divine choice) built into the fabric of creation and that much of value in creation would be lost if nature did not contain this indeterministic aspect.

What is more, I have acknowledged the insight of those who argue that all created entities must embody certain limitations, that they cannot embody contradictory attributes and thus that their potential for good must under certain circumstances constitute a potential for harm. Finally, I have accepted Barth's point that all of nature has a shadow side as well as his view that the essence of evil is choosing what God has negated over what God has affirmed.

I believe that any comprehensive explanation of "natural" evil has to include these insights. But none of these approaches alone constitutes such an explanation. Aside from the other criticisms raised against these various positions, the fundamental problem I isolated in Barth's theodicy challenges all these views and constitutes the principle reason why they are not in and of themselves adequate. They fail to incorporate the possibility that there is a sinister agent(s) who is largely responsible for corrupting nature. None of them seriously enough considered the one whom Scripture traces the origin of all evil to: Satan.

If indeed the world is presently plagued by a menacing force mighty enough to be called the "prince" and even "god" of this age as well as the "principality and power" of the world's spiritual realm (Jn 12:31; 14:30; 16:11; 2 Cor 4:4; Eph 2:2), and if indeed this being exercises a significant influence over the whole world (1 Jn 5:19; cf. Acts 26:18; Rev. 12:9), then we should not be surprised to find that the "natural" order under his influence exhibits diabolic qualities. A creation that is under the strong influence of a cosmic "roaring lion" (1 Pet 5:8) is going to become "red in tooth and claw." When a "cosmic Herod" exercises power over the "Bethlehem" of God's "natural" order, a perpetual "slaughter of the innocents" can be expected.

Along the same lines, if indeed one who had a cosmic level of moral responsibility, together with other angelic beings who possessed high levels of authority, freely chose to reject God's reality in favor of a reality of their own willing ("the nothingness"), then it is no surprise that much of the cosmos manifests the opposite of what we would expect to find coming from the hands of the all-powerful, perfectly loving Creator. Furthermore, if this cosmic rebel is at war with God and his people, as Scripture declares, we should not be surprised when we experience "nature" as a weapon being used against us. As we know from our own experience, the neutral medium of our objective world loses its neutrality in the hands of a morally responsible free agent. It becomes a tool of blessing or a weapon of harm. In the hands of God, it is the former; in the hands of Satan and other evil spirits, it is the latter.

If nature seems like a war zone that is significantly occupied and run by hostile agents, it is because it *is* a war zone and *is* significantly controlled by such agents. This, I submit, is the perspective that best explains the viciousness of nature and the perspective most consistent with the perspective of Jesus and the New Testament. As we have seen, Jesus never attributed genetic mutations, deformities, blindness, deafness, leprosy, blood diseases, fevers, falling towers, barren trees, life-threatening storms or death itself to God's providence or to "natural" features of his Father's creation. He consistently identifies them as evidence of the reign of the kingdom of darkness here on earth, a kingdom that his whole ministry was intended to destroy.

I thus suggest that we have no compelling philosophical or biblical reason to locate the primary cause of tornadoes that kill children, genetic mutations that reduce them to vegetables or mudslides that bury them alive to any other source than the enemy of God. We must now turn to the task of clarifying this position and defending it against objections.

10

THIS AN ENEMY HAS DONE

"Natural" Evil &
the Trinitarian Warfare Theodicy

There is a wild antagonism at the heart of things.
There is a madness there....
The countenance of Satan is indelibly inscribed in nature.
W. E. STUERMANN, *THE DIVINE DESTROYER*

No evil ever came from [God's] hands....
Let this truth be fixed in our hearts ... whenever we are troubled with the thorn or the thistle,
with the poisonous or useless weed, with the noxious beast ...
or with any of the other countless inconveniences and pains of our present condition;
whenever we feel ready to faint by reason of fighting without and fears within,
let us remember that God made all things good,
and avoiding hard thoughts of Him, say, An enemy hath done this.
G. H. PEMBER, *EARTH'S EARLIEST AGES*

Jesus woke up and rebuked the wind.
MARK 4:39

"Where ... did these weeds come from?" He answered, "An enemy has done this."
MATTHEW 13:28

*T*he fundamental flaw in the seven approaches to "natural" evil we examined in the previous two chapters was that they did not incorporate the reality of Satan and other evil spirits in their explanation. While affirming that the source of natural goodness is a good spiritual will (God), they did not accept that the source of natural evil is evil spiritual wills.

In this chapter I will develop this thesis and defend it against objections. I first review how the trinitarian warfare perspective on "natural" evil has been articulated by theologians in the early church and in contemporary times. I then attempt to respond to the various objections that have been raised against it.

Satan and Nature in the Early Church

As unusual as the trinitarian warfare perspective on "natural" evil may seem to some contemporary Westerners, especially in the academy, this was the view uniformly espoused by the early church. Early Christian thinkers assumed that angels, like humans, were created free and given a sphere of influence and responsibility over creation and that, again like humans, angels could use this influence for good, as God intended, or for evil. "The Maker and Framer of the world," wrote Athenagoras, "distributed and appointed . . . a multitude of angels and ministers . . . to occupy themselves about the elements, and the heavens, and the world, and the things in it, and the godly ordering of them all."[1]

"Natural" evil was explained as resulting from these spirits rebelling against God and thus abusing their authority over creation. Hence, for example, Origen argued that famines, scorching winds and pestilence were not "natural" in God's creation; they were rather the result of fallen angels bringing misery whenever and however they were able.[2] These perverted guardians were also "the cause of plagues . . . barrenness . . . tempests [and] similar calamities."[3] "Diseases and other grievous calamities," Tertullian

---

[1]Athenagoras *A Plea for the Christians* 10 (ANF 2:133-34). Again, "Just as with men, who have freedom of choice as to both virtue and vice . . . so is it among the angels. Some, free agents, you will observe, such as they were created by God, continued in those things for which God had made and over which He had ordained them; but some outraged both the constitution of their nature and the government entrusted to them" (ibid. [ANF 2:142]). Origen likewise held that every aspect of nature was under the care of "invisible husbandmen and guardians" (*Against Celsus* 8.31 [ANF 4:651]). Gregory I at a later date states in his *Dialogues* 4.5 the prevailing conviction well when he says, "In this visible world . . . nothing can be achieved except through invisible forces" (*Dialogues,* trans. O. J. Zimmerman, The Fathers of the Church: A New Translation 39 [New York: Fathers of the Church, 1959], p. 199). Still later Thomas Aquinas writes, "Just as the lower angels who have less universal forms are controlled by the higher ones, so also material things are controlled by angels. This is the position not only of the doctors of the Church, but also of all the philosophers who postulate the existence of nonmaterial beings" (*Summa Theologiae,* vol. 15, *The World Order* [New York: Blackfriars/McGraw-Hill, 1970], p. 5 [1a.110-19]).

[2]Origen *Against Celsus* 8.31 (ANF 4:651).

[3]Ibid., 1.31 (ANF 4:409).

added, were the result of demons, whose "great business is the ruin of mankind." When "poison in the breeze blights the apples and the grain while in the flower, or kills them in the bud, or destroys them when they have reached maturity," one can discern the work of these rebellious guardian spirits.[4]

Every army has a captain. Taking their cue from the New Testament, these early theologians understood the leader of the rebel army that ravaged nature to be Satan. In the words of Athenagoras, Satan was "the spirit" originally entrusted with "the control of matter and the forms of matter."[5] This "spirit" unfortunately rebelled against God and now exercised his tremendous authority against God. He abused "the government entrusted to [him]." Given the nature of moral responsibility, God could not simply revoke his sphere of influence when Satan chose evil (recall TWT5). Hence, "the prince of matter [now] exercises a control and management contrary to the good that is in God."[6]

Reflecting the basic vision of the early church, Athenagoras concluded that everything in nature that obviously looks contrary to God's character appears that way because it *is* contrary to God. It did not arise from the omni-benevolent hand of the Creator (as the atheists of his day and ours object) but was due rather to the activity of this evil "ruling prince" and "the demons his followers."[7]

Satan and Nature in Recent Thought

The view that evil spirits are largely responsible for "natural" evil has been suggested throughout church history by many theologians. But due to the influence of Augustine's blueprint model of divine providence, this insight was rarely considered the ultimate explanation for "natural" evil, as it was before Augustine. The assumption was that everything Satan and demons do somehow fits into God's meticulous plan for world history. Because of this, "natural" evil has generally been regarded as a problem of understanding God's providence, not an issue of spiritual warfare.

Modern perspectives on "natural" evil have drifted even further from the warfare perspective of Scripture and the postapostolic church. Under the influence of Enlightenment naturalism, rationalism and biblical criticism, the very notion of evil spirits influencing the physical world became problematic.

---

[4]Tertullian *Apology* 22 (ANF 3:36).
[5]Athenagoras *A Plea for the Christians* 24 (ANF 2:142).
[6]Ibid., 25 (ANF 2:142-43).
[7]Ibid.

Physical laws became the ultimate explanation for anything in the physical world. Hence, as we have seen in the previous two chapters, very few modern theologians—including many who theoretically accept the reality of evil spirits—ascribe any significant role to the devil or demons in explaining "natural" evil.

The need for suprahuman evil free wills. There are notable exceptions to this general trend, however, and we will do well briefly to survey their reflections. William Robinson recognized that any adequate explanation of "natural" evil required the postulation of nonhuman evil free wills. After reviewing the magnitude of "natural" evils that plague humanity, he writes:

> How, then, can we account for the evil in the world which cannot be laid at the door of man's misuse of free will? There seems to be no way of accounting for it but by a way from which some will shrink. We shall have to think of the misuse of free will in some "higher" order of creation than that of man.

The logic of Robinson's conclusion is that if "natural" evil cannot be attributed either to God's will or humanity's will, it must be attributed to the free will of some other agent. This view, Robinson notes, "is the solution which meets us in the pages of the Bible when it is read as a whole." Reflecting the core vision of the warfare worldview, he continues:

> It means that the world is a place where a tremendous struggle is being fought out between the powers of evil and of goodness. The world is a battlefield, and battlefields are rarely comfortable places. . . . Why should this solution be thought to be less satisfactory for *our day* than for other days?[8]

C. C. J. Webb argued along similar lines earlier in the twentieth century. Noting the impossibility of explaining "natural" evil (especially prehumanoid animal suffering) by appealing to a supposedly good design of an omnipotent Creator, he wondered whether it could be better understood as a higher level of moral evil. "That morally evil *human* wills exist, we know," he notes, and "that they affect injuriously the environment of other persons we also know." He continues:

> No new difficulty is added by the thought that superhuman evil wills exist and

---

[8]William Robinson, *The Devil and God* (New York: Abingdon-Cokesbury, 1945), p. 123; cf. pp. 119-20. Concerning angelic evil, Jeffrey B. Russell writes, "There is no reason to assume that the active evil in the universe is limited to humanity. . . . Nor is there reason to assume that the cause of human evil lies in human nature alone" (*Mephistopheles: The Devil in the Modern World* [Ithaca, N.Y.: Cornell University Press, 1986], p. 298). Considering the possibility of nuclear annihilation, he asks, "What is the nature of the force that can contemplate the destruction of the entire universe?" (p. 298).

have injuriously affected the environment of humanity as a whole. And this supposition would go some way towards explaining why it is hard to regard Nature as altogether good.[9]

We have previously demonstrated the need for a neutral medium of relationality if free moral agents are to be able to communicate and affect one another (chapters eight and nine). Because these agents are morally responsible, this medium is subject to their influence and becomes a means for good or evil in their hands. It can be used as a tool or as a weapon. Webb suggests that this applies to "superhumans" as well as human free agents.[10]

Philosopher Terrence Penelhum has also advocated a warfare understanding of "natural" evil. Reflecting the conviction that genuine moral responsibility must be to some extent irrevocable, he concluded that much "natural" evil is due to fallen spirits "who have been allowed [by God] to exercise some of their evil powers on God's creation because they too are free agents whose powers must have an actual sphere of exercise to be real."[11] So too, closely following the view of the early church, Dom Trethowan held that God desires to administer his providence through a hierarchy of morally responsible agents. "Natural" evil is a result of high-level agents within this hierarchy choosing evil. The "disorganization of the material universe" is due to the fall of angels who were entrusted with it. "It is a reasonable theory," Trethowan adds, not only because there is no adequate alternative theistic explanation, but because

> it seems to be an eternal law that the lower orders should be governed by the higher ones, that God's creatures should be arranged in a hierarchy, with a certain dependency of those below on those above. Since God can't be expected

---

[9]C. C. J. Webb, *Problems in the Relations of God and Man* (London: Wisbet, 1911), p. 270.

[10]Webb notes that, though this conclusion is "hardly considered . . . worthy of serious consideration in our day," the view that "the world, as we know it, is depraved through the activity of an evil will or wills antecedent to the appearance of man in it is a very ancient and wisely held view" (ibid., p. 269). He also notes that Plato endorsed something like this with his postulation of an evil world soul just beneath the good Creator (*The Laws of Plato* 10.896.97, trans. T. L. Pangle [Chicago: University of Chicago Press, 1980], pp. 293-99). Nothing over and above a modernist prejudice against the notion of a devil or demons makes it seem implausible in modern times. By "modern times" Webb is referring to the beginning of the twentieth century. His point was far truer then than it is today. Western culture is returning to a worldview in which a belief about nonhuman and suprahuman spirits plays an integral part. The present explosion of interest in angels and supernatural experiences is evidence of this cultural shift. See Gregory A. Boyd, *God at War: The Bible and Spiritual Conflict* (Downers Grove, Ill.: InterVarsity Press, 1996), pp. 61-66.

[11]Terrence Penelhum, *Religion and Rationality: An Introduction to the Philosophy of Religion* (New York: Random House, 1971), p. 246.

to change his all-over plan [that is, revoke the angelic sphere of moral influence], the fallen angels remained powerful, even after their fall.[12]

Finally, and most recently, we must mention the argument of Wallace Murphree. Building on Plantinga's suggestion that "natural" evil could *possibly* be explained by appealing to the devil, Murphree argues that this is the *only* possibility totally consistent with the belief that God is all-good and all-powerful. He argues that: (a) If God is perfectly good, he must do everything he can "properly do" to prevent evil.[13] (b) The only evil God cannot "properly" prevent is evil arising from the willing of a free agent, for preventing this would result in a loss of the greater good of having freedom. (c) "Natural" evil cannot be attributed to any human agent. Hence, "natural" evil must be attributable to a perverse nonhuman agent. Thus, he concludes, "common sense theism is epistemically committed, not only to the affirmation of free will, but to the existence of a devil as well."[14]

A warfare view of animal suffering. This line of thinking has also been applied to the pervasive violence of the animal kingdom. If there is an evil "prince of matter" able to influence all material things at a structural level, then the supposition that the animal kingdom reflects this influence becomes a rational possibility. Indeed, if we accept this much, we have no reason to expect that any aspect of nature, including the animal kingdom, will unambiguously reflect the wisdom and character of the Creator. C. S. Lewis explains violence in the animal kingdom prior to the arrival of humans in this fashion:

> It seems to me . . . a reasonable supposition, that some mighty created power had already been at work for ill on the material universe, or the solar system, or, at least, the planet Earth, before ever man came on the scene. . . . If there is

---

[12]Dom I. Trethowan, *An Essay in Christian Philosophy* (London: Longmans, Green & Co., 1954), p. 128.

[13]"Although God is capable of preventing any evil . . . by means of his own agency, he cannot do so without thereby destroying a power which produces more good that [sic] evil; and this would result in an overall loss of God. . . . [God is] capable of preventing the evil, but [not] . . . capable of doing so properly" (Wallace A. Murphree, "Can Theism Survive Without the Devil?" *RelS* 21 [1985]: 239).

[14]Murphree, "Can Theism Survive?" p. 233. For a discussion, see W. O. Mundia, "The Existence of the Devil" (Ph.D. diss., Boston University School of Theology, 1994), pp. 384-93. I should also mention the view of Brother Andrew ("God's Smuggler"), who held that "many events we call 'natural disasters' are really satanic attacks." For this reason he argued that "we must be ready to pray against the evil forces when such disasters occur" (Brother Andrew and Susan DeVore Williams, *And God Changed His Mind Because His People Prayed* [reprint, London: Marshall Pickering, 1991], p. 169).

such a power, as I myself believe, it may well have corrupted the animal creation before man appeared.

Lewis goes on to explain the nature of this corruption by drawing an analogy with the Fall of humans:

> The intrinsic evil of the animal world lies in the fact that animals, or some animals, live by destroying each other. That plants do the same I will not admit to be an evil. The satanic corruption of the beasts would therefore be analogous, in one respect, to the satanic corruption of man. For one result of man's fall was that his animality fell back from the humanity into which it had been taken up but which could no longer rule it. In the same way, animality may have been encouraged to slop back into behavior proper to vegetables.[15]

Writing around the same time as Lewis, Dom Webb took a similar approach to understanding "natural" evil in general and animal suffering in particular:

> Venomous insects and snakes, the scorpion, the boa constrictor, the octopus with its dreadful tentacles—these, like the subterranean rumblings of an earthquake, the blackened clouds gathering for the storm burst, the tornado, appear dark and sinister.

The sinister quality of these aspects of nature, he argues, cannot be written off entirely as anthropomorphic projections of humans onto nature. Neither can they be cogently ascribed to the benevolent will of the Creator or to some "inherent limitation of created being." Rather, they must be seen as a result of the evil influence of rebellious spirits who were originally put in charge of nature. Reiterating the thinking of the early and medieval church on this point, Webb continues:

> Let us not forget that before man existed there occurred the first and the greatest of all sins, that of Lucifer, considered by St. Thomas to have been the highest spirit in all creation, and also of those lower spirits who joined him in revolt. It is a general principle throughout creation that a higher being can, within certain limits, act upon natures lower than itself. Plants act on the mineral matter which they absorb, and animals act on the plants they eat. So, too, spirits have the power to act both on spirits lower than themselves, and also on material nature.[16]

Toward the end of the nineteenth century G. H. Pember had also argued that

---

[15]C. S. Lewis, *The Problem of Pain* (New York: Macmillan, 1962), p. 135
[16]Dom B. Webb, *Why Does God Permit Evil?* (New York: P. J. Kennedy & Sons, 1941), p. 36. In agreement with the principle of irrevocability (TWT5), Webb notes that the nature of moral responsibility is such that one's sphere of influence is not revoked when the responsibility is abused (p. 37).

the carnivorous nature of the animal kingdom was incompatible with the character of the Creator and so must be the result of the fall of a subordinate cosmic being in charge of nature. He wrote:

> The present state of things, in which animal food is allowed and necessary to man, and carnivorous beasts, birds and fishes abound, testifies to a woefully disorganized and unnatural condition; such a one as would be impossible save in a world at variance with the God of order, peace, love, and perfection.[17]

The philosopher Eric Mascall took the notion further by construing it in an evolutionary perspective. One major effect of the angelic fall, he argued, was "to introduce into the material realm a disorder which has manifested itself in a distortion of [God's] evolutionary plan."[18] Evolution thus reflects both God's creative design and Satan's perverse influence.

Mascall regarded "the twin beliefs that the angels had charge over the material world and that many of them had fallen away from God before the commission of the first human sin" to be a "striking" explanation of "natural" evil. It is, he argued, all the more compelling because these beliefs were not constructed for theodicy purposes. In other words, one cannot accuse the warfare view of being an ad hoc hypothesis generated simply to account for data that is problematic to theism.[19]

But the theologian who perhaps developed this explanation of "natural" evil the fullest was Norman Williams in his 1924 Bampton Lectures. Resurrecting Plato's corrupted "world soul" theory, Williams supposed that God's primal creation, the fundamental "Life Force of the cosmos . . . was created good; but . . . at the beginning of Time, in some transcendental and incomprehensible manner, it turned away from God and in the direction of Self,

---

[17]George H. Pember, *Earth's Earliest Ages* (1876; reprint, Grand Rapids, Mich.: Kregel, 1975), p. 69.

[18]Eric L. Mascall, *Christian Theology and Natural Science: Some Questions on Their Relations* (London: Longmans, Green & Co., 1956), p. 301. Another noteworthy exponent of this perspective (though unfortunately he does not develop his views at length) is Alvin Plantinga. "Natural evil," he argues, "is due to the free actions of nonhuman persons" (*God, Freedom, and Evil* [Grand Rapids, Mich.: Eerdmans, 1974], p. 58.

[19]Mascall, *Christian Theology*, p. 303. Richard Swinburne argues against the warfare view on precisely these grounds. Invoking demons to account for natural evil, he argues, "has the status of an *ad hoc* hypothesis" (*The Existence of God*, rev. ed. ([Oxford: Clarendon, 1991], p. 202). Again, "Fairly clearly many, many years ago theism came to include this hypothesis for just this reason—to deal with the problem of evil" (p. 221). Swinburne is simply incorrect in his assumption. As I demonstrated in chapter one and throughout *God at War*, the belief that Satan and demons were adversely affecting God's creation was around in Western culture long before the problem of evil took on the form it has had since Augustine. The issue is discussed by Steward Kelly, "The Problem of Evil and the Satan Hypothesis" (paper delivered at SCP Eastern Regional Meeting, April 7-9, 1994).

thus shattering its own interior being."[20] He continues:

> We can at least feel sure that this interior self-perversion, which we have hypo-
> thetically attributed to the collective Life-Force which was God's primal crea-
> ture . . . might *a priori* have been expected to appear in the cruelty which
> ravages the animal world, in the unknown maleficent factor which hindered
> the due development of herd-instinct just when the anthropoids were becom-
> ing men. . . . If, in harmony with later Jewish and primitive Christian thought
> . . . we are prepared to admit the existence of evil discarnate intelligences, it
> would doubtless follow that the malevolent nature of such beings was to be
> regarded as the outcome of the pre-mundane Fall of that World-Soul, of which
> they, equally with men and beasts, would be the offspring.[21]

Without endorsing any of the particulars of Williams's speculations, I
would argue that his view is generally consistent with the trinitarian warfare
worldview expressed in Scripture and in the early church. Both he and Mascall are particularly close to the thinking of Athenagoras. The problem of evil
is not a problem of occasional bad things happening on the otherwise pristine stage of God's creation, as it is frequently portrayed. Rather, evil permeates *the structure of the stage itself,* for the one given authority over the
structure (Satan) has become corrupt.

This insight lies at the heart of the trinitarian warfare worldview. Leviathan and Rahab encompass the earth and war against God (e.g., Job 9:13;
26:12-13; 41:1-34; Ps 74:14; 89:9-10; Is 27:1). "Raging waters" of chaos
defying the Almighty and threatening his creation must be kept at bay (e.g.,
Job 7:12; 38:6-11; Ps 74:10-17; 104:7-9; Prov 8:27-29).[22] The entire creation has been subject to bondage and decay, and it groans accordingly
(Rom 8:20-22). A sinister spirit of great power is "the god of this world"
and "the ruler of the power of the air" (2 Cor 4:4; Eph 2:2). An evil
"prince" owns all the kingdoms of this world and indeed controls the entire
fallen world (Lk 4:6; 1 Jn 5:19; Rev 12:9). The being entrusted with over-

---

[20]Norman P. Williams, *The Ideas of the Fall and of Original Sin* (New York: Longmans, Green
& Co., 1927), p. 526.

[21]Ibid., p. 527.

[22]Jon Levenson summarizes the motif well when he notes that passages such as these convey "a
sense of the Sea as a somewhat sinister force that, left to its own, would submerge the world
and forestall the ordered reality we call creation" (*Creation and the Persistence of Evil: The Jewish Drama of Divine Omnipotence* [San Francisco: Harper & Row, 1988], p. 15, cf. p. 122).
Biblical authors are always confident that Yahweh has defeated and will continue to defeat
such forces. But what makes Yahweh's victory *praiseworthy* is that his foes are formidable. See
Levenson, *Persistence of Evil,* pp. 16-17, 47-48; and Adrio König, *New and Greater Things:
Re-evaluating the Biblical Message on Creation* (Pretoria: University of South Africa, 1988), p.
46.

seeing the very structure of matter (as in Athenagoras) has mutinied against the Creator. Or, in the words of Williams, the "Life-Force" originally created to express God's beautiful character throughout the process of his creation has now become perverse.[23] Everything and everyone under his authority has to some extent been affected accordingly.

To be sure, according to Scripture the creation was originally created good, and the glory of God is still evident in it (Gen 1; Rom 1:20). But something else—something frightfully wicked—is evident in it as well. Of their own free will, Satan and other spiritual beings rebelled against God in the primordial past and now abuse their God-given authority over aspects of creation. The one who "holds the power of death—that is, the devil" (Heb 2:14) exercises a pervasive structural, diabolical influence to the point that the entire creation is in "bondage to decay" (Rom 8:21). If this scenario is correct, then the pain-ridden, bloodthirsty, sinister and hostile character of nature makes perfect sense. If not, then despite the valid contributions of a number of thinkers on "natural" evil, the demonic character of nature must remain largely inexplicable.

Objections to the Warfare Theodicy

We have identified persuasive advocates of the trinitarian warfare explanation on "natural" evil from both the early church and contemporary times. We must now address the major objections that have been raised against this explanation.

Objection 1: The warfare theodicy is too vague. The first major objection to the warfare understanding of "natural" evil is that it is simply too vague to be convincing. Though he believed that the warfare understanding of "natural" evil made "more sense than its rivals," Leonard Hodgson expressed this reservation:

> Attempts to work out its implication in detail . . . to trace the connection between [a supposed angelic fall] and the creation of this actual universe which we are trying to understand—all such attempts, 'like the truth' they may be in the Platonic sense, leave us without conviction that they give any record of what actually occurred.[24]

---

[23]Jürgen Moltmann seems to reflect a perspective similar to that of Williams insofar as he holds that sin can affect not only moral action but can pervert the very "creative potencies [that] are intended to make the life processes possible" (*God in Creation: A New Theology of Creation and the Spirit of God,* trans. Margaret Kohl [London: SCM Press, 1985], p. 169). On this see C. Deanee-Drummon, "Moltmann on Heaven," in *The Unseen World: Christian Reflections on Angels, Demons and the Heavenly Realm,* ed. Anthony Lane (Grand Rapids, Mich.: Baker, 1996), p. 54.

[24]Leonard Hodgson, *For Faith and Freedom,* 2 vols., Gifford Lectures, 1955-1957 (Oxford: Basil Blackwell, 1956-1957), 1:214.

According to Hodgson, the warfare view has a certain prima facie appeal to it, but it loses its plausibility when one attempts to develop it in any detail. Many questions remain that, if left unanswered, undermine the credibility of the warfare perspective—at least if we insist on taking it as a nonmythological account of how and why creation exhibits elements of hostility. For these reasons Hodgson himself treated it more as a useful myth than as a credible theory.

To be more specific, if the cogency of any theory is its power to explain phenomena, critics may question exactly *how* satanic forces are supposedly behind earthquakes, famines and the like.[25] They may question how this warfare understanding is consistent with our knowledge of the natural causes of these phenomena. They may also want us to clarify how the animal kingdom has been adversely affected by evil spirits or specify which aspects of the animal kingdom and of nature as a whole are the result of this sinister influence and which are not. If the carnivorous nature of predators in the animal kingdom is demonic, for example, how are we to conceive of hyenas that did not eat antelope? What would creation look like had there not been this corrupting influence? How did this corruption take place alongside particular "natural" phenomena?

Providing this information with any degree of confidence, however, is extremely difficult, if not impossible. How damaging is this to the trinitarian warfare theodicy? In my estimation, not very. Two considerations support this conclusion.

What has and has not been affected? First, I would argue that the request to know exactly which aspects of nature have and have not been adversely affected by Satan is an unfeasible question. One would have to have some experience of *a nonfallen creation* to assess this accurately. However, through divine revelation we *do* have enough information about the character of the Creator, about his original plan for creation, about the fall of angels and the reign of Satan, about the depth of corruption our present creation experiences and about God's eschatological vision for the creation to conclude *that* the creation is polluted with destructive sinister forces. But we lack any experience of precisely what a nonfallen creation would be like. *Everything* we experience on an empirical level has been affected by the fall.

---

[25]So objects David J. Bartholomew to the warfare view: "To attribute [natural evils] to Satan does not really explain anything. It is not particularly difficult to believe in a personal devil or even in demonic forces, but even if such exist it is not easy to attribute to them the power to cause volcanic eruptions or droughts" (*God of Chance* [London: SCM Press, 1984], p. 109).

We thus cannot conceive of a noncarnivorous hyena (if such a species would even exist in a nonfallen world) because the only hyenas we know are carnivorous. Our concept of a hyena is inextricably wrapped up with being a carnivore. Again, we may conclude *that* the carnivorous nature of a hyena is not part of God's original design because it is incompatible with the Creator's character as revealed throughout Scripture. The Bible suggests that the animal kingdom was originally vegetarian (Gen 1:30) and that the animal kingdom will be nonviolent when Christ reigns (Is 11:6-9; 65:25). But this admittedly does not supply the requested information. A hyena in an unfallen world would simply be a very different kind of animal than the hyenas we know in our own.

The mystery of spirit and matter. Second, the mystery of how demonic forces influence nature is no different than the mystery of how the Spirit of God influences nature. Orthodox Christians unanimously believe not only that God *somehow* created the world from nothing but also that he *somehow* perpetually governs it, influences it and occasionally significantly alters it in ways we call "miraculous."

In keeping with Scripture, Christians have always credited God with blessing us with various aspects of nature even though we have had no idea *how* God orchestrated this blessing. We might occasionally thank God for rain, even though we can offer no detailed account of exactly how God, who is Spirit, affected the physical world to produce rain and even though we would not want to thereby suggest that the occurrence of the rain was not also the result of natural causes. Why then should Christians object to blaming the devil for cursing us with a certain aspect of nature (a fatal disease, for example) even if we cannot offer a detailed account of how the devil accomplished the cursing and even though the "cursing" can also be explained in terms of natural causes?[26]

The mystery of how spirit affects the physical world is hardly unique to the trinitarian warfare theodicy; it is manifested in every free action humans perform. For example, one might analyze the neurological processes of the brain that precede all of my actions to understand the mechanics of how my brain affects my body. But scientific analysis is unable to explain how *I* affect these neurological processes or even define what *I* am. In every explanation other than a strictly materialistic one, *I* transcend the physical processes of the brain. *I* make free decisions that *somehow* activate all this neurological activity. But the inherent limitations of our empir-

---

[26]So argues Mundia, "Existence of the Devil," pp. 396-97.

ical methodologies are such that this "somehow" remains a mystery.[27]

We see, then, that the claim that evil spirits can adversely affect our physical environment should in principle be no more controversial to the nonmaterialist than the claim that God can affect our environment or that I can affect my environment. Although we have difficulty explaining *how* spirit influences matter, we have good reasons for believing *that* it does.[28]

Objection 2: The trinitarian warfare theodicy violates Ockham's razor. A closely related criticism that could be raised against the trinitarian warfare explanation of "natural" evil is that it is unnecessary. We know the causes of earthquakes, famines, cancer, tornadoes, and the like, and there is no mystery as to why certain animals prey on others. Proposing supernatural explanations beyond these natural ones violates the principle of Ockham's razor, which stipulates that, all other things being equal, the simplest way of accounting for things is the one most likely to be true. Thus one should not postulate superfluous causes to explain anything.[29]

In what follows I offer several observations that, I believe, negate the force of this objection. In the course of making these observations I further develop several aspects of the trinitarian warfare theodicy, especially as it concerns its relation to chaos theory and quantum mechanics.

What are we trying to know? First, from a scientific perspective we can claim to know the causes of natural phenomena such as tornadoes and earthquakes only because we have *defined* "knowing" in this context as the ability to make predictions. We know that under certain conditions tornadoes or earthquakes are likely to occur. The trinitarian warfare theodicy is not primarily concerned with this knowledge. Rather, it offers a *different kind* of explanation. It addresses the question of *why* the creation is the kind of place where tornadoes and earthquakes occur under certain conditions, given that it is created and sustained by an all-good God. Comparing the explanation

---

[27]On the mind-brain problem see John C. Eccles, *How the Self Controls Its Brain* (New York: Springer-Verlag, 1994); J. P. Moreland and Scott B. Rae, *Body & Soul: Human Nature and the Crisis in Ethics* (Downers Grove, Ill.: InterVarsity Press, 2000).

[28]This is not to say that we can learn nothing about *how* spirit (whether God, demons, angels or humans) affects the neutral medium of our relationality (nature), only that a belief *that* spirit affects nature is warranted even without this information.

[29]See John Hick, *Evil and the God of Love,* rev. ed. (San Francisco: Harper & Row, 1978), p. 13; cf. p. 369. So argues Swinburne, *Existence of God,* p. 202; Michael Martin, *Atheism: A Philosophical Justification* (Philadelphia: Temple University Press, 1990), p. 397; Michael Tooley, "Alvin Plantinga and the Argument From Evil," *Australasian Journal of Philosophy* 58 (1980): 372; Peter Vardy, *The Puzzle of Evil* (Armonk, N.Y.: M. E. Sharpe, 1997), p. 60. Mundia addresses this objection in "The Existence of the Devil," pp. 395-98.

that science gives with the explanation that theodicies offer is comparing apples with oranges. The one *describes* the world as it is; the other asks *why* is it the way it is.

Creation does not have to operate exactly the way it does. Chemicals do not *have* to interact with each other the way they do. Animals, weather patterns, geological plates, genetic codes, viruses and body cells do not *have* to behave the way they do. There is no known reason for why things *have* to die. Indeed, from a strictly scientific perspective there is no reason why there *has* to be a second law of thermodynamics. It is conceivable that the physical cosmos could have tended toward increasing complexity and design rather than degenerating toward randomness. Thus it is reasonable to ask why it does not. If it is all God's handiwork, should it not operate differently? Science has nothing to say about this question.

Some of the apparently ungodly qualities of creation are undoubtedly consequences of metaphysical requirements of any neutral medium of relationality, as I argued in the last two chapters. But no one has effectively argued that the more catastrophic and horrifying features of this medium are metaphysically necessary. Deadly tornadoes, earthquakes, cancer and AIDS are simply not logically mandated by the existence of a neutral medium. If they were, Scripture's promise that nature will not manifest these features in the kingdom of God would have to be considered false. It is Scripture, however, that suggests that these features are not inherent features of God's creation. This observation supports the conclusion that there are personal agents behind these destructive aspects of creation, a point that Scripture also suggests. Indeed, the Bible explicitly identifies death as the result of Satan's influence (Heb 2:14).

How does all this relate to the objection that the trinitarian warfare theodicy violates Ockham's razor? It demonstrates that our theodicy is not unnecessarily adding to the complexity of any scientific understanding of natural phenomena. As David O'Connor says in defense of Plantinga's "Satan Hypothesis":

> Ockham's razor [does not] justify us in preemptively depopulating Plantinga's defense of its devils, for, as described by Plantinga, the work of Satan and Satan's followers duplicates that of no other posited beings.

Thus he concludes:

> it is not illicit to argue, against arguments whose conclusion is that certain facts of natural evil are logically inconsistent with God, for the possibility of

immensely powerful, intelligent, and cunning malevolent spirits who are morally responsible for natural evil.[30]

The question we are addressing, in fact, is unrelated to the scientific question and does not violate Ockham's razor.

The simplicity of the trinitarian warfare theodicy. If considered in terms of the question it does address, the trinitarian warfare theodicy is in principle quite simple. It attempts to provide the simplest explanation for "natural" evil within the context of a biblical worldview. In the trinitarian warfare worldview, as opposed to the blueprint worldview, we do not need to qualify the character or will of the Creator or obfuscate appearances by claiming that what looks like terrible evil somehow contributes to the good from God's perspective. All other things being equal, in the trinitarian warfare perspective we may assume that the source of what appears to be good in creation is a good agent and that the source of what appears to be evil is an evil agent(s). Things are as they appear. The world *looks* like a war zone because it *is* a war zone. In attempting to account for all the evil in the world, no theodicy could be simpler.

The applied complexity of the trinitarian warfare theodicy. This leads to a second observation regarding the trinitarian warfare theodicy and Ockham's razor. While the trinitarian warfare explanation of "natural" evil is simple on the level of general theory, it is admittedly complex in its application. Indeed, regarding the explanation for why any particular evil occurred, the trinitarian warfare theodicy admits that the matter is too complex for us ever to know.

Indeed, as I argued in chapters five through seven, the trinitarian warfare theodicy concedes that one would have to know everything about every free agent who ever existed, everything about all the other variables that determine the "givens" of any particular situation, to know why in any particular instance God did or did not prevent something that was against his will. Does this concession confirm the criticism that the trinitarian warfare theodicy is needlessly complex?

The answer is that it does not. This sort of combination of theoretical simplicity with applied complexity is found in all areas of human knowing. Consider the scientific explanation of tornadoes. On the basis of a few general principles we are able to specify the kind of conditions that produce tor-

---

[30]David O'Connor, *God and Inscrutable Evil: In Defense of Theism and Atheism* (Lanham, Md.: Rowman & Littlefield, 1998), p. 115. Though O'Connor defends Plantinga on this account, he does not himself embrace the "Satan Hypothesis."

nadoes. But these principles will never allow us to predict with absolute precision or explain with absolute accuracy every detail about any particular tornado.

Why is this? Because there are too many variables involved exhaustively to predict or explain any particular tornado. Further, as chaos theory maintains, the slightest alteration anywhere can in principle cause a very significant alteration elsewhere. The result is that, while we can specify the *kinds* of conditions that are likely to produce tornadoes (or any other natural phenomenon), we can never exhaustively predict or understand any *particular* tornado.[31]

Dealing with an unimaginable complexity. If it is always the case that the more exhaustive our exploration is, the more complex our explanation becomes, then we have yet another reason to discard the objection that the trinitarian warfare theodicy is unnecessarily complex. If the attempt to predict or explain the physical causes of a particular deadly tornado ultimately lead to an incomprehensible complexity of variables, the trinitarian warfare theodicy cannot be criticized for appealing to innumerable variables (namely, the society of spiritual agents) to explain why the physical variables often develop into deadly tornadoes in the first place.

As in most scientific explanations, the basic principles invoked in the theological explanation remain simple. The trinitarian warfare theodicy, we have seen, appeals to principles of love, freedom and moral responsibility (TWT1-6). Here Ockham's razor holds. But, as in the sciences, an exhaustive theological explanation of the particulars would be unimaginably complex.

Consider once again the deadly tornado. What role if any did the myriad of free decisions within the angelic society play in the process of bringing about this particular tornado? Moreover, why did the multitude of free decisions in this semidemocratic society impact the world as it did and not otherwise? Providing an exhaustive answer to questions such as these would ultimately require that we possess exhaustive information about every free decision ever made by spirits and every indeterministic variable that ever

---

[31]Even if we concede that the probability of a phenomenon is occasionally close to 100 percent, rendering it virtually certain, we cannot predict its exact characteristics. So, for example, conditions may render it virtually certain that a tornado will form. But we can never exhaustively predict when or where it will form, the exact course it will take, its exact size or velocity, and the like. My point, issuing from chaos theory, is that this inability is rooted in the nature of things. The science of understanding and predicting tornadoes will undoubtedly improve, but it will never be exhaustively accurate.

took place in the history of the world—among other things! All of these variables contributed something, however minute, to the world being the exact world it was at the moment this tornado was generated. These variables thus contribute something not only to why it is that the world is the kind of place in which tornadoes can occur but also why this particular tornado struck exactly when it did, where it did, with the force it did, killing the particular children it did.

Obviously, we do not and cannot possess such information. The reality of the spiritual world we are concerned with is unimaginably complex and mostly inaccessible to our finite, physically oriented perspectives. But note that we are up against an unknowable complexity *whether we admit the existence of free spirits into our equation or not.* Postulating the variable of spirits does not in principle change the situation. We are simply embracing one more *kind* of variable in our equation to broaden the scope of our explanation of a particular deadly tornado.

If this point is considered within the context of a trinitarian warfare worldview, one may conclude that the problem of explaining why a particular "natural" evil occurred is in actuality no different than the problem of explaining why any particular thing occurs. As argued in chapter seven, the mystery surrounding any evil event is in principle no different than the mystery surrounding why two cars are separated by an eight-second interval on a given highway at a given moment of time.[32]

As Yahweh instructed Job, humans simply are not in a position to understand the cosmos fully (Job 39—41). We can discern the *kind* of things that bring about "natural" events, including ones that are evil, such as a deadly tornado. But in terms of understanding the reasons or causes behind any *particular* tornado, deadly or not, we must always come up short. The world is too vast and the variables too complex for us finite creatures to comprehend.[33]

This, I have argued, is the real mystery of evil. It is not the mystery of God's character or of an all-good blueprint that world events meticulously follow. It is, rather, simply the mystery of creation's complexity.

Objection 3: The warfare view of "natural" evil contradicts the biblical creation account. A third objection to the trinitarian warfare understanding of "natural" evil needing to be addressed is that it contradicts

---

[32]Note C. S. Lewis's observations regarding the deceptive nature of simplicity in *Mere Christianity* (New York: Macmillan, 1979), pp. 46-51.

[33]The exception to this, of course, is when God himself tells us in Scripture that he was the source of a natural disaster brought about to punish unrepentant sinners.

the biblical creation account. In the Genesis 1 account, this objection goes, the Creator exercises unopposed control over every aspect of creation and pronounces it all "good." In this respect the Genesis account differs from all pagan and dualistic* renditions of creation. The environment is cursed in Genesis 3 after the Fall of humanity, but, according to this objection, it is God, not Satan, who curses the ground (Gen 3:17-19; Rom 8:20). Further, there is no indication that this cursing perverted the structure of things such as the laws of nature or the constitution of animals. In this respect the Genesis account seems to contradict the trinitarian warfare theodicy.

I believe that the creation account in Genesis 1 can be reconciled with the trinitarian warfare theodicy I am proposing, but before I argue this case, two preliminary points are in order.

The variety of creation accounts. While the creation account in Genesis 1 is the most extensive in the Bible, it is by no means the only biblical account. The very next chapter, of course, offers a slightly different, complementary account. Even more importantly, many additional references are sprinkled throughout the Old Testament (e.g., Ps 74:12-17; 89:1-52; 104:1-35). As I have argued extensively elsewhere, most of these other accounts parallel ancient Near Eastern creation stories that depict creation in the context of a primal cosmic conflict between good and evil forces.[34] These often neglected creation accounts are particularly agreeable with the warfare understanding of nature.

For various reasons, the Judeo-Christian tradition tended to give the Genesis 1 account normative status, but this selectivity was really quite arbitrary.[35] At least if we accept the plenary inspiration of Scripture, the Genesis 1 account should be read as a piece of the whole mosaic of Scripture's view of creation, not as the whole picture itself, and one must assess the adequacy of the warfare view of "natural" evil by its compatibility with the whole of Scripture, not with one passage alone.

The trinitarian warfare theodicy and dualism. However we interpret the details of the Genesis 1 account, there is no tension between the trinitarian warfare theodicy and the belief that the Creator was originally unopposed in bringing forth the world. Nor is there any difficulty in affirming that the original creation was unequivocally good. Indeed, the trinitarian warfare view of creation differs from metaphysical dualism and agrees with the classical view insofar as it holds that all things were created by God and thus that he originally possessed all power. If there are now forces opposing God—and

---

[34]See the discussion in *God at War,* pp. 83-113.
[35]Ibid., pp. 100-101.

there certainly are—this is because he (for reasons I have discussed) gave them the ability to do so. The dualism of the trinitarian warfare theodicy, then, is an ethical and provisional dualism, not a metaphysical dualism.

Be that as it may, we nevertheless must reconcile the view that nature is corrupted by fallen angels with the Genesis 1 creation account, in which God pronounced everything "good" prior to the Fall. In what follows I will consider three viable interpretations of Genesis 1 and attempt to show how the trinitarian warfare theodicy might be rendered compatible with each one.

Evolution and Genesis 1 as myth. The most common scholarly interpretation of Genesis 1 is that it is a poetic myth expressing theological truth. Contrary to all the pagan views of its neighbors, this creation account expresses Israel's conviction that the whole creation comes from Yahweh. He is completely sovereign over it, and it is essentially good. In this view, the details of this inspired mythic poetry cannot be used to dispute the prevailing scientific view that the earth is five billion years old, that all species have evolved from lower species and that suffering has been a part of the evolutionary process for millions of years.

If this interpretation of Genesis 1 is accepted, there is little difficulty reconciling this passage with the trinitarian warfare theodicy. At some point in the prehistoric past, the evolutionary defender of the warfare theodicy could argue, Satan and his angels rebelled. As part of their assault on the Creator, they assailed his work of creation by perverting the responsibility they had as guardians over aspects of this creation. Thus, long before humans existed—perhaps at the beginning of the evolutionary process itself—these agents exercised a corrupting influence on the creation. Insofar as it was within their authority as guardians to do so, they twisted the laws of nature and corrupted the evolutionary process to reflect something of their perverse nature rather than the benevolent nature of the Creator. In short, the animal kingdom and all of nature reflects both the wisdom of the Creator and the violence of his opponents.

A defender of this interpretation could further argue that despite this satanic counterinfluence, God providentially achieved his aim in creating beings in his image. Unlike any of the previous animals, humanity was empowered with morally responsible free will and enabled by the Creator to enter into a loving relationship with him and to participate in his fight against the anticreational forces to regain lordship of the earth. Unfortunately, we freely allowed ourselves to be co-opted by the very power we were commissioned to overthrow. We have thus come under the same bondage as the rest of creation. Through the work of the cross God has sought to defeat his opponents and to restore humans to their original place as guardians of the earth.[36]

A creationist reading. For both biblical and scientific reasons, many scholars reject the theory of evolution or the mythic reading of Genesis 1.[37] Some
of these rather interpret the Genesis 1 account as a mostly literal picture of
creation. Such an interpretation would seem to rule out the view that Satan
and his followers exercised a corrupting influence on the laws of nature and
the animal kingdom before the fall of humanity. But it is not necessarily
incompatible with the warfare theodicy on this account.

One could argue that, whenever the angels fell, they did not begin their
process of corrupting the world until after Satan successfully co-opted the
original parents into his rebellion. When Adam and Eve fell, they surrendered to Satan the authority over the earth that they and their descendants
were supposed to have. Once established as "ruler" and "god" of the world
(Jn 12:31; 14:30; 16:11; 2 Cor 4:4), Satan immediately began to exercise his
own dominion over the earth. Furthermore, in keeping with his character—
one of his names is *Apollyon* ("Destroyer," Rev 9:11, cf. Jn 10:10)—this
dominion was decidedly destructive.

One could argue that God was involved in this cursing, as the Genesis
account says, in the sense that he gave permission to Satan to take over the
dominion intended for humans. It was, after all, the Creator who established
the cosmos as a place within which morally responsible agents can affect oth-

---

[36]Defeating the devil was seen as the primary purpose of Christ's death in the New Testament and
the early church. Only with Anselm (eleventh century) did the substitutionary aspect of Christ's
death come to dominate the Christian understanding of the atonement. See Boyd, *God at War,*
pp. 238-68. Other scholars who recognize the centrality of the warfare motif in the New Testament understanding of the work of Christ are Gustaf Aulén, *Christus Victor: A Historical Study
of the Three Main Types of the Idea of Atonement,* trans. A. G. Hebert (New York: Macmillan,
1969); Karl Heim, *Jesus the Lord: The Sovereign Authority of Jesus and God's Revelation in Christ,*
trans. D. H. van Daalen (London: Oliver & Boyd, 1959); Karl Heim, *Jesus the World's Perfector:
The Atonement and the Renewal of the World,* trans. D. H. van Daalen (Edinburgh: Oliver &
Boyd, 1959); Ragnar Leivestad, *Christ the Conqueror: Ideas of Conflict and Victory in the New
Testament* (New York: Macmillan, 1954); John S. Whale, *Victor and Victim* (Cambridge: Cambridge University Press, 1960). R. A. Greer has traced the transition from the Christus Victor to
the substitutionary understandings of the atonement in "Christ the Victor and Victim," *CTQ*
59 (1995): 1-30. As Robert E. Webber notes, there is now a growing appreciation for the
Christus Victor motif among theologians and in the church (*The Church in the World: Opposition, Tension or Transformation?* [Grand Rapids, Mich.: Zondervan, 1986], p. 267).
[37]On the genre of Genesis 1, see, e.g., Gordon Wenham, *Genesis 1-15,* WBC (Waco, Tex.:
Word, 1987), pp. 54-55; and J. H. Sailhamer, "Genesis," in *EBC,* 2:10-11. On problems with
evolutionary theory on a scientific basis, see, e.g., Michael Behe, *Darwin's Black Box: A Biochemical Challenge to Evolution* (New York: Free Press, 1996). See also the collections in William Dembski, ed., *Mere Creation: Science, Faith and Intelligent Design* (Downers Grove, Ill.:
InterVarsity Press, 1998).

ers for better or for worse. God created the world such that when morally responsible agents fall, everything they are morally responsible for will become adversely affected. This, I have argued (chapter five), is part of the meaning of moral responsibility. Thus, there is no contradiction in saying that God cursed the earth because of Adam's sin and that Satan and his legions also plague the earth because of Adam's sin.

All other facets of the trinitarian warfare worldview could be considered in the same way as the previously discussed evolutionary view, except that on this interpretation all of the corrupting influence occurs after the creation and fall of humanity. It was at this point that the laws of nature became twisted and animals became predatorial. This radical alteration need not have happened all at once; the gradual shortening of human life in the Genesis record perhaps suggests that the corrupting influence took time to saturate the creation. But regardless of how much leeway we ascribe to the genealogies of Genesis 1—5, it must have happened rather quickly, especially in comparison to the time allowed for in the evolutionary view.

The restoration reading. While it is not incompatible with the trinitarian warfare view of "natural" evil, the creationist reading of Genesis 1 is problematic. Among other things, this view contradicts the nearly unanimous consensus of geologists that the earth is billions of years old, as well as the nearly unanimous consensus of paleontologists that animals were devouring one another millions of years before humans arrived on the scene. If creationists are right, one has to accept that dinosaurs and humans lived at the same time and that the original Tyrannosaurus Rex was vegetarian!

A third view may avoid the difficulties of both the first and second readings of Genesis 1 and may be the most compatible with the warfare understanding of "natural" evil. It is called the "restoration" or "gap" theory of creation.[38] In this view, Genesis 1:1 describes the original creation, while Genesis 1:2 describes this creation after it had been corrupted by demonic influences, torn apart by a spiritual war and come under God's judgment. Genesis 1:3-31 then describes (in literal or nonliteral terms) God's work of restoring the earth by refashioning it out of the materials of the previous creation.

In keeping with this reading, we may suppose that over billions of years the original creation came under bondage to destructive spirits, some of whom perhaps had been agents originally entrusted by the Creator with caring for it. These guardians joined Satan's rebellion, however, and began exercising their domain of influence in an anticreational manner. In this

---

[38]For a more detailed exposition and defense of this view, see Boyd, *God at War*, pp. 100-113.

sense, the restoration view is similar to the previously discussed evolutionary warfare perspective. Insofar as these fallen spirits were able (that is, insofar as they possessed irrevocable authority), they twisted the laws of nature governing the cosmos in a destructive direction. They perverted earth's animal inhabitants, perhaps infiltrating the evolutionary process (if such a process was indeed present). Perhaps in a manner remotely analogous to the way deformed hybrid creatures were produced by the mixture of demonic and human natures prior to the flood (Gen 6:1-4), the mingling of demonic influences with the good creative "life-force" (Norman Williams) of God produced hybrid creatures in this world that no longer perfectly reflected the glory of their original Creator. Nature became hostile, creatures became vicious, and the whole planet became subject to God's enemy and was no longer fit for the purposes for which it was originally created.

Eventually God waged war against his foes who now significantly controlled the world. It is perhaps this battle that is echoed throughout the many creation-conflict passages of the Old Testament. Using mythological imagery familiar to ancient Near Eastern people, inspired writers depicted and celebrated Yahweh's battle with and victory over malevolent forces such as the raging sea, the deep, Leviathan the many-headed dragon and Rahab along with her cohorts. Further, as each of these passages proclaims, it was out of this battle that the world we presently inhabit was created. It is not that Satan was destroyed or the entire universe permanently cleansed from demonic influences, but the forces that had seized this earth had been subdued, at least temporarily.

Similar to God's decision to start over with humanity in the days of Noah, God judged and mostly destroyed the previous demon-inhabited war-torn world. As a result of this judgment, and perhaps as a result of the cosmic battle itself, the earth was reduced to the "formless void" we find in Genesis 1:2.[39] Since the concept of "the deep" (*t^ehôm*) was a way of expressing threatening chaos in the ancient Near East, we may interpret the reference to the Spirit (or wind, *rûah*) of God brooding over the abyss as the author's way of

---

[39]Genesis 1:2 can arguably be translated, "Now the earth became [or had become, *hāy^etâ*] formless and empty." It is significant to note also that the terms used to describe the earth in verse 2, "formless and void" *(tōhû wābōhû)*, are almost always used pejoratively. Indeed, the only other time this exact phrase is in reference to the state of the world after God's judgment (Jer 4:23; cf. Is 34:11). Also significant is the fact that Scripture explicitly teaches that God did not originally create the world in a state of *tōhû*, (Is 45:18). So too we should recall that "the deep" *(t^ehôm)* always had an sinister connotation in ancient Near Eastern thought, as is perhaps best expressed by the chaotic figure of Tiamat (whose name, interestingly enough, has the same root as *t^ehôm*) in the Enuma Elish. See Choan-Seng Song, *Third-Eye Theology: Theology in Formation in Asian Settings* (Maryknoll, N.Y.: Orbis, 1979), pp. 35-39.

expressing God's ongoing control of his foes. He had set a guard against "the Sea" and "the Dragon" (Job 7:12). He had assigned the rebel waters "a boundary that they may not pass" (Ps 104:9).

Then, as he did after Noah's flood and as he will do once again when he purges the earth at the end of this age (2 Pet 3:10, 12; Rev 21:1), God began the process of restoring the earth by refashioning it out of the remains of the old one. Keeping the forces of evil at bay, and apparently working at a highly accelerated rate (if we take the Genesis 1 record more literally), God refashioned a new animal kingdom devoid of the meat-eating monsters (e.g., carnivorous dinosaurs) that had evolved in the previous one. In keeping with his universal design to exercise his sovereign lordship through morally responsible administrators, God created humans after his own image to be responsible stewards and guardians of this new world.

The primary responsibility of humans was to preserve and perhaps expand God's "conquest of an evil being who had penetrated into creation," as Franz Delitzsch describes it.[40] They were thus instructed and empowered to "subdue" the earth (Gen 1:28) and to guard the garden (Gen 2:15). They were to exercise a loving lordship over the whole animal kingdom, as represented by Adam's charge to name all the animals (Gen 2:19-20). They were to glorify God by being his viceregents on the earth.

Not only this, but judging from what later transpired through Christ (already foreshadowed in Gen 3:15), it is possible that one of God's original agendas in recreating the earth and establishing humanity as stewards over it was ultimately to employ these earthly guardians in a strategy for overthrowing the rival kingdom once and for all. This was accomplished by the God-man Jesus Christ allowing himself to be crucified by the spiritual "rulers of this world" and by rising victorious on the third day (Col 2:13-15, cf. Jn 12:31; 1 Pet 3:21-22). Empowered by the Spirit of our conquering Head, the church is now to fulfill the role of original humanity: reclaiming the earth from the kingdom of darkness as the domain in which the Creator is King.

In any event, the refashioned paradise apparently did not last long. As soon as he was able, the enemy sought to recapture the earth by deceiving its human rulers and bringing them under his domain of influence. We of

---

[40]Quoted in Erich Sauer, *The King of the Earth* (reprint, Palm Springs, Calif.: R. Hayes, 1959), p. 93. Sauer argues that the cleansing of the newly created world of all demonic influences had not yet been complete and that this was the task entrusted into humans. The garden was to be the home base, as it were, from which the whole world would ultimately be reconquered for Christ.

course do not know how long Eden lasted, but we do know that at some point the enemy discovered a strategy that worked. The viceregents of God and intended stewards of the earth surrendered their authority over the earth to the enemy (Lk 4:6) and joined the satanic rebellion. In doing so they exposed the earth once again to the same corrupting forces of evil that had perverted it in the previous age.

Just as the refashioning of nature had been carried out by God at an accelerated speed, so was its recorruption, it seems. With the lord of death and destruction enthroned once again (Heb 2:14), humans began to die within a millennium. Within a few more thousand years they live for scarcely more than a century. In time, the global average would be less than a half a century.

We can imagine nature and the animal kingdom undergoing the same accelerated process of corruption. Having come once again under the influence of its previous evil anticreator, the laws of nature once again became twisted, the animal kingdom once again became violent, and humans who were originally commissioned to rule the whole planet with the love and power of God became the subjects of the very forces they were supposed to control.

A number of things can be said in favor of this view. Its integration of the creation-conflict accounts of the Old Testament is a strong point in its favor that the other views lack.[41] It explains why angels are not included in the list of things created in Genesis 1, though their existence seems to be presupposed in the first-person plural of Genesis 1:26.[42] It also explains how an evil serpent could appear out of nowhere in Genesis 3 and why the Lord commanded Adam and Eve to "subdue" the earth (Gen 1:28) and to guard the garden (Gen 2:15), even though the world itself had been pronounced good.[43] Finally, it does not require us to reject the consensus of geologists

---

[41]Levenson may be correct when he argues that the Genesis narrative *begins* where other ancient Near Eastern and other biblical accounts *end*, namely, when the battle between God and his foes had just come to an end. More specifically, the author of the Genesis account "begins near the point when the *[Enuma Elish]* ends its action, with the primordial waters neutralized and the victorious and unchallengeable deity about to undertake the work of cosmogony" (Levenson, *Persistence of Evil,* p. 112). Genesis 1:2 is thus a "postbattle" summary, describing "a chaos that . . . resembled the morning after a battle" (Sauer, *King of the Earth,* p. 93).

[42]For a defense of this interpretation of the "us" in Genesis 1:26, see my *God at War,* pp. 107, 131-32.

[43]God's pronouncement that the creation is "good" does not rule out the presence of evil forces. There is no reason to assume any connection between God's evaluation of his refashioned physical creation as "good," on the one hand, and the issue of whether or not there existed at this time beings who were neither physical nor part of this refashioned creation, on the other. God is talking about his new creation when he says "it is good," not the forces he had to defeat to bring this creation about.

and paleontologists regarding the duration and violent nature of the earth before humans arrived on the scene. It thus need not postulate vegetarian dinosaurs contemporary with humans, as does the creationist account. But neither is its coherence undermined if one decides on other grounds that evolutionary theory is implausible.

On these grounds I am inclined, however tentatively, to accept the restoration interpretation of Genesis. Though the plausibility of the trinitarian warfare theodicy does not hang on this, I believe that this interpretation accommodates this theodicy best. Nevertheless, I have attempted to demonstrate that, whatever view of Genesis 1 one adopts, it is possible to integrate a warfare understanding of "natural" evil into it.

Conclusion

In one of Jesus' parables, a farmer discovered that weeds were growing in his field alongside of the crop he had planted. Since he did not plant the weeds, he concluded, "An enemy has done this" (Mt 13:28). The point of this chapter has been that we should cultivate a similar critical discernment regarding the "field" of the Lord's creation.

The mudslide that buries a schoolroom full of children alive; the deadly tornado that snuffs out the lives of young children as they enact an Easter pageant; the disease that slowly incapacitates the minds of three beautiful siblings, thereby crushing the spirits of their parents; the tempest that drowns a boat full of immigrants seeking freedom; the hurricane that kills ten thousand people and leaves thousands more homeless—such "natural" phenomena cannot be regarded as "natural" in a world created and governed by an all-powerful, beneficent Creator. This is not the kind of "seed" that the all-loving God sows. We should in each instance conclude, "An enemy has done this."

Such evils have the same moral quality as the abduction and rape of a young child. While there are a number of variables that must be considered

---

Another possibility, however, is that the whole creation narrative is written from the perspective of the one to whom it is revealed. The author is describing the restoration of the whole cosmos from the perspective of the earth. This view makes sense of the fact that the author records the bringing forth of vegetation on the earth before the appearance of the sun, moon and stars (Gen 1:11-19). It also allows us to integrate the Genesis record with the astronomical fact that the light from stars we presently observe originated billions of years before the earth as we know it was formed. This is no problem if we accept that the Genesis account is written in phenomenological terms. Had one been standing on the earth at the time, it would have looked as though God simply placed the stars in the sky to light up the night. If either of these views is granted, there is no incompatibility with the restoration-warfare reading of the Genesis narrative and God's pronouncement that his creation was "good."

for a comprehensive understanding of such terrible occurrences, their ultimate explanation must lie in the volition of evil agents who abuse their God-given authority. In short, Satan and his legions are directly or indirectly behind all forms of "natural" evil. Satan turns the neutral medium of the natural order into a weapon just as human agents sometimes use rocks, sticks or water as weapons when they choose to do so. This conclusion is the only one entirely consistent with the Bible and the only one that adequately accounts for all the data in need of explanation. It takes seriously the fact that Jesus always considered "natural" infirmities and diseases as directly or indirectly the work of Satan's kingdom. It also squares well with the fact that Jesus treated a life-threatening storm the way he treated demons: he "rebuked" it.[44]

One important difficulty for the trinitarian warfare theodicy remains, however. We need to reconcile our perspective with the biblical and traditional proclamation that the hell that Satan creates for himself and others will endure *forever*. If the temporary suffering of people presents a problem for belief in an all-good and all-powerful God, their eternal suffering presents a much greater one. So it is to this difficulty that we turn in the final two chapters of this work.

---

[44]Boyd, *God at War*, pp. 203-6. The term *phimoō* ("Be still!") literally means "to muzzle" and is applied elsewhere to Jesus' exorcising demons (e.g., Mk 1:25; Lk 4:35). In the words of James Kallas, "If language means anything at all, it appears that Jesus looked upon this ordinary storm at sea, this ordinary event of nature, as a demonic force, and he strangled it" (*The Significance of the Synoptic Miracles* [Greenwich, Conn.; Seabury, 1961], p. 65). Neil Forsyth notes that the Gospel narrative taps into the Old Testament motif of Yahweh "rebuking" the hostile seas (*The Old Enemy: Satan and the Combat Myth* [Princeton, N.J.: Princeton University Press, 1987], pp. 286-87).

11

A CLASH OF DOCTRINES

Eternal Suffering & Annihilationism

When you choose anything, you reject everything else.
G. K. CHESTERTON, *ORTHODOXY*

[The wicked] shall be as though they had never been.
OBADIAH 16

[The devil and his angels] will be tormented day and night forever and ever.
REVELATION 20:10

The clash of doctrines is not a disaster, it is an opportunity.
ALFRED NORTH WHITEHEAD,
SCIENCE AND THE MODERN WORLD

*T*hough the war between God and Satan has raged for eons, it will not continue forever. The victory over Satan and the freedom for God's children that Christ won through his death and resurrection will someday be fully manifested. Then God's creation will no longer be subject to the destructive influence of his archenemy.

John gives us a beautiful picture of this final victorious state when he writes:

> [God] will dwell with them [his church] as their God; they will be his peoples, and God himself will be with them; he will wipe every tear from their eyes. Death will be no more; mourning and crying and pain will be no more, for the first things have passed away. (Rev 21:3-4)

We are now in the midst of "the first things." This is the necessary probationary period that all free agents must experience. Since love requires choice, God intends this stage of existence to function as a prelude to his eternal kingdom. It is the gestation period of our eternal life, the courtship of the heavenly groom and his earthly bride to be, the temporal time of choice that eventually forms our eternal being. But God never intended it to be the battlefield it has become. Though God of course anticipated this possibility, the age-long battle between God and Satan with all the suffering it has caused is not something the beneficent Creator would ever will.

Despite the war, however, God's plan of creating a beautiful bride for his Son who freely receives and reflects his eternal, triune love continues as originally planned. Even the tragic rebellion of his most powerful angelic administrator cannot thwart God's ultimate objective for creation. Thus God patiently carries out his will in these miserable conditions, using even the pain and suffering of this age to his own advantage (Rom 8:28).

And he will succeed. As the spotless bride who has made herself ready, we will sit down with Christ at an eternal wedding banquet (Rev 19:6-10; cf. Mt 25:1-10; Eph 5:25-32). Functioning as the viceregents we were always intended to be, we will reign with our heavenly husband, Jesus Christ, on the earth (Rev 5:10; 22:4-5). At this time, "all things" will be reconciled to God through Christ (Col 1:20; cf. Acts 3:21). "All things" will be made new (Rev 21:5). "All things" will be gathered up in Christ (Eph. 1:10). Then, as it had always been planned, the triune God will be "all in all" (1 Cor 15:28).

This is the ultimate hope the Bible offers. The hope is not that God's will is now being done but that God's will shall *someday* be done "on earth as it is in heaven." The hope is that this probationary period, together with the war that rages within it, will come to an end. The hope is that however terrible our present circumstances may be—and at times they can be unbearable—before long they will all come to an end. Then creation will be what God always intended it to be.

The Problem of Hell

However, Scripture's otherwise magnificent eschatological vision seems to be marred by one thing. According to traditional interpretations, this vision includes the understanding that innumerable angels and people will suffer excruciating pain for all eternity. Rebels will anguish in a lake of fire that will never be extinguished (Lk 16:22-24; Rev 14:10; 20:14-15) and in which they "will be tormented day and night, forever and ever" (Rev 20:10).

How is this perpetual suffering consistent with the proclamation that God

will be altogether victorious, that "all things" will be reconciled to him and
that he will be "all in all"? In the words of Philip Hughes:

> When Christ fills all in all and God is everything to everyone (Eph. 1:23;
> 1 Cor. 15:28), how is it conceivable that there can be a section or realm of cre-
> ation that does not belong to this fullness and by its very presence contradicts
> it?[1]

How are we consistently to conceive of a God who loves and died for every
human who ever existed preserving their existence forever for no other purpose than perpetual torment? Further, how are we to understand the
redeemed enjoying untainted bliss in heaven if alongside of this kingdom billions of people and fallen angels will be experiencing excruciating, unending
anguish?

If the reality of suffering in this probationary period is a problem for biblical theists, the hellish reality of unending suffering is even more so. What is
more, unlike the problem of temporal suffering, it does not seem that the
problem of suffering in hell can be resolved by appealing to the trinitarian
warfare worldview, for in the eschaton, the war will have come to an end.
The necessity of God's self-limitation to allow for freedom in the probationary stage of "first things" will be over. It seems that whatever exists in this
final state *must* exist *because God wills it.*[2]

The problem is exceedingly difficult and extremely important, so it is fitting that we conclude this work on Satan and the problem of evil by addressing it. Our goal will be to arrive at an understanding that is fair to the diverse
teachings about hell in Scripture while also supporting the view of God and
his relationship to the world we have developed throughout this work.

To this end we will examine and critique arguments for two interpretations
of hell that have been offered throughout church history and that are held by
Christians today: the traditional and majority view that hell is eternal, conscious suffering, and the annihilationist* view that hell will ultimately cease to
exist because the wicked will be extinguished.[3] In the following chapter I will

---

[1]Philip E. Hughes, *The True Image: The Origin and Destiny of Man in Christ* (Grand Rapids,
Mich.: Eerdmans; Downers Grove, Ill.: InterVarsity Press, 1989), p. 406.

[2]Thus John Hick argues that the doctrine of eternal hell "renders any coherent Christian theodicy impossible by giving the evils of sin and suffering an eternal lodgment within God's creation" (*Death and Eternal Life* [London: MacMillan, 1990], p. 201). This is a dominant
theme in Jonathan Kvanvig's excellent work, *The Problem of Hell* (New York: Oxford University Press, 1993).

[3]Some argue that universalism should be considered as another viable option. Space considerations allow me only to assert my conviction that I do not see this position as having much biblical or philosophical merit. For various refutations of universalism, see William Crockett, "Will

propose a third possibility that mediates between these two views. It is rooted in Barth's concept of *das Nichtige*. I believe it answers the difficulties of both views while also incorporating their strong points.

The Case for Eternal, Conscious Suffering

The scriptural case for the traditional understanding of hell as eternal, conscious suffering has been effectively presented many times.[4] Therefore, our review of this material will be brief.

The Old Testament on eternal suffering. Among the few Old Testament passages that are cited in support of the traditional view of hell is Daniel 12:2.[5] Here Daniel proclaims that there will be a resurrection of the dead in which some will be granted "everlasting life" while others are condemned to "shame and everlasting contempt." Jesus also refers to a dual resurrection of the redeemed and the condemned (Jn 5:28-29; cf. Mt 25:31-46). The fact that the duration of the shame and contempt in Daniel parallels the duration of the unending life granted to the righteous suggests that hell is to be a place of unending, conscious torment, according to traditionalists. Some traditionalists further argue that it would be exceedingly odd for God to resurrect the wicked only for the purpose of annihilating them.[6]

God Save Everyone in the End?" in *Through No Fault of Their Own? The Fate of Those Who Have Never Heard,* ed. William Crockett and James Sigountos (Grand Rapids, Mich.: Baker, 1991), pp. 159-68; J. D. Bettis, "A Critique of the Doctrine of Universal Salvation," *RelS* 6 (1970): 329-44; Kvanvig, *Problem of Hell,* pp. 73-96; H. Brown, "Will Everyone Be Saved?" *Pastoral Renewal* 11 (June 1987): 11-16; N. M. de S. Cameron, ed., *Universalism and the Doctrine of Hell* (Grand Rapids, Mich.: Baker, 1992). On the other hand, see chapter six, note 3, for some valiant attempts to defend the view.
[4]Several recent philosophical defenses of the traditional position have been strong. See Jerry Walls, *Hell: The Logic of Damnation* (Notre Dame, Ind.: University of Notre Dame Press, 1992); and Kvanvig, *Problem of Hell.* For more popular, largely exegetical, defenses of the traditional perspective, see Larry Dixon, *The Other Side of the Good News* (Wheaton, Ill.: Victor, 1992); Harry Buis, *Doctrine of Eternal Punishment* (Philadelphia: Presbyterian & Reformed, 1957); Jon E. Braun, *Whatever Happened to Hell?* (Nashville: Thomas Nelson, 1979); Robert A. Peterson, *Hell on Trial: The Case for Eternal Punishment* (Phillipsburg, N.J.: P & R Publishing, 1995); and Anthony A. Hoekema, *The Bible and the Future* (Grand Rapids, Mich.: Eerdmans, 1979).
[5]Traditionalist scholars of the past sometimes tried to argue that every reference to *sheol* in the Old Testament (usually translated as "grave" or "underworld") was identical with the New Testament concept of hell (*hades* or *gehenna**)—which, of course, they assumed entailed eternal conscious torment. So, for example, William G. T. Shedd, *The Doctrine of Endless Punishment* (New York: Scribner, 1886), pp. 21-24. Most modern defenders of the traditional perspective are more sensitive to historical-critical considerations and to the progressive nature of revelation. Thus their claims regarding the Old Testament's support of their position tend to be more modest.
[6]Tertullian argued this: "It would be most absurd if the flesh should be raised up and destined to 'the killing of hell,' in order to be put an end to it, when it might suffer such an annihilation (more directly) if not raised again at all. A pretty paradox, to be sure, that an essence must be

Another Old Testament passage frequently cited in support of the doctrine of everlasting torment is Isaiah 66:24. In an eschatological vision in which the Lord expounds on the blessings that will come on the righteous and the judgment that will come on the wicked, the Lord notes that all wicked people will suffer an ignoble fate. The righteous

> shall go out and look at the dead bodies of the people who have rebelled against me; for their worm shall not die, their fire shall not be quenched, and they shall be an abhorrence to all flesh.

Robert Peterson, a defender of the traditional doctrine, comments on this passage:

> The prophet used imagery from the present world to describe the future order. For exposed corpses to be eaten by worms or burned was a disgrace. Here was the ultimate disgrace. In all other cases the maggots would die when they had finished their foul work (cf. Isa. 14:11), and the fire would go out once its fuel was consumed. But in the prophet's picture of God's judgment of those who rebel, the worm does not die and the fire is not quenched! The punishment and shame of the wicked have no end; their fate is eternal.[7]

Eternal punishment as conscious torment. Turning to the New Testament, one of the most persuasive passages supporting the traditional view of hell is Matthew 25:31-46. Here we find Jesus acting as "King" on the day of judgment. To those who knew him (whether consciously or not, Mt 25:37-39) he grants eternal life (Mt 25:34). But those who did not know him (even if they thought they did, cf. Mt 7:22-23) he consigns to eternal punishment (Mt 25:46). The fact that Jesus contrasts the eternal punishment of the wicked with the eternal life of the righteous suggests that the wicked will endure punishment forever (Mt 25:41, 46). If the former state is an unending conscious duration, it seems natural to take the latter as unending conscious duration as well, according to traditionalists. The fact that Jesus explicitly refers to the fire of this punishment as an "eternal fire" seems to confirm this (Mt 25:41).

The parable of the greedy rich man who would not care for Lazarus is also frequently cited in support of the traditional view. After death, the rich man finds himself "in Hades . . . being tormented" (Lk 16:23). In this state he begs Abraham to send Lazarus to "dip the tip of his finger in water and cool my tongue; for I am in agony in these flames" (Lk 16:24). Despite the figu-

---

refitted with life, in order that it may receive that annihilation which has already in fact accrued to it!" (*On the Resurrection of the Flesh* [ANF 3:570], quoted in Peterson, *Hell on Trial,* p. 99).
[7]Peterson, *Hell on Trial,* p. 33.

rative language, the passage implies that the wicked experience torment after death.

Traditionalists also argue that unending conscious torment is evident in Jude's reference to fallen angels who are kept in "eternal chains" (Jude 6). If the chains are eternal, what the chains hold must be eternal as well. The same is true of Paul's teaching that the Lord will in the end be revealed "in flaming fire, inflicting vengeance on those who do not know God." "These," he further says, "will suffer the punishment of eternal destruction" (2 Thess 1:8-9).

This destruction cannot amount to total annihilation, traditionalist argue, for part of it consists of being "separated from the presence of the Lord and from the glory of his might" (2 Thess 1:8-9). It seems one can only be separated from someone else if one continues to exist.[8] In addition, in the preceding verses Paul draws a parallel between the affliction that the Thessalonians innocently suffer at the hands of persecutors and the affliction the persecutors will justly suffer at the hands of God (2 Thess 1:6-7). If the affliction the Thessalonians suffered was conscious—and it obviously was— so must the affliction of the persecutors be conscious.

With the same implication, Jesus taught that the sin against the Holy Spirit is "an eternal sin" (Mk 3:29) that "will not be forgiven, either in this age or in the age to come" (Mt 12:32). While traditionalists debate a number of issues surrounding this passage, all agree that the teaching entails that those who are refused forgiveness eternally must eternally exist to be refused.

A fate worse than death. Traditionalists also argue that many if not most of the images used to speak of the punishment of the wicked suggest that they will consciously suffer in this eternal punishment. When they are cast into "outer darkness" or "into the furnace," Jesus says of the wicked, "there will be weeping and gnashing of teeth" (Mt 13:42; 22:13). To weep and gnash one's teeth, one must be conscious. Recalling Isaiah 66, Jesus also teaches that in this horrid place of torment the worm that devours will never die and the fire will never go out (Mk 9:48), implying eternal suffering, according to traditionalists.

In this same context Jesus teaches that the wicked will be "salted with fire" (Mk 9:49). This unusual expression arguably suggests that the fires of hell will not utterly annihilate the wicked, for the primary function of salt in

---

[8]Scot McKnight argues that Paul has in mind "an irreversible verdict of eternal nonfellowship with God," which means that the "person exists but remains excluded from God's good presence" ("Eternal Consequences or Eternal Consciousness?" in Crockett and Sigountos, eds., *Through No Fault of Their Own?* pp. 155-56; cf. Peterson, *Hell on Trial,* p. 81).

the ancient world was preservation. Hence, traditionalists argue, we must accept that this terrible unquenchable fire burns even while it preserves those whom it burns.

Along the same lines, Paul teaches that while God will grant "eternal life" to all "who by patiently doing good seek for glory and honor and immortality," there will be "wrath and fury" to all who reject God. Then he adds that this fury will cause "anguish and distress" (Rom 2:7-9). This implies conscious torment on the part of those who are judged. Moreover, according to traditionalists, the fact that this judgment is contrasted with eternal life implies that the anguish and distress is eternal as well.

Traditionalists also argue that Jesus' teaching that it would be better to be "drowned in the depth of the sea" than to be cast into hell for being a stumbling block only makes sense if the wicked consciously suffer throughout eternity (Mt 18:6). If hell is annihilation, then it is no different in consequence than being drowned. Likewise, only if hell is eternal in duration does it make sense for Jesus to say that it would have been better for Judas if he had never been born (Mk 14:21). If hell is annihilation, then Judas's fate would in fact be as though he had never been born. But in this case how could Jesus describe his fate as *worse* than nonbirth? Further, how could Jesus describe the fate of some as being worse than others on the day of judgment if indeed all the wicked are to be annihilated (Mt 11:20-24)?

Tormented forever and ever. Perhaps the strongest scriptural arguments for the traditionalist position, however, come from the book of Revelation. At one point an angel proclaims that anyone who worships the beast and its image will "be tormented with fire and sulfur in the presence of the holy angels and in the presence of the Lamb." Most significantly, he adds:

> the smoke of their torment goes up forever and ever. There is no rest day or night for those who worship the beast and its image and for anyone who receives the mark of its name. (Rev 14:9-11)

To argue that the torment and restlessness is temporary while the "smoke of their torment" is unending seems to many to constitute exegetical gymnastics. But, lest there be any doubt, Revelation 20 states explicitly that the devil, the beast and the false prophet were all thrown "into the lake of fire and sulfur," where "they will be tormented day and night forever and ever" (Rev 20:10). Later it is said that "anyone whose name was not found written in the book of life was thrown into the lake of fire," apparently to suffer the same eternal fate as the devil they followed (Rev 20:15).

The eternality of hell and the soul's infinite potential. Beyond the scriptural witness, throughout church history philosophical arguments have been offered in support of the necessary eternality of hell. Following Anselm, some have argued that justice demands that hell be eternal, for sin against God is an infinite offense. Others have argued that hell must be eternal because the soul is inherently immortal. While few put much stock in these arguments any longer, I am not convinced that they cannot be salvaged if construed along certain lines.[9] I wish to offer one revised argument for the eternality of hell on the basis of the soul's innate immortality.

As I argued previously, the nature of morally responsible freedom entails that an agent's potential for good must be proportionate to its potential for evil. This potential, I further suggested, must be irrevocable (TWT4 and 5). If these insights are valid, one could perhaps further argue that since agents enjoy a potential to choose love *for eternity* they must, by necessity, possess a proportionate capacity to choose its opposite *for eternity*. In other words, if opportunity and risk necessarily go hand in hand, then the opportunity for eternal gain must entail the risk of eternal loss. Hence, the risk God must take in creating creatures with the capacity for eternal heaven is that he thereby creates them with the capacity for eternal hell.[10]

If this argument is sound, it answers the most common philosophical objection raised against the doctrine of eternal, conscious suffering, namely, that such an irreversible state is incompatible with the universal loving character of God. Pinnock expresses this objection persuasively:

> How can one reconcile this doctrine [of eternal punishment] with the revelation of God in Jesus Christ? Is he not a God of boundless mercy? How then can we project a deity of such cruelty and vindictiveness? Torturing people without end is not the sort of thing the "Abba" Father of Jesus would do. Would God who tells us to love our enemies be intending to wreak vengeance

---

[9]For a critical biblical review of the philosophical assumption of immortality, see E. Fudge, *The Fire That Consumes: The Biblical Case for Conditional Immortality*, rev. ed. (Carlisle, U.K.: Paternoster, 1994), pp. 32-40. See also Hughes, *True Image*, pp. 398-407.

[10]Richard Swinburne argues in this direction in "A Theodicy of Heaven and Hell," in *The Existence and Nature of God*, ed. Alfred J. Freddoso (Notre Dame, Ind.: University of Notre Dame Press, 1983), pp. 37-54. W. Van Holten also argues along similar lines against universalism, Calvinism and annihilationism in "Hell and the Goodness of God," *RelS* 35 (1999): 37-55. In a similar vein, Walls argues that the eternality of hell is necessary if our moral choices are to be ultimately significant (*Hell*, pp. 136-37). See also the relevant discussion in Kvanvig, *Problem of Hell*, pp. 27-55. All such arguments are rejected by Thomas Talbott on the grounds that there is no conceivable motive for someone choosing eternal misery ("The Doctrine of Everlasting Punishment," *Faith and Philosophy* 7 [1990]: 19-42).

on his enemies for all eternity? . . . What would we think of a human being who satisfied his thirst for revenge so implacably and insatiably?[11]

If God were in fact "torturing people without end," this objection might constitute an insurmountable objection to the concept of eternal, conscious hell. But we need not think of the matter in these terms. Scripture teaches that God does not will anyone's damnation (Ezek 18:23; 33:11; 1 Tim 2:4; 2 Pet 3:9). Why then does God allow any to suffer eternally? Perhaps because this possibility had to be part of the irrevocable freedom and eternal potentiality given to humans. Hell is therefore a risk God *had to take* if his goal was to populate his kingdom with agents who genuinely choose to be there.

I confess that I am myself not entirely convinced that this argument is valid. I consider it a plausible explanation of the scriptural teaching that those who reject God suffer eternally. If I did not have scriptural grounds for thinking that people suffer eternally, however, I could not confidently conclude this simply on the grounds that the potential to choose God eternally must be balanced by an opposite potential to reject him. One could rather argue that the possibility of choosing eternal life is balanced by the possibility of choosing *eternal death*, not eternal suffering.

The Case for Annihilationism
A increasing number of theologians and biblical scholars reject the traditional premise that the Bible teaches that those who reject God suffer eternally. They rather argue that Scripture teaches that those who reject God are ultimately annihilated.[12]

---

[11]Clark Pinnock, "The Conditional View," in *Four Views on Hell*, ed. W. Crockett (Grand Rapids, Mich.: Zondervan, 1992), p. 140. A number of people since the nineteenth century have argued that the doctrine is immoral. See, e.g., John Stuart Mill's essay "Utility of Religion," in *Three Essays on Religion* (London: Longmans, Green & Co., 1923), p. 23. Bertrand Russell argued along similar lines in *Why I Am Not a Christian* (New York: Simon & Schuster, 1957), p. 17. Though the doctrine of everlasting hell is making a comeback in recent times (see "Hell's Sober Comeback," *U.S. News and World Report*, March 25, 1991, p. 56) its clash with modern moral sensibilities led to its demise both within and without the church for the last two hundred years. See Martin E. Marty, "Hell Disappeared. No One Noticed. A Civic Argument," *HTR* 78 (1985): 381-98. Robert Short blames much of the rejection of Christianity in modern times on the doctrine of eternal suffering (*Something to Believe In* [San Francisco: Harper & Row, 1978], p. 34).

[12]The most thorough and compelling exposition of the biblical basis of annihilationism is Fudge's *Fire That Consumes*. A number of reputable evangelical leaders have embraced the annihilationist perspective. See John Wenham, *The Enigma of Evil* (Grand Rapids, Mich.: Zondervan, 1985), pp. 27-41; John Wenham, "Conditional Immortality" in Cameron, ed., *Uni-*

Response to passages suggesting eternal torment. Annihilationists maintain that the passages used to support the doctrine of eternal hell do not teach that hell is *suffered* eternally, only that its *consequences* are eternal. The damned suffer "eternal punishment" (Mt 25:46), "eternal judgment" (Heb 6:2) and "eternal destruction" (2 Thess 1:9) the same way the elect experience "eternal redemption" (Heb 9:12, cf. 5:9). The elect do not undergo an eternal process of redemption. Their redemption is eternal in the sense that once the elect are redeemed, it is forever. Likewise, annihilationists teach, the damned do not undergo an eternal process of punishment or destruction, but once they are punished and destroyed, it is forever.[13]

Annihilationists argue that Scripture's references to an "unquenchable fire" and "undying worm" also refer to the finality of judgment, not its duration (Is 66:24; cf. 2 Kings 22:17; Is 1:31; 51:8; Jer 4:4; 7:20; 21:12; Ezek 20:47-48). The fire is unquenchable in the sense that one cannot hope to put it out before it consumes those thrown into it. Similarly, the worm is undying in the sense that there is no hope that it will be prevented from devouring the corpses of the condemned.[14] Nevertheless, most annihilationists hold that there is a period of suffering for the damned prior to their annihilation, depending on the severity of their wickedness. In their minds, this accounts for passages noted above that seem to ascribe conscious suffering to those who are judged (Lk 16:19-31; Rom 2:8; 2 Thess 1:6).

Finally, concerning the passages in Revelation that speak of torment being "day and night forever and ever" (Rev 14:10-11; 20:10), annihilationists

---

versalism; John Stott in John Stott and D. Edwards, *Essentials: A Liberal-Evangelical Dialogue* (London: Hodder & Stoughton, 1988), pp. 320-29; and Clark Pinnock, "The Conditional View." One of the best *theological* defenses of annihilationism, connecting with the doctrine of the *imago dei,* is offered by Hughes in his outstanding work, *True Image.* See also Richard Swinburne, *Responsibility and Atonement* (Oxford: Clarendon, 1989), pp. 180-84; H. E. Guillebaud, *The Righteous Judge: A Study of the Biblical Doctrine of Everlasting Punishment* (Taunton, England: Phoenix, 1941). For a thorough (but overly enthusiastic and strongly biased) investigation of exponents of annihilationism (or at least of "conditional immortality") within the church tradition, see LeRoy E. Froom, *The Conditionalist Faith of Our Fathers: The Conflict of the Ages over the Nature and Destiny of Man,* 2 vols. (Washington, D.C.: Review & Herald, 1965-1966).

[13]In the words of Philip Hughes, "because *life* and *death* are radically antithetical to each other, the qualifying adjective *eternal* or *everlasting* needs to be understood in a manner appropriate to each respectively. Everlasting life is existence that continues without end, and everlasting death is destruction without end, that is, destruction without recall, the destruction of obliteration. Both life and death hereafter will be everlasting in the sense that both will be irreversible: from that life there can be no relapse into death, and from that death there can be no return to life" (*True Image,* p. 405).

[14]Fudge, *Fire That Consumes,* pp. 62-64.

point out that this a symbolic book whose apocalyptic images should not be taken literally.[15] Indeed, even in the book of Isaiah, which is generally far less symbolic than Revelation, God's judgment could be described in everlasting terms in a context where it could not possibly be taken literally. Isaiah writes that the fire that will consume Edom will burn "night and day" and "shall not be quenched." Its smoke "shall go up forever" and no one will pass through this land again "forever and ever" (Is 34:10). Obviously, this is hyperbolic, for the fire and smoke of Edom's judgment is not still ascending today. If this is true of Isaiah, annihilationists argue, how much less inclined should we be to interpret similar expressions literally in the book of Revelation?

The annihilationists' view, however, does not depend only on how they reinterpret passages traditionally taken to support the doctrine of eternal, conscious suffering. It is based on biblical material that they argue explicitly teaches the annihilation of the wicked. In what follows I briefly overview this material.

Annihilationism and the Old Testament. Whereas contemporary traditionalists do not appeal much to the Old Testament to establish their view of hell as eternal, conscious suffering, annihilationists appeal to it frequently.[16] They argue that the pervasive pattern of divine judgment found throughout the Old Testament narrative is that God allows evil to run its full course and then annihilates it. For example, when the Lord saw that the human race had become hopelessly evil, he said to Noah, "I will blot out from the earth the human beings I have created . . . for I am sorry that I have made them" (Gen 6:7). Again, "I have determined to make an end of all flesh. . . . I am going to destroy them along with the earth" (Gen 6:13; cf. 7:4).

The pattern is repeated in the Lord's destruction of Sodom and Gomorrah (Gen 19:1-29). The people and the land were utterly destroyed. Peter specifically cites the destruction of Sodom and Gomorrah as a pattern of how God judges the wicked. The Lord turned the inhabitants of these cities "to ashes" and "condemned them to extinction," thus making "them an example of what is coming to the ungodly" (2 Pet 2:6). Conversely, the Lord's rescue of Lot sets a pattern for how the Lord will "rescue the godly from trial" (2 Pet 2:9).

---

[15]On the nonliteral nature of apocalyptic language (and how it is often misinterpreted), see N. T. Wright's excellent discussion in *The New Testament and the People of God* (Minneapolis: Fortress, 1996), pp. 280-99.

[16]With traditionalists, annihilationists concede that most Old Testament passages addressing the topic are concerned with the fate of the wicked *in this world*. But against the traditionalists, they maintain that at least some of these passages are eschatological. See Fudge, *Fire That Consumes*, pp. 41-67.

Throughout the Old Testament the Lord threatens the wicked with annihilation. To all who refuse to comply with the covenant God has established,
for example, the Lord vows to "blot out their names from under heaven"
(Deut 29:20). Indeed, he vows to destroy them and the land "like the
destruction of Sodom and Gomorrah . . . which the LORD destroyed in his
fierce anger" (Deut 29:23). Likewise through the prophet Isaiah the Lord
warns that

> rebels and sinners shall be destroyed together,
>   and those who forsake the LORD shall be consumed. . . .
> You shall be like an oak whose leaf withers,
>   and like a garden without water.
> The strong shall become like tinder,
>   and their work like a spark;
> they and their work shall burn together,
>   with no one to quench them. (Is 1:28, 30-31)

Again:

> As the tongue of fire devours the stubble,
>   and as dry grass sinks down in the flame,
> so their root will become rotten,
>   and their blossom go up like dust,
> for they have rejected the instruction of the LORD of hosts. (Is 5:24)

Judgment as destruction in the Psalms. The theme that the Lord will annihilate the wicked is especially prominent in the Psalms. The psalmist says that
whereas those who take delight in the Lord will be "like trees planted by
streams of water," the wicked will be "like chaff that the wind drives away . .
. the wicked will perish" (Ps 1:3-4, 6). They will be dashed "in pieces like a
potter's vessel" (Ps 2:9), torn into fragments (Ps 50:22) and "blotted out of
the book of the living" (Ps 69:28; cf. Deut 29:20). Each metaphor depicts
total annihilation, according to annihilationists.

Similarly, the Lord's plan for evildoers is to "cut off the remembrance of
them from the earth. . . . Evil brings death to the wicked" (Ps 34:16, 21).
The wicked will be so thoroughly destroyed that they will not even be
remembered (Ps 9:6; 34:16). In the powerful words of a later author, the
wicked "shall be as though they had never been" (Obad 16).

With the same force, the psalmist proclaims that the wicked "will soon
fade like the grass, and wither like the green herb" (Ps 37:2). They "shall be
cut off . . . and . . . will be no more; though you look diligently for their
place, they will not be there"(Ps 37:9-10). While the righteous "abide for-

ever" (Ps 37:27), "the wicked perish . . . like smoke they vanish away" (Ps 37:20). The wicked "vanish like water that runs away; like grass [they will] be trodden down and wither . . . like the snail that dissolves into slime; like the untimely birth that never sees the sun" (Ps 58:7-8). Again, "transgressors shall be altogether destroyed" (Ps 37:38; cf. 37:34). In short, the fate of the wicked is disintegration into nothing, according to annihilationists.

Judgment and destruction in other Old Testament passages. The psalmist's emphasis on the total destruction of the wicked has parallels throughout the Old Testament. Daniel, for example, speaks of all who will be crushed by the rock of God's judgment as being "broken." They become "like the chaff of the summer threshing floors," blown away by the wind, "so that not a trace of them [can] be found" (Dan 2:35). Nahum says that in the judgment the wicked "are consumed like dry straw" (Nahum 1:10). Malachi tells us that the judgment day will come "burning like an oven" and that "all the arrogant and all evildoers will be stubble." The judgment thus "shall burn them up" (Mal 4:1). Proverbs tells us that all who hate the Lord "love death" (Prov 8:36) and that when "the tempest" of God's judgment passes, "the wicked are no more" (Prov 10:25). Again, when God's fury rises, "the wicked are overthrown and are no more" (Prov 12:7). Finally, "the evil have no future; the lamp of the wicked will go out" (Prov 24:20). Annihilationists argue that it is impossible to accept that the wicked have no future if in fact they will never cease to experience an eternal future in hell.

Through Isaiah the Lord depicts the destruction of the wicked as a vineyard that will be "devoured," "trampled down" and made into "a waste" (Is 5:5-6). So too the wicked will be "like thorns cut down, that are burned in the fire" (Is 33:12). Zephaniah depicts their fate graphically by noting that "their blood shall be poured out like dust, and their flesh like dung" (Zeph 1:17). In typical apocalyptic hyperbole he proclaims that "the whole earth shall be consumed; for a full, a terrible end he will make of all the inhabitants of the earth" (Zeph 1:18). Passages such as these, argue the annihilationists, are fundamentally incompatible with the view that the wicked consciously suffer endless pain.

The valley of exposed corpses. Finally, while some traditionalists argue that Isaiah 66 supports eternal, conscious suffering, annihilationists argue that it rather supports their position. In this passage the Lord promises life and prosperity to those who keep covenant with him (Is 66:10-14) and fiery justice to all who do not.

> For the LORD will come in fire,
>   and his chariots like the whirlwind,

> to pay back his anger in fury,
>   and his rebuke in flames of fire.
> For by fire will the LORD execute judgment,
>   and by his sword, on all flesh;
> and those slain by the LORD shall be many. (Is 66:15-16)

All the "survivors" (Is 66:19) from among the Jews will go out and bring to Jerusalem (Is 66:20) people from every nation whose hearts are open to the Lord, and they will all behold the glory of the Lord (Is 66:18-21; cf. Rev 5:9-10; 7:9-10; 21:22-26). "All flesh shall come to worship before me," says the Lord (Is 66:23). According to annihilationists, the universal qualifier here is predicated on the extinction of all who would not worship him. *All* people—that is, all who were salvageable and were not slain—will abide forever before the Lord, just as "the new heavens and the new earth, which [he] will make" will abide forever (Is 66:22). They will all behold the results of God's victory:

> They shall go out [from Jerusalem] and look at the dead bodies of the people who have rebelled against me; for their worm shall not die, their fire shall not be quenched, and they shall be an abhorrence to all flesh. (Is 66:24)

To a Jew, the most shameful fate imaginable was to have one's corpse left above ground to rot or to be burned instead of buried (Josh 7:25; Amos 2:1). In this passage the wicked are pictured as suffering such an ignoble fate. Hence they are described as an abhorrence to the living because they are left out for maggots to infest and consume and to have their bodies burned by fire. The worm will not die, and the fire will not be quenched, until the wicked are utterly consumed.

New Testament evidence
The consuming fire. According to annihilationists, the teaching that the wicked will be completely destroyed is even stronger in the New Testament. As in the Old Testament, they are frequently depicted as being destroyed by fire. For example, John the Baptist proclaimed that "every tree . . . that does not bear good fruit is cut down and thrown in the fire" (Mt 3:10). He announced that the Messiah "will clear his threshing floor and will gather his wheat into the granary; but the chaff he will burn with unquenchable fire" (Mt 3:12). Jesus himself repeats the imagery of hell as a consuming fire several times (Mt 7:19; 13:40; Jn 15:6).

The author of Hebrews writes that those who fall away from Christ are like ground that produces only "thorns and thistles. . . . Its end is to be burned over" (Heb 6:8). To all who resist the truth there remains only "a fearful prospect of judgment, and a fury of fire that will consume the adversaries" (Heb 10:27).[17] Annihilationists argue that the term *consume (esthiō)* in this context denotes total annihilation. It is what happens to wood when it is burned up (Ps 83:14; Joel 2:5; Nahum 1:10; cf. Lev 10:2; Ps 59:12-13; Is 26:11; 33:14). As mentioned earlier, Peter seems explicitly to draw this conclusion. When God turned "the cities of Sodom and Gomorrah to ashes" he says, God "condemned them to extinction" and thereby "made them an example of what is coming to the ungodly" (2 Pet 2:6). The "eternal fire" that rained from heaven on these wicked cities was a fire that irrevocably incinerated its inhabitants (Jude 7).[18]

Hell as destruction. The New Testament has many other ways of describing the fate of the wicked. Each of these depict total annihilation, according to annihilationists. Frequently it is said of the wicked that they will be "destroyed." For example, Jesus contrasts the wide gate that "leads to destruction" with the narrow gate that "leads to life" (Mt 7:13-14). Destruction clearly contrasts with life in this passage, and this, annihilationists argue, at least implies cessation of consciousness such as when a person is dead. Along similar lines, Jesus tells his disciples not to fear those who kill the body but cannot kill the soul; rather, "fear him who can destroy both soul and body in hell" (Mt 10:28). The implication is that God will do to the soul of the wicked what humans do to the body when they kill it. This, annihilationists argue, implies that the soul of the wicked will not go on existing in a conscious state after it has been destroyed.

James teaches that God alone is able both "to save and to destroy" (Jas 4:12). Peter teaches that "destruction" awaits false, greedy teachers (2 Pet 2:3), and Paul teaches that the quest for riches can plunge people into "ruin and destruction" (1 Tim 6:9). Moreover, all who are "enemies of the cross" have "destruction" as their final end (Phil 3:18-19; cf. 1:28). Likewise, if anyone "destroys God's temple, God will destroy that person" (1 Cor 3:17).

---

[17]Cf. Isaiah 33:14, where people facing future judgment proclaim, "Who among us can live with the devouring fire? Who among us can live with everlasting flames?" (Is 33:14). Annihilationists argue that the flames are everlasting not in the sense that people will burn in them forever but that they are not going to go out before they do what fire is supposed to do: it consumes all that it burns. For this reason, no one can live in it. The wicked must therefore be warned that they will be incinerated like chaff unless they repent (Is 33:11). See Hughes (*True Image*, p. 402), who argues that the "eternal fire" that was said to have destroyed Sodom and Gomorrah in Jude 7 denotes a fire that "struck and left such devastation from which no restoration could follow."

[18]The "eternal" in this passage is clearly qualitative, not quantitative. On the meaning of *aiōn* and *aiōnios* ("eternal" or "everlasting"), see Fudge, *Fire That Consumes*, pp. 11-20.

With the same force the apostle teaches that "sudden destruction" will come on the wicked in the last days (1 Thess 5:3). This day is elsewhere described as a day for the "destruction of the godless" (2 Pet 3:7).[19] Annihilationists argue that such passages contradict the traditional view that damned souls are in fact never destroyed but rather endure endless torment.

Hell as corruption, perishing and death. Another common way of expressing the fate of the unsaved in the New Testament is to depict them as suffering "corruption" (*phthora*). "If you sow to your own flesh," writes Paul, "you will reap corruption from the flesh" (Gal 6:8). The ordinary meaning of this term in Greek is "ruin, destruction, dissolution, deterioration, corruption."[20] So, at the very least, this term entails a loss of consciousness, according to annihilationists.

On a related note, annihilationists point out that "immortality" and "incorruption" are promised only to the righteous (1 Cor 15:42-44, 50). We "put on imperishability" and "immortality" (1 Cor 15:54). The teaching implies that the unrighteous remain mortal and perishable. Likewise, Scripture teaches that God alone is immortal by nature (1 Tim 6:16); all others receive it as a gift. Believers are given the gift of eternal life (e.g., Jn 3:15-16; 10:28; 17:2; Rom 2:7; 6:23; Gal 6:8; 1 Jn 5:11); they do not have it innately. The "tree of life" that was forbidden to humans after the Fall (Gen 3) is open to them in the eschaton (Rev 22:19). Conversely, annihilationists argue, those who are not given eternal life have only finite life, which is to say, it comes to an end.[21]

The New Testament also frequently expresses the destiny of the wicked by depicting them as dying or perishing *(apollymi)*. John proclaims the good

---

[19] Acts 3:23 may be relevant here. Peter, speaking about Deuteronomy's prophecy regarding the coming Messiah, says that "everyone who does not listen to that prophet will be utterly rooted out of the people." The verb *exolethreuō* means to "destroy utterly, root out" (W. Bauer, W. F. Arndt, F. W. Gingrich and F. W. Danker, *A Greek-English Lexicon of the New Testament and Other Early Christian Literature,* 2nd ed. [Chicago: University of Chicago Press, 1979], p. 276). Though only found here in the New Testament, it was frequently employed in the Septuagint in passages depicting the destruction of the wicked (e.g., Ps 37:9, 22, 28, 34, 38).

[20] Ibid., p. 865. It was used to speak of everything from perishable food to miscarriages. See Fudge, *Fire That Consumes,* p. 158.

[21] This view that immortality is a gift, not an innate quality, arguably is rooted in the Genesis account of the Fall. This passage teaches that Adam and Eve were expelled from the garden precisely so that they would not eat from "the tree of life" and becoming immortal, like God (Gen 3:22). They had been warned that disobedience would result in death (Gen 2:17; Rom 5:12). Not coincidentally, one of the privileges the citizens of the future kingdom of God are given is the "right to the tree of life" that our original parents surrendered (Rev 22:14). We will *put on* immortality (1 Cor 15:54).

news that God sent Jesus so that "everyone who believes in him may not perish but may have eternal life" (Jn 3:16). Paul utilizes this same contrast when he states that, while those who proclaim the gospel are a "fragrance from life to life" to those "who are being saved," they are "a fragrance from death to death" to those "who are perishing" (2 Cor 2:15-16).

Jesus teaches that "those who find their life will lose it, and those who lose their life . . . will find it" (Mt 10:39). To annihilationists, the contrast in these passages between death, losing life and perishing, on the one hand, and life, on the other, is incompatible with the contrast of eternal bliss with eternal pain that the traditional teaching on hell presupposes. Death, losing life and perishing are not easily read as signifying another kind of life, that is, a life of eternal, conscious pain. They rather seem to connote a total loss of consciousness, if not total extinction, according to annihilationists.[22]

Paul also teaches that "the wages of sin is death, but the free gift of God is eternal life" (Rom 6:23; cf. 1:32; 6:21). So too James writes that "sin, when it is fully grown, gives birth to death" (Jas 1:15); thus the person who "brings back a sinner from wandering will save the sinner's soul from death" (Jas 5:20). Likewise, Christ is said to have come to abolish "death and [to bring] life and immortality to light through the gospel" (2 Tim 1:10). Indeed, he came to "destroy the one who has the power of death, that is, the devil" (Heb 2:14). Life and immortality are connected with following God, death with following Satan. In contrast to traditionalists who interpret this death figuratively, annihilationists take it literally and thus conclude that it at least entails loss of consciousness.

God's victory. Finally, annihilationists argue that only this view explains the biblical motif of God's final and ultimate victory over all evil. How are we to envisage God's triune love reigning supreme if at the same time we must envisage multitudes of people and fallen angels in hopeless torment throughout eternity? How can we affirm that Christ will be over all (Eph 1:10, 21-22) and that God will be "all in all" (1 Cor 15:28) when there will be a dimension of reality perpetually opposed to God? How can we accept the scriptural affirmation that all creatures in heaven and earth will bow before the throne (Phil 2:10-11; cf. Rom 14:10-11) and that all things will be reconciled to God (Col 1:20; cf. Acts 3:21) if in fact many creatures will forever exist in hostile rebellion to God? How can we affirm the final and ultimate victory of God's joy and peace and accept that there will be no more tears, sorrow or death (Rev 21:4) if throughout eternity there shall be "weeping

---

[22]"It would be hard to image a concept more confusing than that of death which means existing endlessly without the power to die" (Hughes, *True Image*, p. 403).

and gnashing of teeth" as multitudes suffer an endless second death? The portrait of God's final victory suggested by the traditional view is incoherent, according to annihilationists, for God remains nonvictorious. Instead of a glorious universal kingdom unblemished by any stain, an ugly dualism reigns throughout eternity.

Annihilationists also question how heaven could ever be enjoyed as heaven if we knew that loved ones were at every moment being hopelessly tormented without relief. Only if the wicked have been altogether extinguished as the inhabitants of Sodom and Gomorrah (2 Pet 2:6) and have vanished "like a dream when one awakes" (Ps 73:20) can we ever truly enjoy the bliss of heaven, annihilationists argue. The joy of heaven is only conceivable if the damned have been annihilated and are remembered no more.

Conclusion

When all the biblical evidence is viewed together, it must be admitted that the case for annihilationism is quite compelling. Not without reason have such notable evangelical scholars as Philip Hughes, John Stott, I. Howard Marshall, John Wenham and Clark Pinnock endorsed this view. Nevertheless, even after the full force of the case has been appreciated, many Christians still have reservations about it.

First, it is not the traditional view. This cannot be decisive for all who adhere to the Protestant principle of *sola scriptura*, but as I argued in chapter four, it does put the burden of proof on new perspectives. Though the case for annihilationism is admittedly strong, it is questionable whether it is strong enough to overturn the majority view throughout church history.

Among its weaknesses, the annihilationists' symbolic reading of Revelation 14:10 and 20:10 is not altogether compelling. Revelation is a highly symbolic book, to be sure, but it is difficult to avoid the conclusion that eternal, conscious suffering is implied in its depiction of the punishment of the wicked. The annihilationist account of the parallel Jesus draws between the eternal reward of the righteous and the eternal punishment of the wicked in Matthew 25:46 is less than persuasive as well. It seems that Jesus is contrasting two different eternal *places* in which people will dwell (Mt 25:34, 41). Likewise, when Paul associates the anguish of the judged with the eternal punishment of their judgment, it seems logical to conclude that the anguish of the judged is eternal (2 Thess 1:6-9; cf. Rom 2:6-10).

Where does this leave us? For my part, it leaves me in a conundrum. I do not believe that either the traditional position or the annihilationists' position adequately accounts for all the biblical evidence cited in support of the opposing side's position. Yet I do not believe that Scripture can contradict itself (Jn 10:35). This raises the question: Is there a logically consistent way of affirming both views as essentially correct? Prima facie, this may seem absurd. Either the wicked suffer eternally or they are annihilated. But we must remember that some of the church's most fundamental doctrines have developed as a result of people wrestling with apparent contradictions in Scripture. For example, Scripture teaches that there is only one God but also that the Father, Son and Holy Spirit are each individually fully God. The doctrine of the Trinity resolves the apparent contradiction. Similarly, Scripture teaches that Jesus was fully human but also fully God. The doctrine of the incarnation resolves the apparent contradiction. In keeping with this theological tradition, therefore, I wish to explore whether or not there might be a way in which we can coherently affirm that the wicked are annihilated, in one sense, yet experience eternal torment, in another.

Alfred North Whitehead once opined that "the clash of doctrines is not a disaster, it is an opportunity."[23] Perhaps *this* clash is such an opportunity. In the final chapter of this work I will explore this possibility.

---

[23] Alfred North Whitehead, *Science and the Modern World,* quoted in Peter Coveney and Roger Highfield, *The Arrow of Time* (New York: Basic Books, 1990), p. 260.

12

A SEPARATE REALITY

Hell, das Nichtige *& the Victory of God*

So farewell Hope, and with Hope farewell Fear,
Farewell Remorse: all Good to me is lost;
Evil be thou my Good. . . .
Better to reign in Hell, than serve in Heav'n.
SATAN, IN MILTON'S *PARADISE LOST*

[Hell] is nowhere and has no characteristics,
the fit dwelling for those who have chosen nothingness over reality.
JEFFREY B. RUSSELL, *MEPHISTOPHELES*

The whole difficulty of understanding Hell is that the thing
to be understood is so nearly nothing.
C. S. LEWIS, *THE GREAT DIVORCE*

*T*he six theses that constitute the trinitarian warfare theodicy help explain how God's creation could become the ravaged war zone that it is. They do not in and of themselves explain suffering that continues in hell once the war is over, however. Yet no theodicy can be considered adequate that does not address this topic. In the previous chapter we examined the scriptural teaching regarding the fate of the wicked but found it paradoxical. Both traditionalists and annihilationists can find support for their differing conclusions regarding hell, yet these positions seem contradictory.

In theology, as in all areas of human understanding, sometimes advancements are made when we refuse to accept apparent antitheses as absolute.

We cannot be satisfied with contradictions, for they are meaningless, but we can seek to develop a model in which the antitheses are reconciled, at least to the extent of rendering them paradoxes instead of contradictions. The doctrines of the Trinity and the incarnation are examples of this in theology, as I noted in the previous chapter. The understanding of light as possessing both wavelike and particle-like characteristics is an example of this in science. Though the doctrine of hell is certainly less important than either the doctrines of the Trinity or the incarnation, this is what I will tentatively attempt to accomplish in this chapter. I will attempt to move beyond the impasse of the traditional and annihilationist understandings of eternal punishment and construct a model of hell that allows us to affirm the essence of both perspectives.

Toward this end, I will first make use of Karl Barth's curious concept of *das Nichtige* discussed in chapter nine. I will attempt to construe hell as existing in a peculiar "third way" between being and nonbeing. I will then develop this perspective further by relating it to another concept discussed in chapter nine, namely, that beings need a *neutral medium of relationality* if they are to interact with one another. I will suggest that when God's victory over all his foes is finally manifested, and thus when the Creator finally exercises his right to define all of reality as he wills—in accordance with his triune love—this shared medium of relationality will cease to exist between all who say yes to God's reality and all who continue to say no to it. The result is that those who have rejected God, and therefore reality, cease to exist to everyone except themselves.

[handwritten margin note: his thesis]

[handwritten annotation: Why not cease to exist all together?]

Barth on *Das Nichtige*

As we saw in chapter nine, Barth develops the concept of *das Nichtige* (literally, "the nothing") to account for the origin and nature of evil. Barth supposes that God's yes to that which he creates requires a no to that which he does not create. The act of bringing forth created reality produced an alternative realm of unreality. The divine choice for *this* to exist entails the negation of *that* as something that does not exist. *Das Nichtige* is thus not absolute nothingness, but neither is it existence. It paradoxically exists in a peculiar "third way" as the "reality of unreality." Out of this peculiar ontological status, *das Nichtige* threatens God's creation, according to Barth.

I suggested earlier that this concept, as it is described in Barth's own work, is problematic. Negated possibilities can in and of themselves do nothing and thus can threaten no one. By definition, negated possibilities have no actual being and thus can possess no power to influence, no say-so. These reasons, in addition to Barth's denial of creaturely self-determination, lead me to conclude that Barth's theodicy is incomplete and uncompelling. If self-determining agents can freely choose that which God negates, however, Barth's concept of *das Nichtige* becomes compelling and, I will now argue, quite useful, for now we can construe *das Nichtige* as having the potential to become actualized. Possibilities that God has negated become actualized if wills overturn the divine negation and "impute" reality to these negated possibilities by choosing them. Now "the nothingness" acquires authority, for now a free agent with authority has invested itself into it. *Nothing* has now become *something*.[1] What was negated by God is affirmed by a creature, and thus the possibility of something opposing God—the possibility of evil—becomes actualized.

Choosing das Nichtige. This revised concept of *das Nichtige* may provide the foundation for a theological model that will allow us coherently to bridge the divide between annihilationism and the traditional view of hell.

The model can be developed along the following lines. Because God desires love rather than robotic obedience, he endows creatures with self-determining freedom (TWT1). This freedom must be morally responsible, must involve genuine risk proportionate to the degree of love that can be chosen and must be irrevocable within limits (TWT2-6). On the basis of these theses, we can understand why the omnipotent Creator must for a time tolerate beings who oppose him. Due to this loving self-limitation, God must engage in genuine strategic warfare as he opposes the self-determining say-so of rebel creatures. The prolonged war is not a charade; it *must* be tolerated, given the Creator's objectives for creation.

Now, insofar as created beings choose to oppose God, the content of what they choose is what God has negated. Evil is not a substance that eternally coexists in competition with God, for God is the Creator of everything.

---

[1]In this sense I am in agreement with Lawrence Cunningham when he notes, "We have to think of evil as a nothingness and the incarnation of that evil as a something (Someone)" ("Satan: A Theological Meditation," *ThTo* 51 ([1994]): 360). Søren Kierkegaard makes a related point when he speaks against "the notion that sin is merely a negation to which one can acquire no title, as one can acquire no title to stolen property, a negation, an impotent attempt to give itself consistency, which nevertheless, suffering as it does from the torture of impotence in a defiance of despair, it is not able to do. Yes, so it is speculatively; but Christianly sin is . . . a position which out of itself develops a more and more positive continuity" (*The Sickness unto Death*, trans. W. Lowrie [Princeton, N.J.: Princeton University Press, 1941], p. 237). In short, sinners become the negation they choose. Finally, Arthur Cohen attempts to articulate metaphysically this "nothing-become-something" reality of evil by holding that evil is not "ontological" but "ontic" (*The Tremendum: A Theological Interpretation of the Holocaust* [New York: Crossroad, 1981], p. 33).

To this extent Augustine was correct in his abstract definition of evil as the absence of being. Evil is not eternal. It became a possibility as a result of God's desire to create creatures capable of choosing for or against him. The possibility of choosing against love in favor of what God negates is necessarily entailed by the possibility of choosing love and in favor of what God affirms. Hence, as I have noted, the possibility of love metaphysically entails the possibility of war.

When we choose possibilities that God has negated, when we choose to war against God, we are sinfully fighting for *the right to define reality*. We are rebelliously striving to replace the Creator's purposes for our lives with our own purposes. In Barth's terms, we are seeking to overturn the Creator's authoritative no with our own creaturely yes. We are, in effect, attempting to dethrone God as Lord of all reality and to enthrone ourselves as lords of an alternative reality of our own willing. This is the essence of sin.

According to Scripture, all of us have done this. We have in a multitude of ways said no to God's lordship in our lives. But God did not abandon us. Instead, out of his boundless love, he continued his yes toward creation with a yes of salvation: "While we still were sinners Christ died for us" (Rom 5:8). God freed us from the devil and forgave all our sin. God's redemptive yes is intended for every person. As all were in Adam, so now all are in Christ (Rom 5:18; 1 Cor 15:22; cf. 1 Tim 2:6; 4:10).[2] Yet, God continues to be a God of persuasion, not coercion (Irenaeus). Though the Father lovingly influences every human heart to accept his yes toward them (for we surely would not do it on our own), we possess the capacity to continue saying no to this gracious yes. Just as we rejected God's sovereign defining of us in creation, we can reject his sovereign defining of us in salvation. We can insist on living as though it were not true that we are loved, forgiven and freed in Christ.

Exposing **das Nichtige** *as nothing.* We identify the essence of the model of hell we are exploring when we ask, What becomes of those who say no to God's yes when in the eschaton God's yes reign's supreme? When this probationary period is over and God no longer allows agents to choose what he negates, when all of reality will be defined in accordance with his triune love, what becomes of those who have irrevocably defined their own reality over and against the reality that the Creator wills?

The answer can only be that the reality chosen by rebels must be exposed

---

[2]For an excellent treatment of the "universalist" passages in the New Testament along the lines I am developing, see Neal Punt, *Unconditional Good News: Toward an Understanding of Biblical Universalism* (Grand Rapids, Mich.: Eerdmans, 1980).

as "the nothingness" it is. The only reason *das Nichtige* can be actualized in this probationary period is that creatures who have self-determining say-so are allowed to invest it with their own actuality. But when this preliminary stage of existence is over, when all creaturely power to oppose God has been spent, the nothingness must literally *come to nothing.* The wills that choose this realm of negated possibilities must also become what they have chosen: utter negation. In short, when God's triune love reigns supreme, all that opposes this love must be reduced to nothing. God will be "all in all" (1 Cor 15:28).[3]

The eternal dignity of the creature. Thus far the model I am developing is consistent with annihilationism. But in this model there remains a distinction between the beings who choose *das Nichtige* and *das Nichtige* itself. If my argument in the previous chapter, that the potential to choose *eternal* fellowship with God entails a parallel potential to choose *eternal* separation from God is correct, and if some aspects of the traditional interpretation of Scripture's teaching on hell are correct, then we must conclude that while the entire *content* of what is willed against God is exposed as nothingness, the *will itself* that chooses this negation is not. In this view it can continue to exist, but *this existence can only be the existence of utter negation.*

We may consider this ongoing negative existence as the last remnant of the original dignity of self-determination that God gave the creature. God leaves rebels alone to follow their heart, to choose negated possibilities that can no longer be actualized in the eschaton. In giving creatures the irrevocable potential to accept his love eternally, God gives creatures the irrevocable potential to reject his love eternally. Even when reality will be exhaustively defined by God's triumphant triune love, God grants creatures the right to continue to reject it. However, now, in contrast to the probational period, there is no *real* alternative to his love. When it is no longer possible to actualize *das Nichtige,* the existence of those who nevertheless choose it is impossible. Hence the total content of what rebels choose is unreality.

Why might God allow beings to continue on in their rebel choice? Why does he not end their existence, as annihilationists claim? Two things may be said. First, if my argument in the previous chapter for the inherent immortality of the soul from the principle of proportionality is correct, *God has no choice in this matter.* The potential for eternally saying yes to reality as

---

[3]For a marvelous exposition of the thesis that God's love defines all of reality in heaven, see Jonathan Edwards's sermon, "Heaven Is a World of Love," in *The Works of Jonathan Edwards: Ethical Writings,* ed. Paul Ramsey (New Haven, Conn.: Yale University Press, 1989), pp. 366-97.

defined by the loving Creator metaphysically requires the potential eternally to say no to this reality, just as the creation of two adjacent mountains logically requires the creation of an intervening valley. If this is correct, then, as Peter Kreeft and Ronald Tacelli argue, "To annihilate the souls in hell would be to destroy something God created to be intrinsically and essentially immortal and indestructible—this is [a] . . . self contradiction."[4]

Second, the eternal potential to choose *das Nichtige* is compatible with God's triumphant love. God loves the beings he creates, for he creates out of this love. The core identity and primordial dignity of these beings is their original potential to choose for or against him. God loves this probational potential, for though it is risky it is nevertheless good. Without it, love among contingent beings would not be possible. When creatures actualize this potential by choosing against him, God is of course grieved. But while he detests what they choose, he nevertheless continues to love the dignity inherent in these creatures that allows them to choose it.[5]

Thus, while the *content* of what rebels will must be detested, judged and exposed as being the nothingness that it is—for this content *is* incompatible both with God's love and with his right as Creator to define reality—the fact *that* free beings choose this unreality is not incompatible with God's love. So also we may now understand how it is out of God's love for these rebel creatures that he eternally grants them the dignity of choosing this.[6]

Giving creatures what they want. What supports this perspective is that Scripture sometimes construes God's judgment on sin as a matter of God

---

[4]Peter Kreeft and Ronald Tacelli, *Handbook of Christian Apologetics* (Downers Grove, Ill.: InterVarsity Press, 1994), p. 301.

[5]On the enduring good of free will, even when it has irrevocably chosen evil, see Richard Creel, *Divine Impassability* (Cambridge: Cambridge University Press, 1986), pp. 141-43. In order to avoid the problem of hell eternally frustrating the love of God, Creel supposes that freedom is the goal of God's creation, not simply the means toward the goal of love. In my estimation, this move is unnecessary and ill advised. It protects God from pain by undermining his love. See also Jerry Walls, *Hell: The Logic of Damnation* (Notre Dame, Ind.: University of Notre Dame Press, 1992), pp. 107-10.

[6]Walls makes the case that God refrains from annihilating sinners in hell out of his grace (*Hell*, pp. 137-38). In my view, we should conceive of God's decision to grant rebels the dignity of eternally choosing against him as occurring at creation, not in the eschaton, since the potential to choose eternally against God is metaphysically entailed by their potential to choose for God, a potential given them at creation. Once such beings are created, the "granting" was metaphysically required. I will shortly argue that this granting can be viewed not only as a metaphysical implication of our potential but also as an act of God's love. In fact, it can also be viewed as God's ultimate expression of judging wrath on his enemies. In short, God's love and justice meet at the metaphysical condition of creaturely freedom. Kreeft and Tacelli also argue that it is out of love for the dignity of his creations that God allows the inhabitants of hell to exist (*Handbook*, p. 292).

simply letting sinners reap the consequences of what they have sown. The Creator ultimately defines reality, and when people (or angels) insist on resisting this reality they inevitably bring suffering and death on themselves. James expresses this motif when he writes:

> No one, when tempted, should say, "I am being tempted by God"; for God cannot be tempted by evil and he himself tempts no one. But one is tempted by one's own desire, being lured and enticed by it; then, when that desire has conceived, it gives birth to sin, and that sin, when it is fully grown, gives birth to death. Do not be deceived, my beloved. (Jas 1:13-16)

James construes death as the inevitable consequence of persistently giving in to temptation. Those who reject the source of life, love, joy and beauty, as a natural consequence of this decision, accept death, lovelessness, misery and ugliness.[7] If creatures choose this course for themselves, God allows it.

Indeed, Scripture frequently construes God's judgment on sinners as a matter of letting sinners have exactly *what they want*. For example, we read in the Gospel of John:

> God did not send the Son into the world to condemn the world, but in order that the world might be saved through him. Those who believe in him are not condemned; but those who do not believe are condemned already, because they have not believed in the name of the only Son of God. And *this is the judgment*, that the light has come into the world, and people *loved darkness* rather than light because their deeds were evil. (Jn 3:17-19, emphasis added)

Similarly, Paul understands "the wrath of God" to be "revealed from heaven against all ungodliness" (Rom 1:18) when God decides to let the ungodly Romans do what they want. God "gave them up to a debased mind" and allowed them fully to indulge their desires (Rom 1:28). Along these same lines, Revelation portrays the wicked as being outside the city walls *continuing to do* the same wicked things that prevented them from dwelling in God's city in the first place (Rev 22:15). Indeed, the door to the city is *open*, but they choose to remain outside (Rev 21:25-27).

As C. S. Lewis argues, then, hell is simply a matter of God giving crea-

---

[7]"God does allow men to sin; and misery is the natural, not the arbitrary inflicted, consequence of sin to the sinner. God is the only possible source of beauty and joy and knowledge and love: to turn away from God's light is to choose darkness, hatred, and misery" (Peter Geach, *Providence and Evil* [Cambridge: Cambridge University Press, 1977], p. 138). See also C. S. Lewis. *The Problem of Pain* (New York: Macmillan, 1962), pp. 122-24.

tures who refuse to be saved what they want.[8] If people want to reject reality as God defines it, including (most importantly) the reality of salvation accomplished in Christ, God allows them to do so. If people want to persist in the self-inflicted miserable deception that God did not send his Son for them and that they can exist autonomous from him, God lets them so choose.[9] Indeed, if this prerogative is in fact a metaphysical corollary to the potential eternally to accept God's love, as I have argued, then God must grant free creatures this eternal prerogative in the very act of creating them.[10]

A contentless eternal existence. What can be said about the "existence" of an eternal being who chooses to reject reality? In the eschaton, reality will be exhaustively defined by the triune love of God. Still, the permission to reject this reality remains, for this is not incompatible with God's love, as I argued above. But nothing else is. The fact *that* wills reject God's love remains real, but the total content of *what* they choose does not. When God's yes defines all, those who continue to say yes to his no have an utterly vacuous yes.[11] To put it in Lewis's terms, when God finally defines all reality, the damned will be defined solely by "their rejection of everything that is not simply themselves."[12]

We might conceive of the existence of such wills as a sort of dimensionless

---

[8]Lewis, *Problem of Pain*. This is the dominant theme that Lewis masterfully expresses throughout *The Great Divorce* (New York: Macmillan, 1946). Hence Lewis speculates that "hell is hell, not from its own point of view, but from the heavenly point of view. . . . It is only to the damned that their fate could ever seem less than unendurable" (*Problem of Pain*, p. 126). Lewis grants that "the damned are, in one sense, successful, rebels to the end; that the doors of hell are locked on the *inside*. . . . They enjoy forever the horrible freedom they have demanded, and are therefore self-enslaved" (*Problem of Pain*, p. 128). Walls offers an insightful discussion on this point in *Hell*, pp. 124-38. Thomas Talbott argues that an all-loving God would abandon free will and unilaterally turn his creations to him if not doing so meant that they would experience eternal misery ("The Doctrine of Everlasting Punishment," *Faith and Philosophy* 7 [1990]: 38). In my view (following Lewis and others), Talbott is asking for a metaphysical impossibility. This is the fundamental incoherence in universalism. Love *must* be chosen. See J. Kvanvig's discussion, *The Problem of Hell* (New York: Oxford University Press, 1993), pp. 83-88.
[9]On hell as self-inflicted deception of autonomy, see Walls, *Hell*, pp. 129-30; Lewis, *Problem of Pain*, p. 129.
[10]So too Kreeft and Tacelli maintain that "God does not sustain in existence the souls of the damned by any supernaturally willed act. Rather, his sustaining of souls forever is built into the *nature* of souls. In the act of creating eternal souls in the first place, God sustains them forever" (*Handbook*, pp. 307-8).
[11]I am in agreement with Walls when he writes, "Because they [the inhabitants of hell] are unwilling to admit their sin, they are shaped by a lie rather than the truth. Being so shaped is of the essence of damnation" (*Hell*, p. 174).
[12]Lewis, *Problem of Pain*, p. 123.

point in eternity. In rejecting reality once it has been exhaustively defined by God's yes, the only reality that remains for such a will is negation. It continues to invest itself into divinely negated possibilities that can no longer be actualized. Hence, the only real thing about such a will is that it continues to choose this negation. Its choosing is its only reality. Like an infinitely dense black hole from which light cannot escape, this will has utterly caved in on itself. It can no longer participate in reality, for reality is defined by the divine yes that this will opposes.

This understanding of sin is consistent with the church's traditional teaching on sin as self-enclosure. The nature of love and holiness is *openness* to God and others. The nature of sin is *closedness* to God and others. "The essence of sin," writes Donald Baillie, "is self-centeredness, refusal of divine and human community, absorption in oneself, which kills true individuality and destroys the soul."[13] The model of hell we are exploring represents the zenith of this self-enclosure. In the words of Lewis, in contrast to heaven, which is "reality itself," hell is "a state of mind." For "every shutting up of the creature within the dungeon of its own mind—is, in the end, Hell."[14]

When reality becomes exhaustively defined by triune love, the fact that certain wills choose to curve in on themselves will remain, but the content of what they choose will be nothing to all outside themselves. Only the fact of their choice has reality, for only this is consistent with God's love. They endure, to be sure, but only as infinitely small points that do not interact with those who are real. Indeed, since the only real thing about these wills who say no to God's yes is their negatively defined choice, they could be real to people in the eschatological kingdom only in a way similar to the way antimatter is real to people today. They theoretically exist but are never experienced. They are beings whose entire existence is swallowed up by a hypothetical reality that *used* to be possible *but is no longer so*.[15] In fact, as I will soon argue, from the perspective of reality in the eschaton all that can be said

---

[13]Donald M. Baillie, *God Was in Christ: An Essay on Incarnation* (New York: Charles Scribner's Sons, 1948), p. 204. Both in Scripture and church tradition, sin is often discussed as rebellion, covenantal unfaithfulness, idolatry, unbelief, unrighteousness, sensuousness, selfishness and a violation of the law (David L. Smith, *With Willful Intent: A Theology of Sin* [Wheaton, Ill.: Bridgepoint, 1994]). All of these characterize sin. But the fundamental root and consequence of sin is separation from God. While manifested in a variety of ways, sin originates in a heart closing to God and, if left unredeemed, culminates in a heart irrevocably closed to God.

[14]Lewis, *Great Divorce*, p. 69.

[15]Though his meaning is not eschatological in the usual sense of the word, Paul Tillich nevertheless grasps the logic of this position when he says, "Condemnation can only mean that the creature is left to the nonbeing it has chosen" (*Systematic Theology*, 3 vols. [Chicago: University of Chicago Press, 1967], 2:78).

about those who reject reality must be said in the past tense. They *used to* exist.

[handwritten annotation: yet they still exist as a will? not embodied?]

The Loss of a Shared Medium

In chapter nine I argued that agents need a neutral objective medium through which they can relate. Unless a middle ground exists between free agents, an objective reality that they can affect but not exhaustively define, these agents cannot relate to one another. One is real to another only because both share a third reality.

In the eschaton, the love of the Trinity will define all reality. The medium of all who say yes to God's love will be this love itself. God will be "all in all," for God's own triune social reality will encompass and define all that is. The only thing that will be eternally real in the kingdom, then, is the unsurpassable, ecstatic love of the triune God, all who say yes to this triune love and the sheer fact that there are wills who freely rejected it, choosing unreality over reality.

No shared reality. This entails that ultimately there can be no shared reality between those who say yes to God and those who say no, just as there can be no shared reality between the actuality that God affirms and the possibilities that God negates. Hence Lewis depicts the damned as invisible to the redeemed and as unable to communicate with them.[16]

To be sure, divine love eternally grants creatures the opportunity to say no, as I have suggested, for one aspect of God's yes is the empowerment of creatures to say no. But when God's love is finally victorious and defines everything that is, there can be no real context for this no. The fact *that* love gives a place for a no remains, but the entire *content* of this no does not—except to the self-enclosed rebel who chooses it.

In other words, the illusory content that is chosen as the alternative to love cannot be shared. It is real to no one except the self who chooses it. It is an enclosed reality unto itself, a wholly separate and wholly isolated reality. As Barth says about *das Nichtige,* it exists in a third way between being and nonbeing. It is an unreal reality. In the words of Lewis, hell is "that horrible thing which cannot be, yet somehow is."[17]

Lewis again captures the isolation of damnation when he notes that the unregenerate self-absorbed person

> tried to turn everything into a province or appendage of the self. The taste for
> the *other,* that is, the very capacity for enjoying good, is quenched in him

---

[16]Lewis, *Great Divorce,* p. 91.
[17]Ibid., 78.

except in so far as his body still draws him into some rudimentary contact with an outer world. Death removes this last contact. He has his wish—to live wholly in the self and to make the best of what he finds there. And what he finds there is hell.[18]

The self-enclosed world of those who say no to God's yes is not real in any objective sense of the word, for objective reality is shared reality. Milton was insightful when he depicted hell as "nowhere" in *Paradise Lost*.[19] The content of the illusory world of self-lordship the damned imagine for themselves has no place in the land of love. Outside their own illusory solitary decision, it does not exist. In the words of Lewis, the "damned soul is nearly nothing: it is shrunk, shut up in itself."[20] *But it is something - what?*

Hell is real only from the inside. Even now, in this probationary period, we may observe people moving toward the contentless zenith of the self-curving nature of sin. Allow me to provide one example.

Years ago I worked as a volunteer for a charity organization that delivered presents to shut-ins during the holiday season. On one occasion I had an exchange with an elderly lady that taught me a valuable lesson about the nature of hell. This lady told me about her tragic and pathetic life story.

Sixty years earlier, she informed me, she had been betrayed by her fiancé and sister. They ran off together and were married three days before her planned wedding. Her heart was understandably broken. But even more wounded than her heart was her pride. She had been an exceptionally beautiful woman and, as she put it, "could have had any beau in the county." (Portraits of herself as a young woman hanging on the wall confirmed her claim.) But the one she had chosen to give her heart to had rejected her.

Her heart and her pride were so wounded that she never again seriously considered the possibility of marriage, though many men attempted to convince her otherwise. Nor did she seriously consider the possibility of forgiveness. Some time after their marriage, her ex-fiancé and sister sought forgiveness from her, but she refused. Indeed, she resolved never to speak to

---

[18]Lewis, *Problem of Pain*, p. 123. Trying to rescue a condemned "ghost," a heavenly Spirit pleads, "Friend . . . [c]ould you, only for a moment, fix your mind on something not yourself?" (Lewis, *Great Divorce*, p. 62).

[19]Milton, *Paradise Lost*, 1.420. "This is the beauty of Milton's conception," writes Jeffrey B. Russell. "The place where Satan sets up his throne and with his fallen comrades seeks to raise a new empire is precisely nowhere at all; a perfect metaphor for the absolute nonbeing of evil. . . . It is nowhere and has no characteristics, the fit dwelling for those who have chosen nothingness over reality" (*Mephistopheles: The Devil in the Modern World* [Ithaca, N.Y.: Cornell University Press, 1986], p. 109).

[20]Lewis, *Great Divorce*, p. 123.

them again, and despite repeated efforts on their part to reconcile with her over the course of the next six decades, she never wavered from this commitment. Indeed, in time her bitterness so possessed her that she managed to alienate all of her friends and relatives because they continued to have relationships with these two.

Now this bitter old woman sat alone on Christmas Eve without a person in the world who even knew, let alone cared, that she existed. With a scornful, jaw-stiffened, pridefully triumphant tone, this pitiful woman boasted to me how her sister and ex-fiancé had gone to their graves never having heard her voice again. With an air of victory she told me how "so many times" people had encouraged her to let her hatred go only to have her mock their pleas and eventually disdain them personally as well.

This was her "victory." With the Satan of Milton's *Paradise Lost* she in effect proudly proclaimed, "Better to reign in Hell, than serve in Heav'n."

For more than sixty years this woman chose bitterness over forgiveness, war over love. The result was a life (if one could yet call it such) that was completely curved in on itself, shut off from the land of the living. Again, as Milton depicted Satan in his epic poem, this woman's whole reality was her self-willed hatred, and she was its only lord. This was the reality she wanted and freely chose for herself (Jn 3:19). Indeed, whereas once she could have chosen otherwise, now (as far as any human could discern) she had eternally *become* the hateful decisions she made. Just like Milton's Satan, this woman had become her own hell.[21] This hell was her reality—but it was only hers. To all participants in the real world, she had virtually ceased to exist. Her pathetic victory, and the world she had "won" by this victory, was real *only from the inside.*

The extremity of this case is undoubtedly exceptional in this probationary period.[22] But it illustrates the intensely self-enclosed nature of hell. If indeed

---

[21]Milton has Satan proclaim, "Which way I fly is Hell; myself am Hell" (*Paradise Lost,* 4.75; see also 4.20-23). Walls claims that damned people have closed off every apparent avenue by which good may enter. At every point at which grace could have been accepted, evil was preferred. Where such consistency is achieved, evil gains sufficient potency that the possibility of repentance is all but foreclosed. The persons for whom this is true may be accurately described as thoroughly immune to the grace of God" (*Hell,* pp. 123-24).

[22]Though see Geach, *Providence and Evil,* pp. 138-39. The case I have provided is reminiscent of Napoleon in Lewis's *Great Divorce.* In hell, Napoleon existed in an empire of his own making, separated by light years from all other inhabitants (all inhabitants in hell were continually choosing to move farther from one another in Lewis's allegory). Napoleon's entire existence was consumed in pacing back and forth "muttering to himself all the time. 'It was Soult's fault. It was Ney's fault. It was Josephine's fault. It was the fault of the Russians. It was the fault of the English'. . . . A little, fat man and he looked kind of tired. But he didn't seem able to stop it" (pp. 20-21).

the will is necessarily endowed with an eternal dignity, and if in fact the love of the Trinity will ultimately define all of reality, then the world of the will that says no to reality must be eternally vacuous and eternally miserable.

Love is about relationships, and relationships are about sharing reality. Hence, when in the eschaton reality is exhaustively defined by God's love, the "reality" of any agent who opposes love cannot be shared by anyone else and thus cannot be real to anyone else. It is experienced as real *from the inside* of the one who sustains it by his or her act of willing it. But to all who participate in reality—that is, who are open to God and to each other through the medium of God's love—it is nothing. It is eternally willed nothingness.

We may begin to see how the model of hell as chosen *das Nichtige* might allow us to integrate the two biblical motifs that divide traditionalists and annihilationists. In this model, we are able to affirm that in one sense the inhabitants of hell are annihilated, though they suffer eternally. From the perspective of all who share reality in the eschaton, the damned are no more (Obad 16). They exist only as utter negation. They are like smoke that has vanished in the air, chaff that has been incinerated, a dream when one awakes (Ps 73:20). From the perspective of those locked inside the self-chosen negation, however, "life" goes on. Just like the bitter old lady, they continue to experience torment, but it is a torment of their own pathetic choosing in an illusory reality of their own damned imagining.

Lewis captures the unreality of hell to the participants in heaven when he has a redeemed spirit say to a hell-bound ghost, "All Hell is smaller than one pebble of your earthly world: but it is smaller than one atom of *this* world, the Real World." The condemned ghost replies, "It seems big enough when you're in it, Sir." The redeemed spirit continues:

> And yet all loneliness, angers, hatreds, envies and itchings that it contains, if rolled into one single experience and put into the scale against the least moment of the joy that is felt by the least in Heaven, would have no weight that could be registered at all.[23]

No shared time. The loss of a shared medium entails several other significant things about heaven and hell. For one thing, as C. S. Lewis and several others have suggested, it means that we cannot conceive of heaven and hell existing parallel to each other throughout eternity.[24] The lives of all people parallel each other in this age only because we necessarily share a common

---

[23]Lewis, *Great Divorce*, 122-23.
[24]Lewis, *Problem of Pain*, p. 127. See also Kreeft and Tacelli, *Handbook*, pp. 291, 307.

human nature and a common objective physical reality. We thus share a relatively common time, for time is simply the measurement of change in our shared objective environment.

Even with this much in common, however, our individual perceptions of time may vary significantly from one another. This is true both subjectively and objectively. Subjectively, we all know how "time flies when you're having fun" and how it almost comes to a standstill when we are in pain or profoundly bored. The same train ride can be experienced as a short moment to a person absorbed in a good book but as an eternity to a person with a migraine headache.

Objectively, we now know that the flow of time actually changes as our relationship to our objective environment changes, for our physical relationship to our objective environment is conditioned by the speed of light. It has been both mathematically and empirically demonstrated that if a person could travel close to the speed of light, time would slow down relative to those who are more stationary.

To cite one famous thought experiment illustrating this, Einstein demonstrated that if one twin were able to travel in a spaceship close to the speed of light for a certain period of time he would come back to earth younger than the other twin. Though it would be true that the twins *had* been born at the same time, they would *never again* be the same age because they to some degree ceased measuring time within a shared reality. As long as they shared a common objective world, a common neutral medium of relationality, they were in the same time. When their worlds changed, so did their times. Their lives no longer strictly paralleled each other.

But what if there ceased to be *any* shared medium between two twins? What if the twin who traveled at the speed of light never returned? The twins would no longer exist contemporaneously with one another. All that could be said about their relationship is that they *used to be* the same age and *used to share* the same reality.

This, I submit, is an analogy for how we may understand the relationship—or better, lack of relationship—between those who say yes and those who say no to God's rule in the eschaton. When God's yes defines all of reality, there can be no common medium of relationality between these two camps, and thus no shared time. The participants of the eternal kingdom will all share a common "before" and "after," for they are lovingly open to God and to one another. Their individual lives and thus their experience of time will be lovingly defined by their relationships with God and with each other. But those who rebelliously turned in on themselves and who thus rejected love and relationality will thereby have rejected the whole of reality in the eschaton. They will thus have rejected this shared "before" and "after." Having created their own separate illusory reality, they will have created their own separate illusory time.[25] Hence, it may be said that while those who say yes to God and those who say no to him were once contemporaneous with one another, for they once shared a common reality, in the eschaton we cannot conceive of them paralleling one another at all.[26]

This means that for all who say yes to reality as defined by God in the eschaton, the self-enclosed existence of the damned would remain *in the past*, for the only common ground they have with these beings is what they *used* to share. As with Einstein's twins mentioned above, the sequence of experiences that constituted their lives and their time once intersected within the objective medium of relationality in the probationary period, but they no longer do so. Their relationship to the objective medium has changed; in the case of hell, it has changed to the point where the only relationship is one of negation. Hence, in the eschaton, among the inhabitants of the real world of the eternal trinitarian community, the damned can only be thought of as having once existed. They have indeed become like a dream when one awakes (Ps 73:20; cf. 37:20; 68:2).

Annihilation and eternal suffering. In this light we can understand the scriptural teaching suggesting the annihilation of the wicked. From the vantage point of reality, the wicked *used* to be alive. But now in the eschaton they are corpses with no place in the land of the living (Is 66:24). They are thrown out of the city of the living into outer darkness and into the consuming fires of *gehenna* (Mt 5:22, 29; 8:12; 10:28; 18:9; 22:13). As Scripture

---

[25]One can speculate whether or not the inhabitants of hell will share any reality among themselves. They have their rejection of loving relationality and the self-absorption that results from this rejection in common, and this rejection of a shared reality paradoxically gives them a certain kind of shared reality. But the only "relationships" that could be built on this negative commonality would be negative. As sometimes happens even in this probationary period, we may conceive of the inhabitants of hell as seeing each other, but never really seeing *each other*; talking to each other, but never really communicating *with one another.* All their "relationships" are defined by their relationship with themselves, which is to say that they will not have any *real* relationships. As John Wesley taught, "there is no friendship in hell." John Wesley, "Of Hell," in *Works of John Wesley*, ed. Albert C. Outler (Nashville: Abingdon, 1986), 3:34. On the lack of friendship in hell, see also Walls, *Hell*, pp. 152-53. The only *real* relationships, and thus the only real friendships, are in the heaven, where each individual is defined by a loving relationship with others and with the Creator. C. S. Lewis captures the isolation of the damned with his depiction of the inhabitants of hell as always moving farther and farther away from each other (*Great Divorce*, pp. 19-21).

[26]Peter Geach argues along these lines (*Providence and Evil*, p. 141). See also Kreeft and Tacelli, *Handbook*, pp. 291, 307.

says, they are extinct, reduced to ashes, forever forgotten, and one could not find them even if one looked for them (Ps 1:4, 6; 9:6; 34:16, 21; 37:9-10; Dan 2:35; Nahum 1:10). But we may also accept the scriptural teaching regarding the eternity of the torment of the reprobate. For in this view, all that remains is the sheer fact that free beings chose this destruction for themselves. From the inside of the rebel experience, the nothingness that they have willed is experienced as a something. To all others, it is nothing. Even the choice for this illusion is not contemporary to the inhabitants of heaven. It is forever past.

Drawing together these various implications, we might consider the domain of negatively defined wills as constituting a sort of infinitesimally narrow parameter outside of the kingdom of God that separates reality from unreality, love from war and what once was and could have been from what now is and always will be. In the words of Lewis, hell "is in no sense *parallel* to heaven: it is 'the darkness outside,' the outer rim where being fades away into nonentity."[27]

The remains that are cast out. One final implication of the loss of a shared medium between heaven and hell is that it seems we cannot conceive of the inhabitants of hell as truly human (or, in the case of condemned angels, as truly angelic). Our humanity is part of our shared medium of relationality. When this medium is removed, every semblance of a shared humanity goes as well. C. S. Lewis is our guide once again when he writes:

> To enter heaven is to become more human than you ever succeeded in being in earth; to enter hell, is to be banished from humanity. What is cast (or casts itself) into hell is not a man: it is "remains." To be a complete man means to have the passions obedient to the will and the will offered to God: to *have been* a man—to be an ex-man or "damned ghost"—would presumably mean to consist of a will utterly centered in its self and passions utterly uncontrolled by the will.[28]

The purpose for a shared medium, we have noted, is to develop a capacity to love eternally by God's grace. When we move in this direction, we increasingly become what we were created to be: a community of whole persons

---

[27]Lewis, *Problem of Pain*, p. 127. So too Kreeft and Tacelli argue that because "coexistence implies a common field of some kind of time and/or place in which to coexist," and because the inhabitants of hell share no time or place, we are able to assert that "there is no eternal Manichean dualism, no stalemate between good and evil, only God's final triumph" in the eschaton (*Handbook*, p. 307).

[28]Lewis, *Problem of Pain*, pp. 124-26. See the discussion in Kreeft and Tacelli, *Handbook*, pp. 286-87.

who are mutually defined in the triune community of God's love. This is what it ultimately means to be human and to manifest the image of the triune God whose very existence is social love.

If we choose the opposite, however, we ultimately become what we were not created to be. Our existence becomes a negation. We become nothing real other than a will that does not will reality. Having chosen against love, we have become antilove, antichrist and antihuman. With Lewis, then, it seems that what is cast into the eternal dump *(gehenna)* can only be understood as the remains of what once *could have been* a human being.[29]

Letting Rebels Have Their Way

I have suggested that God allows spirits to choose the unreality of their rebellion over his kingdom of love out of metaphysical necessity and (what amounts to essentially the same thing) out of his love. We may conclude this chapter, and this book, by noting that this very necessity and love may also be understood as God's judgment. God's love and wrath unite in allowing creatures to go their own way throughout eternity.

Paul offers us an insightful inspired picture of what God's wrath looks like in Romans 1, and it fits well with the portrait of hell I am proposing. Because these people had rejected God, they became "futile *[mataiō]* in their thinking" and thus had their "senseless minds" darkened (Rom 1:21). The sin of these people was that they "exchanged the truth about God for a lie" (Rom 1:25). Rather than opening up to reality—wherein the Creator is Lord of all—these rebels turned in on themselves to create their own idolatrous reality. Thus the "wrath" of God burned against them (Rom 1:18).

We do not know how long God's Spirit struggled with these idolaters, but as is always the case, there came a time when their character had become irreversibly sealed (TWT6). Their choices were now choosing them. Their *becoming* had now become their *being*. Their libertarian freedom, in which they could have chosen otherwise, had now become compatibilistic freedom,

---

[29]In this light, we can describe the state of being of these "remains" as being self-conscious only by analogically stretching the term, for they cannot be conscious in the same sense that humans are conscious now. Our present experience of self-consciousness is intrinsically bound up with our connection to a shared medium. We experience ourselves as a relatively autonomous and continuous center of consciousness only because we experience ourselves in relation to people and a world outside of ourselves. It is, in short, our openness to what is other than ourselves that gives us our sense of self. In the view of hell I am proposing, however, all of this is lacking. The self in hell is utterly enclosed in its own unreality. There is no real relationship to anything outside itself.

in which they could choose only according to the solidified character they had freely acquired. Thus, God had no choice but to give up on them. For Paul, this divine abandonment is the execution of God's wrath. He lets rebel people have their way.

> Therefore God *gave them up [paradidōmi]* in the lusts of their hearts . . . because they exchanged the truth about God for a lie. . . . For this reason God *gave them up* to degrading passions. . . . Since they did not see fit to acknowledge God, God *gave them up* to a debased mind. (Rom 1:24-26, 28)

God withdrew his Spirit, just as he had done in the days prior to the flood (Gen 6:3). God let these rebels go their own way. If the rebels recognized anything about this wrath, it would only have been an increased freedom from their previously nagging conscience. They were getting what they wanted. But from Paul's redeemed perspective this increased "freedom" was *the result* of God executing his wrath, for now the possibility of entering into the eternal love and joy of God was forever gone for these people. They were now locked out of the kingdom, cast into outer darkness. They were irreversibly solidified in the lie they chose over the truth.[30]

When God concludes that a soul is hopelessly lost he leaves it to experience the consequences of its own choices. This is the soul's enduring dignity as well as its irreversible damnation. As Earl Palmer noted, in hell people actually get exactly what they want.[31] Indeed, in my view, all they have *is their want*. Their self-enclosed will is the sum of their reality, for outside this rebel willing, their "reality" does not exist. God forever grants them their illusion. Indeed, the dignity of having the capacity to choose in this tragic fashion was given to them out of love at the moment of their creation.

But this dignity is also their judgment now that they have used it in this rebellious fashion. God loves the creature and loves the self-determining dignity of the creature. But now that the creature has irrevocably declared war on God, this dignity, originally given and eternally preserved out of love, must be experienced as God's wrath. The potential blessing becomes an actual curse, and in this case, it is eternal.

---

[30]In response to an objector to the doctrine of eternal hell, C. S. Lewis asks: "What are you asking God to do [for unrepentant sinners destined to hell]? . . . To forgive them? They will not be forgiven. To leave them alone? Alas, I am afraid that is what He does" (*Problem of Pain*, p. 128). See Kreeft and Tacelli, *Handbook*, p. 290, and the relevant discussion in Richard L. Purtill, *C. S. Lewis's Case for the Christian Faith* (San Francisco.: Harper & Row, 1981), pp. 96-100.

[31]Edwin Palmer, *The Five Points of Calvinism* (Grand Rapids, Mich.: Baker, 1972), pp. 36-37.

Conclusion: The Eternal Trivialization of Satan and Evil

Tying these various speculations together, we may once again assert the paradoxical conclusion that hell is the eternal suffering of agents who have been annihilated. It is the unending experience of beings who are really in the past, the unending dignity and damnation of beings who should have been kingdom participants, the infinitesimally narrow parameter of the kingdom of God and of all reality in the eschaton, negatively defining the eternal boundary between what is real and what is illusion, what once was from what shall eternally be.

The lord of this forever past and eternally contentless "outer parameter"—the garbage dump outside the city walls—is Satan. Out of love, God lets this once glorious son have his way, just as he gives free reign to all who want to follow him. If darkness is what one loves, darkness is what one gets (Jn 3:19). But this permission is also the most horrifying expression of God's wrath, for no plan against God can ever ultimately succeed (Prov 21:30).

In the end, the Creator alone defines what is and is not real within the creation, and the unsurpassable love that is the triune God forms the content of this eternal definition. There is no place for anything else. Satan will indeed be the lord of nothing, existing nowhere, as Milton said. The triune God will be "all in all."

We may in this light consider God's judgment on Satan as allowing him to exist as he chooses, but also of annihilating him. Both thoughts, when brought together, produce the insight that God's ultimate victory over Satan is expressed in Satan's absolute, unending and pathetic *trivialization*. He is indeed allowed to be the lord he originally sought to be and for which he has for ages viciously fought to win. But when God's love transforms the kingdom of this world (Rev 11:15), Satan's rule will become an infinitely trivial lordship and he an infinitely pathetic lord.

When God rules, the one who once enthroned himself as god of this age will become god of absolute nothingness. The one who once terrorized the world will cave in on himself and become an infinitely small point, a point so utterly insignificant to people within the real kingdom of love that it will possess no contemporary reality. From the perspective of the kingdom, the most we will be able to say about this loathsome figure is that *he once was* but that he is now so utterly pathetic he does not even recognize this.

Sadly, all who shut out the love of God will be under this rule and part of this pathetic nothingness. Stillborns of the probationary gestation period, these rebels will timelessly endure in the loveless, illusory separate reality that they and their ruler have imagined. As they are forever in the past to the participants of the kingdom of God, the joy and peace of the kingdom that they truly desire and were created to share in must forever lie in an attainable future for them. This torment is their eternal dignity and humiliation, their choice and their damnation, and it expresses God's eternal love as well as his eternal wrath.

To the inhabitants of the kingdom of God, however, there is only divine love. All suffering endured in the probationary period will be behind us. Satan and all humans and angels who followed him will be in the past. Even our memories of them will have been transformed (Ps 9:6; 34:16, 21). There will be no more sin, no more sorrow, no more tears, death or abducted children (Rev 21:4-5). We will forever live in the love and joy of the Father, Son and Holy Spirit. *selfid. of the saved*

Perhaps most importantly for our purposes, the moment the kingdom is ushered in, all of us who have eagerly anticipated it will know in an instant that it was worth it. God's risky creation was a wise, though costly, endeavor. There will be no regrets. Indeed, Scripture has the audacity to proclaim that the glory awaiting us will render all suffering in this present age insignificant (Rom 8:18). In light of the nightmarish suffering that occurs in this present war zone, the eschatological kingdom of God must be one unimaginably beautiful place.

doesn't answer ? about destructive tornado

Appendix 1

REMAINING OBJECTIONS

In this appendix I will briefly consider six objections to the trinitarian warfare theodicy that were not fully addressed in the body of this work. The first four concern God's sovereignty. The remaining two concern methodology.

The trinitarian warfare theodicy undermines belief in God's omnipotence. The problem of evil is the problem of reconciling the reality of evil with a belief in an omnipotent God. It seems that the trinitarian warfare theodicy resolves this problem by logically undermining belief in the omnipotence of God. It is, therefore, an illegitimate theodicy from a Christian perspective.

The trinitarian warfare theodicy does not logically undermine belief in the omnipotence of God. It rather presupposes it. In contrast to Process theology and all forms of finite theism, the trinitarian warfare theodicy holds that God is the original possessor of all power, that all things were created by God, that all power is given by God and thus that God can guarantee that he will be victorious in the war in which he and his church are now involved.

It is true that the trinitarian warfare theodicy holds that God does not *exercise* his omnipotence during this probational epoch, for he desires creatures to enter into his eternal triune love, which requires that they have the power to choose for or against him (TWT1). Giving agents this power further entails that there are constraints God must work around in his providential governing of the world and that things might not always turn out as he would desire. But admitting this does not compromise the omnipotence of God any more than other views of God held throughout church history.

Almost all theologians throughout church history have granted that God cannot do the logically impossible, for no meaning can be given to the notion that God *could* do the logically impossible. In this sense almost all theologians have granted that there are constraints on God. He cannot lie or do anything inconsistent with his character, for example. Nor can he change the past (that is, make it so that something that happened did not happen). Furthermore, classical Arminians have always held that by logical necessity God cannot predestine morally responsible free acts. Most Calvinists, on the other hand, have held that God cannot save all people even though in a very real sense, they insist, he does not desire any to perish (2 Pet 3:9), for his desire to display the glory of his justice in judging sinners constrains his desire to have mercy on all.[1]

The trinitarian warfare theodicy simply applies the principle that God cannot do the logically contradictory in a different (and, I argue, more consistent) manner than these other philosophies. The six theses that structure the trinitarian warfare theodicy are simply logical implications of the view that God created the world for love. The "givens" that constrain God at any moment are simply applications of the six theses. This does not affect the view that God is omnipotent. It simply specifies the conditions that God and others must contend with, given that the omnipotent Creator has chosen to create this kind of world.

The trinitarian warfare theodicy is contradicted by Romans 9. In Romans 9 Paul discusses the nature of God's election by noting that God "loved" Jacob and "hated" Esau "before they had been born or had done anything good or bad (so that God's purpose of election might continue, not by works but by his call)" (Rom 9:11-13). He then uses the example of Pharaoh and Moses to illustrate the fact that God "has mercy on whomever he chooses, and he hardens the heart of whomever he chooses" (Rom 9:18). This raises the charge that God is unjust, for "who can resist his will?" (Rom 9:19). Paul replies, "Who indeed are you, a human being, to argue with God? Will what is molded say to the one who molds it, 'Why have you made me like this?'" (Rom 9:21)?

Some would argue that this entire passage contradicts the trinitarian war-

---

[1]In some sense, John Piper admits, there must be two wills in God. One desires all to be saved, another that many be damned for the greater glory of God. See his "Are There Two Wills in God? Divine Election and God's Desire for All to Be Saved," in *The Grace of God and the Bondage of the Will,* 2 vols., ed. Thomas Schreiner and Bruce Ware (Grand Rapids, Mich.: Baker, 1995), 1:107-32.

fare theodicy, which says that humans and angels decide their own destiny and which explains evil by appealing to the free will of these agents. The trinitarian warfare theodicy locates the mystery of evil in the unknowable complexity of the cosmos, but Paul locates it squarely in the unfathomable sovereign will of God.

Romans 9 is frequently interpreted this way, especially by Calvinists, and I grant that if this reading is correct it contradicts the trinitarian warfare theodicy. But I, along with many other scholars, do not think this interpretation is correct. I will make five comments in response to this interpretation (which I will call the "deterministic interpretation").

First, as a preliminary word, the view that God simply chooses whom he will have mercy on and whom he will harden and that this divine activity decides people's eternal destiny contradicts the clear teaching of Scripture that God's love is universal and impartial (Acts 10:34, cf. Deut 10:17-19; 2 Chron 19:7; Job 34:19; Is 55:4-5; Ezek 18:25; Mk 12:14; Jn 3:16; Rom 2:10-11; Eph 6:9; 1 Pet 1:17) and that God desires everyone to be saved (Ezek 18:23, 32; 33:11; Jn 3:16; 1 Tim 2:4; 4:10; 2 Pet 3:9; 1 Jn 2:2). It also undermines the central motif of Scripture that free agents are morally responsible for their free actions and are thus culpable when they go against God's will (see chapter two). In addition, it arguably contradicts the scriptural depiction of God as one who is altogether holy, just and merciful. He "does not willingly afflict or grieve anyone" (Lam 3:33; cf. Deut 32:4; Hab 1:13; 1 Jn 1:5). For all who hold that Scripture is inspired by God and thus is consistent in what it teaches, this inconsistency should cause us to suspect that something is amiss in the deterministic interpretation of Romans 9.

As a second preliminary word, it is worth noting that this passage was not interpreted in a deterministic fashion prior to Augustine in the fourth century (with the exception of certain Gnostics and the Manicheans).[2] Once the blueprint model of providence became established in the church, the interpretation became common (though prior to Calvin, few carried it through as consistently as Augus-

---

[2]M. Parmentier, "Greek Church Fathers on Romans 9," *Bijdragen* 50 (1989): 139-54; 51 (1990): 2-20; J. Patout Burns, "The Atmosphere of Election: Augustinianism As Common Sense," *JECS* 2 (1994): 325-39; Peter Gorday, *Principles of Patristic Exegesis: Romans 9-11 in Origen, John Chrysostom, and Augustine,* Studies in the Bible and Early Christianity 4 (New York: Mellen, 1983). This in part explains why Calvin, for example, cannot cite ante-Nicene fathers against his libertarian opponents (e.g., Pighius). On Calvin's use of patristic sources, see Wilhelm H. Neuser and Brian G. Armstrong, eds., *Calvinus Sincerioris Religionis Vindex* [*Calvin As Protector of the Purer Religion*], Sixteenth Century Essays and Studies 36 (Kirksville, Mo.: Sixteenth Century Journal Publishers, 1997). Hence, when Calvin debates Pighius on the freedom of the will, he cites Augustine abundantly. I will explore this Augustinian shift more fully in my forthcoming book, *The Myth of the Blueprint.*

tine). This may suggest that the deterministic reading of this passage is at least partially the result of people bringing to the text an assumed worldview (the blueprint worldview) that Paul (and the early postapostolic fathers) did not share.

Third, whenever interpreting difficult texts it is important to pay close attention to the author's own summary of his argument, if and when he provides one. If our conclusions about the author's argumentation differ from the conclusion he himself provides, it is clear we are misunderstanding his argument.

Fortunately, Paul provides us with such a summary in Romans 9. Paul begins his summary by asking, "What then are we to say?" (Rom 9:30). If the deterministic interpretation of Romans 9 were correct, we would expect Paul to summarize his argument by saying something like, "The sovereign God determines who will be elect and who will not, and no one has the right to question him." But this is not at all what Paul says. He rather brings the strands of his argument in this chapter together by concluding:

> Gentiles, who did not strive for righteousness, have attained it, that is, righteousness through faith; but Israel, who did not strive for the righteousness that is based on the law, did not succeed in fulfilling that law. Why not? Because they did not strive for it on the basis of faith, but as if it were based on works. (Rom 9:30-32)

Paul explains everything he has been talking about in this chapter by appealing to the morally responsible choices of the Israelites and Gentiles. The Jews did not strive by faith, though they should have. As Paul reiterates in the succeeding two chapters, the Jews as a nation did not submit to the righteousness of God that comes by faith (Rom 10:3). "They were broken off *because of their unbelief*" (Rom 11:20). *This* is why they as a nation have now been hardened (Rom 11:7, 25), while the Gentiles who seek God by faith have been "grafted in" (Rom 11:23). God's process of hardening some and having mercy on others is not arbitrary: God expresses "severity toward those who have fallen [the nation of Israel] . . . but kindness toward you [believers], provided you continue in his kindness" (Rom 11:22).

Neither Paul's summary in Romans 9:30-32 nor his subsequent discussion in chapters 10 and 11, which emphasize free will, square with the deterministic reading of Romans 9. This is a sure indication that the deterministic reading is misguided.

Fourth, we begin to understand what is misguided about the deterministic interpretation of Romans 9 when we consider its interpretation of the potter-clay analogy that Paul uses in Romans 9:20-23. In the deterministic interpretation, it is assumed that the clay has no "say" in how it is fashioned;

the potter decides everything. This, I submit, is not at all how Paul understood this analogy.

It is important to remember that Paul did not invent this analogy; he found it in the Old Testament. Moreover, the Old Testament passage that is the source of this analogy employs it to make the exact *opposite* point that those who espouse the deterministic reading of Romans 9 think Paul is making with it.[3]

In Jeremiah 18 the Lord shows Jeremiah a potter working on a vessel. "The vessel he was making of clay was spoiled in the potter's hand, and he reworked it into another vessel, as seemed good to him" (Jer 18:4). The Lord then says, "Can I not do with you, O house of Israel, just as this potter has done? . . . Just like the clay in the potter's hand, so are you in my hand, O house of Israel" (Jer 18:5-6).

As we discussed in chapter three, the Lord says that since he is the potter and can do whatever he wants with the clay, he will recant prophecies of fortune or misfortune if the people he prophesies about change for better or for worse (Jer 18:7-11). As a master potter, he reserves for himself the right to rework vessels whenever he sees fit. God can and will change his plans if people change their hearts. Hence the Lord reassures the Israelites that though their sin has "spoiled" the vessel he was making out of them, as a masterful potter he can refashion a new vessel out of them *if they, the clay, will allow him to.* If they repent, he will repent of the judgment he intended to bring on them.

When Paul used this analogy to explain why God had mercy on Moses and hardened Pharaoh, therefore, we need not conclude that this entails that Moses and Pharaoh had no say in how they were made. Quite the opposite. As in Jeremiah, the "clay" Paul is referring to is not some preexistent clay of humanity out of which the Lord arbitrarily fashions individuals to suit his own eternal purposes—that is, to demonstrate his wrath or mercy. It is rather the clay of people's lives *in history.* As in Jeremiah 18, people *make themselves* "spoiled" or pliable, and God *responds* by reworking them in this state "as seem[s] . . . good to him" (Jer 18:4)—always in accordance with their pliable or hardened hearts.

This is why Paul says that God "*endured* with much patience" the vessels he was preparing for destruction (Rom 9:22). Why would he need much patience if the vessel was "spoiled" according to his own design?

---

[3]On the importance of paying attention to the broader context of all Old Testament citations in Paul, see Richard Hayes, *Echoes of Scripture in the Letters of Paul* (New Haven, Conn.: Yale University Press, 1989).

Why would he say, "All day long I have held out my hands to a disobedient and contrary people" (Rom 10:21, quoting Is 65:2) if he was the one molding them to be disobedient in the first place? Finally, one must wonder why an all-holy, all-loving God who "does not willingly afflict or grieve anyone" (Lam 3:33) would intentionally fashion "spoiled" people in the first place.

The patience and frustration of God toward the vessels that he prepared for "destruction" makes no sense on the deterministic interpretation, but it makes perfect sense if we understand them in the light of Jeremiah 18. This understanding of God's use of Pharaoh also squares best with the Exodus narrative about Pharaoh that Paul relies on in using his analogy. It is important to note (as the rabbis of Paul's day frequently did) that the first acts of hardening in the Exodus narrative depicting God as hardening Pharaoh's heart are done *by Pharaoh himself* (Ex 8:15, 32). God simply used Pharaoh's hardening to suit his own providential purposes. He desired "to show his wrath and make known his power" (Rom 9:22) in order to intimidate Israel's future adversaries.

When Paul responds to the charge of injustice by asking, "Who . . . are you, a human being, to argue with God?" (Rom 9:20), he is not thereby appealing to the sheer power of the potter over the clay. He is rather appealing to the rights of a wise and just potter to fashion clay according to his providential purposes and in a manner that is appropriate, *given the kind of clay with which he has to work*. If Israel persists in their rebellion, the potter hardens them and prepares them for destruction. If Gentile and Jewish believers persist in their simple faith, God has mercy on them and fashions out of them a beautiful vessel displaying his own eternal glory (Rom 9:21-23).

This fashioning may *look* arbitrary, especially to hardened Jews who believed that they were the "vessel of honor" simply by virtue of being Jewish.[4] As in Jeremiah 18, however, Paul's use of this analogy demonstrates that this kind of Jewish thinking and the charge of arbitrary injustice that rises from it is incorrect. God's activity in history is not arbitrary; it is just and wise. Moreover, to the offense of many Jews at the time, the possibility of being clay fashioned into a vessel that displays God's glory is open to Jews and Gentiles alike. It all depends on whether or not one is willing to seek after the righteousness of God that comes by faith, not works (Rom

---

[4]Paul's primary concern throughout Romans 9 is to correct this kind of thinking, according to James Dunn. See his excellent discussion in *The Theology of Paul the Apostle* (Grand Rapids, Mich.: Eerdmans, 1998), pp. 499-519.

9:30-32; 10:3-5, 12-13; 11:22-23).

Fifth, and perhaps most importantly, it is crucial that we interpret Romans 9 in accordance with the question Paul attempts to answer with it. The deterministic interpretation of this passage does not adequately do this. Paul is not interested in the question of how God elects or rejects individuals to eternal salvation or damnation. He is not concerned with individuals or eternal destinies.[5] His concern throughout chapters 9, 10 and 11 is only to answer the question, Has the word of God (that is, his covenantal promises) failed (cf. Rom 9:6)?

To Jews who had attached God's promises to their nationality and works, this is precisely what the Christian message of salvation by faith in Christ seemed to entail. If the Christian message was true, then those Jews who had not accepted Jesus as the Messiah were no longer part of God's covenant. But, according to their understanding of the Old Testament, this entailed that God had gone back on his promise to have them as his people.

Paul answers this question in the following manner. He first reveals that though it is a privilege to be a Jew by nationality (Rom 9:4-5), "not all Israelites truly belong to Israel" (Rom 9:6) and "not all of Abraham's children are his true descendants" (Rom 9:7). The true Israelites have always been those who have faith, like their father Abraham did. Abraham believed God, and it was credited to him as righteousness (Rom 4:3). His faith brought about Isaac, the child of promise, and thus, to reiterate the centrality of faith, Paul quotes Genesis 21:12, which says that "it is through Isaac that descendants shall be named for you" (Rom 9:7). Paul argues that faith, not nationality or external adherence to the law ("works"), has always been the condition for being a child of the covenant. God still honors his word, therefore, by remaining faithful to all who simply believe as Abraham did—both Jews and Gentiles.

To Jews who think that election is a privilege attached to their nationality and that righteousness is earned by adherence to the law, this is shocking. So

---

[5]Several examples of exegetes who express this perspective are Dunn, *Theology;* J. D. Strauss, "God's Promise and Universal History: The Theology of Romans 9," in *Grace Unlimited,* ed. Clark Pinnock (Minneapolis: Bethany House, 1975), pp. 190-208; Leon Morris, *The Epistle to the Romans* (Grand Rapids, Mich.: Eerdmans, 1988); Roger Forster and V. Paul Marston, *God's Strategy in Human History* (Wheaton, Ill.: Tyndale House, 1973); and C. E. B. Cranfield, *A Critical and Exegetical Commentary on the Epistle to the Romans* (Edinburgh: T & T Clark, 1979). For defenses of the Calvinistic, individualistic reading, see Thomas Schreiner, "Does Romans 9 Teach Individual Election unto Salvation?" in Schreiner and Ware, eds., *Grace of God,* 1:89-106; and John Piper, *The Justification of God: An Exegetical and Theological Study of Romans 9:1-23* (Grand Rapids, Mich.: Baker, 1983).

Paul sets out to demonstrate that God has the sovereign right to choose whomever he wants as covenant partners. He does this by appealing to the Old Testament narratives concerning Isaac, Jacob and Moses, the three examples that would perhaps be most noteworthy to Jews.

It was not Abraham's nationality or works that caused God to choose Abraham and miraculously give him his son, Isaac. This sovereign decision was based on Abraham's faith (Rom 9:9). As Paul said several chapters earlier, *before* Abraham was circumcised (that is, had done any "works" of the law) God reckoned his faith as righteousness (Rom 4:9-10). The reason for this was so Abraham would be "the ancestor of all who believe without being circumcised and who thus have righteousness reckoned to them, and likewise the ancestor of the circumcised [the Jews]" (Rom 4:11-12). The fact that Abraham's lineage flows through Isaac, a child miraculously birthed through faith, confirms this point (see Rom 4:16-25).

From the very beginning, God sovereignly chose to elect those who believe. Hence, all who believe are descendants of Abraham (through Isaac). While there are certainly privileges to being a Jew (see Rom 9:4-5) and while adhering to the law is necessary for them and beneficial if it flows out of faith, nationality and adherence to the law alone have never been what makes a person a true covenant partner with God.

Paul then demonstrates God's sovereign right to choose whomever he wants by noting how God chose Israel as a nation to carry out his purposes in world history. Using Jacob and Esau as representatives of Israel and Edom, he notes (quoting Gen 25:23 and Mal 1:2-3) how God preferred Jacob over Esau "before they had been born or had done anything good or bad (so that God's purpose of election might continue, not by works but by his call)" (Rom 9:11-12). Paul is not concerned with the individual salvation of Jacob and Esau; he is concerned with showing God's providential sovereignty *in history*, and as with the example of Isaac, the point is that God's choices have never depended "on human will or exertion," such as the unbelieving Jews assume, but "on God who shows mercy" (Rom 9:16).

Finally, Paul demonstrates God's sovereignty in history by appealing to his hardening of Pharaoh and his mercy on Moses (Rom 9:17). It is at this point that he employs the potter-clay analogy discussed above. The master potter knows what he is doing, so however arbitrary it may look to some, his sovereign will must be acknowledged as wise and just. God has the sovereign right to have mercy on whomever he wants and to harden whomever he wants (Rom 9:18). What is shocking to the unbelieving Jews is that despite their privileged nationality and obedience to the law, they now find themselves in the position of their ancient nemesis Pharaoh. They are the ones now being hardened! Moreover, the Gentiles whom they always considered to be outside the covenant are now in the position of Moses!

This "mercy" and "hardening" is not arbitrary, however it may look to unbelieving Jews. God's sovereign choice has always been to accept those who persist in faith and to harden those who, like Pharaoh, persist in their rebellion. The Jews are hardened "*because* of their unbelief" (Rom 11:20; cf. 9:32).

Paul concludes this chapter by showing, through several Old Testament quotes (Hos 2:23; 1:10; Is 10:22-23; 1:9), that God has always intended to make the Gentiles his children and that it is only "the remnant" of the faithful from among the Jews who are truly his children (Rom 9:24-29).[6] He follows this with his summary, discussed above, which explains why the Gentiles have attained God's righteousness while the Jews as a whole have not. The Jews "did not strive for it on the basis of faith, but as if it were based on works" (Rom 9:32), while the Gentiles who "did not strive for righteousness" by works "have attained it . . . through faith" (Rom 9:30).

In all of this Paul seeks to answer the question, Has the word of God failed? His answer is a decisive no. The "word of God" was always conditioned on faith, not works of the law, and thus it is fulfilled whenever anyone is incorporated into the people of God through faith, whether they are Jews or Gentiles. Such a plan seems outrageous and arbitrary to people who trust in their own nationality or works, but this is God's sovereign prerogative. The same God who chooses to bless Abraham with Isaac, to elect Israel over Edom and to have mercy on Moses while hardening Pharaoh chooses to save all who simply confess Jesus Christ as Lord (Rom 10:9).

If read in context, we see, Romans 9 does not contradict the trinitarian warfare theodicy. This theodicy concedes that God has the power and right to shape history however he sees fit and to establish any plan of salvation he sees fit. If God decides to have mercy on all who simply trust in Christ, that is his divine prerogative. If he decides to harden all who persist in unbelief, placing their trust in their nationality or works, that too is his divine prerogative. The trinitarian warfare theodicy's only requirement is that within the historical parameters sovereignly set by God, agents possess some degree of self-determining freedom. This, we have seen, is perfectly compatible with Romans 9.

---

[6]He continues to string Old Testament quotes together, making essentially the same point, throughout Romans 10.

The trinitarian warfare theodicy is contrary to the biblical teaching about exhaustive divine sovereignty. The trinitarian warfare theodicy is fundamentally rooted in the assumption that God's power and human and angelic power are pitted against one another in a "zero-sum game." To the extent that agents are free and morally responsible, God cannot exercise unilateral control over his creation. But some would say that the Bible assumes the opposite. That is, God's power does not "compete" with creaturely power. The motifs of exhaustive divine sovereignty and human (and angelic) responsibility are inextricably interwoven throughout the biblical narratives. The trinitarian warfare theodicy is built on the motif of creaturely freedom, but at the expense of the motif of exhaustive divine sovereignty.

There are two responses to be made to this objection. The first is biblical, the second logical. First, I agree that the motifs of divine sovereignty and creaturely morally responsible freedom are inextricably interwoven throughout the biblical narrative. But I do not see why this divine sovereignty entails *exhaustive* control. To be sure, there are certainly examples in Scripture that explain human actions by appealing to God's initiative. But these examples do not teach or assume that God is *always* behind human (or angelic) action. More important, even in most of these instances it need not be assumed that God is behind the action as the power that causes the action rather than the wisdom that simply orchestrates it.[7]

Second, I argue that the notion that God exercises unilateral control over free actions is not a mystery; it is a contradiction. If the concept of morally responsible freedom has any meaning, it means that the agents are the final cause and explanation of their behavior (see chapter two). To say that God exercises unilateral control over agents means that God must be the final cause and explanation of agents' behavior. Hence, the notion that God exercises unilateral control over agents while these agents are nevertheless free and morally responsible is a self-contradictory notion. It affirms and denies the same thing. No analogies have or can be provided to help us understand what the notion *means* (let alone whether it is plausible or not).

If God genuinely gives creatures say-so, to that extent he surrenders his own unilateral say-so in what they do. What else does it mean to *give* say-so to creatures? If creatures who have been given say-so nevertheless necessarily carry out God's say-so, then in truth they have not been given say-so *of their*

---

[7]The most extensive attempt to demonstrate that the Bible teaches both exhaustive divine control and human responsibility is D. A. Carson's work, *Divine Sovereignty and Human Responsibility* (Atlanta: John Knox Press, 1981). For a discussion of passages used to support this view of sovereignty, see appendix five.

own. Hence, I argue that there is no mystery in the notion that God exhaustively controls free agents, for there is no meaning to the notion that God exhaustively controls free agents.

The trinitarian warfare theodicy is inadequate on a practical level. By emphasizing the autonomy of free agents with their potential to act contrary to God's sovereign purposes, some argue that the trinitarian warfare theodicy undermines trust in God and instills fear in people. It also provides no hope to people in the midst of radical suffering, for it denies that there is a sovereign purpose for their pain. When one transfers the mystery of evil from God to the complexity of the cosmos, a person's suffering may be pointless.

As a pastor, I am sensitive to the concern addressed in this objection. My experience has been that many of those who reject the trinitarian warfare theodicy do so not because the scriptural evidence for it is weak or because it does not adequately explain evil. They do so because they fear its implications. They dread the thought that things can happen to us at the hands of other free agents, things that God did not intend or (in my view) even foreknow with certainty. This is, I admit, a disquieting thought. But I do not believe that this means that the trinitarian warfare theodicy is untrue or that it leaves people who are in the midst of suffering in despair. On the contrary, I believe it empowers us more effectively to provide realistic hope to people in despair. Five things may be said in response to this objection.

First, while it may be less comforting to believe that the world is a real war zone than it is to believe that it is meticulously controlled by God, it is not clear to me how this fact has any bearing on the truth or falsity of the belief that the world is a war zone. Why should we think that our personal comfort is a criterion of truth? We would not appeal to this criterion to decide, for example, whether it is true or false that we are at war with another country or whether or not our bodies are "at war" with cancer cells.

Sometimes the truth is discomforting. Reality often does *not* conform to our wishes. The world in its present state is a scary place. If children can simply disappear, how can anyone think otherwise? Far from being an argument against the trinitarian warfare theodicy, I believe that the discomforting dimension of this perspective actually testifies to its truthfulness, for it means that this perspective conforms to (and explains) what we already know in our hearts to be true about the world. At times it *is* a horrifying place to live.

On a fundamental level (manifested more by what we *do* than by what we *say*), all Christians believe that the world is populated by free agents who can thwart God's will. However controlling Christians' view of God might be, *they still lock their doors at night.* No sane person simply leaves his or her fate "in the hands of God." We take practical steps to protect ourselves and our loved ones from harm. We consistently act as though some of our welfare is up to us and others to decide. What does this say about our core beliefs? It says that in the core of our being we assume that not everything is controlled by an all-loving God and that a world that contains murderers, robbers, kidnappers and rapists is not an altogether safe environment.

In this light I would claim that the trinitarian warfare theodicy *simply articulates and explains what we already believe at a core level.* Just look at how we *act.* This consistency of beliefs and action is not true of the blueprint model of providence and is, I suggest, one more piece of evidence for the truthfulness of the trinitarian warfare view.

Second, it is not clear how affirming that God controls all provides any real comfort in the face of the scary aspects of the world. Suppose several children have been abducted in your neighborhood. You are understandably concerned about the safety of your children. How does believing that kidnappers fit into God's mysterious purposes help you cope with this fear? You are still going to go out and buy a padlock for your door and walk your children to and from the bus stop. You still know this evil *could* happen to you, unless you take precautions. You still know at the core of your being, the core out of which you act, that the world is just as scary *with* your belief as *without* it. So what advantage is your belief?

Indeed, I would contend that your belief actually makes the world a scarier place, for two reasons. First, if God controls kidnappers and kidnappers victimize godly and ungodly families alike (which no one can deny), then it just might be that God has decided from all eternity to have one of these kidnappers victimize *your* family next. If God has decided this, there is nothing you can do about it. Secondly, if God is the sort of God who is capable of ordaining such evils, then there is no character here that you can trust. You have nothing to hang on to. If God ordained that one child will be kidnapped, he may have ordained that your child will be kidnapped. Again, there is *nothing* you can do to change this fact.

If God does not control all things, however, then there *is* something you can do about it. As a morally responsible free person you can make choices that maximize your safety and minimize your vulnerability against other free people (and spirits) who have chosen evil. The world is still scary, but less so than if the Creator himself had the kind of character that made him capable of ordaining child kidnappings "for his glory." Thus I would argue that the trinitarian warfare worldview does not increase people's fear; it simply acknowledges and explains the concerns we already have. The blueprint model of providence, however, may increase our fear while not explaining it.

Third, I believe that in many instances the trinitarian warfare worldview has a practical advantage over the blueprint worldview in comforting and empowering people in the midst of suffering. This perspective motivates believers to exercise faith and prayer in coming against whatever it is that it causing the suffering. This is especially true when the suffering is of a physical nature. While the warfare model grants that the Lord can *sometimes* use a person more in illness than in health (2 Cor 12:7-10), it does not default to this conclusion. Following Jesus' example, it holds that unless we have direction from God to think otherwise, we should in faith oppose the illness as something that is contrary to God's will. The blueprint model of providence does not as clearly provide this motivation. As a result, many people accept suffering as part of God's plan when in fact God would rather have them free from this suffering. It is difficult passionately to pray that the Father's will would be done "on earth as it is in heaven" (Mt 6:10) if one believes that the Father's sovereign will is *already* being done in bringing about the very thing against which one is now praying.

Fourth, it is not the case that the trinitarian warfare theodicy can "offer no hope" to people in the midst of suffering. The trinitarian warfare worldview offers the same comfort that the New Testament offers. With Scripture, the trinitarian warfare worldview affirms that God's character is unambiguously loving and thus that he is on our side when we suffer. In this view, we need not wonder why God has ordained or specifically allowed a child to be kidnapped or a spouse to die in a car crash. Sadly, many people who embrace the blueprint worldview push God away when they need him the most because they assume he is ultimately responsible for the horror they or a loved one are going through. If their blueprint understanding of God's providence is true, this assumption is correct. But the trinitarian warfare worldview provides a different understanding of God's providence, one that encourages people to embrace God in the midst of their suffering rather than pushing him away.

With Scripture, the trinitarian warfare worldview also affirms that, regardless of what happens to us, our eternal relationship with the Lord is secure (Rom 8:31-39). It frankly acknowledges, as Paul does, that bad things may happen. Believing in Christ is no security blanket in the midst of the war zone. But such events cannot separate us from the Lord.

With Scripture, the trinitarian warfare worldview also affirms that whatever happens to us, God will work with us to bring a redemptive purpose out of the event (Rom 8:28). The evil event that happened to us or a loved one may indeed have had no higher purpose; it may have been "pointless." This is part of its evil. But we can be assured that God is able to bring good out of evil with unfathomable ingenuity. He does not will evil, but he can use it. The blueprint model of providence goes beyond this and suggests that the evil itself was ordained or specifically allowed for the purpose that God brings out of it. But it is not clear how this adds anything to our hope.

Finally, and perhaps most importantly, the trinitarian warfare worldview offers people in the midst of suffering the central hope of the New Testament, namely, that in the end it will all be worth it. This horrific war will come to an end and Christ will be victorious over Satan. Justice will be administered, and the ecstasy that the bride of Christ will experience as she participates in the eternal triune love of God will heal all wounds, dry all tears, vanquish all fear and more than compensate for all the nightmares suffered. Even now, in the midst of this ungodly combat, having a focus on heaven can give the sufferer a peace that passes all natural understanding (Phil 4:7).

The trinitarian warfare theodicy is constructed on an ad hoc basis. That is, the appeal to the activity of evil spirits as well as the way the implications of love are fleshed out—the six TWT theses—is determined by aspects of the problem of evil that you believe need explaining.

It is true that I believe that the problem of evil is only adequately resolved when we consider the activity of evil spirits and the metaphysical conditions that make love possible. But this does not mean that the appeal to spirits and the six TWT theses are ad hoc hypotheses conjured up only to explain evil. Two considerations demonstrate that this is not the case.

First, the reality of spirits has always been part of the teaching of the Christian church. Indeed, as I argued in *God at War,* this belief has in one form or another been shared by almost every culture throughout history. Therefore, the appeal to them to account for a dimension of evil in the world is hardly ad hoc. The only novel element of the trinitarian warfare theodicy concerning the existence and activity of spirits is that it attempts consistently to develop the implications of what the church has always believed about these beings.

Second, the appeal to the six conditions that make love possible could only be considered ad hoc if it could be shown that there are no grounds for accepting these conditions other than the fact that they help explain the problem of evil. My argument, however, is that the conditions are to be accepted on the grounds that love in contingent beings is inconceivable apart from these conditions. I argue that we cannot consistently conceive of the possibility of love in finite, contingent beings without conceiving of them possessing freedom (TWT1), without this freedom entailing risk (TWT2), without them having a power to influence others with a proportionate potential for good and evil (TWT3-4), without this power being irrevocable (TWT5) and without this power being finite (TWT6). The plausibility of these conditions is then supported by appealing to the way aspects of Scripture and of our experience are illuminated if they are accepted. They are further confirmed by the fact that the problem of evil is resolved when they are accepted.

One may argue that love is conceivable apart from these conditions or that aspects of Scripture and of our experience are not consistent with these conditions or that the problem of evil remains even when they are accepted. But one cannot justifiably reject the trinitarian warfare theodicy on the basis that it is ad hoc.

The trinitarian warfare theodicy is overly speculative. The trinitarian warfare theodicy leverages a lot of its explanatory power on the activity of Satan, fallen angels and demons, especially in its treatment of "natural" evil. But Scripture does not pay that much attention to these invisible agents and does not explicitly give them the authority the trinitarian warfare theodicy gives them.

I agree that the trinitarian warfare theodicy is speculative, but I deny that it is *overly* speculative. It is in truth no more speculative than any other theodicy one might suggest. Two considerations support my claim.

First, all theodicies inevitably go beyond Scripture insofar as they attempt to resolve certain intellectual problems that Scripture does not resolve. (In this same sense, all church doctrine goes beyond Scripture.) Even those who claim to avoid all theodicies and simply appeal to "the mysterious will of God" go beyond Scripture in claiming this. The fact that the trinitarian warfare theodicy goes beyond Scripture, therefore, should not be held against it.

The question is not whether or not a theodicy or teaching goes beyond Scripture but whether or not it is consistent with and (even better) clarifies Scripture in doing so. In this sense, I have argued, the trinitarian warfare theodicy fares better than alternative theodicies. More specifically, between the speculative choices of attributing evil to God's mysterious blueprint or to the complexity of a creation populated with free agents, human and angelic,

I argue that the latter is the better choice. It not only is consistent with Scripture; it reconciles the scriptural portrait of our loving Father with our experience of horrific evil.

Second, it is simply not true that Scripture does not pay much attention to invisible agents. As I summarized in chapter one (and demonstrated more thoroughly in *God at War*), the activity of evil invisible agents permeates Scripture, especially the New Testament. Further, the Bible gives these agents the same authority the trinitarian warfare theodicy gives them. The trinitarian warfare theodicy admittedly goes beyond Scripture in appealing to them to explain certain kinds of evil (e.g., unanswered prayer and "natural" evil), but it does so in a way that is consistent with Scripture (see, e.g., Ps 82; Dan 10). Finally, as suggested above, the emphasis on these agents in the trinitarian warfare theodicy is understandable, given that we are attempting to answer theodicy questions, while Scripture is not.

Appendix 2

FOUR PHILOSOPHICAL ARGUMENTS FOR THE INCOMPATIBILITY OF EDF & SELF-DETERMINING FREE WILL

For biblical Christians, the final court of appeal regarding the validity of any belief is Scripture. Hence, as was argued in chapters three, four and five, the primary grounds for embracing the open view of the future are scriptural. Still, truth is *one*. Thus, if we are interpreting Scripture correctly it should be consistent with reason, assuming that we are reasoning correctly. From a theological perspective, this is the job of philosophy.

In chapter four I discussed a philosophical argument that attempts to prove that the EDF doctrine (God possesses exhaustively definite foreknowledge) is inconsistent with a belief that agents possess self-determining free will and thus inconsistent with the view that God ever takes genuine risks. In what follows I outline and briefly develop four other philosophical arguments that support this conclusion.

The Meaning of Self-Determination
Premises

P1: Self-determination means that the *self* gives *determinateness* to its actions. In other words, regarding any genuinely free act, free agents themselves ultimately transition a range of *possible* acts into one *actual* act. By definition, they *define* (render determinate) what was previously undefined (that is, indeterminate possibilities). They are the ultimate cause and explanation for the move from "possibly this or possibly that" to "certainly this and certainly not that."

P2: Retroactive causality does not occur. We cannot change the past.

P3: Each created free agent begins in time. It is not eternal.

Conclusion: From P1-3, it follows that the determinateness given to an action by a self-determining agent cannot eternally precede that agent's self-determination. Moreover, if the determinateness does not exist an eternity before the agent creates it, there is no determinateness for God to know an eternity before the agent creates it. Thus, if agents possess self-determination, God does not possess EDF.

Comment: Either the determinateness of my actions comes from me, in which case I am self-determining, or it does not, in which case I am not self-determining. If the determinateness eternally precedes me in the mind of God, it cannot come from me, for I am not eternal (P3) and retroactive causation does not occur (P2). But on the view that God possesses EDF, all future actions are from eternity within this category. Thus, if God possesses EDF, creatures cannot possess self-determining freedom.

The Distinction Between Possibility and Actuality
Premises

P1: The most fundamental feature of the distinction between possibility and actuality is the distinction between indefiniteness and definiteness.

P2: Self-determination is the power to change possibility into actuality, indefiniteness into definiteness, what *might* be into what *is*.

P3: If God possesses EDF, then all events are exhaustively definite before they occur. In God's mind there is no indefiniteness to the future.

Conclusion: From P1-3 it follows that if God possesses EDF, it does not lie within any created agent's power to change possibilities into actuality, indefiniteness into definiteness, what might be into what is. If God possesses EDF, in other words, creatures cannot possess self-determination.

Comment: Regarding P1, if the distinction between actuality and possibility is not located in definiteness, in what is it to be located? No cogent, more fundamental definition has been given. Regarding P2, if self-determination is not to be defined as an ability to render possibilities actual, how are we to define it? No one has suggested a cogent alternative.

If both are granted, however, the possibility of affirming that the content of God's foreknowledge is exhaustively definite while at the same time affirming self-determination is logically ruled out. Unless the future is to some degree ontologically open (not simply *experienced* as open by creatures because of epistemological limitations), then there is simply no "material," as it were, from which agents can determine themselves. Agents cannot turn possibilities into actualities if there are no genuine possibilities. By its very definition, however, EDF does not allow for future possibilities. Hence, if God possesses EDF agents cannot possess self-determining freedom.

EDF and Actual Occurrences

Premises

P1: If God possesses EDF, the definiteness of all events eternally precedes their actual occurrence.

P2: As argued above, actuality is most fundamentally distinct from possibility in that actuality is characterized by definiteness ("definitely this and definitely not that"), while possibility is characterized by indefiniteness ("possibly this and possibly that").

P3: If all events are exhaustively definite in the mind of God before they occur, all events are actual before they are actual.

Conclusion: If it is absurd to say that an event is actual before it is actual, then (*reductio ad absurdum*) events cannot be exhaustively definite in the mind of God before they occur. God does not possess EDF.

Comment: This argument is similar to the preceding one, but somewhat more encompassing. The hidden question in this argument is, What does the actual occurrence of x add to God's foreknowledge of x so as to distinguish the actual occurrence of x from the mere foreknowledge of x? If God's experience of the actual occurrence adds *anything* to God's foreknowledge, then God's foreknowledge cannot be thought of as *exhaustively* definite. He *learned* what it was to *experience* x even if we concede that prior to this he had a perfect prepositional knowledge *about* x.[1] If God's experience of the actual occurrence of x adds *nothing* to God's knowledge, however, then it is

---

[1] Thus, theologians who hold that God's foreknowledge is propositional and not experiential do not in truth believe that God has *exhaustively* definite foreknowledge. In this light open theists' denial that God possesses EDF should not be considered exceptional. They differ only in *the extent* to which they hold that God's knowledge is indefinite.

impossible to render intelligible the distinction between a thing's actual occurrence and its being merely foreknown.

Put differently, if experience is the highest form of knowledge (and it most certainly is), then an exhaustively definite knowledge of x entails an unsurpassably perfect experience of x. Likewise, an exhaustively definite *fore*-knowledge of x must entail an unsurpassably definite experience of x *an eternity before x occurs.*

To salvage EDF, then, one must accept divine timelessness. God must experience the world as an eternal "now." Aside from the fact that this view seems to undermine God's temporal interaction with the world that structures the whole biblical narrative, and aside from a number of other paradoxes that the view generates, the view of God as timeless rules out self-determination on the grounds given in the first and second arguments above as well as in the fourth argument, which follows.

Hence, I once again conclude that if God possesses EDF, creatures cannot possess self-determining freedom.

The Cause of Eternal Definiteness
Premises

P1: Causes precede effects. This is to say, retroactive causation does not occur.

P2: Nothing contingent is uncaused.

P3: The definiteness of the actual world is contingent.

P4: The definiteness of the world is caused (from P1).

P5: If God possesses EDF, the world was perfectly definite (in God's mind) an eternity before the world existed.

P6: If God possesses EDF, the world cannot be the cause of its own definiteness, for it did not exist from eternity.

P7: If God possesses EDF, God must be the sole cause for the world's definiteness, or the world is not contingent.

Conclusion: If God possesses EDF, agents in the world cannot be the ultimate cause of the definiteness of their own actions. That is to say, agents cannot be *self*-determining.

Comment: If EDF is true, the two consistent views regarding the future are the Calvinist view of absolute predestination and Spinoza's view of a wholly necessary world. The future is eternally definite either because the one eternal being *willed* it from eternity to be what it is or because it is logically impossible, and thus eternally impossible, for it to be other than it is.

What is inconsistent, as theological determinists have always argued, is the classical Arminian view that wants to affirm EDF while also affirming self-determination. As Luther argued, "If God foreknows things, that thing necessarily happens. That is to say, there is no such thing as free choice."[2] Conversely, if one grants libertarian free choice, one must deny that God possesses EDF.

The logic here is straightforward. On the one hand, free agents are said to cause the definiteness to their own actions. On the other hand, the definiteness of their actions is held to be eternal (in God's EDF), though the free agent is not eternal. As far as I can see, this position is logically inconsistent. How are we to conceive of a temporal cause producing an eternal effect without granting retroactive causation (that is, deny P1)?

Aquinas (following Aristotle) was more consistent in arguing that what is eternal cannot be contingent, for what is eternal could not have been other than it is. Hence Aquinas construes God as being in every respect the eternal cause of the temporal, contingent world (though both he and Aristotle were less than consistent in working out the omni-deterministic implications of this view).[3] It seems, then, that the cause of the eternal definiteness of God's EDF regarding the totality of contingent world history cannot be the temporal, contingent world history itself.

Some simply argue that there is *no* cause to the eternally definite content of God's foreknowledge. The knowledge is "just there" as an attribute of God's omniscient nature.[4] As was argued in chapter four, however, it is not clear how this view improves the case for the compatibility of EDF with creaturely self-determination. The problem with the EDF account of reality is that the whole of contingent world history is definite—"definitely this and definitely not that"—from all eternity. The question is, *Why* is the definiteness of contingent reality eternally *this* way as opposed to eternally *that* way? Assigning God as the explanation, as Calvinists do, undermines creaturely self-determination, as Arminians have argued. Assigning the future world itself as the explanation, as Arminians do, implies retroactive causation, which most agree is logically impossible (P1). But assigning *no cause* surely does not increase the intelligibility of the position.

For one thing, postulating an uncaused contingent fact denies the princi-

---

[2]Martin Luther, *The Bondage of the Will*, trans. Philip S. Watson, Luther's Works 3 (Philadelphia: Fortress, 1972), p. 149.

[3]Herein lies one of the most fundamental contradictions of the classical philosophical view of God: a necessary eternal cause produces contingent temporal effects, some of which are the actions of free moral agents. I submit that this is incoherent.

[4]William Craig defends this position in *The Only Wise God: The Compatibility of Divine Knowledge and Human Freedom* (Grand Rapids, Mich.: Baker, 1987), pp. 119-25.

ple of sufficient reason. It is by definition absurd. For another, construing the definiteness of my future as eternally uncaused is no more compatible with me possessing self-determining freedom than is construing it as eternally God-caused. The problem here is simply the supposition that the future is definite before I make it so; *how* it became definite is actually inconsequential to this problem.

Conclusion

On the basis of these four arguments, together with the other arguments presented in chapters three, four and five, I argue that there is no way to render intelligible the notion that every aspect of my life is definite (in EDF) prior to my choosing it so, though I am free and morally responsible for the choices I make. Consequently, if one wishes to affirm self-determining freedom, logically one ought to deny that God possesses EDF.

Appendix 3

ON INCOMPLETE
PROBATIONARY PERIODS

A central feature of the trinitarian warfare theodicy is the conviction that love must be freely chosen. While this perspective is the key to understanding the warfare worldview of Scripture and the war-torn nature of God's creation, it also raises a difficult question. What happens to those who die without having a chance to resolve themselves either for or against God's love?

This question is sometimes discussed in terms of what becomes of unevangelized people. While this is an important issue, it is not the one I am presently concerned with.[1] The trinitarian warfare theodicy does not add anything to the stipulation, shared by all Arminians, that the final destiny of unevangelized people must be freely chosen by them, not determined by

---

[1]For an excellent survey of opinions on the matter, see John Sanders in *No Other Name: An Investigation into the Destiny of the Unevangelized* (Grand Rapids, Mich.: Eerdmans, 1992). See also William Crockett and James Sigountos, eds., *Through No Fault of Their Own? The Fate of Those Who Have Never Heard* (Grand Rapids, Mich.: Baker, 1991); E. Osburn, "Those Who Have Never Heard: Have They No Hope?" *JETS* 32 (1989): 367-72; Clark Pinnock, *A Wideness in God's Mercy* (Grand Rapids, Mich.: Zondervan, 1992); Joachim Jeremias, *Jesus' Promise to the Nations* (Philadelphia: Fortress, 1982); R. Blue, "Untold Billions: Are They Really Lost? *BSac* 138 (1981): 338-50; and Millard Erickson, "Hope for Those Who Haven't Heard? Yes, But. . ." *Evangelical Missions Quarterly* 11 (1975): 122-26. Jerry Walls provides an excellent discussion on divine goodness and hell in *Hell: The Logic of Damnation* (Notre Dame, Ind.: University of Notre Dame Press, 1992), pp. 83-111.

divine decree. The issue I wish to address has to do with the fate of humans who for whatever reasons did not arrive at the point where they could make any free decision regarding their eternal destiny. More specifically, what becomes of persons who died in infancy or were mentally challenged to the point of being incapable of making morally responsible decisions in this probational period?

Post-Mortem Developments and the Free Will Defense

Though the point is rarely made and even less frequently discussed, the fate of infants and mentally incapacitated people is crucial to anyone who holds to a free-will defense. The most fundamental claim of this defense is that love requires choice and that choice entails the possibility of evil. But if love indeed *requires* choice, and if heaven is defined as participating in God's love, then it follows by logical necessity that people who never made a choice for love *cannot* participate in heaven, regardless of why it is that they did not or could not make that choice. Nor can such individuals participate in hell, for the state of rejecting love also must be chosen.

Most contemporary Christians assume that all deceased infants and mentally incapacitated persons automatically go to heaven. But this assumption undermines the free-will defense. The conception of self-determining freedom as a precondition for love only explains the reality of evil in the world if it is a *necessary* precondition and is therefore applied *universally* to all persons—including infants and mentally incapacitated people.

Hence, though I would never propose that this conclusion be regarded as anything more than speculation, I argue that those who hold to the free-will defense should logically consider the possibility that those who were unable responsibly and decisively to choose for or against God's Kingdom *before* death must somehow be given an opportunity to do so *after* death. This view is often called the "future probation"* or "probation after death" position.

Given the current prevalence of the free-will defense, it is somewhat surprising that the concept of future probation is rarely given serious consideration among evangelicals. The central reason for this, I suspect, is that Scripture does not explicitly address this matter, and where Scripture is silent, conservative evangelicals often assume that we must also remain silent. The reverence for the authority of Scripture embodied in this position is laudable. But three considerations reveal it to be somewhat misguided in this case.

The prevalence of opinions. First, in point of fact, most contemporary

Christians are not silent on this issue. It is difficult not to hold an opinion about a topic that is this practically important. As noted above, most contemporary Christians assume that all infants and mentally incapacitated persons automatically go to heaven. There is no explicit scriptural support for this position, however, any more than there is for any other option. What is more, Christians rarely held this view until the modern period. Whatever else may be said about the future probation position concerning babies and mentally incapacitated persons, therefore, it should not be ruled out simply on the grounds that there is no explicit support for it in Scripture.

The Bible and church theology. Second, the church has historically been willing not only to repeat what Scripture explicitly says but also to develop what Scripture *logically implies.* Were this not the case we would not have the doctrines of the Trinity or incarnation. Every doctrine of the church and every conviction individual believers hold is the result of going one step beyond Scripture to arrive at *a coherent way of making sense out of Scripture.*

Since this issue is not explicitly addressed in Scripture, we must draw conclusions that are rooted in *other* truths that *are* rooted in Scripture. The destiny of infants and the triunity of God are on a par in this matter.

The destiny of babies in church history. Third, the church has historically entertained various positions about the fate of deceased babies (the fate of mentally incapacitated persons was rarely addressed). Since Scripture is largely silent on the matter, theologians had to struggle with this issue on the basis of other principles they believed to be true.[2]

Hence, for example, on the basis of a particular view of original sin and an understanding of baptism as necessary to wash away sin, the prevailing opinion from Augustine through the medieval period was that baptized babies go to heaven and unbaptized babies go to hell. In the light of a renewed appreciation of the character of God revealed throughout Scripture, however, many in the late Middle Ages softened this view by suggesting that unbaptized babies go to "limbo," a sort of middle ground between heaven and hell.[3] On the basis of their understanding of covenantal relationships, many Christians from the late Middle Ages on have held that the fate of babies was

---

[2]For discussions on this issue, see Benjamin B. Warfield, "The Development of the Doctrine of Infant Salvation," in *Studies in Theology* (New York: Oxford University Press, 1932), pp. 411-44; P. Gumpel, "Unbaptized Infants: May They Be Saved?" *Downside Review* 72 (1954): 342-458 and "Unbaptized Infants: A Further Report," *Downside Review* 73 (1955): 317-46. On this whole issue, see the excellent summarizing report by John Sanders in *No Other Name,* pp. 287-305.

[3]While "limbo" was usually construed as the highest level of hell, it was believed to be devoid of pain.

connected to the faith or unbelief of their parents, not their own baptism. Rooted in a particular understanding of divine election, Reformed theologians have traditionally held that the fate of babies was decided in the same way as the fate of adults. Elect babies are predestined to salvation; nonelect babies are not.[4]

The pervasive view among current Western Christians differs from all of these traditional positions, as noted earlier. Rooted in a robust confidence in the universality of God's love and (sometimes) a peculiar modern sentimentalism about the inherent goodness of humans, all babies and mentally incapacitated persons are believed to automatically go to heaven.

We see that the church has always felt the need to speculate on the fate of babies, because understanding this issue is important for arriving at a coherent Christian worldview. Hence, whatever criticisms might be raised against the possibility of a future probation for deceased babies or mentally incapacitated persons, the criticism that it is not explicitly stated in Scripture cannot be one of them.

Neither can this view be legitimately criticized for being nontraditional. As we have just seen, there is no standard view on this subject in church history. Indeed, in terms of being rooted within church tradition the future probation position fares better than the modern prevailing sentiment. Though it was never widely embraced, the view has had its occasional supporters, both Protestants and Catholics, from the fourth century up to the present.[5]

I thus contend that the view that certain individuals will somehow be given a post-mortem opportunity to accept or reject Christ must stand or fall

---

[4]"That there is an election and reprobation of infants, no less than of adults," says the Synod of Dort, "we can not deny in the face of God, who loves and hates unborn children," cited in *The New Schaff-Herzog Encyclopedia of Religious Knowledge*, ed. S. Jackson (New York: Funk & Wagnall's, 1909), 5:491. It should be noted that this view was usually combined with the covenantal view so that elect parents were assured that their babies were elect.

[5]On exponents of this view, ancient and modern, see G. J. Dyer, "The Unbaptized Infant in Eternity," *Chicago Studies* 2 (1963): 147; Ladislaus Boros, *The Mystery of Death*, trans. Gregory Bainbridge (New York: Herder & Herder, 1965), pp. 109-11; John Hick, *Evil and the God of Love*, rev. ed. (San Francisco: Harper & Row, 1978), 345-48; and John Lawson, *Introduction to Christian Doctrine* (Wilmore, Ky.: Asbury, 1980), pp. 261-63. This view was arguably held by C. S. Lewis (see, for example, *The Great Divorce* [New York: Macmillan, 1946], pp. 67-69). Jerry Walls also holds that "Further spiritual growth could occur after death" (*Hell*, p. 90). The conservative reformed theologian J. Oliver Buswell holds a similar view. He speculated that it may be that "at the moment of death the Holy Spirit of God . . . does so enlarge the intelligence of one who dies in infancy [or in imbecility] that they are capable of accepting Jesus Christ" (*A Systematic Theology of the Christian Religion*, 2 vols. [Grand Rapids, Mich.: Zondervan, 1962-1963], part 3, p. 162).

on the basis of whether or not one accepts the argument that love and moral responsibility require choice. If this is indeed a metaphysical truth, then people who have not chosen must somehow be given the opportunity to do so.

Incomplete Processes and the Future Probation

While one must admit that Scripture does not explicitly address the fate of infants or mentally incapacitated people, it is nevertheless significant to note that Scripture does not *contradict* this perspective. Indeed, while many contemporary Protestants assume that the Bible teaches that every person immediately enters heaven or hell after death—a view that would obviously rule out any future probation—Scripture hints that things may not be this simple.

For example, several familiar passages of Scripture could be understood to teach that certain people were given the chance to decide to follow Christ after death (Rom 10:7; Eph 4:8-10; 1 Pet 3:18-20; 4:6). Other texts suggest that believers whose sanctification is not completed in this life may somehow be completed and made fit for the kingdom of God in the next. Several of Christ's teachings seem to point in this direction. One example must suffice. On the need quickly to reconcile with brothers and sisters, Jesus says:

> Come to terms quickly with your accuser . . . or your accuser may hand you over to the judge, and the judge to the guard, and you will be thrown into prison. Truly I tell you, you will never get out until you have paid the last penny. (Mt 5:25-26)

Jesus is addressing disciples here—otherwise he could never give people hope of "getting out" after they have paid the "last penny." I do not believe that Jesus is literally saying that the person pays for the sin during this time, as though this person is atoning for the sin in "purgatory." Scripture is clear that Christ's sacrifice *alone* atones for sin, and it is sufficient for *all* sin (Rom 3:21-25; Heb 2:17; 9:27-28; 1 Jn 2:2; 4:10). His point may rather be that we either make things right *now* or we get them made right *later*, and getting them right later is *going to take time*.

In other words, this passage suggests that sanctification is *not optional* for disciples. If it does not happen now, it will later.[6] We are not told when or

---

[6]See also Lk 12:47-48, where Jesus taught that the "slave who knew what his master wanted, but did not prepare himself . . . will receive a severe beating. But the one who did not know and did what deserved a beating will receive a light beating." As uncustomary as such a picture is to standard Protestant teaching, in its context (Lk 12:35-46) it seems evident that Jesus is talking about *believers*. For several works that address the topic of the judgment of believers, see D. M. Paton, *The Judgment Seat of Christ* (Hayesville, N.C.: Schoettle, 1993); and Joseph C. Dillow, *The Reign of the Servant Kings* (Hayesville, N.C.: Schoettle, 1992).

how this completion shall take place, but we are clearly taught that all believers will appear before the judgment seat of Christ, and it may be that this completion process is part of this judgment (Rom 14:10; 2 Cor 5:10). Unlike the white throne judgment, this judgment is for believers and is remedial rather than retributive. Here, everything in a believer's life ministry that was not built on the foundation of Jesus Christ is burned up with fire. Paul writes:

> The work of each builder will become visible, for the Day will disclose it, because it will be revealed with fire, and the fire will test what sort of work each has done. If what has been built on the foundation survives, the builder will receive a reward. If the work is burned up, the builder will suffer loss; the builder will be saved, but only as through fire. (1 Cor 3:13-14)

Paul seems to be suggesting that everything that is not consistent with Christ's lordship will be burned up. We do not take garbage into the kingdom. As a majority of church fathers and mothers prior to the Reformation taught, if indeed nothing unclean can enter the kingdom of God (Rev 21:27; 22:14-15), then the refining of believers *must* be completed before they enter into heaven.

This teaching on the believer's judgment in no way compromises the scriptural truth that Christ's death is sufficient for our righteousness before God or that we are saved exclusively by God's grace. God's chastisements that refine our character in this life are done out of love and do not compromise our salvation by grace (Heb 12:5-6; Rev 3:19). Why think differently if similar refining chastisements occur after death before the judgment seat of Christ? It is simply a matter of completing *then* what was left undone *now*.

How does all this apply to the issue of the fate of babies and mentally incapacitated persons? It suggests that there is some precedent in Scripture for suggesting that certain processes that are incomplete at death are completed after death. If this is true of people who die before their sanctification is complete, might something like this be true of people who die before their self-determination for or against Christ is complete?

This conclusion is of course highly speculative and must be developed tentatively. The worst that can be said about it is that it has no more explicit rooting in Scripture and is thus no more speculative than any other position. In the end, the issue must be decided on other grounds. So far as I can see, this view is the only one consistent with the understanding that love must be freely chosen, and thus with a free-will defense.

Appendix 4

A THEOLOGY OF CHANCE

The trinitarian warfare worldview has a different perspective on chance than the one traditionally held by Christians. While the church has traditionally almost always denied that chance is real, the trinitarian warfare worldview acknowledges not only that it is real but that it is an important and advantageous aspect of God's creation. We need to flesh out this perspective more fully than was possible in the body of this work.

The Arbitrariness of Life
In chapters six and seven I argued that the reason God's interaction in the world seems so arbitrary to us is that we are ignorant of the specific variables conditioning this interaction. Like Job, our knowledge of the visible and especially the invisible world is extremely limited, and thus we experience life largely as an arbitrary fluctuation between blessings and curses. Life lacks rhyme or reason, not because God is arbitrary (as Job thought) nor because we are getting punished for wrongdoing we are not aware of (as Job's friends thought). It lacks rhyme or reason primarily because *our perspective on reality is so myopic*. We experience the effects but can never comprehensively discern the causes. Hence our experience of the world and of God *seems* arbitrary.

If the trinitarian warfare worldview is true, however, we must admit that there is a sense in which life not only *seems* arbitrary but *actually is* arbitrary, for it embodies an element of chance. The church has traditionally denied the reality of chance, for it conflicts with the blueprint worldview. But it is important to the trinitarian warfare understanding of God, the world and evil that we affirm its reality and develop some of its implications.

The Definition of "Chance"

An event can be said to have occurred by "chance" if it has either no *reason* or no *cause* sufficient to explain it. The behavior of quantum particles is an example of the former. Given the state of a quantum particle in its superposition, a range of possible behaviors can be predicted. But there is no cause as to why, within this range of possible behaviors, the particle appeared exactly here and not there. To be sure, there is a cause as to why the particle acted *within the range of possibilities* it acted in. But, on the standard interpretation, there is no cause as to why it acted this way as opposed to that way within this range. The precise way it transitioned from an indefinite to a definite state was to some extent a matter of chance.

Two drunk drivers crashing in an intersection is an example of the second, more important, type of chance. In the course of making their free decisions neither of the drivers intended this collision to take place. But by their irresponsible choice to drink and drive they individually set in motion a chain of events that led to this event.[1] Like ripples from two rocks dropped in a pond interfering with one another to create a new set of ripples, the consequences of the decisions of these two people interfered with one another and created a new set of consequences that neither person intended. When two or more agents independently set a causal chain in motion, and these chains intersect to produce consequences that neither agent specifically intended, these consequences can legitimately be said to be "chance occurrences."[2] They

---

[1]On this understanding of chance, see Arthur R. Peacocke, *Creation and the World of Science* (Oxford: Clarendon, 1979), pp. 90-92. If we were to speak precisely, the chain of events that rendered this collision increasingly likely (as the time of the event approached) goes back long before the two drivers decided to drink and then drive. It goes back to every event (including free decisions) that ever influenced them into being the kind of people who would likely choose to drink and drive, at least under the circumstances they actually did so. Indeed, it goes back to all the events (including free decisions) that influenced the events and decisions that in turn influenced them, and to the events that influenced these events, *ad infinitum*. There is an element of chance all along the way.

[2]The phenomenon of interference is found throughout nature. For a discussion on the concept of "interference" in physics, see Ian Stewart, *Does God Play Dice? The Mathematics of Chaos* (Oxford: Blackwell, 1989), pp. 81-83. We might note that this element of chance is largely what gives life its "tragic" sense. As the ancient Greeks knew so well, sometimes even good intentions can mesh

have causes, *but no governing reasons.*

While any version of the blueprint worldview must dismiss chance as simply due to our ignorance, the trinitarian warfare theodicy acknowledges that chance is real. God allows an element of spontaneity to permeate all of created reality, I have argued, and gives creatures morally responsible self-determination. Thus, the manner in which these independent spontaneous and self-determined events interact with other spontaneous and self-determined events will be partly a matter of chance.

To refer to our previous analogy, if there is no governing reason as to where, when and how hard any number of rocks are thrown into a pond, there certainly is no governing reason as to exactly how their ripples will interfere with one another. Likewise if there is an element of nonnecessity in the way humans determine their behavior, there must be an element of nonnecessity in the way in which the consequences of their behavior unfold.

The "givens" of any particular situation will be partly determined by the way the "ripples" from spontaneous events and, more importantly, free decisions interact with each other—and this is partly a matter of chance. God's plan and character is not arbitrary, but the "givens" that constitute the integrity of any given situation to some degree are.

A Cause Without a Reason

This observation has significant implications for our understanding of evil. Consider a tragedy that occurred several years ago. A young couple and their little girl became lost one evening and ended up driving in an unfamiliar neighborhood. The husband and father, who was driving, pulled into an alley in order to turn around when suddenly the car was riddled with bullets on both sides. Both parents were seriously injured and the young girl was instantly killed. It turns out that the couple had inadvertently driven into the middle of a gang-related turf war. One of the gangs apparently thought the car was somehow associated with a rival gang and opened fire on it.

From a classical philosophical perspective one might wonder, What good reason might God have had for ordaining, or at least specifically allowing, this tragedy to occur? What higher purpose did the atrocity serve? How does this occurrence fit into the grand cosmic picture? From the perspective of the trin-

---

with or collide with other good intentions in ways that produce pain. See, e.g., Sidney Hook, *Pragmatism and the Tragic Sense of Life* (New York: Basic Books, 1975), esp. pp. 55-60.

A THEOLOGY OF CHANCE

itarian warfare worldview, however, such questions are not appropriate.[3]

We *could* specify the numerous causes and reasons that led the gang to be located at this particular alley on this particular night. We *could* specify why the gang thought the car belonged to a rival gang and thus why they opened fire on it. We *could* even specify the immediate causes that resulted in this particular unfortunate family being lost in this neighborhood and pulling into this alley. In other words, we could within limits render intelligible each causal chain that brought about this tragedy, for each chain originated in the intentionality of a free moral agent.

But the precise way in which all these causal chains intersected to create this particular tragedy has no *overarching* reason to it. It is a chance by-product of other decisions that were made. Again, there are intelligible causes and reasons that can be specified as to why the little girl was killed, but there is no single *overarching* reason. Her death was not capricious, for morally responsible decisions brought it about. But it was nevertheless largely a matter of chance. She was simply an unfortunate casualty of war.

Who Is and Who Is Not to Blame

Does believing in God alter our assessment of this sad situation? Not necessarily, at least if we are thinking in the context of the trinitarian warfare worldview. We can in this view specify the *sort* of reasons God has for allowing morally responsible agents the freedom to make the kinds of bad decisions that were made leading to this young girl's untimely death, as I previously argued (chapters two through seven). But unless God reveals to us otherwise, we have no reason to believe that there is an overarching divine reason for why the exercise of creaturely freedom unfolded in the tragic way it did in this particular instance.

Regarding all the details of this tragedy—why *this* particular family, *this* particular girl, at *this* particular time, and so on—we must conclude that it was, in the end, simply bad luck. The independently initiated causal chains of

---

[3]As I have maintained throughout this work, it is certainly scriptural that God can *at times* have a specific reason for allowing a particular evil to occur. He may in fact temporarily orchestrate matters such that people's resolve is strengthened so that they act in congruity with their evil character (instead of acting otherwise for ulterior motives), for in this instance the evil they intended would play into God's design, despite the fact that it is in and of itself evil. (I interpret the biblical references to God "hardening" individuals' hearts to mean this. See, e.g., Ex 4:21; 9:12; Josh 11:20; Rom 9:18, see appendix five). The trinitarian warfare theodicy simply argues that (a) this truth cannot be universalized; (b) we ordinarily have no reason to assume that this is the case unless God explicitly reveals it to us; and (c) whether God can do this or not depends on innumerable variables that constitute the "givens" of a particular situation.

moral decisions just happened to converge in this manner.

Note that admitting this element of chance in no way undermines the moral responsibility of the gang members who opened fire on this car, nor the responsibility of all other agents who contributed in one way or another to this event (e.g., parents, peers, lenient judges, demons). We are to some extent responsible for how our decisions ultimately affect others even when this effect was not explicitly intended by us. Indeed, even if we suppose that an evil agent such as Satan had been working for some time to influence wills in this tragic direction, this in no way compromises the human agents' responsibility. Nor does it undermine the element of chance involved in the event. For as long as the humans were free, they could have resisted this influence and this tragic "accident" could have been avoided. Had any of the agents chosen differently, thus altering the "givens" of this situation, things might have flowed differently and this tragedy might have been avoided.

The same holds true for whatever angelic or demonic agents were involved in this event. Indeed, it is possible that as this event was unfolding and a tragedy became increasingly probable, God attempted to inspire various people to engage in intercessory prayer to prevent it (as in Ezek 22:30). It is possible that these people unconsciously resisted his prompting, however. If so, and if their prayers would have helped prevent this event, these individuals unwittingly bear some responsibility for this tragedy. It may even be true that certain angels should have done more to protect the family and thus bear some of the responsibility for this event (cf. Ps 82). Conversely, it is possible that it was because some people prayed and certain angels did intercede that the tragedy was not worse than it might otherwise have been.[4]

In the end, every single agent who directly or indirectly contributed to this tragic collision of causal chains bears some degree of moral responsibility for it. If there is one agent who does not share any of the responsibility for this little girl's death, it is God. True, as Creator, God designed the world

---

[4]This helps explain how apparent miracles can happen in tragedies. After the Columbine shootings in 1999, for example, there were multitudes of Christian testimonies about the "miraculous" way the massacre planned by the two killers was thwarted and "only" fourteen people were killed. Skeptics understandably wondered why *all* were not saved if God was indeed miraculously saving other people. The blueprint worldview can only respond by saying that somehow the deaths of these fourteen people fit into God's grand plan. The warfare worldview can acknowledge miracles that kept this tragedy from being worse without claiming that the deaths of these fourteen people were part of a divine plan. There were miraculous and demonic aspects of this tragedy, just as there are good and evil features of all others aspects of creation. The mystery of why some were killed while others were miraculously saved concerns the infinite complexity of creation (including the activity of good and evil spirits) instead of the arbitrary will of God (see chapter seven).

such that tragedies like this might occur. But if my assessment of the metaphysical conditions of love has been correct, God had no alternative, at least not if his goal for creation was love. A loveless world devoid of choice would have indeed been insured against tragedy. But, as all of us who choose to love despite its risk know, such a robotic world would have been of far less value than the risky one in which we now live.

It must also be said that, though the Creator bears no moral responsibility for the sinful choices of fallen angels and humans, out of his love and mercy he nevertheless accepts responsibility for them. The cross of Calvary demonstrates that there is no risk to which God permitted humans to be subject that he himself was not willing to bear. In order to free us from our sin and from the tyranny of the evil one, Scripture tells us that God accepted the full consequences of our rebellion. The one who deserved it least of all suffered the effects of rejected love the most.

If *he* deemed the risk worth it, we may be sure that it *is* worth it—however clouded this perception may become when the risk of evil becomes reality for us.

The Lord of Chance

We see that in a cosmos populated with free agents, chance must play a significant role in determining what does and does not occur. This contributes to our understanding of the apparent arbitrariness of God's interaction with the world. It may also raise another problem, however, for it might be argued that if the "givens" of a particular situation determine the extent to which God can interact in a situation, and if these "givens" are partly determined by chance, then chance, not the Creator, is the real lord of the cosmos. In short, God seems subject to chance.[5]

The objection is misguided, in my view, for the role chance plays within the cosmos is the general role *the Creator himself allotted it to play*. If God is in any particular situation prevented from intervening to bring about the best possible state of affairs, he is so only because he set up things such that this situation was possible. Had he been a less intelligent, less dynamic and

---

[5]The omnipotent Lord of all creation must, in this view, by definition be in control of all that he has created. The view is expressed succinctly by R. C. Sproul when he writes: "If chance existed, it would destroy God's sovereignty. . . . If chance is, God is not. If God is, chance is not. The two cannot coexist by reason of the impossibility of the contrary" (*Not a Chance: The Myth of Chance in Modern Science and Cosmology* [Grand Rapids, Mich.: Baker, 1994], p. 3). The traditional perspective is summarized well by David J. Bartholomew when he notes that "there is [in traditional theology] something intrinsically evil about chance" (*God of Chance* [London: SCM Press, 1984], p. 113). See also Peter Windt's related criticism against Plantinga in "Plantinga's Unfortunate God," *Philosophical Studies* 24 (1973): 335-42.

certainly less secure God, he would have avoided this possibility. He would have designed an exhaustively predetermined world, devoid of chance and challenges. Instead, the sovereign God wisely, courageously and lovingly chose the risky cosmos we find ourselves in.

It is a cosmos that is only partially predetermined, for an element of spontaneity permeates things and, more importantly, free agents have significant say in what transpires. Hence it is a challenging world where chance has a role and in which things do not always go as God would desire. But for this same reason it is a world that is, by God's grace, capable of love. Hence God chose to create this world rather than the safer but uninteresting world of predestined puppets.

As the Creator of the world that contains chance, it is evident that he is the Lord of chance, not vice versa.

Chance as a Beautiful Mystery

I have thus far spoken of chance as a necessary but largely negative by-product of a free creation. God desires creatures who are capable of choosing love, so he risks the possibility that their free decisions will interact in unfortunate and unplanned ways. But to complete our discussion of chance we should note that it need not and should not be construed only negatively. Because of the dominance of the blueprint worldview, the Western intellectual tradition did not legitimize, let alone appreciate, the positive role and beauty of chance. Once we free ourselves from this Platonic and Stoic legacy, however, we can begin to see both its benefits and its beauty.

Regarding the benefits, a number of philosophers have argued that chance is not simply the by-product of freedom but that freedom would not be possible without it. As was discussed in chapter nine, unless there was an element of indeterminacy in the nature of things, such as we find with quantum particles, there could not be self-determination on a morally responsible level. It has been argued that the sort of intelligence humans enjoy would not be possible were there not an element of indeterminacy woven into the fabric of things. Others who argue from an evolutionary perspective have maintained that there are a host of biological advantages to having a world in which chance plays a role.[6]

Chance has a nonutilitarian value as well. I suspect that, whatever deter-

---

[6]Examples of individuals who argue that indeterminacy at a micro level is necessary for the production of the kind of world we live in, one that includes human free will, are Roger Penrose, *The Emperor's New Mind: Concerning Computers, Minds, and the Laws of Physics* (Oxford: Oxford University Press, 1989); Bartholomew, *God of Chance;* Nancey Murphy and George F. R. Ellis, *On the Moral Nature of the Universe: Theology, Cosmology, and Ethics* (Minneapolis: Fortress, 1996); and Robert Kane, *The Significance of Freedom* (New York: Oxford University Press, 1996). The argument is frequent among Process theorists.

ministic theories they may hold, most intuitively find an element of randomness in things both interesting and beautiful. Is this not why most people
find games that incorporate an element of chance along with skill more
enjoyable than games that are purely skill? Is not part of the beauty we find
in nature the beauty of its randomness? A school of minnows randomly
negotiating the strong current of a stream, a bee haphazardly exploring a
flower bed, a butterfly flittering about in the breeze, the ever-changing and
always unique billowing cloud formations, the shifting patterns in a gusty
snowstorm—do we not find such things interesting and beautiful precisely
because we experience them as incorporating spontaneity? Would not a
world devoid of such spontaneity be a world lacking some significant aesthetic value?

Consider also the wonderful way in which children who previously did
not know each other can gather together and spontaneously create a game
or the interesting way team sporting events or animated conversations
between friends ebb and flow. Is not our delight in such things due largely to
the fact that we are encountering a spontaneously generated social reality
that has, as it were, taken on a life of its own? Individual personalities and
decisions intersect in unpredictable ways and create a reality that no individual agent intended. There is a fascinating beauty to the social role of chance
in human life.

We may thus conclude that a cosmos that includes chance possesses values
that a cosmos lacking chance could not possess. Thus we may understand
that God included chance in creation not only because it is a by-product of
freedom but because it is interesting, potentially beautiful and potentially
beneficial in and of itself. A world without it would be less of a world.

Appendix 5

EXEGETICAL NOTES ON TEXTS USED TO SUPPORT COMPATIBILISM

The trinitarian warfare theodicy presupposes an incompatibilist understanding of free will. It holds that morally responsible freedom is incompatible with exhaustive divine determination. Compatibilists argue rather that morally responsible freedom *is* compatible with exhaustive divine determination. God determines all that occurs, in their view, yet he does so *in such a way* that humans and angels are free and morally responsible for what they do.

In chapters two and three I offered philosophical, experiential and biblical objections to compatibilism. In this appendix I will briefly analyze some of the biblical texts compatibilists appeal to in support of their position. Before doing so, however, I would like to offer a preliminary word on the nature of this debate.

Paradigms and Proof Texts

Most Christian compatibilists agree with Christian incompatibilists on three fundamental biblical teachings. First, they agree that God is all-holy and thus that he never wills evil, for Scripture clearly teaches this. For example, Moses teaches us that "all [God's] ways are just" and that there is no "deceit" in him (Deut 32:4). John tells us that "God is light and in him there is no darkness" (1 Jn 1:5). Indeed, Habakkuk goes so far as to say that God's "eyes are too pure to behold evil" (Hab 1:13).

Second, most agree that because God is perfect in love and holiness, he "does not willingly afflict or grieve anyone" (Lam 3:33). He does not want anyone to suffer damnation. He rather "waits to be gracious" to sinners (Is 30:18) and pleads with everyone to turn to him (Is 65:2; Ezek 18:30-32; 33:11; Hos 11:7-9; Rom 10:21; 1 Tim 2:4; 2 Pet 3:9).

Third, most compatibilists agree with incompatibilists that humans and angels are (or at least were) in some sense free and thus morally responsible for their actions. Throughout Scripture God calls on free agents to choose for or against him (e.g., Deut 30:11-19). It consistently places the responsibility for their choices *on them*. Jesus says that good and evil actions flow *from a person's own heart* (Lk 6:43-45; cf. Mt 15:19).

The two sides fundamentally disagree, however, on how to reconcile these three points with the sovereignty of God. Compatibilists argue that one can affirm that God is perfectly holy, that he does not willingly afflict or will the damnation of anyone and that humans and angels are free, while yet maintaining that God exercises exhaustive control over creation, including the destinies of free agents. This is not a contradiction, they insist, though it is paradoxical. By contrast, incompatibilists argue that Scripture does not teach that God controls all events and that it is logically contradictory to suppose that he does. It is therefore meaningless to affirm that God is all-holy and yet hold that evil is ordained by him, that God wills all to be saved though he ordains the damnation of many and that creatures are free though God predestines their every move.

Incompatibilists do not deny that some verses in Scripture seem to support the compatibilists' position if read in isolation from the rest of Scripture. Every theological position has to deal with difficult texts. However, incompatibilists deny that the compatibilist position makes the *best* sense of the *whole* of Scripture. Further, they deny that the compatibilist position is logically consistent or that it can be reconciled with our experience of ourselves as free moral agents (see chapter two).

The issue comes down to what paradigm a person employs in interpreting Scripture. Do we start with the view that God is all-determining and then interpret verses affirming that humans and angels are free in this light? Or do we start with the view that humans and angels are free and then interpret verses seeming to suggest that God is all-determining in this light? Throughout this work I have argued on scriptural, logical and experiential grounds that the latter is the better position to take.

Nevertheless, it is incumbent on any theological position to account for difficult texts. While I have to some extent done so throughout this work, there are a number of texts often cited by compatibilists that I have not had occasion to address. This is what I attempt to do in this appendix. This list of difficult texts is by no means exhaustive. I only attempt to address those texts that provide the strongest case for compatibilism and that I did not address in the body of my work. Also, my comments about each passage will be brief and are not intended to constitute a full exegetical discussion. For my present purpose it will suffice simply to show that the compatibilistic interpretation of each of these texts is implausible, or at least unnecessary.

Texts Used to Support Compatibilism
Genesis 45:5; 50:20. "Now do not be distressed, or angry with yourselves, because you sold me here; for God sent me before you to preserve life [cf. Gen 45:7]. . . . Even though you intended to do harm to me, God intended it for good, in order to preserve a numerous people."

Compatibilists often argue that these texts, in which Joseph comforts his brothers, illustrate that God ordains evil actions for greater good. While different interpretations are possible, I am largely in agreement with compatibilists on this point. The passage seems to indicate that God intentionally orchestrated the evil intentions of the brothers in order to get Joseph into Egypt.

Does this support the compatibilist claim that all actions fit into God's eternal, sovereign plan? I do not believe so. Consider three points. First, though he probably could have achieved his objectives in a variety of ways, the biblical narrative leads us to believe that a good deal of God's plan for world history hinged on getting Joseph and his brothers to Egypt at this time. In these extraordinary times it should not surprise us to find God involved in extraordinary ways. This text should not be taken as a proof text of how God usually, let alone always, operates.

Second, if we interpret this episode as evidence of how God always operates, we must accept the consequence that this passage always minimizes the responsibility of human agents. This is the conclusion Joseph himself draws from his observation that God used his brothers to send him to Egypt. "Do not be distressed, or angry with yourselves," he tells them, "for God sent me." If this text is taken as evidence of how God *always* controls human action—if God is involved in each kidnapping and murder the way he was involved in the activity of Joseph's brothers—we must be willing to console every murderer and kidnapper with Joseph's words: "Do not be distressed, or angry with yourself, for God kidnapped and murdered your victims." We cannot universalize the mode of God's operation in this passage without also universalizing its implication for human responsibility. No one, of course, is willing to do this.

Third, nothing in these texts indicates that God orchestrated the brothers' activity before creation or even before the brothers developed their characters on their own. The text only suggests that *at some point* in the course of God's interaction with humans, God decided that it fit his sovereign purpose to steer the brothers' intentions in the manner we read in Genesis. It wasn't God's original plan that the brothers would acquire the character they did, but in the flow of history it fit his plan to use these brothers in the way he did.

Thus, while I agree with compatibilists that this text shows that God *may decide* to orchestrate evil actions according to his sovereign will, I deny that this passage supports the conclusion that *all* evil actions occur in accordance with God's eternal, sovereign will.

Exodus 4:11. "Then the LORD said to him [Moses], 'Who gives speech to mortals? Who makes them mute or deaf, seeing or blind? Is it not I, the LORD?'"

According to some compatibilists, this passage teaches that all infirmities are willed by God. However, this interpretation is not required for at least three reasons. First, as a hermeneutical principle, Christians should interpret the Old Testament in the light of the New, not vice versa. Most importantly, Christians should start their reflections about God with their minds fixed on the person of Jesus Christ, for he is the decisive revelation of God to us (e.g., Jn 1:14, 18; 14:7-10). Throughout his ministry Jesus opposed all infirmities and diseases as things that God does not will. Never once did he ascribe these things to his Father's will. Never once did he encourage people to find comfort in the notion that these things were part of God's plan. Rather, infirmities and diseases were consistently rebuked as the result of Satan's activity, which is why Jesus and his disciples always delivered people from them (see chapter one).[1] However we interpret the Exodus passage, it must

---

[1]For a full discussion, see my *God at War: The Bible and Spiritual Conflict* (Downers Grove, Ill.: InterVarsity Press, 1996), chs. 6-8. Bruce Ware repeatedly critiques the open view of the future on the grounds that it cannot provide comfort to believers who suffer because it does not affirm that their suffering is part of God's plan (*The God of a Lesser Glory* [Grand Rapids, Mich.: Baker, forthcoming]). Among other problems with this critique, it is completely inconsistent with the ministry of Jesus. Nowhere does Jesus offer this "comfort." On the practical value of the trinitarian warfare theodicy, see appendix one.

not contradict Jesus' teaching or his example.

Second, it is important to read this passage in context. Moses is arguing against God's decision to use him as his spokesperson to Pharaoh and the Jews in Egypt on the grounds that he is "slow of speech and slow in tongue" (Ex 4:10). God becomes understandably frustrated with Moses (Ex 4:14), for he has just demonstrated to Moses that he can perform enough miracles to convince the Jewish elders that Moses is sent by God. God thus uses emphatic language to emphasize the point (once again!) that as the Creator of the universe he can handle any and all obstacles in the way of delivering the Israelites out of Egypt. Thus he rhetorically asks Moses, "Who gives speech to morals? Who makes them mute or deaf?"

It is also important to note that God speaks of the human condition in general terms in this verse. As Terence Fretheim observes, the passage does not imply that God picks and chooses which *individuals* will be deaf, mute or blind, "as if God entered into the womb of every pregnant woman and determined whether and how a child would have disabilities." The text only implies that God created the *kind of world* where mortals may become disabled.[2] God created a risky world in which natural processes can be corrupted by free agents with the result that mortals are sometimes "flogged" (*mastix,* cf. Mk 3:10; 5:29, 34; Lk 7:21) with infirmities such as deafness and muteness (cf. chapter one). God wanted Moses to know that as Creator he is able to work around such obstacles in achieving his objectives. In the warfare ministry of Jesus, God went further and demonstrated that the presence of his kingdom is evidenced by overcoming such obstacles altogether. Jesus frees these people from Satan's "flogging" (cf. Acts 10:38).

Exodus 21:12-13. "Whoever strikes a person mortally shall be put to death. If it was not premeditated, but came about by an act of God, then I will appoint for you a place to which the killer may flee."

Compatibilists sometimes argue that this passage shows that fatal accidents are intentional acts of God. The Hebrew does not require this, however. It may simply mean that God allows the accident to happen. Hence the NIV translates the phrase, "God lets it happen."

It is helpful to remember that throughout the Old Testament God was laying the foundation for subsequent revelation. The centerpiece of this foundation was monotheism. Against the polytheistic views of Israel's neighbors, God consistently emphasized that he alone is Creator and that he alone is ultimately in control of the whole world. He has no rivals. Given this

---

[2]Terence Fretheim, *Exodus,* Interpretation (Louisville: John Knox Press, 1991), p. 72.

emphasis, Hebrew authors sometimes describe events or states as coming from the Creator, though they do not mean by this that the events or states are directly caused by God and ordained from the beginning of time. Free agents and chance influence how things transpire (Eccles 9:11), but they can only have the domain of influence Yahweh allots them. We can thus understand how an Old Testament author could contrast an intentional murder with a fatal accident that "God lets . . . happen."

Joshua 11:19-20. "There was not a town that made peace with the Israelites, except the Hivites . . . all were taken in battle. For it was the LORD's doing to harden their hearts so that they would come against Israel in battle, in order that they might be utterly destroyed" (cf. Ex 7:3; 10:1; 14:4; Deut 2:30).

Some compatibilists argue that passages speaking of God hardening human hearts demonstrate his absolute sovereignty. He hardens whomever he wills (Rom 9:18). He could just as easily soften their hearts, but for his own sovereign reasons he chooses to do otherwise. It is difficult, to say the least, to reconcile this conception of God with the previously discussed teaching that God "does not willingly afflict or grieve anyone" (Lam 3:33), that he desires and pleads with everyone to turn to him (Is 30:18; 65:2; Ezek 18:30-32; 33:11; Hos 11:7-9; Rom 10:21; 1 Tim 2:4; 2 Pet 3:9) and that evil flows from our own hearts (Lk 6:43-45; cf. Mt 15:19). Fortunately, the compatibilist interpretation of these verses is not necessary.

The root meaning of the Hebrew word "to harden" in Joshua 11:20 *(ḥāzaq)* is "to strengthen."[3] God hardens people by strengthening the resolve *in their own hearts.* Before God hardened Pharaoh's heart, Scripture says that Pharaoh hardened his own heart. Similarly, long before God hardened the Canaanites' hearts, he had been tolerating their freely chosen wickedness and hardness toward him (cf. Gen 15:16). The God of unsurpassable love strives with humans to turn toward him, but there is a point at which humans become hopeless (Gen 6:3-8; Rom 1:24-32). At this point God's strategy changes from trying to change them to using them in their wickedness for his own providential purposes.

God judges people by hardening their hearts. But it could have been—and God wishes it would have been—otherwise. (See the second objection in appendix one.)

---

[3]See the excellent discussion in Roger Forster and V. Paul Marston, *God's Strategy in Human History* (Wheaton, Ill.: Tyndale, 1974), pp. 155-75. On the hardening of Pharaoh's heart, see L. Haines, "Exodus," in *The Wesleyan Bible Commentary,* 7 vols., ed. Charles W. Carter (Grand Rapids, Mich.: Eerdmans, 1964-1969), 1:183-84.

Judges 9:23. "God sent an evil spirit between Abimelech and the lords of Shechem; and the lords of Shechem dealt treacherously with Abimelech" (cf. 1 Sam 16:14; 1 Kings 22:19-23).

Some compatibilists cite this passage to support the view that evil spirits always carry out the Lord's will (though they contend that God is good for willing it and the spirits evil for carrying it out). I argue that this conception is unintelligible and that the interpretation of this passage supporting it is unnecessary.[4]

We should first note that that passage does not imply that evil spirits *always* carry out the Lord's will. We must be careful not to universalize specific historical narratives. Second, the word "evil" in this passage *(rā'a)* can simply mean "troubling" or "disastrous." It does not have to be interpreted as referring to a morally evil spirit. Thus this passage may simply mean that as an act of judgment God sent a spirit to trouble or bring disaster to Abimelech.

Third, even if we conclude that the spirit in this verse was morally evil, the verse may be interpreted as teaching that as an act of judgment God allowed the spirit to do what it wanted to do to Abimelech. It does not warrant the conclusion that evil spirits *always* carry out God's sovereign plan. If this were the case, we would have to accept that God is in conflict with himself when Jesus rebukes demons. Jesus carries out the Father's will in casting out demons who are allegedly present in a person's life because God willed it. Jesus said that he could not be casting out demons by Satan, the prince of demons, because a kingdom cannot be divided against itself (Mt 12:25-28). The same logic leads to the conclusion that Jesus could not cast out demons by the power of God if the demons were themselves present by the will of God. God's kingdom, like Satan's kingdom, cannot be divided against itself.

Ruth 1:13. "It has been far more bitter for me than for you, because the hand of the LORD has turned against me."

Some compatibilists cite this passage, which records Naomi's statement to her two daughters-in-law, to support the conclusion that all misfortune is ordained by God. Several considerations show that this conclusion is not necessary.

First, it is not entirely clear that the opinion Naomi expresses here is endorsed by the inspired author of the book of Ruth. The author may only intend to communicate Naomi's despair over the death of her husband and her two sons. Even if she were to marry again, she is too old to have any more children. She has no means of providing for herself, let alone her wid-

---

[4]See Boyd, *God at War,* pp. 80-81, 154.

owed daughters-in-law. Naomi is "bitter" toward God (cf. Ruth 1:20-21), for she "blames the Lord for bringing about the situation in which she finds herself." She is arguing that it "does not make logical sense for Orpah and Ruth to align themselves with someone who seems to have the hand of the Lord turned against her."[5]

Second, given the Hebraic tendency to emphasize the Creator's general responsibility for the world, we should be reticent to read too much into Naomi's expression. God created the kind of world where bereavement can occur, and in this sense, perhaps, Naomi feels the "hand of the LORD" had "turned against" her.

Finally, even if we conclude that the deaths of Naomi's husband and her only sons were specifically willed by God, this would not justify the conclusion that *all* bereavement comes from God and certainly not that *all misfortune* comes from God. The point of Naomi's complaint has nothing to do with such a general metaphysical conclusion.

1 Samuel 2:25. "They [Eli's sons] would not listen to the voice of their father; for it was the will of the LORD to kill them."

Compatibilists sometimes cite this text as an example of how God determines events for which humans are morally responsible. Eli's sons were evil in not listening to their father, yet it was the Lord who prevented them from doing this. If read in context, however, the passage does not support the compatibilist interpretation.

Eli's three sons had willfully persisted in abusing their priestly office for a long time. The Lord detested their vile activity (1 Sam 2:17), and Eli warned his sons about the severity of their wickedness, but it was too late. God had already decided to bring judgment on them. God's sovereign act of preventing the sons from heeding Eli's warning was an act of judgment and was consistent with the wicked character the sons had freely developed for years.

Now if the passage said that the sons were wicked in the first place because God wanted to judge them, it might support compatibilism. Or if the passage said that the sons were godly people until the Lord changed their hearts and prevented them from heeding their father's words, it might support compatibilism. But this passage does not teach this; indeed, significantly enough, no passage in Scripture teaches this. Scripture rather teaches that God sometimes hardens people to judge them *because* they are persistently wicked. It also uniformly teaches that all wickedness is absolutely contrary to God's will.

---

[5]Kathleen R. Farmer, "Ruth," in *NIB*, 2:904.

2 Samuel 16:10. "The king [David] said [of Shimei's cursing of him], 'If he is cursing because the LORD has said to him, "Curse David," who then shall say, "Why have you done so?"'"

Some compatibilists cite this text to suggest that David regarded even evil deeds, including cursing, as taking place in accordance with the sovereign will of God. If we accept this interpretation and apply it to all evil deeds, we should also accept David's logical conclusion that *nothing should be done about evil deeds* (see above, Gen 45:5). If this conclusion is unacceptable, so is the deterministic interpretation of this passage that gives rise to it.

In point of fact, this text does not support compatibilism. Abishai, who tended to have a hot temper (1 Sam 26:8-9; 2 Sam 3:30, 39), wanted to respond to Shimei's curses by killing him (2 Sam 16:9). David rather "takes this moment of cursing to reflect on his position before God and his trust that it is God's grace and not Abishai's sword that can counter Shimei's cursing."[6] If God is in fact against David—if Shimei is speaking truth—killing Shimei will accomplish nothing. On the other hand, if God is on David's side, killing Shimei is not necessary. David hoped that God was on his side and that his fortune would be reversed in the near future (2 Sam 16:12). The text does not warrant the conclusion that God controls all cursing and thus (thankfully) the implication that we should be passive in the face of evil.

2 Samuel 17:14. "Absalom and all the men of Israel said, 'The counsel of Hushai the Archite is better than the counsel of Ahithophel.' For the LORD had ordained to defeat the good counsel of Ahithophel, so that the LORD might bring ruin on Absalom."

This passage is sometimes cited to support the view that God ordains all things, including how people respond to other people's advice. I submit that this conclusion goes beyond what the passage warrants. In response to David's prayer and in line with his sovereign design to secure the throne of David, God had determined to "turn the counsel of Ahithophel into foolishness" (1 Sam 15:31) and thereby bring judgment on Absalom, King David's wicked son. The passage does not suggest that God had ordained Absalom's foolishness from before creation. What God does in this passage he does *in response* to what humans do. Absalom's wickedness was not part of God's sovereign plan. This was entirely Absalom's own doing. But if Absalom chooses this for himself, God is able to ensure that his wicked schemes will end in his own disaster (2 Sam 18:9-15; cf. Prov 16:9).

2 Samuel 24:1. "Again the anger of the LORD was kindled against Israel,

---

[6]Bruce C. Birth, "1 and 2 Samuel," in *NIB,* 2:1326.

and he incited David against them, saying, 'Go, count the people of Israel and Judah.' "

1 Chronicles 21:1. "Satan stood up against Israel, and incited David to count the people of Israel."

Compatibilists frequently cite these parallel passages—in which one text says that the Lord incited David to count the people, the other that Satan incited David to count the people of Israel[7]—as an example of how Satan always carries out God's plan. God's plan, they insist, is always good, though Satan is evil in carrying it out. The "paradox"—or (I believe) contradiction—this viewpoint creates is unnecessary. These texts do not imply that Satan *always* carries out God's plan, only that he *sometimes* does so. In this case, God planned to judge Israel, so he allowed Satan to bring it about. For editorial reasons, the author of 2 Samuel attributes the judgment to God, while the author of 1 Chronicles refers the action to Satan, who was allowed by God to do what he wanted to do.

1 Kings 8:57-58. "The LORD our God be with us . . . [and] incline our hearts to him, to walk in all his ways, and to keep his commandments."

Compatibilists sometimes cite biblical prayers such as this one, Solomon's prayer at the dedication of the temple, to support the view that God determines the human heart. If this were the case, however, one wonders why humans would have to *pray* for this to happen. In this passage Solomon is simply realizing that the people of Israel will not be faithful to God on their own. Thus he asks God to move on people's hearts. But neither this nor any other biblical passage requires us to conclude that this spiritual influence is coercive.

Job 1:21. "The LORD gave, and the LORD has taken away; blessed be the name of the LORD."

This passage is often quoted as the proper attitude pious people should assume in the face of tragedy, with the implication that all tragedy is the Lord's doing. This teaching lands hard on the ears of many parents who have had their children abducted. Compatibilists often soften its harshness by saying that God *allows* tragedies such as Job suffered for a greater good. But as Calvin and others have admitted, if God indeed ordains all things, speaking in terms of what God allows or permits is an equivocation.[8] Cer-

---

[7]For a fuller discussion, see my *God at War,* pp. 153-54.

[8]Calvin writes, "Why shall we say 'permission' unless God so wills? . . . I shall not hesitate, then, simply to confess with Augustine that 'the will of God is the necessity of things,' and that what he has willed will of necessity come to pass" (*Institutes of the Christian Religion,* ed. John T. McNeill, trans. Ford L. Battles [Philadelphia: Westminster Press, 1960], p. 956 [3.23.8]).

tainly if Job 1:21 is used to support compatibilism, we must admit that the Lord himself "takes away" children when they are abducted just as he "gives" children when they are conceived.

In my estimation, this usage of Job 1:21 (as well as other compatibilistic-sounding texts in Job, e.g., 14:5-6) is fundamentally misguided. Nothing in the text indicates that the author condoned the all-determinative theology Job expresses in 1:21 and in his dialogue with his friends. True, the narrator acknowledges the unblemished character of Job after he utters this statement (Job 1:22), and Yahweh commends Job for speaking truth from his heart, in contrast to his friends (Job 42:7). But this is not the same as endorsing Job's theology.

Much of the theology that Job expresses throughout his dialogue with his friends is clearly *not* theology that the author of this book advocates. Indeed, Job often states a view of God as a cruel, unjust tyrant who controls everything in an arbitrary fashion. For example, Job exclaims:

> When disaster brings sudden death,
>   [God] mocks at the calamity of the innocent.
> The earth is given into the hand of the wicked;
>   he covers the eyes of its judges—
>   if it is not he, who then is it? (Job 9:23-24; cf. 21:17-26, 30-32; 24:1-12)

Again:

> Why are times not kept by the Almighty,
>   and why do those who know him never see his days? . . .
> From the city the dying groan,
>   and the throat of the wounded cries for help;
>   yet God pays no attention to their prayer. (Job 24:1, 12)

Would anyone recommend *this* opinion as the proper attitude of pious people? Clearly not. Yet it is in line with Job's sentiment that the Lord simply gives and takes away regardless of a person's moral stature.

Job's depiction of God is even harsher when he considers the injustice of his own state. For example, Job cries out to the Lord:

> Your hands fashioned and made me;
>   and now you turn and destroy me. (Job 10:8)

> Bold as a lion you hunt me;
>   you repeat your exploits against me. (Job 10:16)

> Let me alone; that I may find a little comfort. (Job 10:20)

You have turned cruel to me;
with the might of your hand you persecute me. (Job 30:21)

And to his friends Job claims:

Surely now God has worn me out;
he has made desolate all my company.
And he has shriveled me up. . . .
He has torn me in his wrath, and hated me;
he has gnashed his teeth at me;
my adversary sharpens his eyes against me. (Job 16:7-9; cf. 11-17)

With violence he seizes my garment;
he grasps me by the collar of my tunic. (Job 30:18)

Are we to believe that these are sentiments the author of this work is *recommending* to his readers? Does not the god Job describes in these passages sound more like "a roaring lion . . . looking for someone to devour," in other words, "your adversary the devil" (1 Pet 5:8)? Far from condoning this impious theology, I submit that the point of this work is to expose its inadequacies.

When Yahweh appears at the end of this work to set the record straight, he *corrects* the thinking of both Job and his friends (Job 38—41). As mentioned in chapter seven, the Lord does not acknowledge that he was the one behind Job's sufferings, as Job claimed, or that he was justly punishing Job, as his "friends" claimed. Rather, God silences *both* Job and his "friends" by revealing how little they (or any human) know about the cosmos he has created. They know nothing of the vastness of creation (Job 38—39) and cannot contend with cosmic forces such as Behemoth (Job 40) and Leviathan (Job 41). Nor do they know anything of what transpires in the heavenly realm (Job 1—2). In the end, the reason suffering seems to be so arbitrary must remain mysterious to finite humans. God does not give Job an answer. But the mystery attaches to the vastness, complexity and warfare nature of *creation*, not to *God's character*.

This is why Job acknowledged that he "uttered what [he] did not understand" after his confrontation with God (Job 42:3). His friends were wrong in reducing the complexity of creation, and therefore the mystery of evil, down to one variable: Job's character. But Job was also wrong in reducing the complexity of creation and the mystery of evil down to one variable: God's character. The truth is that the complexity of creation, and therefore the arbitrariness of suffering, cannot be reduced to any level that we humans can understand.

In the light of all this, I suggest that we ought not to take Job's sentiment that the Lord gives and takes away (Job 1:21) any more authoritatively than we take his sentiment that "God pays no attention to [the] prayer" of wounded victims (Job 24:12). Job was admirably expressing the truth of his pain, but in his pain he was not consistently expressing ultimate metaphysical truth. To discover the proper attitude that believers should take in the face of unjust suffering, we need to center our attention on the person and work of Christ. He never encouraged accepting evil as coming from God. He rather taught us to revolt against it as coming (ultimately) from Satan (see the introduction and chapter one).

Psalm 105:24-25. "The LORD made his people very fruitful, and made them stronger than their foes, whose hearts he then turned to hate his people, to deal craftily with his servants."

Some compatibilists cite Psalm 105:25 as evidence that God meticulously controls human hearts. If so, we must accept the conclusion that even grotesquely wicked hearts like Hitler's and Stalin's were exactly as God willed them to be. Fortunately, the passage does not require this conclusion. It speaks specifically of the Egyptians' hatred of the Jews. God's plan was to develop his people while they were in Egypt for four centuries (Ps 105:24), then to deliver them and bring them into the Promised Land (bringing divine judgment on the Canaanites for four centuries of wickedness in the process, Gen 15:16). At this critical juncture in human history it fit God's providential plan to turn the Egyptians' hearts in this fashion. This display of sovereignty is noteworthy to biblical authors precisely because it is atypical.

Even here, however, we should not assume that God was the *originator* of the hatred in the Egyptians' hearts. It is not as though the Egyptians would otherwise have cherished the Israelites as good neighbors were it not for God turning their hearts. The Israelites were already abused slaves at the hand of the Egyptians. God's "turning" only intensified what was already there. It is similar to God's activity of "hardening" hearts (see Josh 11:19-20 above). God could have done this simply by eliminating other avenues by which the Egyptian hatred of the Jews could have been dissipated or suppressed.

This way of reading the text does not make God a co-conspirator with every wicked person (and angel) and retains the moral responsibility of the Egyptians. Given Scripture's pervasive insistence that God is in no sense aligned with evil and that free agents are responsible for their own inclinations and behavior, it is, I submit, to be preferred over the compatibilist reading.

Psalm 135:6. "Whatever the LORD pleases he does, in heaven and on earth" (cf. Job 23:13-14; Ps 115:3; Dan 4:35).

Some conclude from passages like this that God's will can never in any sense be thwarted. Since Scripture explicitly teaches that God's will *is* in fact sometimes thwarted (Is 63:10; Lk 7:30; Acts 7:51; Eph 4:30; Heb 3:8, 15; 4:7), we must reject this conclusion. These passages certainly teach that the Lord can do whatever he pleases, but they only support the view that God meticulously controls everything if we assume that it pleases the Lord to control everything. There is no basis for this assumption, however. Most parents would not be pleased meticulously to control their children, even if they could. We all know that relating to free persons is infinitely more rewarding than controlling people, though it is also much more risky. Why then should we conclude that God's greatest agenda for creation—what "pleases him"—is meticulously to control it?

Proverbs 16:4. "The LORD has made everything for its purpose, even the wicked for the day of trouble."

Compatibilists often cite this verse to support the conclusion that some people are created wicked for the purpose of being sent to hell. Since Scripture teaches that God is love (1 Jn 4:8, 16), that he loves all people (Jn 3:16) and thus does not willingly afflict anyone (Lam 3:33) or will the damnation of any (Ezek 18:30-32; 33:11; 1 Tim 2:4; 2 Pet 3:9), we should seek an interpretation that does not compromise God's character.

An alternative interpretation is not difficult to find. Proverbs 16:4 uses the language of moral order. God set up creation such that good is (eventually) rewarded and evil (eventually) punished. In this sense the "purpose" for the wicked is found in the "day of trouble" that will come on them. The verb translated in the NRSV as "made" *(pāʿal)* can be translated as "works out" (as in the NIV), an observation that confirms my interpretation. God steers the wickedness of agents so that their end eventually fits the moral order of creation. Moreover, the word translated as "purpose" *(maʿan)* can be translated as "answer."[9] The meaning of the passage, then, is that God works things out so that the end of the wicked "answers" their wickedness. They eventually reap what they sow. We thus need not entertain the gruesome prospect of God creating people for the purpose of having them suffer endlessly.

Proverbs 16:9. "The human mind plans the way, but the LORD directs the steps" (cf. Prov 19:21; 20:24; Jer 10:23).

---

[9]See D. J. A. Clines, "Predestination in the Old Testament," in *Grace Unlimited*, ed. Clark Pinnock (Minneapolis: Bethany House, 1975), p. 116.

Far from teaching that God controls everything, as some compatibilists maintain, this verse *contrasts* what the Lord controls with what he chooses *not* to control. Humans can and do make their own plans, but the Lord directs how those plans get worked out. As Proverbs 19:21 puts it:

> The human mind may devise many plans,
>   but it is the purpose of the LORD that will be established.

This does not imply that God meticulously controls everything humans do as they seek to live out their plans, only that he steers their paths in ways that best fit his sovereign purposes. When the course of action the Lord is steering flows from someone's evil intentions, we may be assured that he wishes it were otherwise.

Proverbs 21:1. "The king's heart is a stream of water in the hand of the LORD; he turns it wherever he will."

Compatibilists sometimes argue that this passage teaches that everything every government official ever does is the result of the Lord turning the official's heart. In light of the hideous things many government officials have done (e.g., Hitler's program of ethnic cleansing), and in light of the fact that Scripture frequently depicts God as outraged by government officials, we should seriously question this conclusion. Fortunately, this conclusion is not required by this passage. Two things may be said.

First, we must consider the genre of this passage. This passage is a proverb. Hebraic proverbs often state general principles in unequivocal terms for emphasis. It was their way of putting an exclamation mark at the end of a teaching. We misinterpret them if understand them as universal laws. For example, Proverbs 12:21 states:

> No harm happens to the righteous,
>   but the wicked are filled with trouble. (cf. Prov 13:21, 25)

If read as a universal law, this passage is nonsense. History and our own experience demonstrate that righteous people frequently suffer great harm while wicked people often live in peace and prosperity. Indeed, Scripture itself repeatedly makes this observation. *As a general principle*, however, righteous living helps one avoid harm while wicked living leads to trouble. The author states the principle in absolute terms to emphasize its importance.

Another example of how Hebraic proverbs state things in absolute terms for emphasis is Proverbs 22:6:

> Train children in the right way,

and when old, they will not stray.

Many godly parents whose children strayed from the path they taught them have been needlessly indicted by a misreading of this passage. As we all know, as children grow up they increasingly become free moral agents who determine their own destinies. There are no absolute guarantees when raising children. Still, as a general rule it is true that consistently training children in the right way will increase the likelihood that they will not stray when they grow up. Again, the author states the principle in unequivocal terms for emphasis.

It is thus not advisable to interpret Proverbs 21:1 as an absolute law. The author is not suggesting that every decision made by every king throughout history was orchestrated by God. He is simply emphasizing God's general sovereignty over kings. We see this sovereignty dramatically depicted elsewhere in Scripture. For example, as an act of judgment (but not an eternally predestined plan) God stirred up the wicked hearts of pagan kings against Israel (e.g., 1 Chron 5:26; Is 10:5-6). Conversely, when he wanted his people to return to their homeland, he influenced Cyrus's heart to let them go (2 Chron 36:22-23; Is 44:28). God is sovereign over earthly kings, but we read too much into this passage if we conclude that he meticulously controls everything they do.

Even when God "turns" the hearts of kings in the direction he desires, he does not *determine the nature of the heart* he turns, which is my second point. As noted above (Prov 16:9), people resolve their own hearts and make their plans either in accordance with God's will or against God's will. This is their domain of irrevocable freedom. But even when they set themselves against God, God still directs their steps. He steers the way they live out their choices so that they further his good purposes for the world as much as possible. He is always at work to bring good out of evil (Rom 8:28), but he does not himself ordain the evil out of which he brings good.

Isaiah 6:10. "Make the mind of this people dull, and stop their ears, and shut their eyes, so that they may not look with their eyes, and listen with their ears, and comprehend with their minds, and turn and be healed" (cf. Mt 13:14-15).

If taken out of context, this passage may sound as though the Lord wants certain minds to be spiritually dull, certain ears to be spiritually deaf and certain eyes to be spiritually blind. Thus this passage is sometimes cited as evidence that some people are hardened to the message of the Lord by sovereign design. How can this passage be reconciled with the universality of God's love and desire for salvation expressed elsewhere in Scripture?

The answer is to be found in the observation that the Lord is not commissioning Isaiah to preach to people who would otherwise be receptive to his message. God never hardens anyone arbitrarily (Lam 3:33). Rather, in this passage God is *responding* to the Israelites' persistent obstinance. (Note that God no longer refers to them as "my people" [cf. Is 1:3] but as "this people" [cf. Is 8:6, 12; 9:16]).[10] He sends Isaiah out *as an act of judgment,* anticipating that the preaching of his word will only serve further to solidify the Israelites in their self-chosen obstinacy. This increased solidification will make them "ripe for judgment." It always grieves the Lord when he has to treat people in this fashion; it is not his perfect will (e.g., Hos 11:5-9). Yet even in judgment the Lord often holds out hope for the future (cf. Jer 29:10-14).

Isaiah 14:24, 27. "The LORD of hosts has sworn: As I have designed, so shall it be; and as I have planned, so shall it come to pass. . . . For the LORD of hosts has planned, and who will annul it? His hand is stretched out, and who will turn it back?"

The fact that Scripture frequently speaks of God's will being thwarted and his Spirit being grieved, as we have seen, should prevent us from interpreting this passage as a universally applicable, absolute law. Scripture's many examples and illustrations of the Lord modifying his "designs" in response to humans—even after he has publicly declared what they are (e.g., Jer 18)—should caution us against this interpretation as well. The point of the passage is not to instruct us about the way God operates at all times and in all places. The context makes it clear that it is simply teaching that when God decides to bring judgment on a nation (in this case, Assyria, Is 14:25), no one can stop him. A careful reading of similar passages that speak of God fulfilling his "purposes" and "plans" reveals that they also "have in view a particular event or a limited series of events" (e.g., Is 25:1; 46:10; Jer 23:20; Mic 4:12).[11] They do not warrant the conclusion that God determines all things.

Isaiah 45:7. "I form light and create darkness, I make weal and create woe; I the LORD do all these things."

Lamentations 3:37-38. "Who can command and have it done if the Lord has not ordained it? Is it not from the mouth of the Most High that good and bad come?"

Compatibilists often argue that passages such as these attribute both good and evil to God's sovereign hand (cf. Amos 3:6). Some nonevangelical scholars argue that this conception of God represents an ancient Hebrew stage of

---

[10]K. E. Jones, "The Book of Isaiah," in Charles Carter, ed., *Wesleyan Bible Commentary,* 3:35.
[11]Clines, "Predestination," p. 122.

religious development where Yahweh was viewed as morally ambiguous. Only later, they argue, was Yahweh seen as all-holy in the eyes of Israelites and was evil attributed to Satan and/or other free agents. In my estimation, the conclusion that God is morally ambiguous if he originates both good and evil is irrefutable. Evangelical compatibilists escape this conclusion only by merely asserting that it is not so.

Fortunately, when read in context, neither text supports the view that God is morally ambiguous. The Isaiah passage addresses the future deliverance of the children of Israel out of Babylon (Is 45:1-6). As a number of scholars have argued, the "light" and "darkness" of this passage refer to "liberation" and "captivity" (as in Is 9:1-2; Lam 3:2). The "weal" and "woe" (or "prosperity" and "disaster") refer to Yahweh's plans to bless Israel and to curse Babylon. In the words of Terence Fretheim, this language

> is not cosmic in orientation, but language typical in the prophets for specific (historical) divine judgments. . . . God's "creating" here is not *ex nihilo*, but action which gives specific shape to a situation of historical judgment.

Thus he concludes, "no claims are made that God is the all-determinative actor in this (or any other) situation."[12]

Similarly, if read in context, Lamentations 3:37-38 does not suggest that Yahweh causes or ordains evil. Indeed, four verses earlier the prophet proclaims that God "does not willingly afflict or grieve anyone" (Lam 3:33). This passage is not concerned with God's cosmic sovereign activity; it specifically addresses prophecy. Both "good and bad" prophecies (i.e., prophecies about blessings and disaster) come "from the mouth of the Most High." As much as it grieves the Lord (cf. Lam 3:31-33), he is prophesying judgment on Israel because "the prisoners of the land are crushed under foot [and] human rights are perverted" (Lam 3:34). Far from suggesting that good and evil are part of God's sovereign plan, the passage highlights God's unequivocal holiness in opposing evil as something that he does not in any sense will![13]

John 6:44. "No one can come to me unless drawn by the Father who sent me."

Compatibilists sometimes argue that this passage teaches that the Father

---

[12]Terence Fretheim, "Divine Dependence on the Human: An Old Testament Perspective," *Ex Auditu* 13 (1997): 6-7. See Fredrik Lindström, *God and the Origin of Evil: A Contextual Analysis of Alleged Monistic Evidence in the Old Testament,* trans. F. H. Cryer, ConBOT 21 (Lund: Gleerup, 1983), pp. 178-99. See also Boyd, *God at War,* pp. 149-50.

[13]On Lamentations 3:37-38 and Amos 3:6, see Lindström, *Origin of Evil,* pp. 199-236; cf. Boyd, *God at War,* pp. 150-52.

chooses and then "draws" certain people to Christ. Those who are drawn certainly come (Jn 6:37), while all who are not drawn remain in their sin. In short, this passage is interpreted to teach particular election.

It is true that the "drawing" Jesus speaks of is not universal, as some Arminians suggest, since Jesus is here *contrasting* those who are drawn with those who are not. But neither this nor any other passage requires us to believe that the Father simply decides who will and will not be drawn. The Father draws people (or not) *in response to* their hearts. God wants all to be saved and is at work in every human heart to get them to accept the gospel. But people can and do resist God's influence and thwart his will for their lives. When a heart has been successfully opened, however, God goes further and draws that person to Jesus Christ.[14] (See chapter two for a further discussion on grace and free will.)

Acts 4:27-28. "Both Herod and Pontius Pilate, with the Gentiles and the peoples of Israel, gathered together against your holy servant Jesus . . . to do whatever your hand and your plan had predestined to take place."

This passage tells us that Herod, Pilate, the Gentiles and the peoples of Israel carried out God's predestined plan, not that they were individually predestined to carry out God's plan. *That* Jesus was going to be killed was settled ahead of time; *who* would kill him was not. (See chapter four for additional discussion on this passage).

Acts 13:48. "When the Gentiles heard this [preaching], they were glad and praised the word of the Lord; and as many as had been destined for eternal life became believers."

Luke does not specify when the Gentiles who believed were "destined for eternal life." Compatibilists rightfully point out that the Gentiles' faith *followed* their being destined for eternal life but mistakenly assume that this destiny was decided by God from before creation. The text only requires us to believe that the Spirit of God had been at work preparing the hearts of all who did not resist him to accept the gospel when they heard it. God knows our hearts before we express them through our words or decisions (Ps 139:2-4). On this basis the Lord could assure Paul before his missionary endeavor at Corinth that "there are many in this city who are my people,"

---

[14]This does not imply that all those who never hear the gospel have hearts that are closed to Christ. On the issue of the salvation of non-Christians, see John Sanders, *No Other Name: An Investigation into the Destiny of the Unevangelized* (Grand Rapids, Mich.: Eerdmans, 1992); Clark Pinnock, *A Wideness in God's Mercy* (Grand Rapids, Mich.: Zondervan, 1992); and William Crockett and James Sigountos, eds., *Through No Fault of Their Own? The Fate of Those Who Have Never Heard* (Grand Rapids, Mich.: Baker, 1991).

that is, whose hearts have been opened and who will therefore believe Paul's message (Acts 18:10). Likewise Lydia listened intently to Paul's gospel because the Lord had already "opened her heart" (Acts 16:14). Those Gentiles who did not resist the Spirit's work in their lives were ripe for the message of Paul and Barnabas. They were already destined for eternal life and thus accepted the good news when it was preached to them.[15]

In my opinion, this is also how we ought to interpret Jesus' words when he tells certain Jews, "you do not believe, because you do not belong to my sheep. My sheep hear my voice . . . and they follow me" (Jn 10:26-27). Jesus is not implying that God unilaterally decides who will and will not be sheep, as compatibilists teach. Moreover, he certainly is not suggesting that this matter was decided before any of these people were born. Jesus' words only imply that *at the time of his speaking* some people were sheep and therefore believed while others were not and thus did not believe. We only create impossible problems for ourselves—such as how God can love all and want all to be saved while predestining many to hell—when we go beyond what Scripture teaches.

Acts 17:26. "From one ancestor he made all nations to inhabit the whole earth, and he allotted the times of their existence and the boundaries of the places where they would live" (cf. Dan 2:21).

In this passage Paul is preaching to Epicurean and Stoic philosophers (Acts 17:18). His goal is to show them that, in contrast to their idols, God created and cares for all people (Acts 17:24-26). Paul says that the reason God gives "times" and "places" to nations is "so that they would search for God and perhaps grope for him and find him—though indeed he is not far from each one of us" (Acts 17:27). The statement certainly implies that God is sovereign over the nations, but it also implies that God does not meticulously control people. God wants to be found and "now commands all people everywhere to repent" (Acts 17:30). Yet many people from every nation refuse to do this. Indeed, most of the philosophers Paul was preaching to rejected his message (Acts 17:32-34). Although God controls the general parameters of human freedom (chapters five and six), he does not meticulously control humans and thus does not always get his way when it comes to the decisions they make.

Romans 9:18. "[God] has mercy on whomever he chooses, and he hardens the heart of whomever he chooses."

---

[15]An alternative, nondeterministic reading of this passage is to suggest that God ordained people to eternal life on the basis of his foreknowledge of their faith. See Charles W. Carter, "The Acts of the Apostles," in Charles Carter, ed., *Wesleyan Bible Commentary,* 4:570.

This is one of the most frequently cited texts in support of compatibilism. If the text implied that people were believers or not as a result of whether God had mercy on them or hardened them, compatibilists would have a point. But if read in context, the passage rather suggests that God has mercy and hardens people *in response* to what they do. Thus Paul summarizes his argument in Romans 9 by noting that Gentiles receive the righteousness of God *because* they have faith, while unbelieving Jews were hardened *because* "they did not strive for [righteousness] . . . on the basis of faith, but as if it were based on works" (Rom 9:30-32). "They were broken off *because of their unbelief*" (Rom 11:20; cf. 10:3). *This* is why they as a nation were hardened (Rom 11:7, 25), while the Gentiles who seek God by faith have been "grafted in" (Rom 11:23).

To Jews who assumed that their standing before God was based on their works or their nationality, this *seems* arbitrary (Rom 9:14, 19). But Paul insists that God has the right to have mercy on people simply because of their faith, if he so chooses: "He has mercy on whomever he chooses, and he hardens the heart of whomever he chooses." (See the second objection in appendix one for a fuller discussion.)

Romans 11:36. "For from him [God] and through him and to him are all things."

Compatibilists sometimes cite this doxology as evidence that Paul believed that every single event in world history is from, through and for God. Since the verses leading up to this doxology address God's genuine frustration with Israel's unbelief (Rom 11:7, 20-23, cf. 9:30-32; 10:3), this seems like an extremely odd conclusion to draw. If the Israelites' unbelief came from God, why would God be frustrated over it? Paul's primary goal throughout Romans 9—11 is to show that even though both Jews and Gentiles can and do resist God's will, God's overall purposes for history will be achieved. It is in this sense that we should understand Paul's doxology. All things—including free will—come from God and, in one way or another, will eventually end up glorifying him.

Ephesians 1:11. "In Christ we have also obtained an inheritance, having been destined according to the purpose of him who accomplishes all things according to his counsel and will."

This text has frequently been used to support the view that all things happen in accordance with God's counsel and will. But this reads too much into the text. This passage says that all that God accomplishes is "according to his counsel and will," not that all that takes place is God's accomplishment in accordance with his counsel and will. Scripture is clear that much of what takes place in this world is not God's will. He detests sin and the gratuitous suffering it produces. But in all things God is at work to advance his sovereign purpose as much as possible. Whatever God accomplishes is consistent with his counsel and will, which Paul specifies as centering on acquiring a people for himself who "have obtained an inheritance . . . in Christ."

2 Thessalonians 2:11-12. "God sends them [those who disobey the truth] a powerful delusion, leading them to believe what is false, so that all who have not believed the truth but took pleasure in unrighteousness will be condemned."

This passage is sometimes cited as evidence that the delusions that unbelievers embrace are as much a part of God's sovereign will as believers' enlightenment. Yet, compatibilists insist, this occurs in such a way that unbelievers are responsible for their delusions, though believers have only God to thank for their enlightenment. There is a less paradoxical (contradictory?) interpretation of this passage available to us.

First, we should note that the passage says that God "sends . . . a powerful delusion . . . *so that* all who have not believed . . . will be condemned." The delusion that God sends does not explain why unbelievers do not believe. It only explains how God *responds* to their unbelief. He condemns it.

Second, it is not too difficult to surmise how God might send a powerful delusion in response to unbelief without directly attributing deception to God. We saw earlier (Judg 9:23; 2 Sam 24:1; 1 Chron 21:1) that sometimes the intentions of evil spirits fit God's intention to judge people. There is a certain poetic justice in letting deceiving spirits delude people who have already demonstrated that they want to believe lies. This conception may lie behind Paul's word to the Thessalonians.

2 Timothy 1:9. "[God] saved us and called us with a holy calling, not according to our works but according to his own purpose and grace. This grace was given to us in Christ Jesus before the ages began."

Compatibilists sometimes appeal to this verse to support the view that God determined who would (and thus who would not) be saved "before the ages began." This interpretation is possible but conflicts with Scripture's affirmation that God loves all and wants all to be saved. If an interpretation is possible that does not pose this contradiction, it is to be preferred. Fortunately, an alternative interpretation is available.

Jews thought about God electing people in corporate terms. God chose the nation of Israel to be his people and wanted them to be his vehicle for reaching the world. Thus, when Paul speaks of God saving and calling people "before the ages began," it is likely that he is thinking about the church, the "new Israel," as a corporate whole.[16] Before the ages God determined to shower grace on all who would believe in Jesus Christ. Paul can therefore say to all who believe that God "saved *us* and called *us* . . . before the ages began." What was decreed for the corporate whole becomes applied to each individual once that person by faith aligns himself or herself with the corporate whole.

Conclusion

Neither the list of verses we have addressed nor the content of this address has been exhaustive. However, I hope it has been adequate to demonstrate that the key texts compatibilists cite to support their position can be given a plausible and often better interpretation. The value of understanding these texts in a noncompatibilistic way is that it frees us from the paradoxes compatibilism poses. We need not accept the paradoxical conclusion that agents are responsible for what God predestined them to do. We need not affirm that God genuinely hates the sin he himself ordained to take place. Finally, we need not believe that an all-holy God who does not willingly afflict or damn anyone nevertheless ordained all suffering, including the endless suffering of multitudes of humans and angels.

Add to this all the passages teaching that God genuinely battles against Satan, demons and people with evil intentions, and you have, I believe, a solid case for accepting something like the trinitarian warfare theodicy.

---

[16]On the corporate view of election, see William W. Klein, *The New Chosen People: A Corporate View of Election* (Grand Rapids, Mich.: Zondervan, 1990).

Glossary of Terms and Concepts and Their Significance to the Trinitarian Warfare Theodicy

This glossary is designed to serve two purposes. First, it provides an introduction to technical terms and concepts for readers unfamiliar with them. Some of these terms are unique to the trinitarian warfare worldview and thus will be unfamiliar to all readers. Second, even for readers already familiar with a given term or concept, the glossary provides a brief review of how the term or concept functions in the trinitarian warfare theodicy. Where appropriate, the chapter in which the term or concept is most relevant is cited after the entry.

actual occasions. The ultimate units of becoming, according to Process thought. Each actual occasion is constituted as a creative synthesis of previous actual occasions. All things, including God, are made up of actual occasions. Their stability over time is the abstract quality shared by the myriad of actual occasions that constitute them. This conviction leads Process theologians to deny that God can exist apart from the world or ever exercise unilateral control over any aspect of the world (chap. nine).

already-not yet tension. The tension between those aspects of Satan's defeat and the coming of God's kingdom that are already accomplished and those aspects that remain to be achieved in the future (also sometimes labeled "realized eschatology"). For example, the New Testament at times depicts Satan as having already been defeated (Col 2:14-15), at other times as yet having control over the earth (1 Jn 5:19). It at times depicts the kingdom of God as having already arrived on earth (Mt 10:7), at other times as yet needing to be brought about (Mt 6:10). The trinitarian warfare theodicy stresses that although Satan was in principle defeated on Calvary, the influence of this fatally wounded foe, together with his minions, yet lies behind much of the evil in the world.

angelic free fall. The biblical teaching that Lucifer and other angels rebelled against God by their own free will. In the view of the trinitarian warfare theodicy, this fall and ongoing rebellion is crucial to making sense of the scope and intensity of evil in the world (chap. two).

annihilationism. The doctrine that eternal punishment (hell) is eternal in *consequence,* not in *duration* (as the tradition has generally taught). In this view the wicked are eternally annihilated, not tormented. The view has strong scriptural support, but for many is not altogether compelling. I tentatively propose a model that affirms the central aspects of both the annihilationist and the traditionalist views of hell, though I do not hold that the trinitarian warfare theodicy is inextricably tied to this solution (chaps. eleven, twelve).

anthropomorphism. A depiction of God in human terms. The Bible is full of anthropomorphic depictions of God, but, I argue, language about God changing his mind, speaking of the future in a subjunctive mode, or being surprised or disappointed are not among them. These expressions are just as literal as expressions of God being loving, faithful or holy. The point is important to the trinitarian warfare theodicy in that it is founded on a dynamic understanding of God who interacts with his creation on a moment-by-moment basis (chap. three).

blueprint worldview/model of divine providence. The view of the world rooted in the assumption that behind every specific event there is a specific divine reason as to why it was ordained or at least allowed to take place. This view contrasts with the trinitarian warfare worldview, which argues that although there is a *general* reason as to why God made free agents (love), the ultimate reason for why they engage in the *particular acts* they engage in is generally found in them, not God. Because freedom must be to some extent irrevocable, God cannot always prevent events he would like to prevent. Hence, in the trinitarian warfare worldview there is no justification for wondering about a specific reason as to why God ordained or allowed a given evil event to take place (introduction; chap. one).

chance. Either an aspect of an occurrence that was spontaneously brought about—it was not necessitated by antecedent causes (e.g., precisely how a quantum particle behaves)—or, more commonly, the intersection of two or more lines of causation initiated by two or more free agents (or somewhat spontaneous events) producing consequences that were not specifically intended by any one of them. The blueprint worldview rules out seeing chance as an ontological category. In this worldview, "chance" can only refer to our ignorance of causes or reasons. The trinitarian warfare theodicy, however, accepts that an element of spontaneity and unplanned intersection of causal chains permeates all of contingent reality. There is an element of chance in all evil occurrences, which in part explains why the explanation for why any evil event occurred must remain mostly unknowable (chap. seven; appendix four).

chaos theory. A broad theory based on the discovery that miniscule differences in the "initial conditions" (e.g., of an experimental situation) often produce major differences in long-range outcomes. The flap of a butterfly wing in one part of the globe can constitute the crucial variable that produces a hurricane in another part of the globe. At the same time, there are far too many variables for us ever to know perfectly the initial conditions. Consequently, there is an element of unpredictability attending to every future state of affairs, however broadly or narrowly defined.

This theory provides an important analogical aspect for the understanding of the mystery of evil within the trinitarian warfare theodicy. The mystery of why any given evil occurred is not to be exclusively (if at all) located in the will of God but in the incomprehensible complexity of the visible and invisible worlds. There are more variables (some of which are relatively unpredictable) that condition creation than we could possibly fathom, let alone account for. The issue, for example, of why a particular little girl was abducted by a particular person at a particular place and time is in principle unanswerable for the same reason that the question of why there is, for example, just this particular interval of time between two particular cars on a freeway at a particular moment is unanswerable. It is not that God's will is so mysterious, for God's will and character is clearly revealed in the person of Jesus Christ. It is rather that the creation is so complex. From a warfare theodicy perspective, this is the central point of the book of Job (chaps. five, six, seven).

chronocentrism. The view that the perspective of our time (*chronos*) is superior to all previous times. This has been a plague of modernity. It believes itself to be "enlightened" and thus judges differing cultural perspectives as "primitive" or "superstitious." It is, I argue, a form of ethnocentrism (our ethnic perspective is the standard by which all others are to be judged). While acknowledging the technological advantages of the Western worldview, I argue that in some respects the worldviews of primordial cultures—and the first-century culture of the New Testament—are superior to the narrow perspective of modernity. Most importantly, their worldview allows them to believe in and experience the reality of spirits and of miracles, whereas the modern, naturalistic, Western worldview does not. Thankfully, this myopic, naturalistic perspective is gradually being discarded as we move into postmodernity (chap. seven).

classical philosophical tradition/theism/view. The tradition that originated in ancient Greek philosophy which holds that divine perfection entails atemporality (God is above time), pure actuality (God is devoid of potentiality), absolute immutability (God is above any change) and exhaustive impassability (God is above suffering or emotions). This philosophical view has exercised a strong influence on the theological thinking of the Christian West since the time of Augustine (though aspects of it are found earlier). I distinguish the classical *philosophical* tradition from the classical tradition as such, for the latter encompasses not only the theological thinking of the West but also the more popular theological formulations of the West (in which God was expressed as involved in time, potentiality, change and emotions). Many aspects of the classical tradition, I argue, are inconsistent with the classical philosophical tradition, though classical theologians often held the two views side by side. The trinitarian warfare theodicy logically precludes the classical philosophical view of God.

compatibilism. The view that freedom is compatible with determinism. For compatibilists, freedom is defined as the ability to do what you want, though what you want is determined by factors outside of you. Theological compatibilists hold that ultimately it is God who determines what individuals want. The trinitarian warfare theodicy holds that such a view of freedom does not render intelligible the fact that free agents are morally responsible. It thus logically undermines the free-will defense. God can be absolved of responsibility for evil in the world only if free agents (human and angelic) are the ultimate cause and explanation of their own free behavior. This presupposes that they are self-determining. See "self-determining freedom" and "incompatibilistic freedom" below (chap. two).

corruptio optimi pessima. A medieval expression meaning "the corruption of the best is the worst." The principle expresses TWT4: *moral responsibility is proportionate to the power to influence.* The more potential someone has for good, the more potential that one has for evil. The principle explains why God must allow agents to have a potential for evil that parallels their potential for good. It thereby explains why God would create a being such as Satan, who unfortunately now exercises such a pervasive, destructive influence throughout creation (chap. five).

covenant of noncoercion. A metaphorical covenant God makes with himself not to microcontrol a free agent he has created. The extent to which God binds himself not to coerce another agent is the extent to which that agent is truly free in a self-determining sense. It defines an agent's quality of freedom (see "quality of freedom" below) at a given moment in time. This concept forms a central aspect of the fifth structural thesis of the trinitarian warfare theodicy: *power to influence is irrevocable.* It explicates why God must tolerate the ongoing destructive existence of Satan, demons and reprobate people. This covenant, however, is not absolute or unconditional. To the contrary, it is conditioned by a number of contingent variables (chap. six).

das Nichtige. Literally, "the nothingness." Karl Barth employed this concept to account for evil in creation. The realm of *das Nichtige* is constituted by all the possibilities that God negated when he decided to create this particular world. These negated possibilities, Barth argues, have a kind of existence that "menaces" creation. I argue that the concept is implausible as found in Barth, for negated possibilities have no power and can do nothing. The trinitarian warfare theodicy amends this concept, however, by postulating free agents who can choose against God's will and thus can invest negated possibilities (*das Nichtige*) with being. When God ultimately wins his war with evil and becomes "all in all" (1 Cor 15:28; cf. Eph 1:10, 22; Col 1:22), the choices of evil beings against him will be exposed as "the nothing" that they are. Hence, hell is eternally chosen nothingness (chaps. nine, twelve).

deism, deistic. A view of God in which he creates the world but then remains (either by choice or by metaphysical necessity) uninvolved in it. Any view of God holding that God does not or cannot miraculously intervene in the world is in that respect "deistic." Though some might argue that the trinitarian warfare theodicy is deistic, since it holds that there is something God cannot do in his relationship with free agents (exhaustively control their use of freedom), in truth the trinitarian warfare theodicy is as opposed to a deistic view of God as any view could be. God is *intimately involved* in creatures' lives for the same reason he refuses to be *exhaustively coercive* in creatures' lives: he desires a *personal relationship* with them. As with all personal relationships, this involves granting the "other" room to exist while also embracing the "other" in a mutually influential (that is, noncoercive) relationship (chap. six).

dualism. The belief that there are two ultimate powers running the world, one good and one evil. Metaphysical dualism (see "metaphysical dualism" below) holds that this sharing of power is built into the nature of things. It could not be otherwise. Scripture clearly rules out such a view, for it consistently depicts God as the single Creator of all that is. What Scripture does not rule out, however, is viewing God *for a period of time* as sharing power with others. This constitutes a *provisional* dualism, which is what the trinitarian warfare theodicy espouses. The omnipotent Creator shares power, not only with Satan but with all free agents. There is no metaphysical necessity to this sharing, except insofar as such sharing was necessary given the purpose for which God created the world (inviting agents to participate in the eternal love that he is). What is more, God did not share with Satan or any other created being a power equal to his own or even more power than he could generally control. Hence, though God must genuinely war against foes in this present age, he is assured of ultimate victory (chaps. one, four, nine).

epistemic distance. A concept employed by John Hick to explain why nature does not unambiguously reveal the Creator's wisdom and character. If our relationship with God is to have a moral quality to it, nature must have an element of ambiguity to it. If God were perfectly obvious, Hick argues, our decision to follow him would for all intents and purposes be coerced. I argue that Hick's point is essentially correct but that the amount and intensity of suffering at the hands of nature far outruns what this principle is capable of explaining. Nature is not only ambiguously good; sometimes it is unambiguously evil. To adequately account for this dimension of "natural" evil, the trinitarian warfare theodicy argues, we must include in our explanation an appeal to Satan and other fallen powers who use their God-given authority over aspects of nature to a destructive end (chap. eight).

eschaton/eschatology. The end times and, by extension, the study of end times. In the trinitarian warfare theodicy, this is the time when Satan and all who freely align themselves with him will be finally defeated. While God's will is not consistently carried out in world history, for this depends somewhat on the free cooperation of free agents, it will be carried out in the eschaton. All who have aligned themselves with God's will shall eternally exist in God's triune presence. All who refuse to do so will be brought to nothing, for in the end there will be no alternative reality to the reality that God wills. See "*das Nichtige*" above (chaps. six, twelve).

exhaustively definite foreknowledge. The classical understanding of foreknowledge that affirms that God eternally knows the future as exhaustively definite. The entire future is eternally and meticulously defined as definitely one way, and therefore as definitely not any other way. In other words, there are no indefinite possibilities—no maybes—for God. This is problematic from a biblical perspective, for the Bible often explicitly depicts God as thinking and speaking of the future in terms of what may or may not happen (e.g., Ex 4:7-9; 13:17; Jer 26:2-4; Ezek 12:3). It also depicts God as experiencing regret over the outcome of his decisions (e.g., Gen 6:6; 1 Sam 15:12, 35) as well as experiencing surprise and disappointment about how events transpire (e.g., Is 5:1-5; Jer 3:6-7, 19-20). Similarly, the Bible depicts

God as testing people "to know" what they shall do (e.g., Gen 22:12; Ex 16:4), as trying to accomplish things that don't come to pass (e.g., Ezek 22:29-31) and as frequently changing his mind (e.g., Jer 18:7-11; 26:2-3, 13, 19; Jon 3:10). These facts are difficult to reconcile with the belief that God possesses eternal exhaustively definite knowledge of all that shall come to pass. The view is also problematic on theological and philosophical grounds.

Open theism (see *open theism* below) has no trouble accounting for this biblical data, for while it affirms that God has exhaustive knowledge of the future, it denies that God has exhaustively *definite* knowledge of the future—not because God lacks any knowledge but because the future does not exist as an exhaustively definite reality for God to know. In the open view, the future is in part composed of indefinite possibilities, and thus God perfectly knows it partly as a realm of indefinite possibilities. Because God is infinitely intelligent, he can attend to and prepare for each of these possibilities *as though* they were the only possibility that could come to pass. But because they are only possibilities, not definite realities, it is not certain that they shall come to pass. This view not only squares with the biblical data, it allows us to ascribe to God genuine risk, for it means that things may not transpire as God would want them to.

future probation. The view that individuals who did not have the opportunity to resolve their wills either for or against God's love during this probationary epoch (see "probationary period/probational epoch" below) will somehow be given the opportunity to do so in a post-mortem state, prior to the full actualization of the kingdom of God. I argue that this is the most logical position for anyone who espouses the free-will defense to hold (appendix three).

gehenna. The most common Greek word for *hell* in the New Testament. It literally referred to the dump outside of Jerusalem, in the valley of Hinnom, which had previously been associated with pagan rituals and sacrifices. The implication is that those who go to hell are, as C. S. Lewis put it, "the refuse of humanity." They are the tragic remains of what is left over when one refuses the Author of life to the bitter end. I argue that there may be a way of integrating Scripture's teaching that hell is eternal with its teaching that the wicked are ultimately destroyed (chap. twelve).

givens (of any particular situation). A concept (adopted from Francis Tupper, *A Scandalous Providence*) that refers to the complex constellation of contingent variables that collectively constitute a particular situation. The metaphysical principles that condition God's interaction with free agents (chaps. six, seven), together with all the particular decisions and chance occurrences that influenced history to arrive at just this situation, constitute the "givens" of a particular situation. The givens constitute that which God is up against in responding to a situation. God always seeks to do as much good and prevent as much evil as possible, given the situation he must work with. The trinitarian warfare theodicy contrasts with the classical philosophical view of God (see "classical philosophical tradition" above) in that in this latter perspective the givens can never be a serious consideration in terms of what God can or cannot do. In the classical philosophical view omnipotence is taken to imply that God always can intervene to prevent situations, if he chooses. Hence the only decisive variable to consider in understanding any particular situation is God's will. This conviction is what grounds the blueprint worldview, which holds that there is a specific divine reason behind every specific event (see "blueprint worldview" above). The trinitarian warfare theodicy holds that God *could have* operated like this if he had chosen to, that is, if he had chosen to create *a different kind of world,* one devoid of free agents and thus one in which he would not have to take into consideration the givens of every situation. But the Creator deemed the benefit of bringing about this kind of world in which love was possible, and thus in which free agents exist, worth the risk that he might have to tolerate situations he does not approve of.

incompatibilistic freedom. The view that creaturely freedom is incompatible with any form of determinism. The ultimate cause and explanation for a free agent's behavior goes back to the agent, no further. This is also called "self-determining freedom." The trinitarian warfare theodicy presupposes an incompatibilistic view of freedom. See "compatibilism" above (chap. two).

kenotic process. Based on the meaning of *kenotic* ("emptying"), a concept that refers to the view of George Ellis and Nancey Murphy that the apparent violence of the animal kingdom reflects the kenotic nature of the Creator, who "emptied himself" when he became a human (Phil 2:5-11). Nature is a kenotic process in that it moves forward by animals sacrificing themselves for others. I argue that nature reflects the opposite. Animals do not offer themselves up for anything; they have their lives violently ripped from them by other animals, people or "natural" processes. This aspect of nature, I suggest, does not reflect the loving design of the Creator but the predatorial design of the anticreator (1 Pet 5:8). Had nature not come under the bondage of Satan, the animal kingdom may have been vegetarian (chap. eight).

mechanistic worldview. The view of the world that rose out of the scientific revolution which assumes that causation governs all things and every particular effect is necessitated by a particular cause. The world is thus conceived of as a mechanism. Among other things, this way of thinking leads to the conclusion that if any particular future event is determined, all the conditions that lead to that event must be determined. Since the Bible clearly depicts some events as predetermined or foreknown (e.g., the crucifixion of Christ, Acts 2:23; 4:28), many who are influenced by this worldview conclude that all people and conditions that happen to bring about these events must be predetermined or foreknown. The assumption that every particular effect is necessitated by a particular cause has been increasingly abandoned in many fields of science, being replaced by a more dynamic understanding of causation in which causes govern more than one possible effect. Throughout the twentieth century we discovered that the stability of the world cannot be exhaustively described in linear terms; we must also employ nonlinear equations to describe it. Relatedly, we discovered that the stability of the world we experience is statistical, not mechanistic. Hence, for example, the solidity of a cup in our hands is ensured by the laws of nature even though the behavior of each of the quantum particles that constitute the cup is somewhat unpredictable. When these insights are combined with the understanding of God as infinitely wise and resourceful, there is no difficulty in grasping how God can predestine and foreknow certain events without predestining and foreknowing the exact means (the behavior of free agents) to their execution (chaps. four, five and six).

metaphysical dualism. Any view that understands the conflict between good and evil to be a matter of metaphysical necessity (i.e., it could not be otherwise). The Christian tradition has rightly always rejected this philosophy as undermining the omnipotence of the Creator. At least since Augustine, the classical philosophical tradition by logical implication tended towards metaphysical monism: the view that only the good is ultimately real and thus the conflict between good and evil is only apparent. The trinitarian warfare theodicy mediates between metaphysical dualism and metaphysical monism by maintaining that the conflict between good and evil is real, but not metaphysically necessary and thus not eternal. It holds that the *possibility* of evil is metaphysically necessary *if* God chooses to create free agents. But there is no necessity to God creating such beings and no necessity to their choosing evil after they are created. The rebellion against God, headed up by Satan, that presently plagues God's creation constitutes a temporary dualism that did not in any sense need to happen (chap. six).

middle knowledge. The view that between ("in the middle of") God's knowledge of all logical possibilities and God's knowledge of what shall come to pass is God's knowledge of all that *would* come to pass in any other world God might create. On the basis of God's middle knowledge of what free creatures would do in any given situation, God creates the world that best suits his sovereign purposes. The main advantage of this view (often called Molinism) is that it grants God maximal control wile avoiding all the difficulties that attend to Calvinism, in which God controls the world by predestining all that comes to pass.

The trinitarian warfare theodicy criticizes the classical Molinist position for limiting the scope of God's middle knowledge to *would*-counterfactuals. We must also consider *might*-counterfactuals. Propositions expressing *might*-counterfactuals have an eternal truth value and thus must be known by God. If we allow that God knows that some might-counterfactuals as well as would-counterfactuals are true, we arrive at a position that can account for the openness motif in Scripture (e.g., God changing his mind, thinking and speaking of the future in terms of what might happen) and which avoids the philosophical problems of classical Molinism (see chap. four and *neo-Molinism* below).

"natural" evil. Usually defined as evil that cannot be attributed to human wills. It is evil that occurs in nature, such as hurricanes, earthquakes, mudslides, diseases, and the like. This category of evil is difficult to explain in most theodicies because "natural" evils seem to occur as a result of nature operating the way God created it to operate. Following the early church, the trinitarian warfare theodicy explains "natural" evil by denying that nature is now operating the way God designed it to operate. There is nothing *natural* about "natural" evil. Hence I put quotation marks around the word "natural" whenever referring to this kind of evil. In my view, "natural" evil is as much the result of the misuse of free will as is evil that comes from human agency. The difference is that most "natural" evil comes from the agency of nonhuman wills, that is, fallen angels. The trinitarian warfare theodicy holds that angels, like humans, can use the physical environment for the better or for worse. It can become a means of blessing others or harming others. This is part of the moral responsibility built into the possibility of love (TWT3-4). "Natural" evil is the result of evil spirits choosing to engage in the latter. This does not mean that there is a specific willing agent behind every specific "natural" evil. But it does mean that nature as it now is has been subjected to corrupting influences by spiritual agents (chaps. eight, nine, ten).

neo-Molinism. The open view of the future. Classical Molinism, named after Jacob Molina in the sixteenth century, affirms that God has significant control over the world even though agents possess libertarian freedom because God knows what agents would do in every conceivable situation (see *middle knowledge* above). The open view substantially agrees with this position but asserts, in contrast, that God also knows what agents might do in certain situations. In otherwords, classical Molinism errs in limiting God's counterfactual knowledge to *would*-counterfactuals instead of including *might*-counterfactuals. In the neo-Molinist view God knows what agents *might* do insofar as agents possess libertarian freedom. And God knows what agents *would* do insofar as they have received from God and through circumstances or acquired for themselves determinate characters. God knows both categories of counterfactuals as they pertain to every possible subject in every possible world throughout eternity. As in classical Molinism, God creates the world (or better, the set of possible worlds) that best suits his sovereign purposes.

Allowing that God knows might-counterfactuals as well as would-counterfactuals enables neo-Molinism to avoid the biblical and philosophical problems that attend to classical Molinism while substantially retaining the theological advantages of classical Molinism (see chap. four).

neutral medium of relationality. The view (espoused by C. S. Lewis and others) that morally responsible free agents can only interact with each other if there is an objective environment between them that is relatively neutral to their desires. It stands over and against them. They must be able to influence it (as when we communicate with our bodies, using air waves, and so on) but not exhaustively control it. Some of the unpleasant aspects of nature are due to this "over-and-against" quality it must have for us to relate to each other through it. I argue, however, that this observation does not account for all "natural" evil. The more horrific aspects of "natural" evil can only be adequately accounted for when we accept that humans are not the only agents who can influence the neutral medium of relationality for better or for worse. If we grant that Satan and other fallen powers exist and can influence nature, "natural" evil may be seen as a category of "moral" evil; thus there is no longer any major difficulty in theoretically accounting for it (chaps. nine, ten).

Newtonian worldview. The worldview that arose largely out of Newton's influence in the scientific revolution of the seventeenth century. The world was seen in deterministic, thoroughly linear terms of natural cause and effect (see *mechanistic worldview* above). Largely as a result of Einstein's relativity theory, quantum theory and, most recently, chaos theory, this view has been replaced in this century by a more nonlinear, dynamistic, indeterministic understanding of reality. Because of its dynamic understanding of God and of free agents, the trinitarian warfare worldview is much more compatible with this understanding of reality than with the Newtonian understanding (chap. three).

ontological possibilities. The view that future possibilities are ultimately real, even to God. Possibilities do not just *appear* real to finite beings because of our limited cognitive abilities. In the trinitarian warfare theodicy as I have developed it in this work, possibilities are ontologically real and thus God knows them as real. Hence God knows the future partly as a realm of "maybes." Consequently, when Scripture depicts God as speaking or thinking in terms of what *might* happen, as it often does, it should be understood literally, not anthropomorphically (see "anthropomorphism" above). I argue that this view of possibilities as real is required if the concept of God as a risk-taker is to be coherent. See "open view of God" below (chap. three).

open view of God/the future. The view that the future in part consists of possibilities and is known by the omniscient God as such. It contrasts with the traditional EDF doctrine (see *exhaustively definite foreknowledge* above). The trinitarian warfare theodicy defended in this work argues that the open view of the future is founded on a more balanced reading of Scripture than the classical philosophical view. It does not have to dismiss as "anthropomorphic" the many passages in which God changes his mind, speaks about the future in terms of what *might* happen, tests people "to know" what is in their heart to do or experience regret, surprise or disappointment. It is also the view that is logically most consistent with the view that agents possess self-determining freedom and thus that God takes a genuine risk in creating such agents (chaps. three, four; appendix two).

possible world. A set of logical possibilities that collectively describe the way a conceivable world (a conceivable creation throughout all time) could be. Every logically possible way the world could be different from the way it actually is, including the totality of the past, constitutes a possible world. There is, for example, a possible world that is identical to this one in all respects except that in that possible world I did not shave this morning, where as in the actual world I did. Every possible choice every agent makes constitutes a different possible world.

The concept of possible worlds is relevant to the trinitarian warfare theodicy in that classical Molinism (see *middle knowledge* above) includes in each possible world counterfactuals of creaturely freedom. God knows how each free agent would choose in every possible world. God chooses which possible world to actualize on the basis of this knowledge. The open view of the future in principle agrees with this (see *neo-*

Molinism above) but adds that counterfactuals of creaturely freedom consist not only in what free agents *would* do but what they *might* (or might not) do. There are would-counterfactuals and might-counterfactuals, and possible worlds that include free agents must contain both. The behavior of free agents in possible worlds is described by might-counterfactuals insofar as they possess libertarian freedom and by would-counterfactuals insofar as their behavior is rendered determinate either by the character God gives them *(habitus infuses)* or by the character they have acquired on their own by the use of their libertarian freedom *(habitus acquirus)*.

In eternally knowing each and every possible world, God knows all of this. As in classical Molinism, the open view holds that God chooses which world to actualize based on his "middle knowledge." But since the possible world that God wants to actualize contains creatures possessing libertarian freedom, the actualization must in part depend on the choices of free agents. In other words, God actualizes the world insofar as he delimits a range of possible worlds for free agents to choose between.

prehend/prehension. The term used in Process thought to explain how present actual occasions experience other (now past) actual occasions. The key analogy to understanding prehension is memory. In memory we incorporate the past in a new context. According to Process thought, every actual occasion "remembers" ("prehends") the past in a novel fashion, and this novelty constitutes an addition to the total content of reality. This also expresses how God relates to the world. He experiences every actual occasion in the world and synthesizes it with his total experience of the world (including his experience of the infinite past). This is why Process theology denies that God can ever exist apart from the world (chap. nine).

probationary period/ probational epoch. The period of time a free agent must go through in order to choose to love or not to love, for love cannot be coerced. I argue that if love was God's aim in creation, there had to, by metaphysical necessity, be a probationary period, for love must be chosen. For humans, this present age is our probationary period. Our individual probationary periods come to an end as our free choices become crystallized in the form of an irreversible character. Ultimately, one is eternalized either as one who is open to God's love or as one who is closed off to it. The probationary period, and the self-determining freedom that accompanies it, comes to an end. This is expressed by TWT6: *the potential to influence is finite* (chap. six).

Process thought. A twentieth-century school of thought, rooted largely in the philosophy of Alfred North Whitehead, that understands God and the cosmos to form two eternal, interdependent realities that are together perpetually in the process of becoming. God is thus *necessarily* limited by the world. The trinitarian warfare theodicy accepts the Process view that God's experience is sequential and that God can experience new things. But it rejects any idea that God is limited by anything outside of himself. In the trinitarian warfare view, God's restrictions are self-imposed. God could have refrained from creating free agents. Once he decides to create a cosmos inhabited by free agents, however, he is metaphysically constrained in certain ways, spelled out by the six theses of the trinitarian warfare theodicy (chap. nine).

quality of freedom. The parameters of self-determination that an agent possesses at a given moment in time. This constitutes the scope of the irrevocable covenant of noncoercion (see "covenant of noncoercion" above) that God makes toward them. In the trinitarian warfare theodicy, an agent's quality of freedom defines one's essential potentiality for good or for evil (TWT4) and thus the range of the agent's moral responsibility. The quality of an individual's freedom is impossible for us to know in detail, for it is enveloped by innumerable contingent variables that condition it (God's will, genes, environment, other agents' decisions, an agent's own previous decisions, and so on). According to hints in Scripture and the explicit teaching of the early church, the human and angelic society of free agents is structured hierarchically with the beings with the greatest quality of freedom having responsibility for beings who possess a lesser quality of freedom (chap. six).

quantum mechanics/physics/theory. The theory and experimental science surrounding the behavior of quantum particles. This is of interest to the trinitarian warfare theodicy in that the behavior of quantum particles is indeterministic. It cannot be precisely predicted. The regularity of the phenomenological world, composed as it is of such indeterministic particles, is a statistical regularity. Among other things, this demonstrates that causation is not rigorously deterministic and that there is no incoherence in the notion that God can confidently govern the world while allowing for an element of openness (chaps. two, four, five, six).

self-determining freedom. The ability of an agent to determine his or her own actions. The agent renders indefinite possibilities ("maybe this" and "maybe that") into definite realities ("certainly this" or "certainly that"). Antecedent and external factors *influence* the agent but cannot *determine* the agent insofar as the agent is self-determining. This view of freedom contrasts with "compatibilist" freedom, which sees human (and angelic) freedom as compatible with determinism. This view is thus sometimes called "incompatibilistic freedom." The trinitarian warfare theodicy is predicated on the conviction that agents possess self-determining freedom (chap. two).

sola gratia. A Latin phrase meaning "by grace alone." The Protestant Reformation emphasized that salvation was solely by God's grace. Some Reformed theologians take this to mean that free will can have no part in a person's salvation. The implication is that God chooses who will (and thus who will not) be saved. This implication, I argue, is at odds with the scriptural teaching that God loves all whom he has created and thus desires all to be saved (1 Tim 2:4; 2 Pet 3:9). I also maintain that the doctrine of salvation by grace alone is not incompatible with the teaching that humans must choose to accept it (chap. two).

soul-making theodicy. A theodicy that arguably goes back to Irenaeus in the second century and has in recent times been popularized by John Hick. In contrast to the free-will defense and other classical philosophical explanations for evil, this theodicy argues that evil and suffering are allowed in creation as a means of developing our moral character (i.e., developing our souls). The trinitarian warfare theodicy agrees that the *possibility* of evil and suffering was necessary if creatures were to have the capacity of making morally responsible decisions and of developing moral characters, but it denies that evil and suffering were ever a necessary part of creation (chap. nine).

superposition. The state of a quantum particle prior to its being measured. The most fundamental thing we can say about it in this premeasured state is that it is possibly this way or possibly that way. It is nothing over and above a realm of possibilities. The act of measurement "forces" the particle to resolve itself and then it becomes a definite particle, capable of being located at a particle time and place. According to the trinitarian warfare theodicy, the future is in part something like a superposition until agents resolve it into a definite thing, at which time it becomes the present, then the past. In other words, the final thing to be said about aspects of the future, even from God's perspective, is that it is possibly this way and possibly that way. God decides aspects of it as he sees fit; other aspects of the future become settled as necessary consequences of the present. But in other ways the future stays in a state of superposition (chap. four).

theodicy. A term coined by Leibniz to describe a means of giving a rational justification for God in the face of evil in the world. Some contemporary philosophers (e.g., Alvin Plantinga) distinguish between a "theodicy," which tries to give divine reasons for all particular evils in the world, and a "defense," which simply attempts to argue that evil in the world is not logically incompatible with a belief in God. As the label indicates, the trinitarian warfare theodicy is attempting to give more than a defense, for I want to posit a plausible (not just logically possible) account of why a world created by an all-good and all-powerful God contains evil. In this sense it is a theodicy and not a defense. But the trinitarian warfare theodicy differs from many other theodicies in that it does not hold that there is a *specific* divine reason for each *specific* evil in the world. To the contrary, at the heart of the trinitarian warfare theodicy is the denial that particular evils have particular divine reasons behind them. The trinitarian warfare theodicy justifies God in the face of evil by maintaining that, generally speaking, the ultimate cause of any particular evil is the free agent, human or angelic, who produced it. The reason why God's creation has evil, therefore, is that God created free agents who (by metaphysical necessity) had the capacity to make it so. God is justified in creating such a world if the aim of creation was worth the risk of evil.

transcendental postulate. The postulation of a reality that to some extent transcends empirical analysis in order to render certain phenomena intelligible. Peirce called this sort of reasoning "abduction" (in contrast to induction or deduction modes of reasoning). I argue that in order to render intelligible our experience of morally responsible freedom, and in order to render intelligible the fact that the world is filled with evil though it is created and governed by an all-good God, we must postulate an agent who is the ultimate cause and explanation of that agent's own behavior. The postulation of such agency is transcendental because the concept of agency cannot be exhaustively reduced to or understood within strictly empirical categories (chap. two).

trinitarian warfare theodicy. The understanding of evil that follows from a trinitarian warfare worldview. It argues that the scope and intensity of suffering and evil we experience in this world are only adequately accounted for when viewed against the backdrop of a cosmic war between God and Satan. Much evil in the world is the result of the earth being caught up in the crossfire of this age-long (but not eternal) cosmic battle. It is in most cases futile, therefore, to search for a specific divine reason for some episodes of suffering, though God will always work with his people to bring good *out of* evil, often with such effectiveness that it may *seem* that the evil was planned all along. The reason why God created a world in which a cosmic war could break out is articulated in the six theses that structure the trinitarian warfare theodicy.

trinitarian warfare worldview. A worldview that combines belief in the Trinity with a recognition of the war-torn nature of this world. A *warfare* worldview is a view of the world that understands that there are good and bad spirits significantly involved in the affairs of this world. Most cultures throughout history have embraced some version of the warfare worldview. The *trinitarian* warfare worldview is unique, however, in that it also affirms the existence of a supreme triune Creator from whom all other gods, and all other things, came. Unlike other warfare worldviews, this view unequivocally affirms that all power flows from the Creator and that the Creator is assured of ultimately defeating all opposing forces. The trinitarian warfare theodicy is the explanation of evil that flows from the trinitarian warfare worldview.

warfare worldview. See "trinitarian warfare worldview" above.

Bibliography

Abegg, M. G., Jr. "Paul, Works of the Law, and the MMT." *BARev* 20.6 (1994): 52-55, 82.

Adams, M. McCord. "Is the Existence of God a 'Hard' Fact?" In *God, Foreknowledge, and Freedom*. Edited by John M. Fisher, pp. 74-85. Stanford, Calif.: Stanford University Press, 1989.

Adler, Mortimer. *The Idea of Freedom.* New York: Doubleday, 1961.

Albritton, R. "Present Truth and Future Contingency." *Philosophical Review* 66 (1957): 1-28.

Alston, William P. "Divine Actions, Human Freedom, and the Laws of Nature." In *Quantum Cosmology and the Laws of Nature: Scientific Perspectives on Divine Action.* Edited by Robert J. Russell, Nancey Murphy and C. J. Isham. Vatican City: Vatican Observatory Publications, 1993.

Anderson, Susan. "Plantinga and the Free Will Defense." *Pacific Philosophical Quarterly* 62 (1981): 5-6nn.

Andres, F. "Die Engel- und Dämonenlehre des Klemens von Alexandrien." *RQ* 34 (1926): 13-37, 129-40, 307-29.

Andrew, Brother, and Susan DeVore Williams. *And God Changed His Mind Because His People Prayed.* Repr., London: Marshall Pickering, 1991.

Anscombe, Elizabeth. "Causality and Determination." In *Metaphysics and the Philosophy of Mind: Collected Philosophical Papers.* Vol. 2. Minneapolis: University of Minnesota Press, 1981.

Aristotle. *The Categories of Interpretation.* Translated by H. P. Cook. LCL. Cambridge, Mass.: Harvard University Press, 1962.

———. *Politics.* In *The Basic Works of Aristotle.* Edited by Richard McKeon. New York: Random House, 1941.

Arnold, Clinton E. *Powers of Darkness: Principalities and Powers in Paul's Letters.* Downers Grove, Ill.: InterVarsity Press, 1992.

Augustine. *Confessions.* Translated by Henry Chadwick. Oxford: Oxford University Press, 1991.

———. *The Catholic and Manichean Ways of Life.* Translated by D. and I. Gallagher. Washington, D.C.: Catholic University of America Press, 1966.

Aulén, Gustaf. *Christus Victor: A Historical Study of the Three Main Types of the Idea of Atonement.* Translated by A. G. Hebert. New York: Macmillan, 1969.

Ayer, Alfred J. "Freedom and Necessity." In *Philosophical Essays.* London: Macmillan, 1954.

Baelz, Peter. *Does God Answer Prayer?* London: Darton, Longman & Todd, 1982.

———. *Prayer and Providence: A Background Study.* New York: Seabury, 1968.

Baillie, Donald M. *God Was in Christ: An Essay on Incarnation.* New York: Charles Scribner's Sons, 1948.

Baker, J. "Omniscience and Divine Synchronization." *Process Studies* 2 (1972): 201-8.

Barrett, W. "Determinism and Novelty." In *Determinism and Freedom in the Age of Modern Science.* Edited by Susan Hook. New York: Collier-Macmillan, 1958.

Bartholomew, David J. *God of Chance.* London: SCM Press, 1984.

Basinger, David. *The Case for Freewill Theism: A Philosophical Assessment.* Downers Grove, Ill.: InterVarsity Press, 1996.

———. "Divine Omnipotence: Plantinga and Griffin." *Process Studies* 11 (1981): 9 n. 15.

————. *Divine Power in Process Theism: A Philosophical Critique.* Albany, N.Y.: SUNY Press, 1988.

————. "Practical Implications." In *The Openness of God: A Biblical Challenge to the Traditional Understanding of God.* Edited by Clark Pinnock. Downers Grove, Ill.: InterVarsity Press, 1994.

Beachy, Alvin J. *The Concept of Grace in the Radical Reformation.* Nieuwkoop, Netherlands: De Graaf, 1977.

Behe, Michael. *Darwin's Black Box: A Biochemical Challenge to Evolution.* New York: Free Press, 1996.

Berry, R. J. "This Cursed Earth: Is 'The Fall' Credible?" *Journal of Science and Christian Belief* 11 (1999): 29-49.

Bertocci, Peter. *An Introduction to the Philosophy of Religion.* New York: Prentice-Hall, 1951.

————. "Personality, Free Will and Moral Obligation." In *The Problem of Free Will.* Edited by Willard Enteman, pp. 19-31. New York: Charles Scribner's Sons, 1967.

Best, W. E. *God Is Love.* Houston: South Belt Grace Church, 1985.

Bettis, J. D. "A Critique of the Doctrine of Universal Salvation." *RelS* 6 (1970): 329-44.

Billheimer, Paul E. *Destined for the Throne.* Minneapolis: Bethany House, 1975.

Birch, Charles, and Lukas Vischer. *Living with the Animals: The Community of God's Creatures.* Geneva: WCC Publications, 1977.

Bishop, J. "Agent-Causation." *Mind* 92 (1983): 61-79.

Blocher, Henri. *Evil and the Cross.* Translated by David G. Preston. Downers Grove, Ill.: Inter-Varsity Press, 1994.

Block, Daniel I. *The Gods of the Nations: Studies in Ancient Near Eastern National Theology.* ETSMS 2. Jackson, Miss.: Evangelical Theological Society, 1988.

Bloom, Howard. *The Lucifer Principle: A Scientific Expedition into the Forces of History.* New York: Atlantic Monthly, 1995.

Blue, R. "Untold Billions: Are They Really Lost? *BSac* 138 (1981): 338-50.

Böcher, O. *Christus Exorcista: Dämonismus und Taufe im Neuen Testament.* BWANT 5.16. Stuttgart: Kohlhammer, 1972.

Boeft, J. den. *Calcidius on Fate: His Doctrine and Sources.* Philosophia Antiqua 18. Leiden: E. J. Brill, 1970.

Bonda, Jan. *The One Purpose of God.* Translated by R. Bruinsma. Grand Rapids, Mich.: Eerdmans, 1993.

Bonjour, L. "Determinism, Libertarianism and Agent Causation." *The Southern Journal of Philosophy* 14 (1976): 145-56.

The Book of Enoch. Translated by Matthew Black. Leiden: E. J. Brill, 1985.

Boros, Ladislaus. *The Mystery of Death.* Translated by Gregory Bainbridge. New York: Herder & Herder, 1965.

Boyd, Gregory A. *God at War: The Bible and Spiritual Conflict.* Downers Grove, Ill.: InterVarsity Press, 1996.

————. *The God of the Possible.* Grand Rapids, Mich.: Baker, 2000.

————. *Trinity and Process: A Critical Evaluation and Reappropriation of Hartshorne's Di-Polar Theism Towards a Trinitarian Metaphysics.* New York: Lang, 1992.

Boyd, Gregory A., and Edward Boyd. *Letters From a Skeptic.* Colorado Springs, Colo.: ChariotVictor, 1994.

Bracken, Joseph. *Society and Spirit: A Trinitarian Cosmology.* Selinsgrove, Penn.: Susquehanna University Press, 1991.

Braun, Jon E. *Whatever Happened to Hell?* Nashville: Thomas Nelson, 1979.

Brightman, Edgar S. *A Philosophy of Religion.* New York: Prentice-Hall, 1940.

Broad, Charlie D. "Determinism, Indeterminism and Libertarianism." In *Ethics and the History of Philosophy.* London: RKP, 1952.

Brockelman, Paul. *Time and Self: Phenomenological Explorations.* New York: Scholars Press, 1985.

Brooks, Robert E. *Free Will: An Ultimate Illusion.* Lake Oswego: Ore.: CIRCA, 1986.

Brown, H. "Will Everyone Be Saved?" *Pastoral Renewal* 11 (June 1987): 11-16.

Brown, Stuart , ed. *Reason and Religion: A Royal Institute of Philosophy Symposium.* New York: Cornell University Press, 1977.

Brueggemann, Walter. *Old Testament Theology: Essays on Structure, Theme, and Text.* Minneapolis: Fortress, 1992.

Brümmer, Vincent. *What Are We Doing When We Pray? A Philosophical Inquiry.* London: SCM Press, 1984.

Buchler, Justus. *Metaphysics of Natural Complexes.* Albany, N.Y.: SUNY, 1990.

Buis, Harry. *Doctrine of Eternal Punishment.* Philadelphia: Presbyterian & Reformed, 1957.

Burns, J. Patout. "The Atmosphere of Election: Augustinianism As Common Sense." *JECS* 2 (1994): 325-39.

Buswell, J. Oliver. *A Systematic Theology of the Christian Religion.* 2 vols. Grand Rapids, Mich.: Zondervan, 1962-1963.

Calvin, John. *Commentaries on the First Book of Moses.* 2 vols. Translated by John King. Grand Rapids, Mich.: Eerdmans, 1948.

————. *Institutes of the Christian Religion.* Edited by John T. McNeill. Translated by Ford L. Battles. Philadelphia: Westminster Press, 1960.

Cameron, Nigel M. de S., ed. *Universalism and the Doctrine of Hell.* Grand Rapids, Mich.: Baker, 1992.

Campbell, Charles A. *In Defense of Free Will.* London: Allen & Unwin, 1967.

Capek, Milic. *The Concepts of Space and Time: Their Structure and Their Development.* Boston Studies in the Philosophy of Science 22. Dordrecht, Holland: Reidel, 1976.

————. "The Unreality and Indeterminacy of the Future in the Light of Contemporary Physics," In *Physics and the Ultimate Significance of Time.* Edited by David R. Griffin. Albany, N.Y.: SUNY, 1986.

Carasik, Michael. "The Limits of Omniscience." *JBL* 119 (2000): 221-32.

Carson, D. A. *Divine Sovereignty and Human Responsibility.* Atlanta: John Knox Press, 1981.

————. *How Long O Lord? Reflections on Suffering and Evil.* Grand Rapids, Mich.: Baker, 1990.

Carter, Ben M. *The Depersonalization of God: A Consideration of Soteriological Difficulties in High Calvinism.* London: University Press of America, 1989.

Carter, Charles W., ed. *The Wesleyan Bible Commentary.* 7 vols. Grand Rapids, Mich.: Eerdmans, 1964-1969.

Chesterton, G. K. *Orthodoxy.* Garden City, N.Y.: Doubleday, 1959.

Chilton, D. *The Days of Vengeance: An Exposition of the Book of Revelation.* Fort Worth, Tex.: Dominion, 1987.

Chisholm, R. "Agents, Causes, and Events: The Problem of Free Will." In *Agents, Causes and Events: Essays on Indeterminism and Free Will.* Edited by Timothy O'Connor, pp. 95-100. New York: Oxford University Press, 1995.

————."Freedom and Action." In *Freedom and Determinism.* Edited by Kevin Lehrer. New York: Random House, 1966.

Clark, Robert E. D. *The Universe: Plan or Accident?* Philadelphia: Muhlenberg, 1961.

Clark, Ronald W. *Einstein: The Life and Times.* New York: Hodder & Stoughton, 1973.

Clark, S. "Is Nature God's Will?" In *Animals on the Agenda: Questions About Animals for Theology and Ethics.* Edited by Andrew Linzey and Dorothy Yamamoto, pp. 123-36. Urbana: University of Illinois Press, 1998.

Clarke, Adam. *The Holy Bible . . . with a Commentary and Critical Notes.* London: T & T Clark, 1810.

Clarke, Randolf. "A Principle of Rational Explanation?" *Southern Journal of Philosophy* 30 (1992): 1-12.

———. "Toward a Credible Agent-Causal Account of Free Will." In *Agents, Causes and Events: Essays on Indeterminism and Free Will*. Edited by Timothy O'Connor. New York: Oxford University Press, 1995.

Clines, D. J. A. *Job 1-20*. WBC 17. Dallas, Tex.: Word, 1989.

———. "Predestination in the Old Testament." In *Grace Unlimited*. Edited by Clark Pinnock. Minneapolis: Bethany House, 1975.

Cohen, Arthur. *The Tremendum: A Theological Interpretation of the Holocaust*. New York: Crossroad, 1981.

Collins, A. Yarbro. *The Combat Myth in the Book of Revelation*. HDR 9. Missoula, Mont.: Scholars Press, 1976.

Collins, J. J. *Daniel*. Hermeneia. Minneapolis: Fortress, 1993.

Colwell, J. "Chaos and Providence." *International Journal for Philosophy and Religion* 48 (2000): 131-38.

Cottrell, Jack W. "The Nature of Divine Sovereignty." In *The Grace of God, the Will of Man: A Case for Arminianism*. Grand Rapids, Mich.: Zondervan, 1989.

Coveney, Peter. "Chaos, Entropy and the Arrow of Time." *New Scientist* 127 (1990): 49-52.

———. "The Second Law of Thermodynamics: Entropy, Irreversibility and Dynamics." *Nature* 333 (1988): 409-15.

Coveney, Peter, and Roger Highfield. *The Arrow of Time*. New York: Basic Books, 1990.

Craig, William. *The Only Wise God: The Compatibility of Divine Knowledge and Human Freedom*. Grand Rapids, Mich.: Baker, 1987.

Cranfield, C. E. B. *A Critical and Exegetical Commentary on the Epistle to the Romans*. Edinburgh: T & T Clark, 1979.

Creel, Richard. *Divine Impassability*. Cambridge: Cambridge University Press, 1986.

Crenshaw, C. I. *Man As God: The Word of Faith Movement*. Memphis: Footstool Publications, 1994.

Crockett, William. "Will God Save Everyone in the End?" In *Through No Fault of Their Own? The Fate of Those Who Have Never Heard*. Edited by William Crockett and James Sigountos, pp. 159-68. Grand Rapids, Mich.: Baker, 1991.

Crockett, William, and James Sigountos, eds. *Through No Fault of Their Own? The Fate of Those Who Have Never Heard*. Grand Rapids, Mich.: Baker, 1991.

Cunningham, Lawrence. "Satan: A Theological Meditation." *ThTo* 51 (1994):12 n. 1.

Cupitt, Don. "Four Arguments Against the Devil." *Theology* 64 (1961): 5 n. 32.

Custance, Arthur C. *Man in Adam and in Christ*. Doorway Papers 3. Grand Rapids, Mich.: Zondervan, 1975.

Daniélou, Jean. *Gospel Message and Hellenistic Culture*. Edited and translated by John A. Baker. Philadelphia: Westminster Press, 1973.

Darrow, Clarence. *Crime: Its Cause and Treatment*. New York: Colwell, 1922.

Davidson, D. *Essays on Action and Events*. Oxford: Oxford University Press, 1980.

Davies, Paul. *About Time: Einstein's Unfinished Revolution*. New York: Simon & Schuster, 1995.

Davis, Stephen. *Logic and the Nature of God*. Grand Rapids, Mich.: Eerdmans, 1983.

Dawkins, Richard. *The Selfish Gene*. New York: Oxford University Press, 1976.

Day, John. *God's Conflict with the Dragon and the Sea*. Cambridge: Cambridge University Press, 1985.

Deanee-Drummon, C. "Moltmann on Heaven." In *Unseen World: Christian Reflections on Angels, Demons and the Heavenly Realm*. Edited by Anthony Lane. Grand Rapids, Mich.: Baker, 1996.

Dembski, William, ed. *Mere Creation: Science, Faith and Intelligent Design*. Downers Grove,

Ill.: InterVarsity Press, 1998.

Dennett, Daniel C. *Elbow Room: The Varieties of Free Will Worth Wanting.* Cambridge, Mass.: MIT Press, 1984.

——. "On Giving Libertarians What They Say They Want." In *Agents, Causes and Events: Essays on Indeterminism and Free Will.* Edited by Timothy O'Connor, 43-55. New York: Oxford University Press, 1995.

DeVries, Peter. *The Blood of the Lamb.* Boston: Little, Brown, 1962.

Dillow, Joseph C. *The Reign of the Servant Kings.* Hayesville, N.C.: Schoettle, 1992.

Dixon, Larry. *The Other Side of the Good News.* Wheaton, Ill.: Victor, 1992.

Dossey, Larry. *Healing Words: The Power of Prayer and the Practice of Medicine.* San Francisco: HarperSanFrancisco, 1993.

Double, Richard. "Libertarianism and Rationality." In *Agents, Causes and Events: Essays on Indeterminism and Free Will.* Edited by Timothy O'Connor, pp. 57-65. New York: Oxford University Press, 1995.

——. *The Non-reality of Free Will.* Oxford: Oxford University Press, 1991.

Dow, G. "The Case for the Existence of Demons." *Churchman: Journal of Anglican Theology* 94 (1980): 6 n. 4.

Dummett, M. "Can an Effect Precede Its Cause?" Reprinted in *Truth and Other Enigmas.* Cambridge, Mass.: Harvard University Press, 1978.

Dunn, James D.G. *The Theology of Paul the Apostle.* Grand Rapids, Mich.: Eerdmans, 1998.

Dyer, G. J. "The Unbaptized Infant in Eternity." *Chicago Studies* 2 (1963): app. 3 n. 5.

Eccles, John C. *How the Self Controls Its Brain.* New York: Springer-Verlag, 1994.

Edwards, David L., and John Stott. *Essentials: A Liberal-Evangelical Dialogue.* London: Hodder & Stoughton, 1988.

Edwards, Jonathan. *Freedom of the Will.* Edited by Paul Ramsey. New Haven, Conn.: Yale University Press, 1957.

——. *Jonathan Edwards: Ethical Writings.* Edited by Paul Ramsey. New Haven, Conn.: Yale University Press, 1989.

Edwards, P. "Hard and Soft Determinism." In *Determinism and Freedom in an Age of Modern Science.* Edited by Sidney Hook, pp. 117-25. New York: Collier Books, 1961.

Eells, Ellery. *Probabilistic Causality.* Cambridge: Cambridge University Press, 1991.

Epperly, Bruce. *At the Edges of Life: Toward a Holistic Vision of the Human Adventure.* St. Louis: Chalice, 1992.

——. "To Pray or Not to Pray: Reflections on the Intersection of Prayer and Medicine." *Journal of Religion and Health* 34 (1995): 7 n. 31.

Erickson, Millard. *God in Three Persons: A Contemporary Interpretation of the Trinity.* Grand Rapids, Mich.: Baker, 1995.

——. "Hope for Those Who Haven't Heard? Yes, But. . ." *Evangelical Missions Quarterly* 11 (1975): 122-26.

Evans, G. R. *Augustine on Evil.* Cambridge: Cambridge University Press, 1982.

Feinberg, J. "And the Atheist Shall Lie Down with the Calvinist: Atheism, Calvinism and the Free Will Defense." *TJ* 1 (1980): 142-52.

Ferguson, Everett. *Demonology of the Early Christian World.* New York: Mellen, 1984.

Fisher, John M. "Freedom and Foreknowledge." In *God, Foreknowledge, and Freedom.* Edited by John M. Fisher, pp. 86-96. Stanford, Calif.: Stanford University Press, 1989.

——. "Ockhamism." *Philosophical Review* 94 (1985): 81-100.

——, ed. *God, Foreknowledge, and Freedom.* Stanford, Calif.: Stanford University Press, 1989.

Flew, A. "Compatibilism, Free Will and God." *Philosophy* 48 (1973): 231-44.

——. "Divine Omnipotence and Human Freedom." In *New Essays in Philosophical Theology.* Edited by Anthony Flew and Alasdair MacIntyre. London: SCM Press, 1955.

Flint, T. P., and Alfred J. Freddoso. "Maximal Power." In *The Existence and Nature of God.*

Edited by Alfred J. Freddoso, pp. 81-114. Notre Dame, Ind.: University of Notre Dame Press, 1983.

Floyd, W. E. G. *Clement of Alexandria's Treatment of the Problem of Evil.* Oxford: Clarendon, 1971.

Foster, John. *Ayer.* London: Routledge & Kegan Paul, 1985.

Forster, Roger, and V. Paul Marston. *God's Strategy in Human History.* Wheaton, Ill.: Tyndale, 1973.

Forsyth, Neil. *The Old Enemy: Satan and the Combat Myth.* Princeton, N.J.: Princeton University Press, 1987.

Fortey, Richard. *Life: A Natural History of the First Four Billion Years.* New York: Alfred A. Knopf, 1997.

Fost, F. "Relativity Theory and Hartshorne's Di-Polar Theism." In *Two Process Philosophers: Ford's Encounter with Whitehead.* Edited by L. Ford. Tallahassee, Fla.: American Academy of Religion, 1973.

Foster, Richard. *Prayer: Finding the Heart's True Home.* San Francisco: HarperSanFrancisco, 1992.

Frankena, William. *Ethics.* 2d ed. Englewood Cliffs, N. J.: Prentice-Hall, 1973.

Frankfurt, H. "The Problem of Free Action." *American Philosophical Quarterly* 15 (1978): 157-62.

Fretheim, Terence E. "Divine Dependence on the Human: An Old Testament Perspective." *Ex Auditu* 13 (1997): 1-13.

———. "Divine Foreknowledge, Divine Constancy and the Rejection of Saul's Kingship." *CBQ* 47 (1985): 595-602.

———. *Exodus.* Interpretation. Louisville: John Knox Press, 1991.

———. "God in the Book of Job." *CurTM* 26 (1999): 7 n. 13.

———. "The Repentance of God: A Key to Evaluating Old Testament God-Talk." *HBT* 10.1 (1988): 47-70.

———. "The Repentance of God: A Study of Jeremiah 18:7-10." *HAR* 11 (1989): 31-56.

Froom, LeRoy. E. *The Conditionalist Faith of Our Fathers: The Conflict of the Ages over the Nature and Destiny of Man.* 2 vols. Washington, D.C.: Review & Herald, 1965-1966.

Fudge, Edward. *The Fire That Consumes: The Biblical Case for Conditional Immortality.* Revised ed. Carlisle, U.K.: Paternoster, 1994.

Gale, R. "Endorsing Predictions." *Philosophical Review* 70 (1961): 376-85.

———. *The Language of Time.* New York: Humanities Press, 1968.

Garrett, Susan. *The Demise of the Devil: Magic and the Demonic in Luke's Writings.* Minneapolis: Fortress, 1989.

Garrigue, M. *Dieu sans idée du mal. La liberté de l'homme au coeur de Dieu.* Limoges: Critérion, 1982.

Geach, Peter. *Providence and Evil.* Cambridge: Cambridge University Press, 1977.

Geisler, Norman. *Creating God in the Image of Man? Neotheism's Dangerous Drift.* Minneapolis: Bethany House, 1997.

———. *Baker Encyclopedia of Christian Apologetics.* Grand Rapids, Mich.: Baker, 1999.

Gentry, Kenneth, Jr. *Before Jerusalem Fell: Dating the Book of Revelation.* Tyler, Tex.: Institute for Christian Economics, 1989.

———. "A Preterist View of Revelation." In *Four Views on the Book of Revelation.* Edited by C. Marvin Pate, pp. 37-92. Grand Rapids, Mich.: Zondervan, 1998.

Gibson, J. C. L. "On Evil in the Book of Job." In *Ascribe to the Lord: Biblical and Other Studies in Memory of Peter C. Craigie.* Edited by Lyle Eslinger and Glen Taylor. JSOTSup 67. Sheffield: Sheffield Academic Press, 1988.

Ginet, C. "In Defense of Incompatibilism." *Philosophical Studies* 44 (1983): 391-400.

———. *On Action.* Cambridge: Cambridge University Press, 1990.

Glass, Leon, and Michael Mackey. *From Clocks to Chaos: The Rhythms of Life.* Princeton, N.J.: Princeton University Press, 1988.

Gleick, James. *Chaos: Making a New Science.* New York: Penguin Books, 1987.

Gokey, Francis X. *The Terminology for the Devil and Evil Spirits in the Apostolic Fathers.* Patristic Studies 93. Washington, D.C.: Catholic University of America Press, 1961.

Goldhagen, Daniel J. *Hitler's Willing Executioners: Ordinary Germans and the Holocaust.* New York: Alfred A. Knopf, 1996.

Goldingay, John E. *Daniel.* WBC 30; Dallas: Word, 1989.

———. *Models for Interpretation of Scripture.* Grand Rapids, Mich.: Eerdmans, 1995.

Goldman, Alvin. *A Theory of Human Action.* Englewood Cliffs, N.J.: Prentice Hall, 1970.

Goldstein, Jeffrey. *The Unshackled Organization: Facing the Challenge of Unpredictability Through Spontaneous Reorganization.* Portland, Ore.: Productivity, 1994.

Good, Edwin. *In Turns of Tempest: A Reading of Job.* Stanford, Calif.: Stanford University Press, 1990.

Gorday, Peter. *Principles of Patristic Exegesis: Romans 9-11 in Origen, John Chrysostom, and Augustine.* Studies in the Bible and Early Christianity 4. New York: Mellen, 1983.

Gorringe, T. J. *God's Theatre: A Theology of Providence.* London: SCM Press, 1991.

Gray, John. *The Biblical Doctrine of the Reign of God.* Edinburgh: T & T Clark, 1979.

Gray, T. "God Does Not Play Dice." *Them* 24 (May 1999): 21-34.

Greer, R. A. "Christ the Victor and Victim." *CTQ* 59 (1995): 1-30.

Gregg, Steve, ed. *Revelation: Four Views.* Nashville: Thomas Nelson, 1997.

Gregory I, Pope. *Dialogues.* Translated by O. J. Zimmerman. The Fathers of the Church: A New Translation 39. New York: Fathers of the Church, 1959.

Griffin, David R. "Introduction: Time and the Fallacy of Misplaced Concreteness." In *Physics and the Ultimate Significance of Time.* Edited by David R. Griffin. Albany, N.Y.: SUNY Press, 1986.

———. "Why Demonic Power Exists: Understanding the Church's Enemy." *LTQ* 28 (1993): 1 n. 11.

———, ed. *Physics and the Ultimate Significance of Time.* Albany, N.Y.: SUNY Press, 1986.

Groothuis, Douglas. "Deposed Royalty: Pascal's Anthropological Argument." *JETS* 41 (1998): 2 n. 60.

Gruenler, Royce. *The Inexhaustible God: Biblical Faith and the Challenge of Process Theism.* Grand Rapids, Mich.: Baker, 1983.

Guillebaud, H. E. *The Righteous Judge: A Study of the Biblical Doctrine of Everlasting Punishment.* Taunton, England: Phoenix, n.d.

Gumpel, P. "Unbaptized Infants: A Further Report." *Downside Review* 73 (1955): 317-46.

———. "Unbaptized Infants: May They Be Saved?" *Downside Review* 72 (1954): 342-458.

Gunton, Colin. *Becoming and Being: The Doctrine of God in Charles Hartshorne and Karl Barth.* Oxford: Oxford University Press, 1980.

———. *The One, The Three and the Many: God, Creation and the Culture of Modernity.* Cambridge: Cambridge University Press, 1993.

Gutiérrez, Gustavo. *On Job: God-Talk and the Suffering of the Innocent.* Translated by Matthew J. O'Connell. Maryknoll, N.Y.: Orbis, 1992.

Hanegraaff, Hank. *Christianity in Crisis.* Eugene, Ore.: Harvest House, 1997.

Härle, Wilfried. *Sein und Gnade: Die Ontologie in Karl Barths Kirchlicher Dogmatik.* Berlin: Walter de Gruyter, 1974.

Hartley, John E. *The Book of Job.* NICOT. Grand Rapids, Mich.: Eerdmans, 1988.

Hartman, Louis F., and Alexandra A. DiLella. *The Book of Daniel.* AB 23; Garden City, N.Y.: Doubleday, 1978.

Hartshorne, Charles. *Beyond Humanism: Essays in the New Philosophy of Nature.* Chicago: Willet, Clark, 1968.

———. *Born to Sing: An Interpretation and World Survey of Bird Song.* Bloomington: Indiana

University Press, 1973.

———. *Creative Synthesis and Philosophic Method.* Repr., Lanham, Md.: University Press of America, 1983.

———. *Creativity in American Philosophy.* Albany, N.Y.: SUNY Press, 1984.

———. "Freedom, Individual, and Beauty in Nature." *Snowy Egret* 24 (Fall 1960): 5-14.

———. "Ideal Knowledge Defines Reality: What Was True in 'Idealism.' " *Journal of Philosophy* 43 (1946): 573-82.

———. *The Logic of Perfection and Other Essays on Neoclassical Metaphysics.* La Salle, Ill.: Open Court, 1962.

———. "Metaphysics Contributes to Ornithology." *Theoria to Theory* 13 (1979): 127-40.

———. *Whitehead's View of Reality.* New York: Pilgrim, 1981.

Hasker, William. "The Necessity of Gratuitous Evil." *Faith and Philosophy* 9 (1992): 23-44.

———. "A Philosophical Perspective." In *The Openness of God: A Biblical Challenge to the Traditional Understanding of God.* Edited by Clark Pinnock. Downers Grove, Ill.: InterVarsity Press, 1994.

Hauerwas, Stanley, and John Berkman. "A Trinitarian Theology of the 'Chief End' of 'All Flesh.' " In *Good News for Animals? Christian Approaches to Animal Well-Being.* Edited by Charles Pinches and Jay B. McDaniel, pp. 62-73. Maryknoll, N.Y.: Orbis, 1993.

Hayes, Joel. *The Foreknowledge of God; or, the Omniscience of God Consistent with His Own Holiness and Man's Free Agency.* Nashville: MECS Publishing House, 1890.

Hayes, Richard. *Echoes of Scripture in the Letters of Paul.* New Haven, Conn.: Yale University Press, 1989.

Heim, Karl. *Jesus the Lord: The Sovereign Authority of Jesus and God's Revelation in Christ.* Translated by D. H. van Daalen. London: Oliver & Boyd, 1959.

———. *Jesus the World's Perfector: The Atonement and the Renewal of the World.* Translated by D. H. van Daalen. Edinburgh: Oliver & Boyd, 1959.

Helm, Paul. *The Providence of God.* Downers Grove, Ill.: InterVarsity Press, 1994.

Hesse, Mary. "Miracles and the Laws of Nature." In *Miracles: Cambridge Study in Their Philosophy and History.* Edited by Charles F. D. Moule. London: A. R. Mowbray, 1965.

———. "Physics, Philosophy and Myth." In *Physics, Philosophy and Theology: A Common Quest for Understanding.* Edited by Robert J. Russell, William R. Stoeger and George V. Coyne, pp. 185-202. Notre Dame, Ind.: Notre Dame University Press, 1988.

Hibbard, Billy. *Memoirs of the Life and Travels of B. Hibbard.* 2d ed. New York: Piercy & Reed, 1843.

Hick, John. *Death and Eternal Life.* Basingstoke & London: Macmillan, 1990.

———. *Evil and the God of Love.* Revised ed. San Francisco: Harper & Row, 1978.

———. "An Irenaean Theodicy." In *Encountering Evil.* Edited by Stephen David. Atlanta: John Knox Press, 1981.

Hillers, D. R. "Revelation 13:18 and a Scroll from Murabba'at." *BASOR* 170 (1963): 65.

Hobart, R. B. "Free Will As Involving Determination and Inconceivable Without It." *Mind* 43 (1934): 1-27.

Hobb, J. "Chaos and Indeterminism." *Canadian Journal of Philosophy* 21 (1991): 141-64.

Hodgson, Leonard. *For Faith and Freedom.* 2 vols. Gifford Lectures, 1955-1957. Oxford: Basil Blackwell, 1956-1957.

Hoekema, Anthony A. *The Bible and the Future.* Grand Rapids, Mich.: Eerdmans, 1979.

Hoffman, Banesh with Helen Dukas. *Albert Einstein: Creator and Rebel.* New York: Viking, 1972.

Hoffman, J., and G. Rosenkrantz. "Hard and Soft Facts" In *God, Foreknowledge, and Freedom.* Edited by John M. Fisher, pp. 123-35. Stanford, Calif.: Stanford University Press, 1989.

Hollinger, Henry, and Michael Zenzen. *The Nature of Irreversibility.* Dordrecht, Holland: Reidel, 1985.

Holte, John, ed. *Chaos: The New Science: Nobel Conference XXVI.* Lanham, Md.: University Press of America, 1993.

Honderich, Ted. *A Theory of Determinism.* 2 vols. Oxford: Oxford University Press, 1988.

Hook, Sidney. *Pragmatism and the Tragic Sense of Life.* New York: Basic Books, 1975.

Horwich, Paul. *Asymmetries in Time.* Cambridge, Mass.: MIT Press, 1989.

Hudson, T. "Measuring the Results of Faith." *Hospitals and Health Networks* 70 (September 1996): 7 n. 39.

Hughes, Philip E. *The True Image: The Origin and Destiny of Man in Christ.* Grand Rapids, Mich.: Eerdmans, 1989.

Inbody, Tyron. *The Transforming God: An Interpretation of Suffering.* Louisville: Westminster Press, 1997.

Jacob, Edmond. *Theology of the Old Testament.* Translated by A. W. Heathcote and P. J. Allcock. New York: Harper & Row, 1958.

James, Willard. "The Dilemma of Determinism." In *The Problem of Free Will.* Edited by W. Enteman. New York: Charles Scribner's Sons, 1967.

James, William. *The Will to Believe and Other Essays in Popular Philosophy.* New York: Dover, 1956.

Janis, Irving, and Leon Mann. *Decision Making.* New York: Free Press, 1977.

Jeremias, Joachim. *Jesus' Promise to the Nations.* Translated by S. H. Hook. Philadelphia: Fortress, 1982.

Jones, Major. *The Color of God: The Concept of God in Afro-American Thought.* Macon, Ga.: Mercer University Press, 1987.

Jung, Leo. *Fallen Angels in Jewish, Christian and Mohammedan Literature.* Philadelphia: Dropsie College, 1926. Repr., New York: Barnes & Noble, 1995.

Jüngel, Eberhard. *God As the Mystery of the World.* Translated by Darrell L. Guder. Grand Rapids, Mich.: Eerdmans, 1983.

Kallas, James. *The Significance of the Synoptic Miracles.* Greenwich, Conn.: Seabury, 1961.

Kane, Robert. *The Significance of Freedom.* New York: Oxford University Press, 1996.

———. Two Kinds of Incompatibilism." In *Agents, Causes and Events: Essays on Indeterminism and Free Will.* Edited by Timothy. O'Connor. New York: Oxford University Press, 1995.

Kant, Immanuel. *Critique of Pure Reason.* Translated by F. Max Müller. Garden City, N.Y.: Doubleday, 1966.

———. *Religion Within the Bounds of Reason Alone.* Translated by Theodore. M. Greene and Hoyt H. Hudson. New York: Harper & Brothers, 1960.

Kaufman, Walter, ed. *Religion from Tolstoy to Camus.* New York: Harper & Row, 1961.

Keel, O. *Jahwes Entgegung an Iob.* FRLANT 121. Göttingen: Vandenhoeck & Ruprecht, 1978.

Kelly, Steward. "The Problem of Evil and the Satan Hypothesis." Paper delivered at SCP Eastern Regional Meeting, April 7-9, 1994.

Kenny, A. "Divine Foreknowledge and Human Freedom." In *Aquinas: A Collection of Critical Essays.* Edited by Anthony Kenny, pp. 255-70. Notre Dame, Ind.: University of Notre Dame Press, 1976.

Kiel, L. Douglas. *Managing Chaos and Complexity in Government: A New Paradigm for Managing Change, Innovation, and Organizational Renewal.* San Francisco: Jossey-Bass, 1994.

Kierkegaard, Søren. *The Sickness unto Death.* Translated by W. Lowrie. Princeton, N.J.: Princeton University Press, 1941.

Kirkpatrick, L. "Subjective Becoming: An Unwarranted Abstraction?" *Process Studies* 3 (1973): 9 n. 9.

Kirwan, Christopher. *Augustine.* London: Routledge, 1991.

Klein, William W. *The New Chosen People: A Corporate View of Election.* Grand Rapids, Mich.: Zondervan, 1990.

König, Adrio. *Here Am I! A Christian Reflection on God.* Grand Rapids, Mich.: Eerdmans, 1982.

————. *New and Greater Things: Re-evaluating the Biblical Message on Creation.* Pretoria: University of South Africa, 1988.

Kreeft, Peter, and Ronald Tacelli. *Handbook of Christian Apologetics.* Downers Grove, Ill.: InterVarsity Press, 1994.

Kümmel, Werner G. *Promise and Fulfillment: The Eschatological Message of Jesus.* 3rd ed. SBT 1.23. London: SCM Press, 1957.

Kushner, Harold. *When Bad Things Happen to Good People.* New York: Schocken, 1981.

Kvanvig, Jonathan. *The Problem of Hell.* New York: Oxford University Press, 1993.

Kyle, Richard. *The Last Days Are Here Again: A History of the End Times.* Grand Rapids, Mich.: Baker, 1998.

Labuschagne, C. J. *The Incomparability of Yahweh in the Old Testament.* POS 5. Leiden: E. J. Brill, 1966.

Ladd, George E. *Jesus and the Kingdom: The Eschatology of Biblical Realism.* 2nd ed. Waco, Tex.: Word, 1964.

Lake, D. M. "He Died for All: The Universal Dimensions of the Atonement." In *Grace Unlimited.* Edited by Clark Pinnock, pp. 31-50. Minneapolis: Bethany House, 1975.

Lamb, D. "On a Proof of Incompatibilism." *The Philosophical Review* 86 (1977): 20-35.

Lathem, Edward C., and L. Thompson, eds. *Robert Frost Poetry and Prose.* New York: Holt, Rinehart and Winston, 1972.

Lawrence, Brother. *The Practice of the Presence of God.* Translated by John J. Delaney. Garden City, N.Y.: Image, 1977.

Lawson, John. *Introduction to Christian Doctrine.* Wilmore, Ky.: Asbury, 1980.

Lazlo, Ervin. *The Systems View of the World: The Natural Philosophy of the New Developments in the Sciences.* New York: George Braziller, 1972.

Leibniz, Gottfried. *Selections.* Edited by P. Wiener. New York: Scribner, 1951.

Leivestad, Ragnar. *Christ the Conqueror: Ideas of Conflict and Victory in the New Testament.* New York: Macmillan, 1954.

Levenson, Jon. *Creation and the Persistence of Evil: The Jewish Drama of Divine Omnipotence.* San Francisco: Harper & Row, 1988.

Lewin, Roger. *Complexity: Life at the Edge of Chaos.* New York: Macmillan, 1992.

Lewis, C. S. *The Great Divorce.* New York: Macmillan, 1946.

————. *Mere Christianity.* New York: Macmillan, 1979.

————. *Miracles.* New York: Macmillan, 1978.

————. *The Problem of Pain.* New York: Macmillan, 1962.

Lewis, Edwin. *The Creator and the Adversary.* New York: Abingdon-Cokesbury, 1948.

Lightfoot, J. B., and J. R. Harmer, eds. and trans. *The Apostolic Fathers: Greek Texts and English Translations of Their Writings.* Edited and revised by M. W. Holmes. Grand Rapids, Mich.: Baker, 1992.

Lindley, David. *Where Does the Weirdness Go?* New York: Basic Books, 1996.

Lindström, Fredrik. *God and the Origin of Evil: A Contextual Analysis of Alleged Monistic Evidence in the Old Testament.* Translated by F. H. Cryer. ConBOT 21. Lund: Gleerup, 1983.

Linzey, Andrew and Tom Regan, eds. *Animals and Christianity: A Book of Readings.* New York: Crossroads, 1988.

Longman, Tremper III, and Daniel G. Reid. *God Is a Warrior.* Grand Rapids, Mich.: Zondervan, 1995.

Loomer, Bernard. "Two Kinds of Power." *Criterion* (Winter 1976): 5 n. 8.

Lucas, J. Randolph. *The Future: An Essay on God, Temporality, and Truth.* London: Basil Blackwell, 1989.

————. "The Temporality of God." In *Quantum Cosmology and the Laws of Nature: Scientific Perspectives on Divine Action.* Edited by Robert J. Russell, Nancey Murphy and C. J. Isham, pp. 235-46. Vatican City: Vatican Observatory Publications, 1993.

Luther, Martin. *The Bondage of the Will*. Translated by Philip S. Watson. Luther's Works 3. Philadelphia: Fortress, 1972.

Mackie, J. "Evil and Omnipotence." *Mind* 64 (1955): 100-15.

Madden, Edward, and Peter Hare. *Evil and the Concept of God*. Springfield, Ill.: Charles C. Thomas, 1968.

Mannoia, J. "Is God an Exception to Whitehead's Metaphysics?" In *Process Theology*. Edited by Ronald Nash, pp. 253-80. Grand Rapids, Mich.: Baker, 1987.

Marina, Jacqueline. "The Theological and Philosophical Significance of the Markan Account of Miracles." *Faith and Philosophy* 15 (1998): 298-323.

Martin, Michael. *Atheism: A Philosophical Justification*. Philadelphia: Temple University Press, 1990.

Marty, Martin E. " 'The Devil, You Say. . .' 'The Demonic, Say I. . .'." In *Heterodoxy/Mystical Experience, Religious Dissent and the Occult*. Edited by Richard Woods. River Forest, Ill.: Listening Press, 1975.

———. "Hell Disappeared. No One Noticed. A Civic Argument." *HTR* 78 (1985): 381-98.

Mascall, Eric L. *Christian Theology and Natural Science: Some Questions on Their Relations*. London: Longmans, Green & Co., 1956.

Matthews, Dale. *The Faith Factor: Proof of the Healing Power of Prayer*. New York: Viking, 1998.

Mavrodes, G. "Is the Past Preventable?" *Faith and Philosophy* 1 (1984): 131-46.

McCabe, Lorenzo D. *Divine Nescience of Future Contingencies a Necessity*. New York: Phillips & Hunt, 1882.

———. *The Foreknowledge of God, and Cognate Themes in Theology and Philosophy*. Cincinnati: Cranston & Stowe, 1887.

McClelland, W. Robert. *God Our Loving Enemy*. Nashville: Abingdon, 1982.

McCloskey, H. J. "The Problem of Evil." *JBR* 30 (1962): 187-97.

McConnell, D. R. *A Different Gospel: A Historical and Biblical Analysis of the Modern Faith Movement*. Peabody, Mass.: Hendrickson, 1988.

McDonald, H. D. *The God Who Responds*. Minneapolis: Bethany House, 1986.

McGill, Arthur C. *Suffering: A Test of Theological Method*. Philadelphia: Geneva, 1968.

McLelland, Joseph C. *God the Anonymous: A Study in Alexandrian Philosophical Theology*. Patristic Monograph Series 4. Cambridge, Mass.: Philadelphia Patristic Foundation, 1976.

Mesle, C. R. "Aesthetic Value and Relational Power: An Essay on Personhood." *Process Studies* 13 (1983): 59-70.

Mettinger, T. N. D. "Fighting the Powers of Chaos and Hell—Towards the Biblical Portrait of God." *ST* 39 (1985): 21-38.

———. "The God of Job: Avenger, Tyrant, or Victor?" In *The Voice from the Whirlwind: Interpreting the Book of Job*. Edited by Leo G. Perdue and W. Clark Gilpin, pp. 39-49. Nashville: Abingdon, 1992.

Miller, Paul M. *The Devil Did Not Make Me Do It*. Scottsdale, Penn.: Herald, 1977.

Mill, John Stuart. *Three Essays on Religion*, 3rd edition. London: Longmans, Green & Co., 1923.

Moltmann, Jürgen. *God in Creation: A New Theology of Creation and the Spirit of God*. Translated by Margaret Kohl. London: SCM Press, 1985.

———. *The Trinity and the Kingdom: The Doctrine of God*. Translated by M. Kohl. San Francisco: Harper & Row, 1981.

Montgomery, Ray. *It's a Wonderful World—Naturally*. Washington, D.C.: Review and Herald, 1982.

Moreland, J. P., and Scott B. Rae. *Body & Soul: Human Nature and the Crisis in Ethics*. Downers Grove, Ill.: InterVarsity Press, 2000.

Morris, Henry. *The Beginning of the World*. El Cajon, Calif.: Master Books, 1977.

————. *The Genesis Record*. Grand Rapids, Mich.: Baker, 1976.

Morris, Leon. *The Epistle to the Romans*. Grand Rapids, Mich.: Eerdmans, 1988.

Morris, Thomas V. *Anselmian Explorations: Essays in Philosophical Theology*. Notre Dame, Ind.: University of Notre Dame Press, 1987.

Morson, G. S. "The Prosaics of Process." *Literary Imagination* 2, no. 3 (2000): 377-88.

Mundia, W. O. "The Existence of the Devil." Ph.D. diss., Boston University School of Theology, 1994.

Murphree, Jon Tal. *A Loving God and a Suffering World*. Downers Grove, Ill.: InterVarsity Press, 1981.

Murphree, Wallace A. "Can Theism Survive Without the Devil?" *RelS* 21 (1985): 8 n. 1.

Murphy, Nancey, and George F. R. Ellis. *On the Moral Nature of the Universe: Theology, Cosmology, and Ethics*. Minneapolis: Fortress, 1996.

Nagel, Thomas. "The Problem of Autonomy." In *Agents, Causes and Events: Essays on Indeterminism and Free Will*. Edited by Timothy O'Connor. New York: Oxford University Press, 1995.

Narveson, J. "Compatibilism Defended." *Philosophical Studies* 32 (July 1977): 99-105.

Nee, Watchman. *What Shall This Man Do?* London: Victory, 1961.

Neuser, Wilhelm H., and Brian G. Armstrong, eds. *Calvinus Sincerioris Religionis Vindex* [*Calvin As Protector of the Purer Religion*]. Sixteenth Century Essays and Studies 36. Kirksville, Mo.: Sixteenth Century Journal Publishers, 1997.

Neville, Robert. *Creativity and God: A Challenge to Process Theology*. New York: Seabury, 1980.

Newlands, George. *Theology of the Love of God*. Atlanta: John Knox Press, 1980.

Nichols, Terence. "Miracles As a Sign of the Good Creation." Ph.D. diss., Marquette University Graduate School, 1988.

Nicolis, Grégoire, and Ilya Prigogine. *Exploring Complexity: An Introduction*. New York: W. H. Freeman, 1989.

Nitecki, Z., and C. Robinson, eds. *Global Theory of Dynamical Systems: Proceedings of an International Conference Hold at Northwestern University, Evanston, Illinois, June 18-22, 1979*. Berlin: Springer Verlag, 1980.

Nozick, Robert. "Choice and Indeterminism." In *Agents, Causes and Events: Essays on Indeterminism and Free Will*. Edited by Timothy O'Connor, pp. 101-14. New York: Oxford University Press, 1995.

————. *Philosophical Explanations*. Cambridge, Mass.: Harvard University Press, 1981.

O'Conner, Timothy. "Indeterminism and Free Agency: Three Recent Views." *Philosophy and Phenomenology Research* 53 (1993): 499-526.

O'Connor, David. *God and Inscrutable Evil: In Defense of Theism and Atheism*. Lanham, Md.: Rowman & Littlefield, 1998.

O'Connor, Timothy, ed. *Agents, Causes and Events: Essays on Indeterminism and Free Will*. New York: Oxford University Press, 1995.

Oden, Thomas C. *The Transforming Power of Grace*. Nashville: Abingdon, 1993.

O'Donnell, John. *Trinity and Temporality: The Christian Doctrine of God in the Light of Process Theology and the Theology of Hope*. Oxford: Oxford University Press, 1983.

Oliver, Harold. *A Relational Metaphysics*. Boston: Martinus Nijhoff, 1981.

Olson, G. *The Foreknowledge of God*. Arlington Heights, Ill.: Bible Research, 1941.

Omnés, Roland. *Physics World*. United Kingdom: Institute of Physics, 1995.

Osburn, E. "Those Who Have Never Heard: Have They No Hope?" *JETS* 32 (1989): 367-72.

Padgett, Alan. *God, Eternity and the Nature of Time*. New York: St. Martin's, 1992.

Pagels, Elaine. *The Origin of Satan*. New York: Random House, 1995.

Palmer, Edwin. *The Five Points of Calvinism*. Grand Rapids, Mich.: Baker, 1972.

Pannenberg, Wolfhart. "Atom, Duration and Form: Difficulties with Process Philosophy." *Process Studies* 14 (1984): n. 9.

Parmentier, Marvin. "Greek Church Fathers on Romans 9." *Bijdragen* 50 (1989): 139-54; 51 (1990): 2-20.

Pate, C. M., ed. *Four Views on the Book of Revelation.* Grand Rapids, Mich.: Zondervan, 1998.

Paton, D. M. *The Judgment Seat of Christ.* Hayesville, N.C.: Schoettle, 1993.

Payne, J. Barton. *Encyclopedia of Biblical Prophecy.* New York: Harper & Row, 1973.

Peacocke, Arthur R. "Chance and Law in Irreversible Thermodynamics, Theoretical Biology, and Theology." In *Chaos and Complexity: Scientific Perspectives on Divine Action.* Edited by Robert J. Russell et al., pp. 123-43. Vatican City: Vatican Observatory Publications, 1995.

————. *Creation and the World of Science.* Oxford: Clarendon, 1979.

Peirce, Charles S. *Collected Papers of Charles Sanders Peirce.* Edited by Charles Hartshorne and P. Weiss, Cambridge, Mass.: Harvard University Press, 1931-1935.

Peitgen, H. "The Causality Principle, Deterministic Laws and Chaos." In *Chaos: The New Science: Nobel Conference XXVI.* Edited by John Holte, pp. 35-43. Lanham, Md.: University Press of America, 1993.

Pember, George. H. *Earth's Earliest Ages.* 1876. Repr., Grand Rapids, Mich.: Kregel, 1975.

Penelhum, Terrence. *Religion and Rationality: An Introduction to the Philosophy of Religion.* New York: Random House, 1971.

Penrose, Roger. *The Emperor's New Mind: Concerning Computers, Minds, and the Laws of Physics.* Oxford: Oxford University Press, 1989.

————. *Shadow of the Mind.* Oxford: Oxford University Press, 1994.

Peterson, Michael. *Evil and the Christian God.* Grand Rapids, Mich.: Baker, 1982.

Peterson, Robert A. *Hell on Trial: The Case for Eternal Punishment.* Phillipsburg, N.J.: P & R Publishing, 1995.

Pike, N. "Over-Power and God's Responsibility for Sin." In *The Existence and Nature of God.* Edited by Alfred J. Freddoso. Notre Dame, Ind.: University of Notre Dame Press, 1983.

Pinnock, Clark. "The Conditional View." In *Four Views on Hell.* Edited by William Crockett. Grand Rapids, Mich.: Zondervan, 1992.

————. "Systematic Theology." In *The Openness of God: A Biblical Challenge to the Traditional Understanding of God.* Edited by Clark Pinnock. Downers Grove, Ill.: InterVarsity Press, 1994.

————. *A Wideness in God's Mercy.* Grand Rapids, Mich.: Zondervan, 1992.

————, ed. *The Openness of God: A Biblical Challenge to the Traditional Understanding of God.* Downers Grove, Ill.: InterVarsity Press, 1994.

Pinnock, Clark, and Robert Brow. *Unbounded Love.* Downers Grove, Ill.: InterVarsity Press, 1994.

Piper, John. "Are There Two Wills in God? Divine Election and God's Desire for All to Be Saved." In *The Grace of God and the Bondage of the Will.* 2 vols. Edited by Thomas Schreiner and Bruce Ware, 1:107-32. Grand Rapids, Mich.: Baker, 1995.

————. *The Justification of God: An Exegetical and Theological Study of Romans 9:1-23.* Grand Rapids, Mich.: Baker, 1983.

Placher, William C. *The Domestication of Transcendence: How Modern Thinking About God Went Wrong.* Louisville: Westminster John Knox, 1996.

Plantinga, Alvin. *God, Freedom, and Evil.* Grand Rapids, Mich.: Eerdmans, 1977.

————. *The Nature of Necessity.* Oxford: Clarendon, 1982.

————. "Self-Profile." In *Alvin Plantinga.* Edited by James E. Tomberlin and Peter Van Inwagen. Profiles: Contemporary Philosophers and Logicians 5. Boston: D. Reidel, 1985.

Plato. *The Laws of Plato.* Translated by Thomas L. Pangle. Chicago: University of Chicago Press, 1980.

————. *The Statesman.* Translated by H. N. Fowler. Cambridge, Mass.: Harvard University Press, 1962.

Polkinghorne, John. "The Quantum World." In *Physics, Philosophy and Theology: A Common*

Quest for Understanding. Edited by Robert J. Russell, William R. Stoeger and George V. Coyne. Notre Dame, Ind.: Notre Dame University Press, 1988.

———. *Quarks, Chaos and Christianity: Questions to Science and Religion*. New York: Crossroad, 1996.

———. *Science and Creation*. Boston: Shambala, 1988.

Popper, Karl. *Objective Knowledge*. Oxford: Oxford University Press, 1972.

———. *The Open Universe: An Argument for Indeterminism*. London: Hutchinson, 1982.

———. *Quantum Theory and the Schism in Physics*. London: Hutchinson, 1982.

Priesmeyer, H. Richard. *Organizations and Chaos: Defining the Methods of Nonlinear Management*. Westport, Conn.: Quorum Books, 1992.

Prigogine, Ilya. *From Being to Becoming*. San Francisco: W. H. Freeman, 1980.

———. "Irreversibility and Space-Time Structure." In *Physics and the Ultimate Significance of Time*. Edited by David. R. Griffin, pp. 232-49. Albany, N.Y.: SUNY, 1986.

———. "Time, Dynamics and Chaos: Integrating Poincaré's 'Non-Integratable Systems.' " In *Chaos: The New Science: Nobel Conference XXVI*. Edited by John Holte, pp. 55-88. Lanham, Md.: University Press of America, 1993.

Prigogine, Ilya, and Michèle Sanglier. *The Laws of Nature and Human Conduct*. Brussels: Task Force of Research Information and the Study of Science, 1985.

Prigogine, Ilya, and Isabelle Stengers. *Order out of Chaos: Man's New Dialogue with Nature*. New York: Bantam Books, 1984.

Prior, A. "The Formalities of Omniscience." *Philosophy* 37 (1962): 114-29.

Punt, Neal. *Unconditional Good News: Toward an Understanding of Biblical Universalism*. Grand Rapids, Mich.: Eerdmans, 1980.

Purtill, Richard L. *C. S. Lewis's Case for the Christian Faith*. San Francisco.: Harper & Row, 1981.

Rae, Alastair. *Quantum Physics: Illusion or Reality?* Cambridge: Cambridge University Press, 1986.

Ratzsch, Del. *The Battle of Beginnings*. Downers Grove, Ill.: InterVarsity Press, 1996.

Reichenbach, B. "Hasker on Omniscience." *Faith and Philosophy* 4 (1987): 86-92.

Reichenbach, Hans. *The Direction of Time*. Berkeley and Los Angeles: University of California Press, 1956.

Reppert, V. "The Lewis-Anscombe Controversy: A Discussion of the Issues." *Christian Scholars Review* 19 (1989): 32-48.

Rice, Richard. "Biblical Support." In *The Openness of God: A Biblical Challenge to the Traditional Understanding of God*. Edited by Clark Pinnock. Downers Grove, Ill.: InterVarsity Press, 1994.

———. *God's Foreknowledge and Man's Free Will*. Minneapolis: Bethany House, 1985.

Ricoeur, Paul. *Freedom and Nature*. Evanston, Ill.: Northwestern University Press, 1973.

Rist, John M. *Augustine: Ancient Thought Baptized*. Cambridge: Cambridge University Press, 1994.

Robinson, William. *The Devil and God*. Nashville: Abingdon-Cokesbury, 1945.

Ross, S. David. *Transition to an Ordinal Metaphysics*. Albany, N.Y.: SUNY, 1980.

Rowe, William. "Two Concepts of Freedom." In *Agents, Causes and Events: Essays on Indeterminism and Free Will*. Edited by Timothy O'Connor. New York: Oxford University Press, 1995.

Royce, Josiah. *The Conception of God*. New York: Macmillan, 1898.

Ruelle, David. *Chance and Chaos*. Princeton, N.J.: Princeton University Press, 1991.

Russell, Bertrand. *Why I Am Not a Christian*. New York: Simon and Schuster, 1957.

Russell, Jeffrey B. *Mephistopheles: The Devil in the Modern World*. Ithaca, N.Y.: Cornell University Press, 1986.

———. *Satan: The Early Christian Tradition*. Ithaca, N.Y.: Cornell University Press, 1981.

Russell, R. J. "Entropy and Evil." *Zygon* 19 (1984): 8 n. 4.

———. "Quantum Physics in Philosophical and Theological Perspective." In *Physics, Philosophy and Theology: A Common Quest for Understanding*. Edited by Robert J. Russell, William R. Stoeger and George V. Coyne. Notre Dame, Ind.: Notre Dame University Press, 1988.

Sabourin, L. "The Miracles of Jesus (II): Jesus and the Evil Powers." *BTB* 4 (1974): 115-75.

Sachs, J. R. "Current Eschatology: Universalism, Salvation and the Problem of Hell." *TS* 52 (1991): 227-54.

Samenow, Stanton. *Inside the Criminal Mind*. New York: Times Books, 1984.

Sanders, John. *The God Who Risks: A Theology of Providence*. Downers Grove, Ill.: InterVarsity Press, 1998.

———. "Historical Considerations." In *The Openness of God: A Biblical Challenge to the Traditional Understanding of God*. Edited by Clark Pinnock. Downers Grove, Ill.: InterVarsity Press, 1994.

———. *No Other Name: An Investigation into the Destiny of the Unevangelized*. Grand Rapids, Mich.: Eerdmans, 1992.

Sarna, Nahum. "Epic Substratum in the Prose of Job." *JBL* 67 (1974): 17-34.

Sauer, Erich. *The King of the Earth*. Repr., Palm Springs, Calif.: R. Hayes, 1959.

Sawyer, John. *Prophecy and Biblical Prophets*. Revised ed. New York: Oxford University Press, 1993.

Schreiner, T. "Does Romans 9 Teach Individual Election unto Salvation?" In *The Grace of God and the Bondage of the Will*. 2 vols. Edited by Thomas Schreiner and Bruce Ware, 1:89-106. Grand Rapids, Mich.: Baker, 1995.

———. " 'Works of Law' in Paul." *NovT* 33 (1991): 217-44.

Schwarz, Hans. *Evil: A Historical and Theological Perspective*. Translated by Mark W. Worthing. Minneapolis: Fortress, 1995.

Scott, M. "The Morality of Theodicies." *RelS* 32 (1996): 1-13.

Searle, John. *Minds, Brains, and Science*. Cambridge, Mass.: Harvard University Press, 1984.

Segerberg, Osborn, Jr. *The Immortality Factor*. New York: E. P. Dutton, 1974.

Sellars, W. "Thought and Action." In *Freedom and Determinism*. Edited by Keith Lehrer, pp. 105-40. New York: Random House, 1966.

Sennett, J. F. "The Free Will Defense and Determinism." *Faith and Philosophy* 9 (1991): 340-53.

———. "Is There Freedom in Heaven?" *Faith and Philosophy* 16 (1999): 69-82.

Shedd, William G. T. *The Doctrine of Endless Punishment*. New York: Scribner, 1886.

Sherburne, Donald, ed. *A Key to Whitehead's Process and Reality*. Chicago: University of Chicago Press, 1966.

Short, Robert. *Something to Believe In*. San Francisco: Harper & Row, 1978.

Skutch, A. F. "Bird Song and Philosophy." In *The Philosophy of Charles Hartshorne*. Edited by Lewis E. Hahn, pp. 65-76. Library of Living Philosophers 20. La Salle, Ill.: Open Court, 1991.

Smith, David L. *With Willful Intent: A Theology of Sin*. Wheaton, Ill.: Bridgepoint, 1994.

Smith, Q. "An Atheological Argument from Evil Natural Laws." *International Journal for Philosophy of Religion* 29 (1991): 159-74.

Soelle, Dorothee. *Christ the Representative: An Essay in Theology After the "Death of God."* Translated by David Lewis. Philadelphia: Fortress, 1967.

———. *The Strength of the Weak: Toward a Christian Feminist Identity*. Translated by Robert and Rita Kimber. Philadelphia: Westminster Press, 1984.

Sokolowski, Robert. *The God of Faith and Reason*. Notre Dame, Ind.: University of Notre Dame Press, 1982.

Song, Choan-Seng. *Third-Eye Theology: Theology in Formation in Asian Settings*. Maryknoll, N.Y.: Orbis, 1979.

Sproul, R. C. *Chosen by God*. Wheaton, Ill.: Tyndale House, 1986.

———. *The Invisible Hand: Do All Things Really Work for Good?* Dallas: Word, 1996.

———. *Not a Chance: The Myth of Chance in Modern Science and Cosmology*. Grand Rapids, Mich.: Baker, 1994.

———. *Willing to Believe: The Controversy over Free Will*. Grand Rapids, Mich.: Baker, 1997.

Stacey, Ralph. D. *Managing the Unknowable: Strategic Boundaries Between Order and Chaos in Organizations*. San Francisco: Jossey-Bass, 1992.

Stannard, Russell. *God for the 21st Century*. Philadelphia: Templeton Foundation Press, 2000.

Stapp, Henry. *Mind, Matter, and Quantum Mechanics*. New York: Springer Verlag, 1993.

Stewart, Ian. *Does God Play Dice? The Mathematics of Chaos*. Oxford: Blackwell, 1989.

Stoffer, D. "The Problem of Evil: An Historical Theological Approach." *ATJ* 24 (1992): 1 n. 16.

Strauss, J. D. "God's Promise and Universal History: The Theology of Romans 9." In *Grace Unlimited*. Edited by Clark Pinnock, pp. 190-208. Minneapolis: Bethany House, 1975.

Strawson, Galen. *Freedom and Belief*. Oxford: Oxford University Press, 1986.

———. "The Impossibility of Moral Responsibility." *Philosophical Studies* 75 (1994): 5-24.

———. "Libertarianism, Action, and Self-Determination." In *Agents, Causes and Events: Essays on Indeterminism and Free Will*. Edited by Timothy O'Connor. New York: Oxford University Press, 1995.

Stuermann, Walter E. *The Divine Destroyer: A Theology of Good and Evil*. Philadelphia: Westminster Press, 1967.

Stump, E. "Sanctification, Hardening of the Heart, and Frankfurt's Concept of Free Will." *Journal of Philosophy* 85 (1988): 395-420.

Surin, Kenneth. *Theology and the Problem of Evil*. Oxford: Blackwell, 1986.

Swenson, Richard. *Hurtling Toward Oblivion*. Colorado Springs: NavPress, 1999.

Swinburne, Richard. *The Christian God*. Oxford: Clarendon, 1994.

———. *The Coherence of Theism*. Oxford: Clarendon, 1977.

———. *The Existence of God*. Oxford: Oxford University Press, 1979. Revised ed. Oxford: Clarendon, 1991.

———. *Responsibility and Atonement*. Oxford: Clarendon, 1989.

———. "A Theodicy of Heaven and Hell." In *The Existence and Nature of God*. Edited by Alvin J. Freddoso. Notre Dame, Ind.: University of Notre Dame Press, 1983.

Talbott, Thomas. "The Doctrine of Everlasting Punishment." *Faith and Philosophy* 7 (1990): 19-42.

———. "The Love of God and the Heresy of Exclusivism." *Christian Scholars Review* 27 (1997): 99-112.

Taylor, Richard. *Action and Purpose*. Engelwood Cliffs, N.J.: Prentice-Hall, 1966.

———. "Deliberation and Foreknowledge." In *Free Will and Determinism*. Edited by Bernard Berofsky. New York: Harper & Row, 1966.

———. *Metaphysics*. 2nd ed. Englewood Cliffs, N.J.: Prentice-Hall, 1974.

Tennant, Frederick R. *Philosophical Theology*. 2 vols. Cambridge: Cambridge University Press, 1928-1930.

Terry, Mitton S. *Biblical Apocalyptics: A Study of the Most Notable Revelations of God and of Christ*. 1898. Repr., Grand Rapids, Mich.: Baker, 1988.

Thalberg, I. "How Does Agent Causation Work?" In *Action Theory*. Edited by Myles Brand and Douglas Walton, pp. 213-38. Dordrecht, Holland: D. Reidel, 1976.

Thistlethwaite, Susan. "I Am Become Death: God in the Nuclear Age." In *Lift Every Voice: Constructing Christian Theologies from the Underside*. Edited by Susan B. Thistlethwaite and Mary P. Engel. San Francisco: Harper & Row, 1990.

Thomas Aquinas. *Summa Theologiae*. Vol. 15, *The World Order (1a.110-119)*. New York: Blackfriars/McGraw-Hill, 1970.

Thompson, I. "Liberal Values and Power Politics." In *Ethics and Defense: Power and Responsibility in the Nuclear Age.* Edited by Howard Davis, pp. 82-102. New York: Blackwell, 1987.
Thorp, John. *Free Will: A Defence Against Neurophysiological Determinism.* London: Routledge & Kegan Paul, 1980.
Tiessen, Terrance. *Providence and Prayer: How Does God Work in the World?* Downers Grove, Ill.: InterVarsity Press, 2000.
Tilley, Terrence W. *The Evils of Theodicy.* Washington, D.C.: Georgetown University Press, 1990.
Tillich, Paul. *Systematic Theology.* 3 vols. Chicago: University of Chicago Press, 1967.
Tooley, Michael. "Alvin Plantinga and the Argument From Evil." *Australasian Journal of Philosophy* 58 (1980):5-6nn.
———. *Causation: A Reality Approach.* Oxford: Clarendon, 1987.
Trethowan, Dom I. *An Essay in Christian Philosophy.* London: Longmans, Green & Co., 1954.
Trible, Phyllis. *God and the Rhetoric of Sexuality.* Philadelphia: Fortress, 1978.
Tupper, Francis. *Scandalous Providence: The Jesus Story of the Compassion of God.* Macon, Ga.: Mercer University Press, 1995.
Twain, Mark. *Letters from the Earth.* New York: Fawcett World Library, 1963.
Twelftree, Graham H. *Jesus the Exorcist: A Contribution to the Study of the Historical Jesus.* WUNT 2.54. Tübingen: Mohr [Siebeck], 1993.
Van Holten, W. "Hell and the Goodness of God." *RelS* 35 (1999): 37-55.
Van Inwagen, Peter. *An Essay on Free Will.* Oxford: Oxford University Press, 1983.
———. "The Incompatibility of Free Will and Determinism." *Philosophical Studies* 27 (1975): 185-99.
———. "When Is the Will Free?" In *Agents, Causes and Events: Essays on Indeterminism and Free Will.* Edited by Timothy O'Connor. New York: Oxford University Press, 1995.
Vardy, Peter. *The Puzzle of Evil.* Armonk, N.Y.: M. E. Sharpe, 1997.
Voltaire. *Voltaire's Candide, Zadig and Selected Stories.* Translated by D. M. Frame. Bloomington: Indiana University Press, 1961.
Wacome, Donald. "Evolution, Foreknowledge and Creation." *Christian Scholars Review* 26 (1997): 5 n. 8.
Waldrop, M. Mitchell. *Complexity: The Emerging Science at the Edge of Order and Chaos.* New York: Simon & Schuster, 1992.
Wallace, Ronald. *The Lord Is King: The Message of Daniel.* Downers Grove, Ill.: InterVarsity Press, 1979.
Waller, B. "Free Will Gone Out of Control." *Behaviorism* 16 (1988): 149-57.
Walls, Jerry. *Hell: The Logic of Damnation.* Notre Dame, Ind.: University of Notre Dame Press, 1992.
Ward, Keith. *Divine Action.* London: Collins, 1990.
———. "God As a Principle of Cosmological Explanation." In *Physics, Philosophy, and Theology: A Common Quest for Understanding.* Edited by Robert J. Russell, William R. Stoeger and George V. Coyne. Notre Dame, Ind.: University of Notre Dame Press, 1988.
———. *Rational Theology and the Creativity of God.* Oxford: Basil Blackwell, 1982.
Ware, Bruce. "An Evangelical Reformulation of the Doctrine of the Immutability of God." *JETS* 29 (1986): 431-46.
———. *The God of a Lesser Glory.* Grand Rapids, Mich.: Baker, forthcoming.
Warfield, Benjamin B. "The Development of the Doctrine of Infant Salvation." In *Studies in Theology.* New York: Oxford University Press, 1932.
Waszink, J. H. *Commentarius: Corpus Platonicum Zmedi Aevi.* Leiden: E. J. Brill, 1962.
Watts, Rikki. *Isaiah's New Exodus and Mark.* WUNT 2.88. Tübingen: Mohr [Siebeck], 1997.
Weatherford, Roy. *The Implications of Determinism.* London: Routledge, 1991.
Weatherhead, Leslie. *Salute to a Sufferer.* New York: Abingdon, 1962.

Webb, C. C. J. *Problems in the Relations of God and Man.* London: Wisbet, 1911.

Webb, Dom B. *Why Does God Permit Evil?* New York: P. J. Kennedy & Sons, 1941.

Webber, Robert E. *The Church in the World: Opposition, Tension or Transformation?* Grand Rapids, Mich.: Zondervan, 1986.

Weber, Bruce, David Depew and James Smith, eds. *Entropy, Information and Evolution.* Cambridge, Mass.: MIT Press, 1988.

Welker, Michael. *Creation and Reality.* Translated by John F. Hoffmeyer. Minneapolis: Fortress, 1999.

Wenham, John. "Conditional Immortality." In *Universalism and the Doctrine of Hell.* Edited by Nigel M. de S. Cameron. Grand Rapids, Mich.: Baker, 1992.

———. *The Enigma of Evil.* Grand Rapids, Mich.: Zondervan, 1985.

Wesley, John. *Works of John Wesley,* vol. 3. Edited by Albert C. Outler. Nashville: Abingdon, 1986.

Whale, John S. *Victor and Victim.* Cambridge: Cambridge University Press, 1960.

Wheatley, Margaret. *Leadership and the New Science: Learning About Organization from an Orderly Universe.* San Francisco: Berrett-Koehler, 1992.

Whitcomb, John C., Jr. *The Early Earth.* Grand Rapids, Mich.: Baker, 1986.

Whitcomb, John C., Jr., and Henry Morris. *The Genesis Flood: The Biblical Record and Its Scientific Implications.* Philadelphia: Presbyterian & Reformed, 1961.

Whitehead, Alfred North. *Process and Reality: An Essay in Cosmology.* Corrected ed. New York: Free Press, 1978.

Wiebe, B. "The Focus of Jesus' Eschatology." In *Self-Definition and Self-Discovery in Early Christianity: A Study in Changing Horizons.* Edited by David J. Hawkins and Tom Robinson, pp. 121-46. Lewiston, N.Y.: Mellen, 1990.

Wiggins, D. "Towards a Reasonable Libertarianism." In *Essays on Freedom and Action.* Edited by Ted Honderich. London: Routledge & Kegan Paul, 1973.

Wilcox, John. "A Question from Physics for Certain Theists." *JR* 41 (1961): 293-300.

Williams, Norman P. *The Ideas of the Fall and of Original Sin.* New York: Longmans, Green & Co., 1927.

Windt, Peter. "Plantinga's Unfortunate God." *Philosophical Studies* 24 (1973): 335-42.

Wink, Walter. *Engaging the Powers: Discernment and Resistance in a World of Domination.* Minneapolis: Fortress, 1992.

———. *Unmasking the Powers: The Invisible Forces That Determine Human Existence.* Philadelphia: Fortress, 1986.

Wolf, Susan. *Freedom Within Reason.* Oxford: Oxford University Press, 1990.

Wolfson, Harry, A. *Philo: Foundations of Religious Philosophy in Judaism, Christianity, and Islam.* 2 vols. Cambridge, Mass.: Harvard University Press, 1947.

Worthing, Mark W. *God, Creation and Contemporary Physics.* Minneapolis: Fortress, 1996.

Wright, N. T. *The New Testament and the People of God.* Minneapolis: Fortress, 1996.

Wright, Nigel. *The Satan Syndrome.* Grand Rapids, Mich.: Zondervan, 1990.

Wright, R. K. McGregor. *No Place For Sovereignty.* Downers Grove, Ill.: InterVarsity Press, 1996.

Wynkoop, Mildred B. *A Theology of Love: The Dynamic of Wesleyanism.* Kansas City, Mo.: Beacon Hill, 1972.

Yochelson, Samuel, and Stanton Samenow. *The Criminal Personality.* 2 vols. New York: Aronson, 1977.

Zagzebski, Linda. *The Dilemma of Freedom and Foreknowledge.* New York: Oxford University Press, 1991.

Zemach, E. and D. Widerker. "Facts, Freedom, and Foreknowledge." In *God, Foreknowledge, and Freedom.* Edited by John M. Fisher, pp. 111-22. Stanford, Calif.: Stanford University Press, 1989.

Zukav, Gary. *The Dancing Wu Li Masters: An Overview of the New Physics.* New York: William Morrow, 1979.

Author/
Subject Index